MUSIC EDUCATION FOR TEEN-AGERS

EXPLORATION SERIES IN EDUCATION

Under the Advisory Editorship of
John Guy Fowlkes

SECOND EDITION

Music Education for Teen-Agers

WILLIAM RAYMOND SUR
Professor of Music
Chairman of Music Education
Michigan State University

CHARLES FRANCIS SCHULLER
Professor of Education
Director of the Instructional Media Center
Michigan State University

HARPER & ROW, PUBLISHERS, NEW YORK

MUSIC EDUCATION FOR TEEN-AGERS, Second Edition

Library of Congress Catalog Card Number: 66-10115

Contents

Editor's Introduction

It is usually held that education—whether of the young or of the old—should provide for the whole person. It is therefore not surprising that music is being given increased attention. More training is being offered in music appreciation and in musical performance.

This increase is also reflected in activities outside of the school, college, or university. Operas, symphony orchestras, choruses, bands, string quartets, and other groups of performing musicians are found not only in the largest cities, but also in the smaller towns and hamlets.

Naturally, more and better teachers are needed. Toward this end Professors Sur and Schuller wrote a book called *Music Education for Teen-Agers,* published in 1958, which was included in The Exploration Series. The reception of the first edition was enthusiastic. Now this work is being revised and polished.

In the Editor's Introduction of the first edition, the following statement was made: "This book should prove both interesting and of invaluable assistance to all those concerned with public school music." This has been the case, and it is indeed a pleasure to present this revised and improved edition of *Music Education for Teen-Agers.*

John Guy Fowlkes

September, 1965

Preface

Music education is concerned with music as an art, as a social force, and as a therapy. In the total school program we believe its function is to meet the needs of the individual pupil and the group. We are concerned in this writing with a broad concept of music education: a concept that takes into account a sustained, reasonable, and ever-growing musical development of girls and boys, a concept in which music is not an isolated area of instruction but a significant part of the education of all the pupils. It is our hope that the material and suggestions contained in this book will enable teachers to bring music into the lives of greater numbers of girls and boys.

Recognition of the value of new media of instruction in educational systems across the nation is reflected in chapters on audio and visual materials and methods for teachers of music. These media are treated as effective means of communication of music concepts, and consequently as integral rather than as exceptional or incidental aspects of the modern music teacher's preparation.

Many of the problems facing junior-senior high-school music teachers would not exist if girls and boys were given adequate music training throughout the elementary grades. Studies of school systems show the need for a balanced and adequate program of music in these early grades, kindergarten through sixth.

Administrators and secondary-school music teachers have an obligation to promote and support music through the beginning years of schooling. The authors, thoroughly convinced of the need for a sound program of music from early childhood through the elementary schools, have included a chapter on Music in the Elementary School. Effectively taught, music in the elementary school has the power to develop in children a receptive attitude toward good music and to promote musical growth. The foundation of success in secondary-school music rests largely on the foundation established in early childhood.

A challenging opportunity for bringing pupils into contact with music and the other arts is found in the new chapter, Regarding Music and the Humanities. In these new chapters, plus the final chapter, Music Educator's Reference File, and revisions of chapters throughout the text, we hope to assist secondary-school music teachers in meeting their problems and improving the quality of instruction in the junior and senior high school.

The professional assistance and cooperation of many persons have made it possible to write *Music Education for Teen-Agers*. The authors appreciate the interest and assistance of John Guy Fowlkes, Professor of Education, School of Education of the University of Wisconsin, in reading the manuscript and in offering his valuable suggestions. Our appreciation is also extended to Lorin Richtmeyer, Assistant Professor of Music, Northern Michigan University, and to Alice Doll Nelson of the Lansing, Michigan, Public Schools for their interest and contributions to the text.

Limitations of space make it impossible to mention all those who have responded to the call for assistance in the preparation of this book. To them we express our gratitude and thanks.

CHARLES FRANCIS SCHULLER
WILLIAM RAYMOND SUR

September, 1965

PART I

The Instructional Program

Lyons Township High School, La Grange, Illinois.

CHAPTER

1

Youth and Music

MUSIC'S HOLD ON TEEN-AGERS

There's music in our teen-age girls and boys. Given the opportunity to make music under the direction of capable teachers, with good equipment and in a favorable environment, they will make the most of that opportunity. They are doing it from Maine to California, in hundreds of cities and towns. Thousands of girls and boys in school bands, orchestras, and choruses are performing everything from Bach to the hit tunes of the week with a skill that is unheard of in any other country.

This widespread interest is not something new in American education. Music has been offered in the schools of most communities for many years, but perhaps we haven't fully realized what a tremendous attraction music has for teen-agers. When you find a school subject that has something to offer every pupil in the school, a subject which appeals to young people so strongly that they willingly give up part of their lunch period or after-school hours for extra rehearsals, you have discovered a subject that can exert a powerful influence for good in their lives.

Some years ago when I was visiting music classes in an Indiana high school, members of the school orchestra, as was their custom, brought their lunch to the noon-hour orchestra rehearsal. The musical future of America is in safe hands when you see teen-agers put down a hamburger to pick up a fiddle bow! Music has that sort of a hold on many youngsters. It is impressing them with the necessity for hard work and the need for working together to get satisfying results.

What music can mean to high-school youngsters was recently discovered in a visit to a high school near Chicago. In this community, parents have joined with the school authorities to provide musical advantages for their sons and daughters. There is a chance for any pupil in this school to make music if he wants to. If he hasn't the money to own an instrument he can borrow one from the school, or the school will rent him one for a small fee.

Six hundred youthful music makers! They play in the school symphony orchestra and in concert and marching bands, or they sing in choruses and choirs.

Sacramento Public Schools, Sacramento, California.

Fig. 1.1. Young players in a junior-high-school festival.

They take part in music, not because someone says they must, but because they love music. They have no fear of the great masters or modern composers of music. With enthusiasm and energy they struggle with the music of the past and present, and in time they gain an understanding and love for music that will be theirs throughout life.

Are these girls and boys unusual? Are they more talented than those in other communities? Not at all. They are just live-wire American youngsters representing many nationalities, colors, and creeds. A glance at the teacher's roll book reveals everything from Brown to Velkoborsky. Together they play and sing and come to know and understand each other through music, the universal language.

About 30 years ago music in this particular school started out very humbly with a drum corps as the main attraction. In time, school and community leaders with a vision of what music could mean to their girls and boys went into action. A large and enthusiastic group of fathers and mothers met and the result was a parents' organization to support the plans for developing the school music program. They learned what was needed to produce good musical groups: instruments and other equipment, qualified teachers, and the backing of the school administration. They went to work to achieve a good music program.

What happened as the needed instruments and equipment were secured was even more than they had hoped for. There was extensive participation and increasing interest in music, and to an extent this was reflected in excellent work at festivals and contests (Fig. 1.1). The orchestra and the band, in addition to appearances at civic functions, began to prepare several major concerts each year for the benefit of the students and the community.

Let's step into the instrumental room and listen while the orchestra rehearses for a concert. They are playing beautifully; every player is alert and watching the conductor. We understand why this orchestra is considered an outstanding organization. Music is fun for young people but they take it seriously. Their fun comes from pitching in and doing the job well (Fig. 1.2).

The music department offers a wide variety of activities in music. There is a story in itself about the chorus, choir, and glee clubs. Their performances of operas, musical comedies, and great sacred and choral works are heard each year. Advanced classes in music theory and appreciation attract the more serious students. Popular music has its place; competition runs high when the call goes

Fig. 1.2. Young people take their music seriously.

Elgin Public Schools, Elgin, Illinois. Courtesy Elgin Daily Courier-News.

Oakland Public Schools, Oakland, California.

Fig. 1.3. Dance bands and youth have a strong affinity.

out for dance-band players. The music teachers show as much interest in the dance band and its soloists as they do in the traditional school musical organizations (Fig. 1.3).

While music is taught primarily for its cultural, social, and educational value, many of these students make music their life work. We find them later in the country's symphony orchestras, the large bands, the dance bands, on radio and television. Many of them have become successful music teachers. And all of them are more intelligent consumers of music for their four years in this high school.

This is an example of what can be done in any high school, large or small. It needs only capable and dedicated teachers, an interested and cooperative administration, and parents who will support a program which will give their children a lifelong love of music. The children will take it from there.

VARIED INTERESTS OF YOUNG PEOPLE IN MUSIC

The diversity of interests of young people in music has resulted in important advances in secondary-school music. Participation in music has a strong appeal to young people. They want to sing and play; they want to listen to music and write music. Music of all ages and styles appeals to them. Their interest and capacity for music is reflected in the large and increasing enrollments in instrumental organizations, choirs, glee clubs, and choruses. In those communities where competent leadership has been provided, the interest of boys and girls has proved to be a motivating factor resulting in outstanding musical achievement —achievement far beyond anything considered possible by the pioneers of school music (Fig. 1.4).

Both photographs from South Bend Public Schools, South Bend, Indiana.

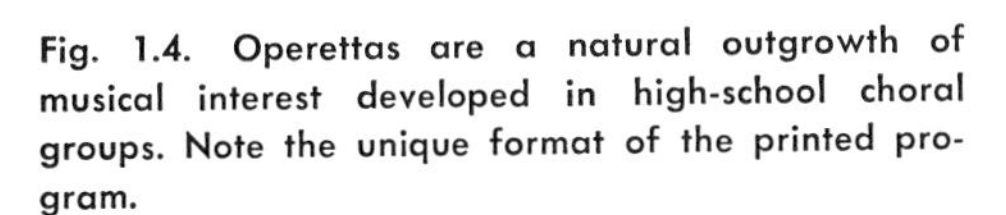

Fig. 1.4. Operettas are a natural outgrowth of musical interest developed in high-school choral groups. Note the unique format of the printed program.

The Development of Interest in School Music

Music as we find it in the modern school had very humble beginnings, according to Karl Wilson Gehrkens. In writing of the start of high-school music, Professor Gehrkens states:

> Many high schools maintained a chorus of sorts and some of these choruses were very good indeed, a few of them venturing to present the *Messiah* at Christmas time. . . . Between 1910 and 1930 there were important developments which had far-reaching effects on school music.
>
> 1. The introduction and acceptance of instrumental music as a regular school subject.
> 2. More general recognition of the fact that teaching music in schools is a complex affair.
> 3. The development of longer and better courses for music teachers.
> 4. The invention and improvement of the phonograph.
> 5. The acceptance of the idea of class instrumental teaching.
> 6. The success of the violin class led to experiments in which all the stringed instruments were taught, to similar classes for wind instruments, and eventually to instruction in "Class Piano."
> 7. The development and rapid spread of the a cappella choir movement.
> 8. The origin and development of the organization now known as the Music Educators National Conference.[1]

The story of the development of school music goes beyond the dedication of the early teachers of school music, to the belief in what music can contribute to the education of the child. The response of boys and girls has been a prime factor in the growth and development of school music. The present-day enthusiastic response to music covers a broad range of activities extending from the jam session to participation in string quartets and the singing of madrigals.

The Research Division of the National Education Association conducted a research study called "Music in the Public Schools."[2] The findings of this study are very encouraging in the light of the increased emphasis on science, mathematics, and foreign languages in the schools. The research covered the five years from 1956–1957 to 1961–1962. According to the data from the reporting secondary schools some conclusions were reached:

1. The trend is toward more music in the public schools, rather than less.
2. All schools of more than 1000 pupils reported that they offered instruction in music.
3. Five per cent of the schools reported an increased percentage of students enrolled in music courses; only 6 per cent reported decreases.

[1] Karl Wilson Gehrkens, "Five Decades of Music Education," *Education*, March, 1956, pp. 395–407.

[2] National Education Association, "Music in the Public Schools," *NEA Research Bulletin*, **41**:2 (May, 1963), pp. 56–59.

Fig. 1.5. Music work and fun mix well in summer camp surroundings.

Arrowbear Music Camp, Long Beach, California.

4. Between 20 and 35 per cent of the schools (depending on size and type) added courses in music; only 6 to 17 per cent dropped courses.
5. Pupil enrollment in extracurricular activities in music increased.
6. The number of full-time and part-time music teachers was increased.

The final paragraph of the study states: "As long as pupils and teachers love to play and sing, music will be an important part of the school program."

Another indication of the response of girls and boys to music is the continued growth of summer music programs for youth. The growth of these summer programs is due largely to the number of junior- and senior-high-school pupils willing to devote a portion of their summer vacation to continuing their study of music in programs sponsored by the local school system, and in music camps and clinics (Fig. 1.5).

The competition-festival which eliminated many of the undesirable features of the early contest movement is another means of estimating the value teenagers place on music. Throughout the nation there are annual state, regional, district, city, and county festivals in which thousands of pupils perform. They elect to participate in solo and small ensemble festivals as well as in those planned for the large instrumental and choral organizations (Fig. 1.6). In the festivals the student is given the opportunity to have his musical performance evaluated, to listen to other performers and organizations, and to share the inspiration that comes from fine music produced by musicians his own age. It is interesting to note that the problem faced by the groups sponsoring the festivals is one of limiting the number of participating students in order to insure the educational value of the festival.

Ann Arbor Public Schools, Ann Arbor, Michigan.

Fig. 1.6. The competition-festival provides a stimulating challenge for high-school students.

The Few—The Serious Amateurs

There are, of course, varying degrees of interest and musical ability to be found among the students in any junior- or senior-high-school student body. A small but significant percentage of any student body will be made up of the serious amateurs. In this group are those students who are capable of outstanding achievement in music because of their intense interest and inherited musical ability, and because of the encouragement of their parents and teachers. Music is vital in the lives of these young people. They need music as a means of communication and of self-expression, and as a means of fostering mental health. From this group will come the future professional musicians and those laymen who will be active in the cultural activities of the community.

A challenging program of instruction will bring outstanding results from this group. These are the gifted and they must not be allowed to drift into mediocrity.

Fig. 1.7. The talented youth of today may become the gifted performer of tomorrow.

West Hartford Public Schools, West Hartford, Connecticut.

They must be inspired and challenged to make the most of their talents and to make the contributions which only they can make to the cultural development of our country (Fig. 1.7).

The Many—Social and Recreational Interests

The larger percentage of the student body is likely to be made up of those students with purely social and recreational interests in music. Within this group are found those of average ability in music. They serve to reinforce the contribution of the highly gifted and make the present-day achievement in school music possible. Music for them is more than an art. It is a social force and, whether they recognize it or not, a therapy. It is one means of escaping the boredom and the routine of the mechanized world in which they live. Music is a means of enriching and humanizing their lives.

In addition to the contribution they make to the school music program, they are likely to be among those who will move into community living as members of the community music organizations. They will be eager to have music in their homes, and from the listening standpoint they are likely to become the discriminating consumers of music. While many of these students appear to have a superficial interest in music as a social and recreational force, a functional school music program may very well bring them into the ranks of the serious amateurs. This group of serious and devoted amateurs plays an important part in community living as producers and consumers of fine music.

The Unknowns

In any school there is a certain percentage of young people who might be classified as "the unknowns," from the standpoint of musical resources. The range of talent and interest varies within this group, and a program of music designed for all the students is essential if we are to broaden their interests and bring the benefits of music into their lives.

Lack of a musical background, no satisfying musical experience in the elementary school or in the home, inertia or timidity may be behind their failure to take part in the musical activities of the school. A musical aptitude testing program covering the entire student body may disclose some very gifted students in this group who are not aware of their ability in music. The needs of this segment of the student body have convinced many school administrators that the music program must be broadened and made attractive to these students. Where guidance, testing, and curriculum development function, many of these girls and boys will respond to and benefit from some part of the music program.

Youth does have varied interests in music, but these interests must be nourished if they are to be sustained during the adolescent years. An inspiring experience with music in the elementary grades is of primary importance if we are to insure the musical growth of girls and boys during the secondary-school years (Fig. 1.8). Enthusiasm for young people and music on the part of teachers, parents, and community does much to encourage teen-agers to bring their vitality and zest to music.

MUSIC IS FOR ALL STUDENTS

Music is many things. It has many styles, types, and classifications. The media of musical expression are extensive and of great variation, and music as a universal language communicates to individuals in many ways. It is difficult to imagine that any but a minute percentage of the students in any school are indifferent to music or reject it in all its forms.

Indifference or rejection of music by young people is likely to be the result of physical defects, poor teaching, unfortunate experience or no experience at all with music in the elementary school, a narrowly conceived curriculum in the high school, parental indifference to music in the home, or a combination of

American Music Conference, Chicago, Illinois.

Fig. 1.8. Musical interest can be nourished by recreational instruments.

these causes. It is generally agreed that preschool and early school experiences are likely to establish the child's attitude toward music for the remainder of his life. It is fortunately true that the number of people who lack sufficient interest in music or the talent to pursue it successfully is extremely small. In a school in which a large percentage of the students are indifferent to the opportunities open to them in music, the music program of that school is failing to meet the needs of the students and an evaluation of the program is in order.

In School Life

In school life music may provide for the student:

1. The key to richer and more effective living through contact with the art of music and its masterworks.
2. Social contacts and recognition through participation in music as a soloist

or as a member of an ensemble. The ability to get along with and work cooperatively with other people can be an outgrowth of the social contacts established through music (Fig. 1.9).

3. An opportunity for service to school and community through participation in school and community activities. This is one factor in developing good citizenship and fine school spirit.
4. Wholesome recreation. Music does not need to be "symphonic focused" to provide recreation and leisure-time activity. The simplest of musical instruments: the harmonica, the ukulele, the autoharp, the recorder and a host of melody and rhythm instruments, as well as recreational singing, have proved their worth as a means of combating juvenile delinquency and providing wholesome activity.
5. Good mental and physical health. Music instruction can do much to promote mental and physical health. Music therapy as an outgrowth of the school music program may be effective in aiding the student to meet the emotional and mental problems of life.
6. An opportunity to discover and evaluate musical talent. The discovery and development of talent is one of the main functions of an educational program. Working in music with the teacher and with other students aids the individual in evaluating his own musical talent and receiving suitable guidance.

Detroit Public Schools, Detroit, Michigan.

Fig. 1.9. The interest these girls have in their ensemble can be seen in their faces.

7. A means of earning a living on a full- or part-time basis. Many students secure a college education or supplement the family income through their ability in music.
8. An opportunity to develop creative capacities.

In Home and Community Life

In home and community living, music may provide:

1. A richer life—a means of securing the vitality and freedom that comes from expressive and creative activity. This is of particular importance in modern living when one considers the dull, mechanical routine which many people face because of the mechanical specialization of our age.
2. A worthy use of leisure time. Music has something to offer everyone regardless of age, race, color, or economic status. It is an art for all the people. The broad field of music provides the means of participation through active and understanding listening or by actual performance as a soloist or a member of an ensemble.
3. A means of unifying family and neighborhood living. An interest in music may serve as a common interest, unifying the family and may also serve to bring neighborhood and community groups together in desirable relationships.
4. A source of personal and social contacts for those people of like interests through participation in church choirs, small ensembles, community and industrial musical activities, and community concerts.

Planning Music for Everyone

Planning music for everyone must be a shared responsibility in the modern secondary school. The music teacher, teachers of other subjects, administrators, parents, and community leaders can help to initiate a realistic and functional curriculum (Fig. 1.10). Such planning brings to the music curriculum the strength and vitality essential to the continued growth of the instructional program as a positive force in the lives of the students. At the same time there must be general acceptance of the fundamental concept that music is an essential element of living in the modern world and, as such, must have a sound educational and functional basis. Music must play an educational role rather than one of entertaining the school and community.

The late Russell Morgan, Director of Music Education in the Cleveland, Ohio, public schools, expressed a basic thesis of functional curriculum planning in the following statement.

American Music Conference, Chicago, Illinois.

Fig. 1.10. When families enjoy music together they are likely to enjoy living together.

One important phase of education is, without doubt, a development of many and varied appreciations. We are chiefly concerned in music with the development of an aesthetic appreciation beyond the power of words to express or the mind to translate into definite thoughts. There is hunger in every man for just this thing whether he knows it or not, and the bitterness and hopelessness of many lives could have been relieved or prevented if a proper introduction had been given to the power of the arts to elevate one above material things.[3]

Enjoyment, appreciation, and participation are key words in the goal of bringing music to larger numbers of pupils. There must be concern for those who do not have the talent for superior musical performance. The message of the late President Griswold of Yale University challenges the music educator: "The arts are as powerful today as the most powerful weapons invented by the scientists . . . and you neglect them at your peril, at the peril of the country." He cited the

[3] Russell Morgan, *Music: A Living Power in Education*, Silver Burdett, 1953, p. 41.

success of performing artists and groups who traveled to Russia as additional evidence of the power of culture to "unlock doors where diplomacy cannot penetrate."

RECOGNITION OF MUSIC AS FUNCTIONAL

The Struggle for Recognition

Like many other areas of instruction, music education has had to struggle for adequate recognition leading to academic respectability. It cannot serve girls and boys and meet their varied needs until it is brought into the curriculum as a functional and regular part of the total school program. Music considered as a special subject in the curriculum or an extracurricular subject cannot make an adequate contribution to the general objectives of education.

Recognition of music as a functional part of the school program came some years ago through the National Association of Secondary-School Principals official publication, *The Bulletin*. An issue of the magazine was devoted to "The Function of Music in the Secondary-School Curriculum."[4] A sustained and expanding interest in the arts was shown in the 1961–1962 major project of the NASSP Committee on Curriculum Planning and Development, through their position paper, "The Arts in the Comprehensive Secondary School." The report supports curriculum development that would provide:

1. Recognition of each art as an academic discipline with an adequate program of course offerings to meet the diverse needs of a comprehensive student body.
2. A place for the arts in other courses such as creative writing in English, the dance in physical education, art and music in history and literature, etc.
3. Experience in performance and creative enterprise through school bands, orchestras, choral groups, plays, operettas, debates, and publications.
4. Art resources in the community and services to the community to supplement the school program. Concerts, lectures and exhibits, and art instruction through adult education are all possibilities.

This report, supporting the belief that *all* secondary-school students need experience in understanding music, the visual arts, the theater arts, the industrial arts, and home economics, calls for increased emphasis on the arts in both junior and senior high schools. The committee recognizes that art courses have traditionally been required in junior high school and recommends general courses in

[4] *The Bulletin*, National Association of Secondary-School Principals, National Education Association, November, 1952, p. 3.

all areas of the arts for all students in senior high school, plus more specialized courses for the talented. The portion of the paper devoted to music for all students follows.

MUSIC[5]

General Goals

Each student, according to his abilities and interests, should have the opportunity to:

1. Develop skills in music so he may:
   a. participate in some kind of musical performance either as an individual or as a member of a group;
   b. listen to music with understanding and enjoyment;
   c. associate the musical score with what is heard or performed;
   d. improvise and create music of his own.
2. Become an intelligent critic of jazz, folk music, popular music, parade music, and the major types of serious music.
3. Develop a sense of responsibility for exercising his critical judgment for the improvement of the musical environment of his community, including offerings on radio and television as well as live performances.
4. Recognize music as an international language and a vehicle of international goodwill.
5. Acquire such knowledge about music as: history of music, form and design of music, symbolism of the music score, the quality of tone and other characteristics of the various musical instruments and the ranges of the human voice, the combinations of instruments and voices, the role of composers in various historical periods, and the relation of music to such other disciplines as science, mathematics, and literature.
6. Understand how emotional expression as a part of normal, healthy, happy living can be enhanced by music.
7. Desire to continue some form of musical experience both in school and following graduation; for example, select and use recordings and tapes, engage in small vocal and instrumental ensemble work, and participate as performers and listeners in community musical activities.

Specialized Subjects

More advanced courses and musical activities particularly for those students with special interests and abilities should be organized. Bands, orchestras, and vocal groups with both large and small ensemble divisions at different performance levels are desirable. Small groups provide the kinds of music experiences that people more frequently have outside of school. So do listening laboratories with high quality sound reproducing equipment.

The following specialized subjects are suggested: Theory-harmony-composition; history and appreciation of music; class instruction in piano and orchestral instruments; individual listening to tapes and records.

[5] "The Arts in The Comprehensive Secondary School," *The Bulletin*, National Association of Secondary-School Principals, National Education Association, September, 1962.

INDIVIDUAL AND GROUP PERFORMANCE

The emphasis on individual and group participation in music has been the foundation of the expansion and development of music education in the secondary-school program. In recent years there has been created in some schools a situation in which group activity tends to eliminate all but the most competent from participation. It is the band, the orchestra, the choir, that counts, and the individual is of importance only as he contributes to the group.

In music education, the organization itself has great value, but its greatest value is the influence it has upon the students as individuals. To justify a significant place in the school program, music must stem from a program broad enough to serve the needs of the individual through emphasis upon the individual as well as upon the group (Fig. 1.11).

In planning music for everyone, thought must be given to the continuing benefits which may come to high-school girls and boys in their home, school, and community life. In school or out of school each child will be a producer of music, a consumer of music, or both. It is impossible in present-day living to escape music. Our aim must be to help young people to become more discriminating consumers and performers of music.

San Diego City Schools, San Diego, California.

Fig. 1.11. These young trombonists benefit individually and collectively in music class.

THE WELL-BALANCED CURRICULUM

Secondary-school music can move forward by means of a well-balanced curriculum which continues to serve the individual and the group as a part of the total school program. Music educators with vision, working cooperatively with school administrators and teachers in other areas of instruction, can further the development of the program. In the light of the educational needs of today there has never been a greater opportunity offered music education for service to youth and to music.

A flexible pattern for curriculum development based on music for all is found in the *Outline of a Program for Music Education,* published in revised form by the Music Educators National Conference in 1951. The following portions of the outline apply equally well to large and small secondary schools.

Junior-High-School Grades (7, 8, 9)

1. General Music Course. Open to all students regardless of previous musical experience. A course offering a variety of musical activities, such as playing, singing, listening, reading music, creative activity, etc.
2. Vocal Music. Boys' and girls' glee clubs, chorus or choir, small vocal ensembles, assembly singing for all students.
3. Instrumental Music. Orchestra, band, small instrumental ensembles, class instrumental instruction in wind, string, and keyboard, for beginners and more advanced students; credit for private lessons available in Grade 9.
4. Special Electives in Music. In some junior high schools there is need for special elective classes in Music Appreciation and in Music Theory, especially in Grade 9.
5. Relating and Coordinating Out-of-School Influences (Radio, Television, Motion Pictures, Church and Home) in all Ways with Those of the Classroom.

Senior-High-School Grades (10, 11, 12)

1. General Music Course. Open to all students, regardless of previous musical experience. A course similar to that described under Junior High School, but adjusted in its content to Senior High School interests and needs.
2. Vocal Music. Boys' and girls' glee clubs, chorus, choir, small vocal ensembles, voice classes, applied music credit for private lessons. Some of the large choral groups selective and others open for election by any interested student, unless the school is too small to allow for more than one group.
3. Instrumental Music. Orchestra, band, small ensembles; class instrumental instruction in wind, string, percussion and keyboard for beginning and advanced students; dance band. Orchestra and band should be divided into beginning and advanced sections, or first and second groups, if the enrollment warrants such division; applied music credit for private lessons.

4. Elective Course Offerings. Music theory, music appreciation, music history. Many high schools find it feasible to offer several years of instruction in each of these fields.[6]

Informal Music Activities

Informal music activities in the junior and senior high school which meet the purely social and recreational needs of students are unfortunately classified at times as extracurricular activities. The assumption is that such activities are extra and not quite as important or respectable in the educational program as the formal curricular activities. Yet there is reason to believe that meeting the social and recreational needs of students through an informal approach may be of equal importance to anything experienced by the pupil in the formal classroom. There are many informal approaches and activities in music. A few of them are found in the *Outline of a Program for Music Education:*

1. Assembly Programs. Music programs with singing by all the students, the appearance of school musical organizations, and appearance of outside artists and musical organizations.
2. Recitals and Concerts by Student Performers [Fig. 1.12].
3. Educational Concerts.
4. Music Clubs. Clubs devoted to those interested in certain phases of music study or related areas: Record Collectors Club, Conducting Club, Folk Dance Club, Recorder Club, etc.
5. Musical Programs in the Community.[7]

Fig. 1.12. Student performances provide both recognition and the satisfaction of musical achievement.

West Hartford Public Schools, West Hartford, Connecticut.

[6] *Outline of a Program for Music Education,* Music Educators National Conference, 1951.
[7] *Ibid.*

A PROGRAM TO MEET THE NEEDS OF ALL STUDENTS

The teacher of music in the modern secondary school must develop a sympathetic understanding of high-school students and their needs. He must be competent musically, and have an interest in music as an art and as a social and a recreational factor in living. He should recognize and accept the need for continuous curriculum planning and revision based on the needs of his particular situation and the trend of the times. He must be in sympathy with the total school program and must bring music into line with the objectives and aims of that program.

Long-Term Planning

Music for all demands the establishment of a flexible, long-term instructional program for the school and the community. It is no longer possible to achieve results with students without considering both community and school needs and resources. The creation of guideposts to instruction that will bring about continuity in the program and point toward a higher cultural level in both school and community should be the objective of secondary-school teachers of music.

Long-term planning for music instruction is essential in our modern schools. If proper teaching materials and aids, equipment, and instructional facilities are to be provided for the pupils, planning for the acquisition of these necessities must proceed in an orderly manner over a period of years. More important than planning for music and equipment is planning for curriculum development that will best serve the pupils. Curriculum planning must come first and proceed year by year with expansion or modification as indicated by the teaching situation, by the needs of the pupils, and by school and community changes.

The Community-School Concept

The community-school concept is one which provides music education with an unusual opportunity for service in bringing the school and community into a closer relationship. This concept can bring music into a position of great importance in the educational program of a community.

In the large school system functioning under the community-school concept, the music program will be based on a continuing study of the musical activities and resources of the area served by the school. It will mean that within a large city or county school system there may be considerable variation in the music curriculum developed for each of the schools of that system. While there will be a basic unity in the overall school music program, each school will be serving its students and its area in the manner which will promote the best possible carry-over of school music into community living. The music teacher, through parent-teacher and child-study groups, through church, community, and industrial organizations, can find the means of strengthening school-community relationships and extending the service of the school into the community.

The community-school concept can also be served through the school music program in the small school system. The teacher of music in the county or in the small school is familiar with community needs and can see that they are reflected in the musical development of a program of instruction that serves both the community and the school.

SUMMARY

The different phases of school music present many avenues of approach to the varied musical interests of young people. School music must reach the few gifted students, the many of average ability, and those whose interest in music has not yet been awakened.

Music provides for the student a richer life, social contacts through participation in music, good citizenship through community service, recreation, and a possible means of earning a living.

A well-balanced curriculum is a flexible pattern based on the idea of music for everyone, in the light of individual interests and abilities. Such a curriculum requires long-term planning for needed instruments and equipment, as well as provision for expansion and modification as times and situations change.

In the community-school concept, music education seeks to study the needs and resources of the area which it serves, and to meet these needs in the manner that will provide the best carry-over of school music into community life.

SUGGESTED ACTIVITIES

1. Check on summer music programs available to youth in your area. Consider opportunities offered by school systems, private organizations, colleges and universities. Report on your findings to the class.
2. Prepare a ten minute speech on "Youth and Music" to be presented to a meeting of junior-high-school parents.
3. Collect pictures and other materials for a bulletin board display showing teen-agers participating in music activities.

4. Visit a meeting of a Music Parents Club. Write a five hundred word article on its aims and achievements.
5. Interview six junior- or senior-high-school pupils playing or singing in school music organizations. Discover why they elect these organizations. Report on your findings to the class.
6. Make a list of sound motion-picture films or filmstrips presenting secondary-school pupils in musical performances. Select one for viewing by your class.
7. As a class project, prepare a set of 2 × 2 slides on any phase of music in the junior high school. Prepare and record a script explaining the slides.
8. In a three minute report tell which music activities were most meaningful to you in senior high school. Tell why they were important to you.
9. Discuss school music with a junior- and a senior-high-school principal. Report to the class on their concept of the role of school music.
10. Drop-outs are a problem facing school music teachers in the junior and senior high school. Interview a vocal and an instrumental teacher to obtain their opinions on this matter. Report to the class.
11. Study the complete report of the NASSP Committee on Curriculum Planning and Development, "The Arts in the Comprehensive Secondary School," for class discussion.

SELECTED READINGS

Benn, Oleta A., "Place of Music in a Technological World," *Music Educators Journal*, February–March, 1956, p. 62.

Britton, Allen P., "Music Education An American Specialty," *Music Educators Journal*, June–July, 1962, p. 27.

Gehrkens, Karl Wilson, "Five Decades of Music Education," *Education*, March, 1956.

Hood, Marguerite V., "Our Changing School Music Program," *Music Educators Journal*, February–March, 1962, p. 49.

Kelner, Bernard G., "The Successful Teenage Student—What Made Him That Way," *The Bulletin*, National Association of Secondary-School Principals, November, 1960, p. 39.

Logsdon, James D., "A Comprehensive Activities Program," *Music Educators Journal*, January, 1963, p. 59.

Music Educators National Conference, *The Music Curriculum in the Secondary Schools* (Frances M. Andrews, Chairman), 1959, 115 pp.

Music Educators National Conference, *Music in the Senior High School* (Wayne S. Hertz, Chairman), 1959, 112 pp.

National Association of Secondary-School Principals, "The Arts in the Comprehensive Secondary School," *The Bulletin*, September, 1962.

Weaver, James D., "The School's Role in the Cultural Renaissance," *Music Educators Journal*, November–December, 1963, p. 99.

Weigand, J. J., "Music in the Junior High School, 1900–1957," *Journal of Research in Music Education*, **IX**:(1) (Spring, 1961), 55.

Dayton Public Schools, Dayton, Ohio.

CHAPTER

2

Music in the Elementary School

THE PLACE OF MUSIC IN THE ELEMENTARY SCHOOL

"The Instructional Program in Music in the elementary grades must be viewed as the foundation for all future endeavors in music."[1] The teacher of music in the secondary school should understand, support, and promote the teaching of music to all children throughout the elementary grades. Nye and Nye maintain that "The preparation of the teacher of music should include a clear concept of the place occupied by music activities in the elementary school."[2]

The place, the goals, and the purpose of elementary-school music have never been more precisely stated than in "The Child's Bill of Rights in Music" prepared by the Council of Past Presidents of the Music Educators National Conference and adopted by the National Conference in 1950:

THE CHILD'S BILL OF RIGHTS IN MUSIC[3]

I

Every child has the right to full and free opportunity to explore and develop his capacities in the field of music in such ways as may bring him happiness and a sense of well-being; stimulate his imagination and stir his creative activities; and make him so responsive that he will cherish and seek to renew the fine feelings induced by music.

II

As his right, every child shall have the opportunity to experience music with other people so that his own enjoyment shall be heightened and he shall be led into greater appreciation of the feelings and aspirations of others.

III

As his right, every child shall have the opportunity to make music through being guided and instructed in singing, in playing at least one instrument both alone and with others, and, so far as his powers and interests permit, in composing music.

[1] O. M. Hartsell, *Teaching Music in the Elementary School: Opinion and Comment*, Association for Supervision and Curriculum Development, NEA, 1963.

[2] Robert E. Nye and Vernice T. Nye, *Music in the Elementary School* (2nd ed), Prentice-Hall, 1964.

[3] Music Educators National Conference, 1950.

IV

As his right, every child shall have opportunity to grow in musical appreciation, knowledge, and skill, through instruction equal to that given to any other subject in all the free public educational programs that may be offered to children and youth.

V

As his right, every child shall be given the opportunity to have his interest and power in music explored and developed to the end that unusual talent may be utilized for the enrichment of the individual and society.

VI

Every child has the right to such teaching as will sensitize, refine, elevate, and enlarge not only his appreciation of music, but also his whole affective nature, to the end that the high part such developed feeling may play in raising the stature of mankind may be revealed to him.

THE MUSIC ACTIVITIES OF THE GRADES

Just what are the music activities for all the children of the grades? Why are they considered to be of such importance? The music program of the kindergarten through the sixth grade in the modern school's educational offering is more than a vocal or singing experience, as it was in the early days of school music. It has developed from a vocal course of instruction with great concentration on sight-singing to a basic or general music program of activities designed to serve all the children of all the grades. It is a program of singing, listening, playing instruments including the piano, rhythmic and dance activities, reading and writing music, learning about composers and styles of composition, relating music to other learning experiences, making musical instruments, creating original songs, dances, and instrumental scores, and using music creatively in all forms of expression. The teaching of music should have continuity through a developmental program planned for the child as he proceeds through the grades (Fig. 2.1).

The long-range aim of this program is, of course, to establish a foundation for future music activities. Properly organized and maintained, it would eliminate many of the problems facing teachers of secondary-school music. The junior- and senior-high-school teachers have a practical and musical responsibility to exert their influence in support of a suitable program of elementary music activities.

The immediate and most important aims of elementary music teaching are to help the child:

1. enjoy music and develop a sensitivity to the spirit of music
2. become a better and happier individual now and in the future
3. develop a receptive attitude toward music that will remain throughout life,

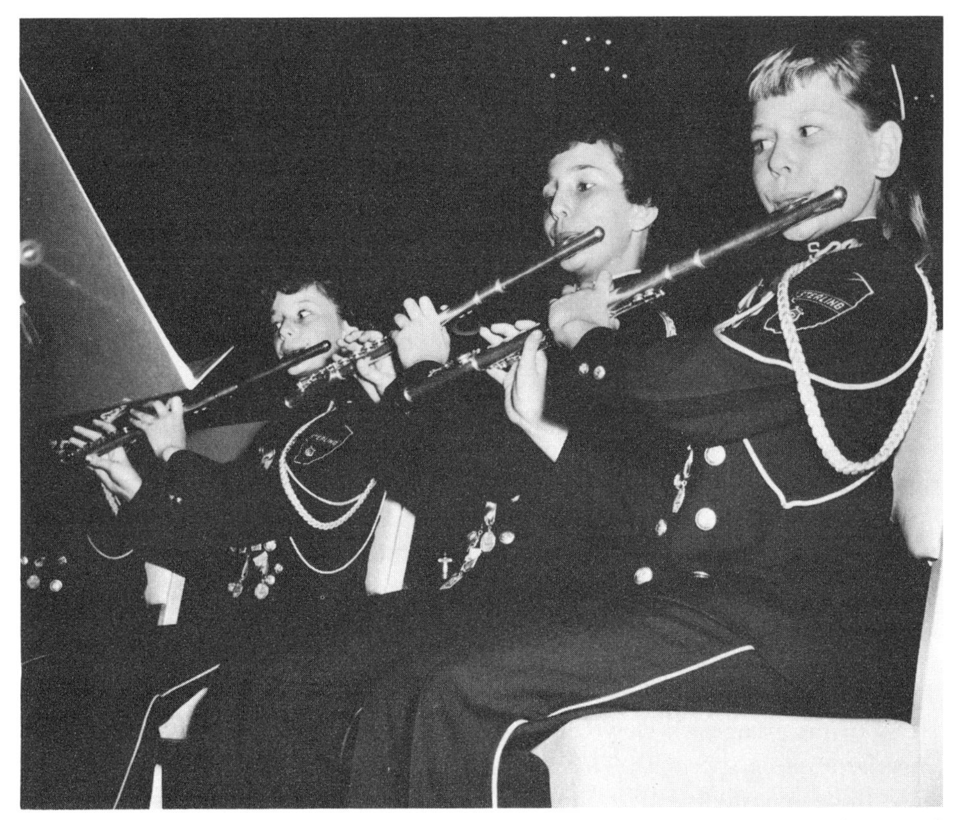

Used by permission, Music Educators National Conference, Washington, D.C.

Fig. 2.1. The children in this elementary-school band are getting an early start in instrumental experience.

an attitude that will encourage the child to make music a part of his daily living

4. develop skill, craftsmanship, knowledge, and understanding that will open the doors for continued participation and enjoyment in music

Primary Grades—The Organization of Instruction

The basic or general music of the primary grades must be viewed as the foundation for musical growth. It is without doubt the most vital part of the musical education of the child. Instruction should not be an informal, hit-or-miss affair, but should be based on a well-organized guide to music learnings developed to fit the children and the particular school situation. Progress has been made in the teaching of music to children in the early grades, but unfortunately instruction at this educational level is, in many instances, the most neglected part of the school program.

Just what can very young children accomplish musically? A large percentage of children entering school are out-of-tune singers. Through their school music they can become tune singers who sing with a good musical tone. They need help with rhythmic and simple instrument experiences, listening to music, developing music-reading readiness, and experiencing many creative activities in music. Instructional materials selected must be of interest to the child and considerate of the physical, mental, and psychological factors of child growth and development as he progresses from grade to grade. Children of the primary grades are eager for music, they react naturally to it. They have the potential for a considerable musical development if they have adequate instruction and opportunity for music in the daily school program.

Who should teach music in these grades? This is a subject of continuing controversy among music specialists. There are those who believe that the music teaching should be handled exclusively by music specialists. In some school systems this is done. There is, however, a long history of music teaching in the grades being the responsibility of the classroom teacher.

While we will not become involved in this controversy, one point must be stressed: the great need classroom teachers have for frequent and regular assistance by a music specialist. This need is urgent for primary-grade teachers who have the responsibility of starting children in their musical development. It is the duty of all music specialists to fill this need. Many classroom teachers secure excellent results in the teaching of music, but many others have had little or no music training and are unprepared for or insecure in the task.

All classroom teachers need the services the music specialist can offer through workshops, class visitations, demonstration teaching, guidance in the selection of teaching materials, etc. It is through the joint efforts of the classroom teacher and the music specialist that an effective program of instruction for the first three grades is made possible. As a result of this teamwork the children of the primary grades enjoy music and are made ready for the musical development possible in the intermediate grades.

Intermediate Grades—The Organization of Instruction

If the child and music are to be considered, it is both logical and obvious that the basic or general music teaching of grades four, five, and six must be a continuation and development of the guide to music learnings suggested for the beginning school years. Again, in those situations where the classroom teacher is responsible for the music teaching in his grade, the services of the music consultant must be freely offered and frequent and regular visitations made available. These will be focused on demonstration teaching, workshops, conferences, evaluation of materials, and other supporting activities.

From the musical standpoint the children of the primary grades should enter the upper grades with a genuine interest in and enthusiasm for music. The out-of-tune singer problem should be virtually eliminated, and rhythms, dancing, listening, and instrumental experiences should have provided a firm foundation for the potential musical growth of the children. Mentally, physically, and psychologically girls and boys are ready for concentration and significant achievement in a broad program of music teaching.

In the last years of the grades emphasis is placed on:

1. Music skills. The children become familiar with staff notation and learn to read music. They learn note and rest values, bar lines, measures, repeat signs, dynamic markings, clef signs, and time and key signatures.
2. Moving ahead in singing by expanding the song repertoire of unison and part songs. The introduction of part singing starting with simple rounds and descants and eventually leading to the use of easy basses and two- and three-part songs.
3. More extensive use of simple melody and harmony instruments such as the recorder, autoharp, ukulele, guitar, and percussion instruments. Continuing the playing of percussion scores. Use of band and orchestra instruments in the classroom. Piano keyboard experience.
4. Rhythms through creative movement, formal dances (Fig. 2.2).
5. Musical form as it becomes familiar to the child through singing, listening, rhythmic, creative, and instrumental activities.
6. Listening as a part of all experiences including particular emphasis on composers, their works and style of writing.
7. Relating music to social studies, foreign language study, science, history, and geography.
8. Preparation for and the start of instrumental instruction on orchestra and band instruments.
9. Experience in school orchestras, bands, choirs, and small vocal and instrumental ensembles.

PROBLEMS IN ELEMENTARY-SCHOOL MUSIC

School Board and School Administrators

Responsibility for the offering of the schools in a community is vested in a local school board advised and guided by school administrators. The result is that there is almost unbelievable variation in the elementary music offerings. The

Chapel Hill Public Schools, Chapel Hill, North Carolina.

Fig. 2.2. Most children love to dance. As part of the music class, the dance serves a double purpose. Both creative dancing (left) and formal dancing (bottom) are basic rhythmic experiences.

Atlanta Public Schools, Atlanta, Georgia.

academic areas of instruction fare much better under this system than do the arts. School boards and administrators have a justifiable concern for the reading, writing, and arithmetic achievement of their pupils. They feel secure and familiar with the needs of children in these subjects. It is just as true that the majority of school administrators and school board members feel insecure in making decisions regarding music instruction. All too frequently they admit that they know nothing about music and can't even carry a tune. Facts from school board sponsored surveys show clearly the need for administrators and school board members to be made aware of the value and place of music in the education of all the children of the elementary grades.

Evidence of Inadequate Music Programs

It is not uncommon in school survey reports to find that:

1. The staff of elementary music specialists is entirely inadequate to serve the needs of the classroom teachers who are expected to teach the music of their grades. In some instances a single elementary music specialist is responsible for the impossible task of serving from twenty to thirty schools. Lack of balance in the music staff is frequently uncovered. For example, one school system had one elementary music supervisor or consultant caring for the entire basic or general music program of 28 schools. The same school system had a staff of seven elementary music specialists teaching class instruments to selected groups of children.
2. No practical plan or guide to music instruction for basic or general music in the grades has been developed by the teaching staff. Music teaching through the grades is a hit-or-miss affair. In some school systems the decision as to whether or not to teach music rests with the classroom teacher, although he has no such right in regard to other subjects.
3. Many classrooms lack the minimum equipment and materials of instruction. They are in need of basic music texts, rhythm, harmony, and melody instruments and recordings.
4. The recommended minimum time allotment for music of 100 minutes per week is unknown or ignored in a number of school systems. In some instances 30 minutes a week is considered adequate for the teaching of music!
5. Class instruction on instruments of the band and orchestra is unfortunately deferred until the junior-high-school years rather than being started in the fourth or fifth grade.
6. Reports from many small communities contain no indication of a basic or general music program. These are usually one-music-teacher school systems with an instrumental teacher charged with the responsibility of developing and main-

taining a high-school band. No music instruction is offered to all the children of the grades.

7. In some school systems no music is offered until the junior- and senior-high-school years.

RELATIONSHIP OF ELEMENTARY MUSIC ACTIVITIES TO SECONDARY-SCHOOL MUSIC

What happens to children without a well-organized and well-directed program of music taught from the first day of school on through the grades? A large number of children in the upper grades will be out-of-tune singers. They will probably continue throughout life in that unfortunate classification. They certainly are not equipped to participate in the choral activities of their secondary schools or the church choirs of their communities. The children have no music reading ability, no knowledge of simple music notation. It follows that they are unable to enjoy part singing. No introduction to the masterworks of music has been theirs; music is not a part of their lives.

Perhaps the most unfortunate result of an inadequate basic or general music program is the attitude developed by the children toward music. In many cases either they are indifferent to music or they reject it. Making music a natural part of the child's world is the most important goal of elementary school music (Fig. 2.3).

While the evaluation of elementary music must not be based on what it contributes to secondary-school music, it must be recognized that failure to develop a basic program in the grades does much to impair music in the secondary school. Where there is no foundation program of music in the grades, usually it is found that general music classes in the secondary school are at a low level of achievement, teachers must devote more time to meeting discipline problems than to teaching music, and recruitment of choral groups is difficult.

Responsibility for Elementary-School Music

Whose responsibility is it to promote and support the elementary music instructional program for all the children of the grades? The answer is well stated by Hartsell, who maintains that "It is precisely because the teaching of music in the elementary school serves as a foundation that it must be the responsibility of *all* educators regardless of the titles they hold. The school administrator and members of the teaching staff can make an ideal group for initiating and maintaining a good instructional program for each of the classrooms in their schools."[4] With

[4] O. M. Hartsell, *op. cit.*

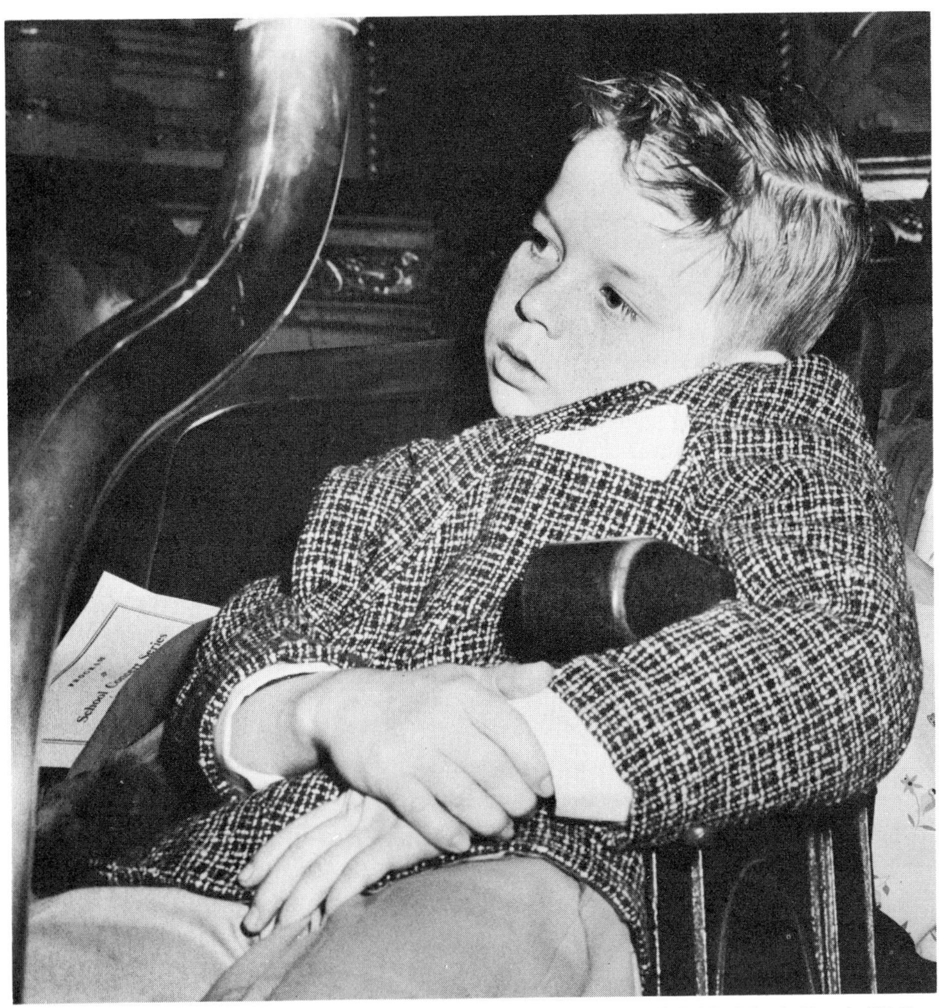

Detroit Public Schools, Detroit, Michigan.

Fig. 2.3. The School Concert Series helps make music a part of the child's world.

the best interests of children and music in mind, the secondary-school music teacher, regardless of his specialization, has the responsibility to bring the school officials and community leaders to an understanding of a good elementary music program.

A RECOMMENDED PROGRAM OF ELEMENTARY MUSIC

For many years the elementary schools of Chapel Hill, North Carolina, have had an excellent program of music. The outline of the program follows.

MUSIC PROGRAM[5]
CHAPEL HILL ELEMENTARY SCHOOLS

Our music program is planned on a broad cultural basis, with the idea of introducing children to music of many different styles in different periods of history. Listening experiences are wide in scope, presenting the music of primitive and ancient civilizations as well as medieval, classic, romantic, and modern developments. Informative materials such as stories, films and film strips, pictures and other visual aids are used to enrich the program.

The music program aims to make musical experiences a part of the child's daily living at school. A major objective is to give every child an opportunity to participate in some form of musical activity *each day*. The activity may vary according to the child's abilities, his interests and his needs, but it is directed towards his continuing growth in understanding and using music expressively.

The attainment of musical skills is the important goal towards which the following activities contribute:

1. Singing
2. Listening
3. Playing instruments [Fig. 2.4]
4. Rhythmic and dance activities
5. Reading and writing music
6. Learning about composers and styles of composition
7. Relating music to other learning experiences
8. Making musical instruments
9. Creating original songs, dances, instrumental scores and using music creatively in all forms of expression

[5] By permission of Adeline McCall, Music Supervisor in the Chapel Hill, North Carolina, Elementary Schools.

American Music Conference, Chicago, Illinois.

Fig. 2.4. Keyboard experience provides an excellent introduction to instrumental instruction.

The music program is planned with a view to continuity, increasing in levels of difficulty, from the first through the sixth grades.

Music in the Primary Grades

In the primary grades teachers schedule music as a regular part of the day's activities, along with reading, number work, physical education, library, social studies, writing, spelling, etc. The State Department Handbook for Elementary Schools emphasizes the need for a flexible program, recommending that a minimum of one hour daily be devoted to "music, art, creative individual or group work." Each teacher wisely plans how to apportion the time for the best interests of the children and the success of her music program. In most primary classrooms musical experiences occur throughout the day—in one form or another—as they fit into the general program.

BRIEF SUMMARY

First grade:
- Learn to sing on pitch, with a light, pleasant tone quality.
- Acquire a repertoire of folk songs, children's songs, Mother Goose songs for classroom singing and group sings.
- Create original songs, and make up original accompaniments with percussion and melody instruments.
- Experiment with sounds and explore instruments, such as piano, guitar, autoharp, psaltery, bells, xylophone, etc.
- Learn to handle and play percussion instruments.
- Play tunes in number notation on melody bells, xylophone.
- Listen to music to develop an understanding of: Form (AB, ABA, AABB, ABC); Dynamics (loud–soft); Tempo (fast–slow); Pitch (high–low); Type (march, waltz, lullaby).
- Composer for intensive study: Mozart.

Second grade:
- Improve sense of pitch, tone quality and diction.
- Acquire a repertoire of folk songs and children's songs for classroom singing and for group sings.
- Play instruments of the percussion and melody type.
- Observe written music to acquire reading readiness.
- Read and play scores for instruments involving use of half, quarter, eighth notes, and rests, 2/4, 3/4, 4/4 meter.
- Experience music of various styles and types through listening and body movement.
- Create songs, instrumental scores, original dances.
- Composer for intensive study: Haydn.

Third grade:
- Continue to emphasize beautiful tone quality and clear diction in singing.
- Acquire a repertoire of songs for classroom singing and for group sings; relate songs to social studies [Fig. 2.5].
- Use song books for beginning reading experiences.
- Read instrumental scores and play many songs on melody bells, psalteries, xylophones —using both number and letter notation.
- Experience music of many different styles and types through listening and body movement.

Fig. 2.5. Social studies and music are naturally related. Here third-graders explore the origin of the trumpet (left) and the horn (right) and their ancestors.

Both photographs from Dayton Public Schools, Dayton, Ohio.

Create songs, instrumental scores, original dances.
Composers for intensive study: BACH and HANDEL.

MUSIC IN THE UPPER GRADES

In the upper grades music is scheduled as a regular part of classroom activities at times which best fit into the general program. It is recommended in the State Department Handbook for Elementary Schools that the equivalent of three forty-five minute class periods weekly be allotted as a minimum. Some teachers prefer to schedule singing each day for a short time, and have longer periods at other times during the week for listening, playing instruments and rhythmic movement. Each teacher knows best, according to her individual situation, how to plan for the interests of the children and the music program.

BRIEF SUMMARY

Fourth grade:

As a foundation for two-part and three-part singing, emphasize rounds, songs with descants and easy basses.

Acquire a repertoire of folk songs, songs related to literature and social studies for classroom and group use.

Play instruments of the percussion type for continued note reading with scores of greater difficulty than those of the previous year; use autoharp chords.

Learn staff notation through playing Tonettes, recorders.

Include children who play violins or band instruments in the classroom instrumental group (write special parts).

Write, read, and play many songs for Tonettes.

Experience music of many different styles and types through listening and body movement; include music related to social studies.

Create songs, instrumental scores, original dances.

Composers for intensive study: GRIEG, BEETHOVEN, MENDELSSOHN, SCHUMANN, SCHUBERT, BRAHMS.

Fifth grade:

Continue singing rounds, two-part songs, songs with descants and easy basses; use autoharp with songs and instruments.

Acquire a repertoire of American folk songs for classroom singing, group sings, and for playing on instruments.

Play instruments of the percussion type with longer, more difficult scores.

Emphasize writing music in notebooks.

Include string, band or other wind instruments in miscellaneous classroom "orchestra" (Tonettes, recorders, bells, autoharp, psalteries, ukeleles, chord bells, etc.).

Emphasize American music of many different styles and types for listening and body movement, but include other kinds.

Create songs, instrumental scores, original dances.

Composers for intensive study: MACDOWELL, STEPHEN FOSTER, and other American composers such as AARON COPLAND, FERDE GROFÉ, LEROY ANDERSON, etc.

Sixth grade:

Continue singing rounds, two-part songs, songs with descants and easy basses; introduce three-part songs.

Acquire a repertoire of songs for classroom singing and group sings; test voices for quality, pitch, and changes.

Continue use of various kinds of instruments, as in fifth grade.

Emphasize improvement in reading; continue to write songs and instrumental scores in notebooks.

Learn simple harmony with autoharp as tool; I, IV, V, V^7.

Experience music of many different styles and types through listening and body movement; relate musical experiences to social studies.

Create songs, instrumental scores, original dances.

Composers for intensive study: RALPH VAUGHAN-WILLIAMS, ELGAR, COATES, PERCY GRAINGER, BENJAMIN BRITTEN, RIMSKY-KORSAKOV, STRAVINSKY, WAGNER, PROKOFIEV, TCHAIKOWSKY, CHOPIN, DEBUSSY, RAVEL, and other contemporary composers, exemplifying modern tonalities. Also: Music of Primitive Man, Middle Ages, Greece, Rome, Egypt.

In all grades:

1. Relate music to geography, social studies, language arts.
2. Use music with various art media—finger painting, paint, clay, etc.
3. Learn to sing simple descants to songs.
4. Play autoharp accompaniments to songs.
5. Read stories about various phases of music composers, etc.
6. Prepare for the North Carolina Symphony children's concert, and for other concerts during the year [Fig. 2.6].

Chapel Hill Public Schools, Chapel Hill, North Carolina.

Fig. 2.6. School children listen to a children's concert performed by a professional symphony orchestra.

7. Plan special musical programs for Christmas, Easter, Thanksgiving, and other holidays.
8. Share children's interests in radio and TV programs.
9. Take trips that relate to musical interests, such as to a TV studio; a music store; a band concert; a library; a museum.
10. Invite musicians to come into the classroom or into the school to play or sing for children.
11. Show films, film strips, and pictures on musical subjects.
12. Create original plays, puppet plays, dance programs based on program music, such as, for instance, "The Firebird," "The Sorcerer's Apprentice," "Coppelia," "Nutcracker Suite," "Peer Gynt Suite," "Sleeping Beauty," "The Bartered Bride," "Lohengrin," etc.

Enjoy music with your children.

SUMMARY

The teacher of music in the secondary school should understand, support, and promote the teaching of music to all children throughout the grades. This requires a basic or general music program in which the teaching of music is a planned developmental program from grade to grade. School administrators need help in understanding the place of music activities in the elementary schools—their needs, benefits, and potentialities. The classroom teacher responsible for the music teaching needs frequent help from a music specialist by means of workshops, class visitations, demonstration teaching, and guidance in the selection of materials. Curriculum development in the elementary grades provides the foundation for future musical growth.

The need for continuity in music instruction through the twelve grades has been recognized for many years by the Music Educators National Conference through its "Outline of a Program for Music Education." It is recommended as a guide in curriculum development and can be found in Chapter 20.

SUGGESTED ACTIVITIES

1. Observe music teaching in a primary grade. Report on the characteristics of the children. In what ways did the teacher show concern for child development and for music?
2. Observe music teaching in a fifth grade. Report on some of the differences observed between characteristics of primary children and those of fifth-grade children. How did the teacher provide for these differences?
3. Study a first-grade book from any of the series of texts for elementary music. What do you learn from the book that will help you in working with very young children?
4. Plan a class debate on the topic "We not only teach music—we also teach children."
5. Offer to assist with a beginning music class for elementary classroom teachers in training. Report on the musical needs of the students.
6. Make a comparative study of two series of elementary music texts. What do you consider to be the strengths and weaknesses of each?
7. Report on a recent elementary music course of study or guide to music learnings developed by a city school system.
8. Visit a series of lessons in class instrumental teaching. Report on what you learned about the recruiting, scheduling, and development of instrumental instruction.

SELECTED READINGS

Andrews, Dorothy E., "Comparative Study of Two Methods of Developing Music Listening Ability in Elementary School Children," *Journal of Research in Music Education*, Spring, 1962, p. 59.

Benn, Oleta A., "Excellence in Elementary Music Programs," *Music Educators Journal*, November–December, 1962, p. 34.

Hartsell, O. M., *Teaching Music in the Elementary School: Opinion and Comment,* Part One: "Music in the Education of Children," pp. 1–11, Association for Supervision and Curriculum Development, NEA, 1963.

Hartsell, O. M., *Teaching Music in the Elementary School: Opinion and Comment,* Part Two: "Elementary School Music: Questions, Opinions and Comments," Association for Supervision and Curriculum Development, NEA, 1963.

Hoffer, Charles R., and Catherine A. English, "The Music Specialist and the Classroom Teacher," *Music Educators Journal,* September–October, 1961, p. 45.

Leonhard, Charles, "The Place of Music in Our Elementary and Secondary Schools," *Music Educators Journal,* February–March, 1964, p. 53.

Nye, Robert E., and Vernice T. Nye, "Music and Child Development," *Music in the Elementary School* (2nd ed.), Prentice-Hall, 1964, chap. 2, pp. 14–45.

Zimmerman, George H., "Listen," *Music Educators Journal,* June–July, 1961, p. 29.

Courtesy of Standard School Broadcast, Standard Oil Company of California.

CHAPTER

3

The General Music Class

WHAT IS THE GENERAL MUSIC CLASS?

One teacher who has achieved notable success in her work with junior-high-school students describes the work in her General Music classes as school music in action. She feels that at no other level of music instruction are participation and action so important and each class so challenging to the teacher. To her, action means that each pupil has many opportunities to participate in class activities by producing music. Singing is, of course, the most natural means of musical expression and is considered by many teachers of General Music to be the heart of the program.

In her school, seventh-grade General Music classes are scheduled as required courses for two 50-minute periods a week throughout the year. There are separate General Music classes for boys and for girls. In the boys' classes there are times when singing cannot be very satisfactory. At the time we talked with this teacher she had one boys' General Music class in which no boy could sing over five tones and very few boys who could sing the same five tones together! The boys in her classes participated in and made their own music by:

1. Having keyboard experience through which they learned to play simple melodies and to chord simple accompaniments, thereby gaining an understanding of, and familiarity with musical notation.
2. Playing the autoharp as an accompaniment for whatever unison or part singing was possible with a particular class (Fig. 3.1).
3. Playing Song Flutes, recorders, and bells as a means of teaching music reading while enjoying the fun of playing tunes.
4. Playing rhythm instruments as an aid in working out rhythmic problems. They used tom-toms, maracas, claves, castanets, and tambourines (Fig. 3.2).
5. Singing in unison and in parts. Many of the arrangements for part singing were made by the teacher to fit the class situation.
6. Listening as a part of the program with recordings from the school library and recordings brought in by pupils.

Both photographs from Lansing Public Schools, Lansing, Michigan.

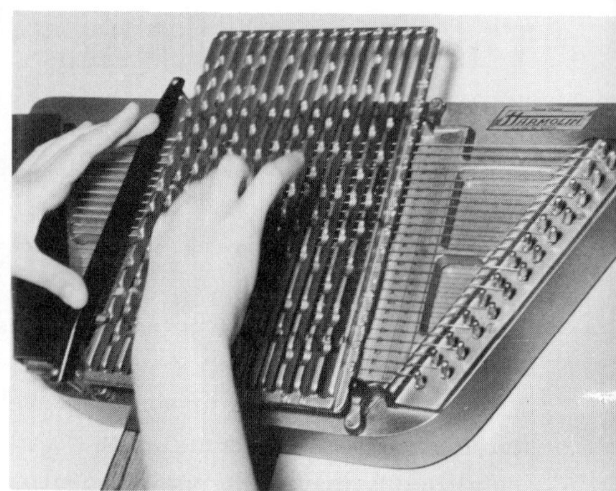

Fig. 3.1. The autoharp (left) and the Harmolin (right) provide opportunities to develop harmonic sensitivity with no previous knowledge of music.

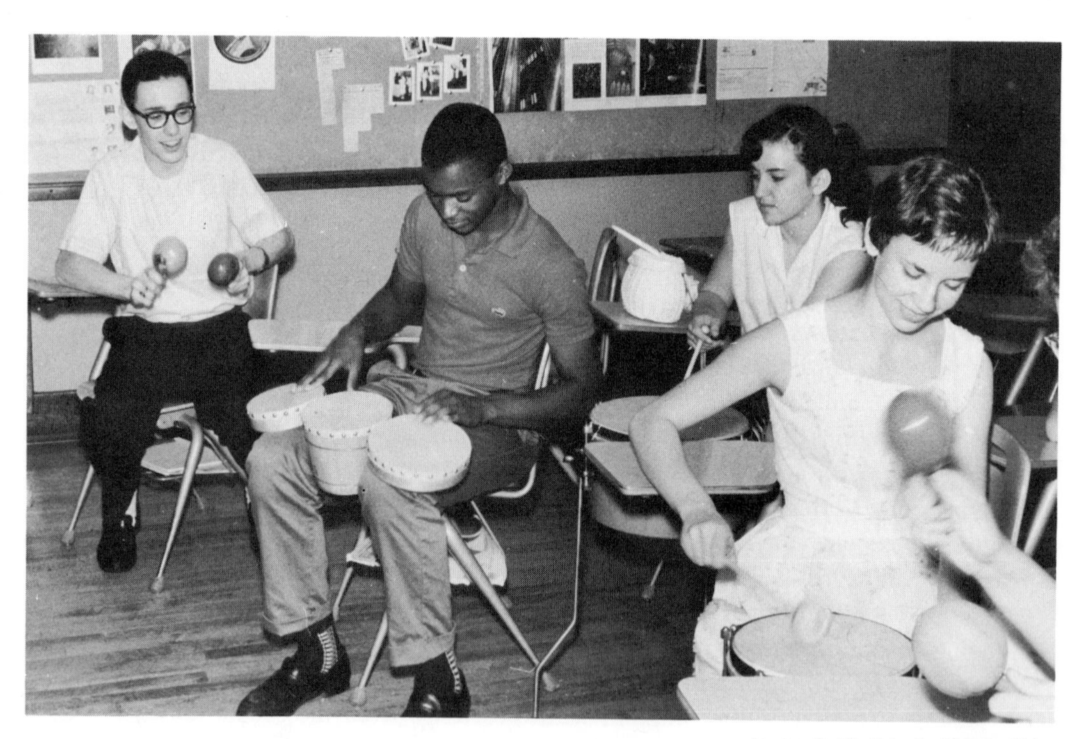

Dayton Public Schools, Dayton, Ohio.

Fig. 3.2. Rhythm instruments provide an absorbing outlet for creative expression as well as knowledge of the rudiments of music.

In working with the girls' General Music classes all of the above musical activities were used. The girls devoted more time to singing, since in their case a more satisfactory singing experience was possible. When given the opportunity by their teacher to list the General Music activities they enjoyed most, the pupils in this school rated keyboard experience above all the other activities, and the instrumental experience of playing autoharp, bells, and rhythm instruments next in order of preference.

GENERAL MUSIC IN THE SCHOOL PROGRAM

General Music as a course in the junior high school is not easily defined. We think of it as a pupil-centered program of singing, listening, rhythmic, creative, and instrumental activities with the content of the course determined by the needs and interests of the pupils enrolled in the class. General Music is the foundation of a sound music education program—the keystone upon which other music courses and activities may be based. It is founded upon a broad concept of music education for teen-agers which recognizes the importance of the orchestra, the band, the choruses, and other ensembles, but which, in addition, provides an opportunity for all pupils, regardless of their previous experience in music, to become more familiar with and receptive to music as performers and consumers (Fig. 3.3).

The junior-high-school General Music class with its variety of activities will fit into the school program by aiming at these objectives:

> . . . (a) arouse and develop interest in music, (b) give further contact with music and some experience in producing it, (c) give information about music that the well-informed person should have, (d) provide exploratory experience in singing, listening, and playing, (e) further desirable musical skills, and (f) provide opportunities to discover musical skill.
>
> There should be (a) singing of interesting songs of all classifications, songs with strong melodic or rhythmic appeal are especially desirable; (b) enough voice training to enable each pupil to use good tone quality and good diction, and to understand the possibilities in the use of his singing voice; (c) use of attractive materials and attractive illustrative materials of all kinds; (d) use of varied techniques of teaching this course, for example: demonstrations, discussions, programs by visiting artists and speakers, class concerts, and class expeditions to places of musical interest; (e) a tie-up of subject matter as far as possible with the pupils' in- and out-of-school interests such as topics or projects which interest them in social studies, English, art, and modern languages, including music they have heard and enjoyed in radio, television, concert performances, church, or motion pictures; (f) frequent use of audio-visual aids and other new teaching devices including informal instruments—melodic, harmonic and rhythmic.[1]

[1] Vanett Lawler (ed.), *The Function of Music in the Secondary-School Curriculum*, Music Educators National Conference, 1952, pp. 21–22.

Dayton Public Schools, Dayton, Ohio.

Fig. 3.3. Students in the foreground examine the xylophone and metalaphone from Germany. Such instruments as these are used by the school children in Germany and Austria for creating their own music.

Traditionally, the junior-high-school grades have been considered the place for exploratory courses. There is a justifiable trend toward maintaining exploratory courses in the senior high school. General Music is also offered in the senior high school as an elective course. It has proved a successful practice to schedule a class section for those without previous background in music. Another section offers those more interested and gifted an opportunity to do advanced work in music theory and literature. Both sections will profit by work at the piano keyboard in addition to continued exploration of some of the instruments mentioned previously. Some objectives of keyboard experience:

1. Get acquainted with the keyboard
2. Introduce students to triads in root, first, and second inversions
3. Play the triads in several keys
4. Introduce the V^7 chord
5. Help pupils select chords to accompany a song
6. Introduce the class to block-chord style, broken-chord style, and other simple types of piano accompaniment.

WHAT DOES THE GENERAL MUSIC CLASS OFFER THE PUPIL?

What the General Music class offers the teen-age girl or boy is much more easily understood if we are familiar with the characteristics of pupils at this period in their lives. Camilla Low, in her studies on child development, found that individual differences encountered at all ages exist to an exaggerated degree at the junior-high-school age.[2] A visit to a junior high school clearly reveals the variations of individuals as to weight, height, sexual maturity, and physical skills, social acceptability, emotional adjustment, intellectual and other interests (Fig. 3.4). Observation of pupils in their classes also shows that in general the junior-high-school girl is more mature than the boy the same age.

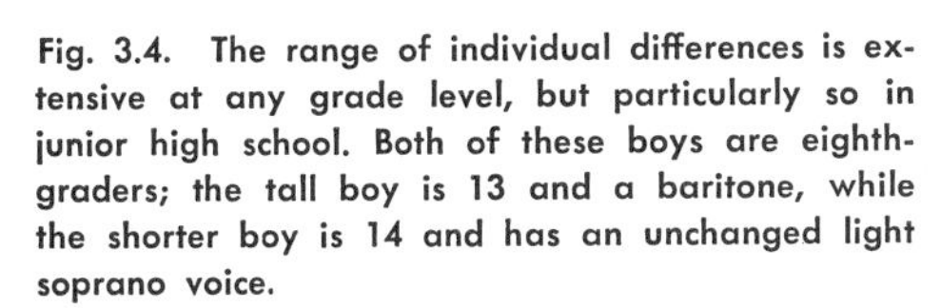

Fig. 3.4. The range of individual differences is extensive at any grade level, but particularly so in junior high school. Both of these boys are eighth-graders; the tall boy is 13 and a baritone, while the shorter boy is 14 and has an unchanged light soprano voice.

Lansing Public Schools, Lansing, Michigan.

[2] Camilla Low, "Tasting Their Teens," *NEA Journal*, September, 1953, pp. 347–349.

As we observe junior-high-school pupils it is helpful to keep in mind that there is a wide range of growth levels within each individual pupil. For example, arms and legs may be growing more rapidly than the trunk, bones more rapidly than muscles, etc. Miss Low reminds us that "wise teachers are interested, therefore, in how each pupil is growing with reference to his own particular growth pattern, rather than what his present status is as compared with others of similar chronological age."[3]

A Guided Exploratory Experience

As we face the pupils in the General Music class we find ourselves guiding a sensitive, energetic, restless group of girls and boys seeking action and variety in everything they do. The restlessness is often related to a feeling of insecurity in the junior-high-school situation with its variety of classes, new teachers and new classmates. Noticeable aggression may give evidence of overpowering anxiety. For example, when things pile up, the child strikes back at anything for relief of frustration. Or there may be a submissive or withdrawn behavior in a pupil indicating that he has a hopeless view of the situation, and therefore thinks or dreams about things more pleasant. These girls and boys are awkward and easily embarrassed and their emotions are intense.

The General Music class of the junior high school with its activity, participation, and exploration is well suited to these boys and girls. They respond readily to guidance by teachers sincerely interested in them and in music. The nature of the General Music class makes it possible for the teacher:

1. To help girls and boys be like others their own age. They rebel against anything that will make them appear to be different. For example, boys want to be seated with other boys, not among girls, even though they may still have unchanged voices. The experienced teacher mentioned at the beginning of this chapter recognizes the teen-agers' rebellious reaction to anything that might be embarrassing. You will recall that when no boy in one of her boys' General Music classes could sing over five tones she made extensive use of keyboard, instrumental, and listening experiences in which they all could participate successfully (Fig. 3.5).

2. To help these young people in their struggle for freedom from adult controls. They want to be grown up and to be recognized as individuals. They follow examples which are set. If the teacher is enthusiastic for music, some of his enthusiasm will rub off on the pupils. They respond to teacher-pupil planning, guidance rather than dictation, and they accept responsibility.

[3] *Ibid.*, p. 349.

Lansing Public Schools, Lansing, Michigan.

Fig. 3.5. Keyboard experience enables everyone to participate actively.

A Program for the Performer and the Consumer

The General Music class may be adapted to the interests and needs of both the performer and the consumer of music. It offers all pupils the chance:

1. To broaden their musical interests and to increase their understanding and appreciation of fine music and musical performance. For instance, a functional approach may be made to the mastery of the rudiments of music, which will, of course, be an aid to anyone interested in music. The opportunity is at hand to introduce girls and boys to the masterworks of music through recordings, films, and live performances by capable musicians and musical organizations. The teacher's sincerity, enthusiasm for good music, salesmanship, and the competitive instincts of pupils used as motivation will foster the musical growth of the pupils as performers and consumers of music.
2. To offer community service. Teen-agers are eager to explore and broaden their interests. The General Music class provides an opportunity to relate school and community activities.
3. To experience the pleasure and benefits of participation in vocal and instrumental music through class singing or playing, as members of small groups from within the class, or as soloists performing for or with the class. If the teacher thinks in terms of vocal and instrumental participation for all of the pupils in his General Music class, he will make use of informal recreational music and instruments as well as the piano and band and orchestra instruments.
4. To discover their musical interests, strengths, and weaknesses.
5. To recognize and make use of the leisure-time possibilities inherent in music.
6. To learn and practice audience etiquette. Class recitals, listening periods, preparation for concerts make excellent practice sessions.

Guidance Based on Achievement and Aptitude Testing

Guidance is an important function of the teacher of music. The General Music class is an advantageous center of guidance and counseling in music. Many pupils in the class may like music but have no idea what they want or should do in music. At this time, when elective subjects, speech classes, plays, athletics, and other school activities are to some extent competing for his time, the junior-high-school pupil is in need of guidance based on sound judgment. He needs exposure to the many experiences in music possible in the General Music class. He needs to have his work in music evaluated and to have the benefits of aptitude testing.

For the junior-high-school pupil this is a decision-making period. Should he continue to elect music in school? Does he have the talent in music to attain reasonable success? If so, should he elect choral or instrumental music? He is interested in instrumental music; what instrument should he play? Should he start or continue private lessons? What about music as a career? All of these questions need to be answered objectively and the consideration of them is appropriate to the General Music class. The teacher must make a particular effort to discover the talented student who should continue music study in the school organizations, elect courses in music theory and music literature, and be guided into private music study.

A good introduction to guidance in the course may be the administration to the entire class of an aptitude test such as the *Seashore Measures of Musical Talent;* Whistler and Thorpe's *Musical Aptitude Test;* Gaston's *Test of Musicality;* or the *Kwalwasser Music Talent Test.* A detailed list of aptitude and achievement tests will be found in Chapter 20.

Guidance opportunities abound in the singing, playing, and creative experiences of the class in General Music. All of these experiences produce evidence of individual interest and achievement that is useful in helping pupils to make right decisions in regard to the study of music. Exploratory opportunities with keyboard, melody, and harmony instruments, or with the instruments of the band and orchestra are interesting to girls and boys. At the same time they enable the teacher to guide the pupils intelligently.

CLASS ORGANIZATION

Class organization has much to do with the success or failure of the General Music class, particularly in the junior high school. In some schools, classes are organized to accommodate 65 to 100 pupils. In such large classes one is not likely to achieve the real values of General Music. The characteristics and the needs of junior-high-school pupils are such that organizing classes for mass handling of pupils may be detrimental rather than beneficial to them. Thirty-five pupils or less in a class is the desirable enrollment which permits the teacher to know the pupils individually and to achieve reasonable success in instructing them.

Enrolling large groups of pupils in General Music classes without regard for academic ability, musical background, talent, and interests of the individual pupils defeats the purpose of General Music. It is possible for teachers to develop academic and musical standards for sectioning of General Music classes. Ability or interest grouping is not intended to eliminate any pupil. It is intended to match learning activities to the level of the pupil, instead of trying to match the pupil to the level of the class. English, mathematics, and other areas of instruction have proved the effectiveness of ability grouping in class organization.

In a section of General Music composed of low academic achievers with little or no background, talent, or interest in music, reasonable outcomes of instruction can be achieved only by a realistic course of study based on the singing of easy unison songs, rounds, and descants and easy melody and harmony instrumental activities. The class will be geared to the potential capacity of the students. In a section composed of interested, talented, and academically capable students, considerable emphasis may be placed upon music theory, music reading, more difficult part-singing, and more demanding instrumental activities. Class sectioning is the key to improved instruction.

In the Junior High School

There is no established pattern in the scheduling or requiring of General Music in the junior high school. The classes meet from two to five periods a week and, in most schools, contain both boys and girls. There are some schools which have boys' General Music classes and girls' General Music classes. Teachers appear to agree that scheduling the class for less than two periods a week is unsatisfactory.

A plan which appears to be gaining favor is to offer General Music as a part of an exploratory program required of all pupils in one of the junior-high-school years. A typical program of this character schedules a pupil for five periods a week for nine weeks in different areas of instruction which includes General Music, Art, Home Economics, and Industrial Arts.

Should General Music be required or elective? Some schools require General Music in Grades 7, 8, and 9; others require it only in Grade 7, and others maintain the course on an elective basis. There is no right answer to this question.

Fig. 3.6. Interest in music can be developed and sustained through the changing voice period even though the youngster may not sing or play well. Simple instruments such as these are an excellent means of heightening interest.

Both photographs from Lansing Public Schools, Lansing, Michigan.

There is, however, one factor that should be considered by teachers when faced with this problem. The boy's changing voice and his natural inclination at this age to consider music "sissy" may result in a boy's dropping out of music permanently unless General Music is required for a period long enough to carry a boy through a good portion of the changing voice period (Fig. 3.6). If the class is organized on a practical basis with a realistic approach to music and to children, and is not dominated by academic or professional pressures, the interest of many boys and girls in music will be sustained and they will continue in music after junior high school. When attitudes and interests determine procedure and course content, General Music appears to make its best contribution to the individual and to the group.

In the Senior High School

Organization of the General Music class in the senior high school may have the same basis as in the junior high school, with a change in approach to instruction to accommodate the difference in age level. The class should be open to all pupils regardless of their musical background. It proves to be of value in school situations such as rural areas where large numbers of pupils enter the senior high school from elementary schools offering little or no music.

In other situations the senior-high-school General Music class places emphasis on such subject matter as music literature and music theory for more advanced, more experienced, and more interested pupils. This offering is particularly desirable in the small senior high school which may be unable to offer full elective courses in music theory or music literature.

The General Music class in both the junior and the senior high school offers unusual opportunities for a logical expansion of music education conceived in terms of all the pupils. It can very well be one of the most important contributions music education can make to raising the cultural level in our communities.

PLANNING INSTRUCTION

Planning instruction for General Music is a challenge to the teacher. Instruction in the course is on broad lines appropriate to the individual and to the group. The type of instruction and the materials which produced results last year may not be suited to the individuals or groups taking the course this year. Ideas and resources for instruction may be gathered, but planning instruction for a particular class is a developmental project for teacher and pupils together.

Many educators are now advocating required music courses in the senior high school. "The Arts in the Comprehensive High School" clearly justifies this trend toward required music beyond that traditionally offered to junior-high-school pupils.[4] The interest in a Humanities Program in both junior and senior high schools offers one possible solution. In planning instruction for General Music, here is an opportunity for the teacher or a team of teachers to experiment with new approaches involving the other arts and other subject areas. As the planning proceeds, however, the teacher must continue to be concerned with the smaller percentage of those pupils who want to increase their musical understanding and skill. The planning of instruction has as one of its goals the encouragement of these girls and boys. Another goal, and possibly the most important of all, is to meet the needs of the large group of students for whom the General Music

[4] "The Arts in the Comprehensive High School," *The Bulletin*, National Association of Secondary-School Principals, National Education Association, September, 1962.

class will be the end of formal music instruction in the schools. They are not the most gifted students, but they will be consumers of music. The goal in planning for them should be to bring them to a recognition and perception of fine music and musical performance.

Teacher-Pupil Planning

The adolescent needs to know that someone has a plan and can help him, but at the same time he responds, enthusiastically and with the will to learn, to the call for assistance in instruction-planning. General Music classes have failed in some schools because the teacher treated the boys and girls as a captive audience and imposed on them a program of instruction based only upon *his* interests in music. Objectives, units of instruction, and all phases of instruction will be more effective when they are developed by the teacher and his pupils working cooperatively. There are many ways to teach General Music, and boys and girls can offer valuable suggestions to the teacher.

As the teacher plans with his pupils, he becomes bewildered by the vast amount of material that could be included. What and how much should he teach? This is not the place for him to decide that his pupils are going to learn music fundamentals or else. It is the place to select with the pupils a few areas of music that can be handled well. If the pupils assist in the selection and are guided by the teacher they will select areas of music that are meaningful to them. In practice, teachers have found that this approach to course content is an important factor in maintaining interest and discipline. It even helps to sustain the interest in music of the less musical pupils after completion of the course.

Pupils may also bring vitality to the course by locating community and other musical resources which will serve to enrich the course content. There are many examples of local resources not known to the teacher which become available to the General Music class through teacher-pupil planning. The set of beautiful rosewood recorders that were brought to school by a boy helping to plan a "Music in the Home" unit is one of the many discoveries made by pupils working with the writer in course planning. Each teaching unit becomes alive and meaningful when its inclusion in the course and its development are experiences shared by the pupils.

Possible Units and Activities

As a help to teachers and students in planning study units, a few units are suggested here. These units are in use in schools having traditional Grades 7 and 8, and in those having departmentalized junior high schools. There is an exceptional opportunity for correlation with social studies in the production of study units when the music teacher and the social studies teacher plan coöperatively. More than musical knowledge is needed. The music teacher must be reasonably well informed about the habits, customs, and traditions of the people in the countries upon which a unit is based.

The State-Wide Junior High School Music Education Committee of Wisconsin made available to teachers units based on "Music: A World Art" as a help to seventh- and eight-grade music classes.[5] The seventh-grade units are based on Australia and New Zealand, Southern and Eastern Asia, South Africa, Latin America, and Arabia. The eighth-grade units are based on the United States, American Colonial Days, Music in the Missions, The Fight for Freedom, Westward Ho and the Gold Rush, and Modern Music.

Other teachers are working with the following units:

America at Work
America at the Concert
America Marching
America Worships
Music in Our Town
Music as a Career
The Keyboard Instruments
Musical Terms
Instruments of the Band and Orchestra
How a Composer Works
Notes and Rests
Work Songs of the Railroad
Music Is Sound
Music of Our Southland
Music That Tells a Story
Music in Our Lives
Experimenting with Band and Orchestra Instruments
Music of the People
Dance Forms in Music
Look, Listen, and Learn Music
Music of Latin America
Songs of Many Nations
Ancient Music
What Is Music?
Composers
The British Isles
Spain
France
Countries of the Middle East
Countries of the Far East
Ancient Rome and Modern Italy
Hearing and Harmonizing
Stage Music
Music in Recreation

Following are a number of class projects and activities that have been well received by pupils:

Making Instruments:
Jugs, bottles, glasses
Shepherd's pipes
Rhythm instruments
Bottle chimes (a rack from which are hung eight 8-oz. pharmaceutical bottles

[5] State Department of Public Instruction, Madison, Wisc., *Curriculum Bulletin No. 25*, 1954.

tuned to the F scale, three 12-oz. bottles tuned down to low C, and two 6-oz. bottles tuned up to high A. Exploratory uses of these chimes include finding familiar tunes, or making up short tunes and repeating them. This [project] "is one of the earliest checks as to whether a child is really hearing (imaging) what he is singing. If he cannot find the tune on the chimes, he has not connected up his ears and his singing)."[6]

Compiling Scrapbooks:
- Pictures of instruments, composers, and performers
- List of recordings
- Concert programs
- Favorite music
- Current musical events
- Cartoons, drawings, paintings about music

Charts Made by Teacher and/or Pupils:
- Songs we have learned
- Recordings we have heard
- Musical terms
- The piano keyboard
- Chord charts for autoharp
- Rhythm patterns
- The scale
- Circle of sharps and flats
- Seating plan of band and orchestra
- Our voices
- Drawings and paintings on music we have heard

Bulletin Boards:
- Flat pictures of composers, instruments, and performers
- News stories on musical events
- Cartoons about music
- Recording folders
- Lyrics of songs
- Programs
- Reproductions of paintings
- Architecture
- Book jackets
- Suggested reading
- Musical events to come
- Themes from masterworks

[6] Music Education Staff, *Growth Through Music: A Teaching Guide for Grades 1–12*, Dallas, Tex., Independent School District, 1952, p. 34.

Miniature Stage Sets

Puppets

Soap Carvings of Instruments

The Playing of Instruments:

- Autoharp (demonstration of chords, their sounds and sequences. Start simple song with two or three chord changes.)
- Ukulele; guitar (same procedure as with autoharp.)
- Keyboard experience (same procedure as with autoharp.)
- Recorder (solo or ensemble performance.)
- Shepherd's pipe
- Rhythm instruments
- Instrumental ensemble formed of class members who play

Field Trips:

- To local radio or television station
- To a church to see how an organ is constructed
- To a community symphony orchestra rehearsal

As an example of a complete unit used in Grades 7 and 8, the following is presented as a guide:

MUSIC IS SOUND[7]

General Music Unit (for Seventh or Eighth Grades)

Music is a part of the vast amount of sound we have about us all of the time. Your ears and their connection with your brain are truly remarkable, for you are able to hear many different sounds at the same time and to identify and receive meaning from each. When you drop your pencil on the desk, play a tone on the piano or talk to someone, a great many things happen all around you that you may or may not be able to see with your eyes. Through a few experiments with sound we will be able to understand the principles of sound better.

Singing

The songs for this unit were selected for their word content mainly. The songs are about sound, imitate sound, street cries, use the spoken word in combination with the singing voice, sound and echo effects. The textbooks are those widely used in the seventh grade and eighth grade.

Berg, Richard C., *et al.*, *Music for Young Americans, Book Seven*, American Book, 1961:

Above the Fields	Down By the Riverside
The Band Played On	The New River Train
Blow, Ye Winds	Patrick on the Railway

[7] Developed and used by Dr. Alice Nelson, Chairman, Music Department, Walter French Junior High School, Lansing, Michigan, and reprinted here with Dr. Nelson's permission.

The Riflemen at Bennington
Singing Is Good for You
Stodola Pumpa
Tiritomba
When Johnny Comes Marching Home
With a Roll of His Drum

Berg, Richard C., *et al., Music for Young Americans, Book Eight*, American Book, 1961:
Camptown Races
Chairs to Mend
Go, Team, Go
Grandfather's Clock
High-School Cadets
Hollahee, Hollaho
Selections from *Mikado*
La Raspa
The Street Called Straight
Tarantara
Tum-Balalayka
Vreneli

Cooper, Irving, *et al., Music in Our Life*, Silver Burdett, 1959:
The Appenzeller
The Army Goes Rolling Along
Big Corral
The Charcoal Man
Chumbara
Deep in the Heart of Texas
Dude Ranch Cowboy
Good Friends, Good Fellows!
Gospel Train
The Happy Wanderer
Holla Hi, Holla Ho!
While Strolling Through the Park

Cooper, Irving, *et al., Music in Our Times*, Silver Burdett, 1959:
Along the Navajo Trail
An Malzel
Bagpipe Chorus
Hey, Ho! Nobody Home
A Hot Time in the Old Town Tonight
Long John
O Whistle and I'll Come to You, My Lad
Once in Love with Amy
The Railroad Cars Are Coming
Timber-r-r!
Yo Ho, Ahoy
Waiting for the Robert E. Lee

Ehret, Walter, *et al., Time for Music*, Prentice-Hall, 1959:
Can't You Dance the Polka?
Fiesta
Goodbye, Old Paint
The Happy Wanderer
Hayride
Hear Our Voices Ring!
Land of the Silver Birch
The Peddler
Sambalele
The Swazi Warrior
Ta-Ra-Ra Boom-Dee-Ay!
Whistle, Mary, Whistle

Ehret, Walter, *et al., Music for Everyone*, Prentice-Hall, 1959:
Alleluia
Boola, Boola
The Church in the Wildwood
Deep in the Heart of Texas
Go, U Northwestern!
Holla-Le! Holla-Lo!
Mardi Gras
Paddy on the Railway
Spin, Spin
Timber
Troika
Whoopee Ti-Yi-Yo!

Ernst, Karl D., *et al., Birchard Music Series, Book Seven*, Summy-Birchard, 1958:
Above the Plain
Bagpiper's Carol
Caisson Song
Chiapanecas
Chick-a-Hank-a
If I Had the Wings
The Jolly Coppersmith
I'inverno è passato

Pat-a-Pan
The Peddler
The Volga Boatmen
Toviska
Walking at Night
The Weggis Dance

Ernst, Karl D., *et al.*, *Birchard Music Series, Book Eight*, Summy-Birchard, 1958:

Fum, Fum, Fum
The Happy Wanderer
Kuckuck
My Spanish Guitar
The Old Chisholm Trail
The Orchestra
La Raspe
Sacramento
The Swan Song
Vreneli
While By My Sheep
While Strolling Through the Park

Pitts, Lilla Belle, *et al.*, *Singing Juniors*, Ginn, 1961:

Angeline
Chiapanecas
Deaf Woman's Courtship
Little Tommy Tinker
The Meek Old Cow
Selections from *The Magic Flute*
The Orchestra
The Orchestra Song
La Spagnola
The Tuba and the Alto Horn
Whippoorwill
Whoo-Pee-Ti Yi Yo

Pitts, Lilla Belle, *et al.*, *Singing Teen-Agers*, Ginn, 1961:

Big Corral
Caisson Song
Cockles and Mussels
French Cathedrals
Hello! Hello!
John Brown's Baby
Johnny Schmoker
Orchestra Song
She'll be Comin' 'Round the Mountain
Sing-a-Ling-a-Ling
Song of the Bells
Sweetly Sings the Donkey

Richardson, Allen L., and Mary E. English, *Living with Music, Book I*, Witmark, 1956:

Fum, Fum, Fum
Heidelidom
I Can't Do the Sum
I Love a Parade
The Metronome
Patsy Orey-ay
The Shepherd
Strike up the Band
That's an Irish Lullaby

Richardson, Allen L., and Mary E. English, *Living with Music, Book II*, Witmark, 1956:

Calypso Band
Chiapanecas
Eddystone Light
Mi Chacra
Hey Ho! Nobody Home
Norwegian Sailors' Song
Sing a Merry Madrigal
Salomon Levi
Sumer Is Icumen In
Tamale Joe
When Yuba Plays the Rumba on the Tuba

Singleton, Ira C., and Emile H. Serposs, *Music in Our Heritage*, Silver Burdett, 1962:

Ein Ton
Laredo
Masters in This Hall
Me Gustan Todas
Night Bells
Tambourine Dance
While Strolling Through the Park

Sur, William R., *et al., This Is Music, Book 7,* Allyn and Bacon, 1963:

Coventry Carol
Ding Dong! Merrily on High
The Elfin Knight
From Ship to Shore
Herdsman's Song in Spring
How Well I Remember
I'm Going to Sing All the Way
Night Herding Song
Now Is the Month of Maying
Shanty-Man's Alphabet
The Tortilla Vendor
With the Guard on Duty Going

Sur, William R., *et al., This Is Music, Book 8,* Allyn and Bacon, 1963:

The Army Goes Rolling Along
Can't You Line It?
The Dutch Company
Echo Hymn
Han Skal Leve
I'm Going to Sing All the Way
I'm Gonna Sing
Jolly Old Roger
Nobody Home
The Oompadoodle Canon
Sing Together
When Johnny Comes Marching Home

Wolfe, Irving, *et al., Music Sounds Afar,* Follett, 1958:

Awake, You Lazy Sleeper
The Derby Ram
The Flower Peddlars
The Happy Wanderer
The Keeper
The Lone Star Trail
Nancy Lee
The Orchestra
Sourwood Mountain
Suliram
Thumbalaika
Tumba

Wolfe, Irving, *et al., Proudly We Sing,* Follett, 1958:

The Animal Fair
The Blacksmith
The Frog and the Mouse
The Little Brown Church
Pat on the Railway
The Shoemaker
Shoo Fly
Sweet Betsy from Pike
Tinker's Song
Wait for the Wagon
When Johnny Comes Marching Home
Winter Sports

RHYTHMIC ACTIVITIES

Dramatize songs. Use appropriate actions with the songs. Freely interpret songs with simple actions of hands or body movement. Use simple rhythm instruments with the songs. Substitute clapping and tapping for certain words or phrases in the songs.

AUDIOVISUAL MATERIALS

Recordings:

Adventure in Hi-Fi (RCA Victor)
Classics in Full Dimensional Sound (Capitol)
Hi-Fi Demonstration Record (Urania)
The Science of Sound (Folkways)

Compare recordings made before and after the recent developments of hi-fi.

Films:

Musical Notes (United World Films, 1951, 12 min.)

Nature of Sound (Coronet, 1956, 11 min.)
Pen Point Percussion (International Film Bureau, 1951, 7 min.)
Science in the Orchestra, Part 3: Looking at Sounds (McGraw-Hill, 1952, 10 min.)
Sound (McGraw-Hill, Junior Science Series, 1957, 13 min.)
What Is Sound? (Young America Films, 10 min.)

Creative Activities

Create sound effects to accompany the songs. These can be done with the singing and speaking voice or with the fingers, hands or feet, or by the addition of bells, pipes, xylophone, autoharp, drums, simple rhythm instruments, string bass, ukes, guitar, or instruments which the children can make.

Build instruments with definite and indefinite pitch.

Bring all types of materials and listen to the sound. Is it noise or a musical tone that is produced?

Play a game by dividing the class in half. The two groups turn their backs and take turns identifying the object that is making the sound as in a spell-down.

Organize the class as a Calypso band.

Experiments

Experiment with sound and the principles dealing with sound, to show: vibrating objects produce sound; sound travels at different speeds in different substances; our ears identify vibrations from 16 to 20,000 times in a second; some sounds cannot be heard; reflected sound is called an echo; sound is both noise and musical tone; we can produce both noise and musical tone with our vocal chords; a musical tone has pitch, dynamics, duration and quality to describe it; resonance will give a sound carrying properties; a scale can be made from flower pots, glasses or bottles with or without water. See also the section "For Those Who Are Interested."

Helpful Words

acoustics	eardrum	larynx	quality
amplitude	echo	music	resonance
duration	frequency	noise	vibration
dynamics	intensity	pitch	vocal cord (fold)

Suggested Readings

Bear, Marian E., *Sound, An Experiment Book*, Holiday House, 1952, 127 pp.
Beeler, Nelson F., *Experiments in Sound*, Crowell, 1961, 122 pp.
Brandwein, Paul F., *et al.*, *You and Science*, Harcourt, Brace, 1955, pp. 519–524.
Freeman, Ira N., *All About Sound and Ultrasonics*, Random House, 1961, 129 pp.
Kettlekamp, Larry, *The Magic of Sound*, Morrow, 1956, 64 pp.
Knight, David E., *The First Book of Sound*, Watts, 1960, 90 pp.
Leeming, Joseph, *The Real Book of Science Experiments*, Garden City Books, 1954, pp. 91–104.
Sur, William R., *et al.*, *This Is Music, Book* 8, Allyn and Bacon, pp. 38–40.

For Those Who Are Interested

Illustrate the experiments on sound in your notebook.
Discuss with a panel of classmates what music has contributed to your life and to the lives of the people who have lived before you.
Make a tape recording of various types of sounds you are able to produce with your vocal cords, those the class can produce together, and the songs found in this unit with added sound effects.
Identify and describe sound effects you have heard on TV and radio. The commercials will give you a wealth of material.
Write the instrumentation and sound effects for your songs on a score.
Test the acoustics of the school auditorium, the cafeteria and the halls and classroom.
Read further on the acoustics of music, hi-fi, and binaural and stereophonic sound.
Read on the history of pitch.
Practice producing pure tones with the stroboscope.
Set up experiments [similar to those in Fig. 3.7] to illustrate how sound travels and how the vibration rate of strings is related to their length.

The following three units have been prepared for use in General Music classes that are scheduled 35 minutes daily for a 9-week period:

MUSIC OF AMERICA

Unit for Seventh Grade[8]

Reading

McGehee, Thomasine C., and Alice D. Nelson, *People and Music,* Allyn and Bacon, 1963, pp. 375–403.
Howard, John Tasker, and George Kent Bellows, *A Short History of Music in America,* Crowell, 1957.
Stearns, Marshall W., *The Story of Jazz,* Oxford, 1956.

Songs

Sur, William R., *et al., This Is Music, Book* 7, Allyn and Bacon, 1963:

America The Beautiful (with descant)
Erie Canal–Work Song
The Sea–Edward MacDowell
Loading Bananas in Ecuador–Calypso
Maple Leaf Forever–Canada
In That Morning–Spiritual
Shanty-Man's Alphabet–Lumber song
New River Train–American Folk
America's Creed–Kelley
The Tortilla Vender–Chilean Folk
Shady Grove
Some Folks Do–Stephen Foster
John Henry–Railroad Work Song–Copland

[8] A suggested start for unit development. Explore other sources of material to develop the unit further.

Fig. 3.7. Experiments with sound waves and vibrations demonstrate practical application of scientific principles to music. Top left: a row of marbles in a channel reveal how sound waves travel; top right: vibration principles are illustrated by swinging identical weights at the ends of different lengths of string—the shorter strings will swing faster than the longer strings. These principles are applied by use of the bass viol, tuning fork, and piano (bottom).

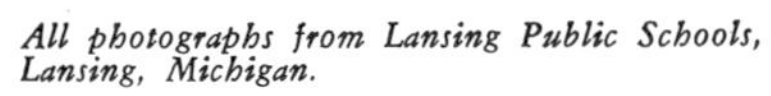
All photographs from Lansing Public Schools, Lansing, Michigan.

Mexican National Song–Mexico
You're a Grand Old Flag–Cohan
Balm in Gilead–Spiritual
Henry and Lizzie–Pennsylvania Dutch
My Gypsy Sweetheart–Victor Herbert
Chester–Billings

Listening

Adventures in a Perambulator–Carpenter
John Henry and Billy The Kid–Copland
Music of Mexico–Chavez
Rhapsody In Blue–Gershwin
Grand Canyon Suite–Grofé
Symphony No. 4, "Folksong"–Harris
Music of Victor Herbert–Herbert
Through the Looking Glass, "Suite"–Taylor
Bachianas Brasileiras No. 7–Villa-Lobos

Film Suggestions

Introduction To Jazz (International Film Bureau, 1952, b/w, 12 min.)
Appalachian Spring (Rembrandt Contemporary, 1959, b/w, 31 min.)
Folk Songs of American History (Coronet, 1959, b/w or color, 13½ min.)
Three Songs by Susan Reed (Brandon, 1954, color, 9 min.)
Music In America (McGraw-Hill, 1946, b/w, 17 min.)

Keyboard

Have some piano student describe to a nonplayer how to find middle C. The piano student should not be able to see the piano. They find this very difficult, but it is wonderful to see the expressions on the faces of students who have never before had an opportunity to press down keys. Then have nonplayer find chords.

Bulletin Boards

Display of pictures of American composers, conductors, and performers
Pictures of young Americans prominent in music
Develop a pictorial music map of the United States

Discussion Topics

What is a folk song?
The origin and development of Jazz
Listen to a composition by Copland and one by Harris. Discuss the differences you notice in their style of composition.

PLAINSONG–CHORALE–CANON–FUGUE

Unit for Grade Eight[9]

Reading

McGehee, Thomasine C., and Alice D. Nelson, *People and Music,* Allyn and Bacon, 1963.
Sur, William R., *et al., This Is Music, Book 7,* Allyn and Bacon, 1963.

Songs

Sur, William R., *et al., This Is Music, Book 8,* Allyn and Bacon, 1963.

O Come, O Come Emmanuel–Plainsong
Fugue for Voices–Niblock
Come Gracious Spirit–Chorale, Bach
From Proverbs–Canon, Niblock
Double Canon–Mozart

[9] This is a suggested start for unit development. Explore other sources of material to develop unit further.

Listening

Passacaglia and Fugue in C minor for Organ—Bach
Schola des Pères du Saint Esprit—Gregorian Chant
A Mighty Fortress—Chorale

Film Suggestions

Little Fugue in G Minor (Teaching Film Custodians, Inc., 1937, b/w, 5 min.)
Voice of a Choir (United World Films, Inc., 1952, b/w, 24 min.)

STUDY OF THE PIANO

Unit for Seventh or Eighth Grade[10]

Reading

Barr, Lawrence, *et al., You and Music, Book Two,* Prentice-Hall, 1959, pp. 47–54.
McGehee, Thomasine C., and Alice D. Nelson, *People and Music,* Allyn and Bacon, 1963, pp. 202–204, 264–265.
Sur, William R., *et al., This Is Music, Book 7,* Allyn and Bacon, 1963, pp. 126–127.
Sur, William R., *et al., This Is Music, Book 8,* Allyn and Bacon, 1963, pp. 133, 139.

Film Suggestions

Pianorama (Wurlitzer, 1956, b/w or color, 28 min.)
Piano Recital (University of Michigan TV, 1957, b/w Kinescope, 30 min.)
Artur Rubinstein (Mills, 1951, b/w, 26 min.)
Grieg: Piano Concerto in A Minor (Screen Gems, b/w, 21 min.)
The Harpsichord (Almanac, 1951, b/w, 10 min.)
Myra Hess (Contemporary, 1947, b/w, 10 min.)
Paderewski Concert (Official, 1946, b/w, 10 min.)
Vronsky and Babin (Mills, 1948, b/w, 25 min.)
Wanda Landowska (Encyclopaedia Britannica Films, Inc., 1957, b/w, 30 min.)

Discussion Topics

Vibrations
Tuning forks. Boys love this for the scientific connection
Types of pianos: spinets, uprights, grands. Sizes of grands
Care of the piano
Concert artists and careers
Change the piano sound by adding thumbtacks to the hammers, making sure it is an *old* piano. This gives a sound similar to the harpsichord.

[10] This is a suggested start for unit development. Explore other sources of material to develop unit further.

Bulletin Boards

Pictures of early instruments (cf. *People and Music, op. cit.*)
Pictures of performers (*Young Keyboard Junior*)

MATERIALS AND EQUIPMENT

Teaching materials and other aids to instruction in the General Music class need to be extensive to meet the demands of a course as varied and flexible as General Music. Adolescent pupils are interested in collecting things, and they will assist in securing flat pictures, magazine and newspaper articles, and many other items of use in class projects and activities. Teachers should acquire books, vocal and instrumental music, recordings, film strips, charts, maps, lists of available motion pictures and, in time, create a considerable amount of readily available material.

General Music in both the junior and senior high schools requires materials for use in all areas of music instruction. Lists of materials and sources of materials for use by both teachers and pupils will be found in Part II. It should be made clear that many teachers are successfully teaching General Music courses with a limited amount of equipment, but the following items are suggested as desirable:

Piano keyboard charts
Phonograph and collection of recordings
Melody and harmony instruments: autoharp, Harmolin, tuned resonator bells, recorders, Song Flutes or other end-blown flutes, ukuleles, guitars, harmonicas, ocarinas, Melodicas
Rhythm instruments: wood blocks, drums, maracas, triangles, tambourines, gongs
Band and orchestra instruments available as needed
Projectors: 2 × 2 slide, opaque, motion picture (available from school audio-visual equipment)
Recording equipment: tape recorder
Classroom bookshelf
Bulletin board
Flannel board

SUMMARY

In the General Music class, participation and activity are important. Singing is the most natural means of expression but other experiences must also be stressed, particularly with junior-high-school boys. Keyboard experience, playing of simple instruments and rhythm instruments, listening, creative music, and music fundamentals are all a part of the General Music class.

In this class the pupils are enabled to broaden their musical interests and increase their understanding of good music, participate in vocal and instrumental music, and receive guidance.

The General Music class is most successful when it is small enough for the teacher to be able to know the pupils, when the course content is based on individual needs and interests, and when the study units are planned coöperatively by the teacher and the pupils.

SUGGESTED ACTIVITIES

1. Develop a plan for introducing keyboard experience in a General Music class.
2. Make up a list of ten well-known songs suitable for Grades 7 or 8 which require not more than three chord changes on the autoharp.
3. Discuss music activities with a number of junior-high school boys taking General Music. Report to the class their reactions to various activities.
4. Examine a course schedule of a junior high school. Is there competition for the pupil's time? What guidance implications come from your investigation?
5. Make a list for class presentation of what you consider to be the strengths and weaknesses of two standardized aptitude tests and two standardized achievement tests.
6. Work out a brief outline of what you feel should be included in a senior-high-school General Music class devoted primarily to music literature and music theory.
7. Plan a class debate on the merits of teacher-pupil planning.
8. Examine several junior-high-school social studies texts and list the ways you believe correlation between music and social studies may be encouraged.
9. Divide your present class into small committees, each committee to work out in detail a unit of instruction.
10. Collect bulletin board material for use with any one of the following units: Worship Through Music, American Composers, Music, How a Composer Works.

SELECTED READINGS

Barton, Clement A., "Challenges of Teaching Music in the Secondary Schools," *Music Educators Journal,* February, 1960, p. 15.

D'Andrea, Frank, "Music and the Adolescent," *Music Educators Journal,* February–March, 1961, p. 75.

Ernst, Karl D. (Ed.), "The Report on General Music," *Music Educators Journal,* June–July, 1960, p. 21.

Gerzina, Frank J., "Listening Develops Musical Taste," *Music Educators Journal*, April–May, 1963, p. 133.

John, Robert W., "The General Music Program," *Music Educators Journal*, February–March, 1961, p. 55.

McCutcheon, Marjorie F., "Why So General About Music?" *Music Educators Journal*, September–October, 1961, p. 87.

McGehee, Thomasine C., and Alice D. Nelson, *People and Music*; Unit I: "Your World of Music," Allyn and Bacon, 1964, pp. 3–15.

Mills, Donn, "Teach Composition in Your General Music Class," *Music Educators Journal*, April–May, 1963, p. 43.

Paullin, Charlene, "Team Teaching in General Music Classes in San Diego, California," *The Bulletin*, National Association of Secondary-School Principals, January, 1962, p. 203.

Phillips, B. D., "Teaching the Large General Music Class," *Music Educators Journal*, February–March, 1964, p. 142.

Rossi, Nick, "Music Listening in the General Music Class," *Music Educators Journal*, January, 1963, p. 33.

Schnoor, Lois L., "Physics of Sound in Junior High School," *Music Educators Journal*, February, 1941, p. 27.

Weigand, J. J., "Music in the Junior High School, 1900–1957," *Journal of Research in Music Education*, **IX**:(1) (Spring, 1961), 55–62.

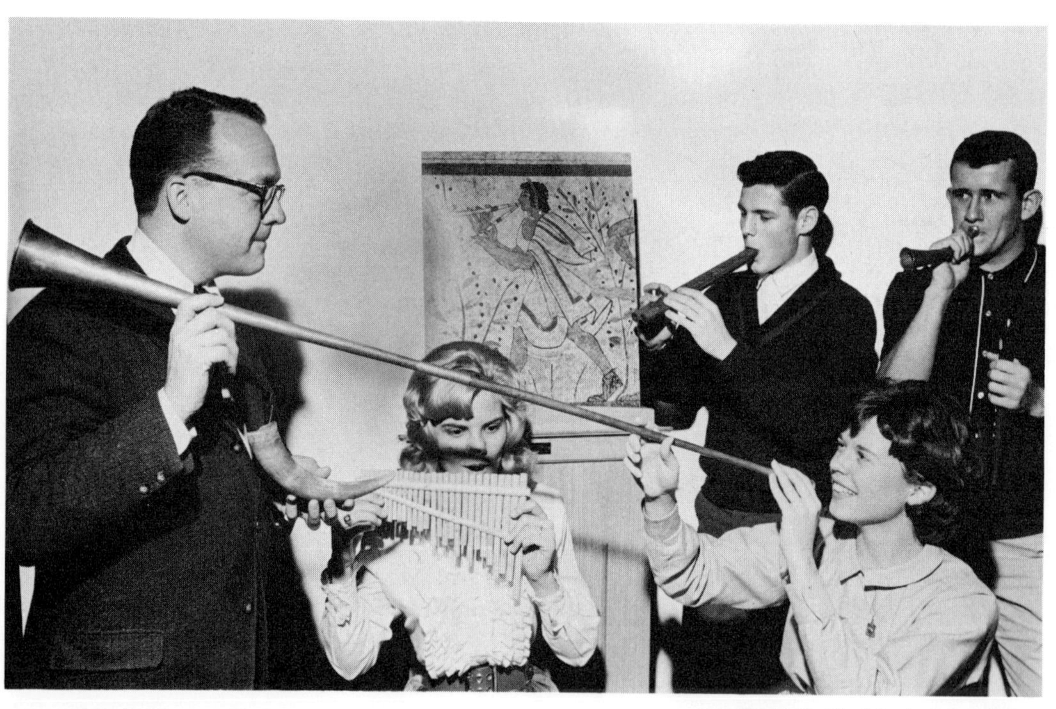

Dayton Public Schools, Dayton, Ohio.

CHAPTER

4

Regarding Music and the Humanities

THE MUSIC TEACHER AND THE HUMANITIES

A music teacher asks, "Why should high-school music teachers be concerned with the humanities? Haven't we enough to do with our sharps and flats, band shows, operettas, budgets, schedules, and equipment? Do we not have enough students in our classes playing and singing each day? It would seem that there is no time and no need to be concerned with Plato, the Age of Enlightenment, nor the impressionistic era of painting."[1]

For many years the program of study in music has been directed largely toward the development of student performers. It must be understood that the developing and continuing interest in music's place in the humanities poses no threat to this program; rather, it reinforces it. Performance skill is the foundation on which the choral and instrumental activities and organizations must rest. Any study that broadens a student's understanding of music and the other arts makes the student increasingly aware of the need for higher standards of performance on his part, individually and as a group member. This is a growing experience, not a competing one.

We have always believed in the value of music for all students, performers and consumers. Music in the humanities program not only reaches the music student and deepens his understanding of what good music is and what it takes to produce it; it draws into music the students presently not touched by the music offerings in the school. Here is an opportunity for music to become more closely related to other areas of instruction, creating a learning experience that broadens the education of all who participate in it.

There are varying patterns of instruction in humanities courses in different schools. The difficulty of securing teachers who are sufficiently qualified in all the areas of instruction has prompted the development of team teaching. The music teacher may join with teachers of art, English, history, languages, and literature to establish objectives and make up a syllabus. Enthusiasm for this

[1] Robert Pratt, "Music and the Humanities," *Michigan School Band and Orchestra Association Journal*, November, 1962, pp. 6–9.

project grows as one becomes involved in it. Teachers find that as they accept responsibility for teaching in the humanities program they develop their own knowledge of other arts to the place where they can go beyond their own area of specialization and work in other parts of the program. Many music teachers have found the humanities program a stimulating experience far beyond the fact that it is another opportunity to bring music into the lives of greater numbers of pupils (Fig. 4.1).

As the title of this chapter suggests, there are no ready-made definitions or formulas that have passed the test of time, upon which we can build today's humanities programs. Although pilot studies are under way in many elementary and secondary schools, they vary in scope and range, and are largely experimental programs which are constantly being evaluated, improved, and revised. The purpose of this writing is to support music as a part of the humanities program, and to describe briefly a few of the courses now being offered as experimental and developmental programs. From this information music teachers may get some idea of the challenge and opportunity for music to contribute to the humanities program.

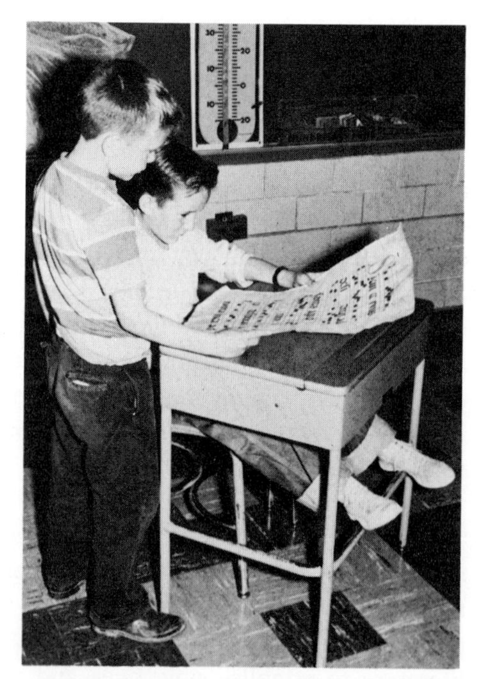

Both photographs from Dayton Public Schools, Dayton, Ohio.

Fig. 4.1. In relating history to today's culture, a high-school senior investigates the inner workings of a spinet (left), and elementary-school children examine an old church music manuscript (right).

DEFINING THE HUMANITIES

From the dictionary we learn that humanities may be: (1) Languages and literature, especially the classical Greek and Latin; and (2) the branches of learning concerned with human thought and relations as distinguished from the sciences, especially literature and philosophy, and often the fine arts, history, etc. This is a broad and all-inclusive definition obviously beyond the scope of any course which might be developed. Teachers faced with the problem have recognized the need for a definition that establishes reasonable, suitable, and manageable limitations to the program. In answering the question "What are the humanities?" Pratt states: "Basically they are the areas of history, literature, and the fine arts, taught either separately or in some combination. The humanities deal with the "why" of human existence, not so much with the "when," "where," or "how." The sciences are interested in the "why" also, but in a more quantitative way. The humanities is concerned with the "why" in a qualitative manner."[2] The defining of humanities and the scope of the program are not fixed or established. There is freedom of choice—subject to evaluation and revision—which rests with teachers establishing the course.

THE RISING INTEREST IN THE HUMANITIES PROGRAM

Interest in improving existing humanities programs and establishing new ones is impressive. Active support comes from educational leaders on the local, state, and national levels. Financial support has come from many foundations, such as the John Hay Fellows program. Workshops, institutes, and internships are being offered or organized in increasing numbers by colleges and universities to study and establish training programs for teachers who desire to qualify for teaching in the humanities. This interest is not new, and it is not the result of a demand for educational change. It comes from a long-felt need to create an educational experience which will broaden the student's horizon beyond that of traditional subject matter offerings.

In the field of music education, conference and leadership sessions and articles in professional publications have long stressed the contribution music can make to the humanities program. Teachers of music have shown a continuing interest in these sessions, recognizing the potential that the program offers. Realizing that the development of performers is the heart of the music program in our schools, an increasing number of music teachers also recognize their responsibility to the larger group of pupils who, because of other important academic

[2] *Ibid.*

interests, will never become performers. As consumers of music in the present and the future, they cannot be ignored. They should have the benefits of music in the humanities.

High standards of musical performance demand that class and rehearsal time be devoted primarily to developing musical skills to their highest possible level. In addition, the pressure of public performance leaves little time to bring students to an adequate understanding of musical form, styles of composing in the various periods, or the language of music. From the viewpoint of the music teacher, Pratt comes directly to the point in his statement: "If we want people to listen to the music we perform, we must educate them to see the expressiveness of the musical art. Too many people look upon music as the private speech of a small group of performers rather than a discipline connected with the history of man and his knowledge of himself and his world."[3]

The specialized instructional programs developed over the years are essential in the education of our young people. However, because of departmental barriers and the limitations of subject-matter concentration, these programs have not always contributed to a unified learning experience. The humanities course frees us from the traditional curriculum limitations. We are able to guide pupils in discovering and exploring the great ideas, books, and masterworks of music and art which have become a part of our cultural heritage through the centuries. Proper relationships are established between the various art forms and periods so that they may become a meaningful and enriching part of the lives of young people. We do not abandon specialization in the curriculum; we broaden experience and through the humanities program with its comprehensive approach we open the door to better living (Fig. 4.2).

HUMANITIES FOR ALL PUPILS OR FOR SELECTED PUPILS

There is no general agreement on the answer to this question. It will be noted that in some schools enrollment in the humanities course is restricted to those pupils capable of high academic achievement. In other schools the course is open to or even required of all students. Realizing the problems involved, we feel that the larger group of girls and boys who are not academically gifted have perhaps a greater need for study of the humanities than those who are highly successful academically. Certainly the student for whom the senior high school is the terminal point in his education needs consideration if we are concerned about the

[3] *Ibid.*

All photographs from Dayton Public Schools, Dayton, Ohio.

Fig. 4.2. Historic and ethnic studies are an excellent and comprehensive way of relating music to the humanities. Top left: musical bells have long been a part of our cultural heritage; top right: this double flute from Jugoslavia, with its beautiful hand-carved designs, has seven finger holes; bottom left: the bagpipes are one example of how the culture of nations is reflected in their musical instruments: bottom right: seventh-graders examine wooden shoes in a project on other countries and other times.

cultural level in this country. Offering vocational training is not enough for the people who will have fewer hours to work than the people of any previous generation.

It seems wise to think of the humanities course as being of more than one kind and serving all pupils. Literature, foreign languages, social studies, history, music, and art have a place in the education of the nonacademic achiever as well as the much smaller number of the high achievers. Not only the top 25 percent of our student body grows up, the other 75 percent grow up too; they also marry and have children, serve on school boards, vote, and by their decisions as citizens affect the development of our cities and our school programs. We cannot afford to give them less than the best we have to offer.

SOME REPRESENTATIVE HUMANITIES PROGRAMS

There is a great deal of similarity among the various humanities programs offered in the schools. There are also many differences. The objectives, although expressed in varying terms, are essentially the same: to produce future adults who have a deeper understanding of themselves and of the world they live in; who have developed an awareness of their historical and cultural heritage and a sensitivity to its aesthetic values; and who have, as a consequence, an improved critical judgment of their world and their times. There are as many different ways of reaching these goals as there are teachers, classrooms, and school systems. Subject matter varies; some courses include only the fine arts, some integrate the fine arts with literature, others add history and social studies; some programs begin with history and social studies and other phases are added to give emphasis and meaning to the original areas.

Scheduling, credits offered, team or individual teaching, prerequisites—these are matters worked out in terms of particular school situations, student abilities and interests, and teacher capabilities. As a guide and a challenge to your thinking, we offer brief summaries of ten humanities programs in progress in various parts of the country. They range from a suggested course of study for a state-wide program in the allied arts and a county-wide program in English, art, and music, to programs for large city schools, small city schools, suburban schools, and junior high schools. The programs are, for the most part, new and still in the experimental stage, constantly being evaluated and revised. More material was available for some programs than for others, but we have tried to give as clear a picture as possible of what the programs are trying to accomplish and how they are doing it.

THE ALLIED ARTS

A High-School Humanities Guide[4]

Purposes of the Course

First, the course will actively involve the student by making him aware of the artistic aspects of the world around him. Art History, valuable as a study in itself, is not a major part of this course. Music or Art Appreciation, concerned with specific works and masters in these areas, is likewise reduced in importance. Where necessary to a clear understanding of the art, both historical style and study of master works will be touched on. But the main emphasis of the course does not lie here. Instead, the concern of the Allied Arts course is largely with the *principles* of the arts and their operation in the everyday world. If the principle under investigation should be "line" the student might expect to learn about line as it operates in fashion design, in popular music, in the literature of both poets and advertising men, in cars and houses, and of course in the best examples of all of the arts as well. If "balance" is being studied, the focus will be on the role played by this principle in both the visual and the auditory arts, again with many everyday examples. The student will become actively involved because he is concerned with his own immediate world. Once it has been pointed out that his own clothes reflect artistic principles (or the lack of them) he will never be quite the same person. By contrast, one might study the arts of the Renaissance and very likely never apply the lessons learned to one's own life.

Second, the Allied Arts course must show proof of its effectiveness in some changes, responses, or new attitudes on the part of the student. The teacher will find many suggested assignments with each unit which are designed to do just this. They should not be just busywork but should challenge the student to become aware of his environment and to do something about it artistically. The sort of art, literature, or music course which allows the student to go home through a cluttered town to a tastelessly furnished home and listen to cheap music while reading a comic book—that sort of education has been largely wasted.

Third, the student's attitudes, responses, and opinions should be permanently changed if the course is to be of lasting value. For this reason, the Allied Arts should aim at improving the critical judgment of the student. This aim is not so lofty or unattainable as it might first seem. A girl who makes her first dress in home economics class has permanently improved her critical judgment of all dresses. The boy who has once taken a motor apart and reassembled it has taken a long step forward in becoming a competent judge of automobile motors. In the Allied Arts, the student will be both "taking apart" and "constructing" many of the arts, from lines of poetry and phrases of music to local building designs, statues, and paintings. Each experience will sharpen his critical judgment of how such arts are constructed. We know that a sandlot ball player can appreciate the professional game better than the non-player can because he has tried it, even though with little success. Similarly, each attempt to put the principles of the arts into practice, feeble though it may be, brings about a greater understanding and sharper critical judgment than before. And this increasing sharpness of judgment is a

[4] Reproduced from *The Allied Arts*, a High School Humanities Guide for Missouri, with the permission of the Missouri State Department of Education.

lasting effect because the student will be constantly seeing and hearing the same kinds of artistic examples as the course works with, even if he never attends a symphony concert or art gallery the rest of his life.

The Allied Arts, then, is designed to plunge the student into the great profusion of art in everyday life—to open his eyes and ears to this fascinating world, and to enable him to form his own opinions about it based on something more than "I don't know anything about art, but I know what I like."

Organization

There is nothing in this Guide about class scheduling, credits, prerequisites, etc. This is a study guide only, and may be organized in any way, to fit each individual school.

Brief Summary of Course

Unit 1. Purpose of the course
Unit 2. Subject in the arts
Unit 3. Sources of art subjects
Unit 4. Function in the arts
Unit 5. Mediums of the arts
Unit 6. Mediums of the visual arts
Unit 7. Mediums of the Time-Arts
Unit 8. Elements of the visual arts
Unit 9. Elements of music
Unit 10. Elements of literature
Unit 11. Organization in the visual arts
Unit 12. Organization in architecture
Unit 13. Form in music
Unit 14. Types of literature
Unit 15. Creativity
Unit 16. Historical styles
Unit 17. Judgment

ART—ENGLISH—MUSIC SEMINAR[5]

A Guide for a County-Wide Humanities Course

The English—Art—Music seminar is a reflection of the County Public School System's recognition of the need for providing a flexible course which will enrich a student's background and extend his intellectual horizons. This recognition and the varied cultural resources available in the Washington area created the atmosphere in which a humanities course was developed. The arts—literature, art, and music—are expressions of life, expressions alerting a student to ideas and ideals through which he becomes acquainted with intellectual and philosophical concepts. They are also a way for a student to learn a little better who he is and what he is.

The English—art—music seminar represents a team effort of three faculty members. One member teaches the academic core of the course, literature and composition; and the other members teach in the enrichment areas, one in art, and one in music. Since

[5] Arlington County Public Schools, Arlington, Virginia.

a specific aim in this program is to meet the needs of the individual student and to encourage him to work up to capacity, it was decided to use the seminar method of instruction in groups of fifteen to eighteen students.

Seminar discussions are based on broad concepts which become specific as individual masterpieces are studied. The students are reminded that great art is a reflection of the culture in which it is created and that a real appreciation of this art is based on both an understanding of culture and the way in which artists, as they create for themselves, react to forces within the culture. Since the aim is to have the students develop not only a feeling for an artistic creation but also an understanding of it, the curriculum is constructed around such broad questions as the following:

1. What is art?
2. To what extent do literature, art, and music reflect the spirit of an age?
3. What are the various approaches to or treatments of tragedy and comedy in the arts?
4. What are the enduring qualities that are inherent in classics and that account for their universal appeal?
5. When has prose been the predominant mode of literary expression?
6. When has poetry been the predominant mode of literary expression?
7. How do trends in prose and poetry relate to the art and music of the day, and in what way?
8. What conclusions can be related to the world in the twentieth century?

These questions given to the students during orientation week serve as a set of objectives for the year's work.

The seminars are organized so that the discussions structured around these objectives will stimulate independent thinking:

1. Class sessions are round-table discussions of an informal nature, the purpose of which is to foster an interest in sharing intellectual ideas.
2. Joint monthly meetings of the seminars from the three schools provide an opportunity for enrichment activities and an exchange of ideas.
3. Attendance at programs which include a variety of experiences is encouraged: The theatre, symphony, ballet, opera, and art exhibits are examples of opportunities available.

Organization

SCHEDULE

Ten periods per week two semesters. Class can be scheduled in either of two ways:

English—two periods on Mondays and Wednesdays
Art—two periods on Tuesdays
Music—two periods on Thursdays
Fridays—seminar sessions or field trips
or
English—one period on Monday, Tuesday, Wednesday, and Thursday
Art—one period on Monday and Wednesday
Music—one period on Tuesday and Thursday
Friday—both periods for seminar sessions or field trips

CREDIT

One credit for twelfth grade English, one-half credit each for art and music.

CLASS SIZE

Maximum of 25.

REQUIRED OR ELECTIVE

Elective.

PREREQUISITES

Senior standing with C or better in tenth- and eleventh-grade English.

TEACHING STAFF

One member teaches the academic core of the course, literature and composition; and the other members teach in the enrichment areas, one in art and one in music. The class is taught by more than one plan, depending on the team of teachers, with the same objective for all.

Suggested Summary for Course

September 5–October 5: Introduction
October 5–November 5: Greek
November 5–November 20: Medieval
November 22–December 22: Renaissance
January 3–February 1: 17th Century
February 1–March 1: 18th Century
March 1–April 15: 19th Century
April 15–June 15: 20th Century

FINE ARTS ADVENTURE[6]

A Fine Arts Course of Study for the High Schools of a Large City

Objectives

Broadening the student's aesthetic horizons through relating the major achievements of our cultural heritage to his experiences [Fig. 4.3].
Pointing up the interrelationship among the arts.
Developing critical evaluation of the arts in their worldly setting through directed training of the eye and the ear.
Assisting the student in developing aesthetic values which may serve as guides in his adult life.
Developing sensitivity to artistic creations in contrast to or as affected by the mechanical and utilitarian aspects of societies.
Guiding the individual person toward a greatly enriched life based on deep pleasure and life-enhancing aesthetic values.

[6] *Fine Arts Adventure*, Art and Music for Senior High School, Detroit Public Schools, Departments of Art and Music, Detroit, Michigan.

Detroit Public Schools, Detroit, Michigan.

Fig. 4.3. Mischa Mischakoff and his daughter Anne appear together with select students from the Detroit public schools on a School Concert Series program.

Organization

SCHEDULE

Class meets daily for one semester. Nine weeks for music, nine weeks for art, the first and last weeks music and art are combined.

The music group and the art group meet at the same time.

First week—orientation—the groups are combined.

For the rest of the semester they meet in two-week periods, one group studying art and the other music, then reversing.

Last week (summary)—classes again combined.

CREDIT

Two and one-half credits.

REQUIRED OR ELECTIVE

Elective.

PREREQUISITES

Academically talented eleventh- and twelfth-grade students whose intellectual and emotional capacities make it possible for them to appreciate quality music and art.

TEACHING STAFF

Two teachers from the Fine Arts Department, one from the art department, one from music.

Brief Summary of Course

AREAS OF ART

Modern Art (Post World War I: 1919 to today)
Roots of Modern Art (1880–1920)
Romantic, Neo-Gothic (1880–1900)
Gothic, Romanesque, Byzantine
Neoclassic, Classic, Renaissance
Baroque (1600–1750)

AREAS OF MUSIC

Contemporary (Post World War I: 1913 to today)
Contemporary Impressionism (1880–1920)
Romanticism (1820–1900)
Classicism (1720–1820)
Baroque (1600–1750)

BASIC CONCEPTS[7]

A Four-Year Program for a City High School

Vital education is more than an exposure to a small fraction of the courses offered in a comprehensive high school. Education at a secondary level must lay a broad, basic foundation of general knowledge. The program begins with simple Orientation. This is followed in the second year by a more difficult course in Mathematics and Science, which includes most of the areas not found in the average high school textbook. The third year is devoted entirely to backgrounds of American Civilization, to give students familiarity with the roots of our present social, economic and political problems. The fourth year is a Humanities course based largely on the Encyclopaedia Britannica Films.

Objectives

1. To place a new emphasis on education
2. To make students aware of our cultural heritage
3. To assist our students in developing a positive philosophy towards life

[7] *Basic Concepts* as a form of team teaching in Fairview High School, Dayton, Ohio.

4. To introduce our students to certain prototypes (the dictator, the politician, the reformer, etc.) and thereby assist them in recognizing the various kinds of appeals that are made by such persons
5. To develop a better understanding of and appreciation for our democratic heritage
6. To realize the importance of the social sciences and social grades in the struggle for survival (Man shall not survive by mathematics and science alone)
7. To add to the regular curriculum the "special items" and thereby enrich the educational experience of all students
8. To give all students the opportunity to hear the teachers and resource personnel who are specialists in certain areas

Organization

SCHEDULE

Four classes, one for each year, meeting one period a week on a rotating basis:
Freshman–Orientation
Sophomore–Mathematics and Science
Junior–Backgrounds and Foregrounds of American Civilization
Senior–Humanities

CLASS SIZE

Mass lectures, followed by smaller discussion groups

REQUIRED OR ELECTIVE

Required of all students
Humanities required of all seniors.

TEACHING STAFF

A member of the English department is director of the Humanities course. Special talents of all teachers are utilized, giving students the opportunity to hear teachers and resource personnel who are specialists. In addition to teachers presenting the program, other teachers who have free periods attend and help with the checking of pupil attendance. Most of the faculty are used in some area.

Brief Summary of Course

As motivational material, the guide for the course is basically a much expanded presentation of the Encyclopaedia Britannica films on the humanities which deal with the various aspects of man's search for truth as seen through three dramas: Thornton Wilder's *Our Town*, Sophocles' *Oedipus Rex*, and Shakespeare's *Hamlet*. With these twelve films the class witnessed the passing of history and the interrelation of the arts: art, architecture, drama, music, the dance, language and custom as it relates itself to mankind. (The Encyclopaedia Britannica films are listed in Chapter 22 under "Motion Picture Films.")

ENGLISH–HUMANITIES PROGRAM[8]

An English–Art–Music Program

Objectives

KNOWLEDGE

A student should gain knowledge of human behavior.

UNDERSTANDING

A student should develop an understanding of:
- Himself and others
- The natural world as revealed through the arts
- Basic moral principles intrinsic in the good life
- Creative arts
- Man's esthetic cultural heritage
- The value of free exchange of ideas and opinions in promoting harmony among groups

INTERESTS

A student should develop an interest in:
- Formulating a sound philosophy of life
- Satisfying personal needs and aspirations through the arts
- Others beyond his immediate environment
- Esthetic experiences
- Continuing his learning throughout life
- The worthwhile use of leisure time

SKILLS

A student should develop skill in:
- Critical analysis of various forms of human expression
- Various forms of communication, verbal and nonverbal democratic procedures

ABILITIES

A student should develop ability:
- To express himself in standard English
- To discriminate between what is important and what is not
- To recognize the other person's point of view
- To adjust flexibly to new situations
- To express with integrity and clarity thoughts and emotions through the arts
- In self-direction

ATTITUDES

A student should begin to develop some attitudes basic in a sound philosophy of life:
- Self acceptance
- Self-respect

[8] *English–Humanities*, Edsel Ford High School, Dearborn, Michigan.

Respect for others
Integrity
Courage
Responsibility
Sense of humor
Justice
Truth
Faith in intelligence
Creativity
Humaneness
The dignity of work

HABITS

A student should develop the habit of:
Good workmanship
Listening critically
Expressing himself effectively
Thinking critically and reflectively
Reading critically and analytically
Caring for physical and mental health

ORGANIZATION

SCHEDULE

A three-year course for all students in Grades 10, 11, 12, meeting daily:
English—three periods per week
Art—one period
Music—one period

CREDIT

Regular English credit. There are other English courses which can be taken in addition to the English-humanities course, but they may not be substituted for it.

SECTIONING OF CLASSES

Classes are grouped according to ability as determined by intelligence quotient, reading level, and past achievement.
Three groups are set up on this basis: A for the more gifted, B for the high average, and C for the average and below average.

REQUIRED OR ELECTIVE

Required for all students in Grades 10, 11, 12

TEACHING STAFF

English teachers teach the course. For the first several semesters they observe while specialists teach their art and music classes. After one or two semesters of observation, they begin to assume responsibility for all three areas—fortified by a weekly conference with the chairman of each of the other two departments.

Brief Summary of Course

TENTH GRADE

This course serves as a foundation for the next two years.
Three major goals:
To help the student toward improvement of his skills in communication
To guide him to the discovery of the function of the artist in revealing life
To aid him in understanding characteristics common to all humanity and in understanding himself as part of humanity

English
Unit 1. Enjoying vicarious experience
Unit 2. Understanding self through others
Unit 3. Understanding the human qualities of the individual
Art
The role of function in both the useful and fine arts in that it was planned to begin with the analysis of works in which the Utility factor is very important and to end with works in which the concept of function has become that of conveying ideas, emotions, or feelings. Moving from the simple to the complex, and from the known to the unknown.
Music
Tone color, rhythm, melody

ELEVENTH GRADE

Additional goals: the understanding of cause and effect relationships in human behavior and the appreciation of the democratic way of life.

English
First Semester—man's relationship to man in the American democracy as revealed through American literature
Second semester—understanding the moral and social values in man's relationships in a democratic society
Art
The graphic arts, sculpture, architecture, painting [Fig. 4.4].
Music
Understanding of the first three elements is developed further.
Teacher helps students follow and describe the accompaniment to a melody, to follow rhythms in compound meter; to become familiar with melodic structure, tonality, basic harmony, and the texture of music.

TWELFTH GRADE

In addition to communication skills and the function of the artist is the development of an understanding of the various relationships of man and his world.

English
Unit 1. Man's relationship to nature
Unit 2. Man's relationship with man

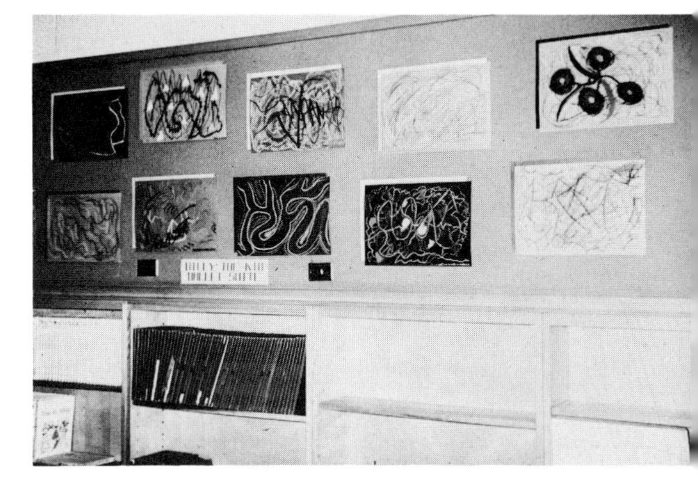

Fig. 4.4. The "Billy The Kid Ballet Suite" is illustrated by pupils in free-form impressionistic designs created while listening to the recording.

Kalamazoo Public Schools, Kalamazoo, Michigan.

Unit 3. Man's relationship with society
Unit 4. Man's relationship to a higher power

Art

A concentrated study of some of the more abstract and nonobjective art forms
A sequential study of some of the major art forms which have evolved from the year 1830 to 1930
A study of contemporary architecture

Music

In addition to further work in the four elements of music, works of music as a whole are considered in terms of structure, with emphasis being placed upon repetition and variety, and in terms of style, with emphasis on the classical, the romantic, and the modern.

The role of instrumentation and arrangement, conception of quality in performance and some concept of what music style is in terms of composer, performer, period, and nationality.

SEMINAR IN THE ARTS[9]

Art, Literature, and Music in the High School

Objectives

To show principles common to art, literature, and music
To present possibilities of the arts in everyday living
To provide tools for understanding the pertinent concepts
To introduce assorted works while giving an opportunity for thorough and complete study of certain selected examples.

[9] *Seminar in the Arts*, Parma Public Schools, Parma, Ohio.

Organization

SCHEDULE

Two semesters

CREDIT

One-half credit each semester

REQUIRED OR ELECTIVE

Elective for either one semester or two.

PREREQUISITES

Junior or senior standing. May be taken by academically talented students who are recommended by a teacher of music, art or English, or by a counselor.

TEACHING STAFF

Three teachers, one each from art, music, literature. Guest lecturers.

Brief Summary of Course

FIRST SEMESTER

Organized chronologically: Prehistoric and Egyptian art, Greek period, antiquity period, Renaissance period, Baroque period, Romantic period, impressionistic art, modern literature, contemporary composers.

SECOND SEMESTER

Offers more detailed study to acquaint students with many forms:
In literature—poetry, allegory, drama, and the novel
In art—painting, sculpture, and architecture
In music—the symphony, oratorio, opera, concerto, and sonata

A PILOT COURSE IN HUMANITIES[10]

A High-School Humanities Course

Objectives

We intend to open some doors to intellectual awareness, to awakening, to the discovery that living and thinking are conscious processes which demand perceptiveness, enthusiasm, and judgment. Charles Keller, Director of the John Hay Fellows Program, uses the phrase "demonotonization" of education to describe that experience. Thus, our

[10] *A Pilot Course in Humanities*, Ann Arbor High School, Ann Arbor, Michigan.

first and perhaps major objective is to create an educational experience that will encourage the student's sense of discovery, his pleasure in studying ideas and arts from several cultures, and that will suggest to him the possibilities of a life governed by intellectual vigor.

Humanities to us will include intellectual history, philosophy, literature, the spatial arts, and music. And our second objective will be integration of these subject matters around a political, intellectual, and moral center. We will attempt to be honest and judicious in the integrations and not integrate where such synthesis is beyond us. But, wherever relationships can be drawn which will help students to understand a philosophy, a culture, a man, an art form, we will draw them. Further, we expect that the student will relate whatever of these experiences he sees as applicable to his own life.

A third major objective is to provide the student with first-hand experience of subject matter—not descriptions about, but work with materials at first hand. Thus, he will read some philosophy, not only about philosophers, and some literature in the best translations. He will study music forms and listen to music. He will study art forms and look at art reproductions [Fig. 4.5].

A fourth objective, related to the first of intellectual stimulation, is to teach students respect for artistic forms. Men as creative beings impose form upon materials. A novelist does not use the same techniques as the writer of sonnets, nor does the sculptor render his ideas in the same ways as the painter in oils. Form is not merely a series of techniques but is a rational and imaginative ordering of ideas and techniques into an object or system that other men can perceive. This creative power is man's greatest gift and from it has come all the great physical constructions, the governments, the arts, the laws. Students not only need to be intellectually excited but to see the discipline by which the "brainstorm" becomes a philosophy or an artifact.

Dayton Public Schools, Dayton, Ohio.

Fig. 4.5. First-hand experience with subject matter can be provided by having students examine unusual instruments such as this harp.

The Humanities Committee then lists the following objectives:

1. To awaken students to the excitement inherent in human history, to show the force and vigor of thought, to "demonotonize" education
2. To present to the serious secondary student some of the significant ideas and arts in human history in primary forms
3. To give students brought up in a materialistic society the humanist viewpoint
4. To show students the value of intellectual exercise, its expression in forms, its power to increase appreciation of life
5. To present challenges to students which will bring forth a curiosity and critical judgment about the world
6. To present to a larger number of students more of the fine arts, music, etc., than are currently available in the curriculum
7. To give students who may enter rigid vocational programs in college or who may not attend college at all the beginnings of a liberal arts education
8. To give students some variety of the educational experiences which they may encounter in college life: lectures in large groups—small discussion groups—independent study, some intensive research in area of student's own interest
9. To present to the students some outstanding resource people, "experts" in fields like philosophy, cultural anthropology, logic, ethics, religion

Organization

SCHEDULE

Two semesters; two hours a day, five days a week: four hours of lectures; four hours in recitation sections of the disciplines; and two hours for the student's independent study.

CREDIT

English credit given, a separate grade determined by the English teacher.

CLASS SIZE

Ninety seniors were selected, by invitation of the teaching team and the principal. Sectioned in recitation and discussion groups.

REQUIRED OR ELECTIVE

Elective. Students may drop the course with permission.

PREREQUISITES

At least C+ academic record; one year's acceleration above grade-level norm in reading. Teaching team, before invitation, considers grades in English and history, general attitudes, and work habits of the students.

TEACHING STAFF

Six teachers—two from English, two from social studies, one from art, one from music. Guest lecturers, one from foreign language department to act as advisor on continental literature, etc., assistant teachers. The lecturer conducts recitations in his field.

Brief Summary of Course

Unit 1. Orientation to humanities study
Unit 2. Ancient civilizations and pre-Hellenic cultures
Unit 3. Greco-Roman
Unit 4. Medieval Europe
Unit 5. Renaissance
Unit 6. The seventeenth century—age of rationalism
Unit 7. The eighteenth century—the enlightenment
Unit 8. The nineteenth century
Unit 9. The twentieth century—the age of anxiety

HUMANITIES

A Humanities Course for the High Schools of Birmingham, Michigan

Objectives

To demonstrate the interrelationships of all knowledge and human expression, and to avoid segmentation of knowledge
To help students become better human beings through understanding human aspirations, questions, and forces that have shaped man's answers in each period
To explore creativity in mankind by bringing the fine arts into realistic focus
To set students on fire with interest and intellectual curiosity about the great ideas and creativity of man
To stimulate interest in ideas rather than in things as a counter-action to today's materialism
To prepare college-bound students for a humanities course in college
To enlarge the experience and horizons of the noncollege bound
To enhance the school program. An outstanding trend of today's modernization of schools, reports NEA's Press and Radio Relations Division, is adoption of high school courses in the humanities and world literature.

Organization

SCHEDULE

Two semesters; one hour a day, five days a week. Three meetings a week are lectures.

CREDIT

One credit. Class can be a substitute for English 4, or an elective, depending on the student's program requirements. It is recommended that if an eleventh-grade student substitutes the course for English, he take English 3 in twelfth grade. The committee feels that the Humanities course is an appropriate substitute for English 4.

CLASSES

Students are scheduled homogeneously in two sections of 27 students each.

REQUIRED OR ELECTIVE

Elective, open to anyone interested. Seniors and, enrollment permitting, juniors.

TEACHING STAFF

One English teacher, with art and music teachers called in for special presentations.

Brief Summary of Course

FIRST SEMESTER

Introducing and defining the humanities (establishing criteria of aesthetic judgment, developing a point of view, and establishing research techniques):
Primitive man and his folklore
Early recorded history in Sumer
The Hebraic tradition
Greece
Aristotle
The Roman conquest
Origins of Christianity

SECOND SEMESTER

The Baroque Age, its major stylistic aspects, its major figures, the changing role of the monarchy, the changing face of education
The Restoration, the Enlightenment, the major figures
The Age of Revolution, the Victorian Age, the twentieth century
In the Humanities English emphasis (substituting for English 4) is placed on language development, growth of literary style, scholarly research techniques. Evaluation papers and a major term paper required.

AN INTRODUCTION TO THE HUMANITIES[11]

Eighth-Grade Literature, Art, Music, in an Intermediate School

Objectives

An "Introduction to the Humanities" is a study of man, his ideas, and the cultural reflection of these ideas from prehistoric times to the present. We approach this through the evaluation of the historical, social, economic, religious, moral, ethical, and cultural position of man at a given period of history. Man has questioned, probed, and reflected in his search for the truth, and we have concerned ourselves with this search.

We hope that students will gain a beginning of a liberal-arts education. They should learn to do independent research and have experience with stimulating and provocative mental exercise. Since we cannot protect students from false doctrines, it is hoped that they will acquire the tools of reason with which to reject that which is false. The

[11] *An Introduction to the Humanities,* Washington Intermediate School, Bay City, Michigan.

student should gain a frame of reference with which to associate later learning, human, and cultural experiences. Finally, we hope, the student will have some basis to judge and think for himself with the help of as much of the knowledge and experience of human history as he can assimilate and appreciate.

Organization

SCHEDULE

A one-year course in eighth grade, meeting three times a week for the year.

REQUIRED OR ELECTIVE

The class is not required. Since this class has been an experiment and not formally scheduled, it can be offered to only the students who can afford to miss other classes and still maintain high scholastic achievement.

PREREQUISITES

Offered to 30 academically talented eighth-grade students.
A future class, it is hoped, will be offered to all eighth-grade students with average reading skill.

TEACHING STAFF

Three teachers: one literature teacher, one in art, one in music.
Many outside experts.

Brief Summary of Course

We begin a unit with a historical study of a particular period of time. From this we select the main ideas from the period. During the year we will have considered such ideas as rationalism, humanism, materialism, feudalism, and many others. We then consider how an idea was reflected in the various art forms of a given period.

The class will spend approximately one month on a given unit; however, this can vary depending on the historical period. Some of the units included in the syllabus are prehistory, early civilizations, Greece, Rome, and the Middle Ages.

FINE ARTS COURSE

A Fine-Arts Course for Seventh and Eighth Grades
in a Suburban Junior High School, Replacing General Music

Objectives

To fill an educational gap that apparently exists at all levels—the evident lack of knowledge, understanding, and sense of unity of that variety of aesthetic experiences and artistic creation commonly and vaguely termed the fine arts.

Organization

SCHEDULE

Two periods a week for two years, seventh and eighth grades

REQUIRED OR ELECTIVE

Required of all students, replaces the General Music course

Brief Summary of Course

SEVENTH GRADE

Music
Jazz, folk music, the basic symphonic forms
Painting
The variance of style, the idea of visual expression, the various mediums
Architecture
The general concept of line and utility, of purpose and expression
Dance
Style, technique, training, and expressive intentions
Sculpture
As in painting, an explanation of how the work was created
Literature
Teachers of English include literature of the major artistic periods as the classes reach them in the Fine Arts Course

EIGHTH GRADE

Symbolism
Opera, American musical theater
Historical survey of the fine arts from ancient Greece to the present (this unit takes half the year)

SUMMARY

The secondary-school humanities program is a challenge and an opportunity for the music teacher. It is a program that reaches out and touches students presently not participating in the traditional music program of the school. Through the humanities, both music and music teachers become more closely related to other areas of instruction, creating a learning experience that broadens the education of all who participate in it. Experimental studies by teams of teachers vary in range and scope, demanding constant evaluation and revision. There are no ready-made definitions, formulas, or programs which have passed the test of time; study and research must continue to establish the program on a sound basis. It is essential that we design humanities programs of more than one kind. There is justification for programs planned for pupils of high academic achievement and even greater justification for developing programs for those pupils classed as nonacademic achievers and for whom education terminates with high school. We have an obligation to serve *all* of the pupils.

SUGGESTED ACTIVITIES

1. Use the Encyclopaedia Britannica film, narrated by Clifton Fadiman, "The Humanities; What They Are and What They Do," as the basis of a class discussion.
2. Study a syllabus for a high-school course in the humanities. As a music teacher, report on the contribution you could make to such a course.
3. Develop an outline of projects and activities in music which you feel would be appropriate for use in the humanities program.
4. Study your college catalog and list courses outside the field of music that would help prepare you for teaching in the humanities program.
5. Report on the resources of your community which would be of use in teaching the humanities.
6. Read and give a class report on Aaron Copland's *What To Listen for in Music.*
7. Invite a composer to class for a discussion of "How a composer works."
8. Plan a class discussion on how to evaluate a course in the humanities.
9. Prepare a listening lesson for a humanities class, introducing the pupils to music in unitary, binary, and ternary form.
10. Select a 16 mm. film featuring a symphonic masterwork for class presentation. How would you prepare the class for the listening and viewing? How would you follow up this lesson?

SELECTED READINGS

Arberg, Harold W., "Music and the Humanities," *Music Educators Journal,* June–July, 1963, p. 79.
"The Arts in the Comprehensive Secondary School," *Music Educators Journal,* November, 1962, p. 25.
Block, H., "The Humanities and General Education," *The Journal of Higher Education,* December, 1954, p. 468.
Booker, Florence, "English–Art–Music Seminar," *Music Educators Journal,* November–December, 1962, p. 110.
Britton, Allen P., "Music Education in the Nineteen Sixties," *Music Educators Journal,* June, 1961, p. 23.
Ernst, Karl D., "Music in the Schools," *Music Educators Journal,* January, 1962, p. 46.

Foster, R. N., "Music in the Humanities," *Dissertation Abstracts,* **23,** Pt. 2 (November, 1959), p. 2323.

Geoghegan, William D., "A Use for the Humanities," *Liberal Education,* May, 1960, p. 197.

Hanson, Howard, "Education Must Give High Priority to the Humanities," *Musical America,* February, 1959, p. 22.

Hartshorn, W., "The Study of Music as an Academic Discipline," *Music Educators Journal,* January, 1963, p. 25.

Hood, Marguerite V., "Our Changing School Music Program," *Music Educators Journal,* February–March, 1962, p. 49.

Howerton, George, "Music As One of the Humanities," *Music Educators Journal,* September–October, 1962, p. 62.

Isenberg, Meyer, "The Emphasis on Music and the Fine Arts in General Education," *Journal of General Education,* January, 1958, p. 51.

Jarrett, James L., "Music As a Fine Art," *Music Educators Journal,* June–July, 1961, p. 27.

Kallich, Martin, "Liberal Arts for All," *School and Society,* February 15, 1958, p. 80.

Kerman, Joseph, "Music: The Case for Basic Education," *Music Educators Journal,* April, 1960, p. 43.

Kintzer, F. C., "General Education and the College Music Program," *Journal of Research in Music Education,* Spring, 1954, p. 49.

Peterson, Georgiana, and Rodney Borstad, "Integration of the Arts in the Curriculum," *Music Educators Journal,* April–May, 1964, p. 37.

Phillips, Norman, "Cultural Enrichment at the Junior High Level," *Music Educators Journal,* April–May, 1964, p. 99.

Trillingham, C. C., "Creative Arts in American Education," *Music Educators Journal,* November, 1959, p. 19.

Weaver, James D., "The Schools' Role in the Cultural Renaissance," *Music Educators Journal,* November–December, 1963, p. 99.

York, Roy J., "Humanities in the High School," *Music Educators Journal,* February, 1959, p. 44.

Tulsa Public Schools, Tulsa, Oklahoma.

CHAPTER

5

Participation in Vocal and Choral Music

Do teen-agers like to sing? Of course they do—they like all forms of music. They are full of rhythm; they dance wherever there is room to move two feet; they listen to music and they have very definite tastes in the records they listen to and buy; they sing at picnics, around the fire, at school pep sessions, and wherever they can be sure they won't be conspicuous. They are sometimes shy at this age about admitting that they can sing, but when we hear the fine work that is being done by school choral groups all over the country we know that the love of music and the love of singing is deep in their hearts and minds. It needs only a capable and understanding teacher to channel this enthusiasm and receptiveness into a familiarity with and love for good music. Youngsters like the music they know. Help them to know the worth-while music of the world.

TYPES OF CHORAL GROUPS

The choral program of the large or small junior and senior high school can bring participation in music to pupils of varying levels of interest and talent. Choirs, choruses, glee clubs, solo and small ensemble activities play a large part in bringing music to all students.

The curriculum in choral music is not the same in all junior and senior high schools. The minimum choral offering in many secondary schools is a chorus of unselected voices whose membership is based solely on a desire to sing. The ideal minimum of choral activity should include this group, but there should be a selective organization for the more gifted and interested students. Boys' and girls' glee clubs may also be offered, serving as training groups pointing toward membership in the advanced selective group, or choir (Fig. 5.1). Solo and small ensemble experiences add opportunities for the gifted. Once a teacher is established in his work, he usually has a voice in determining what the curriculum shall be. The size of the school does impose certain limitations on its choral

Arsenal Technical High School, Indianapolis, Indiana.

Fig. 5.1. Good vocal work comes from the heart as well as from the voice. Both are important for choral groups such as this.

activities but, if a good attitude toward singing in school organizations has been fostered in the elementary grades, even the smallest high school may offer a rather extensive music curriculum for all pupils.

CHORAL MUSIC IN THE JUNIOR HIGH SCHOOL

In the junior high school the scope of the choral offering is largely determined by the vocal resources at hand. If the school contains Grades 7, 8, and 9, it is possible to organize and maintain a broad program, including a well-balanced mixed chorus, glee clubs, and small ensembles.

The number of grades constituting the junior high school in a community is more or less dependent on the instructional facilities available. While the junior high school at the beginning was thought of as a school containing Grades 7, 8, and 9, there are situations in which the junior high school has only Grades 7 and 8. The type and number of choral groups possible in a junior high school are to a degree related to the age of the pupils in that school. It is more difficult, for example, to maintain a well-balanced mixed chorus in a school enrolling only pupils in Grades 7 and 8 because of the number of pupils with changing and unchanged voices (Fig. 5.2).

Fig. 5.2. What voice problems frequently face the director of a group like this seventh-grade mixed chorus?

Kansas City Public Schools, Kansas City, Missouri.

The Mixed Chorus

The junior high school which includes Grades 7, 8, and 9 can maintain a mixed chorus which adequately provides for changed, changing, and unchanged voices of both boys and girls. Securing enough boys is always a problem, but a relatively small number of boys on the baritone and tenor parts will balance the immature quality of tone produced by girls at this age.

In selecting music for the mixed chorus, consideration must be given to the range limitations of all singers. Music which imposes strenuous demands at the extremes of the vocal range is not recommended and, if used, may do harm to the voices of individuals.

The Boys' Chorus

The all-boy junior-high-school chorus or glee club can produce very satisfying results. It is an organization which boys feel is their own and they quickly give it their loyalty. No matter how well the girls sing, a choral group of boys is likely to receive a more enthusiastic audience response than one composed of girls. A well-developed boys' glee club or chorus in the junior high school does much to offset the negative attitude toward singing that many boys have at this age (Fig. 5.3). The fine boy choirs of churches and the concert world give evidence of the musical potential of these youngsters.

San Diego City Schools, San Diego, California.

Fig. 5.3. The boys' glee club has particular appeal in junior high schools. Why is this true?

As we listened recently to an all-boy choir singing a mixed chorus composition, it was obvious that they were enjoying their singing and were growing musically. The singing was beautiful. The soprano tone had the pure and brilliant quality which identifies the young male soprano voice which blends so effectively with other male voices. The lack of girls in the group was undoubtedly a help to the teacher in being realistic about the changing voice problem. The boys were classified as sopranos and altos and there was no embarrassment or sensitivity on their part. Boys unhesitatingly asked to have their voices tested when they encountered vocal difficulties.

The same boys recently presented a Gilbert and Sullivan operetta with marked success. The boys with unchanged voices carried the girls' parts in the performance effectively. The boys' interest in music and their loyalty and pride in their organization was unmistakable. This junior-high-school organization is a strong factor in retaining boys as participants in choral music through the voice-changing period and into adult life.

Krone states that "they [the boys] are especially conscious of their sudden growth, their gangling arms and legs, their awkwardness and the uncertainty of their voices. It is therefore easier to work with them by themselves in a boys' glee club. It is even easier to do an operetta in junior high school with boys taking the girls' parts, for all of the above reasons."[1]

The boys' glee club or chorus may be either an elective or a selective organization. A minimum rehearsal allotment of ninety minutes, or two periods a week, is considered essential if significant work is to be accomplished. Many junior high schools schedule glee clubs for five periods a week.

The Girls' Glee Club

Girls' glee clubs are offered on either an elective or selective basis. They are usually scheduled for from two to five periods a week with ninety minutes a week considered the minimum time allotment. The girls respond well to music and in a group of their own they are not handicapped by the vocal limitations of the boys. Experienced teachers feel that the girls' singing should be for the most part confined to unison, two- and three-part music. Four-part arrangements for junior-high-school girls tend to demand too much use of the lower tones of the alto range.

Small vocal ensembles such as duets and trios are a part of almost all junior-high-school choral programs. From both the educational and the musical standpoints the value of small-ensemble experience is unquestioned.

CHORAL MUSIC IN THE SENIOR HIGH SCHOOL

The choral activities of the senior high school may be broad in scope or may be limited to a choir or a girls' glee club. The response of senior-high-school students to choral music enables even the school with a small enrollment to offer a full program of choral activities. The extent of the choral curriculum is largely dependent upon the teacher.

In one school, the teacher has remained in the position long enough for a choral tradition to develop in the school. Students are eager to be in the choral groups. They are attracted to the organizations because of the competence, understanding, and personality of the teacher.

In another school, choral music is not attracting pupils. The teacher in this school is gifted musically but he has little interest in boys and girls and makes no effort to understand them. He has left three school systems after short terms

[1] Max T. Krone, *The Chorus and Its Conductor*, Neil A. Kjos, 1945, p. 8.

of service. Actually, he could have been successful in any of these schools had he made the effort to understand his pupils, had he realized how vital it is to interest them in music, and had he stayed long enough to achieve something of value upon which a choral tradition might be built.

The Choir Program

The choir has played a unique role in stimulating interest in choral music in the senior high schools. There is a vast amount of music of fine quality available for its use. Teen-agers' interest in choir singing is such that many high schools offer an advanced choir and one or more training choirs. A training-choir program presents the opportunity for choir participation by many students and at the same time establishes achievement levels demanded for membership in the advanced choir.

The stigma of belonging to a second or training group is lessened in schools which name their choirs. Students who would not continue in a second choir will enroll in the same organization if it is named "The Central City Singers" or some similar title.

One administrator who is friendly to school music expressed a feeling that four years' membership in a choir should mean more in terms of musical growth than learning "pieces." There is in the training-choir program the chance to insure the musical development of pupils and to place participation in the school choir on a sound educational and musical basis. Mediocrity is encouraged when only one choir, open to all students, is maintained. The choir program with one or more training choirs contributes much to the high quality of choral performance possible in senior high schools of all sizes.

Boys' and Girls' Glee Clubs

Boys' and girls' glee clubs are found in the majority of senior high schools. They may be on an elective or selective basis, depending upon the local situation, and are scheduled to rehearse from two to five periods a week. A boys' glee club is of tremendous advantage in focusing the attention of the student body and the community on choral music. A boys' vocal ensemble, large or small, has an audience appeal which is invaluable in promoting participation in the choral program. Both the boys' and the girls' glee clubs are important from the social and musical viewpoints and are capable of fine musical performance (Fig. 5.4).

Many senior-high-school music teachers feel that girls and boys should be exposed to more than one type of choral experience. They see that this is possible

West Hartford Public Schools, West Hartford, Connecticut.

Fig. 5.4. Vocal ensembles provide keen interest, challenge, and fine opportunities for advanced singers.

Arsenal Technical High School, Indianapolis, Indiana.

by scheduling the boys' glee club two days a week, such as Monday and Wednesday, and the girls' glee club two days, on Tuesday and Thursday. It is then possible to bring both groups together on Friday for mixed-chorus singing.

Small Vocal Ensembles

Solo and small vocal ensemble opportunities abound in the senior high school. In these grades, trios, quartets, and madrigal groups may function as a regular part of the choral program. In organizing these groups, the teacher seeks to bring together pupils whose voices blend and who are both willing and musically equipped for ensemble singing. While the soloists and ensemble singers need guidance from the teacher, for the most part they rehearse by themselves. Many small ensembles work well without an accompanist but it is advisable to assign an accompanist to work with these groups (Fig. 5.5).

Nicolet High School, Milwaukee, Wisconsin.

Fig. 5.5. A capable accompanist is an important factor in getting a new ensemble off to a good start.

A number of combinations of voices are possible for a madrigal group, but for a high-school ensemble we suggest a group consisting of two first sopranos, two second sopranos, two altos, two tenors, two baritones, and two basses. A group of this size and make-up fits well into the traditional seating around the table and is suited to the literature they will interpret.

Whether it be instrumental or choral music, we cannot emphasize too strongly the educational and musical contribution achieved through small-ensemble experience. The small ensemble appeals to pupils and carries school music into home and community activities. It is one of the most fruitful experiences offered to pupils participating in choral music.

Voice Class

There are a number of senior high schools which offer voice class as a regular part of the music curriculum. Typically the class is given without cost to the pupils and scheduled during the regular school hours. Teaching is done by the teacher of choral music in the school. Enrollment is on a selective basis. Auditions are scheduled for interested pupils and only those who give evidence of being talented both musically and vocally are allowed to enroll. In some schools

20 to 25 pupils must be enrolled in a class before it can be offered, but classes will of course be much smaller in a small high school. Because of the multitude of problems facing a teacher working with adolescent voices, instruction is more effective when separate classes for boys and girls can be organized.

There is a distinct advantage in the gifted young singer's being able to start vocal instruction at this period of his or her life. The voice class aims to guide the pupil in the care and development of his voice and the production and control of tone. Pupils will be concerned with correct posture for singers, breathing and diction for improved tone production, and development of the musicianship essential to good singing, stage deportment, and song presentation.

Whether or not voice class is made available to boys and girls in a school is dependent upon the competency of the teacher. The teacher should be a singer, a student of the voice, and a capable musician. In addition, the teacher must know the possibilities and the limitations of the adolescent voice. While music in the home, in the church, and in other community activities will benefit, the voice class is offered for the individual vocal development of the pupils and *does not have public performance as its primary objective!* (Fig. 5.6)

THE INITIATION AND DEVELOPMENT OF CHORAL ACTIVITIES

Whenever a teacher takes a new position it should be with the desire to strengthen the existing program, and there is always the possibility of doing so, regardless of the size of the school or the present state of the program. This is illustrated in the following example of a new teacher's work in a school with a well-established choral curriculum.

When the teacher started his work, choral music in the school was a popular activity, and a boys' glee club of 40, a girls' glee club of 60, and a mixed choral organization of 25 represented the vocal side of the school's musical life.

Fig. 5.6. Voice class offers appropriate opportunities for the talented.

Flint Public Schools, Flint, Michigan.

Five years later the boys' glee club had grown until it was necessary to divide it into a junior group of 60 and a senior group of 50 singers. The girls' glee club was sectioned into a junior club of 75 and a senior club of 50 girls. The mixed chorus become a choir of 80 members, and two new groups were functioning, a boys' quartet and a girls' double quartet. These two quartets contained the finest ensemble singers in the school.

Four levels of choral music were available to the students, and any pupil was eligible for any of these groups according to his interest and ability in music. Another advance made in the five-year period was the recognition of the choral groups as curricular rather than extracurricular activities. They were scheduled for five periods a week with the same amount of credit as that given for mathematics or any of the traditional secondary-school subjects.

Another teacher had a different experience, although she started out well. She failed to recognize the importance of understanding young people and of guiding them with enthusiasm and imagination toward the goals she had set. She started teaching in a school which did not have a strong tradition in choral music, and she was able to interest 48 boys in enrolling in a boys' glee club. This in itself was a great accomplishment. But before six weeks had elapsed, all but seven had dropped out. The reason the boys gave was very pointed and entirely justified: they wanted to sing, but most of the rehearsal time was spent on learning how to read music. The teacher was so interested in music reading that she lost sight of the boys' reason for being there—their desire to sing. Music reading is part of choral music teaching but it should not dominate the program. A rote-note approach to the learning of song material would have brought the boys gradually to the place where they could see the need for music reading and they would have remained enthusiastic singers. These 48 boys will probably never voluntarily enroll in another choral music class. For them, a poor teacher proved to be worse than no teacher. They had expected music to be fun; now they felt that it wasn't.

Whether it is a junior or a senior high school, the initiation and development of choral activities is basically the same. In some junior high schools, choral music is required for as short a period as one semester to as long as three years. In other schools, all choral music is treated on an elective basis. Some senior high schools require a minimum amount of choral music, but usually it is elective.

Promoting Student Interest

What response is the teacher likely to get in recruiting singers? Girls readily respond to choral activities. A great deal more of the teacher's attention and effort is required to overcome the boys' idea that singing is sissy, but it must

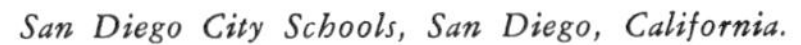
San Diego City Schools, San Diego, California.

3M Company, St. Paul, Minnesota.

Lansing Public Schools, Lansing, Michigan.

Fig. 5.7. Good and well-presented work is in itself a stimulus to increased participation. Top left: selected high school choir; top right: a dress rehearsal recording session of an operetta; bottom: a Madrigal Choir.

be done if enough boys are to be secured to fill out the bass and tenor parts of the mixed chorus or boys' glee club (Fig. 5.7).

The successful teacher promotes his program in many ways, and the first and most important way is to be sincerely interested in pupils, both in the field of music and in other school activities. In addition, the choral activities must be frequently brought to the attention of the entire student body. Bulletin boards can feature choral activities in the school, in other schools, professional and community group performances, and church choir presentations; displays should be arranged with student cooperation and assistance. Pupils interested in journalism and story-writing may prepare stories about the choral groups for the school paper. Every opportunity for the choral groups to perform at school assemblies or community functions can be used to advantage. Teachers who are able to interest ever increasing numbers of pupils in choral participation do not just assume that all the students know what the choral program can mean to them. Well-planned and constant promotion of the program is a part of their work.

How well does the choral group look when it appears in public? This factor is important from the standpoint of student interest and of audience reaction in general. The day has passed when it was possible to line up a group of children on a bare stage and know that people would listen to them and enjoy them, regardless of how they looked. Youngsters and adults alike have seen enough well-produced television shows to be very conscious of the visual side of public performance, and they are inclined to be critical of carelessness in this respect. This does not imply that elaborate robes, lighting, or stage sets are necessary, but a reasonable degree of showmanship combined with a pleasing performance will bring a favorable reaction from the students in any school. The members themselves are a source of many ideas which can be used in dressing up the stage. Art and drama teachers are usually willing to make suggestions and help in producing a simple but attractive stage set.

A high quality of self-expression is perhaps the strongest motivating force for choral activities. Emphasis placed on fine performance of good music develops a loyalty and respect which makes for a strong and continued interest in school music. Where programs have been selected with care and where pupils and teachers have spared no efforts to make performances outstanding, an interest in singing is likely to spread throughout the school.

Enrolling the Needed Boys

How can the teacher get the boys that are needed for the mixed chorus and the male chorus? The teacher who interests boys in singing is first of all interested in boys and their activities. Athletics mean a great deal to most teen-age boys, and the teacher's interest in athletic activities and his attendance at games brings him into contact with many boys who have never enrolled in choral music. Getting to know the boys by attending a football or basketball practice session is half the battle.

In a school where each teacher was asked to be a club advisor, one music teacher made it a point never to be an advisor for the Music Club. Advising a club such as the Boosters' Club or the Photographic Club made possible many contacts with boys not enrolled in music and proved helpful in bringing the boys into the choral groups. The teacher did not campaign to secure more boys in these club meetings, but the boys became acquainted with the teacher and liked him and decided to elect choral music. Another choral teacher put on an all-boy Variety Show each year. Any boy in the school was urged to try out for the show. Many new boys did, and the result was a substantial increase in enrollment in music classes (Fig. 5.8).

The members of the choral groups can do much to increase the enrollment of boys in the classes. Where good use is made of pupil-teacher planning and where students share the responsibility for the organization, they will be effective recruiters.

John Merrill,[2] whose boys' glee club in a medium-sized high school grew in one year from 15 curious and somewhat disinterested boys to a stimulating glee club of 60 members, always makes it a point to know boys and determine their interests. Just as the salesman knows his product and selects a correct approach to the customer, Merrill feels that one must study the boy, recognize his interests, and offer him something to meet his needs. He had the usual experience of having a small turnout after the first call for boys. As is his practice in first meetings with boys, he started them out singing one or two easy songs. His

San Diego City Schools, San Diego, California.

Fig. 5.8. High school boys can be interested in singing, as illustrated in this all-male chorus.

[2] John Merrill, "The High School Boy and the Male Chorus," unpublished research problem, Michigan State University, 1948.

enthusiasm for singing was contagious and the boys readily agreed to help him interest other boys in singing. Together they mapped out an active recruiting campaign, complete with posters proclaiming, "We Don't Care If You Can't Carry a Tune in a Bucket, Join The Male Chorus," and "If You Like to Sing in the Bathtub, Join The Male Chorus." These and other slogan posters did attract boys and insured a good supply of male singers for the choral groups.

Sometimes the appearance of a boy's quartet or a faculty men's quartet at an assembly will bring about an immediate response to the call for singers. The quartet should be uniformly dressed if possible. Of course, if the teacher is fortunate enough to secure some athletes for the quartet, the impact on the boys in the audience is much greater and the idea that singing is for girls is quickly dispelled. The author will never forget the prestige music enjoyed in one high school where the football coach had a magnificent bass voice and on Sundays directed one of the finest church choirs in the city. The boys in that school never considered singing sissy! Cooperation from other faculty members, homeroom teachers, and administrators is always helpful in interesting boys in singing.

Once boys enroll, it is necessary to let them sing music that interests them, and to impress upon them the fact that they need not be gifted singers. As soon as they learn one or two easy numbers, getting them before an audience is important in sustaining their interest. Boys at this age are more concerned with immediate results than long-range objectives. Many of the strongest boy singers we know had to be "high-pressured" into boys' chorus and eventually were able to qualify for advanced choir work.

THE ADOLESCENT VOICE

The choral teacher in the junior and senior high school must become thoroughly familiar with the voices of adolescent girls and boys. For proper classification and use of the voice, and for proper vocal development, the teacher must

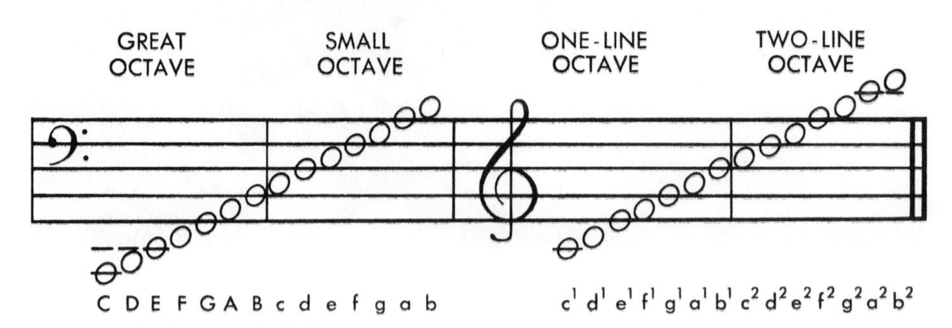

Fig. 5.9. Use this accepted marking to identify pitch.

VOICES OF SECONDARY - SCHOOL PUPILS

Voice	Sex	Range	Quality and Characteristics	Limitations
Soprano	Girls		Girls - light and thin flute-like	1st Sop. c^1 - g^2 2nd Sop. c^1 - e^2
	Boys		Boys - Unchanged voice increasing brilliance until change occurs	1st Sop. e^1 - f^2 2nd Sop. c^1 - d^2
Alto	Girls		Lacks resonance, somber, but richer and broader than soprano. Real alto quality rather uncommon	Best use of voice from d^1 - b^1
Alto	Boys	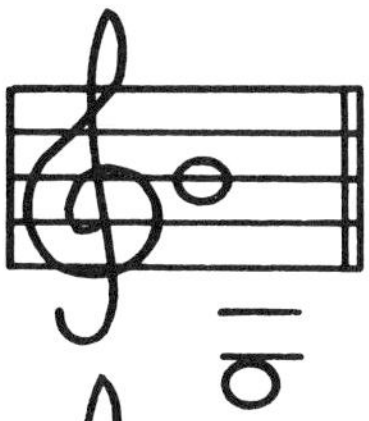	Rich, smooth, mellow velvety Unchanged voice	Avoid sustained singing at extremes of range
Alto-tenor	Boys	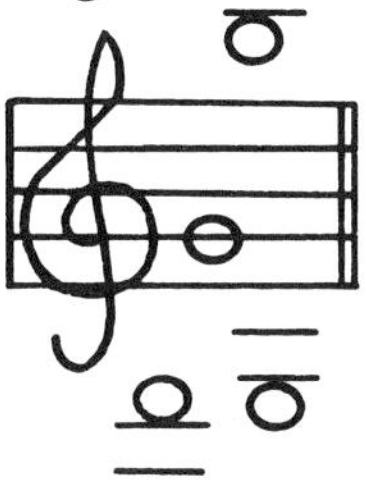	Reedy quality. A changing voice. Boy may give impression that he has a cold.	May be restricted for a time to four or five tones such as f - c^1
Tenor	Boys	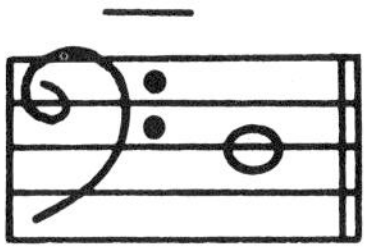	Thin, immature. Lyric or dramatic quality evident throughout range. Judge by quality Rarely found.	Best use of voice in middle of range.
Baritone	Boys	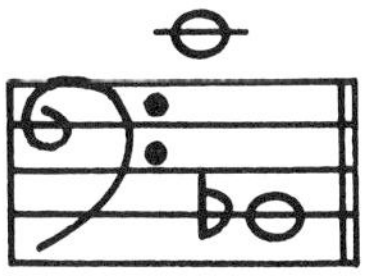	A changed voice sometimes lacking stability	Range sometimes limited but increases as voice settles
Bass	Boys		Deep - heavy, manly tone uncommon	May be limited to a few tones at first, but range will widen in time.

Fig. 5.10. This chart shows the normal range, quality, and limitations of teen-age voices.

have an adequate knowledge of the voice and of choral technique as they are related to the unchanged, changing and changed voice of the teen-ager. Many specialists have written on the adolescent voice and choral technique in greater detail than the limitations of this writing permit. The treatment of the subject here should be considered merely introductory.

Vocal Range

How important is range in classifying the voices of our pupils? Range is only one of the factors which must be considered in assigning pupils to singing parts. For example, it is known that junior-high-school girls have a fairly uniform range (Fig. 5.9) from b flat to f^2. Often the quality and range of these voices is such that for the time being many girls may have the experience of singing either the alto or the soprano part. As you listen to them sing, neither their range nor the quality of their voice definitely classifies them as either sopranos or altos. The very few girls whose range and quality do identify them as either sopranos or altos can be immediately assigned to their respective parts (Fig. 5.10).

Vocal Quality

As has been indicated, vocal quality is the key to proper classification of voices. A teacher who has developed the ability to recognize vocal quality aurally has a distinct advantage in classifying voices. Range charts and descriptions of vocal quality are helpful, but hearing singers of many types and classifications is the best way to gain familiarity with vocal quality and learn to identify voices. This is particularly true of the alto-tenor, cambiata, or changing voice.

If the vocal quality is tenor or alto, the pupil should be singing the tenor or alto part, regardless of the extent of his or her range. The girl with soprano quality whose range is wide and who finds she can sing the alto part should still be assigned to the soprano section, no matter how great the need for altos may be. All pupils should be instructed not to sing those tones which are difficult to produce and which cause vocal strain. No student should be classified as a soprano or alto purely on the basis of her ability to sing the part.

Soprano voices of girls in the junior and senior high school are very much alike. The senior-high-school soprano may sing with a slightly more mature quality, but as a rule her voice is light and thin. When more volume is needed it may be safely secured by increasing the number of singers rather than urging the girls to force their voices.

Alto voices will be well protected and will develop normally when choral parts they are asked to sing fall largely in the middle section of the range. A suitable alto part will not require singers to make great and continued use of the lower parts of the range.

As we look at junior high school boys, their physical appearance may give a clue as to which of them have changed voices (Fig. 5.11). A downy skin, heavier facial features, enlarged larynx, or a boy's stature may be indications of a changed or changing voice. Teachers usually find the speaking voice a reasonably reliable clue as to what part the boy should sing.

The boy soprano has a range close to that of the girl soprano, but there is a marked difference in vocal quality. When practical, it is suggested that the soprano part in the glee club, choir, and the like, be carried by either boys or girls but not both. In classes or choral groups where boy and girl sopranos are used together, boy sopranos should be seated together and near other boys.

The junior-high-school boy abhors anything that implies that he is "sissy." For that reason the soprano part of many choral arrangements for junior-high-school boys is called "First Tenor"; the part sounds as it is written on the staff. The alto is then called "Second Tenor," the alto-tenor or cambiata becomes the "First Bass." This voice may, for a time, be limited to a very few tones such as f to c^1, but the alto-tenor should be encouraged to sing those tones he can sing easily.

Fig. 5.11. What are the probable ranges of these junior high school singers? What visible clues are there?

Green Bay Public Schools, Green Bay, Wisconsin.

The baritone voice, called "Second Bass" in arrangements for junior-high-school boys, may not become settled for a time and may be difficult for the boy to control. The lower tones such as B flat or c may not be easily produced when he starts singing the part.

The problem of the unchanged, changing, and changed voice is centered in the junior-high-school years, but it continues to a considerable degree in the choral activities of the senior high school. The mature tenor voice is not usually found among boys in the junior-high-school grades. Tenors and low basses are not found in great numbers in the senior-high-school grades, but it is possible to secure a satisfactory balance in the secondary-school choral groups with the vocal resources available, since a few basses and tenors will balance the group reasonably well.

Individual differences are such that many exceptions may be found to these comments on the adolescent voice. Vocal development does not follow a fixed pattern. Race and nationality, for example, are responsible for some of the variations. A frequent and careful voice-testing program is most essential if the pupil's voice is to be properly classified and safeguarded.

TESTING VOICES

Voice testing can be an ordeal to pupils, or they may accept it as a routine part of their work in music. The importance of voice testing in both the junior and senior high school is such that the teacher who can secure the cooperation of the pupils in classifying the voices will have a good start in the development of good choral organizations. If the teacher is in a school where he must use all pupils who appear for choir, chorus, or glee club, voice testing as a preliminary for membership not only classifies the voices properly, but it also has the advantage of making pupils feel that they have been selected for the group. People like to be among those selected, and they are likely to be less interested in a group to which anyone can belong.

Preparing for Testing

When teachers help girls and boys to understand the changing voice as a normal part of growing up, and the need for voice classifications and for safeguarding their voices by testing at frequent and regular intervals, the program of testing and tryouts makes sense to them and much of their resistance disappears. Just how successful a teacher has been in securing a positive attitude toward voice testing becomes evident in the number of pupils who request that their voices be checked when they meet vocal difficulties in singing their parts.

Testing and tryouts need to be organized efficiently and carried out with a minimum of delay and embarrassment for the pupils. Cards for recording information on each pupil are designed by many teachers to suit their particular needs. The card contains the pupil's name, homeroom number, year in school, voice classification, ability to sing in tune, previous experience in music, and any other information the teacher may desire. Additional remarks can be made on the back of the card.

Testing Individual Pupils

When it is feasible, there is a distinct advantage in scheduling individual and private tests for pupils. Combining the test with an informal conference with the pupil not only helps put him at ease, but may be a source of helpful information about his interest and background in music (Fig. 5.12).

When the pupil is asked to sing, place him in a position where he cannot see the piano keyboard. If the pupil is totally unaware of the location of the pitch being sung, the results of testing are likely to be more accurate than if he or she decides the pitch being played by the teacher is too high or too low.

In testing a girl's voice, start in the scale of G major, using the syllable "ah." Begin on g^1, continue up to g^2, then down to g and return to g^1. The singing of the scale, or arpeggios if you prefer, should be continued until you have determined both the range and, more important, the quality of the voice.

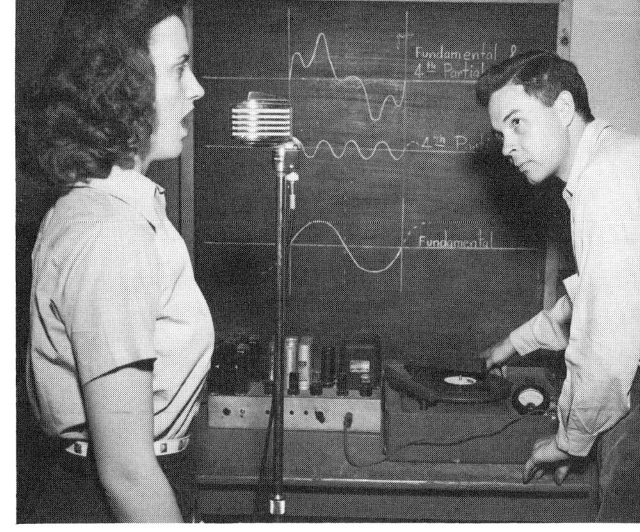

Fig. 5.12. There may be value in recording some voice tests for later study and indications of progress.

Used by permission, Music Educators National Conference, Washington, D.C.

Have the young boy sing the G-major scale, accompanied, after hearing you play it, from g^1 descending to g and returning to g^1. If the quality of the voice thins out as it reaches the lower tones, the voice is probably the unchanged soprano. The boy with unchanged soprano voice is usually able to sing up to f^2 with ease. If any vocal strain is noticeable in the upper tones, protect his voice by advising him not to sing the high tones or by placing him on the second-soprano part.

With a boy who appears to be more mature, a clue to his voice classification may be found, as previously mentioned, in the speaking voice. An informal conversation with him may well reveal the identity of his voice. Ask him to sing the G-major scale slowly from g descending to G, on "ah." He will respond more readily when the teacher accompanies him on the piano.

Group Testing

There are times when a boy or girl would be more at ease in his or her voice test if two or three were tested at the same time or if the teacher sang during the test. Every effort should be made to accommodate those pupils unduly disturbed by voice testing (Fig. 5.13).

When it is necessary to test the voices of groups of pupils, student assistants may be used to keep the testing program moving. The plan recommended by Dr. Irvin Cooper[3] and described by J. Dayton Smith suggests that the teacher follow this procedure:

a. Pitch "Old Folks at Home" in the key of B flat and start the group singing, telling them beforehand to sing in the range that is easiest for them. Move along each row, listening to the individual voices. In the process, ask each boy singing the *lowest* octave to drop out. These are the young baritones.
b. Pitch the same song in the key of G flat for the balance of the group, excluding the baritones, and repeat the listening procedures, asking those boys singing the higher octave to drop out. These boys are still sopranos.
c. The remaining group is of the cambiata classification.

The voice classification given above should not be thought of as permanent. Periodic retests of the boys' voices should be made to keep up with the changing process. It will be necessary from time to time to move young singers from the changing voice group to the baritone section.[4]

[3] Dr. Irvin Cooper, School of Music, Florida State University, Tallahassee, Florida. See listing of books on choral technique in Chapter 21.

[4] J. Dayton Smith, "More About the Boy's Changing Voice," *Fischer Edition News*, September–October, 1956, p. 2.

St. Louis Public Schools, St. Louis, Missouri.

Fig. 5.13. Informal group testing can be accomplished around the piano with familiar songs of good range.

SEATING PLANS FOR CHORAL GROUPS

Intonation, balance, and blending, as well as appearance, are to be considered when making out a seating plan for a choral group. The seating plan should be worked out to facilitate the hearing of closely related parts by the singers. In the organizations of mixed voices, boys, as earlier recommended, should be seated together. For instance, in the junior-high-school choral seating plans, boy sopranos should be seated with boys and not assigned to places among the girls. As individuals are assigned seats for singing, both the individual and the group will benefit by placing the most capable singers next to those who are not as capable and need the support and reassurance that comes from working near an experienced singer.

An established seating plan is also an advantage in promoting good discipline. Pupils who work well together can be seated together while those who need to be separated can be kept apart.

More than one seating chart should be made. One should be on the conductor's music stand to assist him in identifying the pupils by name, and one should be posted in the music room to remind pupils of their location in the organization. The student secretary should have access to a chart at the time the roll is to be taken. The plans which are given below are suggestions only. You may adapt them to the size of your groups, available space, and seating requirements such as number of rows and the like.

BOYS' GLEE CLUB–JUNIOR HIGH SCHOOL
40 Voices

PLAN A

Altos 12	*Sopranos* 14	*Baritones* 6	*Alto-Tenors* 8
x x x x x x	x x x x x x x	x x x	x x x x
x x x x x x	x x x x x x x	x x x	x x x x

Some teachers recognize the boys' desire to be "grown up" and call altos, second tenors; sopranos, first tenors; baritones, second basses; and alto-tenors, first basses.

PLAN B

Higher Unchanged 14	*Lower Unchanged* 12	*Changing* 8		*Changed* 6
		Higher	*Lower*	
x x x x x x x	x x x x x x	x x	x x	x x x
x x x x x x x	x x x x x x	x x	x x	x x x

Higher Unchanged may be called Firsts, Lower Unchanged may be called Seconds, Changing may be called Thirds, and Changed may be called Basses, as suggested by Haydn Morgan.[5]

GIRLS' GLEE CLUB–JUNIOR HIGH SCHOOL
40 Voices

First Sopranos 12	*Second Sopranos* 16	*Altos* 12
x x x x x x	x x x x x x x x	x x x x x x
x x x x x x	x x x x x x x x	x x x x x x

For two- or three-part singing. For two-part singing the second-soprano section may be divided, with some asked to sing the upper part and others the lower part.

[5] Haydn Morgan, *Songs for Young Gleemen*, Schmitt, Hall & McCreary, 1948, p. 2.

CHOIR–MIXED VOICES–JUNIOR HIGH SCHOOL

25 Voices

Plan A

Sopranos 8	*Altos* 7	*Alto-Tenors* 5	*Basses* 5
x x x x	x x x	x x x	x x
x x x x	x x x x	x x	x x x

Plan B

Altos 7	*Sopranos* 8	*Basses* 5	*Alto-Tenors* 5
x x x x	x x x x	x x	x x x
x x x	x x x x	x x x	x x

BOYS' GLEE CLUB–SENIOR HIGH SCHOOL

25 Voices

Second Tenors 5	*Alto-Tenors* 4	*First Tenors* 5	*First Basses* 6	*Second Basses* 5
x x x	x x	x x	x x x	x x x
x x	x x	x x x	x x x	x x

GIRLS' GLEE CLUB–SENIOR HIGH SCHOOL

50 Voices

First Sopranos 18	*Second Sopranos* 13	*First Altos* 12	*Second Altos* 7
x x x x x x x x x	x x x x x x	x x x x x x	x x x x
x x x x x x x x x	x x x x x x x	x x x x x x	x x x

This seating arrangement is satisfactory for both three- and four-part singing.

CHOIR–MIXED VOICES–SENIOR HIGH SCHOOL

40 Voices

Sopranos 14		*Altos* 10		*Tenors* 6		*Basses* 10	
1st sop. 8	2nd sop. 6	1st al. 4	2nd al. 6	1st ten. 3	2nd ten. 3	1st bass 5	2nd bass 5
x x x x	x x x	x x	x x x	x	x x	x x	x x x
x x x x	x x x	x x	x x x	x x	x	x x x	x x

SUMMARY

Teen-agers do like to sing. The fine junior- and senior-high-school choral groups being developed in large and small schools throughout the nation give evidence of the enthusiasm and receptiveness the teen-ager has for choral music. Through choirs, choruses, glee clubs, solo and small-ensemble activities, participation in choral music may be made available to pupils of varying levels of interest and talent.

A high quality of self-expression is perhaps the strongest motivating force for choral activities. Emphasis placed on fine performance of music can very well lead to an interest in singing which will spread throughout a school.

The choral teacher in the junior and senior high school must develop an adequate knowledge of the voice and choral technique as they are related to the unchanged, changing, and changed voice of the teen-ager. It is important that the teacher develop the ability to recognize vocal quality aurally if he is to classify properly the voices of junior- and senior-high-school pupils.

SUGGESTED ACTIVITIES

1. Visit a large and a small junior high school. Observe the choral groups rehearsing, and arrange a conference with the choral teacher to discuss the organization and development of choral music in the school. Report on your visit to the class.
2. Make a selection of 10 choral compositions suitable for use with a junior-high-school mixed chorus of 40 singers. Do the same for a senior-high-school choir of 60 singers. Report on the criteria you used in selecting this music.
3. Develop three bulletin board displays and design three posters which you feel would interest boys in joining the male chorus.
4. Outline a program of instruction that could be used for the training choir of a small senior high school. What would you plan for pupils to prepare them for membership in the advanced choir?
5. Design a simple stage set for a choral concert the theme of which is "Music of the Americas."
6. As a class project, plan an all-boy variety show that could be produced in a small high school.
7. Secure the cooperation of a junior- and a senior-high-school music teacher in recording on tape a voice test given to a number of boys with unchanged, changing, and changed voices. Follow the suggestions made in this chapter for the testing of individual voices. As a class, classify the voices recorded.
8. Classify the speaking voices of three young junior-high-school boys and three more mature-looking junior-high-school boys. Have the boys sing for you. Is the speaking voice a satisfactory guide in classifying these voices?

9. Design a card that you would like to use for developing information on pupils whose voices you have tested. Include all information you feel would be of value to you.
10. Outline a plan that you would use for organizing and developing a choral program in a small junior or senior high school. What choral groups would you include at the start? How would you promote student interest in choral participation? Select 12 compositions that you feel would be suitable for use in a beginning mixed chorus.

SELECTED READINGS

Andrews, Frances, and Joseph A. Leeder, "Junior High School Singers," in *Guiding Junior High School Pupils in Music Experiences*, Prentice-Hall, 1953, pp. 138–177.

Conrad, Robert M., "Developing the Boy's Changing Voice," *Music Educators Journal*, April–May, 1964, p. 68.

Cooper, Irvin, "The Boy's Changing Voice," *Educational Music Magazine*, September–October, 1955, pp. 23, 48–52.

Cooper, Irvin, "Changing Voices," *Music Educators Journal*, February–March, 1962, p. 148.

Cooper, Irvin, "The Junior High School Choral Problem," *Music Educators Journal*, November, 1950, p. 20.

Cooper, Irvin, *Letters to Pat*, Carl Fischer, 1954.

Cooper, Irvin, "Realizing General Music Outcomes Through Singing," *Music Educators Journal*, January, 1964, p. 87.

Garretson, Robert L., *Conducting Choral Music*, Allyn and Bacon, 1961.

Krone, Max T., "Choosing Your Singers," in *The Chorus and Its Conductor*, Neil A. Kjos, 1945, pp. 18–37.

Liemohn, Edwin, "Intonation and Blend in the A Cappella Choir," *Music Educators Journal*, June–July, 1958, p. 50.

Mack, Gerald R., "Vocal Training in the High School," *Music Educators Journal*, February–March, 1964, p. 188.

Nordholm, Harriet, and Ruth V. Bakewell, "Elective Groups," in *Keys to Teaching Junior High School Music*, Schmitt, Hall & McCreary, 1953, pp. 98–107.

Phillips, Norman, and John Scott, "Organizing a Junior High School Elective Chorus," *Music Educators Journal*, April–May, 1963, p. 109.

Rice, William C., "Young Singers: Handle with Care," *Music Educators Journal*, June–July, 1963, p. 75.

Swanson, Frederick, "The Proper Care and Feeding of Changing Voices," *Music Educators Journal*, November–December, 1961, p. 63.

Van Bodegraven, Paul, and Harry R. Wilson, "The Choral Rehearsal," in *The School Music Conductor*, Schmitt, Hall & McCreary, 1942, pp. 75–89.

Wassell, Albert W., "An Unusual Choral Group," *Music Educators Journal*, June–July, 1963, p. 67.

Wikstrom, Thomas N., "Changing Voices," *Music Educators Journal*, February–March, 1962, p. 149.

San Diego City Schools, San Diego, California.

CHAPTER

6

Participation in Instrumental Music

Visualize a famous professional woodwind quintet playing a concert for an audience of girls and boys from neighboring large and small communities. The audience may be made up entirely of music students or may be a combination of students from the general school populace; important is the fact that this rich instrumental experience is happening in their own community. In addition to hearing a finished performance, the music students anticipate the expert guidance and instruction they will receive in the clinic sessions that follow the concert.

Throughout the country this type of concert-clinic experience is being brought to an ever increasing number of boys and girls in community schools. Professional and college musicians are now taking a greater interest in the school music program, because they realize that the future of music in America is to a great extent dependent upon the breadth and quality of musical performance experiences in school curriculums.

The men in the quintet are all members of a great symphony orchestra and received their early training in the school music program. Thus they are in a position to realize the importance of imparting their best experiences to the new generation of school youngsters. They perform in concert, then during the clinic that follows they give additional demonstrations and the best of their professional advice and experiences to aspiring young performers. In effect, these professional musicians are reinforcing the contribution that school instrumental music is making as a social and cultural force in our nation.

Children's concerts by community symphony orchestras are also a part of the music education program of many schools. Before the concert, the children are made familiar with the music to be heard, and afterwards provision is made for them to hear again the music by recordings in the classroom. The response of pupils to these concerts has been enthusiastic. In a way, cooperation between the school and the local symphony orchestra is one of the best means of bridging the gap between school and community music (Fig. 6.1).

Detroit Public Schools, Detroit, Michigan.

Fig. 6.1. Selected high-school students appear with the bass section of the Detroit Symphony Orchestra in a School Concert Series program. John Van de Graaf, Principal Bass.

THE INSTRUMENTAL CURRICULUM

The instrumental curriculums of the junior and the senior high school have much in common. The best curriculums offer a wide range of activities well suited to the musical, mental, physical, and emotional development of the teenager. While bringing instrumental experiences to many pupils, consideration is also given to the discovery and development of the most interested and talented girls and boys. The successful secondary-school instrumental music curriculum is characterized by a continuity of instruction which challenges and inspires pupils throughout their years in junior and senior high school.

The instrumental curriculum does not follow a set pattern; it varies from one school or community to another. The content and general success of the program in any school will depend upon the abilities and the attitudes of the teacher, the school administration, and the community. We have placed the teacher first in this sequence of responsibility because there are countless examples of complete and well-balanced instrumental programs functioning in junior and senior high schools primarily because of the educational leadership and vision of the teacher.

The instrumental curriculum may involve many pupils. It may also be so limited in scope that it serves only the most talented. There is no reason why a program of instrumental music in a secondary school cannot be based on a broad concept of music education which meets the needs of the larger group of pupils while it provides for the most talented pupils by presentation of appropriate higher steps on the instructional ladder. There should be reasonable standards of musical achievement established for membership in the top instrumental organizations of both the junior and the senior high school, but the curriculum should be designed to accommodate pupils with varying degrees of interest and musical talent.

In listening to instrumental groups perform in district and state festivals, one hears junior- and senior-high-school bands and orchestras with large memberships play poorly because too many pupils who are musically inadequate to the performance requirements of the group are allowed to participate. Permitting boys and girls to become members of selective instrumental ensembles for which they are not musically equipped fosters musical mediocrity, tension, frustration, and a misconception by the pupils as to what is good and bad in music. There is a need in the instrumental curriculum for a graded program of instruction that will make possible the proper placement of pupils in training organizations.

The instrumental curriculum which fits the total school program is broad and flexible. It offers to youth instrumental participation ranging from the informal recreational instruments to the woodwind quintet and the string quartet. Proper guidance by the teacher places pupils in the situation best suited to their musical development and talent. An instrumental curriculum in the secondary school may include:

1. Exploratory instrumental classes
2. Class instrumental lessons
3. Band and/or orchestra, intermediate and advanced
4. Solo and small-ensemble experience
5. Instrumental instruction by the private teacher
6. The dance band

Just how much of an instrumental curriculum should be offered in any particular junior or senior high school cannot be determined by a theoretical approach. The teacher's personality, enthusiasm, competence in music, knowledge of successful methods and practices, organizational ability, and length of service in the school—all have a direct influence on the breadth and depth of the instrumental curriculum. Other determining factors are the opportunity, or lack of opportunity, for instrumental study in the elementary grades; administrative, parental, and community interest and support of the program; and economic conditions in the school community. A well-developed curriculum should meet the needs of all children in a manner consistent with both quality of performance and recognition of individual interests and abilities.

EXPLORATORY INSTRUMENTAL EXPERIENCES

Exploratory instrumental experiences are generally considered a part of the music program of the elementary grades and should be available to all students. They should be offered in the junior high school for those pupils who have an interest in instrumental study and were unable to have instruction earlier.

In some schools exploratory instrumental experiences are included in the General Music course of the junior-high-school grades by:

1. Aptitude and achievement testing
2. A check of the interests of pupils as they become acquainted with the appearance and sound of the instruments of the band and orchestra
3. The use of bulletin board displays of instruments and instrumental activities
4. Instrumental performance in class by class members, the teacher, and visitors
5. The use of motion pictures or film strips such as the film strip and recording, *You Can Make Music*[1]
6. The introduction of melody and harmony instruments such as the recorder and the autoharp
7. Keyboard experience (Fig. 6.2)
8. Letting pupils try real instruments with the guidance of the instrumental specialist.

Common practice in the schools is the maintenance of classes for the study of the recorder or similar melody instruments, for keyboard experience, or for an introduction to the instruments of the band and orchestra by playing experiences with these instruments.

For example, in the Kalamazoo Public Schools:

> Exploratory string and wind experiences are offered in Grade 7 when students show serious interest and have missed these experiences in Grades 4 or 5. Other instruments (i.e., viola, cello, trombone, tuba) are often offered at this time if available in the school inventory. Exploratory instruments (in multiple unit cases) are brought to each school on a weekly schedule and all practicing on them is done under the guidance of the teacher. Classes are organized as homogeneous units of 10–12 violins and heterogeneous units of 10–12 cornets and clarinets (5–6 each), and receive a maximum of 12 weeks of group instruction. Mouthpieces are sterilized between classes.[2]

[1] *You Can Make Music*, American Music Conference, Chicago. Supplied without charge as a school service.

[2] "Instrumental Music Grades Four Through Twelve," *Resource Guide In Music*, The Curriculum Department, Kalamazoo, Michigan, 1954.

Kalamazoo Public Schools, Kalamazoo, Michigan.

Fig. 6.2. Keyboard experience is an important preliminary step for pupils desiring to play another instrument.

In the exploratory instrumental experience, more important than the type of instruction is its availability to all pupils. Instrumental teachers seem to agree that this start of instrumental study is the most important part of the program. For them it has proven its effectiveness and is the first step in the building of fine musical organizations (Fig. 6.3).

Weber summarizes the aims of the exploratory or pre-instrument class as follows:

a. To create a love for music.
b. To create a desire to play a real instrument.
c. To function as a talent test to determine which pupils have the ability, interest, ambition and perseverance for successful instrumental music study.
d. To provide every pupil with an inexpensive introduction to the study of instrumental music.
e. To assist the student in selecting a suitable instrument.
f. To help the student acquire a working knowledge of some fundamentals.
g. To determine parental interest and backing.[3]

[3] Fred Weber, "The Elementary and Junior High School Band Program," in *Building Better Bands*, Belwin, 1957, p. 5.

M. Hohner, Inc., Hicksville, L.I., New York.

Fig. 6.3. Exploratory instrumental experience with a variety of simple instruments is also used in other countries, as shown in this music class in a German Volksschule. The children are playing Melodicas, recorders, ocarinas, harmonicas, and bells.

CLASS INSTRUMENTAL LESSONS

The great progress made in instrumental music in the schools may be attributed to the success of class instruction in instruments. Instrumental class instruction for beginners and more advanced pupils is offered in Grades 7, 8, and 9 of the secondary school, as well as in the elementary grades. The classes are usually scheduled to meet one to three times a week and in some schools are limited to a minimum enrollment of six and a maximum of twenty pupils. Class instruction for a pupil may be limited to one year or may be continued for longer periods, depending on school policy. Usually those pupils showing promise of success in instrumental study are urged to transfer from class instruction to private instruction as soon as practical.

The decision must be made as to whether classes should be of like instruments or classes of mixed instruments. In schools where only a single class of beginners is possible, the class must be of mixed instruments. Where a number of beginning classes are possible, classes of like instruments may be organized. From his experience Weber states, "The problem of dealing with classes of mixed abilities is much greater than that of dealing with different instruments."[4] He favors, as do many other teachers, mixed class instruction supplemented by encouraging as many pupils as possible to take private lessons.

In organizing instrumental classes, constant attention must be given to the maintenance of adequate future instrumentation in the bands and orchestras. In schools where this is considered and where careful records are kept, the large performing ensembles are not likely to be weakened by lack of proper instrumentation. Since the balance in the advanced instrumental groups is dependent upon the flow of players from the instrumental classes, it is the teacher's responsibility to maintain the supply of various instruments to insure for the future the needed instrumentation.

There are a number of ways of keeping a close check on instrumental resources, but teachers seem to favor instrumentation charts showing the number of players on each instrument, their year in school, and other information indicating just what replacements are to be available for a balanced membership in the ensembles. Teachers make considerable use of these charts in guiding pupils in the selection of instruments and thus they can protect the organizations from setbacks due to the loss of instrumental personnel by graduation.

Experienced instrumental teachers are well aware of the possibilities of doing more than teaching music in class instruction. While these classes are thought of as the foundation of fine bands and orchestras, the teacher's satisfaction and success comes from both the musical and social development of his pupils. This is reflected by a teacher who reported: "A few case examples from the present class might show why we enjoy the opportunity of helping people.

Case "A" is an eighth-grade boy who failed several subjects last year. He is a quiet, shy type who surprised us when he registered for the course of his own accord. He is not advancing rapidly but has shown enough progress to be promoted to the "B" Band next semester. He seems happy with his instrument.

Case "B" is a ninth grader, who we understand is a low-mentality student but a well-mannered and quiet boy. He chose the course of his own accord and managed to dig up a cornet from the family closet. He is happy in the class and has acquired some degree of success with the instrument."[5]

The social and musical aspects of class instrumental instruction mean a great deal to pupils of junior-high-school age. Many teachers recognize these extra by-products of instrumental class instruction, and they group pupils in sections according to their musical ability and interests. Pupils who are properly sectioned have an opportunity to be successful in the study of music, and the possibility of creating frustrations and tensions for slower achievers is greatly reduced.

[4] *Ibid.*, p. 6.
[5] Frank Woost, Fremont Junior High School, Pomona, California.

The Pomona Unified School District uses the following type of letter and materials each fall, after an instrumental demonstration assembly in each school. This school system starts class instrumental instruction in the elementary grades, which is the best place to start the instruction when it is possible.

POMONA UNIFIED SCHOOL DISTRICT[6]

We are taking this opportunity to call to the attention of parents of children in the Pomona public schools that the total elementary school program includes instruction in the playing of the regular band and orchestral instruments.

Purpose of the Classes

To place within the means of all parents the opportunity of giving their children a foundation in the study of a musical instrument.
To afford an opportunity for children to have a broader experience with music.
To prepare children for participation in the instrumental organizations of the elementary schools, the junior high schools, the senior high schools and the community.
To supplement private lessons. It is not the purpose of the class lesson to take the place of private instruction. The child's interest and progress in the class program will be a good guide to the parent in deciding whether private lessons would be justified.

Facts About the Classes

This is a regular public school offering, therefore there will be no charge for lessons.
Classes will meet once a week during the school time.
Each pupil must be provided with a satisfactory instrument.
Classes will be organized for all regular band and orchestral instruments such as violin, 'cello, viola, string bass, flute, clarinet, saxophone, cornet, French horn, trombone, baritone, tuba, and drum.
The playing of a regular instrument is best begun in the elementary school.
Violin, 'cello, or string bass may be started in grades 4, 5, or 6. Flute, clarinet, saxophone, cornet, French horn, trombone, baritone, tuba, and drum may be started in grades 5 and 6.
It would be to the advantage of the student to have his own instruction book for home practice. The cost of such material should not exceed $2.00 for the year.
More detailed information about the materials will be given during class meetings.
As soon as sufficient advancement is made, students will have the opportunity of playing regularly in one of the selected All-City groups.

Selecting an Instrument

The beginning student needs a good instrument. Much discouragement and waste of energy can be avoided with an instrument which plays easily and is in good adjustment.

[6] John R. Keith, Music Coordinator, Pomona Unified School District, Pomona, California.

Local music dealers are in a position to give helpful advice on the purchase or rental of instruments and offer repair service to keep the equipment in good playing condition.

The instructors have had a wide range of experience with the instruments in band and orchestra. They will be glad to confer with you and recommend an instrument.

If at all possible the student should be given an instrument to which he is best adapted because only then will he take the most interest and make the best progress. This should take into consideration the physical maturity and mental development of the child as well as the possibilities for continued use in the schools or in the community after graduation.

While almost all of the wind instruments can be played in their normal size by elementary school children, there are half and three-quarter size string instruments available for those children who cannot yet handle the full size.

Factors to be considered when selecting a wind instrument include: good physical condition generally, jaw and mouth formation, lips, teeth, and size of the player.

According to experience in the past years, all stringed instruments can be used continuously throughout the junior and senior high school. There is need for more viola, 'cello and string bass players than in recent years.

Of the wind instruments the following are to be particularly encouraged: flutes, trombones, baritones, French horns. A word of caution is in order for the selection of trumpet or cornet, since the supply of players usually exceeds the demand in junior and senior high school.

John R. Keith
Music Coordinator

Approved:
LeRoy Allison
Superintendent

THE BAND

The band in the junior and senior high school has stimulated a great deal of interest in school music. It is bringing participation in music to thousands of boys and girls in large and small communities, and is promoting a healthy relationship between the school and the community (Fig. 6.4).

The band has a strong appeal for teen-age pupils. Their physical, social, emotional, and intellectual development is well suited to this ensemble with its uniforms, color, marching, prominence in school and community, and its variety of activities. It provides new and interesting experiences. Its relationship with the school athletic program provides an organization to which pupils readily give their loyalty. The unique contribution the band can make to the adolescent, and to the total school program, is one that is not underestimated by school administrators and music educators. Because of its far-reaching effects, the band program has become an integral part of school life.

The Junior-High-School Band Program

Just what should be the band program of the junior high school? We would like to suggest, since junior-high-school pupils respond enthusiastically to the school band program, that the band be more than a "feeder" organization for the senior high school. The outstanding performance of many junior-high-school bands points to the high level of achievement possible with pupils at this period of their musical training.

The aim of instruction through the junior-high-school years is to further the musical development of the individual and the group. Teachers use audition, challenge, tryout programs, merit systems, and every possible means of encouraging home practice and achievement. These procedures are also used as a means of evaluating the progress made by individual pupils for appropriate placement in the instructional program.

When the school enrollment permits, a training band in the junior high school will foster not only the musical development of the individual, but also quality in the first or advanced band. In schools where it is possible for pupils to move from class instrumental instruction to training band and finally to be admitted to the first band on the basis of their achievement, the quality of musical performance will be high.

Duluth Public Schools, Duluth, Minnesota. Courtesy of Jon, photography.

Fig. 6.4. Multiply this splendid concert band membership by many hundreds and you begin to get an idea of the impact of band work on high-school curriculums all over the United States.

Junior-high-school bands are scheduled from three to five periods a week. One hundred and thirty-five minutes of rehearsal time is considered to be the minimum time allotment if reasonable standards of achievement are to be maintained.

In some instances there is considerable time devoted to the marching band in the junior high school. Experienced teachers point out that the quality of musical performance suffers when at this level a band attempts to carry out a full marching program and a concert program. They feel that sufficient marching experience will be provided if junior-high-school bands learn the fundamentals of marching and do not get involved in complicated band maneuvers and band shows. Such activities as concerts, marching appearances, and trips may well be limited at the junior-high-school level. In certain situations the activities of junior-high-school organizations are so extensive that pupils fail to respond to the senior-high-school band with marked interest or enthusiasm.

The Senior-High-School Band Program

The instrumental curriculum in the senior high school may provide a limited band program or it may contain a broad program of ensemble activities including training band, advanced band, marching band, and pep band. Advanced band is scheduled for three to five periods a week of rehearsal in school time. Less than three periods of rehearsal a week is not recommended. The scheduling of other activities in the band program depends upon the time available in the school program and the teaching assignment carried by the instructor.

The problem which faces many instrumental teachers is that of planning a program of instruction which devotes sufficient time to the musical education of girls and boys while at the same time supplying the entertainment requests of the school and the community. Decisions in this respect need to be made in terms of what is best for the students. The beginning teacher will do well to seek the advice of the high-school principal in establishing policies which will safeguard the educational aspects of the band program while serving school and community needs.

The Training Band and the Advanced Band

The training band is important to any band program and can be a part of the instrumental curriculum of most schools. When the training band is well organized, participation will be a profitable and satisfying experience for students. In this group, motor skills and general musicianship may be developed which will insure a higher quality of performance than would otherwise be possible in the advanced band.

The effectiveness of the training band is dependent upon the standards of achievement established for the entire band program. One senior high school has a large advanced band and also maintains a training band. The teacher has never established any minimum requirements for membership in the advanced band. The training band in this school is made up of those pupils considered to be "problem" cases and who are moved from the advanced band to the training band as a disciplinary measure. Visits to rehearsals of the training band are disappointing; the group is small and has an instrumentation that makes satisfying musical performance impossible. Morale of its members, as would be expected, is low.

The musical and educational potentialities of a training band are not being realized here. Established standards of achievement in the band program of this school would make possible a training-band program that would provide experience for the less advanced students and at the same time upgrade the quality of performance of the advanced band. In many schools, pupils are expected to be members of the training band until they meet the standards established for membership in the advanced band. Usually the length of service in the training organization is not specified; a talented and industrious pupil may qualify for advanced-band membership at certain times in any school year.

The idea that membership in the advanced band is not open to everyone is psychologically and educationally sound. It causes pupils to develop respect for achievement in music and to make the most of their musical ability. It provides an incentive for them to work harder in the training band, and when membership in the advanced band is finally achieved it is much more meaningful to them (Fig. 6.5).

Names and labels have assumed an importance to some people, a fact which must be recognized if the training band is to be attractive and satisfying to pupils. Titles such as "Training Band" or "Second Band" have aggravated the drop-out situations in some schools. For that reason many teachers have used such titles as "Activity Band," "Blue" or "Red" band, or "A" and "B" Band, and have been successful in reducing the number of drop-outs and the rejection of the training band as an "inferior" organization.

The Marching Band

The marching band is an essential part of the instrumental program of most high schools. It is a demanding program that requires many hours of planning and rehearsing on the part of teachers and students. It can be both entertaining and educational (Fig. 6.6). When the marching band performs it carries a responsibility to the entire music program. Usually the community and pupils hear and see more of the marching band than of any other musical organization

Duluth Public Schools, Duluth, Minn. Courtesy of Duluth News-Tribune.

Fig. 6.5. A good percussion section is an important part of the band, whether it is the training band or the advanced band.

of the school. The aim of this organization should be not only to march and execute maneuvers well, but also to present the best possible musical performance.

While the marching band is recognized for the part it plays in the band program, it should be kept in its proper relationship with the advanced band. For example, one high-school instrumental teacher was extremely successful for years in developing "band shows." The people in the community and the student body of the school were proud of their band and the organization received many citations for its performance on the field. Yet each year a large percentage of the students dropped band at the end of the first semester when the band was about to concentrate on concert performance. This is an example of overemphasis on the marching band which will be avoided by teachers of good judgment and sound musicianship. Throughout the country there are countless examples of superior marching units that also maintain superior ratings in concert performance and have something of musical value to offer their members.

Nicolet High School, Milwaukee, Wisconsin.

Milwaukee Public Schools, Milwaukee, Wisconsin.

Muskegon Public Schools, Muskegon, Michigan.

Fig. 6.6. Precision, color, and attractiveness characterize the good marching band.

The Pep Band[7]

Just when the pep-band movement began as an organized part of the band program is a matter of speculation. Perhaps it has been an outgrowth of the crowded conditions that exist at most indoor athletic events, or it may have been the result of either small beginning instrumental programs or an overcrowded performance schedule for the large band. In any event, the pep band has become, in many schools, one of the busiest and most important groups in the band program. It usually performs at the weekly pep rallies and, in addition, takes the place of the large band at basketball games where space is at a premium. Its smaller size also simplifies the transportation problem. Its many public appearances keep the pep band well occupied and serve as a strong link between the music department, school activities, and the public.

The instrumentation varies with the size of group desired, the type of music played, and the number of the more advanced players available. Such a group might include the following instruments: one piccolo, two clarinets, one alto sax, one tenor sax, one or two cornets, one horn, two trombones, one baritone, one tuba, and two drummers. This size could range from a larger number, if possible, down to perhaps the minimum of one clarinet, one cornet, one trombone, one tuba, and two drummers.

One of the advantages of this group is that with a little training it can sever itself from the director's apron strings, thus giving the students a chance to develop more initiative, learn the consequences of responsibility, and at the same time relieve the director to do other work.

The initial membership is usually chosen by the director from the better musicians in the band, since in a small group it is essential that each member be able to do his part. If more qualified musicians are available than are needed, a rotating schedule may be devised so that all may have the experience. It should be kept in mind that, while worth-while training is obtained from participation, this group is essentially a performing group, not a training one, and the members should be made to feel it is an honor to belong. Extra credit in some form should be given, such as points toward a higher grade or band letter. A student leader should be elected and tryouts held by members themselves to determine new membership. Many such groups even purchase special sweaters rather than wear the regular band uniform.

The repertoire of the pep band is somewhat limited because of its small size and its basic function. The music most needed is, obviously, marches and school pep tunes, since it is the main function of the pep band to do what its name implies, to generate pep and enthusiasm among the players and the student body.

[7] This discussion of the pep band was prepared by Lorin Richtmeyer, Music Department, Northern Michigan University, Marquette, Michigan.

Other types of music do fit into this category, however. Some of the swing marches such as "St. Louie Blues March," "Steppin' High," and the many Dixieland arrangements now available to small groups add a pleasant variety for both the audience and the players. The current popular hits, on the other hand, do not necessarily fit into the excitement and hilarity of athletic events, and in most cases are better avoided. In addition to playing suitable music for the occasion, most pep bands also work with the cheerleaders in devising band-audience yells. Many such cheers are published and the band members themselves have a chance to do a little creative work of their own.

THE ORCHESTRA

If we think in terms of the musical development of students, the orchestra is assured of a place in both the junior and the senior high school. We cannot agree with those who attack the school band program as an obstacle in the way of the school orchestra. There is need for both the band and the orchestra in the educational program, and an increasing number of schools are making progress in developing both organizations.

Competence on the stringed instruments takes a longer period of time to develop than on the wind instruments; thus in most schools the orchestral program is dependent upon the opportunities available for the study of stringed instruments in the elementary grades. Where class lessons on the stringed instruments are offered in Grades 4 and 5 of the elementary school, the development of orchestras is greatly facilitated. In those places where instrumental instruction is first offered in Grade 7 of the junior high school, class lessons on the stringed instruments are capable of producing the players essential to the junior- and senior-high-school orchestra (Fig. 6.7, left).

It is not a question of whether or not the orchestra should be a part of the secondary-school music program. The place of the orchestra in the world of music is of such recognized importance that no program of music education can be complete without stringed instrumental instruction and orchestral training in the secondary schools.

Whether or not there is an orchestra in the junior and senior high school is often a matter determined by the teacher. School boards and school administrators are generally receptive to suggestions that broaden opportunities in music for the pupils in their schools. Colleges and universities, recognizing the need to encourage the development of string players in the high schools, are prepared to advise and assist schools with the instructional program. It is recommended that as much study of the stringed instruments as is possible be done by the teacher in training. It is not necessary to be a string specialist to produce fine

Oakland Public Schools, Oakland, California.

Marshall Public Schools, Marshall, Michigan.

Fig. 6.7. String instruction in the elementary grades can produce capable musicians in the junior high school (left). Student directors like the young lady demonstrating bowing to classmates can help in sectional rehearsals (right).

school orchestras. A large number of superior junior- and senior-high-school orchestras are the result of the efforts made by brass, woodwind, and other specialists who recognize the significance of the orchestra as an integral part of the school music program (Fig. 6.7, right).

Scheduling is often a deterring factor in the organization of school orchestras, particularly in the small junior or senior high school. It is difficult to offer orchestra in a school where the band meets five or more times a week. An arrangement of the scheduling of both band and orchestra can be worked out, with the band meeting three periods a week and the orchestra twice a week during the first semester when marching consumes so much of the band's time. In the second semester the allotment of time might be reversed, with the orchestra rehearsing three periods a week and the band twice a week. The larger secondary schools are in a position to schedule both band and orchestra more easily.

The Development of Youth Orchestras

Some years ago a certain county school system made up of small rural and consolidated schools demonstrated that a county school symphony orchestra could be the means of promoting an unusually strong interest in the string program. For some time the county instrumental teachers had been traveling through the county each week, teaching instrumental classes and, eventually, some of the schools were able to develop bands. But string players, too, need the experience and challenge of playing with a large ensemble, and no one school could supply enough strings to fill this need. A county school symphony orchestra was established, rehearsing each Saturday morning of the school year in a school building at the county seat. In time the orchestra had a complete symphonic instrumentation, and the string program was carried on with enthusiastic community support.

The Youth Orchestra movement has proven to be, perhaps, the most successful means of advancing the study of stringed instruments and maintaining interest in orchestral playing. Youth orchestras functioning throughout the school year can offer playing experience to pupils beyond that which even the largest high schools can give. This can be done in any community that has a group of teachers who will work as a team and who are determined to see that pupils have the

Duluth Public Schools, Duluth, Minnesota, Photo by Gallagher.

Fig. 6.8. Well-developed school orchestras contribute talent to all types of interschool orchestras.

benefits that come from playing with such a group. Teachers who have initiated such a move have found no difficulty in securing the enthusiastic support of school administrators and parents.

The Youth Orchestra movement is effective in the small-school situation, but it is equally effective in the metropolitan area of the largest cities (Fig. 6.8). The founding and growth of the Youth Orchestra of Greater Chicago is an example of what can be done when teachers, school officials, parents, and friends of music join together to bring fine orchestral experience to young people.

In the latter part of 1946, a group of high-school girls and boys who had played together in a student orchestra during their summer vacation had found the experience so stimulating and inspiring that they frequently talked about it during the fall. Their sincere and enthusiastic comments encouraged their parents to bring together a group of people interested in both fine music and in youth, and

who were willing to foster and support a Youth Orchestra. It was quickly apparent that a Youth Orchestra could be organized and managed successfully only if the project commanded the interest of the high-school music directors in the Greater Chicago area. Accordingly, all directors in the area were invited to attend a luncheon. Those who attended were so interested that the original group of friends and parents proceeded to form the Youth Orchestra. On November 14, 1947, the first concert of the Youth Orchestra was held in Orchestra Hall, with 200 students representing over 30 high schools in the Chicago and suburban area. The students rehearse on Saturday mornings and play two or three concerts each year. Conductors have included high school and university music department heads and local symphony conductors.

In 1962–1963, 15 Chicago high schools and 37 suburban schools were represented in the Youth Orchestra of Greater Chicago. Two hundred and thirty-six students competed for the 48 vacancies created in the orchestra by that year's graduates. All members of the Youth Orchestra must be students in high school and members in good standing of their high-school orchestra or band. Former members of the Youth Orchestra are now playing in 61 symphony orchestras throughout the United States, including the Chicago Symphony Orchestra, The Lyric Opera Orchestra, and the Grant Park Symphony in Chicago. One student also played with the Hamburg Symphony in Germany and another with the Edinburgh Festival Orchestra in Scotland.

The goals of the Youth Orchestra point the way for advancing the development of school orchestras in sparsely as well as densely populated areas, and of all-city, county, or district orchestras. Such orchestras can:

1. Provide an opportunity for musically advanced high-school boys and girls to play the world's best music together with others of their own age under competent leadership,
2. Serve as an inspiration to all boys and girls so that they will feel that membership in the Youth Orchestra is really worth striving for—something to be looked upon as an accomplishment—something to hold to—something to protect.

SOLO AND SMALL ENSEMBLES

In one small school system the teacher requires every boy and girl participating in instrumental music to learn several solos and to play in a small ensemble. He guides them in the selection of materials and the pupils perform their solos and play in the small groups at regular intervals during the school year. Prior to the solo and ensemble district festival, an adjudicator or two is invited to hear the soloists and the ensembles with the teacher. They decide which pupils should enter the district festival.

The emphasis in this school on the individual work of pupils as soloists and in the ensembles is probably the reason for the excellence of the music program. The band and orchestra are exceptionally fine, the attitude of the pupils toward participation in music is at a high level, and the school superintendent is pleased with the carry-over of school music into the community. Graduates of the school and those still in school are continuing to sing and play in their homes and churches, and with community groups.

The individual pupil can be lost in the full ensemble, but in the solo and small-ensemble activities he assumes an importance and a responsibility which is fruitful to him both as a musician and as an individual (Fig. 6.9). In some schools there are many solos assigned and small ensembles formed just prior to the festivals, and after the festivals this phase of instrumental participation is dropped. Actually, a continuous program of solo and small-ensemble activity may be the key to the development of better musicianship and to the greater significance of music in the lives of larger numbers of students.

PRIVATE INSTRUMENTAL INSTRUCTION

The success of class teaching of instruments has been mentioned as a valuable factor in the organization and development of bands and orchestras. The need to supplement class instruction by private instruction on the various instruments is not to be overlooked. In several small communities lacking private teachers the school instrumental teacher has made arrangements for private

Arsenal Technical High School, Indianapolis, Indiana.

Fig. 6.9. The string quartet is a small ensemble activity which develops the musicianship of pupils.

instrumental instruction on Saturdays by capable student teachers from a nearby college. The more talented and interested pupils frequently travel miles for a private lesson every week or two.

On boy who was extremely interested in music arranged for a private lesson on every other week end with a member of the music department in a university. Each time he appeared for his lesson he brought a tape recorder to the studio and recorded the entire lesson. On his return home he had not only a record of the playing done by him and by his teacher, but the benefit of rehearing the teacher's suggestions. Over a period of time he had, through the tape, the basis for an evaluation of his progress.

The private teacher and private music instruction are a necessary part of the instrumental instructional program. The teachers of school music are indebted to the private teachers for much of the achievement in music by teen-agers.

Senior-high-school credit for private music study has been made available to pupils for many years in a large number of states and communities. College entrance requirements and other factors do put some limitations on the amount of music credit a pupil may use for graduation from high school. Most teachers feel that it is probably best to use the allowed credit for the large school ensembles and in most cases consider credit for applied music study over and above the credits usually counted for graduation.

Where credit is granted for private music study, the pupil usually makes application to the high-school principal for permission to take the work for credit, study with an approved teacher, make monthly reports on practice (signed by the parents), and pass an examination by a jury or an approved examining committee at the end of each semester. The teacher must make regular reports and evaluations on the lessons taken and assignments given the pupil. College entrance requirements are broader than they were at one time, and it is now possible for many senior high schools to give serious consideration to granting credit for private music study.

THE DANCE BAND

The question of whether the dance band should be part of the school instrumental program is debatable. There seems to be general agreement that if it is offered it should be reserved for the senior high school and be considered a non-credit music activity. Recognition of service in the dance band is made by some schools by annual awards of pins or uniform chevrons.

There are a number of competent school instrumental teachers who feel that having a dance band maintained by the school and under the supervision of the school music director makes it possible for the school to direct the energy and enthusiasm of these young dance-band members toward good musicianship and toward wholesome musical growth. Dance-band performance standards should be maintained on as high a level as those of the concert band.

Students in the dance band become experienced in playing difficult and unusual rhythms, carrying an independent part, sight reading, and tone development. They certainly become increasingly aware of the importance of proper phrasing and the blending demanded in such an ensemble (Fig. 6.10).

Stansell, in studying the high-school dance band, indicates that "the selecting of music for a high school dance band is somewhat of a problem. The stock arrangements are many times difficult to play, and even at that, they are sometimes not good arrangements. They usually have a jump chorus that provides the various soloists a chance to *ad lib*, but on the high school level it is pretty rare to have any players that can improvise a solo and keep a unified line going for a whole chorus."[8] There are now appearing on the market high-school dance-band arrangements suitable for use in the senior high school. Arrangements for dance bands should not be made by the teacher or his students without written permission of the publisher of the composition. To make such arrangements is an infringement of the copyright law.

Schools which accept the dance band in their music program frequently supply the instruments and other equipment, such as front lights and music. There are

Gadsden Public Schools, Gadsden, Alabama.

Fig. 6.10. Dance music has a natural appeal for high-school students. It also has rigorous musical requirements if done well.

[8] William F. Stansell, "A Study of the High School Dance Band," unpublished research study, Michigan State University, 1956.

schools which allow the dance band a fee, established by the school administration, for performance. This fee frequently is placed in the school general fund or the music fund and applied toward the purchase of music and equipment, or for financial assistance to pupils for summer music camps or college and university scholarships. There is a definite policy expressed by teachers working with school dance bands: they must not in any way compete with the commercial dance bands. Competition with the professional musician is prohibited by the *Code of Ethics* jointly agreed to by the Music Educators National Conference, the American Federation of Musicians, and the American Association of School Administrators (see Chapter 20).

HANDBELLS IN MUSIC EDUCATION

In the past fifteen years there has been a tremendous increase in handbell ringing. It has been estimated that more than a thousand groups of handbell ringers, a large percentage of them of school age, meet regularly to enjoy this instrumental activity. Handbell groups have been organized in public schools, some mental hospitals, schools for the blind, and colleges and universities. An individual participating in the group is not responsible for playing the entire melodic line but for the playing of a given number of bells covering specific notes assigned to him as part of the group. In one group a player may be responsible for the playing of from one to three bells; at times a single player has been assigned to control as many as thirteen bells. When more than two bells are assigned to a player, a table is needed to hold bells not in use. For the young player, responsibility for two bells challenges his mental agility sufficiently.

The musical score may be placed on a placard large enough for all to see (Fig. 6.11), but it is more desirable to have each player have a score of regular size. Individual scores identify a player's part by color markings. Each player must be accurate in the reading and performance of rhythmic values and the comprehension of the musical relationship of his part to the whole.

DROP-OUTS FROM INSTRUMENTAL PARTICIPATION

Drop-outs from instrumental instruction in the junior and senior high schools present a real problem to the teacher of instrumental music. Exploratory work with instruments, class instruction, testing, and auditioning provide opportunities for the teacher to counsel and guide pupils and in turn reduce the number of drop-outs.

Potomac English Handbell Ringers, Washington, D.C.

Fig. 6.11. Junior members of the Potomac English Handbell Ringers of Washington, D.C., perform in Elizabethan costumes.

Bergan found that students drop instrumental music because:

1. They are improperly motivated through (a) high pressure tactics, (b) influence of friends, (c) pressure from parents.
2. They are not selected by test methods which will increase their chances of making progress.
3. The music teachers do not establish positive working relations with the parents of their students.
4. The objectives of music education are not made clear.
5. Of the lack of orientation and cooperation between the elementary, junior high and senior high schools.
6. Of the discouraging junior high school practice of transferring instruments.
7. Of the low quality of school-owned instruments.
8. Of poor pupil-teacher relationships.
9. Of the selection of low motivating materials.
10. Of poor methods of evaluation.
11. Of lack of recognition in the group.
12. Of unrealistic demands upon their time.

13. Of the influence of others who drop.
14. Of problems of class schedules.
15. Of the desire and necessity to spend their time earning extra money.[9]

Guidance of pupils in any area of education is recognized as a part of the teacher's responsibility. The waste of both the pupils' and the teacher's time and the economic factors involved indicate the need for a constant check on drop-outs. An up-to-date record of those leaving the work, including their reasons for doing so, should provide information that will lead to the reduction in the number of pupils dropping instrumental study.

SUMMARY

The future of music in America is to a great extent dependent upon the breadth and quality of musical performance in the junior and senior high schools. The instrumental curriculums of these schools have much in common. They offer a wide variety of activities well suited to the musical, physical, mental, and emotional development of the teen-ager. While bringing instrumental experiences to many pupils, they are at the same time concerned with the discovery and development of the most interested and talented boys and girls.

The instrumental curriculum does not follow a set pattern, but varies from one school or community to another. It may include exploratory instruments, class instrumental instruction, the training band, the marching band, the pep band, the concert band, the orchestra, the dance band, solo and small-ensemble experience, and private instrumental instruction. The curriculum should meet the needs of all children in a manner consistent with both quality of performance and recognition of individual interests and abilities. Exploratory instrumental experience should be available to all pupils. Class instrumental instruction is also a very important part of the program. The great progress made in instrumental music in the schools may be attributed to the success of class instruction. Permitting boys and girls to become members of selective instrumental ensembles for which they are not musically prepared fosters musical mediocrity, tension, frustration, and a misconception by the pupil as to what is good and bad in music. The idea that membership in the advanced band is not open to everyone is psychologically and educationally sound.

If we think in terms of the musical development of students, the orchestra is assured a place in both the junior and senior high schools. Private music instruction and the private teacher are also necessary parts of the instrumental program. Solo and small-ensemble experience gives a child the opportunity to assume an importance which is fruitful to him both musically and as an individual.

[9] Hal A. Bergan, "A Study of Drop-outs in Instrumental Music in Five Selected Schools," unpublished doctoral dissertation, Michigan State University, 1957.

SUGGESTED ACTIVITIES

1. Study and report on the instrumental curriculums offered in nearby Class A, B, C, and D senior high schools. How broad are the programs? What do they offer the talented pupil? What percentages of the student bodies participate in instrumental music?
2. Attend a rehearsal of a junior-high-school band or orchestra. Evaluate the work being done by these pupils. What strengths do you find? What weaknesses? Is the membership of the group selective enough, or is it being handicapped by pupils not ready for participation in the organization?
3. Investigate the possibilities of keyboard experience in instrumental music. Report your findings to the class.
4. Make a list of films and filmstrips that could be valuable instructional aids to the teacher of instrumental music.
5. Observe instrumental instruction classes of various sizes and types. Discuss with the teachers in charge their feelings as to the type of instruction best suited to the junior and senior high school.
6. Make an instrumentation chart for Grades 4 through 12 that will show the instrumentation resources necessary for a 40-piece orchestra and a 60-piece band in the senior high school.
7. Study the program of instrumental music in a junior high school maintaining both a band and an orchestra. Report how the groups are scheduled, and how the membership in both organizations is maintained.
8. As a class project, examine the music available for all types of junior- and senior-high-school ensembles. Classify the numbers as to difficulty.
9. Prepare a report on credit allowance for private music instruction in the senior high school.
10. Organize the class for a debate on the subject, "The dance band is an essential part of instrumental instruction in the senior high school."
11. Discuss the problem of drop-outs with several instrumental teachers. Report their comments to the class.

SELECTED READINGS

Andrews, Frances, and Joseph A. Leeder, "The Junior High School Instrumental Program," in *Guiding Junior High School Pupils in Music Experiences*, Prentice-Hall, 1953, pp. 265–299.

Bondurant, Dorothy, "Instrumental Music Is a Part of the Total Music Program," *Music Educators Journal*, November–December, 1956, pp. 38–43.

Hjelmervick, Kenneth, and Richard Berg, *Marching Bands—How to Organize and Develop Them*, Barnes, 1953.

Hovey, Nilo W., *The Administration of School Instrumental Music*, Belwin, 1952.
Ivory, Paul S., "Band Programs in Minnesota," *Journal of Research in Music Education*, Music Educators National Conference, Spring, 1953, pp. 3–10.
Loken, Newt, and Otis Dypwick, *Cheerleading and Marching Bands*, Ronald, 1956.
Miller, Rosemary, "Are They Learning To Read Music?" (Idea Exchange), *The Instrumentalist*, October, 1956.
Rue, Robert A., "The Place of the Dance Band in High School Music," *The Instrumentalist*, November, 1953, pp. 50–51.
The String Instruction Program in Music Education, Music Educators National Conference, 1957.
Sur, William R. (Ed.), *Keyboard Experience and Piano Class Instruction*, Music Educators National Conference, 1957.
Weber, Fred, "The Elementary and Junior High School Band Program," in *Building Better Bands*, Belwin, 1957, pp. 3–26.
Wersen, Louis, "The Pros Can Help Your Orchestra," *Music Educators Journal*, September–October, 1961, p. 54.
Westcott, Wendell, "Handbells in Music Education," *Music Educators Journal*, February–March, 1962, p. 109.
Wiedenmeyer, Clement, "Dance Bands in High Schools," *The Music Journal*, March, 1952, p. 41.

Used by Permission, Music Educators National Conference, Washington, D.C.

CHAPTER

7

Musicianship

WHAT IS BASIC MUSIC THEORY?

Basic music theory in the junior and senior high school is a study of the fundamentals of music. We think of it as being a functional and vitalized study of the elements, the structure, the texture, the terminology, and the notation of music. Through participation and experience the student gains an appreciation and a working knowledge of the staff, lines and spaces, key and time signatures, major and minor scales, and other fundamentals which lead to more intelligent listening, improved musical performance, and greater enjoyment of music. Basic music should be a part of the music education of all students. It is of equal importance to consumers of music and to those who may look forward to a career in music.

The content in a course in basic music varies with the needs of individual students and classes. One school system may have a well-organized and well-taught music program for all the children in the elementary grades. These children are likely to enter the secondary school with a fine attitude toward and some competence in music. Singing, rhythmic, playing, and listening experiences have made the staff, scales, notation, and terminology useful and important to them as musicians. They are ready for advanced work in music fundamentals.

In another school system where there may be little or no music taught in the elementary grades, many of the children entering junior high school are still nonsingers. The staff, scales, notation, and printed music are a mystery to them. For the most part, these girls and boys are naturally interested in music. They want to play and sing. In this situation the teaching of music theory must start where the students are and carry them on as far as they can go. At the same time the teacher must foster and maintain the students' interest in and enthusiasm for music (Fig. 7.1).

WHY BASIC MUSIC IS IMPORTANT

As we listen to young people play and sing, the value of basic music theory training becomes clearer. For example, a certain high-school band has gained a well-earned reputation as a superior marching unit. The school and the com-

San Diego City Schools, San Diego, California.

Fig. 7.1. The study of music notation holds the interest of students.

munity are outspoken in their praise of this group and its band shows. But as we listen to its annual band concert we find the musical performance of the group sadly lacking. Its tone quality leaves much to be desired, its intonation is poor, wrong notes are frequent, rhythms are inaccurate at times, and phrasing is faulty. These children are musical; they are enthusiastic about their band. What is wrong? The fault lies in the fact that from the beginning of instruction the emphasis has been primarily on marching rather than on music and musicianship.

Another school band has an enviable reputation as a marching unit and a concert organization. As we listen we realize that from the start the teaching of fundamentals was given proper emphasis. Its playing is accurate and musical. The members of this band have developed a musical vocabulary which makes the language of music understandable to them. A sight-reading number is included in their concert and as we listen to the playing of this composition we know that the printed page of music has meaning for these boys and girls. Their musical growth through the study of music fundamentals has given them the power to work independently in music. They know that there is good reason for learning about rhythm, melody, harmony, notation, and form, and they know that the result is a superior musical organization.

As one listens to junior- and senior-high-school choral groups in classroom and concert performances, the widespread tendency to rely mainly on the rote approach to learning becomes apparent. A large percentage of these choral groups "learns" pieces year after year. Continued membership in the groups means "learning" more pieces for performance. Little attention is given to the development of useful skills, appreciations, and competencies. Continuity of instruction aimed at musical growth through basic music theory is one means of assuring desirable outcomes of instruction in music. These outcomes are of both immediate and lasting value to students.

Effective music instruction at any level must incorporate some degree of music theory. The pupil may or may not know that he is being taught music theory, but it is inherent in the development of both his skills and his appreciations. Just as a coach must stress the fundamentals of the game, so must a music teacher make certain, if his pupils are to progress, that music fundamentals are thoroughly learned and understood.

OBJECTIVES OF BASIC MUSIC TEACHING

The objectives of basic music teaching are centered primarily in the development of necessary skills, understandings, attitudes, and appreciations which contribute to all-around musical comprehension and competence. Improved musical performance is certainly a natural outcome of the study of basic music theory. In adjudicating the content performance of junior- and senior-high-school pupils it is readily apparent which of the groups have gained a working knowledge of music fundamentals. Technique, intonation, interpretation, and all of the attributes of superior performance are in evidence (Fig. 7.2).

Basic music theory teaching seeks to accelerate the learning of new music and the reading of music through ear and eye training. A great deal of the laborious and inaccurate learning of music is due to the continued use of rote teaching in both the vocal and instrumental areas of instruction. In basic music theory the rudiments of music are related to every music lesson in a functional manner, with the goal always in mind: the development of each student's musicianship and the power to produce his own music, independent of the teacher and of rote teaching.

The speed of progress in music is of great importance when working with adolescents. They want results; they want to advance rapidly; they want to be able to work independently; and they want to be successful in their work. Acceleration of learning leading to greater achievement is an outcome of good instruction in basic music theory.

Duluth Public Schools, Duluth, Minnesota. Courtesy KDAL, Duluth, Minnesota.

Fig. 7.2. The importance of good musicianship is immediately apparent in the performance of choral groups like this one.

The contribution made by basic music theory to the vocational and avocational interests of pupils is also significant. Among junior- and senior-high-school students there are those who will be serious amateur performers and consumers of music, and there will be those who will look forward to a career in music or to a closely related occupation. Basic music theory training naturally is essential for these students, as it is for all young musicians.

TYPES OF BASIC MUSIC TRAINING

There are many types of basic music training and many possible approaches to musicianship. The types and approaches used are for the most part limited only by the creative ability of the teacher. In any type of basic music theory training a functional approach to the work is recommended. As the teacher relates the teaching of music fundamentals to the music being played or sung, students begin to see why a mastery of fundamentals is important to their progress in music. Once students accept and appreciate the fundamentals of music as a help to them, a readiness and a willingness to learn prevails.

Ear and Eye Development

Ear training is the first step in musical development. The ease with which young people learn by rote and make effective use of their ears in learning may be either an asset or a detriment to their progress in music. Evaluation of instruction at regular intervals is essential to be sure that understanding and skill accompany ear development.

The teacher's preparation should include a detailed analysis of the music to be studied in all music ensembles and classes. Such an analysis by the teacher will make clear the need for ear and eye training dealing with lines and spaces, notation, key and time signatures, clefs, scales, modes, melodic line, intervals, harmonies, rhythms, form, and terminology. From this analysis the teacher is then able to plan for basic music instruction over an extended period of time and to incorporate some teaching of fundamentals in every lesson or rehearsal.

Success in music reading hinges upon the student's ear and eye development. It is not necessary for junior- and senior-high-school choral groups to be dependent upon rote learning. The ability to read an easy melody and to do two-, three-, and four-part music reading is well within the capacity of most pupils, provided ear and eye training is sustained. Such training from the beginning of instrumental study also will bring about a reasonable mastery of the musical score.

Music teachers dedicated to the idea of teaching music to children rather than exploiting children in the name of public performance are aware that the power gained in music reading is the key to musical growth, and should increase as the pupil progresses from year to year. Through competence and skill gained in ear and eye training, the student learns more quickly and the standards of performance improve.

At one time a group of church choirs in England, meeting in annual festivals for adjudication, felt the need of freeing themselves from the handicap of rote singing. The members of these choirs were untrained in music and, since they were not in a position to study music as individuals, ear and eye training was made a part of their rehearsals. In this instance great reliance was placed on the moveable "do" system of learning to read music. In a short time the ability of the individual choir members to read music improved greatly and a higher standard of performance followed. Likewise, once provision for ear and eye training is made, progress in music reading is possible with junior- and senior-high-school students or with adults.

In a school visit a few years ago we stepped into the music room of a junior high school. Were we in the right place? What were these boys and girls doing with scrap metal, scrap lumber, and old bottles and glasses of every size and shape? The teacher, Mr. Carl, noticing us, came quickly to the door and welcomed us to the General Music class. He said, "I don't blame you for hesitating. This room looks like a shop when we make instruments from the materials we have collected." An informal atmosphere prevailed as we moved about the room, but there was no discipline problem. Each one of the eighth-graders was completely absorbed in selecting materials or constructing the instrument of his own choice. Some were working with bottles and glasses, some with pieces of metal, and some with wood.

We awaited with interest the end of the period when we could visit with Mr. Carl. We wanted to know his objectives in this unit and if he felt that the time spent making instruments was worth while from the musical standpoint. His reply was enlightening. "In the first place," he said, "this unit is motivated because it satisfies the collector's instinct these youngsters have. You noticed how absorbed they were in their work. They like to work with their hands on a project of their own selection. We help each other and in time each child will have his own instrument. As they struggle with construction and tuning problems they learn a great deal about music and musical instruments, and that really meets the objectives we have in mind.

"When the instrument is finished and tuned they naturally want to play it. They want to play the pieces they know and learn to play music we have in school. At this point they discover that they need to know something of the staff and printed music. Music fundamentals make sense to them and they ask for help with them.

"The project takes a lot of time and patience and requires valuable cooperation from the industrial arts teacher. When the unit is completed the attitude of the students toward music and music fundamentals has changed. When we sing and play in the class they are ready for more work in fundamentals as the need arises."

Keyboard Experience

By virtue of its unique contribution, keyboard experience is becoming increasingly important to music education. It is a tool in the general music program of the school, a tool which facilitates the development of musicianship, promotes music literacy, and makes it possible for every child to have an effective means of applying and experimenting with the essential elements in music—melody, harmony, and rhythm.

Keyboard experience may be incorporated in the General Music class of the junior and senior high school or it may be integrated with other areas of the music curriculum. It requires little equipment and can be made available to pupils in any class with the use of one piano and a number of inexpensive keyboards (Fig. 7.3). The teacher who desires to use keyboard instruction in either choral or instrumental classes does not have to be a pianist. Many vocal and instrumental teachers who are not pianists have been successful in handling keyboard instruction in their classes. Keyboard experience should not be confused with class piano. It does not have for its primary objective the development of pianistic skills, but rather it aims to provide the pupil with a firm foundation in the rudiments of music by means of effective ear and eye training.

Fig. 7.3. Keyboard experience promotes basic musicianship.

American Music Conference, Chicago, Illinois.

The following paragraphs indicate the aid which keyboard experience can bring to music theory teaching.

> It is generally agreed by junior high school teachers that if the General Music class is to be a continuation of the music development of the pupils, a thorough review of the fundamentals of music learned in the elementary grades is desirable. The use of keyboard experience opens the way for an interesting and motivated approach to the review of the fundamentals of music. . . .
>
> Acquaintance with the keyboard is begun by rote. Next the relationship between music notation and the keyboard is developed. Further understanding of the relationship between notation and the keyboard is established through the use of songs which all the group know. Keyboard experience in the General Music class is not only a means of motivating the review of the fundamentals of music; it will lead to better music reading, part-singing, and understanding of simple form and design in music. . . .[1]

Exploring music by means of keyboard experience in the General Music class might start with the distribution of keyboard charts to all the students, time being given them to become familiar by sight and sound with the function of the white and black keys. As soon as possible the pupils should be given an opportunity to go to the piano, and should be encouraged to:

1. Play by ear the melodies of songs they know.
2. Play some of the easier songs from the school music books. The student should

[1] William R. Sur (Ed.), *Keyboard Experience and Piano Class Instruction*, Music Educators National Conference, 1956, p. 14.

start by playing the melody at first and then add other parts as familiarity with the keyboard increases.

3. Continue playing songs in a variety of keys, and to transpose by ear.
4. Accompany songs by ear at the piano by using simple harmonies. The student should be taught to divide the chord tones between hands, playing the I and V^7 chords, using the left hand for the root of the chord and the right hand for the remainder of the chord tones.
5. Continue chording with the class, learning the I, IV, and V^7 chords and progressions.

EFFECTIVE BASIC MUSIC TRAINING

Basic music training in the fundamentals of music is recommended as a part of the instruction received by all students in choral, instrumental, and General Music classes.

Planning for Effective Instruction

Mindful of the variations that exist in elementary-school music programs and of the individual differences of the students in a class, we face the question of how the teacher can determine what music fundamentals are to be covered in a particular situation. At the start of instruction the teacher, in planning for effective music training, is in need of information about the musical achievement and background of individual pupils. The cumulative music-record card can be an effective means of securing such information. An example of such a card is one used in the schools of South Bend, Indiana (see Fig. 7.4).

Also of considerable value in planning for effective instruction is the standardized achievement test in music. A number of these tests are listed in Chapter 20. For the most part they deal with knowledge of music symbols and terms, recognition of syllable names, detection of pitch errors in a familiar melody, detection of time errors in a familiar melody, recognition of pitch names, knowledge of time and key signatures, knowledge of note and rest values, and recognition of familiar melodies from notation.

For both students and teachers to receive the maximum benefit from the use of standardized achievement tests it is suggested that they be given at the start of the school year and at the end of each semester's or year's work, to determine the extent of musical development. Information from tests given semiannually in all music classes of both the junior and senior high school is materially helpful in the effective planning of music instruction.

JUNIOR HIGH
CUMULATIVE MUSIC RECORD

1. Name__________Age______Grade______Home Room______
2. Musical Experience Instrumental__________Vocal______
3. School Previously Attended__________
4. Singing Ability______Quality______Range______
5. Reading Ability______Listening Attitude______
6. Personal Behavior Traits__________
7. Estimate of Musical Ability__________
8. Music Interests of Members of the Family__________
9. In your home do you have a radio______ phonograph______ television______ piano______
10. Remarks__________

South Bend Public Schools, South Bend, Indiana.

Fig. 7.4. A cumulative music record.

Continuity of Instruction

Another valuable characteristic of an effective music program in the secondary school is continuity of instruction, which may be secured by means of a logically planned and flexible sequence of training. Such a plan must be based on the outcomes of the music experiences of the elementary school and at the same time must give consideration to the individual differences of students. It will be useful to the teacher as a guide to music learnings but is not to be used as a set of fixed standards of achievement for all students. The guide should be helpful in determining just what basic music theory is to be considered as a part of the General Music class, the beginning and advanced instrumental and choral groups, and the senior-high-school course in music theory. It may be advantageous in planning progressive instrumental and choral instruction, which brings to the students more advanced music instruction as they continue their work from year to year (Fig. 7.5).

Detroit Public Schools, Detroit, Michigan.

Fig. 7.5. This seventh-grade general music class is laying the foundation for advanced music instruction.

The instrumental and choral groups and the General Music class may support continuity of instruction through:

1. The use of standardized achievement tests as guidance instruments to determine which fundamentals of music need emphasis in a lesson, in a rehearsal, or in a year's work.
2. The teacher's detailed analysis of each composition to be studied. Incorporating into the projected lesson plans the related theoretical material needed by the students as they prepare for performance.
3. The study of the cumulative music record of each student in order to meet his needs and evaluate his work.
4. The development and use of a guide to music learnings that will be of benefit in avoiding useless repetition and overlapping of instruction. The aid that a teacher receives from developing and using such a guide leads to logical continuity of instruction.

BASIC MUSIC THEORY AS A HIGH-SCHOOL ELECTIVE

A course in basic music theory as a two-semester senior-high-school elective offered five periods a week and given full academic credit is not new to the curriculum of the secondary school. The credit received may be used for admission to many colleges and universities, regardless of the choice of curriculum for collegiate study.

In the large high school, sufficient enrollment may be secured annually to schedule a course in music theory. In the small high school the practice is to offer such a course in alternate years. A number of senior high schools are successfully meeting the enrollment problem by offering Advanced General Music as an elective. This substitution limits the offering in music theory; but with the opportunities it provides for experience in singing, rhythms, listening, and music theory, it contributes immeasurably to the all-around musical development of the student (Fig. 7.6). The Advanced General Music class, designed to serve students of varying interests, usually attracts enough students to be offered each year.

Values

Some values of basic music theory training in a senior-high-school elective course, or as a part of an advanced general music course, are:

1. It brings to the performer and consumer of music an understanding and appreciation of the elements of music.
2. It is the means of securing a working knowledge of music notation and terminology.

Fig. 7.6. Appropriate field trips are a part of advanced general music experience. These band members visit a museum to see primitive drums prior to a concert.

Used by permission, Music Educators National Conference, Washington, D.C.

3. It offers the student a means of improving musicianship and a preparation for advanced study.
4. It acquaints the student with musical form, design, and various styles of composition.
5. It makes possible a sustained emphasis on ear and eye training and other skills essential to the development of musicianship.
6. It provides an opportunity for a creative approach to music through part-writing and composition. It is the opportunity for the teacher to make the most of the student's desire to invent and create.
7. It has guidance possibilities in that it is a means of discovering and encouraging the gifted student.
8. It is course work that serves the avocational and vocational needs of students.

A Representative Course Outline

The senior-high-school elective course in music theory must necessarily be adaptable to a variety of situations. The course outlined on page 167 is merely suggestive and in most situations will have to be modified. The approach to instruction and the content of the course will depend on many factors, among them the previous preparation and competency of the members of the class. If students in their junior-high-school General Music class and in their work in various ensembles have gained a mastery of basic music fundamentals, they may be ready to start their study of theory with elementary harmony and chord structure. In this circumstance they can be given considerable opportunity for advanced ear and eye training. Regardless of the level of instruction, it is desirable that students be encouraged to do as much original writing as possible.

In the majority of senior high schools, a large part of the high-school theory course is devoted to fundamentals of music such as key and time signatures, notation, scales, intervals, rather easy melodic and rhythmic dictation, and terminology. In each school and with each class it is the responsibility of the teacher to discover how elementary or advanced the course in music theory should be.

For example, one senior-high-school teacher gave his class in music theory a chance to write original compositions as a week-end assignment. On Monday one of the girls in the class went to the piano and played a minuet she had written. Musically the work was acceptable. Suggestions were made by the teacher and members of the class for minor changes that would improve the writing. During the discussion the comment was made by a boy in the class that their high-school orchestra ought to play the composition. The teacher told the students that before the piece could be rehearsed and performed by their school orchestra, an orchestration of the minuet would have to be prepared. Later a conductor's score would have to be made and parts copied for the various instruments. He suggested this as a class project.

The response to the teacher's suggestion was immediate. Everyone wanted to take part. Skillfully taking advantage of the motivation generated, the teacher introduced elementary orchestration and writing for transposing instruments. The students became intensely interested in the range, the technical possibilities and limitations of the orchestral instruments. In time the minuet was orchestrated, the conductor's score made, parts copied, and all was in readiness for rehearsal and performance of the composition by the school orchestra. The student composer was invited to conduct the work in rehearsal and in concert.

How much learning took place? While it is difficult to determine precisely the extent of learning taking place when students are encouraged and guided in creative activity of this kind, good teachers know that independent study and research undertaken voluntarily by students are highly profitable from the learning standpoint. Furthermore, projects of the type described bring about a natural integration of theory and application, a highly desirable and effective result. The vitality and enthusiasm generated can exert a strong positive influence throughout the entire secondary music program.

A representative course outline is given below:

MUSIC FUNDAMENTALS

Section One: Notation of Pitch
- Musical alphabet, staff, clef signs, notes
- Leger lines, 8va sign
- Accidentals

Section Two: Notation of Duration
- Relative duration of tones, tie, dotted notes
- Bar line, measure
- Time signature, classification of time signature
- More complex problems of duration

Section Three: Tonality
- Basic scales, major scale
- Key signature
- Minor scales

Section Four: Chord Structure
- Basic triads
- Major triad
- Minor triad
- Diminished triad
- Augmented triad
- Intervals

Each unit should be thoroughly mastered from the standpoint of (1) written theory; (2) aural theory; and (3) keyboard drill. For example, it is not sufficient that the student be able to write a major scale; it is very important that the scale be identified by ear, and played (not necessarily with correct fingering) at the keyboard (Fig. 7.7).

Similarly, *all* the above material must be integrated with melodic and rhythmic dictation and keyboard drill. The student must be able not only to spell a major triad correctly, but he should also learn to identify aurally the soprano and bass position of the chord and find it on the piano keyboard. When this material is well integrated with the student's instrumental or vocal study, he will achieve the maximum benefit from the study of music fundamentals (Fig. 7.8).

The approach to keyboard experience in the senior-high-school music theory class is similar to that used in the General Music class of the junior high school. Interest in keyboard work may be heightened by a functional approach to the keyboard in which the students become familiar with the keyboard, play favorite tunes by ear, read and play melodies from their school song books, and gradually add other parts, transposing and chording.

Senior-high-school students enjoy experimenting at the keyboard by attempting to play folk tunes or popular songs in a number of keys. They like working with major and minor scales, starting with a song like "Joy to the World," whose melody follows the scale line, and trying chords in root position and inversions.

Detroit Public Schools, Detroit, Michigan.

Fig. 7.7. The harmony class makes an important contribution to all other areas of music instruction.

Fig. 7.8. The piano can do more to bring music into the home and daily living than any other instrument.

Steinway & Sons.

Enthusiasm for keyboard work usually runs high when developmental accompaniment figures such as waltz bass, broken chord, Alberti, and arpeggio are introduced to chord patterns such as I, IV, V^7, I, and I, VI, IV, II, I^6_4, V^7, and I. It is not uncommon in keyboard practice to find high-school students working away at the harmonies and accompaniments to "Our Boys Will Shine Tonight" and "Hail! Hail! The Gang's All Here" without prodding from the teacher. They will enjoy improvising the accompaniments to the following familiar songs and carols:

Using Chords I, V^7:

- Lightly Row
- Augustine (*German*)
- Clementine
- Long, Long Ago
- Skip to My Lou
- Swanee River (Old Folks at Home)
- Believe Me If All Those Endearing Young Charms
- Annie Laurie
- Auld Lang Syne

Using Chords I, IV, V^7:

- Good Night Ladies
- Our Boys Will Shine Tonight
- For He's a Jolly Good Fellow
- Carry Me Back to Old Virginny
- Goodbye, My Lover, Goodbye
- Little Brown Church in the Vale
- There's Music in the Air
- My Old Kentucky Home
- Camp Town Races
- Beautiful Dreamer
- When Love Is Kind
- Juanita

Polly Wolly Doodle
Old MacDonald Had a Farm
Hail! Hail! The Gang's All Here
Merrily We Roll Along
(*from* Good Night Ladies)
Caisson Song (*army*)
Home on the Range
Oh! Susanna
Li'l Liza Jane
Yankee Doodle
Pop Goes the Weasel
Silent Night
The First Noël
Jingle Bells
Away in a Manger

Using Chords I, IV, II, V^7:
Dixie
Old Black Joe
Old Oaken Bucket
Drink to Me Only with Thine Eyes
Swing Low, Sweet Chariot

INSTRUCTIONAL MATERIALS

Instructional materials of many kinds are necessary in an effective educational program. The music teacher needs good text and reference materials, tests, and a liberal supply of appropriate audio-visual materials as well. Investigation should be made of the new programmed-teaching texts.

Text and Reference Materials

The selection of a text for use by students should be made by the teacher with consideration for the age level, needs, musical ability, and background of the students enrolled in the class. It is important that the teacher become familiar with the various texts and be prepared to make a change when the make-up of a class indicates that the use of a certain text will facilitate learning. A representative list is offered in Chapter 21. The texts listed are not necessarily superior to others which may be available; an evaluation should be made by the teacher. In addition to the text selected for use by all students, the school library should have a representative selection of books on music theory available for use as reference materials by students and teacher.

Standardized Aptitude and Achievement Tests

The first widely known aptitude test in music was *Measures of Musical Talent* by Carl E. Seashore of the University of Iowa, 1919. Since that time the names of Kwalwasser, Drake, Whistler and Thorpe, and Gaston have become familiar to teachers of music because of the excellent tests they have developed. We must recognize the fact that the perfect test of musical aptitude has not been developed, and put to good use the testing materials available to us at this time. They are extremely valuable in the search for musical talent and in discovering basic reasons for failure of music students to reach high levels of performance. Perhaps the most important reason for a teacher to use aptitude tests is to have some means beyond his personal opinion to guide parents and pupils in making decisions concerning music study.

Many standardized achievement tests in music have become available for use by teachers during the last forty years. Most of these tests are concerned with the student's progress and mastery of basic music theory or fundamentals of music. They are also an excellent means of improving instruction in both the elementary and secondary schools. They are the key to developing a mastery of key and meter signatures, music notation, music terminology, intervals, and scales, all of which contribute to better performance by the young singer or instrumentalist. They also offer the teacher a means of checking the effectiveness of his own teaching. Use of these tests by school music teachers is recommended on all levels of instruction. A list of standardize aptitude and achievement tests will be found in Chapter 20.

Audiovisual Materials

Audiovisual materials are of considerable assistance in the teaching of basic music theory when they are properly selected and used. Record players, recordings, tape recorders and tapes for use by students needing additional practice in melodic, harmonic, and rhythmic dictation can be of great value (Fig. 7.9). Similarly, the motion picture, the 2 × 2 slide, and the opaque projector are valuable instruction tools under appropriate circumstances. The opaque projector, for example, is particularly valuable in class viewing and discussion of part-writing exercises and original compositions for discussion and performance.

Considerable use may also be made of flash cards calling for identification of key and time signatures, pitch names, note and rest values, melodic and rhythmic patterns, like and unlike phrases, and many other items. Flash cards can be made by the teacher for his specific needs.

Charts of every type and description have been developed for use in music teaching. Music rooms generally contain charts of the piano keyboard, the staff, the Great Staff, the circle of keys, and examples of musical form and design ranging from simple binary and ternary form to charts which show in detail sonata and other musical forms. Charts are also used for examples of harmonic and

3M Company, St. Paul, Minnesota.

Fig. 7.9. Hearing one's performance on a tape recorder is a unique and valuable means of self-improvement.

contrapuntal writing, rhythmic patterns, transposition, and the range of band and orchestra instruments.

Teachers are making interesting use of the feltboard in teaching music theory. Staff, notes, rests, and a number of cutouts may be made in school or secured from commercial sources. With these teaching aids, clever display-teaching situations can be devised and many useful teaching ideas originated. A feltboard is shown in Fig. 7.10.

It is important for the music teacher to recognize that audiovisual materials are basic tools of effective teaching rather than interesting extras to be used if time and convenience permit. The good teacher uses the tape recorder, record player, filmstrips, and other audiovisual media as integral parts of his teaching technique—and uses each where it makes a particular contribution to the learning experience. Because of its importance to the whole field of music instruction, the subject of audiovisual materials is discussed in detail in Chapters 17 and 18.

Fig. 7.10. The feltboard is useful in teaching music fundamentals as well as providing a variety of other learning experiences.

Lansing Public Schools, Lansing, Michigan.

SUMMARY

The study of basic music theory is one important and definite step in the direction of sound musicianship. It is a study of the fundamentals of music—a functional study of the structure, texture, terminology, and notation of music, presented in terms of the background, needs, and interests of the individual and the class.

Growth in musical competence, skills, and understanding is a result of continuity of instruction in basic music training. As the teacher relates the teaching of music fundamentals to the music being played or sung, boys and girls realize why a mastery of fundamentals is important to their progress in music. Continuity of instruction may be secured by means of a logically planned and flexible sequence of music theory training in both the junior and the senior high school.

Full use should be made of the motivation to be derived from opportunities offered for students to do original composition. Keyboard experience as a tool for use in the General Music class of the junior high school, and in the senior-high-school course in music theory helps provide the foundation for the development of musicianship. Audiovisual materials and equipment such as record players, tape recorders, projectors of various types, charts, filmstrips, flash cards, and feltboards can contribute much to the effective teaching of music theory.

SUGGESTED ACTIVITIES

1. Make a study of concert programs, articles about music and musicians, books on music, and musical scores. From this study, develop a list of the most commonly used musical terms.

2. Administer a standardized achievement test to a group of junior-high-school students and analyze the results. Where are they lacking in their knowledge of music fundamentals? Where do their strengths lie?
3. Construct an achievement test for use in planning basic music theory instruction in a junior or senior high school. Administer the test, analyze the results, and seek to strengthen the test you have constructed.
4. Report on a secondary-school rehearsal or concert with respect to evidence of weaknesses and strengths of the students in basic music theory.
5. Observe several junior- and senior-high-school music classes and determine what steps you would take to vitalize and make functional the teaching of music theory.
6. Design a set of charts or flash cards for use in a junior-high-school General Music class or in a senior-high-school Music Theory class.
7. Plan and demonstrate the use of keyboard experience in promoting musical growth in a senior-high-school Music Theory class.
8. Make a study of the admission requirements of 12 colleges and universities to determine the entrance credit they allow for music study. Do they recognize credit earned in music theory?
9. Discuss the representative course outline in basic music on page 167. What do you consider its strengths and weaknesses?
10. Report on a comparative study of two of the following texts for the teaching of music fundamentals in the junior high school: Cass, Elliot, Reed, Tilson (see Chapter 20 for bibliographical information).
11. Preview and evaluate several motion pictures or filmstrips offered for use in the teaching of music fundamentals.
12. Try to secure for study and discussion several examples of original compositions written by junior- or senior-high-school students.

SELECTED READINGS

"Authoritative Statement on Teaching Machines," *Music Educators Journal*, January, 1962, p. 90.

Henderson, Robert, "On the Musicianship of Conductors," *Music Educators Journal*, June–July, 1964, p. 57.

Horn, Dorothy D., "Music Theory for High School Students," *Music Educators Journal*, January, 1960, p. 74.

Jackson, Sadie I., "Ear and Rhythmic Training," *Music Educators Journal*, September–October, 1963, p. 133.

Lewis, Philip, "Teaching Machines Have the Beat," *Music Educators Journal*, November–December, 1962, p. 94.

Mills, Donn, "Teach Composition in Your General Music Class," *Music Educators Journal*, April–May, 1963, p. 43.

Murphy, Howard A., *Music Fundamentals*, Chandler, 1962.

Pace, Robert, "Keyboard Experience in the Classroom," *Music Educators Journal*, February–March, 1962, p. 44.

Sur, William R. (Ed.), *Keyboard Experience and Class Piano,* Music Educators National Conference, 1956.
Thomas, Ronald B., "Learning Through Composing," *Music Educators Journal,* February–March, 1964, p. 106.
Walton, Charles W., "Three Trends in the Teaching of Theory," *Music Educators Journal,* November–December, 1961, p. 73.

Steinway & Sons, Long Island City, New York.

CHAPTER

8

The Exceptional Child

MUSIC INSTRUCTION AND THE ATYPICAL CHILD

Education in a democracy is education for all children. In the junior and senior high schools are the boys and girls who will be the adults of the future. They are important as a group and as individuals. Some of them are gifted or talented, many are average pupils, and others are handicapped in some way; they all have the right to an education according to their needs and abilities. They all have a right to participate in a music program in the secondary school. Music can serve all children as an art, as a social force, or as a therapy. A broad concept of music education should produce an instructional pattern not only for average children but for those who are especially endowed with mental ability or talent, for the physically handicapped, for the maladjusted, and for the mentally retarded.

The Search for Talent

Giftedness is many-sided, many-patterned. Among the intellectually gifted we find persons talented in many different fields. Different patterns of personality have been noted among children with different kinds of talent—scientific, artistic, musical, leadership ability. Giftedness may take many forms depending upon the particular circumstance.

Gifted children are far from being a homogeneous group; there are wide individual differences among childen designated as gifted.[1]

Lewis M. Terman indicates that:

. . . both interest patterns and special aptitudes play important roles in the making of a gifted scientist, mathematician, mechanic, artist, poet or composer. I am convinced that to achieve greatly in almost any field, the talents have to be backed up by the kind of general intelligence that requires ability to form many sharply defined concepts,

[1] Ruth Strang, "The Nature of Giftedness," in Nelson B. Henry (Ed.), *The Fifty-seventh Yearbook of the National Society for the Study of Education*; Part II: *Education for the Gifted*, University of Chicago Press, 1958, p. 64.

to manipulate them, and to perceive subtle relationships between them: in other words, the ability to engage in abstract thinking.[2]

Just what is a gifted child in music? A panel on "Music and the Exceptional Child" felt that "the gifted child has superior aural sensitivity and sensory equipment, well above average mentality, imagination, and an outstanding singing voice and/or digital manipulability."[3] If we agree with Strang that "giftedness may take many forms," the definition is useful. However, we must be alert for the wide differences among the talented in music. The future composer, musicologist, school music teacher, for example, may not have an outstanding voice or digital manipulability. As valuable and desirable as these qualities are, there will be pupils gifted in music with all the qualities needed for a success in music who are not outstanding performers. There is probably no definition of giftedness in music which would adequately serve all situations. The teacher must try to appreciate and understand the various kinds of giftedness in music (Fig. 8.1).

The search for the boy or girl who is gifted or talented in music is one of the opportunities of those who work in music education. Garrison is of the opinion that "the gifted child is often neglected, and this may considerably affect his

Lansing Public Schools, Lansing, Michigan.

Fig. 8.1. These ninth-grade girls are rehearsing a song that the girl at the piano has composed.

[2] Lewis M. Terman, "The Discovery and Encouragement of Exceptional Talent," *American Psychologist*, **IX** (June, 1954), 221–230.

[3] Pennsylvania Music Educators Association Convention Report, *P.M.E.A. News*, December–January, 1956–1957, pp. 19–20.

mental, social and normal life."[4] New York City was aware of this problem when in 1936 it established the High School of Performing Arts. Such a school challenges the gifted pupil, and the environment for a creative approach to learning stimulates the promising young musician. The environment for learning creates a climate in which mediocrity cannot take over. Each class, each day of schooling, is a challenge to the individual and the group.

Few cities are in a position to provide a school similar to the High School of Performing Arts in New York City. Just how does the teacher of music in the typical junior or senior high school conduct a search for talent? He does it as a normal part of his work—through testing, auditions, tryouts, and the development of a broad program of music education, a program that will attract a large percentage of the student body to some phase of music instruction. The teacher observes, listens, and evaluates as he works. All of these activities are a part of the continuous search for talent.

The Effectiveness of Music with the Handicapped

There are many handicaps with which pupils must live and work. Some are more serious than others and require attendance at a residential school or in special education classes in the local school situation. We are concerned here with those pupils with physical and mental handicaps, or perhaps with a combination of these, who are able to participate in the regular music program of the junior and senior high school.

Scheerenberger, in his writing based on personal experience in working with the mentally retarded, feels that music "by its very basic emotional and aesthetic nature, its potentiality for the inclusion of a variety of themes, lyrics and physical responses, is adaptable to almost any mental age, interest level, or degree of physical development."[5] Thus we have an opportunity to serve both the handicapped and the gifted child through music.

Music which is effective with handicapped girls and boys is more than entertainment or education. It serves as a social force or therapy. Music may bring to the pupil a needed outlet for self-expression; it may assist him in learning to work with others; it may help him to develop and maintain mental and physical health; and it may function as a leisure-time activity.

The effectiveness of teaching the handicapped is not judged solely in terms of musical achievement. Those who seek high levels of musical performance from these children as the sole objective of music teaching are likely to be disappointed.

[4] Karl C. Garrison, *The Psychology of Exceptional Children* (rev. ed.), Ronald, 1950, p. 219.
[5] Richard C. Scheerenberger, "Presenting Music to the Mentally Retarded," *Music Educators Journal*, November–December, 1954, p. 13.

There will be some handicapped children who are capable of superior musical performance, while for others the effectiveness of music experience should be judged on the changes brought about in the child's behavior or attitude. Success is frequently measured in terms of answers to such questions as these:

1. Has there been improvement in muscular strength or coordination?
2. Has there been improvement in speech?
3. Is the pupil successfully fitting into the group?
4. Is he doing his part according to his abilities?

FULFILLING THE NEEDS OF ATYPICAL CHILDREN

The atypical child is the one who is different. In one way or another we all may be atypical, but our reference here is to the child who is different, or atypical, to a degree that makes special consideration necessary to fit him into regular classes. He may be handicapped, physically or mentally, or he may be gifted. Whichever he is, he needs particular attention.

The Teacher's Attitude Toward the Child

The role of the teacher is of even greater significance in working with the atypical child than with the typical child. The teacher is of great importance in fulfilling the needs of atypical children. Personality, training and study emphasizing child growth and development and educational psychology, and experience with atypical children are all of value in meeting the real needs of the pupils. Cooperation with teachers trained in Special Education is essential.

A creative approach to instruction is the basis for teaching which is challenging, and inspirational to the individual child. In such an approach, the pupil will be given as much freedom as possible for experimentation and exploration. The teacher will be interested in research findings and in improving instruction through practical research and experimentation in his work with pupils. Guides to instruction will replace fixed courses of study. New paths to learning will be explored. What is done will be done in terms of what is good for the individual and the group.

The needs of the atypical child can be met in the regular music courses offered in a school. There are innumerable opportunities in choral, instrumental, and other music classes to provide additional projects and assignments which will challenge the gifted and keep them working up to the level of their ability. The choir may sing an original composition by a member of the group, or the woodwind or brass ensemble may perform an arrangement or an original work by a pupil. Opportunities are plentiful for solo and ensemble participation by the gifted.

The needs of the handicapped also can often be met in the regular music classes. A study of the capabilities of the individual will reveal where he can make a contribution to the choral or instrumental organization. The development of an objective attitude by teachers toward handicapped pupils is a strong factor in successful achievement by the handicapped.

A choral teacher, while auditioning a partially sighted boy, discovered that he was very musical, had a good voice and remarkable power of concentration. Although unable to read printed music, he quickly mastered the bass parts of the choir music and was able to take his place as a regular member of the choir. In another situation a boy with a malformation of the right hand was encouraged to experiment with a school-owned alto-saxophone. The teacher worked with the boy and in time was able to admit him to the school's first band.

The handicapped child wants more than anything else to do the things that other children do. He does not want to be set aside and considered different. It is fortunate that the field of music is broad enough to make it possible for the teacher to find ways and means of meeting the needs of the handicapped through the singing, listening, playing, rhythmic, and creative experiences of music in the junior and senior high school (Fig. 8.2).

The teacher's attitude toward the child is of vital consequence in serving the needs of the atypical child. Pupils quickly sense the interest and sincerity of their teachers. The teacher who is sincerely interested in his pupils and approaches them with a belief in the importance of making the most of their abilities has already made a positive step toward fulfilling their needs.

Fig. 8.2. Music is particularly meaningful in the lives of the blind.

Michigan School for the Blind, Lansing, Michigan.

NAME ______________________________ GRADE ________
LAST FIRST

STUDENT'S DAILY ATTITUDE REPORT

		1ST. WK.	2ND. WK.	3RD. WK.	4TH. WK.	5TH. WK.	6TH. WK.	7TH. WK.	8TH. WK.	9TH. WK.	AVERAGE
1ST. SEMESTER	1ST. 9 WEEKS										
	2ND. 9 WEEKS										
2ND. SEMESTER	3RD. 9 WEEKS										
	4TH. 9 WEEKS										

STUDENT'S SIGNATURE

1ST. 9 WKS. ____________________
2ND. 9 WKS. ____________________
3RD. 9 WKS. ____________________
4TH. 9 WKS. ____________________

East Lansing Public Schools, East Lansing, Michigan.

Fig. 8.3. All students use this self-evaluation form which focuses the student's attention on his progress and assists the instructor in his own evaluation.

Understanding Capabilities

Understanding the capabilities of each child is basic to the teacher's approach to the problem of the atypical child. Since we are concerned with music as an art, a social force, and a therapy, it is evident that understanding the child's capabilities is more than knowing what he can do in music. In one school the teachers are asked to include as a part of the child's cumulative record a series of anecdotes about the individual pupil. Such anecdotes can be extremely helpful in understanding the capabilities of the pupils and are far more revealing than the grade record.

In another school, confidential card files are kept to record the progress of each student from year to year. These cards are forwarded to the teacher of music as the child advances on the educational ladder. Separate grade cards for music are made out each grading period, recording the number of times the pupil was absent or tardy, the number of lessons and rehearsals in the grading period, the number of times he has forgotten his music, as well as his grades in conduct, care of instrument, and musical progress. The cards are enclosed with the school's regular report card and sent home for the parent's signature.

A rather interesting plan for learning more about students has been initiated by the Vocal Music Department of the East Lansing, Michigan, Junior High School. This plan has the pupils rate themselves daily. They ask themselves two questions.

VOCAL MUSIC REPORT CARD

NAME ______________________________
LAST FIRST

	PERCENT OF FINAL GRADE	1ST. 9 WEEKS	2ND. 9 WEEKS	1ST. SEM. AV.		3RD. 9 WEEKS	4TH. 9 WEEKS	2ND. SEM. AV.
ATTITUDE								
MUSICIANSHIP								
MUSICOLOGY								
VOICE								
FINAL GRADE								

PARENT'S SIGNATURE:

1ST. 9 WEEKS ______________________________

2ND. 9 WEEKS ______________________________

3RD. 9 WEEKS ______________________________

4TH. 9 WEEKS ______________________________

East Lansing Public Schools, East Lansing, Michigan.

Fig. 8.4. In this report form, note the emphasis on the breakdown of the various factors involved in effective music work.

1. Have I contributed as much as possible to the success of this rehearsal by being alert and following directions? *Yes* or *No*
2. Have I shown a spirit of teamwork and consideration of others? (This involves both musical response and citizenship.) *Yes* or *No*

If both answers are *Yes,* the grade is recorded as "A"; if one is *Yes* and one *No,* the grade is "C"; if both answers are *No,* the grade is "F."

The interesting thing about this rating and self-evaluation plan is that the pupils had voted on whether or not they wanted it. At the end of the grade period they sign their name to the report and turn it in to the teacher, to whom it is a significant help in making an evaluation. It should be remembered that this report does not go to parents. A sample of the form used is shown in Fig. 8.3.

The Vocal Music report card used in this junior high school is also an aid in evaluating pupils and planning for their instruction (see Fig. 8.4). It will be noted that musicology is listed on the card. In this instance musicology refers to musical style, knowledge of composers and history, form and design in music. It may not be musicology in a strict sense but it has a value in terms of student interest. The term musicology seems to fascinate the pupils because it makes them feel grown up, and when the teacher in this particular department was asked about it she said, "The kids love musicology."

Inspiration and Challenge

Both inspiration and challenge must be present as one attempts to meet the needs of the gifted and the handicapped. The creative approach to teaching provides a continuous and natural source of inspiration and challenge. Inspiration stems from an enthusiasm for girls and boys and for music. It is contagious. Challenge is the result of a positive approach to teaching, free of pity or "spoon feeding." It is a stimulating and motivating approach to instruction. The inspirational teacher is one who uses the emotional and intellectual resources of music and who does not interfere with the language of music. The teacher who makes greater use of music than of speech in the classroom is the one who will stimulate and challenge pupils through the language of music.

The Teacher's Knowledge of His Pupils

There are standardized and other aptitude and achievement tests available for use by the music teacher (see Chapter 20). They are, of course, only one means of knowing students. Testing is helpful, but it should be supplemented by a knowledge of the home and community life of the pupils and their life within the school. Participation by the teacher in parent-teacher activities and in community and all-school projects is an important aid to knowing students. Testing, the evaluations of festival judges, and the opinions of music staff members in colleges and universities may make possible an objective evaluation of a pupil's potential ability in music.

Testing and Guidance

Dr. Ruth Larson reports on a 25-year guidance program in the Rochester, New York, public schools.[6] It is a program designed to help find talented pupils and

[6] Ruth C. Larson, "Finding and Guiding Musical Talent," *Music Educators Journal*, September–October, 1955, pp. 22–25.

to encourage them in music to the degree which their talents and interests warrant. She suggests that guidance is a cooperative project involving the music teacher, the school administrator, and others concerned with the pupils.

As the guidance program developed, certain policies were adopted which in the minds of the Rochester staff have been a factor in the success of the program. Among these policies was, first of all, the recognition of each child's right to some music. It is of great importance to the teacher to learn the kind of participation and the degree of encouragement best suited to the individual child. All testing and guidance was done with a positive attitude. Boys and girls were encouraged in music to what ever extent seemed appropriate, but caution was used when test results indicated that a pupil should not participate in special music activities. The Rochester schools have a city-wide policy of being careful not to hurt any child, and it should be borne in mind that a student can be hurt by unwarranted encouragement as easily as he can be hurt by discouragement.

Children are not given information on the results of the tests. Instead of grades, the results are classified as Encourage Strongly, Encourage, Encourage Conditionally, and Not Recommended. In addition to test results, recommendations are based on teachers' estimates of musical excellence, on average grades in music, academic abilities, physical limitations, and other appropriate data.

In Rochester, as a result of guidance and testing in music, performance standards have risen and it has been possible to maintain classes and musical organizations for students of varying talents. There is less tendency for teachers to give a rigid and inflexible curriculum as their reason for not supplying opportunities for all the children in music. Dr. Larson says in her conclusion, "Guidance in music can be best given when there is no underlying cause for exploitation; a successful program will be sufficient reward."[7]

MUSIC THERAPY

Robert Unkefer, Chairman, Music Therapy, Michigan State University, writes:

In the last two decades there has come a gradual, consistent, and growing interest in the therapeutic uses of music. The use of music in the treatment of certain illnesses or for those persons with special handicaps is not new, but dates from earliest history. Music has served many cultures as a means of releasing tensions and allaying fears, for influencing moods, and for affirming religious faiths. It has served individuals as a powerful outlet for fulfillment through self-expression. Only in the last twenty years, however, have careful students seriously considered just how music and music activities can directly aid in the treatment of the nontypical segments of our society.

The hospital musician, once a kind of "Jack-of-all-Music," has grown professionally, and by now has achieved status with the right to the title of *music therapist.* He has become a recognized member of the treatment team in psychiatric treatment, in the

[7] *Ibid.*, p. 25.

education of the mentally retarded, and in the rehabilitation of the physically disabled. His position is gratifying and challenging. He does not "cure" his patients by teaching them to sing or to play instruments. He uses a variety of music and music teaching skills to build a relationship to fulfill patients' particular psychological needs. He must be well trained in music and in treatment techniques. He must learn to know himself well enough to be objective in evaluating his patients' needs and the progress toward treatment goals.

The music therapist provides a variety of opportunities in music for his patients. With some he adopts a completely accepting and giving attitude, with others, when indicated, he will assert both firm and direct guidance. He will teach patients in the private studio; he will also direct varying kinds of music groups. He will provide creative, educational, and recreational activities in music for his patients.

Many registered music therapists work in adult psychiatric treatment centers, others work in children's hospitals and schools for the mentally retarded and the physically disabled. A new area of work is that of a music therapy consultant for special education classes in the public schools. Positions in this new area in music are plentiful if the applicant is able to move to the place where the job is open. Probably at no time will there be a position for a Music Therapist in every single community in the nation. Education and clinical training standards have been determined by the National Association for Music Therapy, Inc., through the National Association of Schools of Music. The Bachelor's degree program spans four academic years plus six calendar months internship in a psychiatric clinic training center. Approved courses are now offered in a dozen universities in this country. Graduate training at the Master's level is available at some universities. The Bachelor's degree in Music Therapy is prerequisite to entry into a graduate training program. Registration of Music Therapists is governed by the Certification-Registration Committee of the National Association for Music Therapy.

Career brochures and other pertinent information may be obtained from the Central Office of the Association at Post Office Box 15, Lawrence, Kansas.[8]

According to a prominent psychiatrist:

> Growth, maturation, development and learning are predetermined by heredity, physical and mental constitution, early environment and many other factors such as prevailing customs, cultures, traditions and styles. It is precisely in the realm of the arts, and especially music, that these factors make themselves felt keenly.

There are situations throughout the country where handicapped children are educated in the regular classes of the local school systems. It is not easy to find teachers who have a working knowledge of the part that music may contribute to the development or rehabilitation of these individuals. The music teacher who desires to make use of music as a therapy will prepare himself by a study of psychology, sociology, the influence of music on behavior, and by consultation with specialists in music therapy.

While the use of music as a therapy requires specialized training, the teacher sensitive to the needs of the handicapped will find many ways of using music for this purpose. For instance, the maladjusted child who responds to a certain type

[8] Specially written by Robert Unkefer for this book.

of music is not apt to be harmed by having extensive opportunities in the area of music that appeals to him. It may be that through a listening, rhythmic, singing, or creative experience, rehabilitation will be facilitated (Fig. 8.5).

PLANNING INDIVIDUALIZED INSTRUCTION

Individualized instruction as a part of group instruction is feasible in music education. In practice it has had a long and successful history in the one- and two-room rural schools of this country. Education for the handicapped, for the gifted and, in fact, for every pupil is largely a matter of planning all teaching with the individual's abilities and real needs in mind. The school instrumental teacher plans his work with an eye to improving the clarinetist who sits in the last chair of the clarinet section as well as the improvement of the first-chair solo clarinetist.

Fitting the Handicapped into the Program

In one school system there are special braille classes and other learning activities developed for blind pupils (Fig. 8.6). But as far as possible the blind students are assigned to classes with sighted children. In these classes there are also partially sighted students of varying degrees of ability. The teachers know their students and what to expect from them. They use a project approach to instruction, and projects are planned with individualized instruction in mind. This approach has made it possible to prepare pupils for advanced work in college

San Diego City Schools, San Diego, California.

Detroit Public Schools, Detroit, Michigan.

Fig. 8.5. In many school systems handicapped children participate in a balanced music program for therapeutic purposes as well as for training and enjoyment.

Detroit Public Schools, Detroit, Michigan.

Fig. 8.6. Braille music is available for vocal work and for all instruments.

or for special training in the vocational field. The teachers' attitude toward their pupils is positive and friendly; they give each child a chance to reach his highest level of achievement while working in a normal classroom situation.

As a handicapped child enters the music class it is possible, through individualized instruction, to help him make the most of his abilities and recognize his true limitations. Much more important than performance will be participation and enjoyment, for he is learning to live happily while working with others. Social adjustment will result from the acquisition of ideals, attitudes, and emotional control. His life will be enriched through games, sports, good books and music, and the formation of friendships.

The child is helped to take his place in the program without being conspicuous. As the work of the child is evaluated, it is important to avoid defeating the child in the name of standards. Garrison urges that while "high standards of scholarship are desirable they should not be used as a means of depriving students of the opportunities for educational growth in harmony with their abilities and needs."[9] Pupils who are handicapped or of mediocre ability should have the opportunity to enrich their lives through an appreciation of music.

[9] Garrison, *op. cit.*, p. 159.

Providing Opportunities for the Gifted

A fixed course of study, a routine use of materials, and a mechanical approach to teaching tend to condemn the gifted to mediocrity. There is little logic in assuming that the gifted will rise to their potential achievement in spite of the school situation. Among the gifted there are many sensitive children who may be overlooked because of less musical but more aggressive pupils. How can we provide the opportunities which will challenge the gifted?

The talented young pianist who serves as accompanist for the Girls' Glee Club may be challenged and may enjoy working out more difficult accompaniments, such as that of the Brahms' *Far and Wide*,[10] or by being the featured soloist in the spring concert. Piano study is recognized as being of great value to both the amateur and the professional musician. Many junior and senior high schools make it possible for the talented student to devote some of his time to piano study by offering practice facilities and class piano instruction.

At one time in the University of Wisconsin High School, an Honors course was established for talented young musicians. The title was used as an administrative convenience because the Honors course in music was not a course in the usual sense of the word. Students in the Honors program were given freedom from some rehearsals and music classes to work on individual projects. Four students were in the first group and each was doing advanced work in music. Two were interested in the study of the string quartets to be played by the Pro-Arte String Quartette which was in residence at the University of Wisconsin that year. They were listening to recordings of representative quartets and analyzing them. Another student was writing a composition for the school orchestra to play at its spring concert, and still another was practicing the first movement of the *Concerto for Piano in A Minor* by Edvard Grieg for performance later in the year. No extra credit was given for the work, but credit and grades seemed to be relatively unimportant to the students. The offering of Honors sections in science, mathematics, languages, and other areas has become well established recently in both small and large high schools. Honors sections should also be made available for those who are highly talented in music.

PLANNING FOR ALL TO PARTICIPATE

Planning for all to participate is planning in terms of the musical growth of boys and girls. If we want all children to participate in music there will be a wide range of singing, playing, rhythmic, listening, and creative activities. A broad

[10] Johannes Brahms, *Opus 103, No. 9*, transcribed and edited by Clara Tillinghast, M. Witmark and Sons.

program of opportunities in music tends in itself to attract students of all types. A narrowly conceived program tends to concentrate on one phase of the music program and reduces the number of pupils participating in music to a small percentage of the student body. The narrow type of program may produce superior music, but its neglect of the majority of students represents a serious weakness both educationally and musically.

In one small Wisconsin town the music teacher had a large percentage of the pupils of junior- and senior-high-school age participating in vocal and/or instrumental music. He spent only two days a week in this school, but his keen enthusiasm for music led him, even in that limited time, to provide something in music for everyone. There were boys from dairy farms who played the guitar, the Swiss bells, or the accordion, besides many others who played band or orchestra instruments or enjoyed singing. It seemed as if all the pupils in that school played or sang. Each year the band of this school received a superior rating in the district and state festivals. The end result was strong interest and support from community and students alike—interest and support which led naturally to consistently fine vocal and instrumental organizations.

Instrumental Opportunities

In the instrumental field there are opportunities for both typical and atypical children to do many things. They may play simple instruments such as the ukulele and the recorder, study the piano at school, or play one of the instruments of the band or orchestra. Some teachers make use of the percussion instruments for handicapped children. Bongos, congas, maracas, castanets, finger castanets, cymbals, and timbals make it possible for many children to participate in music because of the simple manipulative skills required.

There is the possibility, as shown in Fig. 8.5, of organizing an instrumental group for handicapped children. The dance band, the solo and small-ensemble combinations such as the string quartet or the woodwind quintet offer opportunities in music in addition to other scheduled offerings.

Choral Opportunities

Many possibilities likewise exist for participation in choral music. Solo and ensemble groupings such as a girls' trio or quartet, a barbershop quartet, madrigal singers, choir, glee clubs, choruses, assembly singing, and operettas are made available to pupils in many schools. The music curriculum can accommodate all who want to sing, regardless of their gifts or limitations in music. An important advantage of choral music for the typical and the atypical child is the fact that within a relatively short period of time it is possible for a group of junior- or senior-high-school pupils to sing a very creditable program of choral music.

SPECIAL ACTIVITIES FOR THE GIFTED

The music curriculum of the modern school can provide a variety of activities which are beneficial and attractive to students with special talents. It is important that they be guided by their teachers so that they will receive not only a good musical education but a well-balanced academic education as well. The enthusiasm and interest of the gifted music student may, without guidance, lead him to an overemphasis on music at the expense of a well-rounded academic and social development.

John is an example of a talented high-school musician who needed guidance. He played clarinet and intended to make music his career. While in high school he took a private lesson on the clarinet each week, rehearsed five hours a week in the school band, five hours a week in the school choir, two hours a week in the school orchestra, and averaged about a hour a week playing in the high-school woodwind quintet. He graduated from high school with far more credits in music than he could use for admission to college, and with an academic record that was a handicap to him. Too many hours a week devoted to music and too many music activities had not only caused him to achieve far less than his potential in music, but had resulted in poor study habits and poor academic achievement. Talented students like John are constantly in need of guidance. It is important that they have sufficient time for practice on their major instrument and for the development of musicianship, but it is also very important that their program of special activities in music be directed in such a way that they have time to do other things well. There are many musicians who feel that overspecialization at the high-school level is to be avoided.

Student Conductors

At the beginning of a college course in conducting it is always interesting to note that a small number of students conduct easily and effectively. Most of these students have had an opportunity to do some conducting in the secondary school. They are familiar with scores and have learned to express themselves musically when conducting. One high-school teacher we know always has a number of student conductors in training. He feels that the conducting they are able to do under his guidance is one of the best experiences he can give them in music.

They are given some responsibility in the public performances of the music organizations, and over the years a number of them who have not gone into music professionally have, however, become conductors of local choral and instrumental groups, thus helping to stimulate community music activities.

Credit for Private Music Study

Credit for class or private music instruction is a well-established practice. In many states and communities such credit has been allowed over a period of more than 30 years. In states where credit is granted and approved by the state department of public instruction, a state course of study is generally formulated to be used as a guide by teachers and administrators.

The amount of credit granted for such study varies greatly, but common practice in the schools permits a student to count toward graduation one or two of the credits earned in private music study. Most colleges and universities permit a student to count for entrance one or two credits in applied music, particularly if such study requires the student to pursue theoretical courses in music in connection with his instrumental study. The number of states granting credit for applied music study is increasing; this, of course, presents an opportunity for the gifted student.

The National Association of Schools of Music, realizing the desirability of establishing definitions of achievement in applied music and theory expressed in secondary-school units, has made available a bulletin[11] helpful to those seeking guidance in planning for or evaluating applied music instruction in the secondary schools.

The Music Major in the High School

The music major in the senior high school is not new to American education; it has been offered by a number of the larger high schools for many years. In such a major a pupil is usually allowed to substitute music for one academic course each year. In this way he is able to include in his course work a music program consisting of Applied Music, Music Theory, Music History, Music Literature and participation in ensembles. In some of the larger high schools it is possible for a student to accumulate in music half of the number of credits required for graduation. In a four-year high-school course a student might easily earn seven or eight of the 15 or 16 credits or units required for graduation in music.

Regardless of the musical advantages in such a program, however, a complete

[11] *Specimen Examination for Applied Music at the Secondary School Level,* National Association of Schools of Music, Memphis, Tennessee, Southwestern College, 1945.

and balanced curriculum of academic studies must be required of the girl or boy gifted in music or he cannot expect to be admitted as a music major in a college or university. The Committee on Music in the Senior High School Curriculum of the Music Educators National Conference states in its report: "For the pupil who plans to pursue music as a career, in a large highly organized high school it might be possible to obtain half the credits necessary for graduation in music. It is doubtful if such a practice is wise, however, for the pupil may wish to go to college, and few colleges will accept more than four units in music for entrance, and many of them less."[12]

It is in the interest of developing well-rounded individuals that the colleges restrict the amount of credit in any one field that may be used for entrance. Furthermore, the professional musician, the teacher, the physician, and workers in other fields need the type of education that will help them fit into their places in society, and to make the greatest possible contribution to the community. In order to do this they must be familiar with the history and mores of the group. This fits clearly into two important modern educational trends: (1) the emphasis on the individual's relation to the group, and (2) the emphasis on general education.

Most colleges in the various associations of secondary schools and colleges require for college entrance a minimum of 12 units in general academic fields. Since they demand a total of 15 to 16 entrance units, this would leave for other fields, such as music, a maximum of three or four units. In all cases it is suggested that the teacher of music guide the student in such a way that he devotes most of his time in high school to general rather than special subject fields.

High-school credit is measured in units. This unit is usually defined as the credit obtained through attendance at a class meeting five times a week through a period of 36 weeks, each class being 40 minutes in length, with an equal amount of time spent in preparation outside the classroom. Classes that carry no outside preparation earn only half the credit given one which demands both classroom attendance and outside preparation. On this basis, laboratory work is given only half credit. Regular classes in harmony, music appreciation, general music, and theoretical subjects that demand both attendance and preparation may be given a full unit for a year's work. A high-school credit schedule is given below:

90 minutes a week (2 periods of 45 minutes)	1 period daily, 5 days a week	2 periods daily, 5 days a week
¼ unit	½ unit	1 unit

At the present time most colleges and universities offer advanced training in music, and a student wishing to major in music after high school must meet university admission requirements. While most colleges and universities have

[12] Vanett Lawler (Ed.), *Function of Music in the Secondary-School Curriculum*, Music Educators National Conference, 1952, p. 22.

become more liberal in their acceptance of music credits for admission to their music departments, they still demand a broad academic background in addition to whatever experience in music the candidate may have.

As an example, one music teacher majored in music in high school. In order to carry the required music courses, one academic course was eliminated each year from his program of studies. After graduation he found difficulty in securing admission to a university. If he had decided to change his major after leaving high school, he would have the equivalent of one year of academic education to make up. Considering the gifted pupil's individual needs and the admission requirements of the institutions of higher learning, it would appear that majoring in music should be postponed until after the pupil has finished his high-school education.

NEW OPPORTUNITIES FOR THE TALENTED

Addressing parents, Joseph E. Maddy, founder and president of the National Music Camp and the Interlochen Arts Academy, and long associated with creating proper educational opportunities for talented youth, states:

> Parents should recognize and guide youthful talent into appropriate channels for service to humanity. Youth comes but once in a lifetime. Youth's opportunities cannot be postponed. . . . Educators are beginning to realize that the student of superior talent and intelligence must have specialized educational opportunities to provide the challenge and motivation he needs.[13]

The advance toward suitable educational opportunities for the young musician has developed from the offering of a vocational music course in some large high schools, and the growth of summer music study for youth, to the more recent opening of the Interlochen Academy operating throughout the academic year (Fig. 8.7).

Physical development—the acquisition of muscular skills and coordination must start at an early age in the education of the talented. Recognizing this basic need in the education of pupils of demonstrated talent in music, art, drama, dance, or creative writing, the Academy instructional program starts with grade eight and continues through grade twelve. The Academy has as its goal a sound academic program combined with a superior artistic curriculum. Two academic programs are offered:

1. College preparatory—for students who wish to enter a liberal arts college and to use music or one of the fine arts as an avocation later in life.
2. Preprofessional—for students who wish to attend music conservatories, art

[13] J. E. Maddy, *Bulletin*, Interlochen Arts Academy, Interlochen, Michigan, 1963–1964, p. 3.

Interlochen Arts Academy, Interlochen, Michigan.

Fig. 8.7. Boys and girls at the Interlochen Arts Academy benefit from living and working with other talented young people.

schools, or colleges where first priority in admission requirements is given to performance skills as well as an academic background.

The Annual Congress of Strings, organized in 1959 by the American Federation of Musicians, is another advance in opportunities for talented youth through summer study (Fig. 8.8). After successful sessions in Greenleaf Lake, Oklahoma, and in Puerto Rico, the Congress came to the campus of Michigan State University in 1961. Each student wins his scholarship in one of the hundred scholarship try-outs in one hundred different localities in the United States. The individual local unions of the United States and Canada organize, publicize, and handle the contests. Each scholarship winner is provided eight weeks intensive instruction under noted string teachers from the nation's foremost symphony orchestras. Also included are free transportation from the sponsoring local's headquarters city to Michigan State University and return, meals, housing, music lessons, and recreation. In daily practice sessions conducted by great conductors such as Eric Leinsdorf, Josef Krips, and Eugene Ormandy, regular symphony orchestra repertoire is studied as well as chamber music. The idea behind the congress is to discover and encourage the best young string players as part of a continuing AFM campaign to win greater public support for live music.

Emphasis on creativity in schools is the goal of the six-year Ford Foundation grant made to the Music Educators National Conference. The program has two main parts. The first part consists of the selection and assignment of young composers to write music for performance by the orchestras, bands, choruses and

Both photographs from International Musician, *Journal of the American Federation of Musicians of the United States and Canada.*

Fig. 8.8. (Left) Mishel Piastro teaches a gifted young student and Eugene Ormandy conducts a concert (right). The Annual String Congress draws a group of talented young scholarship winners from all parts of the country.

other ensembles of the public secondary-school systems to which they are sent for a period of time in residence. This continues the Young Composers Project initiated by the Ford Foundation in 1958. The second part includes a variety of activities: contemporary music seminars and workshops in the schools in which senior composers, young composers, and music educators will participate, pilot projects to identify creative talents among elementary and secondary students.

SUMMARY

A broad concept of music education can produce an instructional pattern to fit the typical child and the atypical: the handicapped, the maladjusted, the retarded, and the talented or gifted. The role of the teacher is of even greater significance in working with the atypical child than it is with the typical child. For music to be effective with handicapped girls and boys it must be more than entertainment or education in music, and its effectiveness cannot be judged solely in terms of musical achievement. There are innumerable opportunities in music to provide the additional projects and assignments which will challenge the gifted and keep them working up to the level of their abilities. Since we are concerned with music as an art, a social force, and a therapy, it is evident that understanding the child's capabilities is more than knowing what he can do in music. Testing is only one means of knowing students; it should be supplemented by knowledge of the home and community life of the pupils and their life within the school.

While the use of music as a therapy needs specialized training, the teacher sensitive to the needs of the handicapped will find many ways of using music as a therapy.

The narrow program of music may produce superior music, but its neglect of the larger number of students in the school can hardly be justified in terms of democratic education.

SUGGESTED ACTIVITIES

1. Visit a class or a residence school for handicapped children. Report how the teacher fits the music activities to the handicapped child.
2. Do you believe that the effectiveness of music teaching with the handicapped should not be judged in terms of musical achievement? If so, why?
3. Report the findings and recommendations of one research study on music for the gifted child.
4. Develop four music projects that might be appropriate for pupils with exceptional talent in music.
5. Examine and administer three aptitude tests in music. Which do you prefer? On what do you base your preference?
6. Work out a proposal for an Honors program in music to be submitted to the school administration for approval.
7. Prepare a report on the amount of credit in music which any six colleges or universities will accept for admission.
8. Arrange for a conference with a specialist in the field of education for atypical children in order to learn what function he thinks music may have in the rehabilitation of handicapped children.
9. Evaluate the film "Music: a Career or Hobby?" Is it suitable for use in the junior high school, the senior high school, or both?
10. Plan several bulletin board displays which seek to interest the handicapped and the talented pupils in music activities.

SELECTED READINGS

Abraham, Willard, *Common Sense About Gifted Children*, Harper & Row, 1958, chaps. II and V.

Cheslik, Deloris, "Music Instruction for the Visually Handicapped," *Music Educators Journal*, November–December, 1961, p. 99.

Educational Policies Commission, *Education of the Gifted*, National Education Association, 1950.

Gallagher, James J., *Teaching the Gifted Child*, Allyn and Bacon, 1964, chaps. I and VIII.

Harbert, W. K., "Some Results from Specific Techniques in the Use of Music with Exceptional Children," *Music Therapy*, 1952, pp. 147–151.

Hartshorn, William C., *Music for the Academically Talented Student*, NEA and MENC, 1960.

Larson, R. C., "Finding and Guiding Musical Talent," *Music Educators Journal*, September–October, 1955, pp. 22–25.

May, Elizabeth, "Music for Deaf Children," *Music Educators Journal*, January, 1961, p. 39.

Menninger, W. C., *Self-Understanding: A First Step to Understanding Children*, Science Research Associates, 1951.

Murphy, James F., "Student Conductors for High Schools, A Musical Resource," *Music Educators Journal*, April–May, 1960, p. 47.

Newacheck, V., "Music and the Slow Learner," *Music Educators Journal*, November–December, 1953, pp. 50–54.

Nordholm, H., "Music for the Cerebral Palsied Child," *Music Therapy*, 1953, pp. 91–94.

O'Toole, Catherine N., "Music for the Handicapped Child," *Music Educators Journal*, June–July, 1962, p. 73.

Patrick, Nelson G., "The Music Teacher and Vocational Counselling," *Music Educators Journal*, September–October, 1961, p. 97.

Reeves, V., "Music to Aid the Handicapped Child," *Music Therapy*, 1951, pp. 10–15.

Scheerenberger, R. C., "Presenting Music to the Mentally Retarded," *Music Educators Journal*, November–December, 1954, pp. 23–25.

Van Bodegraven, P., "Equality of Opportunity in Music Education," *Music Educators Journal*, September–October, 1952, pp. 20–21.

Weir, L. E., "Music Therapy for Retarded and Artistic Children," *Music Therapy*, 1952, pp. 129–132.

University City Public Schools, University City, Missouri.

CHAPTER

9

Music Assemblies

A PROGRAM FOR ALL STUDENTS

Assembly programs are deeply rooted in the structure of secondary education in the United States. The idea of bringing all the students together in a morning chapel service in the early schools was the forerunner of the assembly program series in the modern school. A series of music assemblies for all students should be conceived in terms of the total school program and present-day educational practice.

Objectives of the Assembly Program

One of the first questions that must be answered is, what are the objectives of the assembly? Secondary-school administrators would like to have their school assemblies contribute to significant educational objectives. According to Thompson:

> One of the primary objectives of the assembly is the building of genuine school spirit—a feeling of individual loyalty to *all* activities of the school. School spirit is not the high emotional pitch of pep sessions, nor is its measure in the volume of gate receipts. It is the feeling of the individual belonging to the school coupled with the oneness of all facets of school life. There is no better way to acquaint the student with the school and to gain respect and meaningfulness for all parts of its program than to demonstrate what the school has to offer through the assembly.
>
> Another main objective of the assembly is the integration of the whole program of the school—curricular and extra curricular. Classroom studies, guidance, subject matter fields, and clubwork may be correlated, motivated, and co-ordinated by means of the assembly.
>
> A third aim of the assembly is to enlarge the cultural background of the student and thereby broaden his interest in life. The goals are to introduce the student to the arts and enhance his appreciation of them and to provide an opportunity for attending programs of higher calibre than are ordinarily available and lift the level of entertainment in the community thereby.

A fourth outcome that may be expected of the assembly is the orientation of the student toward life. Assemblies should add to his fund of information and understanding about the world around him—its people, its places, its wonders.[1]

A Unifying Factor in School Life

Many school administrators endorse the assembly series as a unifying factor in school life. In addition to extending the influence of music throughout the student body, the music assembly unites all students in a pleasant and purposeful activity. The assembly may serve girls and boys by:

1. Improving school spirit and morale
2. Improving behavior and citizenship
3. Fostering understanding and tolerance
4. Relieving tensions
5. Developing, by practice, proper audience etiquette—the habits and behavior of an intelligent audience
6. Attracting gifted students to the regular course offerings in music
7. Bringing the spiritual and inspirational values of music to all students
8. Opening new horizons to students as they are guided into the world of music

An interesting example shows the possible influence of a series of music assemblies in a small high school. One high school was without a principal during an entire school year. A faculty committee was responsible for the administration of the school and, while the committee functioned efficiently, school spirit and morale dropped to a low level. At the start of the school year the administrative committee approved a plan suggested by the music teacher for a series of music assemblies. In the homerooms it was made clear to the students that these assemblies were their programs and their responsibility and that every student was expected to participate as a listener and in group singing. Many students were involved in the planning and organization of the programs. Parents and faculty members were invited to attend the assemblies and take part in the program. As time went on, students, faculty, and parents joined together in other school projects; school spirit and morale rose to a high point. The music assembly series proved to be a strong factor for good in the life of that school.

The Student Body and Music Assembly Series

At one time in the history of school music all students participated regularly in music assemblies. One could walk into a school building and hear the entire student body join together in unison and part-singing. The more recent emphasis

[1] Nellie Zetta Thompson, "School Assemblies," *Bulletin of the National Association of Secondary-School Principals*, February, 1952, p. 157.

on the musical development of a small and select group of students in the performing organizations has had a tendency to minimize the importance of the music assembly.

The interested and gifted students are well served by the experiences available to them in choral and instrumental organizations. Such experiences are an important part of the educational program and must be maintained. In this manner music education meets its responsibility by guiding the gifted boys and girls to high levels of achievement in choral and instrumental music. But what about the thousands of pupils who are not in the musical organizations? Does not music education have a responsibility to them? Should it not be concerned with the general education program of the school? In a democratic society the answers to these questions must be affirmative. School administrators, recognizing the importance of music in education, look for music to reach larger numbers of students and contribute to the general education program of the school. They look for music to continue the development of the finest possible performing groups, but they ask for more than this from music. They seek a broadened and expanded program of music education for *all* students.

The music assembly can contribute to general education. It is one means of

Lansing Public Schools, Lansing, Michigan.

Fig. 9.1. Excellent group coordination and a high degree of interest in choir work are apparent in these high-school singers.

meeting music education's obligation to all students. A broad and expanding concept of music education will include the music assembly and make it an integral part of the general education program of the school. As such, assemblies become educational rather than entertainment projects.

Through the music assembly every student identifies himself with music as a consumer and/or a producer of music. He expresses himself musically as a part of a group; he cooperates with others and learns to respect their achievement (Fig. 9.1). The assembly contributes to education for citizenship. It satisfies the student's aesthetic needs and brings an appreciation of moral and spiritual values. Music serves the student as an art and as a social force.

A contribution to music education is a natural outcome of the music assembly. Through it the student becomes familiar with the music activities of his school. In an assembly he is moved by the playing of "Huldigung's March" from *Sigurd Jorsalfar Suite* by Grieg, or the singing of the Mozart "Ave Verum." This experience may well be the start of a deeper and continuing interest in music. In the music assembly there will be the chance to participate in singing and listening activities for all students, regardless of their previous background and experience in music.

PREPARATION FOR THE MUSIC ASSEMBLY

General acceptance of the assembly program as an integral part of the total curriculum brings to music education a unique opportunity to serve the school staff, students, and people of the community in the preparation and planning of a series of music assemblies. Music serving the assembly in this role becomes more than an entertainment feature or a special subject for the few. All students share common desirable educational experiences in music, and thus music is in a position to make a contribution to the total educational program.

Administrative Planning

A first step toward smooth operation of the music assembly series is careful regard for the details of administrative planning. The administrative responsibility for the annual assembly series varies with schools. The organization of a school may place the assembly programs under the direction of a faculty director of assemblies, a director of school activities, a faculty committee, or the school principal. Since the music assembly series is only one part of the school's total assembly program, preliminary preparation and planning for the series is done with the person or persons responsible for the direction of the school's assemblies.

Just before the start of school, or as early as possible in the school year, plans are sufficiently developed to secure administrative endorsement and cooperation. Long-range planning is essential at this point and its aim is variety, balance, and a desirable sequence of learning in the music programs. Administrative action is initiated on scheduling the assemblies, frequency of assemblies, time allotment, financing the series, the use of school and other musical resources, use of the assembly room for rehearsals, the rehearsal schedule, publicity, and other items related to school operation and policy.

Many of the persistent problems of the assembly may be anticipated and eliminated through cooperative administrative planning by the music teacher and those responsible for directing the school assembly program. Those given the responsibility for the school's assemblies usually know both the school and the community. They are in a position to suggest to the music teacher procedures for improving student audience behavior and to recommend methods of effective group planning and group presentation. Their counsel and cooperation is of great value to the music teacher as he carries out administrative planning for a successful series of music assemblies.

Teacher-Pupil Cooperation in Planning

Planning for the production of a series of music assemblies is a responsibility which ideally lends itself to teacher-pupil cooperative planning. Student committees have contributed substantially to the improvement of the secondary-school assembly in recent years. Through discussions, surveys, workshops and other projects they have been helpful in making recommendations for program content and use of school and community resources, have applied their understanding and knowledge of their classmates in securing desirable audience reactions, and have assisted in the preparation for assemblies in the activity periods, the homerooms, and the classroom.

If teacher-pupil planning is adopted, the question arises: What pupils and how many are needed to serve on the committee for music assemblies? The answer to this question will differ with various schools but it is safe to proceed on the basis that membership on the committee should include representatives of each grade, students from the vocal and instrumental organizations, and students not in the music organizations or classes. The chairman might well be a student, with the teacher serving as a counselor and guide.

Some of the responsibilities of the assembly committee might be to:

1. Suggest and discuss the general and specific objectives of the assemblies. No assembly series should be planned without carefully considered aims and

objectives. To justify its existence, cost, and time allotment, the series must contribute to the education of all the students.

2. Suggest a theme or themes to be followed through the year. The theme should provide continuity that will facilitate learning and be a contributing factor in meeting established objectives.
3. List for reference the available resources for programs in both the school and the community.
4. Asssit in the planning of individual programs.

Preparation in Music and Other Classes

Where the school assembly functions and is recognized as a part of the curricular offering, preparation for the programs is centered in the classroom and activity periods of the regular school day. There are, of course, many junior and senior high schools where before-school, after-school, noon-hour and evening periods must be used for rehearsal purposes. Since the music used for performance in the music assembly frequently includes the compositions used as a part of regular instruction, preparation for the assemblies is easily concentrated in the rehearsal hours of the ensembles.

Singing as an experience for all students is suggested for the majority of the programs. Rehearsal for this singing may be incorporated in all the music classes of the school without serious interference with the regular work of the group. In one small junior high school all the vocal and instrumental ensembles and the General Music classes were asked to assist in the assembly programs by learning the songs to be sung by the entire student body. For the first assembly they learned "America the Beautiful," "God of Our Fathers," "Drink to Me Only with Thine Eyes," and "Santa Lucia." A few minutes spent on singing the songs in class sessions over a period of two weeks brought about considerable improvement in the singing. At the assembly featuring the film *Andrés Segovia*[2] the pupils who had learned the songs in their classes sang with assurance and brought about a better response from those who were being asked to sing the songs for the first time.

Preparation in music classes for performance in assemblies has another advantage in that it promotes staff approval and cooperation. Rehearsal of music for assemblies in the music classes does not interfere with the time allotted to other areas of instruction. Consideration on the part of the music teacher for the time assigned to other classes and activities is imperative if a favorable attitude toward any phase of school music is to be generated in the school staff and administration.

There will be some assemblies devoted entirely to the listening experience (Fig. 9.2). If we consider training the listener as a major part of music education's

[2] *Andrés Segovia*, #106, Mills Picture Corporation, Beverly Hills, California.

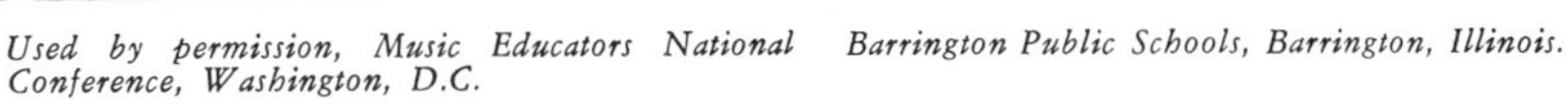

Used by permission, Music Educators National Conference, Washington, D.C.

Barrington Public Schools, Barrington, Illinois.

South Bend Public Schools, South Bend, Indiana.

Fig. 9.2. Performance at assemblies is an outgrowth of classroom instruction. Top: School band and orchestra performances can contribute profitable listening experiences; Bottom left: By presenting sections of operettas, ticket sales and interest in forthcoming choral productions can be stimulated.

responsibility to students, we will be concerned with the student's participation in active and intelligent listening. Music classes, possibly homerooms, noon-hour and afternoon invitational meetings may be used to prepare students for listening. The recently introduced film, *Study Guide,*[3] and the "Keyboard Jr."[4] recordings are examples of the many teaching materials and aids we now have at our disposal for such use.

A university faculty chamber orchestra, following its annual custom, recently presented a program of music by master composers to a number of junior and

[3] William C. Hartshorn, "The Trio #107 Rubinstein, Heifetz, Piatigorsky," Mills Picture Corporation, 1956.

[4] *Keyboard Jr.*, Recordings, 1956.

senior high schools. They played compositions by Handel, Bach, Haydn, Mendelssohn, Mozart, Saint-Saëns, and Debussy. Preparation for an assembly of this type involves participation through active listening, and presents a host of opportunities for preparation in the music classes.

We seek for audience participation either through song or listening in all music assemblies. Electronic devices, organized sports, some forms of professional music all contribute to the tendency to let the other fellow do the job. The school music assembly can counteract that tendency by preparation for listening or making music centered in the music classes and expanded to homerooms, classrooms, and noon-hour or after-school sessions open to voluntary attendance by interested students.

SUGGESTIONS FOR AN EFFECTIVE ASSEMBLY SERIES

Types of Programs

The types of programs scheduled have a direct bearing on the effectiveness of the series. The response to various kinds of programs will not be uniform from school to school. Thompson lists the following types of programs which have found wide acceptance and are suggested as a guide to teachers and pupils in planning assemblies for their schools. Suggestions are included for fitting these classifications of programs into the music series.[5]

Orientation

A program designed to acquaint students with the opportunities open to them in music through vocal and instrumental study, classes in General Music, Music Literature, and Music Fundamentals.

Demonstration

Programs which help students identify instruments of the band and orchestra by sight and sound; a program featuring a study project developed in General Music class such as "Music in Our Community"; a musical production assembly based on all or selected portions of an opera, operetta, or cantata; the presentation of a music program of exceptional merit by pupils of a neighboring school.

Audience Participation

Music assemblies bring audience participation through singing or listening. The effectiveness of audience participation is more certain when the participa-

[5] Thompson, *op. cit.*, p. 167.

tion is planned with proper regard for the musical background and competency of the students. Some programs may be included in the series exclusively for audience participation. The listening experience may be given particular emphasis in a program introducing a musical masterpiece with *brief* explanatory or descriptive comment using understandable terminology. Thematic material, information about the voices or instruments used, comments on the form, design and style of the music or the composer and his work may be used in program building for listening.

Preparatory and follow-up sessions for assemblies devoted to the listening experience are suggested. Noon-hour and after-school programs may be scheduled for those students who elect to come to the music room or auditorium. The only requirement is to listen and observe concert etiquette.

Informational

Possibilities for this category are programs on careers in music; the use of music as a therapy in hospitals and other institutions; the use of music in industry; the use of music in the home; community music activities; music in foreign lands; music and worship; music in recreation, such as the use of easy instruments like the autoharp, the harmonica, the ukulele, the guitar, the recorder, the Melodica, or barbershop singing.

Inspirational

While all music assemblies aim to be inspirational and to create in students a desire for more and better music, this classification emphasizes the need for making the world's great music and musicians known to all students. Programs by a talented performer or performers from the school or outside the school may be initiated into the series. Talent from outside the school not engaged in music as a profession has great inspirational possibilities. The inspirational program where music as the universal language speaks for itself is not difficult to arrange. At the Christmas season, inspiration may come from a program based on Menotti's *Amahl and the Night Visitors,* or at another time from Mendelssohn's *Violin Concerto in E Minor.*

Audiovisual

Audiovisual materials and equipment may be used to provide a complete program or serve to enrich any or all types of music assemblies. They are extremely useful in introducing fine music and musicians to students through the use of the amplification system, the phonograph, and the tape recorder. Slide and opaque projectors open up new program possibilities for audience viewing of pictures, scores, charts, thematic material and other listening aids. Radio and television programs of merit are becoming increasingly available for assembly use.

Commemorative

Programs recognizing the contribution to mankind of the folk songs, the spirituals, the great hymns of all faiths, the works of the music masters of all times and nations. (Fig. 9.3).

Cultural

It should be possible to classify most music programs under this heading, but here might be considered some possibilities in addition to the music resources of the school. The school might schedule performances by the local symphony orchestra, faculty and student soloists of colleges and universities, soloists and ensembles offered for school assembly appearances by concert and assembly bureaus.

Music fits naturally into each type of program reported as having wide acceptance in secondary schools. The listing does make possible combining one or more types of programs to secure variety which will maintain student interest and promote continued interest in the programs.

Used by permission, Music Educators National Conference, Washington, D.C.

Fig. 9.3. Christmas and other holiday programs are a natural part of assembly activities.

Promoting Student Interest in the Assembly

The transition from the teacher-dominated assembly series to the present practice of planning and producing programs with students has fostered student interest and cooperation in the programs. When students have had a part in developing and producing programs by means of student committees and workshops they willingly accept responsibility for performance, audience participation, continued program planning, announcing, presiding, publicity, and the many functions essential to the operation of the programs. The project becomes a creative experience for the pupil. It is an experience which brings life and vitality to the programs.

Preparation for production involves many matters of consequence to the promotion and maintenance of student interest. The best possible use must be made of the facilities and equipment available for assemblies. Assembly room facilities differ from school to school. The school building with a functional stage and auditorium provides a wide range of production possibilities for enriching the programs not open to the school limited to a gymnasium-auditorium for its programs. Music assemblies can be effectively produced in whatever facilities are available when the situation is studied to determine its best use in the production of music.

Student interest and the educational effectiveness of the assembly are heightened when some attention is placed on showmanship in the production of the programs (Fig. 9.4). While showmanship is advantageous, it should be carried out in a manner consistent with good taste and quality of musical performance. Simple but attractive stage settings and lighting may be worked out by students. When more elaborate stage presentations are scheduled, students assist with the construction and painting of sets, costuming, make-up, care of properties, and other details. It is not implied that stage settings and lighting should be as elaborate for assemblies as those which are used for major school productions, but the stage should present an interesting appearance.

Stage sets, lighting, the tuning of musical instruments, seating arrangements, song sheets or books, projectors, and all other properties and equipment need to be checked and tested before students arrive for the start of the program. Scheduling as much rehearsing as can be arranged in the assembly room is imperative. Acoustics and other conditions are different in an auditorium from those in a classroom, and music rehearsed only in the classroom may be performed very poorly in the auditorium unless students become accustomed to playing or singing the program there. If instrumental accompaniment by band or orchestra is planned for choral music, the instrumental organization should thoroughly rehearse the music as a part of its own preparation as well as with the singers in the auditorium.

Alexandria Public Schools, Alexandria, Minnesota.

Fig. 9.4. Christmas programs offer special opportunities and settings for the high-school choir.

The timing of the program is a responsibility given to students in many schools. Programs should be timed in rehearsals as carefully as they are for commercial radio and television. If the program is slow moving, discipline problems may be expected. Overtime assembly programs do not further good faculty relationships.

There should be an objective evaluation of the musical performance and stage presence or deportment of individuals and groups considered for assembly appearance. The high-school audience of today hears and sees music well performed in theatres and on radio and television programs. Students are interested in the capable and well-prepared amateur performance selected for its appeal to the majority of the audience. They are not inclined to tolerate poorly planned and inadequately prepared programs of limited interest. The performers in the assembly must have something worth while to offer from the musical standpoint or they should not be programed.

Publicity has proved itself of value in creating both student and parent interest in assembly programs. Concert and assembly bureaus supplying talent for "paid assemblies" are conscious of the advantage of well-organized publicity and, as part of their service, forward publicity materials to schools scheduling their programs. Posters, pictures, notices, news releases, and advance copies of the program may be produced and distributed by students for use in homerooms and classrooms, on bulletin boards, chalkboards, in display cases, and in the school paper. The extent to which publicity is used and the types of publicity developed are questions best answered in terms of the local situation. Organization for publicity is another step toward wider pupil participation in the assembly series and has interesting educational possibilities for interdepartment projects and cooperation.

Part-Singing in Assemblies

Whether or not there should be part-singing in assemblies depends to some extent upon the experience in music the pupils have had in the elementary school, as well as upon the teacher's creative approach to the problem. If the elementary school experiences in singing have successfully emphasized part-singing, junior- and senior-high-school teachers should not hesitate to introduce it. The introduction of part-singing in this case will be made when the teachers feel that the students are ready for it. If part-singing was not included in the elementary-school experiences, teachers with a creative approach to the problem will use descants, rounds, and simple harmonic patterns to start the part-singing program. Part-singing is a worthy goal of the assembly series. Inexpensive song books are available for use and, though there are copyright restrictions on many compositions, sufficient choral music is in the public domain to make practical the use of school produced slides. There are many junior and senior high schools in which part-singing in assemblies is one of the most inspiring and enjoyable parts of the program (Fig. 9.5).

Voice testing must be done quickly and efficiently if it is attempted. In the small school, testing of all voices can be done in the usual manner through a schedule of individual voice testing in the music room or the auditorium during activity periods or at times when pupils may be released from study halls for a

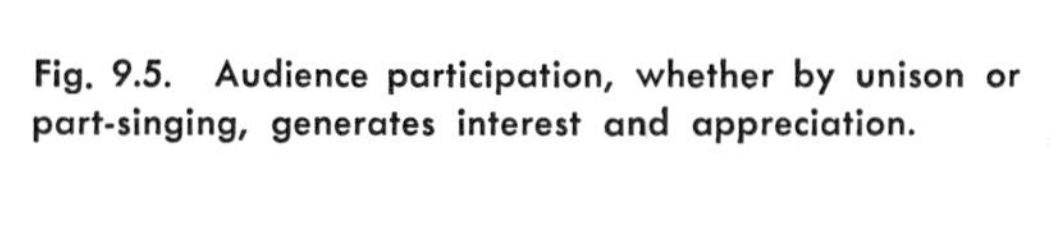

Fig. 9.5. Audience participation, whether by unison or part-singing, generates interest and appreciation.

Detroit Public Schools, Detroit, Michigan.

few minutes. Testing should be scheduled over a considerable period of time and organized in a manner to avoid disrupting other school activities. Students from the choral groups can help by acting as recorders and as assistants in other ways. In the large school, individual testing of voices may not be practicable, but part-singing is possible even when students are not seated according to the parts they sing. Testing boys' voices will be free of many problems if individual tryouts are scheduled during the boys' free periods. Frequent repetition of the invitation to report to the music teacher for a retest is recommended for students experiencing difficulty with the vocal demands of the part to which they are assigned.

Seating plans for music assemblies are helpful because they promote better part-singing, make possible seating adjustments that solve discipline problems, and offer opportunities to assign experienced singers from the choral groups to seats where they may use their ability in part-singing to the best advantage. In the small school a precise seating chart may be made with the help of student assistants, while in the large school a seating chart may be developed on a block system. Each block of seats in the auditorium will be clearly marked with the name of the part to guide students to proper location.

The Importance of the Accompanist

Good assembly singing, whether it is done in unison or in parts, needs in addition to enthusiastic and inspiring leadership a good accompanist at the keyboard. Not all good pianists are good accompanists. Many piano students, when given the opportunity for experience and training as accompanists, eventually develop

South Bend Public Schools, South Bend, Indiana.

Fig. 9.6. Accompanists must be developed through training and experience.

into capable accompanists. By giving as many pianists as possible the chance for experience in accompanying the large and small ensembles, many schools always have available a good supply of students skilled in the art of accompanying (Fig. 9.6).

The leader should plan his music so that the accompanist may be thoroughly prepared and thus be sensitive to the needs of the singers and the conductor. There are times when the mood of the assembly audience indicates the need for a change in the music selected for use on that day. It is therefore advisable to have the accompanist learn a number of accompaniments to care for unexpected changes of song material. A competent accompanist who can transpose, play by ear, and sight read contributes a great deal to the success of group singing in assemblies. There are many teachers who are experienced accompanists and who find it possible to secure fine results in group singing by leading the singing from the keyboard as they accompany.

EXAMPLES OF SUCCESSFUL PROGRAMS

In the Small School

In a small high school with only one music teacher on the staff, in charge of both vocal and instrumental music, the unison and part-singing in its assemblies were outstanding. Every student in the school was given an individual voice test for assembly singing, the tests being scheduled during the free periods in the students' schedules and carried on from the opening of school in September until the middle of October. The faculty gave full cooperation to the voice testing program and were very helpful in excusing students for the test if it proved to be necessary.

After the testing of voices was completed, the teacher, aided by a number of students, made a seating chart of the school auditorium and assigned each student in the school to a seat for music assemblies. Copies of the assignment sheets were sent to the homerooms for posting. Students in the musical organizations who could read music and had part-singing experience were assigned seats throughout the auditorium to positions where they could assist those not experienced in music. A number of faculty members volunteered to take assigned seats and do what they could to encourage part singing.

At the time of the first assembly there was little confusion in getting the group seated and ready for work. A special seating plan for the music assemblies was particularly beneficial in this school. School tradition had been established that the seating for assemblies be according to class rank, with the seniors in front seats and the juniors immediately behind them, etc. Some small groups of students abused their seating privileges and constantly created a serious discipline problem in the regular assembly periods. The seating plan for the music assemblies with assignments made according to the part sung broke up the traditional seating arrangement and eliminated that particular discipline problem.

Student assistants prepared the auditorium for the assemblies. There was a stage crew responsible for preparing the stage for the school orchestra or whatever group was performing on the stage. Another crew of students placed song books in each auditorium chair and then took stations throughout the room to assist in any manner possible. Both of these crews took the responsibility for the return of the song books to the music room and for clearing the stage. This program of assemblies would not have been possible if students had not been willing to assume a large share of the work involved.

The music assemblies in this school were not set on a fixed time schedule. Dates for the assemblies were worked out by the principal and the teacher with the approval of the faculty. Another interesting feature of the program was that the faculty granted the teacher complete freedom in determining the length of any particular assembly except that the assembly must not last more than one school period of 50 minutes. Since this school had both junior- and senior-high-school students, freedom to determine the length of any program was of great help to the teacher. If the students were unusually restless or if their audience etiquette was unsatisfactory they could be returned to regular classroom work even if the assembly had been in session only a relatively short time. The time limitation was not used as a means of threatening students with the loss of assembly time to secure good behavior and response, but it was surprising how soon the students realized that the length of the assembly was in their hands. After one or two early dismissals the remainder of the assemblies always ran the full period.

The assembly programs involved the entire student body in group singing and in a listening period of five to ten minutes. This period was usually devoted to music performed by the students (Fig. 9.7). Themes for the assemblies were used from time to time, but the variety and flexibility of the programing made titling restrictive in many cases and therefore it was not always used.

One of the most interesting and effective programs presented by this school came in the period just before the students were to be dismissed for the Christmas holidays. It featured *The Childe Jesus*, a Christmas cantata which contains well-known and not so well-known carols linked together with original music.[6] The cantata was sung by the school choir and soloists, with the audience singing in parts the harmony of the familiar carols. At the close of the work a student read the Christmas story from the Bible and, following that, everyone joined in singing

[6] Joseph Clokey and Jean Kirk, *The Childe Jesus*, Summy-Birchard.

Detroit Public Schols, Detroit, Michigan.

Fig. 9.7. Capable vocal groups provide good listening experiences in assemblies.

"Silent Night." The quieting effect on the students was amazing. They left the auditorium in an orderly manner without the boisterousness of the usual vacation dismissal. The program was uplifting and inspiring.

In the Large School

One junior high school is fortunate to have the musical and lyrical talent of many colored children, who make up 40 percent of the enrollment. There are two music teachers in the school, both of whom are assigned to vocal and instrumental music.

In addition to the native talent of the pupils and other contributing factors, we believe that the success of the assembly sings was due largely to cooperation and teamwork. Together the two teachers selected and studied songs, and came to exact agreement on tempo and interpretation. After teaching these songs in all the classes, the groups were combined occasionally. One teacher directed and the other accompanied and both teachers knew how the numbers were developing in each other's classes. Songs were never used in assembly until they were well known, and words were projected on the screen.

The teachers were constantly on the alert for good and interesting music, trying to secure songs that youngsters would enjoy. Variety was the watchword. Ordinary as well as unusual spirituals, folk songs, art songs, camp songs, popular pieces and rounds were used. In all the songs, singing in harmony was encouraged. A short list of some of the songs used follows:

My Soul's Been Anchored in de Lord
Listen to de Lambs
Go Down Moses
Travelin' Shoes
Trampin'
Joshua Fit de Battle
Schubert's Ave Maria
Holy City
Brahms' Lullaby
Nobody Knows
There's Music in the Air
(*with counterpart*)
Duna
Danny Boy
Little Bit of Heaven
Mother Machree
John Henry—Mac's Band
Irish Lullaby
Come to the Fair
Arkansas Traveler
Waltzing Matilda
God of Our Fathers
Holy, Holy, Holy
Day Is Dying in the West
Dayenu (*in Hebrew*)
Battle Hymn of the Republic
Hope and Faith
Navajo Trail
Hiking Song
I've Been Working on the Railroad
Bells of St. Mary's
College football songs
Red River Valley

The programs were not held too often, nor were they on a regular schedule. Sometimes there were three "sings" in a month, and then there might not be one for five or six weeks. Five to nine songs were sung at one performance, and the assemblies often ended when the students were eager for more. Enthusiasm, infectious and stimulating, was the order of the day on all sides. The children were eager, the music teachers were devoted, while the rest of the faculty lent their moral support ungrudgingly.

It was felt that the all-out cooperative labor on the fertile soil of the children's talents and inclinations resulted in a rich and abundant fruit. These really artistic sings gave the youngsters a feeling of success and importance; they were rightly proud of themselves and they loved to sing. It followed from the singers being so inspired, that school spirit was perhaps better welded by means of excellent singing than by any other factor in the school.

MATERIALS FOR USE IN ASSEMBLY PROGRAMS

There are many materials for use in music assemblies that have proven their usefulness in enriching programs and in aiding learning. Resourceful teachers will find it possible to produce successful programs and stimulate participation by all the students with a minimum expenditure of funds.

Materials selected for singing by the entire student body must be chosen with thought for the students' background and experience in music and the vocal resources of the school. There are materials such as school songs, hymns, folk songs, popular songs, patriotic and seasonal songs that are suitable for use in all school situations. They may be considered as a basic repertoire for assembly singing and are included in "Suggestions for a Cumulative Song List" (see Chapter 23), compiled by music educators from all parts of the country.[7]

With the wealth of well-graded and classified vocal materials published for use by schools, it is possible to secure music suitable to any school situation and expand this cumulative song list. Music for assembly singing must be selected with the limitations of the junior- and senior-high-school unchanged, changing, and changed voices in mind. Experienced song leaders, as they add to the list, are inclined to select music for group singing which is relatively easy for their students. They have learned that insuring their student body a satisfying and successful experience in group singing is basic to the success of the assembly program. The standards set for the selection of music should be flexible, but the music introduced into the assembly should be of such quality that it will enrich the lives of the students.

SUMMARY

A series of music assemblies for all students must be conceived in terms of the total school program and many school administrators endorse the assembly series as a unifying factor in school life. In the music assembly the chance to participate in singing and listening activities will be given to all students, regardless of their previous background in music.

Planning for the production of a series of music assemblies is a responsibility which lends itself ideally to teacher-pupil cooperative planning. The transition from the teacher-dominated assembly series to the present practice of planning and producing programs with students has fostered student interest and cooperation in the programs. Interest and educational effectiveness of the assembly

[7] Hazel Nohavec Morgan (Ed.), *Music in American Education*, Music Educators National Conference, 1955, p. 319.

is heightened when reasonable attention is placed on showmanship in the production of the program.

Part-singing is a worthy goal of the assembly series. Good assembly singing, whether it is done in unison or in parts, needs in addition to enthusiastic and inspiring leadership, a good accompanist at the keyboard.

Materials selected for singing by the entire student body must be chosen with thought for the students' background and experience in music, and music used should be of such quality that it will enrich the lives of the students.

SUGGESTED ACTIVITIES

1. Plan a music assembly on "Instruments of the Band and Orchestra" for use in a junior high school.
2. Add four songs to each classification of the "Cumulative Song List." What is your basis for selecting these songs?
3. Prepare posters for publicizing in the school a music assembly on "Music in Our Community."
4. Prepare a check list for the evaluation of music assemblies.
5. Report on what you would include in the agenda for the first meeting of a student-assembly planning committee.
6. A university string quartet is scheduled to appear in a music assembly. Prepare several news stories for the school paper to promote interest in the program.
7. Plan a music assembly designed to acquaint students, particularly junior-high-school students, with the opportunities open to them in senior-high-school music.
8. Investigate and report on possible uses of audiovisual materials and equipment in the music assembly.
9. Survey the stage of an assembly room and design a simple stage setting for a Christmas assembly to be presented on that stage.
10. Visit a school assembly and evaluate the program from the standpoint of audience participation.
11. Examine several song books. Which of them would be most suitable for junior-high-school assembly singing? On what do you base your opinion?
12. Part-singing in assembly may be introduced by the use of rounds, descants, or simple harmonic patterns. Study song materials and compile a source list of songs for the introduction of part-singing.

SELECTED READINGS

Dykema, Peter, and Hannah Cundiff, *School Music Handbook* (new edition), Summy-Birchard, 1955, pp. 419–420.

Dykema, Peter, and Karl Gehrkens, "The Music Assembly," in *The Teaching and Administration of High School Music*, Summy-Birchard, 1941, pp. 41–53.

Scott, Jean Calvert, "Lecture Series for Young Listeners," *Music Educators Journal*, January, 1960. (Elementary school, but valuable idea for secondary school.)

Van Bodegraven, Paul, and Harry R. Wilson, *The School Music Conductor*, Schmitt, Hall & McCreary, 1942, pp. 134–136.

Ward, Arthur E., "Assembly Singing," in *Music Education for High Schools*, American Book, 1941, p. 49.

Wilson, Harry R., *Lead a Song*, Schmitt, Hall & McCreary, 1942.

Wilson, Harry R., "The General Assembly," in *Music in the High Schools*, Silver Burdett, 1941, p. 69.

Coronet Instructional Films, Chicago, Illinois.

CHAPTER

10

Music Literature, a Source of Musical Growth

NEED FOR THE TEACHING OF MUSIC LITERATURE

One of the major functions of school music is to guide young people, through varying musical experiences, to an expanding understanding and appreciation of music. The development of musical perception cannot be left to haphazard cultivation by the individual pupil; it is a part of general education as well as of music education. Since all girls and boys are and will always be consumers of music, music educators must be concerned with the musical growth of all students, performers and nonperformers alike. This is the challenge and the responsibility of the music educator.

Modern science and technology have brought music into the lives of all people. The influence on musical taste of the music heard through broadcasts, telecasts, recordings, and films intensifies the need for every school to broaden its music curriculum in order to serve the entire student body. The electronic equipment of the present day may be the means of attracting students to the music offering of the school, and the school must recognize and use these resources. Failure to do so means that electronic mediums take over the school's function, and in a sense become the curriculum makers. Shall we delegate to television, radio, and juke boxes the privilege of molding and developing the musical taste and cultural level of our young people, while we concentrate on the relatively few gifted students?

The musical standards, discrimination, and taste displayed by high-school graduates will be determined to a large degree by the effectiveness of the school music program throughout the elementary and junior- and senior-high-school years. Emphasizing the study of music literature as part of both the general education and the musical education of children during these years provides one key to raising the cultural level of both the school and the community.

Bringing girls and boys into a school environment in which music instruction is designed in terms of the needs of all students is a means of assuring the carry-over of school music into adult. It is a step toward bringing more music into the home, and toward the stimulation of community music activities, concert support and attendance. Bringing worth-while music literature to all students enables them to grow from year to year in musical perception and appreciation of music—a primary objective of music education.

The Literature of Music Instruction

The term "literature of music instruction" as used here means all music which is used for instructional purposes. This literature, particularly that selected for use in choral and instrumental instruction, must be chosen with more in mind than the development of technical skill. Significant as is the development of technical skill, of even greater importance is the growth of musical perception involving melody, harmony, rhythm, musical design or form, tonal beauty, and interpretation, in cultivating the musical sensitivity of students.

To bring to students the meaning and beauty of the masterworks through teaching materials demands that all music selected for use with school groups be of good quality and within the physical, mental, and musical capacities of the students. The use of good music and attention to the ear training essential to musical growth will provide a proper basis for appreciation of music literature.

The child as a performer or as a consumer of music becomes sensitive to musical sound and combinations of sound. It is also possible for him to develop a musical memory through ear training. Ear training thus becomes a stepping stone to a gradually increasing understanding of more complex musical forms such as sonatas, tone poems, and symphonies.

The junior- and senior-high-school music organizations can contribute effectively to the improvement of musical taste in the school and the community (Fig. 10.1). In addition to the preparation they make for school assemblies, concerts, and community functions, the rehearsals of the organizations can provide liberally for the reading of compositions with which the students should become familiar. To restrict rehearsal periods to music scheduled to be performed is to deprive pupils of an essential part of their musical education. They should be permitted to sight-read a great deal of music which they may never perform in public. This not only contributes to their knowledge of music literature and improves their music reading ability, but it helps build the self-confidence that is essential to good musical performance.

To bring teen-agers to a broad and well-balanced acquaintance with the great music of the past and present requires additional opportunities for exploration and study of music literature. The many practical factors which limit the repertoire of the band, orchestra, or choral organizations also limit their contribution to the teaching of music literature. Thus every student, performer or not, should be guided when possible into the General Music class of the junior high school and the Music Literature class of the senior high school.

The Music of Radio, Television, Recordings, Motion Pictures, and Concert Hall

Use of the modern contributions to the reproduction of music facilitates the teaching of music literature in the school. Student interest in music may be heightened by posters and announcements concerning the best in music offered by recording releases, radio, television, and motion pictures which have superior background music or which feature musical masterworks or great artists. When exceptionally good musical offerings on radio or television are announced, class time devoted to some preliminary hearing and study of that music does much to foster enjoyment and appreciation of the programs. This is one way teachers can use music of the outside world to fortify work done in the school.

Records and phonograph equipment are a basic means of bringing into the classroom that music literature which is beyond the performance capacities of students. Recordings may be the only contact with music for students who have no interest in performance but who do like to listen to music and are interested in learning more about it. Adequate phonograph equipment and recording libraries are essential auxiliaries to all junior- and senior-high-school music programs and they should be continuously expanded for use by all students. They can be the means of bringing an interest in good music to thousands of boys and girls presently not touched by the school music offering. The use of recordings by the students in a school may also be a means of evaluating the influence of the music instruction of that school.

Concerts for school children by soloists and groups of performers from within and outside the school are used in many schools as a vital extension of the music program. To see and hear musicians in an auditorium, rather than on a screen or by means of recordings, is an experience which must be a part of the education of boys and girls if we are to have the music of the school carry over to the concert hall. In spite of the electronic devices which surround us, the performance of live music is our only perfect means of hearing, recognizing, and appreciating the true vocal or instrumental tone.

The encouraging increase in the number of community orchestras functioning in American cities and the number of performing faculty members and young artists available through colleges and universities makes it possible for live concerts to be brought to even the smallest schools. Cooperation between school-

Detroit Public Schools, Detroit, Michigan.

Fig. 10.1. High-school students perform with members of the Detroit Symphony orchestra at a School Concert Series program. Select string players with Mischa Mischakoff, concertmaster, prepare for the concert.

teachers and community leaders can bring to the school and community music that will interest students and adults in regular concert attendance.

For concert attendance to contribute to music growth it is necessary that girls and boys have an opportunity to become familiar with concert music by advance preparation in school. It is equally important that after a concert there be an opportunity for discussion and review of the music heard. Encouraging students to attend concerts should not be limited to those enrolled in music. Extension of the curriculum through concerts is a part of the general education program and, as such, concerts are to be brought to all students in the school whenever possible.

Students as Consumers of Music

The function of music in the secondary school is threefold. It must be conceived in terms of the consumer, the performer, and the person endowed with creative ability. While a relatively small percentage of students electing choral or instrumental music are likely to become professional musicians or perhaps even amateur performers as adults, they will continue to be consumers of music throughout life. Thus curriculum development in the music courses and activities of the secondary school must be directed primarily toward meeting the musical needs of all students as consumers of music.

Teen-age students are interested in music. They need the teacher's understanding and guidance in discovering and exploring great works of music as listeners and participants. They need to be made conscious of the characteristics of fine musical performance. They need to be given a background knowledge of all kinds of good music, not only the great masterworks, but also the vast amount of good lighter music. For example, the student who takes part in a Gilbert and Sullivan operetta in school will always have a friendly and sympathetic feeling toward all Gilbert and Sullivan music (Fig. 10.2). A child who feels at home with good music will not be satisfied with popular music in his adult life; he will want more than that. We often hear people say, "I don't understand that music—it's too deep for me." They seem to feel that anything beyond the lightest music is a closed book to them. It need not be that way: give a child, through playing or listening, an intimate knowledge of one symphony and as an adult he will not stand in awe of the symphony and other complex musical forms.

This knowledge of and familiarity with music should be made available to every child. The music room and library facilities should be open to everyone for listening to recordings; there should be attractive assemblies and concerts, both in and out of school. Through the regular course offerings in music, including Music Literature, the informal music activities of the school, and the immersing of the student body year by year in a musical atmosphere, the music program of the secondary school can discharge its obligation to general education and to music education, and most important of all, its obligation to children.

MUSIC LITERATURE—A COURSE BASED ON PUPIL INTERESTS

In addition to participation in music through the performing groups, large and small, the curriculum can provide another avenue to musical growth—the study of music literature. In the junior high school this will be included in the General Music class, required or elective, meeting two to five periods a week. It is de-

Both photographs from Lyons Township High School, La Grange, Illinois.

Fig. 10.2. How does participation in school operettas benefit the student? These are scenes from the Gilbert and Sullivan operetta **Patience,** in which the young cast has learned to understand and appreciate the characteristics of fine musical performance. These young people will always be able to experience the joy of recognition upon hearing Gilbert and Sullivan music.

signed for pupils in Grades 7, 8, and 9 as an introduction to music as an art, and is open to all students. The course will include a variety of experiences in music such as singing, playing, listening, rhythms, music reading, fundamentals of music, and music literature. It must be structured in terms of the musical backgrounds and needs of the students in the class. It is an exploratory course, with the development of music appreciation its ultimate goal.

For the senior high school, Grades 10, 11, and 12, there is the Music Literature class, required or elective, meeting two to five periods a week and offering a minimum of one-half credit. It is a survey course in music literature, open to all students regardless of musical background, and designed to promote musical understanding and appreciation. The small high school can offer this course in alternate years to assure sufficient enrollment if the course is offered as an elective.

What are the musical interests and backgrounds of high-school children? What kind of elementary schools do they come from: did the schools have strong music programs or did they offer little music? Have many students had instrumental experience in grade-school bands or orchestras? Have they had class piano experience? Do many of them take piano lessons or study other instruments? How many have participated in operettas? Have they sung in junior church choirs? How many own record players and what kinds of records do they buy? What are some of the records their parents have and play? Do they sing or play at home? Do they go to many concerts? What are their favorite radio and television programs and performers?

The differences which are found in the musical tastes of individuals will supply a clue to their musical interests and knowledge and hence to an acceptable and stimulating approach to class work. Discovery of a starting place which will motivate students is based on study and evaluation of the experiences of the students with music in the elementary school, the home, and the community. Once the teacher finds the appropriate starting place for a particular class, he can chart the course for a cumulative and expanding experience in music.

Starting with the students' knowledge and interests uppermost in mind precludes the development of a fixed course of study in music literature for either junior or senior high school. Each class will be different and the course of study to be developed must be flexible and adaptable to the particular needs and interests of that group.

Use of Current Popular Music

The teacher of secondary-school music sometimes turns to the use of current popular music as a natural means of establishing contact with the musical interests of his pupils (Fig. 10.3). To ignore popular music or to condemn it as all trash places an impassable barrier between the teacher and the class. There are few classes of junior- or senior-high-school students who wouldn't embark on a study of the origins and history of popular music. Such a study fits naturally into

West Hartford Public Schools, West Hartford, Connecticut.

Fig. 10.3. A popular vocal quintet specializes in close harmony. How can this type of singing be regarded as contributing to the musical education of these students?

the listening pattern of teen-agers, and besides establishing a fine relationship with the teacher, it provides a stepping stone to the introduction of light classics and more serious music.

Dr. Howard McKinney, in his chapters, "Jazz Begins" and "Jazz Hot and Hybrid," presents material of particular value to the junior- or senior-high-school music teacher who senses the importance of making contact with the musical interests of pupils through popular music.[1] In another chapter, "Popular Music in the Americas South of Us," he presents an additional means of catching the interest of pupils—through the introduction of the rumbas, zambas, guaraches, and other representative Latin-American dance music. The introduction of these dance forms and the instruments of the rhythm section such as timbals, bongos,

[1] Howard McKinney, *Music and Man*, American Book, 1948.

claves, and maracas catch the attention of the teen-ager and interest him in the music of our southern neighbors.

Light music of real quality with an uncomplicated approach to melody, harmony, and rhythm is available to the teacher who will search for it; when properly presented to young people it has an immediate appeal. The teacher could have his students study a Gilbert and Sullivan operetta for a few weeks, not for performance, but merely to learn some of the catchy tunes that they will be hearing the rest of their lives. If the teacher prefers to start with instrumental music, compositions such as *The Moldau,* a Smetana piece, or "Scherzo" from Mendelssohn's *Midsummer Night's Dream Music* have proven useful and attractive to students. Good light music is a natural approach to widening the musical horizons of students. It is music which has gained a place in what might be considered the permanent music of the world, and provides the start of a knowledge of music literature which is enduring rather than transient.

The Media of Musical Expression

Young people have a natural interest in vocalists and instrumentalists, the solo instruments, and the instruments of the band and orchestra. The resourceful teacher can use this interest to build enthusiasm and hold attention as the Music Literature class progresses.

There are many ways to develop effective teaching through the introduction of the media of musical expression. Live music performed by members of the class, the school musical organizations, and individuals and groups from outside the school should be used whenever possible. Some suggested class sessions in which live music may be presented include:

1. Demonstrations of band and orchestra instruments by members of school musical organizations or community music groups.
2. Lecture-concert performances for the class by pianists, harpists, or other instrumentalists; class interests may be heightened by time devoted to a study of the construction of the instrument which is being played (Fig. 10.4).
3. Solo and small-ensemble performances of vocalists demonstrating the characteristic qualities of the various male and female voices.
4. Performance of instrumentalists demonstrating the characteristics of the string quartet, the woodwind quintet, and other combinations.
5. A class concert by such small ensembles as the madrigal club and the girls' and boys' vocal ensembles.
6. The scheduling of solo performers from the class and, when practical, the development of small vocal or instrumental performing groups within the membership of the class.

Detroit Public Schools, Detroit, Michigan.

Fig. 10.4. Group playing of unusual instruments introduces pupils to seldom-heard music literature.

Suggested Study Units

In the junior-high-school General Music class, integrated course work makes it possible for the teacher to give emphasis to music literature as a part of the singing, playing, listening, and rhythmic experiences regularly included in that class. Units of instruction are ideally suited to this type of class and may be selected by the teacher or by the teacher and students together. The following units suggest the type of unit that may be used successfully with junior-high-school pupils:

- Keyboard Instruments and Keyboard Music
- Musical Stories
- Music and Worship
- The Language of Music
- The Folk Music Singer
- Masters of Music
- Music of the Western Plains
- Music of Our Southern Neighbors
- We Go to a Concert
- Nationalism in Music

In the Music Literature class of the senior high school many teachers prefer to approach the subject by starting with music of the past and working up to the present. Others feel that by starting with music of the present they can make contact with their students more readily and secure an effective response. Good teachers in both groups frequently make use of a unit plan of instruction, incorporating such units as the following:

Musical Form and Design	The Symphony
The String Quartet	Contemporary Music and Musicians
Program Music	Contrast in Music
The Music of America	Musical Terms
Magic in Music	Operatic Gems
The Symphonic Poem	Folk Song and Art Song
Romantic Composers	

PREPARATION FOR LISTENING WITH UNDERSTANDING

Teacher Preparation

Success in teaching music literature through listening experience requires thorough preparation by the teacher. This preparation includes not only a complete knowledge of the music to be presented, but also an understanding of the students in the class and their probable receptivity to the music, as determined by their musical background, interests, and community environment. Many music teachers use the first two weeks of classes for orientation before launching into a planned course of work.

Boys and girls of junior- and senior-high-school age respond readily to music. The teacher who understands the emotional and intellectual reactions of his students will be able to secure a favorable response to serious music through their active imaginations and their facile memory for musical themes and rhythmic patterns. With interesting, successful musical experiences they can be guided into a lifelong interest in the literature of music.

Emphasis should be on directed listening, which requires that active attention and listening be cultivated. To secure active listening, attention must be focused on the rhythmic, melodic, and harmonic content of the composition; on the composer's use of thematic material; on tone quality of voices or instruments; and on the form or design of the music. In addition, the teacher must have interesting information about the composer and his contribution to music, and about the significance of the music to be heard from the standpoint of style, of design in music, and of music and world history. Some helpful suggestions in planning listening lessons may be found in the following practices used by experienced teachers of music.

Muskegon Public Schools, Muskegon, Michigan.

Fig. 10.5. Solos by members can enhance the class listening experience.

1. When presenting a new composition, start by playing through without comment the entire work or a movement of a large composition such as a symphony.
2. Plan for several presentations of the composition to the class. Each presentation should introduce one major aspect of the music.
3. Use short periods of directed listening. With students of this age, extended periods of listening are not likely to be very fruitful from an educational standpoint.
4. Make presentations simple and to the point, emphasizing one aspect at a time. In one lesson, for example, consider the thematic material and the use the composer has made of it. Play a theme or two to give the students a familiar melody to look forward to and recognize, but keep it simple. In another lesson, review the thematic material, then show how the composer has woven the themes together and made something different of them.
5. When introducing factual material about the composition or the composer, limit it to a few facts that will be remembered. Music is to be heard, not talked about.
6. To add variety and interest, plan several musical works of contrasting types for each listening lesson. With individual tastes in mind, try for something familiar and something new in each lesson.
7. Aim for a variety of approaches to the music to obtain student interest and

assure renewed interest in the work on repeated hearings. Perhaps there are solos or other instrumental or vocal excerpts that could be used, either live or recorded (Fig. 10.5).

8. Follow directed listening with the playing of a familiar composition to which the class listens without comment by the instructor.

Pupil Readiness

Pupil readiness for exploration in music is at its peak in the junior- and senior-high-school years. Boys and girls are physically, mentally, and emotionally matured sufficiently for serious study in music. Their readiness and their sensitivity to beauty at this age combine to make them receptive to music and to the guidance of the teacher (Fig. 10.6). Their active interest in music and their need for guidance and instruction are demonstrated by their enthusiastic support of popular music.

Duluth Public Schools, Duluth, Minnesota. Courtesy Duluth News-Tribune.

Fig. 10.6. The teacher goes over fine points in the score with students from the high-school choir.

To direct this innate love of music into more serious channels and to cultivate readiness and receptivity in pupils, there are many approaches to the teaching of music literature. Start with music pupils know and enjoy; try group singing of folk songs used by a composer in his writing; demonstrate the instruments of the band and orchestra or present a film on the instruments; have pupils play the easy melody, harmony, and percussion instruments; present descriptive or program music. Interest may be further heightened by bulletin board displays of attractive pictorial material such as pictures of instruments, composers, performers, and colorful illustrated jackets from music books and recordings.

Readiness in pupils will be recognized by a change in their attitude toward music. They will ask questions, bring recordings to class, request repetition of compositions, show satisfaction in recognizing themes and instruments, and respond when asked to participate. The teacher can capitalize on the readiness of pupils when he approaches the teaching of music literature with vitality and inspiration.

FACILITIES AND EQUIPMENT FOR TEACHING MUSIC LITERATURE

The teaching of music literature as a part of all music instruction in the school can be carried on in those facilities assigned to band, orchestra, and choral rehearsals, and to other curricular offerings. Practice rooms and other space devoted to individual and small-group practice periods can be equipped with record players for use as listening rooms when they are not in use for practice.

Listening Rooms

When a new school building is being planned, the music teacher should make his needs known. The building and equipment needs of the music department should be planned in terms of an expanding curriculum which will serve the needs of all students. For music literature instruction a sufficient number of small rooms suitable for practicing and listening to music may be included in the plans (Fig. 10.7). A listening room may be planned either as a part of the school library or as a part of the music section of the building.[2] Where listening facilities are included as a part of the school library they are more likely to be of service to all students and departments.

[2] See *Music Buildings, Rooms and Equipment,* Music Educators National Conference, 1955, p. 66.

Fig. 10.7. Appropriate music listening facilities are an important part of the music literature program.

Lyons Township High School, La Grange, Illinois.

Piano, Phonograph, and Recording Equipment

The piano, phonograph, and recording equipment, while standard equipment for music instruction, take on added significance when the teaching of music literature is emphasized throughout the school program as a part of both music education and general education. Such equipment must be of excellent quality and durability. This is important both for performers and consumers, since good sound quality is essential for the development of appreciation.

A sufficient number of instruments and recorders is needed to make them readily available for all who would like to use them. Some of these instruments may be available through the audiovisual service of the school or the library. The music rooms should, of course, be properly equipped at all times.

The importance of the piano and its contribution to the musical growth of students cannot be overestimated. As a solo or accompanying instrument, as a means of studying the fundamentals of music or analyzing musical compositions, as a means of bringing music from the school into the home and the community, the piano stands ready to serve the students and the teacher. The piano, through the live musical performance it makes possible, is an essential part of the instruction equipment in the teaching of music literature if a proper balance between the live and the "canned" music heard by students is to be established.

The Library of Books and Recordings

The school library is designed to meet the needs of all students, all areas of instruction, and the total school program. Its services to the music department first of all consist of a representative number of books for use in the General Music class, the Music Literature class, and other music classes. The school library should contain books on music and musicians, careers in music, musical performance, music theory, music history, and related subjects. In addition, there should be available for student use a music dictionary, one or more standard reference works, and at least one periodical dealing with current events in music.

The modern school library can contribute much to the general and music education programs of the school by expanding its services through the acquisition, organization, and maintenance of a library of recordings. With recordings now used in the teaching of history, social studies, language arts, foreign languages, and science, as well as in the teaching of music, the school's collection of recordings is appropriately a part of the school's teaching materials center, audiovisual center, or the school library. Recordings included in the school library or other centers serving the school are easily distributed and are readily accessible to students and teachers. The turntable equipped with earphones makes it possible for recordings to be used without disturbing other students or library functions. It is important that music teachers be interested in the resources of the library and maintain a cooperative relationship with the school librarian.

Audiovisual Materials

Audiovisual materials may be used as a means of motivation in the teaching of music literature in all music classes. The number and types used depend upon the nature of the subject matter and the creative imagination of the teacher and the students (Figs. 10.8 and 10.9). Prepared visual materials may be purchased, but there is a unique opportunity for the resourceful teacher to guide students in producing their own materials for specific purposes:

Charts:

- Large keyboard
- Instruments of the band and orchestra
- Musical terms
- Thematic material
- Rhythmic patterns
- Form and design in music (sonata form, fugue, etc.)
- Composers of various nationalities and schools

Fig. 10.8. The tape recorder can bring the world's great music to high-school students.

Muskegon Public Schools, Muskegon, Michigan.

Coronet Instructional Films, Chicago, Illinois.

Fig. 10.9. Books, records, and films on the lives of great composers are essential to the development of understanding and appreciation of good music. The above scene is taken from a film on the life of Franz Liszt.

Maps:
- Countries and continents
- Music maps

Display boards:
- Current musical events
- Material related to study units
- Cartoons and clippings on music
- Book covers
- Pictures
- Keyboard Jr.

Flat pictures:
- Composers
- Masterworks of art
- Artist and student performers
- Musical organizations
- Instruments

Flash Cards:
- Themes—melodic and rhythmic
- Instruments
- Compositions
- Musical terms
- Composers

Musical Games:
- Note—O (Lyon and Healy, Chicago)
- Maestro (Gamble Hinged Music Co., Chicago)

Classroom music corner:
- Instrumental display
- Models and puppets
- Music books
- Pictures
- Music
- New and interesting recordings

MUSIC LITERATURE IN THE CURRICULUM

A broad concept of music education is the key to bringing music literature into the curriculum, with the emphasis on music for all students. Such a concept is basic to the general and the music education programs of the junior and senior high school. A broad concept of music education is designed with both the performing and nonperforming student in mind, and aims to fulfill the needs of individual students as consumers of music. Its greatest strength lies in a flexibility which makes it possible to meet the particular needs of the pupils and the varying situations to which the concept must be applied. In the school with a broad concept of music education, the music specialist is more than a music director or a conductor. The teacher of music in such a school becomes a guide and music consultant to students, faculty, parents, and community leaders.

Integration With Other Subject-Matter Areas

Integration of music with other areas of instruction, such as English, social studies, art, and foreign languages, permits an opportunity for curriculum development which can bring music into the lives of greater numbers of students. Junior- and senior-high-school teachers are willing to include music in their teaching, if they are given help and encouragement. The music specialist serving as a consultant is in a position to give teachers confidence in working with music and to help them in the selection of appropriate and authentic music and recordings. Units of instruction, for example, must be produced cooperatively. Music should fit naturally into a unit rather than be imposed upon it artificially. Integration of music with other subjects is possible anywhere in the secondary school, but it meets with particular success in the junior high school because of the inherent curiosity and enthusiasm of students at this age level.

An instructor in the University of Wisconsin High School writes:[3] "I consider singing a vital, integral part of language learning and most essential on the junior high school level." In her classes students often sing French folk songs and listen to recordings of folk songs, operatic airs, and other compositions by French composers. Festivals such as Christmas are made of greater interest to her students through the introduction of the beautiful music of that season into the language class.

Integration is a two-way responsibility. There are inestimable possibilities for educational growth when the teacher of music approaches integration, convinced both of the value of music in the teaching of other subjects, and of the value of other subjects in the teaching of music. Units of instruction in General Music, Music Literature, and other music classes must, when possible, implement the work done by students in other subject matter areas. Teachers of other subjects should be encouraged to enrich their offerings through the use of music. Properly handled, all areas can benefit from the exchange of related offerings.

Integration of music with other subjects does not mean that music will lose its identity; it will not lower the standards of performance or retard the develop-

[3] Miss Laura Johnson in a letter to William R. Sur, October, 1956.

ment of necessary skills. It does mean that music assumes a position of greater importance in the curriculum, in the total school program, and in the lives of boys and girls.

Music integrated with other subject areas should mean more than merely listening to recordings. Recordings should be used for instructional purposes, but whenever possible students should produce their own music and hear music sung or played by other musicians. A music session in a foreign language class can be made truly inspirational when a choral class is combined with it to assist in the singing of folk music, art songs, and choral works. Vocal and instrumental soloists brought into the class add much to the learning situation.

Robert Pooley suggests some specific applications of music in the teaching of literature:

1. Folk songs and ballads. These belong to many periods in the literature of England and of the United States, and with their traditional airs are always interesting to students. We have often dramatized some of the work songs and the students have always enjoyed the types that have the shouting refrains. My American literature texts have always had a section on the folk ballad and the work song and also the Negro spiritual. Either in the text or in a supplementary leaflet we have given the music for many of these.
2. The musical settings for the songs in Shakespeare's plays. In the upper-level classes of any high school there is generally at least one Shakepeare play read in each academic year. In the comedies especially, there are songs that have been set to music by well-known composers. I think particularly of "Twelfth Night" and "As You Like It." It has always interested students to hear recordings of these songs with instrumental accompaniment, especially with the lute, if I can secure such a recording.
3. The use of music to illustrate the artistic point of view of a particular period of literary history. In this connection I have used music of the 17th century, particularly the part-song and madrigal to show the music that Samuel Pepys and the men of his age would have been familiar with. I play some Purcell for the close of the 17th century and the introduction to the 18th century, and follow this up with Handel and Haydn. In a senior high school English literature course I have even introduced some of the operatic music of Buononcini for them to see something of the rococo ornamentation of this style. This in turn would be followed by examples of the early romantic movement and then something of the realistic music of the later 19th century.
4. For poetry of the 19th century and current times there are quite a few musical settings. I think particularly of such things as Kipling's "Recessional," Tennyson's "I Shot an Arrow into the Air," and some of Browning's lyrics. In America some of Longfellow and Whitman, as well as Edna St. Vincent Millay have been set to music. These would generally be used as recordings in the classroom, the students listening to the record while they follow the words in their text.
5. Finally, I have used orchestral music for the creation of mood for creative composition. Just as a student might look at a scene or a picture and derive from it an impression which would lead him to write something, so I have had them listen

to the playing of an orchestral piece and write what their imaginations were aroused to create from this experience. Sometimes the results from this are extremely interesting.[4]

There are opportunities for music to be used in the teaching of science at the time classes are learning and experimenting with basic information on sound waves and acoustics. There is a relationship between music and science which opens interesting possibilities for the science and music teachers. Schnoor has found that the physical aspects of music appeal to the mechanical interests of the adolescent.[5] She has had success with discussions, demonstrations, and experiments on the characteristics of tone as shown in experiments with pitch, tone, quality, resonance, vibration, duration, type of tone, air-column vibration, and the voice.

In presenting tone quality to students, Schnoor seeks to show that the quality of each tone heard is affected by the number of upper partials present. This is done by a demonstration using the piano in which the keys of the harmonic series are held down while the fundamental is struck. The project could be continued by having the same note or series of notes played on brass, reed, double reed, bowed, or plucked instruments. Such demonstrations show how the manner in which a tone is produced affects its tone quality. Similar demonstrations can show that the size and shape of an instrument affect its tone quality as well as its pitch.

Music Literature as an Elective Subject

In a junior or senior high school where the music program is well organized to serve all the students and where boys and girls have had the benefit of an effective basic music program from Grades 1 through 6, there is reason to question the additional requirement of music in the junior or senior high school. In determining whether these courses should be elective or required, a careful study of the particular school situation is necessary. The teacher and administrators must take into consideration the musical experience and background of the students, anticipate scheduling problems, and estimate the class size and the class load of the teacher. There are strong arguments both for requiring General Music or Music Literature or for placing them on an elective basis. These offerings can prove to be extremely effective in developing in young people a lifelong interest in music. Whether the course is required or elective has a great influence on the results which may be expected from the course, and it is a decision that must rest with the teachers of each particular school.

[4] Robert C. Pooley, Chairman, Department of Integrated Studies, University of Wisconsin, in a letter to William R. Sur, October, 1956.

[5] Lois L. Schnoor, "Physics of Sound in Junior High School," *Music Educators Journal*, February, 1941, pp. 27, 57.

SUMMARY

To bring to students the meaning and beauty of the masterworks of music through music literature, all music selected for use with school groups must be of recognized quality and within the physical, mental, and musical capacities of the students. The influence on musical taste of the music heard through radio, television, recordings, and films intensifies the need for every school to broaden its music curriculum to serve a larger percentage of the student body. Music has an important function in both the general and the music education programs of the school.

The function of music in the secondary school is threefold: it must be conceived in terms of (1) consumers, (2) performers, and (3) those endowed with creative ability. In the junior high school, integrated course work makes it possible for the music teacher to give emphasis to music literature as a part of the singing, playing, listening, and rhythmic experiences regularly included in the General Music class. Integration of music with other subject means that music assumes a position of greater importance in the total school program, with greater numbers of girls and boys receiving the benefits of music instruction.

SUGGESTED ACTIVITIES

1. For use in the junior high school make a selection of choral or instrumental materials which you consider worthy from the musical standpoint. Make a similar selection for the senior high school.
2. Prepare a bulletin board display on such topics as "Men in Music," "Music of Latin America," or "American Composers."
3. Develop a list of books on music and musicians suitable for reading by junior-high-school pupils. Develop a similar list for senior-high-school pupils.
4. You have a budget allotment of $200 for the purchase of a phonograph. Study the specifications and prices of several offered for sale for school use. Which do you believe to be most desirable? Why?
5. Prepare a lesson plan for introducing Dvorak's "New World Symphony" to a senior-high-school Music Literature class.
6. Make a study of folk song collections. List those folk songs you would like to use in a junior-high-school General Music class, and in a social studies class studying the Western movement in America.
7. If you planned to make a thorough study of one complete symphony for use in a senior-high-school Music Literature class, which symphony would you select? Give your reasons.
8. Interview a dozen junior-high-school students to learn something of the music they know and like. Report your findings to the class.

9. Prepare a unit of study on the origins and history of popular music.
10. Preview and evaluate three films that would enrich the teaching of music literature in the junior or senior high school.
11. You are establishing a library of recordings for use in a senior high school of 400 pupils. Your purchases are limited to $200. List the recordings you would select. Do the same for a junior high school.

SELECTED READINGS

Altshuler, Blanche, "*Carmen*—A Study in Depth," *Music Educators Journal*, April–May, 1961, p. 90.

Andrews, Francis, and Joseph Leeder, "The Listening Experience," in *Guiding the Junior High Pupils in Music Experiences*, Prentice-Hall, 1953, pp. 184–245.

Gaston, E. Thayer, "Aesthetic Experiences in Music," *Music Educators Journal*, June–July, 1963, p. 25.

Gerzina, Frank J., "Listening Develops Musical Taste," *Music Educators Journal*, April–May, 1963, p. 133.

Joio, Norman Dello, "The Quality of Music," *Music Educators Journal*, April–May, 1962, p. 33.

Newman, William S., "The Pursuit of Music," *Understanding Music*, Harper & Row, 1953, pp. 267–280.

Stevens, Halsey, "Youth and New Music," *Music Educators Journal*, September–October, 1963, p. 49.

Tooze, Ruth, and Beatrice P. Krone, *Literature and Music as Resources for Social Studies*, Prentice-Hall, 1955.

Youngberg, Harold C., "Contemporary Music in the High School," *Music Educators Journal*, September–October, 1962, pp. 51–54.

Zimmerman, George H., "Listen!" *Music Educators Journal*, June–July, 1961, p. 29.

San Diego City Schools, San Diego, California.

CHAPTER

11

Recreational Music

As there are many ways in which music may be used for recreation, there is no single definition for recreational music. Many people find recreation through music by playing the piano for their own enjoyment, playing in a string quartet or community orchestra, singing in a church choir, or perhaps listening to recordings of concertos, symphonies, or operas. Others secure their pleasure and relaxation from singing, playing, or listening to popular music of the day or from playing simple instruments.

The recreational music with which we are concerned here has been called "The music of the people." It is the simple music of immediate appeal which brings relaxation and satisfaction to an individual without the need for extensive study, great talent, or particular experience. It is music which supplements but does not supplant existing music opportunities in the school or the community. Thus recreational music can be and often is combined with other school activities.

Informal vocal and instrumental music and music activities have always contributed pleasure to people. The barbershop quartet movement, the playing of records by a university professor, the boy by the campfire who strums his favorite tunes on the guitar, are typical of the vocal and instrumental interests that may be encouraged among junior- and senior-high-school students. They are participating activities which bridge the gap between what pupils sometimes think of a "real" music and the music played and sung in the school. The school activity period, the assembly, before- and after-school periods and music classes are used in many secondary schools to make the most of teen-agers natural interest in informal music activities.

The music teacher who aims for a music offering in which all may participate finds that recreational music lends itself naturally to the music program. It brings to boys and girls a vehicle for creative expression, teamwork, sociability, and recreation. Music becomes available to all, regardless of the amount of interest manifested, talent, or financial status. The expanded music program which includes recreational music is consequently in a position to attract and serve a majority of pupils.

WHY RECREATIONAL MUSIC?

The basic objectives of music in the junior and senior high school are recognized to be aesthetic, social, and therapeutic in nature. As we move forward to meet these objectives, every child should receive both the encouragement and the opportunity to participate in music. It is not expected that all pupils will continue with music performance. The power which music has to serve the personal and social needs of the adolescent emphasizes the function recreational music may have in music education.

Music as a Social Force and a Therapy

The value of recreational music as a social force is recognized by teachers of music, recreational leaders, and youth workers. The use of music as a therapy is also recognized by the school music specialist who teaches music in terms of what it can do for boys and girls.

Juvenile delinquency, the exceptional child, and other problems at the junior- and senior-high-school level need for their solution the combined efforts of those who work with young people. The reason for recreational music in the school program and a glimpse of its potentialities is illustrated in this anecdote.

A few years ago at a national school music conference the program stressed the need for emphasis on recreational music in the school music program. A newspaper man made quite a point of reporting the interest of music educators in the singing of recreational songs and the playing of simple melody, harmony, and rhythm instruments.

A local judge voluntarily came forward to express his endorsement of simple recreational music activities for boys and girls. He said, "I've been on the juvenile court bench for many years and I have learned what the simple recreational music activities can do for teen-agers." The judge explained that he was not a musician, but for his own pleasure he had learned to play the harmonica. For some years he had been returning to the courthouse on Saturday mornings to teach the harmonica to delinquents whom he had interested in the instrument. The judge said:

Our city schools have an excellent program of music for boys and girls. The junior and senior high schools have instrumental classes, bands, orchestras, choirs and choruses, yet there are a great many pupils who simply don't fit into that program. Music has something for them if we turn to recreational music activities. I've seen youngsters take the harmonica and with a little help from me, shortly play a tune. To the trained musician this sort of thing may not seem important but to these young people it was extremely important. They responded to a chance to learn some music as all children do when properly approached by someone interested in them. The really important thing was that without much training or practice they could play a tune—they were successful in something. You must remember that the larger number of boys and girls who must appear before me in court rarely have gained the security and satisfaction that come from achievement. They are in trouble at home and in school. Recreational music activities provide one very effective means of guiding and encouraging them to make the most of their abilities.

Student Guidance

Junior and senior high schools interested in a program of music for all students find that informal vocal and instrumental activities have a unique drawing power for the teen-age pupil. These seemingly inconsequential music activities are a means of contact with many pupils who under ordinary circumstances would not be touched by the music program. It is through them that musical growth may be generated and the youth may be helped with his problems as an individual.

There are unlimited opportunities for student guidance as a result of a recreational music program. Perhaps the informality of the activity, the relief from anxieties and tensions, or just the security and sense of achievement that come with informal participation tend to develop a wholesome relationship between the teacher and the pupil. Once this relationship has been established through recreational music, the music teacher is in a much better position to supply other types of guidance to girls and boys.

DEVELOPING A PUPIL-CENTERED RECREATIONAL MUSIC PROGRAM

A pupil-centered recreational music program will vary with situations, but in all cases it is a program based on the interests of young people. Eugene Gilbert, President of the Gilbert Youth Research Company, indicates that group singing and playing the piano and the guitar are tops in musical activities. He quotes a high-school girl as explaining it in this manner: "When we kids all sing and play the uke or guitar, we get the most wonderful feeling. Like being part of a big happy family. It makes me feel all warm inside."[1]

[1] Eugene Gilbert, "Music Gains Popularity as Hobby by Teen-agers," *The State Journal,* Lansing, Michigan, November 4, 1956, p. 8.

Informal Group Singing

With the help of students, informal group singing may be brought into music classes by the introduction of folk songs, action songs, singing games, well-known songs, songs with descants, hymns, camp and campus songs. Much of the singing will be unison singing, but "barbershopping" may be encouraged to stimulate an interest in part singing.

Interest in informal singing is increased when piano, autoharp, ukulele, guitar, accordion, and rhythm instruments such as tambourines or castanets are used for accompaniments suggested by the pupils (Fig. 11.1). Violin, clarinet, cornet, and other orchestra and band instruments may also be used for the playing of simple harmonic accompaniments.

Informal group singing is usually singing without a conductor. There is a lead-off person to get the singing started, but formal conducting and rehearsing are the exception rather than the rule. Once pupils are introduced to this type

American Music Conference, Chicago, Illinois.

Fig. 11.1. Nearly everyone would like to be able to play a ukulele and contribute to social gatherings.

of singing, their enthusiasm for it will be contagious. It will find its place in the school assembly, the activity period, the homeroom, and in music and other classes. School camps and trips are natural settings for spontaneous informal singing.

An assembly may be organized to feature small ensembles selected by tryouts from the groups of pupils who have been singing together. Such an assembly stimulates student interest in getting together to sing for fun, and interests other pupils in recreational singing.

Simple Instrumental Activity

There are many simple instruments which pupils may use, such as the shepherd's pipe, the harmonica, jugs and bottles, the autoharp, the guitar, the ukulele, the drum, rhythm instruments, recorders, and other melody and harmony instruments. Demonstration of the instruments in music classes, assemblies, or in school clubs will bring forth an immediate response from the students. Displays of simple instruments in the school's showcases and in the music room produce fine results when accompanied by an invitation for any boy or girl interested in learning to play an instrument to stop by the music room.

The teaching of simple instruments may be conducted before and after school, at the noon hour, or in classes specifically organized for that purpose. In a number of junior high schools it is incorporated into the General Music class as a part of the course. Teachers frequently make use of other students as assistants for teaching the instruments. In one school an approach to simple instrumental activity was made by offering lessons on different kinds of recreational instruments each semester. At the beginning of one semester, for those who wanted to play the ukulele a simple start was made by having the pupil learn two chords, the tonic and the dominant. Before the first class period was over, the pupils were playing their own ukulele accompaniment to "Down in the Valley" and "The Lonesome Cowboy." They left that class period with a list of songs which needed only the two chords they had learned, such as "Paw Paw Patch," "Goodbye Old Paint," "Li'l Liza Jane," and the like. No one had to urge them to practice. They came back to the class with all the suggested songs learned, plus a number of others that needed only "their" two chords for accompaniment.

As has been indicated, very little motivation on the part of the teacher is needed when working with recreational instruments. They are not difficult to play and a tune or an accompaniment can be produced by all pupils in their first attempts. Once the pupil successfully produces music on the instrument, interest is easily sustained.

The State Journal, *Lansing, Michigan.*

Fig. 11.2. More recordings are being bought by more people today than in the whole history of recorded music. Recreational music interests of young people play a significant role in record sales.

The number of students who are attracted to these simple instruments and who eventually elect to study an instrument of the band or orchestra can be significant. These instruments carry music throughout the school and into the out-of-school activities of pupils. They may easily be the means whereby many pupils start on a program of a serious study of music.

Recordings, Films, Books, and Displays

Much interest in recreational music may be generated by recordings, films, books, and displays of recreational music (Fig. 11.2). Recordings are important to the program, for the listening experience is a part of the recreational music offering. Boys and girls need to be guided in their listening. It is suggested that help be given them in knowing what to listen for and that they be given the opportunity to become acquainted with music of all types and styles. The school library of recordings should be available for use by the pupils in their free hours.

An increasing number of sound motion pictures and film strips are becoming available for school use. Films such as *Percussion Group*[2] are both educational and entertaining and bring life and variety to the listening experience. The use of films in assemblies, music classes, and clubs can contribute much toward interesting pupils in music.

[2] *Percussion Group*, Sound B & W, EBF Film, 11 min. This film demonstrates with orchestral accompaniment the playing of tympani, tom-tom, drums, cymbals, gong, castanets, triangle, bell, xylophone, celesta; it includes excerpts from Tschaikovsky, Wagner, and Schubert.

Many books may be brought to the attention of pupils.[3] It has become the custom in some schools for the teacher of music to supply the English teacher with a list of books on music and musicians. These books are then included on the class book list for book reports.

Displays on the bulletin boards may be planned by pupils. Flat pictures, cartoons, news items, and notes of general interest on music and musicians have a strong appeal to teen-agers. Displays should be aimed at informing other students of the part music can play in their lives and inviting them to participate in music through singing, playing, or listening.

DESIRABLE SCHOOL FACILITIES AND EQUIPMENT

No unusual facilities are needed for a program of recreational music. It is a program well suited to both the large and the small school, and may be fitted into almost any type of school program. In the modern school, practice rooms, the stage and other parts of the school auditorium, and classrooms are suitable for instruction on the simple instruments. To encourage pupils to listen to music, a reasonable number of phonographs as well as the library of recordings should be easily accessible to students.

Equipment and instructional materials need not be extensive or expensive. A representative library of recordings is desirable. In addition, it would be helpful for the school to secure for display, demonstration, and in some cases for loan to students, the following instruments

Set of harmonicas
Set of rhythm instruments
Song Flutes, Tonettes, Flutophones
Set of standard ukuleles
One baritone ukulele
Set of chromatic bells
One 4-string tenor guitar
Two 6-string guitars
Set of soprano or descant recorders
One tenor recorder
One bass recorder
Twelve- or 15-bar autoharps
Set of soprano and alto Melodicas
One Piano 26 Melodica
Set of shepherd's pipes and set of materials for making a pipe

The school music library might well include collections of various types of music for recreational singing, instruction books for learning the simple instruments, and solo and ensemble material for all of the simple instruments. To encourage recreational music activity outside the school, these materials, insofar as it is practicable, should be offered to pupils on a loan basis.

[3] See, e.g., Thomasine C. McGehee and Alice D. Nelson, *People and Music*, Allyn and Bacon, Inc., 1963; and Delos Smith, *The Music in Your Life: Lives of the Great Composers*, Harper & Row, 1957.

SIMPLE INSTRUMENTS

A large amount of equipment is not required for recreational music activities; schools with very limited resources have developed recreational music programs without great expense. In fact, many children purchase their own instruments and music to have them for their use at home. The information which follows is to give some idea of the simple instruments which have been found worth while for school use.

All simple instruments may be purchased at low cost, but many of them may also be made by the pupils. Annett emphasizes the evidence that a child with mechanistic ability is often more interested in music after he has constructed his own musical instruments.[4] Further, Coleman has demonstrated in her experimental studies that children can be successful in making tom-toms, tambourines, various types and styles of drums, bamboo pipes or shepherd's pipes, and simple stringed instruments.[5] While making the instruments, the child not only maintains his interest in music but also increases his knowledge of music. As the pupil makes the instrument, the fundamentals of tone production, pitch, scale structure, and tuning of the instrument are learned. Among the simple instruments with which junior- and senior-high-school pupils will want to become acquainted are rhythm, melody, harmony, and both harmony and melody instruments.

Rhythm Instruments

These can be purchased or made from collected materials, and include drums, claves, rattles, tom-toms, castanets, woodblocks, maracas, triangles, pebbles in gourds, tambourines, and shakers (Fig. 11.3).

Melody Instruments

Shepherd's Pipe

An inexpensive musical instrument that may be made out of a piece of bamboo with the simplest of tools.[6] It may be used as a solo instrument or, with other members of the pipe family, may be played in a shepherd's pipe ensemble. The treble pipe may be constructed in the key of D to fit the range of the unison and part

[4] Thomas Annett, *Music for Recreation*, La Crosse, Wisconsin, 1952.
[5] Satis Coleman, *Creative Music for Children*, Putnam, 1922.
[6] Source of supply: Bamboo and Rattan Works, 901 Jefferson St., Hoboken, N.J. In ordering and securing prices, specify bamboo for shepherd's pipes and give length desired. Minimum shipment is ten pieces.

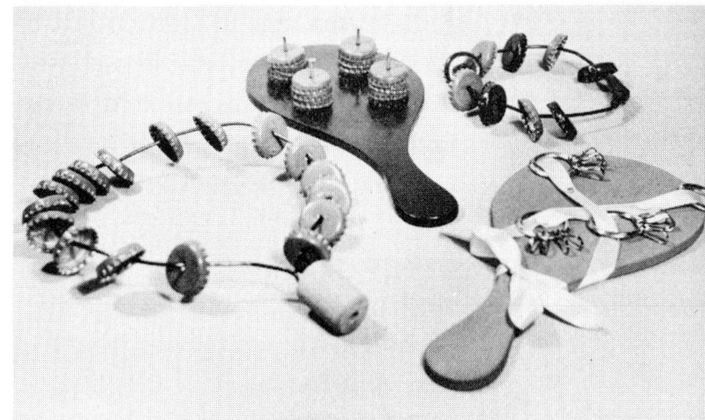

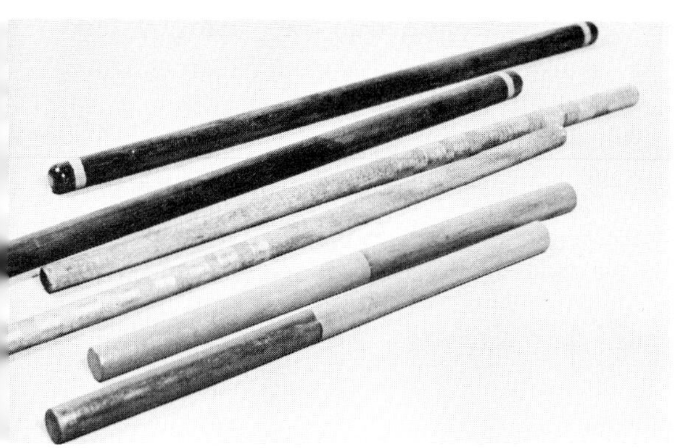

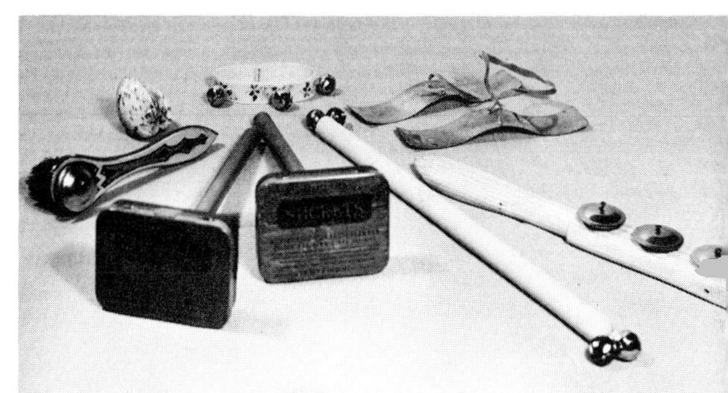

Fig. 11.3. These instruments were made by students. What values are there for the student in making such instruments?

songs. Some make and tune their treble pipes to the key of C to make it possible to perform with the harmonica or treble recorder in C. The alto pipe is tuned to the key of A, the tenor pipe to the key of D, one octave below the treble pipe. The bass pipe is tuned to the key of G. Augustus D. Zanzig has written an inexpensive booklet on the shepherd's pipe (see Chapter 21) which gives complete directions for making pipes. This booklet also contains a few pieces for pipers and a list of piper music. A great deal of interest in the pipes has been shown in this country and abroad. There is a Piper's Guild in England and one in the United States.[7]

Recorder

The recorder, an end-blown flute not to be confused with the modern transverse or side-blown flute, was popular from the time of Shakespeare through the Bach and Handel period. A revival of interest in the instrument and its music about

[7] Information on the American branch of the Piper's Guild may be obtained from Miss Jennie Cossitt, Director, 2800 Tola Ave., Altadena, California.

thirty years ago in Europe has brought recorder solo and ensemble playing into the lives of school children as well as of families and adults throughout the world. The recorder is a non-transposing instrument with a chromatic range of over two octaves. Instruments are now made of plastic and a variety of woods, with pear and maple wood most commonly used. The Baroque or English fingering is preferred rather than the German fingering which favors the basic scale but makes more complex fingering for other scales. The instrument has a unique appeal to students of junior and senior high school are. In addition to its recreational potential, it can contribute to note-reading skills, rhythmic feeling, pitch consciousness and harmonic sensitivity. Successful teachers of beginners strongly recommend that piano accompaniment be frequently used as a means of securing good intonation. The usefulness of the instrument is recognized in the playing of folk tunes with or without autoharp, guitar, or ukulele accompaniment, themes from listening lessons, descants, rounds with voices, bells, or other recorders. It is recommended that the solo and ensemble literature by Bach, Handel, Telemann, Mozart, Gluck, and an increasing number of contemporary composers be performed by secondary-school students.

Instruments of the Recorder Family (Fig. 11.4)

Sopranino in F

Used only for special ensemble requirements.

Soprano or Descant in C

The least expensive recorder, very practical for the start of school instruction.

Alto or Treble in F

An excellent solo and ensemble instrument.

Tenor in C and Bass in F

Frequently purchased by schools to promote ensemble playing.

Flutophone, Song Flute, Tonette, Melody Flute

Inexpensive plastic or metal instruments. Easy to play, they may be used to play the melody, descants, or perhaps the harmony parts.

Ocarina

A simple instrument. The alto ocarina is recommended for beginners.

Meloharp

A chromatic psaltery and melody companion to the autoharp; may be played in any key.

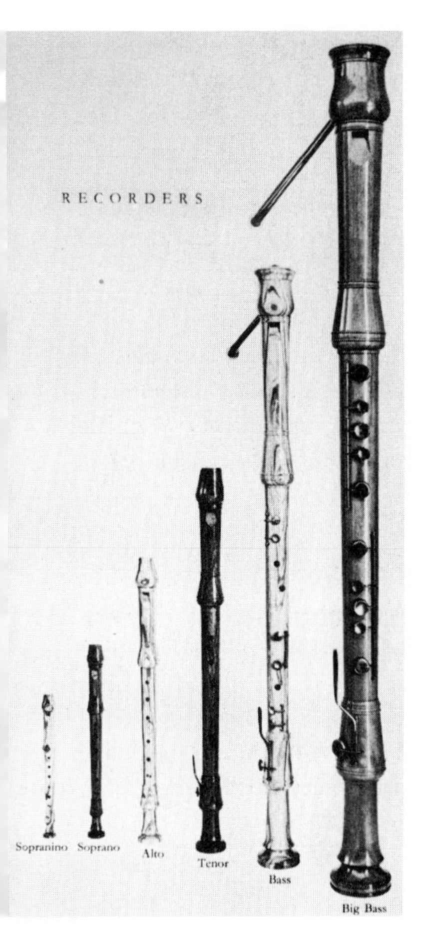

Courtesy of Hargail Music, Inc., New York.

Fig. 11.4. The recorder, an instrument popular in Elizabethan times, lends itself to recreational music because of its uniqueness and the ease with which it can be learned.

Michigan State University.

Harmolette Psaltery

A thirteen-string instrument.[8]

Harmony Instruments

Autoharp

An accompaniment instrument for indoor or outdoor use. It combines well in ensembles with other autoharps, melody bells, Tonettes, and rhythm instruments. Five-, twelve-, and fifteen-bar autoharps are available. For junior and senior high school students the larger twelve- and fifteen-bar instruments present a very

[8] The Harmolette Psaltery is obtainable from The Harmolin Company, San Diego, California.

satisfactory range of accompaniment possibilities. The use of the autoharp as a melody instrument supplying its own accompaniment has not received deserved attention from teachers and pupils.

Harmolin

An instrument similar to the autoharp.[9]

Ukulele

A favorite among recreation workers. Wooden rather than plastic ukuleles are recommended. The standard or small ukulele and the larger baritone ukulele with its deep, rich tone quality make excellent accompaniment instruments. With the use of the inexpensive capo, accompaniments in a number of keys can be played with a small combination of chord fingerings.

Harmony and Melody Instruments

Bells

There are too many types of bells available to list here. Your music magazines and local dealers can supply information on bells to fit every need.

Piano

Simple keyboard experience through the playing of simple melodies and chords has unlimited possibilities for recreational music.

Guitar, Mandolin, Banjo

All of these instruments have a place in recreational music. The guitar is the most popular and has an unusual appeal to young people (Fig. 11.5). There are four- and six-stringed guitars. The tenor guitar is a four-stringed instrument which may be fingered in the same way as a baritone ukulele. Because the player of the tenor guitar can eventually make an easy transfer to the six-stringed instrument, it is preferred as a starting instrument by some teachers. The six-stringed guitar with a round hole in the center of the instrument's body uses steel or nylon strings and produces a soft, mellow tone. The six-stringed guitar with "f" holes

[9] Information on the Harmolin and the autoharp may be obtained from: Montgomery Ward Co., Chicago; Oscar Schmidt-International, Inc., 89 Ferry St., Jersey City, N.J.; Peripole Products, Inc., 2917 Avenue R, Brooklyn, N.Y.; National Autoharp Sales Co., Des Moines, Iowa; The Harmolin Company, San Diego, California, or from a local music dealer.

Fig. 11.5. Interested students frequently graduate from the ukulele to the guitar and derive much pleasure from it.

American Music Conference, Chicago, Illinois.

and using steel strings produces a brilliant tone. The guitar is an instrument with great melodic, harmonic, and rhythmic possibilities. It has a wide range and is capable of many variations in tone color. It is not the easiest instrument to play, although common accompaniment chords can be rather easily mastered and can make the playing of the instrument very satisfying.

Harmonica

For beginners the single reed instrument in C is suggested.

Melodicas

A new family of piano-keyboard instruments recently introduced by M. Hohner, Inc. These instruments present many opportunities for recreational and classroom music. The soprano model has a range of two chromatic octaves up from middle C and the alto model is pitched a fifth lower. Tone is produced by gently blowing into the instrument and depressing the desired keys. The tone blends well with the recorder, xylophone, and the Metallophone. Melodicas will play single notes or full chords with equal ease, and respond, for rhythmic passages, to the tongueing techniques of the woodwinds and brasses. Mouthpieces are interchangeable and washable. A larger model of the instrument called the PIANO 26 MELODICA is similar to the smaller models but the keyboard permits normal piano fingering (Fig. 11.6).

Instructional materials (books, music, song, game, and dance materials) and sources for recreational music will be found in Chapters 21 and 23.

M. Hohner, Inc., Hicksville, L.I., New York.

Fig. 11.6. The Melodica is a new instrument with great potential for playing in combination with other instruments, for use alone as personal recreation, and for introductory keyboard experience.

SUMMARY

Recreational music is the simple music of immediate appeal which brings relaxation and satisfaction to an individual; it supplements but does not supplant existing music opportunities in the school and community. It is well fitted to serve the personal and social needs of the adolescent and is available to all pupils, regardless of the amount of interest manifested, talent, or financial status.

There are unlimited opportunities for student guidance in the recreational music program and, as a result, many students who are attracted to simple instruments eventually elect to study an instrument of the band or orchestra.

The listening experience is a part of the recreational music program. Folk songs, action songs, singing games, songs with descants, hymns, and camp and campus songs bring informal group singing into the classroom (Fig. 11.7). Schools with limited resources can develop recreational music programs without great expense, since although all of the simple instruments may be purchased, many of them can be made by the pupils.

Westport Public Schools, Westport, Connecticut.

Fig. 11.7. The barbershop quartet serves worthwhile personal and social needs of teen-age boys.

SUGGESTED ACTIVITIES

1. Plan an assembly program to introduce a number of recreational instruments such as the harmonica, the ukulele, the recorder, and the Melodica.
2. Outline a plan for the introduction of recreational music activities into both the curricular and extracurricular offerings of a junior high school.
3. From the collection of songs available to you, select six songs that appeal to you as being unique, and be prepared to teach them to the class.
4. Make several charts which would be of assistance in the first lessons on how to play the ukulele.
5. Preview several motion pictures and select one that will further an interest in recreational music. State the reasons for your selection.
6. Prepare and present a five-minute talk on the function of recreational music as a social force.
7. If a chapter of SPEBSQSA exists in your community, arrange an interview with several members to learn what the organization means to them as individuals.
8. Prepare a bulletin board display on how to make a Shepherd's Pipe.
9. Orchestrate a short song for several harmony and melody instruments.
10. Score a composition of your own choice for rhythm instruments.
11. Prepare four song slides for use in informal group singing.
12. As a class, plan the format and outline the contents of a recreational song book.

SELECTED READINGS

Davis, Erma, "Come, Some Music! Come, The Recorder–," *Music Educators Journal,* June–July, 1961, pp. 82–84.

Forty Approaches to Informal Singing, New York, National Recreation Association.

Gerrish, C. L., "A Family Program for Voices," *Music Educators Journal,* February–March, 1962, pp. 98–99.

Grossman, Raphael, "The Classical Guitar, Its Place in the American School," *Music Educators Journal,* February–March, 1963, pp. 140–142.

Kaplan, Max, *Music in Recreation,* Stipes, 1955.

Mandell, Murial, and Robert E. Wood, *Make Your Own Musical Instruments,* Sterling, 1957.

Smeck, Roy, "Take Your Pick and Play," *Music Journal,* March, 1961, p. 24.

Thorne, Marie, "The Case for the Informal Instruments," *Music Journal,* October, 1961, p. 75.

Wechsberg, Joseph, "The Music of Friends," *Music Educators Journal,* June–July, 1963, pp. 32–36.

Zanzig, Augustus D., *How to Make and Play a Shepherd's Pipe,* New York, National Recreation Association, 1950.

Lyons Township High School, La Grange, Illinois.

CHAPTER

12

The Rehearsal

The rehearsal is the heart of the music education program. What happens here determines how well we serve the individual, the group, and the total school program. Musical growth and achievement are determined by the effectiveness of the teacher in the rehearsal schedule.

SCHEDULING THE REHEARSAL

Mr. Harper is troubled, and rightfully so. He has lost two French horn players and the first oboist from the band, and some of the key singers in the choir must drop music because of conflicts in their schedules. What can he do about it? In this case, after Mr. Harper explained his problem, the principal checked each of the student's schedules and made adjustments in their programs which enabled them to continue in music. The principal then explained the changes to the pupils and made them effective as soon as they were approved by the pupils and their parents. As indicated by this case, the scheduling of rehearsals is a constant problem facing junior- and senior-high-school principals and their music teachers.

The problem is more acute in the small high school than in the large one, for in the small school it often is not possible to offer more than one class in certain required subjects. Competition between elective subjects, the tendency of secondary schools to reduce the number of daily class periods, and school bus schedules aggravate the situation. Principals and teachers recognize the fact that there is no simple solution to this problem. Each school must reach its own solution as a result of cooperation between the music teacher and the principal, proper guidance of students in the choice of electives, and schedule planning designed to anticipate and prevent conflicts.

A successful method of class scheduling has been used for years in one medium-sized high school. Each year in May all students, with the help of counselors, elect their programs for the coming year. By June the music teacher has assigned to music students for the coming year those subjects and classes best fitted to their individual abilities and interests.

Fig. 12.1. Classes such as this orchestra, which cuts across age group lines, need scheduling assistance from the school office.

Lansing Public Schools, Lansing, Michigan.

With music classes assigned, the school office then completes the schedules, fitting the other classes around the music schedule. In case of a conflict, a conference is called and the student makes the final choice. This method could apply in any subject matter or activity area in which certain large organizations cut across class lines and make scheduling difficult. It can be used in schools of any size; it has functioned effectively over a period of years in many large city systems. With the offering of Honors sections in English, mathematics, science, and other traditional fields, scheduling music classes first offers one of the best solutions (Fig. 12.1).

Time of Day for Rehearsal

The period of the day used for rehearsals of musical groups varies, and there is no evidence to indicate that any particular hour of the day is better than another for instrumental groups. Achievement in music does not depend on the hour of the day a rehearsal is scheduled; the important thing is what is accomplished in the rehearsal.

Mr. Smith's orchestra and band always rehearse during the lunch period. On the day we visited his school, the boys and girls came to the rehearsal room with their lunch boxes. They quickly ate their sandwiches and in a few minutes the rehearsal was under way. Mr. Smith knows music and he understands boys and girls. His rehearsals would accomplish a great deal regardless of what hour they were scheduled, and the lunch hour rehearsal time seemed to be no handicap here. We do not advocate a rehearsal schedule that penalizes the pupil interested in music, but we do feel that there are fewer limitations on the scheduling of instrumental music than on choral music.

Choral groups are best scheduled for the last half of the morning or for the second or third period after the lunch hour. A certain choir was badly handicapped at one time by a school schedule that set the rehearsal immediately after the lunch hour. A good percentage of the choir members ate their lunch at a drug store near the school. During the noon hour they burned up energy in typical teen-age fashion, and most of the choir period was spent either calming the group down after their noon-hour hilarity, or keeping them awake and alert enough to establish a mood which would make reasonable music achievement possible (Fig. 12.2).

In the scheduling of sectional rehearsals, teachers sometimes make use of the rotating or staggered schedule in which the rehearsal hour moves to a different period each week. This plan of scheduling is helpful to the musical organizations but it has definite disadvantages. Other teachers in the school rightfully resent a rehearsal plan that periodically takes students out of their classes. For students who may be failing or having difficulty in their other work, the music program may be subject to serious criticism by parents, faculty, and the school administration.

Fig. 12.2. Study this picture of an eighth-grade chorus. What implications does it have for scheduling?

Courtesy Hays from Monkmeyer.

A plan which has been favored by some vocal and instrumental teachers is to schedule the rehearsal for the first period in the morning or the last period in the day. Thus it may be possible to begin the rehearsal a half hour before the start of school or extend it for a half hour after school. This plan makes a period and a half available for the rehearsal which is sometimes organized in such a way that the additional half hour may be used for sectional rehearsals. Scheduling problems vary from school to school. The responsibility for scheduling rests with the school principal. The music teacher must understand that he may make recommendations but he may not dictate what the scheduling must be.

Length of Rehearsal

Length of rehearsal is a consideration in both the junior and the senior high school and usually must coincide with the length of the period established for the entire school. Extended rehearsal periods or special rehearsals with boys and girls of junior-high-school age probably should not exceed 40 to 50 minutes. Fatigue, tension, and restlessness may well cancel out the effectiveness of a longer period for younger pupils.

An informal check of festival ratings received by choral groups indicates that there may not be too much connection between the number or type of rehearsal periods and the musical success of the organization. Reasonable rehearsal time is necessary, but it appears that the teacher, rather than the number or type of rehearsals, is the important factor.

In this survey some of the choirs and glee clubs rehearsed five full periods a week; others had two and three rehearsals each week. About 30 percent of the groups had sectional rehearsals in addition to full rehearsals. The adjudicators' ratings of "superior" tended to go just as frequently to organizations with few rehearsals as to those with a very favorable rehearsal schedule.

While no conclusions can be developed from an informal study of this problem, it does point up the need for both choral and instrumental teachers to be more concerned with self-evaluation and the effectiveness of their rehearsals than with their type or frequency.

The Full Rehearsal

There are two kinds of full rehearsals, the regular full rehearsal, and the dress rehearsal for soloists and large and small ensembles scheduled for performance. Organization of both rehearsals have much in common. Some pointers for the dress rehearsal are given later in the chapter. The full rehearsal of a choral or instrumental organization is a unifying factor. It is a rehearsal which permits an emphasis to be placed on interpretation, and which contributes to the production of a satisfying music experience that is inspirational as well as instructional. It is here that the boy or girl learns that performance of music is more than playing the right notes and rhythms.

Conducting a full rehearsal is a great responsibility. If the individual performers are to benefit, the conductor must be prepared to inspire, to teach, and to make every minute count. Before the rehearsal he analyzes the scores, considers proper tempos, diction, foreign language pronunciation and translation, dynamics, and anticipates difficult passages. He must be thoroughly familiar with the music and the problems it presents to his students. Frequent taping of rehearsals is recommended to increase rehearsal efficiency. Routine playing or singing completely through each piece each time it is scheduled for rehearsal wastes time, for many choral and instrumental works contain sections requiring a minimum of practice. The professional scheme of rehearsal, concentrating on difficult or unusual sections, can be used to advantage by school organizations.

The *Adjudicator's Comment Sheets*[1] for choral groups may be used as a guide to the possibilities of the full choral rehearsal. A great amount of attention may be given to improving the intonation of the entire organization. Interpretation and artistic effect of performance with concern for tempo, unity, contrast, proportion, phrasing, tone quality, color, balance, blend, diction, sight reading, posture, and the manner of presentation are part of the work of rehearsals for the entire choral group. The full instrumental rehearsal will be concerned with the problems of tonal development, intonation, technique, interpretation and artistic effect, ensemble discipline, posture and appearance, and as much sight reading of music as possible.

It is in the full rehearsal that choral and instrumental conductors bring their pupils and organizations to the highest level of achievement. The full rehearsal is based on a balanced plan in which no aspect of musical training will be overemphasized and none neglected. In one school the band director became so concerned with the development of music reading ability in his students that all full rehearsals of the band became reading sessions. The pupils did become unusually fine music readers, but their performance left much to be desired in intonations, tone quality, and artistic effect.

Inspiration and encouragement must be considered essential ingredients of the full rehearsal with teen-age boys and girls. A junior-high-school principal became alarmed when after the first three weeks of school some of the most interested and musically talented pupils wanted to drop out of the band. The band director was a capable teacher and musician and for a time the principal was unable to discover what the real difficulty was. Conferences with the pupils finally brought the difficulty to light. They had been giving the band director their best efforts but he had taken such a serious approach to his rehearsals that

[1] National Interscholastic Music Activities Commission, Music Educators National Conference.

he had given not a word of encouragement to the band members. The conclusion of the pupils: we can't please him, so what's the use of trying? The band director was surprised when the principal talked with him about the pupil reaction to the rehearsals. He had been pleased with what the pupils had accomplished, but had neglected to place sufficient importance on the pupil's need for inspiration and encouragement. A few words of encouragement from time to time solved the problem.

This is a universal need—the need for encouragement and recognition. From the beginning of your teaching, develop the art of recognizing effort and accomplishment and of building up instead of tearing down. You will find your groups performing to the limits of their capacity.

The Sectional Rehearsal

A sectional choral or instrumental rehearsal meeting one or more times a week makes possible the improvement of the individual members of the group. Here the teacher has an opportunity to know his pupils and learn their interests, their limitations, and their potential achievement. In the sectional rehearsal the pupil has the chance to seek help and to receive it. Successful teachers believe in the sectional rehearsal as a means of improving the technical ability and musicianship of both the individual and the group (Fig. 12.3). The inexperienced conductor finds the sectional rehearsal an aid to him in mastering the musical score and taking a diagnostic approach in evaluating the performance of his students. The diagnostic approach locates the difficulty and treats it. If the tenors are singing wrong notes, the clarinets are playing out of tune, or the sopranos are having difficulty with a rhythmic pattern, mere repetition will not correct the mistake. The trouble must be located, pointed out to the students, and a remedy suggested before repetition of the passage will be of value. Difficult parts are marked to improve home practice.

A variation is possible in the type of sectional rehearsal. In the choral group, tenors and basses or sopranos and altos may work together, or a teacher may prefer to have separate sectional rehearsals for each voice part. In instrumental music, a variety of groupings may be used as needed. The sectional rehearsal may call for stringed instruments, woodwind instruments, brass or percussion instruments, or the teacher may feel the need of separate sectional rehearsals of first violins, second violins and cellos, etc., in the orchestra; or of the first clarinets, second clarinets, horns, and trombones, etc., in the band.

Careful planning of the sectional rehearsal is necessary to make the best use of the pupil's time and to raise the standards of musical performance. The author can well remember the endless waste of time in his high-school orchestra days when the teacher took time in full rehearsals to help individuals and sections of

Community Music School, Stockholm, Sweden. Used by permission, Music Educators National Conference, Washington, D.C.

Fig. 12.3. Sectional rehearsals contribute to individual and group proficiency. How can sectional rehearsals be arranged without sacrificing rehearsal time for the full orchestra?

the orchestra while the remainder of the group waited impatiently to continue their work.

The sectional rehearsal may also make it possible for the teacher to enrich the music offering by broadening the program to include the rudiments of music and the introduction of music literature. In addition, the sectional rehearsal lends itself to the evaluation and grading of individual pupils. With smaller groups of students there is sufficient vocal or instrumental performance by individuals to enable the teacher to check on achievement in a given grading period. It is also possible in the sectional rehearsal to give written tests on the rudiments of music essential to musicianship.

The Dress Rehearsal

There must be *at least* one dress rehearsal in the auditorium where the performance is to take place (Fig. 12.4). Some important details to be taken care of at this time are the following.

Lansing Public Schools, Lansing, Michigan.

Fig. 12.4. Many problems can be taken care of in dress rehearsal to make the performance go smoothly.

1. Staging with every detail worked out in advance. The stage manager and crew should know their responsibilities and should know exactly how the stage is to be set. Chair and music-rack placements may be marked with tape.
2. Performance timing should have been worked out previously. A last check should be made at this time, particularly if the program is to be broadcast or televised.
3. Lighting practiced according to plan worked out earlier. Careful attention should be paid to spotlights and footlights, so that soloists or students in the front are not in the dark, standing or sitting in front of the stage lights. View this critically from the auditorium.
4. Ventilation, air conditioning, heating checked.
5. Tape recording should be organized, recorders in place, experienced operators on hand for last-minute instructions, and equipment checked.
6. Concert dress exactly as for performance.
7. If there is to be a printed program there should be enough lights left on in the auditorium so that the program may be read.
8. Make sure the programs are on hand.
9. Strive for the same mental alertness you would have in the actual performance.

The dress rehearsal will be much more valuable if you have one or two faculty members or several very reliable students sit in the auditorium to view and listen to the performance from the viewpoint of the audience. They should make notes and the director should check carefully with them to correct any faults.

PLANNING FOR INSTRUCTION

Planning for instruction is a must if a teacher is to achieve success in the rehearsal period. Planning has a threefold significance: to the pupil, to the teacher, and to the total school program.

The first steps in planning are to know your pupils and to be thoroughly familiar with the music you expect to use. The rehearsal period is not the time for the teacher to sight-read music or start to know his pupils. Study and analysis of the musical score should precede the rehearsal period and serve as a basis for planning the rehearsal.

Teacher-Pupil Planning

Many teachers make use of teacher-pupil planning in setting up rehearsals. Such planning may function advantageously in all secondary-school musical organizations; there are students in all the groups capable of helping the teacher in planning. Such students are frequently aware of performance weaknesses and other faults that may have escaped the teacher's notice. They also may serve as a means of communication between the teacher and the students in the group.

Teacher-student planning is particularly useful to the teacher starting a new position. Recommendation by the principal of a few interested and reliable students who are in the musical organizations has assisted many music teachers in the start of their work. Bringing students into planning may well provide important benefits for the students in addition to music learning. Through the responsibility which they assume, student planners will grow in musicianship, in citizenship, and in the ability to work with others.

Teacher-student planning was utilized by an instrumental teacher who accepted a position in a high school noted for its discipline problems. Before school started, this teacher worked out rules and regulations for rehearsal conduct with several students recommended by his principal. These rules were duplicated and distributed to the members of the band and orchestra at their first rehearsals. The students were told how and why the regulations were formulated and were invited to suggest changes through their representatives, the student planners. The change in behavior of these students was immediate. They felt that they had had a voice in establishing the rules, and in a relatively short time discipline problems in the musical organizations were no longer significant. This teacher has continued the plan in both the junior and the senior high school because of its demonstrated effectiveness.

Use of Rehearsal Patterns

The rehearsal patterns used by many teachers help to develop a routine which enables the group to make the most of the class period. A variation of rehearsal patterns stimulates the students and helps avoid the boredom and inertia resulting from the constant use of the same organizational approach. The crowded schedule and the frequent interruptions of the school day in most junior and senior high schools necessitate a creative and flexible approach to rehearsal routine. The mood of the students on a particular day is influenced by the restlessness brought on by athletic victories, an assembly, weather conditions, or the imminence of a vacation period. Any of these situations may demand a variation in rehearsal procedure if anything is to be accomplished. The rehearsal patterns used by many vocal and instrumental teachers follow these general outlines:

Instrumental rehearsal

1. Tuning
2. Warm-up exercise (some teachers prefer the slow playing of scales and arpeggios while others prefer the slow playing of a chorale, a hymn, or a folk tune for the warm-up period)
3. Tuning
4. Rehearsing of new compositions
5. Sight reading
6. Review of music already prepared.

Alexandria Public Schools, Alexandria, Minnesota.

Fig. 12.5. A warm-up period of vocalizing starts this high-school choir off to a good rehearsal.

Choral rehearsal

1. Warm-up period of vocalizing or the singing of a chorale (Fig. 12.5)
2. Detailed work on concert material
3. Sight-reading
4. Singing of numbers requested by students, or other learned concert material.

In both instrumental and choral rehearsals it is very often wise to close the rehearsal with a choice of selection made by the students. They many times show a preference for certain types of music that the director might overlook.

PREPARATION FOR REHEARSALS

Preparation for rehearsing is at the start of the year largely a matter of evaluating the interests, performance ability, and musicianship of individual students. Some teachers schedule individual tryouts, and also check available records on the student's work in music and other subjects. Other teachers administer a written examination in the rudiments of music to all students. Regardless of what preparatory steps are taken, it is important for the teacher to know something of the performance ability and musicianship of his students before determining their musical needs and before selecting the music to be played.

Clearly Defined Goals

What do we want to accomplish in our rehearsals? What are our goals? We want to improve the performance ability and musicianship of each individual. We hope to help him to improve his ability to read music, his vocal and instrumental technique, and to increase his love of music. As we move from one rehearsal to the next, we will endeavor to introduce students to as much fine choral and instrumental literature as possible. These are the long-range goals of rehearsing that lead to the development of discriminating performers and consumers of music (Fig. 12.6).

There should, however, be specific goals which will be realized in each rehearsal. For example, in a choral rehearsal the goal on a particular day might be to check on the group's ability to sing from memory the numbers scheduled for performance. Or it might be to make progress in improving the tone quality of the group. Short-term as well as long-term goals are necessary.

Detroit Public Schools, Detroit, Michigan.

Fig. 12.6. These selected high-school students have an immediate or short-term goal, appearance with the Detroit Symphony on a School Concert Series program. Valter Poole, conductor, and James Tamburini, trumpet.

Physical Arrangements

Physical arrangements which make efficient rehearsing possible should be completed before the students arrive in the room or auditorium. At the start of the school year, student assistants may be selected to prepare the music room for rehearsal.

Music and Instruments in Order

Music and the large instruments should be in place and ready for use. A great deal of work must be done by librarians and other students before the rehearsal period, such as posting the order of rehearsal and the seating chart, and checking lighting, heat, and ventilation.

Having the music and instruments in order in advance is time-consuming but essential to the success of the rehearsal. Student librarians and assistants accept this responsibility in most junior and senior high schools. The duties of a music librarian include the selection of dependable pupils who recognize the need for complete attention to small details. A good music librarian is one who has grown in musical understanding as a player or singer and has learned the job by experience. For this reason it is not uncommon to find a student librarian training several assistants.

Instruments must be checked and in order. Large instruments are frequently placed in position to avoid confusion when the pupils arrive for rehearsal. Keeping all instruments in good playing condition is a problem with beginners as well as advanced pupils. For minor repairs, a repair kit becomes standard equipment in the rehearsal room. Minor repairs may be handled by the teacher, but the services of an expert repairman should be used for all major repairs. Consult Chapter 19 for more information on this subject.

Program on Chalkboard

The rehearsal program and all announcements are posted on the chalkboard where they can be seen by all pupils. Wittich and Schuller recommend a location on the chalkboard which gives as many pupils as possible a "front view." They suggest that the teacher:

> . . . Write a few words or draw a simple sketch on each chalkboard panel. Walk around the room and view the entire chalkboard space from at least five key positions in the seating area. The presence of glare caused by unfortunate angles of light and seating will be apparent. On the basis of your test, determine the space on which the words and drawings are completely and comfortably visible.[2]

Sun curtains, changes in seating, and additional artificial lighting are possible means of correcting light glare in the music room.

Room in Order

That the music room be in order may appear to the reader to be an unnecessary recommendation, but it is a suggestion which needs particular emphasis. In one junior high school we visited, the band room was a confused mass of chairs, music racks, folders, instruments, and instrument cases. In repeated visits we noted that this rehearsal room was never in order and ready for the students. Valuable time was lost at the start of every rehearsal and the situation was unnecessarily chaotic for both pupils and teachei.

In another junior high school the band room was in perfect order before the

[2] Walter Wittich and Charles Schuller, *Audio-Visual Materials* (rev. ed.), Harper & Row, 1957, p. 50.

Interlochen Arts Academy, Interlochen, Michigan.

Fig. 12.7. The players in this orchestra have no lighting problems to hamper their work.

pupils arrived, a seating chart and the rehearsal program were posted, chairs and music racks were in place. The teacher stood quietly in the front of the room and the rehearsal was soon under way with no discipline problems and no time wasted.

Lighting and Ventilation

Lighting and ventilation may detract from or contribute to the effectiveness of the rehearsal (Fig. 12.7). *Music Buildings, Room and Equipment* gives some reasons why lighting problems of the music room need to be checked.[3] The visibility of printed music is concerned with details, variations in manuscript paper, ink, and sizes of music symbols. Distance from the eye to the music, determined by the size of the instrument or the sharing of music, may create problems. The seating arrangement for musical organizations may place students in positions where glare or distractions hamper vision. Risers with pupils on several levels cause lighting problems which must be considered.

Good lighting helps the pupil to read the music rather than play or sing by ear, and also aids him in following the conductor. Standard practice in school lighting recommends 50 foot-candles as a minimum for sewing, drafting, and typing rooms; this minimum is considered appropriate for the rehearsal room.

To produce good music the student must be alert. Ventilation and tempera-

[3] Elwyn Carter (Ed.), *Music Buildings, Rooms and Equipment*, Music Educators National Conference, 1955, p. 45.

ture affect the mental and physical condition of pupils. Healthful and comfortable playing conditions during the rehearsal require a temperature range of from 68° to 72° F.

SUGGESTIONS FOR EFFECTIVE REHEARSALS

Relieving the Tensions of Music Learning

Meyer Cahn, in dealing with the problem of fostering good mental health as well as musical growth, establishes some of the sources of tension in the learning of music.[4] Individual differences of students participating in a rehearsal are a source of tension. There are frustrations that arise from the necessity for much repetition in rehearsing, or from the pupil's inability to master a technical problem. A teacher who is tense and dictatorial invariably generates tension in the rehearsal. Whatever the cause, such conditions make for an unhealthy learning situation.

If we are to relieve the tensions of music learning there must be, according to Cahn, a work-rest plan to prevent fatigue, irritation, and frustration. More time might be allowed for each part of the rehearsal and a reasonable limit placed on expected achievement. Understanding, patience, and encouragement on the part of the teacher as he works with girls and boys contribute to a healthful atmosphere in the rehearsal, an atmosphere which is conducive to both pleasure and accomplishment.

Using Student Assistants

Student assistants have been mentioned previously, but their part in the effectiveness of the rehearsal needs particular emphasis. The teaching load of a successful high-school music teacher is such that student accompanists, librarians, business managers, property managers, conductors, and sectional leaders should be used to free the teacher of many routine duties. The teacher is then in a position to concentrate in those areas where he is most needed. The many responsibilities which may be carried by students in the music program also broaden their educational opportunities. They learn how to accept responsibility, how to work with others, and they develop a leadership in music which may be carried into community music activities.

[4] Meyer Cahn, "The Tensions of Music Learning," *Music Educators Journal*, April–May, 1954, p. 24.

Keeping the Rehearsal Moving

"Keep the rehearsal moving" is valuable advice for the young teacher in avoiding discipline problems and in making the best use of rehearsal time. Proper preparation for the rehearsal and knowledge of the music to be used prepares the teacher for quick thinking and a diagnostic approach to teaching which will make the rehearsal move along. Those teachers who know what they want to do in the rehearsal and know the music at hand make the most of each rehearsal, regardless of the musical limitations of their students. There are no awkward pauses or delays. The rehearsal starts and stops on time and everyone is occupied during the entire period. When such organization is planned and carried through, progress is made.

Using Recording Equipment

The use of recording equipment by school music teachers has increased with the introduction of the tape recorder. The teacher can now record rehearsals on tape and later review the recording for more accurate analysis of the students' work and needs. He can also play the tape for the students so that they may evaluate their own performance. Small ensembles or students rehearsing solos may record their playing or singing for evaluation and suggestions by the teacher.

There are a great many uses of recording equipment in music instruction. We know an instrumental music teacher who has improved his rehearsal techniques by recording each rehearsal and by preparing rehearsal plans which are based on his analysis of the recorded material. Portions of the recording can be played for the band, and remedial treatment then suggested.

Tape recordings of the choral and instrumental music found in the required and selective lists of compositions used in varicus states for the annual festivals have been made available to junior and senior high schools by some colleges and universities. These recordings have proved to be excellent teaching materials. The use of tape recordings is discussed in detail in Chapter 17.

SUMMARY

The rehearsal is the heart of the music education program, since what happens there determines how well we serve the individual, the group, and the total school program. There is no simple solution to the problem of scheduling the rehearsal; it is an administrative problem which must be worked out by principal and teacher together. Achievement in music does not appear to be dependent upon the hour the rehearsal is scheduled or the type of rehearsal. What the teacher does in the rehearsal is the vital consideration. The use of teacher-pupil planning is of value in the classroom and in the development of students. Planning and setting goals for instruction are important if the teacher is to achieve success in the rehearsal period. Rehearsals may be made more effective if tensions are relieved and a healthful atmosphere for learning is created.

SUGGESTED ACTIVITIES

1. Study the complete schedules of several small junior or senior high schools. If possible, talk to the principals and music teachers of the school on how they meet their scheduling problems. Summarize your results for the class.
2. As a class project, secure permission to attend a concert by a junior- or senior-high-school musical organization and, using the *Adjudicator's Comment Sheets*, evaluate the performance. Discuss in class the variations in adjudication that result.
3. Examine and evaluate several books on the rudiments of music theory that might be used in connection with the sectional rehearsal of a choral or instrumental program.
4. Tape a rehearsal of a junior-high-school boys' glee club and prepare a list of the strengths and weaknesses of the group.
5. With the assistance of some junior- or senior-high-school students, develop a list of rules and regulations for student conduct in rehearsals.
6. Observe several rehearsals of junior- or senior-high-school music groups. What suggestions have you for making these rehearsals more effective?
7. What supplies and equipment would you include in an instrument repair kit?
8. Demonstrate how to select and prepare a chalkboard panel for use in the rehearsal.
9. Make a report to the class on the importance of adequate lighting and ventilation in the rehearsal room.
10. Study the teaching load of several music teachers. Visit their classes and determine how student assistants might relieve the teacher of routine duties.
11. Make a list and describe recordings useful in teaching music to junior- or senior-high-school pupils.
12. In preparation for a senior-high-school rehearsal, write an analysis of a major choral, band, or orchestral composition.

SELECTED READINGS

Cahn, Meyer, "The Tensions of Music Learning," *Music Educators Journal*, April–May, 1954, p. 24.

Carter, Elwyn (Ed.), *Music Buildings, Rooms and Equipment*, Music Educators National Conference, 1955, chaps. II, VIII, IX, X.

Chapple, Stanley, "The Study of Music Through Performance," *Music Educators Journal*, November–December, 1962, p. 43.

Dunlap, J. W., "Why Rehearse?" *Education Music Magazine*, January–February, 1953, pp. 25–28.

Hansen, Louis A., "A Study of Score Reading Ability of Musicians," *Journal of Research in Music Education*, Fall, 1961, pp. 147–156.

Helbig, Otto H., "Improving Instrumental Rehearsal Effectiveness," *Music Educators Journal*, November–December, 1962, p. 43.

House, Robert, *Instrumental Music in Today's Schools*, Prentice-Hall, 1964, chap. V.

Johnson, M. O., "Listening with the High School Band," *Music Educators Journal*, January, 1964, p. 83.

Kuhn, Wolfgang, *Instrumental Music*, Allyn and Bacon, 1962, chap. 6.

Lambson, Arthur Ray, "An Evaluation of Various Seating Plans Used in Choral Singing," *Journal of Research in Music Education*, Spring, 1961, pp. 47–54.

Long, Newell H., "More Minutes for Music," *Music Educators Journal*, November–December, 1953, pp. 30–33.

National Association Teachers of Singing, *Choral Techniques*, 1959.

Poole, Reid, "Rehearsal Procedures for the Half-Time Show," *The Instrumentalist*, October, 1956, p. 25.

Van Bodegraven, Paul, and Harry Wilson, *The School Music Conductor*, Schmitt, Hall & McCreary, 1942, chaps. 4–8.

Welke, Walter C., "Baton—Friend or Foe," *Music Educators Journal*, February–March, 1964, p. 129. April–May issue contains Part 2 of this article.

Wright, A. G., "Rehearsal Techniques," *The School Musician*, June, 1955, p. 13.

Used by permission, Music Educators National Conference, Washington, D.C.

CHAPTER

13

Public Performance

Mary Smith was very much upset one day early in October. She was a capable young first-year teacher, but she was distressed because her principal was insisting that the Girl's Glee Club sing at the November meeting of the Parent-Teacher Association. She felt that the glee club was not ready for public appearance. Mary was beginning to feel the pressure of public performance and was just becoming aware of its importance and of the need for planning for it from the start of the school year. She met the situation by introducing into the rehearsals of the glee club a group of numbers that they could learn quickly and sing well. The girls in the club looked forward to the performance with enthusiasm and did their part to make the appearance successful.

Public performance is a challenge to girls and boys. It is important to the parents, the school, and the community. In a very real sense, it is music education in action. It is one means of bringing music to all pupils and of helping to raise the cultural level of the community by stressing the artistic elements of music (Fig. 13.1).

OBJECTIVES OF PUBLIC PERFORMANCE

How can reasonable objectives of public performance be determined? A superintendent, in answer to this question, said, "Our staff sets up educational objectives in terms of what we consider best for the boys and girls of this community." Another approach was taken by representatives of the Music Educators National Conference when they prepared a report which was accepted by the North Central Associations of Colleges and Secondary Schools. This report recommends that public performance by school musicians should:

1. Emphasize the artistic in music.
2. Lead to outstanding programming and achievement.
3. Promote continued interest in and enthusiasm for music in the school and in the community.
4. Bring to parents and others in the community an understanding of the significance of music in education.

College of the Desert, Palm Desert, California; Robert E. Johnson, Photography

Fig. 13.1. Small ensemble experience is a challenge to students.

5. Improve the standards of musical taste in the school and the community.
6. Be a means of stimulating creative, artistic, and social growth of pupils.[1]

These aims are indicative of what public performance can mean to children and to music in education. In practice they serve well in guiding teachers in planning their schedules of public performances. Out-of-school performances by musical organizations should be fully discussed by the music teacher and administrators prior to making overtures to or commitments with other staff members for financial or other support for school music groups, community groups, or professional organizations. Decisions concerning out-of-school performances by school music organizations will be concerned with size of group involved, effect on the school program, travel involved, finances, instructional benefits to be derived by students and teachers, opportunities for gifted students, and broadening experiences for all students.

PROFESSIONAL STAGE PRACTICE

Producing the finest possible music is the aim of every music teacher. The reception of fine musical performance can be greatly enhanced if the teacher and the students realize what professional performers have long known: Their success is dependent on superior music plus a smooth, polished stage appearance that is a result of careful attention to details (Fig. 13.2).

[1] "Extra-Curricular Music Activities," a report of Music Educators National Conference to the North Central Association of Colleges and Secondary Schools, 1951.

Used by permission, Music Educators National Conference, Washington, D.C.

Fig. 13.2. A high-school choir sings for the Music Educators National Conference in a large hotel.

What are some of these details, why are they important, and how can they be mastered? Part of the training of all secondary-school performers should include practice in what might be termed professional stage manners, to enable students to appear at their best. Miss Arcola Clark, a graduate student at Michigan State University, who had this type of training through high school, emphasizes the need for the teacher to set an example of good stage deportment, and through regular practice to bring pupils to an awareness of the need for proper dress, make-up, pleasant facial expression, good posture, the correct manner of walking on and off the stage, practice in bowing to acknowledge applause, etc. These details will become good habits through practice at every opportunity, at rehearsals, class performances, and dress rehearsals. Miss Clark suggests some guidelines for teachers:

1. Students should be helped to understand why professional action is an asset to their appearance.
2. A public performance must be orderly. Every pupil must know what he is to do, when he is to do it, how, where, and why he is to do it.
3. Walking on stage needs practice, particularly if the girls are not accustomed to heels. Walk at a moderately slow pace with dignity; do not run or shuffle.
4. Remember the need for good posture. When you walk on the stage, keep eye contact with the entire audience. Do not stare at one individual, your goal should be to make each member of the audience feel that you are looking at him.

5. Facial expression is important. A natural smile puts the audience at ease, improves the appearance, and relaxes facial muscles.
6. Practice bowing. Students need practice in gestures of gratitude and graciousness to acknowledge applause received when entering or leaving the stage. This means of saying "thank you" must be practiced enough to become a part of one's person. On entering the stage a simple lowering of the head is satisfactory. The bow need not be elaborate, but it must be graceful, leisurely, and sincere.
7. Girls should dress appropriately:
   a. Wear heels and hose. Usually medium heels are desirable. Flats are not dressy enough and do not flatter the feet. Hose of a uniform type and inconspicuous shade.
   b. Jewelry must be conservative. Glittering jewelry can be very distracting to the audience, and its use is in bad taste.
   c. If formal dresses are worn, skirts of floor length are more desirable than short skirts. Some schools have found a long black skirt and a white blouse inexpensive and desirable for performing groups. If floor length dresses are not used, skirts should be a little longer than for street wear. Sheaths and strapless gowns are more appropriate for evening wear than for stage performance.
   d. Hair styles should be conventional rather than radical.
   e. Make-up can usually be a little heavier and more accented for the stage, except for lipstick. Stage lighting must be considered in determining proper make-up.
8. Boys should dress properly:
   Suits or uniform jackets and slacks, and ties of the same type should be chosen. Hair should be of conventional appearance, not with a radical type of cut. Shoes should be shined.

PUBLIC PERFORMANCE AS AN OUTGROWTH OF CLASS INSTRUCTION

Public performance is not the primary aim of school music instruction, but rather an outgrowth of class instruction. It is in the classroom that the success or failure of public performance is determined. When selecting music the successful teacher does not rely on graded lists. He analyzes a great deal of music. He is constantly searching for and evaluating music in terms of the strengths and weaknesses of his students. He asks himself, is this worthwhile music? Will it contribute to their musical growth? Is it literature the students should know, even though they may never be able to play it well enough for public performance? Much of the music selected for classroom use will be sight-reading material to challenge the students. But all music used should be of such quality that if it lies within the performance capabilities of the class it can be presented as literature worthy of presentation to an audience.

Young players and singers are under pressure when appearing before adjudicators or the public. They need practice in public appearance. They should not be expected to perform music not suited to their training, experience, and musical skills. Pupils fail to measure up to their potential when they must perform music with repeated intricate technical passages, face unusual key, rhythmic, and range problems, handle slow sustained passages with good intonation and tone, sing or play pianissimo passages at extremes of range, or perform music written in a style they do not understand.

The repertoire of the classroom and rehearsal is an important factor in determining what music students should play in concert or contest. It is in the classroom that they become familiar with music of the various periods and styles and acquire the skills necessary to perform it. If the teacher is skillful in selecting music suited to his students' capabilities, and if he makes sure that instruments are kept in top playing condition, programming concerts will be a natural outgrowth of the classroom work, and will be presented with a minimum of extra rehearsals and disruption of the regular schedule.

Education Rather than Entertainment

Education rather than entertainment is the primary purpose of music in education. This purpose has important implications if music is to be recognized as an essential feature of the school program.

For example, in one large high school the choir is called upon to sing at many civic functions. The programs of this choir are made up chiefly of compositions which have become popular through radio, television, and the theater. All of the music selected for this choir is purchased with a view to entertaining the audience rather than contributing to the musical development of the choir members. Each year these students learn more pieces by rote. The audience has been entertained, but the choral works of Palestrina, Bach, and their followers are unknown to these students. It is difficult to justify this type of music education. In fact, this is not music education, but largely entertainment. Real music education can and should be both educational and entertaining.

In the instrumental field the band has made a tremendous contribution to the development of school instrumental music. The entertainment possibilities of the marching band through the "band show" have made the program in some schools both educational and entertaining in character, while in other schools it has been purely entertainment (Fig. 13.3).

Michigan State University, East Lansing, Michigan.

Fig. 13.3. Precision work by marching bands can be both attractive to the crowd and worth-while experience to the participants.

A Means of Extending the Music Program into the Community

Public performances by students draw the school and community into closer relationship. Concerts, public appearances by groups at civic functions, demonstrations of school music teaching, and festivals featuring music which has been learned in the classroom can have a strong influence on the people in the community.

Weidensee suggests that a good variation of the annual concert is a program which helps the people in the community to understand something of the methods used in teaching music to children. "Many times parents ask," he writes, " 'Just how do you get children to perform so well?' The parents do enjoy the finished product but they would also like to learn how we go about starting to work on something that finally becomes the finished product."[2] Many teachers use this type of teaching-methods program with considerable success. It is a strong factor in extending the music program into the community (Fig. 13.4).

[2] Victor Weidensee, "About Programs," *Oregon Music Educator*, May–June, 1956, p. 12.

Arsenal Technical High School, Indianapolis, Indiana.

Fig. 13.4. An actual rehearsal of this boys' chorus would make interesting program material for a PTA program.

THE CONCERT

Choral or Instrumental

Planning the concert appearance should be based on what the concert will do for the boys and girls participating. In the choral or instrumental concert, quality of performance must be of prime importance. Dr. Van Bodegraven says, "Concert mechanics, that is, right pitches and rhythmic values; good ensemble, playing or singing together; balance of parts; good tone quality; good intonation; all of these and more are familiar to you—but that is because you are trained musicians."[3] In continuing, he points out that the beginners in our classes are not aware of these things, but we can and must develop in our students a growing awareness of good performance. A school concert of superior quality indicates the development of lasting values which will make our boys and girls better performers of music, and in the years to come, more intelligent consumers of music.

[3] Paul Van Bodegraven, "The Development of Musical Understanding Through Performance," *Music Educators Journal*, April–May, 1955, pp. 29–30.

Recently a junior high school presented a string ensemble and orchestra concert for the purpose of encouraging further interest in the stringed instruments. The girls and boys played with a poor tone, intonation was exceptionally bad, and the playing was mechanical. Inspiration and quality of performance were entirely lacking. In consequence, the concert failed to increase pupil interest in stringed instruments.

The organization of the concert program must consider the capabilities of the pupils and the interests of the audience. The aim is to present a program which is justifiable from the educational viewpoint, and which will impress the audience and interest it in future concerts. The concert should not last longer than ninety minutes; have the audience leave wishing there were more. What about the music to be performed?

1. It should be of good quality, suited to the performers, and within their performance potential.
2. Open the program with a composition of vitality and strength which the students enjoy and sing or play with ease. The concluding number should be stimulating and dramatic.
3. There should be variety and unity in the selection of music. A good program will have music of different forms, styles, keys, and rhythmic content. Some compositions will be light and some more serious.
4. The vocalist or choral group should make the words understood by the audience.

Program building is an art deserving proper attention. Programs which attract large audiences to hear choral and instrumental groups provide the finest kind of motivation for girls and boys. They are morale builders.

Parents, of course, are interested in hearing their children perform in any school concert. Parental enthusiasm and community support and approval are excellent means of stimulating music activity. Fine quality of performance in concert situations is most helpful in developing constructive support for the music program (Fig. 13.5).

Combined Choral and Instrumental

In many small junior and senior high schools, the combined choral and instrumental program is a practical way to provide boys and girls with the benefits of public performance. In a program of this sort no one ensemble is burdened with more performance responsibility than it can handle well. Instrumental and choral organizations cooperatively producing an annual concert may well be a

Fig. 13.5. Concert appearances provide specific goals to work toward, and the confidence which comes with successful achievement.

Marshall Public Schools, Marshall, Michigan.

means of increasing the interest and support of both parents and pupils in the entire school music program.

Suitable materials for combined instrumental and choral concerts at the secondary-school level are available though not readily identified in most music publishers' catalogs. In searching for appropriate compositions of this nature, Moffat, an instrumental director from Pasadena, found most of them to be listed under choral rather than instrumental music.[4] Teachers may want to edit or modify the compositions or arrangements to make them more suitable for use with their organizations. Combining choral and instrumental forces in the performance of such compositions as Howard Hanson's *Song of Human Rights* for senior-high-school mixed chorus is of great inspirational value to both students and audience. For a list of choral compositions with instrumental accompaniment see Chapter 23, p. 561.

MUSIC CONTESTS AND FESTIVALS

There are many kinds of contests and festivals for junior- and senior-high-school music students: competitive and noncompetitive festivals; city, county, district, and state festivals; festivals for bands, orchestras, stringed instruments, choruses, choirs, glee clubs, small ensembles, and solos; festivals for junior-high-school groups, senior-high-school groups, and combinations of both. It would be difficult to estimate the value of the contest or festival in the history of school

[4] See Dana Moffat, "Combined Choral and Instrumental Concert Programs," *Music Educators Journal*, April–May, 1955, pp. 31–32.

music. Both the contest and the festival have been important factors in the development of secondary-school music.

Music education is passing through a stage in which the contest with its highly competitive character is giving way to the festival in which emphasis is placed upon the development of musical interests as well as competencies. In the original contests, a single school could win first place, another second place, and so on. Festivals tend to eliminate hard and fast competitive ranking and emphasize instead the coming together of young musicians to play for mutual inspiration and benefit.

The competition-festival is a combined form which attempts to achieve the principal benefits of both contests and festivals. It retains the inspirational aspects of the festival but also establishes division ratings which permit any number of schools to achieve a first, second, or third divisional rating. Thus, in a small competition-festival where seven orchestras were entered, their work was evaluated as follows: two orchestras were given Division I ratings, three were classified in Division II, and two were classified in Division III. In some instances rating is optional; a school may ask for the judge's comments only.

The division-rating pattern is used in the *Adjudicator's Comment Sheets* prepared by the National Interscholastic Music Activities Commission, and distributed by the Music Educators National Conference. Divisional rating makes it possible for schools to move from the purely competitive contest plan to the competition-festival which seems to represent good education in music rather than to promote the winning of a championship.

There is no particular agreement in educational circles regarding music festivals or interschool competition. The considerable amount of research that has been done in this area is inconclusive. Miller, in his Oregon study, arrived at the following conclusions:

1. The music directors of Oregon appear to be approximately evenly divided in their support of and opposition to the competition-festival as an interschool music activity for large groups (bands, orchestras, choruses) in the districts.
2. There is a trend toward acceptance of the non-competitive festival as an approved type of large group music activity in the districts.
3. There is no longer sufficient demand for the state-final competition-festival for large groups to justify an attempt to revive it.
4. There is a definite demand for solo and ensemble competition on both the district and state level.
5. The present districts seem to be satisfactory as the sponsoring units for interschool music events.
6. There is evidence that competition is being used as a motivating influence by slightly more than half of the directors of Oregon high school music groups. There is also evidence that a nearly equal number believe that motivating influences other than competition are sufficient.

7. Adequate public support of the non-competitive types of music activities seems to be indicated.
8. Many of the criticisms and problems of the competition-festival would be removed by eliminating the judges' ratings. (This would, in effect, transform the event into a non-competitive festival.)[5]

Miller also makes the following recommendations in his study:

1. All districts planning interschool music events should provide for those schools which do not approve of the competition-festival. Those favoring competition should be permitted to enter their groups for judges' ratings, but those who wish only judges' comments should not be placed under unfavorable pressure.
2. The Oregon Music Educators Association should present a studied and documented request to the Oregon School Activities Association for reopening consideration of a state-final competition-festival for soloists and ensembles.
3. In view of the fact that 53.4 per cent of the directors who replied to the questionnaire feel that the competitive element is needed as a motivating factor in securing a high standard of performance, it is suggested that a study be made which might yield evidence that such a motivating force is, or is not, educationally desirable.[6]

The Kansas Music Educators Association, like many other state music education associations, has long been interested in improving its state music festival program. The Music Education Research Council organized a questionnaire on music festivals to which 117 Kansas music teachers responded.[7] A summary of the answers indicates that the KMEA would like to continue music festivals with more judges and more judging time allowed for large groups, sight-reading to be included in the festivals, schools divided into classes for small ensembles and solos, and classes of schools to attend the state festival on different days.

These and other studies of this kind indicate a continuing interest in the festival movement as a factor in music education.

VARIETY SHOWS, OPERETTAS, AND OPERAS

Operettas and variety shows are used in many high schools as a means of enriching the music program and broadening it to include all students (Fig. 13.6). In an Indiana city famous for its athletic program, and particularly for its state championship basketball teams, the music teacher found it difficult to secure school or community interest in the school music programs. He decided to develop a variety show involving a large number of junior- and senior-high-school students. The first step was to announce talent tryouts open to all students, and the

[5] Howard F. Miller, "The History and Present Trends of Inter-School Music Competition in the High Schools of Oregon," unpublished Master's thesis, University of Oregon, 1953.

[6] *Ibid.*

[7] "Results of the MERC Questionnaire on Music Festivals," *Kansas Music Education Review*, Kansas Music Education Association, February, 1955, pp. 31–32.

Westport Public Schools, Westport, Connecticut.

Fig. 13.6. Music, art, physical education, and dance students combine in these scenes from (top) "King and I" and (bottom) "Polovetsian Dances."

response was surprisingly good. It included singers, instrumentalists, dancers, and other performers who had never appeared in music classes or musical organizations. The tryouts were convincing arguments as to the value of this type of production in revealing hidden talent. A student-faculty committee selected the performers, and cooperatively determined what the program should be. Solos and small vocal and instrumental ensembles were scheduled for performance along with the school glee clubs and orchestra. Publicity in the school and local newspapers, posters throughout the business section, and a skit in a school assembly aroused considerable interest in the city and the schools.

Some popular songs were included in the program but for the most part the music was semiclassical. It was well performed before the largest crowd that had ever attended a school music program in that community. The show was short, limited to an hour and ten minutes, and as people left the auditorium they were asking when there would be another program. For the first time, students as well as people in the community were enthusiastically talking about music in their schools. As gratifying as this response was to the music teacher, the really important result was the large number of boys and girls who enrolled in music organizations because of their participation or interest in the production. Girls and boys, and particularly boys, who had rejected anything but popular music came into the school vocal and instrumental groups and in time became interested in fine music. One experienced teacher summed it up by saying that although the variety show was a lot of hard work and perhaps not as satisfying musically as some other types of programs, it had revealed enough talent and aroused enough community interest to warrant scheduling it as an annual event.

The Mikado, *Pirates of Penzance*, and other Gilbert and Sullivan operettas have long been favorites for senior-high-school production. The publication of simplified versions of these operettas and some of the light operas has made them available for use in the junior high school. The list of musically worth-while operettas that may be produced in the secondary school is rather limited and for that reason some junior- and senior-high-school teachers have written and produced their own operettas with considerable success.

The choral director in the Mt. Clemens, Michigan, High School approached the production of an operetta in an interesting and rewarding way. Several goals were set up in the planning of production. The first step was to select an operetta of musical worth which would present opportunities for the participation of a large number of pupils, plus, for the talented pupils, possibilities for solo performance, song writing, script writing, and some student direction. Furthermore, the production needed to be one that would appeal to the townspeople. A student committee was formed, and the members decided that they would like to use a short published operetta, Kurt Weill's *Down in the Valley*,[8]

[8] Kurt Weill, *Down in the Valley*, G. Schirmer.

and develop a short operetta of their own to go with it. This was a sensible decision because the students had never attempted a creative project and they were wise to limit the scope of their first effort.

The committee guided by the teacher discussed the project with the school choir members, and requested a plot which would include three male leads and three or more female leads. While students were skeptical of their ability to write an original work, they were willing to try. Several members of the choir went into action, and in time a student plot was selected and given the name *Festival.*

Then followed many after-school script writing sessions by three of the most talented and interested students (Fig. 13.7). Meanwhile students and teacher composed songs to go with the script. When the material was ready, the school printer multilithed copies for rehearsal and the production was under way. From start to finish, this operetta project was a creative experience rich in opportunities for learning.

Mount Clemens Public Schools, Mount Clemens, Michigan. Daily Monitor-Leader.

Fig. 13.7. An operetta in the process of creation by students and teacher at Mt. Clemens, Michigan.

Operettas in this school are more than entertainment; they are truly education. Robinson has these suggestions for teachers planning operettas or variety shows:

1. Operetta production should be attempted only when the vocal and choral parts of the work can be well performed.
2. Choose the operetta to fit your singers. Look for a good plot and good music; consider the length of the operetta—too short rather than too long; number of male and female leads required; royalty fees; whether to use the orchestral or piano accompaniment. In *Festival*, the original operetta, piano accompaniment was used. An alumni-student orchestra accompanied *Down in the Valley*.
3. Ask yourself, "Why am I putting on this operetta?" If you can't justify your production from an educational standpoint, choose some other type of public performance. Don't put on an operetta just for the show!
4. Advertise. To stimulate ticket sales, use posters, bulletin boards, school assemblies, the school paper, local newspapers, radio, and television if possible. The best performance will lose its punch if no one comes to see it.
5. Eliminate ticket sale problems by using a ticket with a stub. The stub is exchanged by the seller for a reserved seat, and when the reserved seat is delivered to the customer the sale is completed.
6. Involve a lot of "know how" people in your production. They enjoy it and it gives the production a professional touch.
7. Keep to your schedule. After you set the schedule of vocal and orchestral rehearsals, know just what you want to complete at each rehearsal. Revise your plans occasionally to fit the needs of the moment but keep a planned schedule going.
8. Recognize those who have helped in your printed program and by thank-you notes.[9]

The variety show and the operetta may be used to considerable advantage in both the junior and the senior high school. They appeal to the teen-ager and are frequently the beginning of a serious interest in music. A list of operettas for use in junior and senior high schools are found in Chapter 23, pp. 564–565.

Opera

An innovation for consideration by the high-school teacher is the field of contemporary opera.[10] These works do not require elaborate staging or costuming. They are short, up-to-date, and, for the most part, written by excellent composers. There is a new idiom in opera called "Demi-opera," a diminutive form similar to the chamber opera, usually without chorus and with a small number of roles. Many of these are within the grasp of high-school students. "The Reunion," by Jeanellen McKee, for baritone and soprano, is excellent for high school production, as is "Tuesday's Three" for alto, mezzo, and lyric soprano

[9] Gerald W. Robinson, "High School Operetta Writing and Production," Unpublished Research Problem, Michigan State University, 1954.

[10] Courtesy of Loren Jones, Music Department, Michigan State University, East Lansing, Michigan.

voices, by the same composer. Samuel Barber's "A Hand in Bridge" is a fine example of contemporary music for baritone, tenor, soprano, and alto. The setting requires only four chairs and a table. The teacher interested in contemporary music will find this very rewarding.[11] There are a number of values to be found in the contemporary chamber opera:

1. Direct association with contemporary idiom.
2. Absence of lavish sets and costumes.
3. Acquaintance with modern theatre practices.
4. Smaller groups and more intimate relationship with the sponsoring teachers.
5. Rehearsal time is more concentrated, allowing for adequate attention to each individual.
6. More complex music demanding greater understanding and appreciation of music.
7. Less time demand on the teacher, less massive concentration of extracurricular duties.
8. Opportunity for early discovery of opera, pointing toward development of appreciation of the medium.
9. Development of individual initiative in overcoming the technical and musical problems of young people.

A list of operas of proven value in secondary education will be found in Chapter 23, pp. 564–565 (Fig. 13.8).

THE MARCHING BAND

The marching band is a powerful force for focusing attention on school music, for it has a natural appeal for people regardless of their age or background in music. This appeal of the marching band has been responsible for arousing the interest of many teen-age girls and boys in music. It invites them to play an instrument and become a part of the musical organization which, through its many activities, is most closely associated with both school and community life. Thus the marching band, particularly valuable in relation to school athletic events, has had much to do with the willingness of schools and communities to broaden their support of school music.

The marching band started its school appearances in the stands at athletic events, and then moved onto the field or the floor of the gymnasium as a marching unit. These developments led to the present-day band shows at both high-school and college events (Fig. 13.9).

[11] Complete lists of such works are available from Interlochen Press, Interlochen, Michigan, 49643.

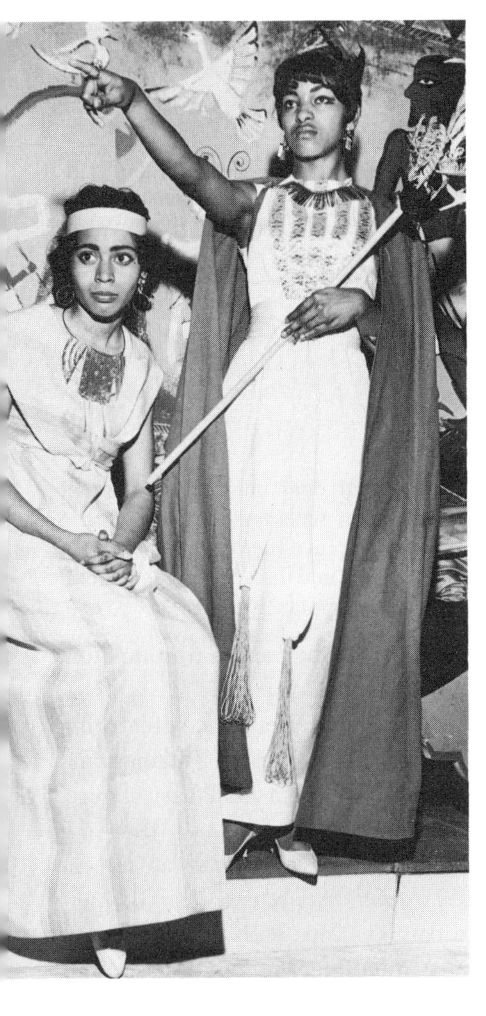

Both photographs from Detroit Public Schools, Detroit, Michigan.

Fig. 13.8. Aida (left) and Carmen (right are favorites of high school students. Even small portions of these operas make worth-while music programs.

There are many types of band shows. One is the vaudeville type of performance which in itself is likely to be cheap entertainment and promotion rather than art or education. Cantrick suggests that band directors, in planning their half-time shows, make use of the best that has been gained from experience over the years. He reminds us of the step forward that was made by the band directors who brought unity into the marching band production by using a central theme. He points out that the way to artistic production is to make use of music and movement: "The theme must be a tune or a visual pattern." His suggestions for possible themes are given here:

Do you have a favorite march? Is there a certain maneuver which has always seemed beautiful to you when well executed? Does a certain folk tune tug at your heart strings? Have you ever seen a band appear dramatic just by standing in a certain formation?

Muskegon Public Schools, Detroit, Michigan.

Fig. 13.9. The lighted cross is a black-lighted marching band formation illustrating "In Flanders Fields the Poppies Grow."

These are the kinds of ideas which can serve as themes. It does not matter whether you start with a tune and invent maneuvers to go with it, or whether you start with a maneuver and invent music (or adapt music) to go with it. In either case the way to begin is to trust your own innate sense for beauty of sound and beauty of movement, in and of themselves, divorced from all association with popular symbols.[12]

The marching band in its public performance can further art and education. Its contribution artistically and educationally is up to the director.

"Patterns of Motion" is a new concept of marching performance, featuring the evolution of designs.[13] Beginning with the basic staging design (formation), which then evolves through other designs, and concludes in a final basic figure, the predetermined sequence of movements results in patterns, and thus the title, *Patterns of Motion* (Fig. 13.10). All maneuvers are conceived as an enlargement of the performance of the *four-man squad.* A pattern may be performed by squads in unison, in sequence, or in combinations with other patterns, from a variety of facings and built upon any compatible staging design. This technique of planning is applicable to any size group that is a multiple of four. By functioning in squads of four, rather than as individuals, the bandsmen integrate their efforts as a team, resulting in greater precision in performance.

When the various marching fundamentals have been mastered, these may be assembled in any order for any squad, or group of squads to provide unlimited possibilities for the evolution of designs. One very important factor in using "patterns" or "kaleidoscopes" is that the audience can see and comprehend what is being done from any position around the field. Unlike "pictures" that must face in one particular direction, a pattern maneuver may be appreciated from the end zone, as well as from the 50-yard line (note Fig. 13.10). They may be recognized from any viewpoint. To illustrate this, hold the page at different angles.

[12] Robert Cantrick, "The Marching Band as an Art," *Music Educators Journal,* September–October, 1954, pp. 35–38.

[13] William C. Moffitt, Assistant Director of Bands, Michigan State University, *Patterns of Motion Series,* Book I: "Patterns"; Book II: "Kaleidoscopes," Hal Leonard Music, 1964.

Another advantage of pattern performance is that once the fundamental techniques have been mastered, presentations are easier to plan and considerably easier to teach.

RADIO AND TELEVISION PERFORMANCE

Radio and television are important to music education as media for public performance, and their potentialities are great. The teacher of music with the backing of the school administration can work cooperatively with the staffs of

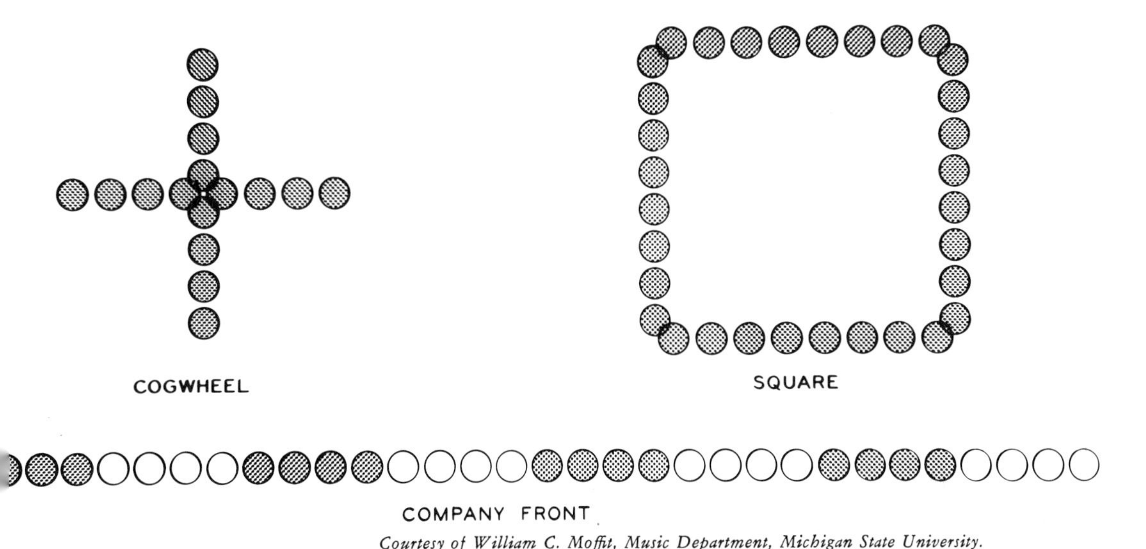

Courtesy of William C. Moffit, Music Department, Michigan State University.

Fig. 13.10. These "Patterns of Motion" can be recognized from any place on the field.

the local radio and television stations to develop programs of benefit to students, the school, and the community. For example, a series of programs on a theme such as "Music and Your Child" might be a means of focusing the attention of parents and others on the value of music in the school program.

The tape recorder enables the school choral and instrumental groups to be heard on radio without the problem of transporting pupils to the unfamiliar surroundings of a studio. With the recorder available as a regular part of the school music equipment, you can produce, under normal school conditions, tapes which can be used by radio stations as a part of their community and educational services. Recording music for this purpose is a good means of motivating students and is a part of the public performance schedule of the school. Be sure, however, that the quality of the recording is adequate.

Television appearance by school groups emphasizes the need for showmanship and musicianship on the part of the teacher. In this case, "How do you look?" is a question which cannot be ignored. Ellis comments, "What an audience sees is secondary, but the appearance of the stage and the artist on it can either help the audience concentrate on the music or provide distraction and irritation."[14] The stage setting and the appearance of the students contribute much to the success of the program. When possible, rehearsals in the studio should be planned with advice from the station staff and attention to details such as camera and microphone location and timing instructions.

A Guide to Teaching Music by Television and Radio suggests that the teacher prepare a brief cue sheet to be used by the program director.[15] The cue sheet contains the names of compositions to be performed, their composers, and some ideas as to what good camera shots are possible. For the station with a music director, a marked copy of each musical score is desirable. Timing the program is necessary, with allowance for station breaks and announcements. A script should be prepared and memorized. For prompting during telecasts, cues are put on chalkboards, on large cards placed behind the cameras, or on teleprompters. If the announcer is not familiar with music terminology, time should be spent helping him with the pronunciation of musical terms and the names of composers. For broadcasting and telecasting, it is necessary to have a list of the compositions, their composers, and publishers prepared in advance to facilitate the clearing of these numbers for station use. If there is a possibility of any compositions having to be changed, the list of music submitted to the station should include complete information on alternate compositions. As in professional broadcasting, appropriate opening and closing themes may identify and set the mood for your programs. In telecasting, an identification card for the group is necessary and specifications may be secured from your station.

This brief summary of television performance requirements is purely introductory. The wise teacher of music will do well to make a particular study of the subject before attempting programs on television. The tremendous potential of this medium is well worth the time and effort involved.

BUSINESS ASPECTS OF PUBLIC PERFORMANCE

Preparation for public performance is more than planning a rehearsal schedule and setting a performance date. Details involving stage settings, lighting, seating arrangements, uniforms, costumes, robes, rental or purchase of music, organi-

[14] Brodbury Pearce Ellis, "How Do You Look?" *Music Journal*, November, 1951, pp. 11, 53–55.

[15] Richard Berg (Ed.), A Guide to Teaching Music by Television & Radio, Music Educators National Conference, 1954.

zation and preparation of copy for the printed program, photographs, ticket sales, publicity, transportation of equipment and students, and a multitude of other details make public performance more than a one-man job. These details are of concern to the teacher whether the program is to be a concert, an operetta, an assembly, an appearance at a competition-festival or on television.

Arrangements cannot be left to chance. In many schools they are cared for cooperatively by students and faculty. Some years ago the writer observed the Elkhart, Indiana, High School orchestra as it appeared for performance at a district music festival. Teachers and students who had been assigned responsibilities worked together, and through teamwork the organization was prepared for performance with a minimum of confusion.

An operetta involves many business details from the beginning of the production to the end. The teacher can prepare a check list for an operetta, a concert, or any other public appearance. Such a list will be of great value in keeping details under control, in securing assistance, in delegating authority, and in avoiding the confusion and tensions that interfere with good performance. The chief value of a check list is in the fact that it makes it possible for the music teacher to delegate authority and still keep administrative control over the concert, the festival, or the operetta. Good business management of performance is not a one-man responsibility; it is the responsibility of a team working with a leader who knows how to let others help carry the load.

HIGH SCHOOL OPERETTA CHECK LIST

First Steps

1. Select and clear dates with administration, athletic department, civic organizations.
2. Secure information on public performance rights, royalties of possible productions.
3. Secure rental costs of orchestrations.
4. Secure estimates on rental costs for costumes, lights, scenery.
5. Secure estimates on printing costs for programs, tickets.
6. Set up an operetta budget for administrative approval.
7. Selection of the operetta by faculty-pupil committee.
   a. Is the music suitable? yes no
   b. Is the plot suitable? yes no
   c. Can our students meet production requirements? yes no
   d. Are facilities and equipment available for production? yes no
8. Tryouts by faculty-pupil committee for leads and understudies.
   a. Set date far in advance.
9. Rehearsal schedule set for leads, chorus, dancers, instrumentalists, stage crew.
   a. Check with administration.
   b. Check with athletic department.
   c. Check with instrumental teacher.
   d. Check with accompanists.

10. First meeting of complete cast and production crew.
    a. Distribute story of plot and simple sketch of sets. yes no
    b. Distribute copies of complete rehearsal schedule. yes no
    c. Distribute assignments to stage crew and others. yes no
11. Order costumes, properties, and scenery.
    a. Personally check and inventory costumes on arrival. yes no
12. Plan publicity.
    a. posters b. news releases
    c. bulletins d. radio, television
    e. skits f. photographs
13. Plan ticket sale with faculty business manager; arrange for complimentary tickets to be sent to school officials.
14. Prepare printed program.
    a. All names on program? Spelling checked? yes no
    b. All acknowledgements of cooperation? yes no
15. Arrange for ushers and ticket collectors.
16. Mark important locations on stage with tape.

For the Performance

1. Assignments of dressing rooms for chorus, dancers, leads.
2. Prompters set? Stage crew set? yes no
3. Piano in tune? yes no
4. Stage setting, lighting, properties in place and functioning? yes no
5. Chorus ready? Leads ready? Dancers ready? yes no
6. Ushers and ticket takers functioning? Programs on hand? yes no
7. Heat, air conditioning, ventilation working properly? yes no

After the Performance

1. Check and return costumes, properties, equipment, rented music.
2. Thank-you letters to people who assisted: administrators teachers custodians merchants parents.
3. Clean up ticket sales.
4. Pay all bills.
5. Prepare business report for school administration.

Publicity

Professional concert management has proved the value and necessity of showmanship and publicity in the presentation of fine programs. The school concert may be sung or played beautifully and be a credit to the community, but it is not a complete success if poor publicity fails to interest people in attending the program. Motivation of pupils and sustained interest in music is a natural outcome of well-attended public performances. There are several proven sources and types of publicity available to the school music teacher.

The School and Local Newspapers

Timing of publicity is a factor. The professional concert manager has a carefully timed series of interesting press releases on the concert. Several releases on the school concert may be prepared by the school music teacher or a school journalist. Get acquainted with the newspaper people in your community. There may be reporters properly qualified and interested in school music who will prepare from your notes what is needed. However, except for the large city papers it is unusual to find a reporter able to do justice to music publicity. In these larger cities a music critic may be excellent in writing news stories on professional musicians. The same critic, lacking sufficient background to fairly evaluate a performance by school pupils can, through his writing, have a destructive influence on all the progress that has been made by the young performers. Familiarizing the local newspaper people with your work and cultivating their support opens the door to effective publicity.

You can learn to write news stories by studying your newspaper. The articles need not be long. Newspapers are interested in:

1. Pictures of students. Pictures of individuals or small groups in action are preferred to pictures of large ensembles.
2. Guest and student conductors, soloists, members of small ensembles, student composers and arrangers, first chair players, etc. Interesting notes about these people will suffice.
3. A review of the concert by an understanding person.

TV and Radio Publicity

Announcements are usually possible. Far more effective are several very short performances by some of the capable students scheduled to appear in the concert. It may be possible to use tapes or other recordings of previous programs for use by radio stations. Careful timing and clearance of the music is a must.

Service Clubs

Short performance by a few students and announcement of the program is a good form of publicity.

School Building Publicity

Posters, chalkboard notices, sample of program in assembly, bulletin board displays showing groups and performers, copy of the program, P.A. announcements, hand bills are various forms of announcement.

Publicity can also be gained through school-related organizations such as Music Parents, P.T.A. Telephone calls announcing school activities are sometimes made by these groups.

SUMMARY

Public performance is a challenge to girls and boys. It is important to parents, to the school, and to the community, and it draws the school and the community into a closer relationship. The objectives of public performance must be established in terms of what is best for the young people involved.

The instructional material used in the vocal and instrumental classes may supply the public performance needs of the school if such material is chosen with quality of music and students' performance abilities in mind, for the concert is the one place where quality of performance is of prime importance.

Public performance can be used in many ways to further the music program in the school. The cooperative production of an annual concert by the instrumental and choral organizations is one means of increasing the interest of parents and pupils in the entire music program. Operettas and variety shows are of use in broadening and enriching the music program for all the students. The marching band is a powerful force for focusing the attention of pupils and community on school music. The potentialities of radio and television for music education have never been fully realized.

The business aspects of public performance are very important, and consequently make cooperation between teachers, students, and administration a necessity.

SUGGESTED ACTIVITIES

1. Set up your own list of objectives of public performance. Is your list in agreement with those set forth to the North Central Association of Secondary Schools by the MENC (see p. 285)? What differences would you propose?
2. Select some instructional materials for a junior-high-school band or chorus and organize a concert program using these materials.
3. Collect a number of junior- and senior-high-school programs. Evaluate each in terms of its quality as education or pure entertainment.
4. Plan a demonstration of school music teaching that may be used as a public performance.
5. Attend a junior- or senior-high-school concert. How does your own reaction to the program compare with that of the parents? If there is a difference of opinion, what implications are there here for school music?

6. Develop a list of choral compositions with instrumental accompaniment for a Class A, B, C, or D school.
7. Evaluate an instrumental or a choral festival. What do you feel are the strengths and weaknesses of this activity?
8. Study the *Adjudicator's Comment Sheets* prepared by NIMAC. Use them in judging a performance in your school.
9. Collect and study the format of a number of operetta programs to help you in designing a program.
10. Examine and evaluate a number of operettas suitable for use in the junior and senior high school. What criteria will you use in evaluating these works?
11. Plan a marching-band show in accordance with the suggestions made by Cantrick (see p. 301).
12. Interview a radio or television staff member in regard to the preparations that should be made by a high-school teacher readying his groups for appearance at the station. Report your findings to the class.
13. Prepare a check list for use with a band traveling on an overnight trip to play at a state music festival.
14. Write a series of newspaper releases for a coming school concert.

SELECTED READINGS

Bachman, Harold B. (Ed.), *Sight Reading Contests for Bands, Orchestras, Choruses*, National Interscholastic Music Activities Commission, Music Educators National Conference, 1954.

Cantrick, Robert, "The Marching Band as an Art," *Music Educators Journal*, September–October, 1954, pp. 35–38.

Dello Joio, Norman, "The Quality of Music," *Music Educators Journal*, April–May, 1962, pp. 33–35.

Eaton, Quaintance, *Opera Production: A Handbook*, University of Minnesota Press, 1961.

Ellis, Brodbury Pearce, "How Do You Look?" *Music Journal*, November, 1951, pp. 11, 53–55.

Hannahs, Roger C., "Adventure in Opera," *Music Educators Journal*, September–October, 1963, pp. 75–76.

Hughes, Gervase, *Composers of Operetta*, St Martin's Press, 1962.

Lawler, Vanett (Ed.), *The Function of Music in the Secondary-School Curriculum*, Music Educators National Conference, 1952, chaps. XIV, XV, XX.

Mason, Lawrence, "A Summer Theatre for Youth," *Music Educators Journal*, June–July, 1963, pp. 70–71.

Miller, Howard F. (Ed.), *Standards of Adjudication*, National Interscholastic Music Activities Commission, Music Educators National Conference, 1954.

Moffitt, William C., *Patterns of Motion Series*, Book I: "Patterns"; Book II: "Kaleidoscopes," Hal Leonard Music, 1964.

Pearman, Martha, "Working Creatively for Performance," *Music Educators Journal,* April–May, 1954, p. 75.

Tatum, Frances, "Should Opera Be Taught in High School?" *Music Educators Journal,* January, 1963, pp. 84–86.

Van Bodegraven, Paul, "The Development of Musical Understanding Through Performance," *Music Educators Journal,* April–May, 1955, pp. 29–30.

Van Bodegraven, Paul, and Harry Wilson, *The School Music Conductor*, Schmitt, Hall & McCreary, 1942, chaps. IX, X, XI.

Used by permission, Music Educators National Conference, Washington, D.C.

CHAPTER

14

The Teacher and His Responsibilities

What do we look for in the teacher of music? What are his responsibilities in music and in education, his responsibilities to the pupil, to the school, and to the community? While these are complex questions to which there are no final answers, we need to give them our serious consideration. Times change, education changes, and the answers change. The responsibilities of the teacher of music have broadened. He must have competence in music, he must understand children, and he must know both the school and the community. Perhaps we can best approach the subject by taking a look at a good music teacher in action.

Miss Norris is the kind of teacher we are thinking about—the kind of teacher who devotes herself to a continuous study of music, children, school, and community. She changes with the times and adapts herself to the growing responsibilities of her profession. Recently we watched her work with a class of seventh-grade boys and girls in General Music. Their response to her leadership was excellent, for her interest in children and her understanding of them was apparent in every move she made. She knew the girls and boys in this class; she was aware of the problems some of them were facing in school, home, and community life; she knew how to motivate and interest them in their work.

Miss Norris is a gifted pianist. She has spent many years developing her performance ability and musicianship, and to maintain and expand this musicianship she keeps up her study of the piano and finds satisfaction in playing for school and community functions. She considers herself a teacher of music, and while choral music is her major interest, she cooperates with and encourages instrumental study.

Miss Norris considers professional activities to be very important and she has a genuine interest in solving professional problems. At present she is serving on faculty committees evaluating the curricular offering of the school, and on a committee working for the improvement of school-community relationships. She is active in the professional and music education associations and is advancing professionally through study during the summers.

She and her colleague in instrumental music have done much to improve the status of school music in this community. Music is meeting its responsibility to the total school program and to the community. It is no longer regarded as a special or extracurricular activity but rather as a regular part of the educational program for all students.

PREPARATION BASED ON NEEDED COMPETENCIES

The pattern of teacher education is a changing pattern, designed to meet the complexities and challenges of a changing world. Social and economic trends in community and family life have influenced curriculum development, and expansion of school services have brought the school and community into a close and realistic relationship. Teachers now need many competencies, for successful teaching requires that all secondary-school teachers have a broad general education in addition to thorough training in their field of specialization. The modern teacher has school and community responsibilities which bring with them a need for greater emphasis on general education in the preparation of teachers. The teacher of music must know more than music.

Cultural Preparation

Preparation for teaching should bring to the teacher a familiarity with and appreciation of the cultural heritage of the world he lives in. The successful teacher is first of all a well-educated person cognizant of his cultural heritage. This prerequisite, plus a knowledge of people and of girls and boys in particular, is a necessary foundation which gives meaning and effectiveness to the teaching of music. In addition to sound training in music, the teacher of music should have a background based on studies in English grammar and composition, English and American literature, the humanities, and the natural and social sciences. These and other cultural studies are of great value to the music teacher, for present trends in secondary education will demand even greater emphasis on his general education. He must be able to converse intelligently and easily with his colleagues and with people in the community about topics other than music and children in order to do his best work with music and children.

Musical Preparation

Details of the musical preparation of the teacher of school music as they are recommended by the Music Educators National Conference and the National Association of Schools of Music will be summarized later. Musical growth is a

Fig. 14.1. Getting students interested, encouraging their best efforts, and guiding their musical development are the major responsibilities of the music teacher.

Duluth Public Schools, Duluth, Minnesota. Courtesy Duluth News-Tribune.

slow development which cannot, by concentrated study or any other means, be accelerated. The teacher of music in the secondary school must meet his responsibilities to the gifted students who are interested in music as a profession, and also to the larger percentage of girls and boys who will be consumers and amateur performers of music. All of these students must be encouraged to make the most of the opportunities for musical development available through private vocal or instrumental study, election of courses in general music, music literature, and music theory, and participation in the school musical organizations (Fig. 14.1).

One competency which deserves special mention is keyboard facility and a functional approach to piano playing. This ability has immeasurable value in the teaching of school music, and should be given greater emphasis in the preparation of teachers and in the guidance of prospective candidates for music teaching. The musical competence of many school music teachers is limited because of their failure to recognize the piano as the instrument basic to all music instruction (Fig. 14.2).

In the musical training of the teacher of junior- and senior-high-school music there has been a tendency toward too much specialization within the field of

Los Angeles Public Schools, Los Angeles, California.

Fig. 14.2. Ability to play the piano is a valuable asset to any teacher of music.

music. The vocal major needs to have a good foundation in instrumental music and the instrumentalist similarly needs a reasonable mastery of vocal music. While the larger secondary schools will always have some need for highly specialized music teachers, the trend in junior- and senior-high-school music is toward the use of teachers with competencies in both fields.

Among the competencies in music which should be developed through course work and independent study by pre-service and in-service teachers of music are the following:

For all music teaching:

1. The ability to sight-read and perform well as a singer or on a major instrument.
2. The ability to play the piano, with keyboard facility developed for the playing of simple accompaniments, community songs, and the playing of parts from the open score.
3. A thorough knowledge of conducting techniques, with expressive conducting as the goal.
4. A functional knowledge of vocal and choral technique.

5. A basic knowledge of instruments and instrumentation, including an understanding of orchestra and band scores.
6. The development of musical perception and aural ability to judge tone production, blend, balance, intonation, and rhythmic response.

For choral teaching:
1. A knowledge of the quality, range, and characteristics of unchanged, changing, and changed voices.
2. The ability to select and assign singers to secure proper balance and blending of voices.
3. A knowledge of correct vocal production as a means of securing correct breathing, phrasing, attack, release, enunciation, pronunciation, good tone production, and intonation. This knowledge should enable the teacher to diagnose vocal problems and correct them.
4. The ability to read and analyze the vocal score.
5. A background in music history and literature with emphasis on choral literature of the various periods in order to insure a knowledge of proper choral style and performance.
6. Familiarity with the materials available for use with unchanged, changing, and changed voices.

For instrumental teaching:
1. Sufficient knowledge of and performance ability on all instruments to be able to demonstrate the instrument and teach beginning students (Fig. 14.3).
2. Ability to read and analyze the full band and orchestra score.
3. A working knowledge of transposition and instrumentation.
4. A background in music history and literature, with emphasis on the instrumental literature of the various periods, and teaching materials for the several types of instrumental ensembles and levels of instruction.

Enthusiasm and interest in music on the part of the teacher are assets to the motivation of girls and boys, but enthusiasm and interest are not enough. The teacher must know music before he can teach it. There is no substitute for a thorough knowledge of music, for success in the teaching of junior- and senior-high-school music depends upon it.

Professional Education

The expansion of music in the total school program and the educational leadership expected of a teacher places importance on competency in the areas comprising professional education. New ideas and practices in secondary education

Used by permission, Music Educators National Conference, Washington, D.C.

Fig. 14.3. Knowledge of instruments and of how to teach them are prerequisites for the instrumental teacher.

are constantly being proposed. These must be interpreted in terms of the total school program, as well as in terms of junior- and senior-high-school music, by those with a background in professional education. The study of such areas as the history, principles, and philosophy of education, general and educational psychology, and child growth and development provide the teacher with the essential knowledge and background to understand, discuss, and evaluate educational proposals and practices. These foundation courses become particularly meaningful and functional to the music teacher when they are related to music education.

Professional education offers many elective courses which are of practical value to the experienced teacher or to the candidate in training for the teaching of junior- and senior-high-school music. Courses in audiovisual instruction, school administration, curriculum construction, methodology, counseling and guidance, to mention a few, are useful to the teacher who desires to make a more effective use of methods and instructional materials. These courses help the teacher to fit music education into the school program in such a way that it will best serve girls and boys.

Many teachers who are competent from the standpoint of knowledge of music fail in teaching because of their inability to adjust to the school and community situation. We believe that the teacher of music with a genuine interest and sound background in professional education is better equipped to adapt himself to the type of program demanded in a specific situation. His training in professional education will assist him in securing desirable changes in a music program so that it will meet the real needs of girls and boys. This requires a willingness on the part of the music educator to be an informed educator, one who will work cooperatively with others for the improvement of curriculum and instruction.

Course of Study Recommended by the MENC

The Standard for the Evaluation of the College Curriculum for the Training of the School Music Teacher is based on the development of competencies which have been demonstrated to be essential to successful music teaching in the schools.[1] The standard may well be used as a guide for the prospective teacher in evaluating his progress toward professional competency. The report stresses the importance of precollege training in music. It makes the following recommendations with respect to preparation for secondary-school music teaching for those students who are gifted and are interested in the professional study of music:

1. The development of functional ability on the piano.
2. The development of some proficiency on a minor instrument.
3. The development of as much performing ability as possible on a major instrument.
4. The opportunity to elect courses in the fundamentals of music and music history and literature.

A summary of recommendations for the music education program as a whole in the college or university suggests the following curriculum pattern:

1. General Culture
   The minimum requirement for the courses which contribute to general culture should be at least one-third of the total credits required for the undergraduate degree.
2. Basic Music
   The minimum requirement in the field of music theory should be about 15 percent of the total credits required for the undergraduate degree.

[1] Hazel Nohavec Morgan (Ed.), *Music in American Education,* Music Educators National Conference, 1955, pp. 147–150.

3. Musical Performance

   The minimum requirement in musical performance is one third of the total credits. The following courses are included in this area: Conducting; ensembles, large and small; functional piano facility; major performance area (voice, violin, cornet, clarinet, etc.); minor performance area.

4. Professional Education

   The minimum requirement suggested is 20 percent of the total credits required for graduation. In addition to courses in general professional education, this area is to include music education methods and materials, observation and student teaching. When the student is qualified, he should do student teaching in both vocal and instrumental music.

PERSONAL QUALIFICATIONS OF THE TEACHER

Personal Appearance and Characteristics

The personal appearance and characteristics of the teacher of music are factors of considerable importance for the prospective teacher of school music. They have an important bearing on the effectiveness of music in the classroom, the school, and the community (Fig. 14.4). Those who would set themselves apart by dress or mannerisms erroneously assumed to be the distinctive mark of the "artist," are likely to hinder the progress of music in the school and community and strengthen the unfortunate classification of music as a special or extra subject.

The personal characteristics of the teacher of music in the junior or senior high school should make him as personally and socially well qualified to be a regular member of the school staff, rather than one who is different from others. The teacher of music who fits well into the school and the community is in a better position to enhance the music program as a whole.

HOW STUDENTS RATE THEIR HIGH SCHOOL TEACHERS[2]

. . . they like being worked hard
. . . they dislike snap courses

What do students most admire and most dislike in their high school teachers today?

This was the subject of a study of selected Michigan high school graduates who did well enough in high school to earn and keep scholarships at Michigan State University in 1961.

[2] By Beulah M. Hedahl, Assistant Professor, Counseling Center and Gordon A. Sabine, Vice President, Michigan State University. Additional copies may be obtained without charge by writing Mr. Sabine at Michigan State University.

Lawrence Township Schools, Trenton, New Jersey.

Fig. 14.4. Good personal appearance and an agreeable personality are of the greatest importance in music teaching.

From a list of personal characteristics, the students were asked to check the five items best describing the best teacher they had in high school, and another five best describing the worst teacher they had had. Anonymity was guaranteed, and responses came from about two-thirds of the 298 to whom questionnaires were mailed.

Their best teachers, 20 percent said, accepted criticism of their teaching, explained the grading procedures thoroughly, supported student activities, permitted class members to disagree with them, encouraged their students to go to college, explained the purposes and goals of the course being taught, were open-minded, were well thought of, were able to give directions, were considerate of others, were businesslike, showed students how to study for the course, and used many illustrations in their teaching.

Their worst teachers they remember as having lost control over the class in arguments, telling too many jokes, making students feel they didn't like them, changing test grades under pressure, being critical of others, acting too important, being domineering, being unfriendly, and making fun of other teachers.

Their best teachers, 40% said, seemed to understand them, were fair in their grading, spent time with students who needed help after school, answered questions willingly, had a good sense of humor, were persons the students would like to be like, were frank and honest, were respected by others, were enthusiastic, and taught the students how to take notes from a lecture [Fig. 14.5]. Their worst teachers expected them to memorize what they told them, were suspicious that their students cheated, were dictatorial, were cold and unfeeling, were frequently angry, did not assign work to be done outside of class, embarrassed students who were unprepared, and gave better grades to the popular students.

Their best teachers, 60% reported, made classes interesting, were well-informed on subjects other than those they taught, were firm but just, gave fully of themselves, worked hard for students, and gave a tough course. And their worst used sarcasm often,

San Diego City Schools, San Diego, California.

Fig. 14.5. Genuine concern for pupils' progress is always a teacher's responsibility.

made students dislike the subject they taught, liked some students better than others, never had time for questions, were annoying, were lazy, were not able to tell when a student was bluffing.

Nearly 80% said their best teachers were those who set high standards for their students, who made students think for themselves, and who knew their subject matter well. The same number described their worst teachers as never admitting they were wrong, being overly impatient with others' mistakes, giving a snap course, and not requiring much outside work for a passing grade.

Encouragingly, many students responded with "I didn't have any teachers who were really bad." Discouragingly, one student wrote, "Sometimes my worst teacher drowsed off in class." Many students criticized teacher-coaches for "playing the ball game over again in class," but others countered with "if it weren't for this teacher, I never would have been here in college."

The questionnaire also asked for general comments the students would make to their former high school teachers. Some sample replies follow.

"Give the students more opportunity for independent, original work."

"Teachers should stop trying to be good buddies. They should be firm, fair, and reasonable, but maintain their position."

"Don't make a high school class like nursery school. Don't make your class a big joke. Teach a hard course."

"I respected most those teachers who ran their classes on the assumption that students were willing to work at the task of learning."

"Don't underestimate the American student. We have as great a capacity for hard work and creative work as any nation's youth."

"Give more tests, preferably college-type tests. Sneak in a lecture once in a while so they don't come as such a shock in college."

"Each teacher should be prepared to give as much of himself as the ability and personality of the student demands."

"Take it for granted your students do know something and show them how to find out for themselves the things that puzzle them. Don't explain everything—help them to figure it out for themselves."

"I wish that teachers would do more for high standards and morals in our high schools. Some students don't realize how important good and high standards are. If only the teacher could incorporate in his or her life and lessons a way to get students to realize this and then live their lives accordingly, this would help our country greatly. A haphazard idea and attitude toward high school today does not help our country's future."

"Far too many teachers are cowards and ignore and thereby encourage cheating."

"Nothing destroys the productivity of a student's mind quicker or more thoroughly than a few caustic or thoughtless remarks dismissing his opinion as worthless."

"My best teacher's whole job was teaching, and he spent hours and hours of time in preparation. His was not an 8-hour job, but a life's dedication. Because of his dedication, I have found that my life will be dedicated, no matter what occupation I choose."

"My worst teacher possessed many qualities usually thought of as desirable, but all his personal qualities deserved infinitely less consideration than the main fact that he did not know what he was talking about."

"Be truthful and frank but speak the truth with love."

"Nobody should teach who is not filled with the simple and noble desire to know everything. Learn, learn, learn!"

"In addition to the immense knowledge of my best teacher, I most admired his belief that education should take place everywhere, not just in school, and that education ends not with a diploma, but with a death certificate."

Ability to Work with Others

The success of the teacher of music in the modern school also depends to a great degree on his ability to work with others. The music teacher is called upon to work with teachers and students on assembly programs, with the athletic department in connection with music at games, and with committees studying the curriculum and other aspects of the school program. The music activities of

FAITH OF AMERICAN TEACHERS

GLADLY do I teach—for I believe in the personal worth and potential ability of every child and youth.

REVERENTLY do I teach—for the guidance of the young toward high ideals and great achievement is a sacred trust.

CONFIDENTLY do I teach—for professional and cultural studies enable me to meet the complex tasks of teaching.

PROUDLY do I teach—for the story of our nation and the history of mankind reflect the wholesome influence of many teachers.

HOPEFULLY do I teach—for the teaching profession is gaining in public esteem and education is advancing toward new and challenging opportunities.

National Education Association, Washington, D.C.

Fig. 14.6. Five hundred classroom teachers, administrators, and specialists employed in schools and colleges throughout the country shared in the drafting of this statement of faith prepared by the National Education Association.

the school involve him in a variety of community activities where he acts as a representative of the school system. He works with service clubs, churches, and with groups of parents and community leaders in connection with community projects or the development of the music program. The successful music program in the school is dependent upon the good will, the interest, and the cooperation of school administrators, teachers, students, parents, and community leaders. The most successful music teachers are those who know and understand children, who know and love music, and who have also cultivated that very important ability to work with others–in short, the most successful music teachers, just as the most successful persons, are those who can "win friends and influence people" (Fig. 14.6).

Leadership

Leadership of the music educator in the school and the community is a challenge for those who are sincerely interested in the school and its program and in those civic responsibilities which make for better community living. Active participation in the work of the service clubs, the Chamber of Commerce, the churches, and community projects contributes not only to the growth and influence of the school music teacher as a person, but to the school and its music program as well. The essence of professional leadership is the willingness to shoulder school and civic responsibilities, even those not directly connected with the music program.

Leadership must be conceived by the teacher in terms broader than the local horizon. There are opportunities for leadership at the state, divisional, and national levels. Interest, work, and a sustained and constructive support of the state and national educational organizations is the duty and privilege of every music teacher. The leadership and interest of the teacher of music should not be confined to those organizations concerned chiefly with school music. There is a need for leadership which will serve those organizations whose interests encompass the entire curriculum. The music educator can contribute much to them and they in turn have much to offer him. This type of leadership can be a source of strength and inspiration to the music teacher. As he returns to his local situation he can more clearly evaluate what is being done and envision the possibilities for the improvement of instruction in his own school (Fig. 14.7).

Glosser, in his writing on leadership in music education, states that the complexity and uniqueness of each social setting make it impossible to express any

Used by permission, Music Educators National Conference, Washington, D.C.

Fig. 14.7. Active support of state, divisional, and national programs of the Music Educators National Conference is an opportunity and a responsibility of every professional music educator (left). Planning meetings of music teachers permits a joint attack on common professional problems (right).

universal formula for leadership through human relations.[3] Although he recognizes the value of certain principles and technics which contribute to effective leadership, he feels that the music educator must be concerned with human values before these principles and technics can be applied effectively. Leadership calls for the music teacher to have respect for the individual and the group. It is first a leadership of people and secondly a leadership of band, orchestra, or chorus.

Thus, leadership in music education requires more than a wide background of musical experience and training. It requires ability to work with and for other people, ability to communicate effectively with others in conversation, in speaking before school and community groups, and in writing. The leader is also one who listens well to others and who learns through listening. How much music should he know? He cannot know too much about the art of music and the science of sound, unless it is known at the expense of knowing people.

General Efficiency

Junior- and senior-high-school music teaching involves more than the assigned schedule of classes. The teacher carries, in addition, a large administrative and organizational responsibility. Purchase, care, and rental of band and orchestra instruments; purchase and handling of band uniforms and choir robes; maintenance of music and recording libraries; preparation for classes, rehearsals, and performances; preparation of annual budget requirements; reports to the superintendent and the school principal; and a host of other administrative details are necessary to the efficient functioning of the music department.

In recognition of the far-reaching effects of good business management on the school music program, the Music Industry Council has for a number of years published for free distribution to the profession *The Music Educator's Business Handbook.* This handbook stresses the fact that "today's successful music educator is businesslike and efficient in the planning of his work. He is more than a musician or a teacher. His greatly enlarged program of music education activities demands efficient organization and administration."[4] The handbook deals with getting acquainted with representatives of the music industry; business correspondence; orders in general; accounts; "on approval" orders; general shipping instructions; contests, clinics, festivals; order forms for instrumental music; broadcast permission; copyright law; musical instruments; uniforms; teacher's agencies and extended works. It is extremely useful as a guide for the efficient operation of the music department.

[3] Mort Glosser, "Leadership and the Music Educator," *Ala Breve,* Alabama Music Education Association, December, 1956, p. 2.

[4] Music Industry Council, *The Music Educator's Business Handbook,* Music Educators National Conference, 1962.

The teacher of music who recognizes the need for general efficiency in the teaching and administrative aspects of music will find that efficiency of operation will enable him to devote more time to music and music teaching.

PROFESSIONAL INTERESTS OF THE TEACHER

The Music Teacher and Research

What has research to do with the effective music teacher? A great deal. While in the past relatively little attention has been paid to findings in educational research, alert supervisors and teachers are beginning to realize that an exciting challenge is to be found here. We have come a long way in education since Mark Hopkins and his famous log. Part of this progress has been achieved through costly trial and error. Much of it, in recent years, has come through the findings of scientific research and their practical application in the classroom.

In spite of propaganda to the contrary, we know that Johnny can read, add and subtract, express himself orally or in writing, and score on achievement tests in almost any subject better than his father or mother could 25 years ago at the same point in their schooling. Much of this improvement is due to the application of educational research findings in our schools.

It is still true that we know much more than we put into practice in many areas of education and this is particularly true in school music. All the more reason, however, why we should seize opportunity by the forelock. In no field does greater or more rewarding opportunity exist than for the enterprising, courageous music teacher. He recognizes that, far from being unrelated to his work, research can be the key to a whole new and exciting era of music teaching.

There are unanswered questions confronting the music teacher every day. How can we teach music reading so that it really works? How can we make the orchestra as attractive as the band to the high-school student. What is the best way to motivate home practice? Find new and better ways of doing things and tell others about them; find out how others have solved their problems—that is the purpose of professional magazines.

For example, the report of success in teaching music fundamentals as told in *Keyboard Experience and Class Piano Instruction* can be of help to you.[5] *The Journal of Research in Music Education* has as its chief goal the reporting of projects on research in music education.[6] Make use of the ideas and successes of other teachers in the field.

[5] William R. Sur (Ed.), *Keyboard Experience and Class Piano Instruction,* Music Educators National Conference, 1956, pp. 9 ff.

[6] *Journal of Research in Music Education,* Music Educators National Conference. Copies can be secured from 1953, its initial year of publication.

Active Interest in and Support of Professional Organizations

The Music Educators National Conference is the Department of Music of the National Education Association and, as such, serves as the recognized voice for music education in the United States. Its headquarters is at 1201 16th Street N.W., Washington, D.C. Its publications, conferences, projects, and other activities have been to a great extent responsible for the establishment of music education as a profession, and for the development of music as a part of the school program in this country.

The MENC is organized on a member-service cooperative basis with state, divisional, and national units, concerned with all phases of music education on all levels of instruction. Many colleges and universities have been granted charters to organize student chapters of the MENC which serve as an excellent means of introducing students to the many professional activities of the state, divisional, and national conferences of music educators. It is in these chapters that the music education student has an opportunity to serve and to develop an active interest in a professional organization which can mean much to his professional future.

It must also be emphasized that the interest and support of the music educator must not be confined only to organizations of music teachers. Participation in state and national education associations interested in the total school program is highly desirable for the welfare of the teaching profession as a whole. It is well to remember that progress in a music program can best be made in a school which is steadily improving its total educational program. Thus it behooves the teacher of music to have broad educational interests, both for the sake of his own professional growth and for that of his music program. In the process such participation will not only make him a better teacher, but will also provide maximum benefits for his students.

Interest in Both School and Community

The relationship between the school and the community is so close that the music teacher cannot help being interested in both his school and his community. Music education provides a natural link between the school and the community through public performances of large and small instrumental and choral ensembles. Since this relationship is so close, junior- and senior-high-school teachers can gain much as they become actively involved in the life of their communities. They will know and understand their students better if they are familiar with the economic situation, the home life and the religious life of the people they serve. They should know the music resources of their town and county. They must recognize the contribution made by the private teachers of music and work cooperatively with them. They have an opportunity to enhance their teaching by bringing into their classes persons who actively support the music of the community, persons who are interested in music but who do not earn their living through music. This is a particularly fine means of enriching the classroom or assembly program.

Another aspect of the teacher's interest in the school and community concerns the increasing number of fund-raising projects. Community residents have readily responded to calls for financial assistance by school music teachers when there was a need for funds for new choir robes, band uniforms, travel costs to accept an invitation to perform at bowl games, etc. The increase in the number and frequency of these drives is shown in the increasing number of exhibitors at state and national conferences offering candy, cake, and magazine sales possibilities to teachers.

Fund raising, when approved by school officials, is legitimate if it does not cause the teacher to neglect his teaching responsibilities and if it improves the instructional program for the pupils. The teacher has an obligation to the school and the community to consider these aspects of the projects:

1. Can long trips to play at bowl games, conventions, etc., be justified from an educational viewpoint? Such trips should not be considered unless they provide sufficient opportunity for the group to perform. They should also be approved by the state administrators organizations responsible for travel by high-school pupils. Invitations that would deprive the professional musician of employment should not be accepted.
2. As far as possible, funds raised by these projects should be used to secure instruments and other equipment necessary to improve the music teaching in the local schools.
3. Community relations must not be allowed to deteriorate because of constant selling drives by pupils. The business man who must support the schools through taxation has cause for complaint when school groups offer products in competition with him. Families in the community support many neighborhood fund drives. Their good will toward school music will suffer if they are faced too often with door-to-door sales programs.

Dedication to Human Service

Much of what has been said in this chapter can be summed up thus: good teaching is a high order of service to humanity. The teaching profession deals not primarily with things or commodities, but with human beings who look for guidance and inspiration. Music can contribute significantly to the life of the child, as an individual experience or a social opportunity, as an agency for growth or as a moral force.

In the junior and senior high schools we work with adolescents whose emotional characteristics and sudden emotional changes must be sympathetically understood by the teacher of music. He must be fully aware of the possibilities for the release of emotional tension through music. Because of his understanding of these pupils, he will select his music with care and regard for the sensitivities of these students.

The adolescent needs to know that someone has an interest in him and is ready to help him in his endeavors and with his problems. "A child learns best when his failures are viewed constructively by a teacher who likes and respects him, and when appropriate remedial or corrective measures are worked out with him."[7] The instrumental and choral groups and the General Music classes, under the guidance of teachers who are devoted to human service, can ideally provide for experiences in music which emphasize human as well as musical values.

Human values and human resources are of the greatest importance in democratic education. One aspect of music work which is particularly dedicated to human service is the field of music therapy. The distinction between music education and music therapy is primarily one of purpose and consequent application. The contributions which music therapy can make to our knowledge of the effect of music on human beings is of particular importance to those who are working with adolescents. Dedication to human service brings about stability in employment, for the teacher must stay with the job for a long enough time to bring about the changes he strives for. He becomes a member of a school team composed of administrators, teachers, students, and parents who unite in their efforts to bring better things through music to girls and boys.

THE TEACHER AND THE COMMUNITY

Attitude Toward the Cultural Level of the Community

The cultural level of the community is a matter of deep concern to teachers of music. In a very real sense it is a factor which influences the music curriculum, the attitude and response to music by students and adults in the community, the type of music used in instruction, and that much discussed subject, the music budget! For effective school work that will bring about desirable changes in girls and boys, teachers of secondary-school music should develop

[7] Camilla M. Low, *N.E.A. Journal*, January, 1955, pp. 17–20, adapted from the *1955 Yearbook of the Association for Supervision and Curriculum Development*, chap. IV.

an awareness of what goes on musically in the "real" world—in community living. They should be aware of the relationship of music to life. It is important in curriculum planning and in guiding young people that teachers know about music in the homes, the churches, the civic institutions, the clubs, and the local industries. They should also be familiar with the racial, religious, and nationalistic backgrounds of the people in their community. Planning for instruction with full knowledge of the people, their musical interests and resources, and the culture of the community is basic to a music program which accepts its full responsibility and aims to improve the cultural level.

Community study on the part of music teachers may disclose unusual musical resources which can be the means of awakening an interest in all kinds of music. Such a study frequently reveals, also, that the cultural level is on a higher plane than first investigations may have indicated. Music teachers who know the community, who know the people, and who have gained their friendship and respect can be most influential in raising the cultural level of the community to new and unexpected heights. The teacher's enthusiasm for music and people may be the spark needed to bring about a movement to develop community music groups. The subject of the music teacher's community relationships is discussed in detail in Chapter 15.

Parents Need Your Help

One of the most encouraging aspects of school music is the strong interest parents have in providing music for their children. It is not uncommon to learn of parents depriving themselves of necessities in order for their children to be able to study music privately or to participate in school music organizations. The enthusiasm of parents for the musical education of their sons and daughters is seen in the support of school music activities through Parent-Teacher Associations, Music Parents, and other similar groups.

It is the responsibility of teachers to include in their plans various ways of guiding and assisting parents in understanding school music and in making correct decisions in matters musical as they affect their children. The secondary-school music teachers do participate in many meetings with parents, but in most cases they appear as conductors of ensembles. The value of such service is clearly recognized, but there should be a number of times each year when the school music teacher devotes himself to the task of informing parents. A few of the questions that parents would like answered are:

1. What does the school music program offer which is of value to my child?
2. What is an adequate program of music for the children in this community?
3. What instrument should my child play?

4. What opportunities does music as a career present?
5. What do other schools offer boys and girls in the music program?[8]

There are many ways to develop communication between teachers and parents: the instrumental demonstration, school visitation by parents, parents sitting in on rehearsals of school groups, parents participating in the school organizations with their sons and daughters, talks by the teacher at civic and school clubs, and conferences with individual parents. All of these are effective in bringing about good school-community relationships and influencing the cultural level of the community.

Audiovisual materials are becoming an increasingly important part of the educational program and can be of great assistance in working with parents. At one time the music teachers of the East Lansing, Michigan, public schools planned a series of 2 × 2 color slides based on the theme "Music for All." The series shows children singing and playing in the classroom. It shows them progressing from the beginning music classes in vocal and instrumental music to membership in the more advanced ensembles the school has to offer. A complete coverage was given to the various areas of music education, thus providing the staff and other interested people with a picture story of instrumental and vocal music on the elementary and secondary levels of instruction. The use of the slides had the advantage of permitting the teacher to hold a particular slide on the screen when questions were asked or when she felt the necessity of giving a detailed account of something presented on the screen. Another possibility in working with slides is the development of an explanatory recording which may extend the usefulness of the slides by making it possible for the program to be handled by community groups without the teacher being present.

Another source of information for parents which has been overlooked in many communities is the music section of the public library. Librarians are always interested in learning of books that would be of interest to parents. The music section of many libraries is not developed and the librarians would welcome the music teacher's recommendations of appropriate books.

Community Music Groups

The increased interest and activity in adult education provides a natural and important carry-over from school to community resources. In many localities the teacher with missionary zeal pushes for the organization of community bands, choruses, and orchestras and often serves as the musical director of one or more of these groups. In other situations the teacher may plant the idea of com-

[8] William R. Sur, "Parents Need Your Help," *Educational Music Magazine*, September–October, 1953, pp. 10 ff.

munity music organizations and cooperate in their formation, but not serve as music director of the organizations.

Music for Everybody is a helpful guide to those interested in promoting community music activities. It urges the development of a local music association representing all community interests concerned with music. The association would have as its aim active participation in music by as many people as possible. No medium of musical expression would be considered too lowly:

> Such a local organization, if so planned, is a clearing house or coordinating office for all things musical in the community, serving as a civic and social agency in this respect. It also motivates the development of additional musical activities in which persons of all ages, races, creeds, and economic and social levels may have a neighborly part. The fullest functioning of such an organization involves cooperation of all musical organizations, and also such institutions and groups as industries, mercantile establishments, lodges, schools, home service clubs, women's clubs, hospitals, etc.
>
> We should keep in mind that community music is not a kind of music; rather it is all kinds of music. The successful community music plan is designed primarily not to demonstrate what people do with music, but what music does to people. Participation in the performance of music eliminates, or minimizes, the consciousness of differences in religious creed, political faith, economic status, social position, or age. From the social standpoint music is an ideal common medium since boys, men, girls and women may, separately or in combination, join in singing or playing.[9]

The task of developing and sustaining community music organizations is rewarding and carries with it many responsibilities, which may well be shared by a group of leaders who represent all segments of the community and who are capable of securing united and effective action (Fig. 14.8). School music teachers should do what they can to promote musical activity among adults, but their first and foremost responsibility is to the boys and girls in their classes. Leadership must be found and developed to direct and carry on the community music activities. The American Music Conference as a part of its free service to communities offers a how-to-do-it manual for community leaders who desire community betterment through music.[10]

SUMMARY

Secondary-school teachers must have, in addition to their specialized training, a broad general education and a thorough professional education to enable them to think and act in terms of the total educational program. Furthermore, the vocal teacher needs to have a good foundation in the field of instrumental music, and the instrumental teacher needs a reasonable mastery of vocal music. The

[9] Claude B. Smith, *Music for Everybody*, MENC, 1950.
[10] *Manual for Developing a Music Council*, American Music Conference.

Used by permission, Music Educators National Conference, Washington, D.C.

Fig. 14.8. Members of the Community Symphony Orchestra provide an instrumental demonstration for a group of pupils.

musical competency of many music teachers is limited because of their failure to recognize the piano as the instrument basic to all music instruction.

The music teacher needs to be sufficiently enthusiastic about teaching to find better ways of securing results through an experimental approach to instruction. He will also find that efficiency of operation will enable him to devote more time to music and music teaching. The secondary-school teacher needs, more than any other one thing, the ability and the willingness to work with other people for the good of the children, the school, and the community.

School music teachers should do what they can to promote community music activities, but their first responsibility is to the girls and boys in their classes.

SUGGESTED ACTIVITIES

1. Interview a school music teacher and a school administrator. Report on what they believe to be the music teacher's responsibilities to music, to education, to the schools, and to the community.

2. Make a study of teacher placement calls in music. Discuss your study in relation to the preparation of candidates for teaching music in the secondary schools.
3. Check the list of competencies for choral or instrumental music teaching (see p. 317). What changes or additions would you make? Justify your suggestions.
4. Develop a class discussion on what a study of child growth and development contributes to successful teaching by the junior-high-school music teacher.
5. As a class project, study the total school program of a small senior high school. Indicate how music can best serve the objectives of that school program.
6. Interview a school administrator or a teacher placement officer on the subject, "Why Teachers Fail." Report your findings to the class.
7. Evaluate the "College Curriculum for the Training of the School Music Teacher" recommended by the MENC. What do you consider to be its strengths and weaknesses?
8. Invite representatives of music dealers, musical instrument manufacturers, and music publishers to discuss before the class the business aspects of music education.
9. Select a research study in music education. Report on the practical application of the study.
10. Make a study to determine some of the ways the MENC has contributed to the advancement of music education.
11. Investigate and discuss the relationship between music therapy and music education. What are the implications of music therapy for music education?
12. Do you agree that "Parents Need Your Help"? Talk to parents of several junior-high-school students contemplating music study for their children. What help do you think they need?

SELECTED READINGS

American Music Conference, *Manual for Developing a Music Council* (free).

Bradac, Francis, "Time To Clean House?" *Music Educators Journal*, June–July, 1963, p. 77.

Britton, Allen P., "The General Theoretical Foundations of Music Education," *Music Educators Journal*, April–May, 1964, p. 44.

Fisher, W. Allen, "The Obligations of a Music Educator," *Music Educators Journal*, June–July, 1963, p. 55.

Flora, Frank E., "Successful Administrative Relationships Make Successful Music Programs," *Music Educators Journal*, April–May, 1961, pp. 66–67.

Harrison, Russell M., "Human Relations in Teaching," *Music Educators Journal*, February–March, 1962, p. 122.

Hoffer, Charles R., "Research and the Music Teacher," *Music Educators Journal*, November–December, 1954, pp. 20–22.

McGill, Ralph, "Bands vs. Bands," *Music Educators Journal*, June–July, 1963, p. 77.

Miller, Kurt, "The Three-Way Team for an Effective Music Program," *Music Educators Journal*, January, 1961, p. 37.

Pickett, R. E., "You Can't Teach It if You Don't Know It," *Music Educators Journal*, November–December, 1951, p. 28.

Riddle, Bruce, "Professional Growth of the Music Educator," *Music Educators Journal*, November–December, 1958, p. 64.

Simpson, Ray H., "Music Instructors' Use of Self-Evaluation Tools," *Music Educators Journal*, April–May, 1964, p. 82.

Sparling, Edward J., "Music for the Masses," *Music Educators Journal*, November–December, 1956, pp. 28–30.

Music Educator's National Conference, Washington, D.C.

CHAPTER

15

School Music and the Community

The universal appeal of music makes it a natural bridge between the school and the community. The spring concert, the marching band, the high-school operetta, and the music festival are activities which bring pleasure and pride to parents and students alike. Yet if our concept of community relationships should encompass something beyond performances for the public, accomplishments far more important can be realized. Through effective use of school music, both schools and communities can be improved. Let us examine the subjects of communities and community schools, and then look into the roles of school music in this context.

THE CHANGING COMMUNITY

The nature of communities has changed rapidly in recent decades. The movement of large population segments from rural to urban-industrial areas has created a nation of city dwellers. Conversely there has been an increasing movement from cities to suburban areas for living (Fig. 15.1). Increasingly we work in the city and live away from it. The effort involved may be extensive. Many New Yorkers, for example, spend from an hour and a half to three hours a day commuting between their homes and their work.

Within cities, people also tend to congregate in groups according to nationality, income, color or, occasionally, occupations. Each of these congregation areas is a community. Each is also part of a larger community—the South Side, the borough, the city as a whole, the state, the region, and the nation. People are Americans. They are also Michiganders, commuters, members of a particular church, Midwesterners, suburbanites, music lovers, Dodger fans, adolescents, lawyers, and so on. Each group is a kind of community in terms of interests, location, status, racial patterns, or other factors. Each is likewise changing in meaning and significance as time goes on.

Thus communities are something more than simple geographic areas. They are complex, heterogeneous combinations of people. One common characteristic

All photographs from the Encyclopaedia Britannica Film, The Living City.

Fig. 15.1. Large cities and suburban areas provide homes for more than half our population. The kinds of communities we have are determined, in part, by how we live.

is that they are based upon interdependent human relationships of several kinds. An appreciation of this interdependence is gained occasionally when the electric power fails or when a strike stops the telephone service. Similarly, people in a community depend upon the state government to help finance their schools and to maintain their highways. Uncle Sam delivers their mail and maintains their armed forces. In local communities the grocer, butcher, milkman, and paperboy play important though unobtrusive roles in their daily lives. Each of these agencies, in turn, is dependent upon the people it serves for some kind of support—political, financial, or social, and usually a combination of these. Modern living is highly interdependent and it is becoming steadily more so. And, as communities change in this and in other respects, schools must adjust and change with them or fail in one of their major functions.

THE SCHOOL AND THE COMMUNITY

The school is a part of the community it serves. It is, or should be, an *integral* part of this community, responsive to its needs and active in serving them. This is part of what school administrators mean when they say that schools will be what their communities want them to be. If this is true, it becomes evident that schools have a leadership function in their communities.

Without active educational leadership in a community, the people's concept of what their schools ought to be doing tends to become static. In consequence, progress in school programing or practice is likely to be slow. In such a situation people are also more easily influenced by those who would attack the public schools for one reason or another. Occasionally we have an aroused public reaction about the effectiveness with which the 3 R's are being taught, about the need for a new bond issue, subversive influences in the schools, or waste of the taxpayers' money on "frills."

The music teacher, through the nature of his work, has a particularly good opportunity to exert an accepted and appreciated kind of educational leadership in the community. If he does a good job, his own program benefits as well as that of the schools as a whole (Fig. 15.2).

If schools have a positive role to play in community affairs, the community likewise has a significant stake in its schools. Neither can progress satisfactorily for long without the other. This is why good administrators work constantly for closer school-community relations. One outgrowth of this effort has come to be known as the community school or community-centered school.

THE COMMUNITY SCHOOL

What is a community school? How does it differ from other schools? Some of the differences are subtle, being identifiable chiefly by the degree to which one school emphasizes its community relationship functions more than another. Other differences are pronounced variations from traditional school patterns. Cook and Olsen observe that *any school* is a community school to the extent that it:

a. educates youth by and for participation in the full range of basic life activities (human needs, areas of living, persistent problems, etc.)
b. seeks increasingly to democratize life in school and outside
c. functions as a community service center for youth and adult groups
d. actively cooperates with other social agencies in improving community life
e. uses community resources in all aspects of its program
f. educates teachers for community leadership[1]

[1] *Encyclopedia of Educational Research* (rev. ed.), Macmillan, 1952, p. 1075.

Oakland Public Schools, Oakland, California.

Fig. 15.2. Christmas music is broadcast from a downtown bank by the Castlemont High-School Choir in Oakland, California. Business goes on as usual and shoppers listen through loudspeakers placed outside the building. This kind of community service by the schools is a natural good-will builder.

Some of the techniques employed in community-centered schools include:

1. Life activity experience curriculums
2. Participation programs involving pupils, teachers, school administrators, parents and community groups on a democratic basis
3. Use of the school plant and school personnel in a community service center
4. Coordinating councils of educators and laymen to plan basic school policy and related programs (these councils frequently extend beyond the immediate school community to include representation from and consideration of needs in area, state, regional, and national communities)
5. Utilization of community resources through field trips, resource visitors, field studies, community surveys, documentary materials, work-experience projects, etc.

6. In-service teacher education activities directed toward the philosophy, programs, procedures, and problems of community-centered education

What does all this have to do with you as a teacher of music? Two things, probably. First, with a better understanding of what good schools are doing to foster community relationships and the reasons for this emphasis, you have an improved basis for planning and for judging the effectiveness of your own music-education program. Secondly, the techniques employed by community-centered schools may suggest a number of specific ways in which you can be an asset to the school program as a whole and to your music program at the same time. It is worth remembering that you are first of all a teacher, and secondly a teacher of music. Your special field and those of your colleagues are of importance primarily in terms of how much and how well they contribute to the overall educational job to be done.

Before going further into community relationships and their importance to you and to the schools, one simple but fundamental point should be stressed, namely, *that the students are your most vital communications link with the community.* If you do a good job of teaching, if your students learn readily and enjoy their work with you, they will be your best emissaries in the school and in the community. Mistakes or omissions in your own relations outside of the school can hamper your program and limit your success. But no amount of public relations can offset a poor job of teaching. Good community relations begin with a superior educational product.

Teacher Relations with Community Groups

A teacher's satisfaction in school work stems from many things. Most important of these is the genuine pleasure he receives from working with young people and helping them to develop. Closely related to this is his enjoyment of the community (or communities) in which he lives and works. One does his best work in surroundings which are conducive to normal, happy living, where he is accepted as a respected member of the community, and where he has friends in the community in addition to students and other teachers. In order to achieve this status, however, he must earn it.

The Development of Good Community Relations

Good community relationships do not just "happen." A teacher—any teacher—has certain advantages when he first comes to a job. His position is respected. Parents depend upon him to work effectively with their children. Times have changed since schoolteachers were looked upon as somewhat different from other people. This change of view is a happy one brought about largely by a generation of normal, healthy teachers who were able to break down many of the artificial barriers which tended to isolate them from other people. It is now more difficult than formerly to spot a teacher by appearance, mannerisms, or aloofness from community affairs.

Good teachers have come to recognize that good education must thoroughly involve the community. To accomplish such involvement, they must know the people and have the people know them as individuals. Music teachers are in a particularly good position to get acquainted in their communities. The church, civic clubs, recreational activities, fund drives, and the like are a few of the avenues. It is essential in these efforts that you be sincere and that you exercise a kind of sensitivity in human relationships which we call *social intelligence.*

Should you happen to teach in a community-centered type of school, you will find it easier to establish friendly and cooperative relationships in the community. But whatever the type of school, such relationships are important to you and your music program; we turn next to a consideration of how they can be developed.

Some Types of Community Relationships

What are some of the organized groups through which school-community relations can be established or improved? These groups are of several types, each of which includes a somewhat different segment of the community's people. In a sense these people represent a variety of communities. Within a church group, for example, will be found individuals of some wealth and others of limited means; businessmen, professional people, farmers, and laborers; people from adjacent neighborhoods and others from rural areas. On the other hand, each church group, service club, or women's club has a particular area of common interest. Most of the people in a community and usually all of the community leaders are to be found in one or more of these community organizations. Accordingly, each organization is important both to the school and to the individual teacher in their efforts to build a strong educational program.

Parent Organizations

Parent-teacher organizations have a power for good which is difficult to overestimate. First established in 1897 as The National Congress of Mothers, the PTA has become the largest and most influential citizens' group with a vital concern in public school affairs (Fig. 15.3).

Detroit Public Schools, Detroit, Michigan.

Fig. 15.3. Illustrative of the kind of support which can be expected when a community becomes interested in the school's music program is this group of parents, teachers, and community leaders in a planning session for a city-wide choral festival.

The National Congress of Parents and Teachers, as the PTA is officially known, is built upon thousands of units tied to individual schools in which parents and teachers know one another, and focus their interests on individual pupils and the educational programs of the school. Coordination and strength are achieved through its organization. Each school's PTA is a member of the community Congress and community groups are members of districts, which in turn are functioning parts of a state Congress of Parents and Teachers. At the top of the organization is the National Congress of Parents and Teachers with a program of activities and influence nationwide in scope and which has made itself felt today in every important piece of legislation affecting the public schools.[2]

It is perfectly natural that the teacher, after a hard day's work, should look with something less than enthusiasm to an evening PTA meeting. And it has

[2] Malcolm S. MacLean and Edwin A. Lee, *Change and Process in Education*, Holt, Rinehart and Winston, 1956, pp. 464, 495–496.

been correctly pointed out that all too often the parents in attendance are not the ones who most need to be there. Yet for the teacher who sees the value of interpreting his music program to the public, there is no organization more directly suited to his needs than the PTA (Fig. 15.4). As MacLean and Lee observe, public interest in the schools as exemplified in PTA organizations, "is an interest on the part of intelligent men and women whose children are in the schools, and whose fundamental desire is that their children shall be afforded the best education which can be devised. Such interest is always sought, and frequently stimulated, by wise principals and superintendents, who know that good schools and good citizens generally go together."[3] In a word, don't sell your PTA short. Here is a good place to start effective community relations.

Occasional performances of school music groups or ensembles on PTA programs are pleasing to parents and good musical experience for students. Some-

San Diego Public Schools, San Diego, California.

Fig. 15.4. San Diego has evening piano classes for parents who use the same instructional materials which their sons and daughters use during the day. A joint recital given by children and parents is featured in the spring.

[3] *Ibid.*, pp. 463–464.

times the music teacher can arrange for a program in which he demonstrates how music is taught, what problems exist, or why music experience is important for all children. He may wish to volunteer to lead or play for group singing for the adults. Generally speaking, he should try to be as cooperative and helpful as he knows how to be in all phases of PTA activities, and not only in those involving music. This, incidentally, is a sound principle of public relations in any organization to which one belongs.

Music Boosters

At some stage of music development in most high schools, some type of parent group has played an important role in support of school music. Most commonly the support at the outset has been financial. When young musicians require new uniforms, new choir robes, several additional sousaphones or other special equipment above and beyond normal budget allowances, Music Mothers' groups have risen to the occasion. White elephant sales, benefit bridge parties, ticket sales to movies and concerts, and a host of other fund-raising devices have been employed, invariably with success. In some high schools, music-booster groups are a part of the PTA organization. At the Cleveland Heights, Ohio, High School, for example, "Band and Orchestra Mothers," "Choir Mothers," "Drama Mothers," and even "Athletic Fathers" are all committees of the PTA. They function under the framework and control of this organization and are required to belong to it. Thus both groups benefit and close relationships are maintained with the school through the school principal who actively works with the PTA.

As with PTA's, there is more of potential value to booster organizations than may appear on the surface. They reflect a keen interest on the part of the community in one of the school's activities. Properly nurtured and channeled, such support can lead to broader interest, understanding and support of the total music program. This is an opportunity which the alert music teacher will not miss (Fig. 15.5).

While it is true that band equipment, uniforms, and choir robes should normally be purchased by the board of education as a legitimate part of the school program, we are considering here the community relationship aspects of the music boosters and similar organizations. The interest and enthusiasm of such groups are evidence of what can be done when parents and teachers get together on projects both recognize as important.

Service Clubs

The music teacher has frequent opportunities to present vocal and instrumental groups at civic club meetings. This is good from a music standpoint, but

San Diego Public Schools, San Diego, California.

Fig. 15.5. This attractive group of young musicians is "jamming" because they enjoy it. More to the point, is the fact that a bandstand in the Bay recreation park has been named for and dedicated to their Mission Bay High-School Band in recognition of its community service.

is of even more importance in terms of the community relations which can be developed. Looked upon in this light, several considerations must be kept in mind:

1. A civic club is usually a cross section of the business community. Some members are parents, all are taxpayers, all are important to the school which the music teacher represents.
2. A variety of musical tastes and backgrounds is inevitably found in groups of this kind. Consequently, the program should be chosen to please the majority—neither too heavy nor too light. And what is selected should be performed *well.*
3. Most adults are naturally interested in children. Thus a group presentation with a number of young people involved is usually better than two or three soloists.
4. Service clubs normally have a strict time schedule. Find out exactly how much time you have and stay within it. They will appreciate this and will be glad to have you back again.

In general, clubs and civic groups offer excellent opportunities to get acquainted with many fine people whom you might otherwise never get to know. It is a good idea, both personally and professionally, to join at least one such organization and to work at it actively. Get to know other members *personally.* Help them with their programs. A key opportunity is to provide music programs at various clubs when asked. Do it well, neither too much nor too little, and by all means emphasize the youngsters. Don't be apologetic or diffident about your work. You have every reason to be proud of it. Get acquainted with the program chairman and help out wherever you can—as a song leader perhaps, but in other capacities as well.

Remember, many community leaders are active in civic organizations. Their understanding and support are important to the schools and to your music program. Seek to earn their respect for you as a person.

Women's Clubs

Women's organizations, like service clubs, appreciate assistance with their programs. They are important to the school music teacher in that the feminine portion of the community usually wields considerable influence. As mothers, their interest in the schools is frequently more immediate and specific than that of their husbands.

Furthermore, a tremendous potential for constructive activity exists in many women's clubs. One has only to consider the hundreds of school bands that have gotten their uniforms through the efforts of band mothers' groups. Not infrequently other women's organizations cooperated actively. In some instances, most of the community became involved in one way or another. And often the leaders in the music mothers' organizations are also leaders in their church and women's club activities.

It is perhaps unnecessary to add that women's clubs can be a powerful influence upon the cultural development of a community. One may wince slightly at some of the misguided efforts which are occasionally made to eulogize culture for its own sake rather than for the richness it can bring to the lives of people who have been readied for it. But dedicated teachers of all the fine arts have as part of their mission in life the development among those with whom they work, of appreciation, enjoyment, and standards of taste for good music, good art, and good theater. Few stronger allies in this endeavor are to be found than the women's clubs of any community. Properly guided, women's organizations can be of inestimable value to the music teacher in his work with the schools and the community.

As an example, a highly worthwhile project, called *Men Who Make Music,* was initiated by the Junior League in Charlotte, N.C. With the cosponsorship of the Charlotte city schools and a local broadcasting company, a series of 13 symphonic programs by the Charlotte Little Symphony and the Jacksonville Symphony Orchestra were recorded on tape and made available to schools. An excellent Teachers Manual includes suggested art activities, correlated history assignments, biographies of the composers, music vocabulary, and a list of related books, records, and films.

Community Music Groups

Another segment of the community can be reached through music organizations outside of the school. These can provide both personal enjoyment for you and excellent opportunities to win understanding and support for your school music program.

The Community Chorus

The community chorus is normally made up of people who are there because they enjoy singing. If there is a chorus in your community, you may want to join. It is a good idea, in any case, to get acquainted with the director and to cooperate in whatever way seems appropriate. Be sure to avoid any suggestion of moving in and taking over. This is the wrong way to win friends and influence people!

Adult music organizations should have some contact with school music activities. Among other interests their members might have, one is that the schools provide the kind of music training which will result in more and better-trained members for their groups in the future. Joint performances of school and adult music organizations are a possible way to establish good community relationships and, at the same time, to provide useful experience for school music pupils (Fig. 15.6).

Church Choirs

The church choir is a type of adult music group in which interested high-school students are usually most welcome. Here is another proving ground for the kind of musical training provided in the high school. While the music teacher may wish to establish a music affiliation with his own church group, it will be well to get acquainted also with the pastors of other churches. Should assistance with their music problems be requested, it should be given when it can be without undue interference with your work at school or without spreading yourself too thin.

Civic Bands and Orchestras

Bands and orchestras are found less frequently in smaller communities than in large cities, but where they exist they are apt to represent the most sincere

Cleveland Heights Public Schools, Cleveland Heights, Ohio.

Fig. 15.6. At the annual concert in Cleveland Heights, Ohio, over 200 high-school alumni, many in their 30s and 40s, come up and join the choir for the grand finale.

and influential music lovers of the community. All that has been said concerning cooperation with community chorus and church choir groups applies here with equal emphasis. While opportunities for participation may be fewer with instrumental groups, they should be explored and utilized whenever appropriate.

A good example of community-school cooperation occurs regularly in Detroit. The board of directors of the Detroit Symphony makes it possible for school pupils to enjoy a specially arranged symphony concert at very low cost. Teachers and pupils prepare in advance for good listening by discussing the composers, hearing records of some of the program numbers, and studying the stories behind the compositions. Local stores and newspapers give special publicity to the event. The Board of Education arranges for bus transportation and pupils flock to the concert by the thousands (Fig. 15.7).

Summer Music Programs

Still another aspect of community life which is important to the high-school music teacher are summer music programs. Such programs frequently take the form of Concerts Under the Stars, camp programs including musical activities, community sings, and instructional programs in choral or instrumental music.

Detroit Public Schools, Detroit, Michigan.

Fig. 15.7. Each year thousands of Detroit youngsters enjoy symphony concert series at Ford Auditorium through the cooperation of civic groups, community leaders, and the schools.

Where summer music programs are professionally organized and conducted, the music teacher's activity may be confined to promoting interest in attendance on the part of his students and their families. In other cases, encouragement for a more active participation may be in order. The point is that summer music programs can provide a kind of continuity to the school music program as well as a measure of cultural interest and enjoyment of music in the community.

Schools often maintain a music activity program as part of their summer session (Fig. 15.8). Activities may be offered for credit, but often they are part of a recreational program which includes hobbies, crafts, sports, and, in some instances, summer camping opportunities.

Where the program is recreational in nature, our previous discussion of recreational programs applies. While you may be away during the summer months, you will none the less have an interest in what goes on. For a valuable measure of the long-range success of your music work in both the school and community is the extent to which music becomes an enjoyed and appreciated part of the lives of people *outside* of school.

Other Community Organizations

Recreational Programs

Recreational programs of some type are found in most towns and cities. While many such programs emphasize sports, increasing numbers today stress well-rounded programs of recreation which also include social activities, hobby groups, arts and crafts, music, and camping. Sometimes these are all-community projects under a qualified recreation director. In other cases, churches or schools

West Hartford Public Schools, West Hartford, Connecticut.

Fig. 15.8. This summer music center orchestra includes pupils of all ages. What benefits can come from summer music groups of this kind?

are the principal initiating agencies. In either type there is usually an out-of-school flavor which appeals to teen-agers through the informality and freedom to take or "leave alone" which characterize good recreation programs (Fig. 15.9). Thus there is a premium on the development of genuinely interesting activities for junior- and senior-high-school boys and girls.

In any case, music has a role which the music teacher will wish to enhance as best he can. If there is a director of recreation, the natural course is to get acquainted with him and offer to assist in any appropriate manner. In the case of church or school recreation programs, the approach may differ but the purpose is the same. Once communication has been established, suggestions may be made. A community "sing" may be in order for some occasion, a Hi-Fi Club might appeal to a certain group of young people, or a dance band might be a welcome addition to the program. You can assess the possibilities for recreational programs as you become familiar with what is going on.

A note of caution is in order here. It is not assumed that the high-school music teacher is going to become personally involved in all of these activities. To do so might be unwise and would certainly be impractical. But when one knows his community well, he can assist many worthwhile developments by suggesting other competent persons who will enjoy doing them. In any case, his awareness and interest will be appreciated.

Detroit Public Schools, Detroit, Michigan.

Fig. 15.9. Music plays a role in an informal "sing" at a metropolitan youth center.

Davis summarizes it well in saying:

> Sally is going to work for the people of the community of Metropolis. She wants them to understand that she is at their service, yet she must never forget her professional standing and dignity. She must keep in touch with all affairs having to do with music in the community and at the same time not assume so many responsibilities that she will be unable to carry on her work effectively.[4]

Public Libraries

Good record collections and listening rooms for use of individuals or groups are frequently found in public libraries. The expanding concept of libraries today gives them a more active role in community life than has been true in the past. From a depository for books and magazines and hushed reading rooms,

[4] Ennis Davis, *More Than a Pitch Pipe*, C. C. Birchard, 1941, pp. 36–37.

the library in many communities is developing as a center for discussion groups, for 16 mm. film circulation and, in some cases, for musical activities. Where this is true, the possibility of working cooperatively with the public library is one which should be explored by the teacher of music as another means of bringing music to the community.

In Michigan, for example, public libraries in 18 cities circulate phonograph records, and a number of these libraries have listening-hour programs for the public at scheduled times each week or month. In the Detroit, Lansing, and Ann Arbor areas, radio and television programs on musical subjects are actively supported by the public libraries. In other cities, libraries extend their facilities to community groups and assist in sponsoring programs dealing with the history or appreciation of music.

Although the pattern for library participation in musical activities is just beginning to emerge in most communities, the opportunity for giving assistance and direction to such development in terms of community needs may be highly worthwhile. In any case, this is one of the agencies to be investigated in the community in which you teach.

Community Music Associations

Much of the present chapter has been devoted to the development of school-community relations from the standpoint of the teacher of school music and of the school music program. In many cities and towns across the nation, community activity in music has been rapidly increased through Community Music Associations which represent and encourage all of the musical interests of the community. These activities include everything from rhythm bands to symphony concerts.

One of the first Community Music Associations was organized in Flint, Michigan, in 1917 to function as a clearing house for all things musical in that city which might enrich the lives of the populace. The Flint Association is typical of many now operating throughout the United States. Working through existing agencies such as industries, service clubs, women's clubs, churches, schools, hospitals, etc., the Association provides stimulation and assistance to music groups and activities of all kinds.

The Flint group is now a Community Chest agency operating primarily in the recreation program of the city. The Los Angeles Municipal Bureau of Music provides a director and accompanist for a large number of youth and adult choruses sponsored in various parts of the city by civic organizations who defray most of the other costs. Independence, Missouri, has a Community Music Association which supports an orchestra having a regular concert season, sponsors a multiple-piano ensemble, and annually stages a festival of school concerts and a church choir festival.[5]

The organization of community music associations and councils is an important part of the program of the American Music Conference. Working closely with the Music Educators National Conference and with other organizations of professional and amateur musicians, and with education, recreation, and community welfare groups, the AMC has a professional field staff to assist in community music workshops and similar projects. Printed and audiovisual materials on the subject are available from the AMC for the asking.

Music on a community-wide basis is an ultimate goal of any well-conceived music program in the schools (Figs. 15.10 and 15.11). The AMC committee states the following, given on p. 157.

Cleveland Heights Public Schools, Cleveland Heights, Ohio.

Fig. 15.10. Attendance at public concerts is one measure of community interest in the school music program. This annual concert in Cleveland Heights, Ohio, is reported always sold out with 2000 paid admissions.

[5] These and other community music association programs are described in *Music for Everybody*, an illustrated report of the Committee on School-Community Relations and Activities of the Music Educators National Conference, a Department of the National Education Association, 1950, pp. 10 ff.

Fig. 15.11. As an inducement for excellence, high-school students are occasionally invited to play with the Detroit Symphony on a "School Concert" program.

Detroit Public Schools, Detroit, Michigan.

. . . the contemporary music educator realizes he can secure the most permanent good and the best ultimate results in the music education program by cooperating in the over-all musical activities of his community. To the modern music educator, there is no dividing line between the classroom and the community, so far as musical affairs are concerned, because people in the community and people who are still in the schools share and share alike in opportunities to listen and to participate—if a music program is so set up that this is possible.[6]

THE CODE OF ETHICS FOR SCHOOL MUSIC TEACHERS

One mark of a profession is a code of ethics which is understood and practiced by its members and recognized by the lay public. It is understood and accepted, for example, that one can safely reveal confidential matters to his lawyer or minister. He knows that his doctor will not discuss his ailments with

[6] *Ibid.*, p. 14.

anyone not entitled to know. These are matters of professional integrity. Similarly, in accepting a teaching position, the teacher accepts a code of ethics. This code has been developed over generations of teaching and is based upon the experience and judgment of thousands of teachers.[7] The code governs music teachers as it does all other teachers. Because of the special conditions of their work in communities, teachers of music have additional ethical considerations which they must practice in their daily work. Several of these have been discussed earlier in this chapter in another context. Since your welfare as a teacher and the success of your music program are so dependent upon your knowledge and practice of appropriate ethics, give particular attention to this section.

Relations with Professional Musicians

In general, the professional musician is as interested in music as a social and cultural force in the community as is the music teacher. Both have essential roles to play in music. The music educator fosters, as best he can, the study of music among young people and develops interest in better music among all the people of the community. The professional musician strives to improve musical taste by performing musical works with the utmost artistry and skill at his command. His organizations serve as inspiration to young musicians and help maintain their later interest as patrons of musical performance.

Both the music teacher and the professional musician are "pro's" in a very real sense, but an essential difference exists between them in the fact that the professional musician depends upon performance opportunties for his livelihood. While the music educator should also be an accomplished musician, he has chosen teaching rather than musical performance as his profession. Thus, were he or his school music organizations to undertake performances which might otherwise have served as employment for professional musicians, a basic conflict of interest would inevitably occur.

The distinction between the province of the music educator and that of the professional musician has been worked out with considerable care by the MENC, the American Federation of Musicians, and the American Association of School Administrators. The result is a Code of Ethics authorized and agreed to by executive action of both musical organizations and by the American Association of School Administrators. In essence it says that music education, including teaching, demonstration, and performance for nonprofit, noncommercial, and noncompetitive functions, is the province of the music educator; and that

[7] For a clear statement of ethics for teachers see *N.E.A. Handbook for Local, State and National Associations, 1948–1949*, National Education Association, 1949, pp. 384–390; also Robert W. Richey, *Planning for Teaching*, New York, McGraw-Hill, 1952, pp. 255–260.

the field of entertainment, irrespective of the nonavailability of funds, is the province of the professional musician.

In order that definitions may be clearly understood with respect to what specifically is and is not included under the headings of music education and entertainment, and in order that the conditions under which the Code applies may likewise be understood, it is recommended that the complete statement of the Code on pp. 509–511 be read with care. In effect, this Code is a part of your contract to teach music in any secondary school in the United States.

Relations with Music Merchants

Music teachers work with expensive equipment and frequently with large amounts of it. This equipment is usually ordered from a dealer or distributer suggested by the music teacher. Some dealers give better service than others, are more convenient, or perhaps have a better understanding of what is needed. Occasionally there is one retailer whose stock is far superior to any other in the area. In such situations, the music teacher may unintentionally get himself and his school into an embarrassing position unless he is aware of what is expected of him.

The first thing expected is that he will recognize as unethical any transaction in which he personally profits, directly or indirectly, from the sale of instruments to his pupils. Commissions of any sort are to be scrupulously avoided. Accordingly, he refuses to become personally involved with any manufacturer, jobber, or dealer, or to recommend to his students or to outsiders one make or dealer over another. To do so is to invite suspicion of his integrity or, at best, of his good judgment. A teacher's reputation is one of his most valuable and irreplaceable assets. His good name must be above reproach or he undermines the confidence of his associates, his students, and the community. Without such confidence, his effectiveness as a teacher becomes impaired to the point where his continued usefulness to the school may be questioned.

Does this mean that he should refuse advice to students and parents in the matter of instrument purchases? On the contrary, he should give whatever reasonable assistance he can, including suggestions of several good makes and sources of suitable instruments. Furthermore, he can legitimately examine and test the suitability of all musical instruments and merchandise purchased by his pupils. Should any be found deficient, he not only may but very definitely *should* get in touch with the dealer and expect immediate adjustment.

The retail dealer also has a Code by which he is expected to abide. Should he fail, neglect, or refuse to cooperate with school music teachers in satisfactorily fulfilling their or their students' legitimate needs, the teacher may and should direct such business elsewhere. Details of the Code for Relations with Music Merchants will be found on pp. 511–512.

Relations with Private Music Teachers

Several ethical considerations apply to relations with private music teachers in the community. One can recommend two or more competent private teachers when requested by parents, but not one above others unless, of course, there is only one who teaches a particular instrument.

As a public employee, the school music teacher is seldom justified in giving private lessons on the side. To do so is to compete with private teachers depending on such work for a livelihood. Where conditions appear to justify private teaching by the school music teacher, it should be undertaken only with the approval of the appropriate school administrators.

Finally, it is unethical and in poor taste to discuss with pupils or parents the work of another music teacher, public or private, in such a manner as to deprecate or otherwise injure his professional reputation. Less obvious but equally important is the careful avoidance of claims for full credit for the achievement of pupils who are or who were also under instruction from another music teacher. The ethical teacher in music or any other subject scrupulously avoids reflections or implications of discredit upon a predecessor or a colleague. A detailed statement of the Code of Ethics in relations with private music teachers is given on pp. 512–513.

SUMMARY

The community is something more than a town or a city. It is a complex—and, in these times, a rapidly changing—combination of people and interests. There are, in fact, a number of different communities within the service area of any school having more than a few pupils. Good schools and good school systems are integral parts of the communities they serve, and should be both responsive to their needs and active in serving them. The community school is based upon the concept that schools and communities benefit mutually and substantially from working closely together. A significant factor in the success of this relationship is the success of individual teachers in becoming an effective part of the communities in which they teach.

The school music program is particularly affected by the kind of community relationships which the music teacher can establish. Parent-teacher organizations, music boosters, service clubs, community music groups, church groups, women's clubs, public libraries, and community recreation programs, among others, are natural and important avenues for building good will and support for music activities both in and out of school. Many cities and towns across the nation have established community music associations to coordinate and encourage all musical interests of the community. The good music educator cooperates and assists in the development of community music interests to the best of his ability, because he knows that the most permanent benefits to the school music program will be served through strong community support of the schools and the school music program.

In his community and professional relationships, the school music teacher is guided by clearly defined ethical considerations which he must understand and observe. Besides the code of ethics applying to all teachers, the teacher of school music has codes of ethics governing relationships with professional musicians, with music merchants, and with private music teachers.

SUGGESTED ACTIVITIES

1. A close friend is going to your home-town high school to teach music next year. What could you tell him about the community, its people, churches, and organizations that would help him to get a good start as a teacher there?
2. What differences would you expect to find in a community school as compared with a school of the more traditional type? Consider probable differences in atmosphere and activities within the schools as well as differences in community relationships.
3. As a music teacher, plan a suitable school music program for a Rotary Club luncheon meeting in a community which you know. Give reasons for the solos, ensembles, or groups used, the selections played or sung, and the length of program planned.
4. Do the same thing for a PTA program in which the chairman has given you the major portion of an evening program.
5. As a new teacher of music you make a point of getting acquainted with the music retailers in your city. A few weeks later a representative of one of the dealers calls on you and offers to donate a new sousaphone for the band. What action would you take, and for what reasons?
6. As you are a talented pianist (or other instrumentalist), several mothers appeal to you to give private lessons to their children even though there are private music teachers in the town. How would you handle this situation?
7. The level of interest in music in the community in which you go to teach is quite limited. Analyze the situation and suggest steps for you to take over a two-year period to help bring about an increase in the community's musical interests.

SELECTED READINGS

Barnes, John B., "Barriers to Community Leadership for Teachers," *Phi Delta Kappan*, November, 1956, pp. 59–61.

Basic Concepts in Music Education, 57th Yearbook, Part I, National Society for the Study of Education, 1958.

Graham, Floyd F., *Public Relations and Music Education*, Exposition Press, 1954.

Lake, Ernest G., "The School Staff—Each Member an Ambassador," *Association of Secondary School Principals Bulletin*, September, 1960, pp. 39–43.

Leeder, Joseph A., and Wm. S. Haynie, *Music Education in the High School*, Prentice-Hall, 1958, pp. 206–212, 295–300.

MacLean, Malcolm S., and Edwin A. Lee, *Change and Process in Education*, Holt, Rinehart and Winston, 1956, pp. 329–335, 463–469, 471–490.

Melby, Ernest O., *Administering Community Education*, Prentice-Hall, 1955, pp. 36–57, 238–258, 281–311.

Music for Everybody, Music Educators National Conference, National Education Association, 1950, pp. 1–60.

Music and Public Relations, Music Educators National Conference, National Education Association, 1958.

Pierce, Truman M., Edward C. Merrill, Jr., Craig Wilson, and Ralph B. Kimbrough, *Community Leadership for Public Education*, Prentice-Hall, 1955, pp. 3–38, 59–95.

Seay, Maurice F., and Ferris N. Crawford, *The Community School and Community Improvement*, Lansing, Michigan, Supt. of Public Instruction, 1954, pp. 7–16, 186–190.

Snyder, Keith D., *School Music Administration and Supervision*, Allyn and Bacon, 1959, pp. 133–155.

Van Camp, Leonard, "Public Relations and the Secondary School Music Educator," *Music Educators Journal*, November–December, 1961, pp. 81–89.

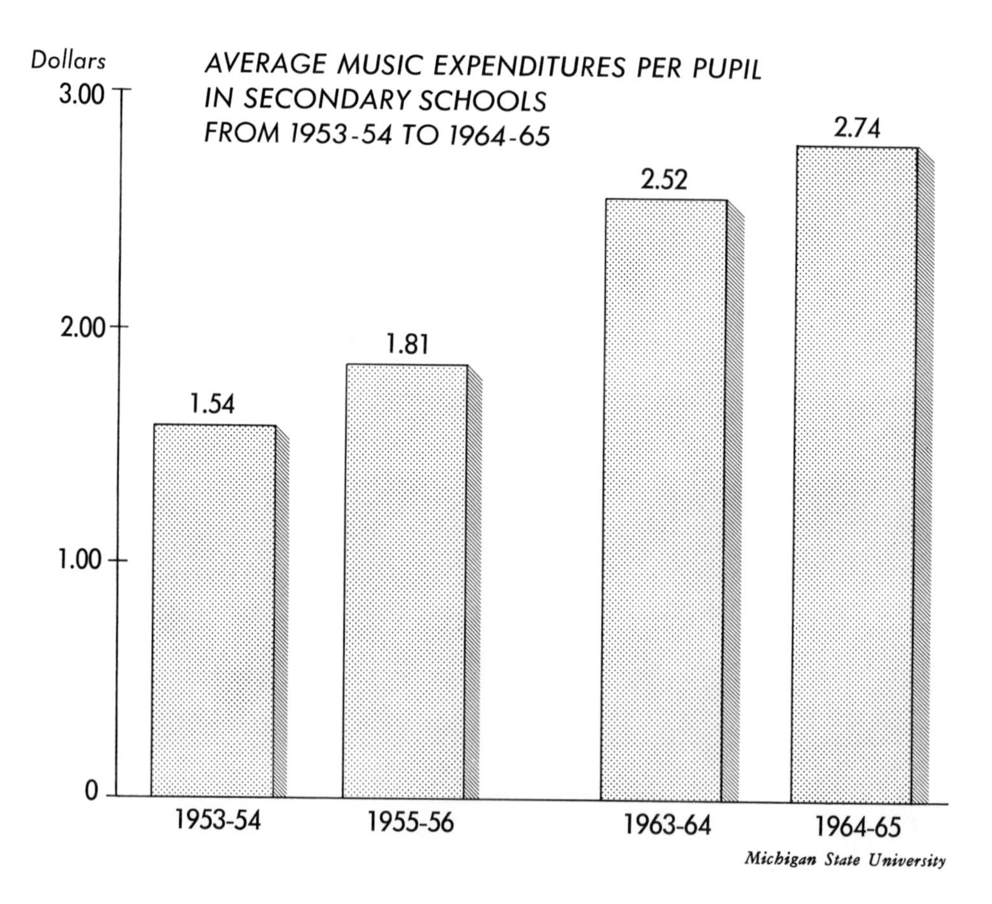
Dollars
AVERAGE MUSIC EXPENDITURES PER PUPIL
IN SECONDARY SCHOOLS
FROM 1953-54 TO 1964-65
3.00
2.00
1.00
0
1.54
1.81
2.52
2.74
1953-54
1955-56
1963-64
1964-65
Michigan State University

CHAPTER

16

School Administration and the Music Program

As you turn to this chapter you may wonder why, as a teacher of music, you need to be concerned with the subject of school administration. The answer is simple. You will be a much more effective teacher with a more successful music program if you understand your school's administration. This understanding will enable you to work more intelligently and more effectively with your principal and superintendent as well as with other supervisors and teachers. If you understand the roles played by the board of education, the superintendent, and other school officials, and what is expected of them, you will know a great deal more about the whole educational "team" of which you are an important part. Many uncertainties about your own role can be avoided, and you can proceed with added confidence and pleasure in your work.

STRUCTURE OF RESPONSIBILITY IN THE SCHOOL SYSTEM

One of the first points to note is that education is basically a function of the state rather than of either the local or the national government. The original constitution of the United States made no provision for education, thus leaving this responsibility to the several states. Each of the 50 states has, therefore, established its own educational system. Almost every state delegates a large amount of its responsibility for schools to smaller governmental units such as the county, the city, or the school district. The state normally sets the standards for schools, accredits teachers and administrative officers, and establishes the laws under which schools must operate. Many states likewise provide substantial amounts of financial support for the schools to insure that minimum standards can be met.

One might ask at this point why the state does not attempt to operate the public schools as it does state colleges and universities. Hawaii *does* have a state system of public education, and Alaska operates a system for about one third of the public school enrollment. In twelve states, the county is the principal administrative unit for the public schools, but in 36 states some form of local school district continues to be the chief unit under which such schools are organized and operated.[1]

Reorganization of School Districts

Since the mid-1940s thousands of small local school districts have combined or consolidated with adjacent school districts so as to provide a broader tax base and sufficient enrollment for an improved educational program. The "little red schoolhouse" is rapidly becoming extinct except in remote areas. In spite of the promise of better schools, however, parents and other citizens stubbornly resisted consolidation for many years. Prominent among the various reasons for this resistance was a strong feeling that local operation and control of the schools was somehow right and proper.

That feeling had a strong historical basis. In the early days of our nation the first public schools were built, financed and operated by the people of local towns and villages. As the nation moved westward the people established schools on the frontier in the same way. Thus, a pattern of local control developed which was destined to persist for a century or more.

The State and Federal Role

Later, in the early 1900s, states began providing financial support to local districts in order that minimum standards could be met. The federal government also helped the states with money for special programs such as agriculture and home economics for high schools under the Smith Hughes Act of 1917, the Civilian Conservation Corps and National Youth Administration programs of the depression years, and the hot-lunch program which still is found in schools across the nation. State departments of education administered and dispensed the state funds and, as a rule, the federal funds to local school districts.

States thus began to play increasing roles in local school affairs. Additional developments in reorganization of local school units during the 1940s and 1950s, steadily increasing fiscal support from the state to local school districts, and the administration of stepped-up federal support under the National Defense Education Act of 1958 have further increased the direct participation of the state government in local school affairs. Throughout this period of development and

[1] See Bureau of the Census, *Public School Systems in the United States, 1961–1962*, Preliminary Report No. 3, Washington, D.C., U.S. Department of Commerce, 1962, p. 1.

change, the importance of local support and participation in public school affairs has not been questioned. Even as state and federal participation have increased steadily, these agencies, as well as professional educators have strongly encouraged adult education, community school programs, citizens committees and other means of enlisting and developing local participation in school affairs. In the final analysis, the schools belong to the people and, so long as inequities can be avoided, school systems tend to function best under the close relationships possible within local or community school districts.

State institutions, while created and maintained by popular assent, are inevitably more remote from the individual citizen. Instead of the few hundred or few thousand people from a local area who are involved in a school-board election, hundreds of thousands of voters may go to the polls in a state election. This mass of people in itself tends to impart a more impersonal quality to state institutions than to local agencies. Also, the fact that the state capitol is usually some distance away from most of the state's people helps contribute to the apparent remoteness of state agencies from individual citizens.

Thus, because schools have been locally operated since colonial times; because the people like it that way and have a personal interest in their schools; because local interest and participation are necessary for good schools; and, finally, because most states are too large in both population and area to maintain a high level of public interest and support for public schools if they were state operated—such schools have remained largely local institutions even though education is inherently a state rather than a local function.

The Board of Education

Occasionally, when you go for an interview in a small or medium-sized community, the superintendent introduces you to one or more of the school-board members. They are local citizens with a keen interest in the schools. Usually they are community leaders and think of themselves as representatives of the people of the community although they are also agents of the state and must operate in accordance with state laws.

It is the board's function to see that the schools are well and properly operated, but it is *not* its function to operate or administer the schools themselves. Like the board of directors in a corporation, they hire the best executive they can find—the school superintendent—and allow him, as the professional expert, to administer the schools. He is directly responsible to the board of education, and the board is directly responsible to the people of the school district. The board, with the superintendent's assistance and guidance, establishes the general policies on which the schools are to operate, and the superintendent then administers them accordingly (Fig. 16.1).

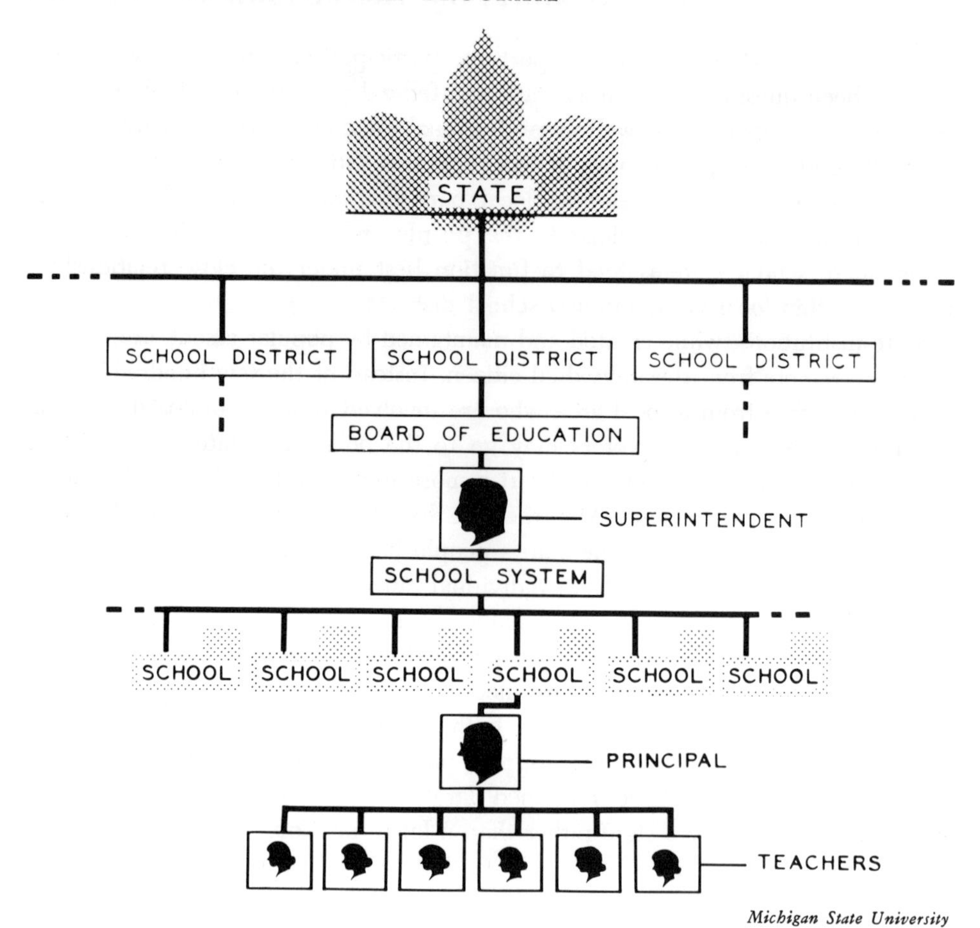

Michigan State University

Fig. 16.1. Legal responsibility for the schools in most states flows from the state to some form of local or county school district. Boards of education in these districts hire superintendents to run the school system and authority is delegated by them to principals and teachers in individual schools.

Thus the board of education sets the school budget, passes on salary schedules, decides on the school calendar, and determines, upon the advice of the superintendent, such matters as whether or not the high-school band should accept an invitation to play at the state basketball tournament. It is the board which issues teachers' contracts, determines when new buildings are to be built, and goes to the people with a bond issue campaign. All of these matters and many more are carried on in accordance with state laws and regulations.

The Superintendent of Schools

The superintendent is the top executive officer of the local school system and as such is directly responsible for all that goes on in the schools. As you can readily appreciate, this is a large order. It means that the superintendent must be a competent professional educator, businessman, administrator, and public relations expert—all rolled into one. It means also that many of his responsibilities must be delegated. Actual supervision of the educational program, for example, is left largely to the principals assisted by supervisors and coordinators. In large systems there is apt to be a business manager, a curriculum director or director of instruction, and a corps of special coordinators and consultants. City systems of more than 100,000 population frequently have several assistant superintendents who are delegated such responsibilities as elementary education, secondary education, instruction and in-service education, business management, and the like.

It is not difficult to comprehend the magnitude of the superintendent's responsibilities. Nor is it hard to understand the very real concern of many superintendents that the increasing complexities of modern school administration are forcing them further and further away from contact with the most important aspect of the school's program—what goes on in the classroom.

Principals, Supervisors, and Coordinators

Classroom activities fall largely within the immediate province of the administrator of the individual school—the school principal. He is assisted by a number of special supervisors who go from school to school and who are directly under the superintendent or one of his assistants. Within the school the principal may also have the help of building coordinators of audiovisual materials, librarians, guidance counselors, and others. In most cases such coordinators also have teaching responsibilities.

The primary responsibility of principals, supervisors, and coordinators is the instructional program itself. The principal conducts faculty meetings on instructional problems, develops in-service education programs for his teachers, plans curriculum-committee organization, and frequently consults with teachers on matters of classroom instruction. He is the administrator having more direct contact with teachers than any other official of the school system. Thus it is the principal with whom the music teacher or supervisors should discuss and implement music plans for the individual school.

The Music Coordinator

The music coordinator's responsibilities vary according to the size of the city or school system. In the small community with one or two elementary schools, he is likely to do all of the teaching of music and is more a traveling teacher than a supervisor. In medium-sized cities the music coordinator's time is spread more thinly. Since there are more classes than he can possibly teach himself, he must help the regular elementary teachers teach most of their own music lessons. This assistance is normally given through teachers' meetings, demonstration lessons, song outlines, and manuals or courses of study to be used as guides. The music supervisor continues to teach some classes on a traveling schedule.[2]

In large city systems there is frequently a director or supervisor of instrumental music, a director or supervisor of vocal music, and a supervisor of elementary music. In very large cities, each of these may have one or more assistants. It is important to note, however, that all of these positions are under the general supervision of a director of music education and all must work together in the support and development of the total music program of the schools.

No situation works well for long without a clear delineation of responsibility and authority. In short, there have to be both "chiefs and indians" for satisfactory results. Accordingly, where there is more than one person involved in a secondary-school music program, it is normally best to have one designated as being in charge and the others as his assistants in specific areas.

STAFF RELATIONSHIPS AND RESPONSIBILITIES

In the small system the music teacher frequently has to wear several different hats. As a teacher of music classes he is directly responsible to the school principal. If he is called upon to assist, also, with the elementary-school music program, he becomes a coordinator or supervisor under the superintendent or director of instruction. In the latter circumstance, or should he have an assistant in some phase of the music work, he may become in addition the director of music for the school system. In order to work effectively in all of these capacities, it is important for him to clearly understand his responsibilities and the staff relationships involved.

The Superintendent of Schools

The superintendent of schools is administrative head of the school system, as we have noted previously. Thus it is his responsibility to make final recommendations to the board of education on the budget, on new positions needed, on new programs to be established, and on a host of other matters. It is important that he be well informed about your music program and willing to support it warmly. The superintendent's information on what you are accomplishing comes from a number of sources: your principal or supervisor, the community,

[2] See *Music in American Education*, Music Educators Source Book No. 2, Music Educators National Conference, 1955, p. 29.

parents, other teachers, and perhaps students themselves. It also comes from observation of your concerts, your reports and recommendations, and in smaller systems, from an occasional personal conference with you. Unless you are working directly under the superintendent, it is usually inappropriate to go to him directly with requests, recommendations, or complaints. To do so is to "go over your superior's head. Unless the latter consents or suggests that you do so, this is one of the surest ways of engendering mistrust and a poor relationship with the individual whose confidence and support you most need.

The School Principal

Principals and supervisors have distinctly different types of responsibilities. The principal is the chief administrative officer of an individual school and is responsible both for its administration and its educational program. All principals operate their schools in accordance with principles and practices set forth by the superintendent, who, in turn, executes the policies established by the board of education for the entire school system. Thus, the line of responsibility extends from the people to the board of education, to the superintendent, to the principals, and to the teachers in individual schools.

It might appear from this explanation that the administrative organization of a school system is military in nature—that the superintendent gives an order, the principal passes it down, and the teacher jumps to obey. This is quite contrary to actual practice in any good school system. The successful school administrator today recognizes his chief responsibility as being one of educational leadership in which not only teachers, supervisors, and principals, but also the students and people of the community participate actively in the determination of what their schools shall be and how they shall be operated. Under such conditions of democratic administration, constructive suggestions and creative ideas are sincerely encouraged, and decisions are worked out cooperatively where possible, with maximum benefit to all concerned.

Supervisors and Coordinators

The supervisor or coordinator of school music frequently has important administrative duties, particularly in small school systems. He may conduct meetings of classroom and music teachers and guide the selection of materials and techniques so that all music work is well coordinated in terms of the total music program. With other teachers and administrators he helps determine standards of performance, class schedules, music budgets, equipment requirements, and other music needs of the school system. He is likely to have extensive responsibility for record-keeping, maintenance of instruments, support of community music programs, suitable publicity and other promotional work for music activities, and general development of the music program.[3]

In addition, there is the important task of helping other teachers do a better job of music teaching. This is the meaning of supervision today. Because the terms "supervision" acquired some unpleasant connotations in years past (such as inspection and teacher-rating), many school systems have adopted the title of *Music Coordinator* or *Music Consultant* instead. While there is no fine line of distinction between administration and supervision in the broad meaning of the terms, there is an important distinction in the staff relationships of individuals performing these functions.

Supervisors, as such, have no administrative authority over the teachers with whom they work. The supervisor's function is one of service of a high professional order. His objective is to help bring about the best music instruction possible. Since in a school system of several schools he cannot do all of the music teaching himself, his success as a supervisor is largely dependent upon his ability to work well with other teachers (Fig. 16.2). This relationship is a precious thing

Michigan State University

Fig. 16.2. The music coordinator's ability to work well with teachers is a major factor in the success of the music program.

[3] A succinct and helpful statement of the administrative duties of music directors in small and large city school systems is given in *Music in American Education, op. cit.*, pp. 18–20.

based upon mutual respect, a sympathetic understanding and regard for people, and a high degree of competence both in music and in teaching. As in almost all lines of work involving people, human relations are of paramount importance in music teaching. For the supervisor, good working relationships are vital. "Success in the music-education field is firmly grounded in two major areas: (1) self-confidence in the technical mastery of music, and (2) the ability to get along with people."[4]

Where a number of schools are involved, the supervisor is normally on the staff of the superintendent of schools. He may, and frequently does, teach a regular schedule of classes, however, and in this capacity he is responsible, like any other teacher, to the principal of his school. His supervisory relationships with other school principals are, as with their teachers, of a permissive and professional-service nature. The music supervisor needs the confidence and cooperative support of the principal of a school in order to work effectively with the teachers in that school.

INSTRUCTIONAL NEEDS FOR MUSIC TEACHING

Teachers as a group are dedicated to their work with young people. The challenges of such work and its rewards are substantial in any area of teaching. The young man or woman who enters the field of music teaching, however, has certain demands and, if successful, a degree of satisfaction and pleasure which are somewhat unique.

On the one hand, the instructor of music is usually called upon for more hours of teaching, more public performances, and more community activity than are teachers in other fields. On the other hand, his primary objective is the pleasant one of helping people throughout the school and community to enjoy music through successful participation. Much hard work is involved in reaching such a goal. But a good job elicits ready appreciation by students and parents alike to a degree found less frequently in other fields of educational work (Fig. 16.3).

Staff Competencies

Joe Walters came into the small community of Middlebury as a band man. With much zeal and energy he dug into the task of developing the high-school band. He gave class instrumental lessons, started a training band, and had frequent sectional rehearsals. Within six months he had achieved considerable prog-

[4] Floyd F. Graham, *Public Relations in Music Education*, Exposition Press, 1954, p. 18.

Oakland Public Schools, Oakland, California.

Fig. 16.3. The degree of interest in music as an important function of the schools is well illustrated in this junior-high-school music festival in Oakland, California. An orchestra of 270 pieces and a chorus of 1200 perform before an audience of 8000 people.

ress. It appeared that Middlebury would do much better in the spring music festival this year.

Mr. Johansen, the superintendent, called Joe in one day, complimented him on the progress the band was making and then added, "Joe, it bothers me that we have no other music emphasis in our high school than band. Shouldn't we be doing something with vocal music and possibly orchestra?" Somewhat surprised at the question because it had not been raised when he was being interviewed for the band position, Joe none the less agreed that the present music program was one-sided and that a choir and one or more glee clubs were needed to give it better balance. Mr. Johansen then indicated that he knew an additional teacher should be hired to take on the vocal work, but since that would not be possible for another year or two, would Joe be willing to do what he could about it?

Joe would. He had done some rapid mental arithmetic while the superintendent was speaking. By reducing the sectional rehearsals somewhat (the sections were coming along pretty well now and could perhaps spare a few of the extra rehearsals), he could work in one vocal group, maybe two. And Mr. Johansen was right—there should be vocal groups in the music program. Only—well, Joe didn't know much about vocal work, though perhaps it was enough to get started. He'd try.

Is this an isolated example? No. Less than half of the nation's high schools are large enough in enrollment to employ two full-time music teachers. Thus if there is to be a well-rounded music program, one teacher will be largely responsible for it. If it is to be a good program for all pupils, the music teacher must be competent in more than one phase of music education.

Joe worked hard. In fact he worked harder than would have been necessary had he possessed a background of vocal as well as of instrumental music. The results in the vocal work were unsatisfactory to him and he knew that the band was not as good as he was capable of making it. Worry, strain, and constant work took much of the pleasure and satisfaction from his teaching and reduced his effectiveness generally. After two years he resigned to take a position in another small school system.

What is the moral of Joe's experience? Not that he was wrong to try. That was something that neither he nor his superintendent could in good conscience avoid. The problem lay in Joe's own musical preparation and perhaps in the college he attended. He was overly specialized for his own personal and professional good. In consequence, Middlebury's students and Joe both suffered.

There is no substitute for a solid foundation in any field of professional work, and music is no exception. Even had Joe Walters not been asked to start a vocal music program, with a broad musical background he would have been more successful as a music teacher. This general knowledge would enable him to work more intelligently in a music program in either a small or a large school system. It would also be important to the possible consideration of him as a department head or music director at some later time.

Another type of preparation important to the prospective music teacher is work in education. The once widely held belief that anyone could teach who knew enough about his subject is becoming recognized for the fallacy that it has always been. Communicative ability of a high order; imagination and a personality which is pleasing to adolescent pupils; a sense of humor; understanding; respect and affection for pupils and an ability to command their respect and affection—all are qualities which a good teacher possesses. The teacher of music is no exception (Fig. 16.4).

It is not enough that he [the music teacher] knows music—he must know how to *teach* music. He must be sensitive to the qualitative and the quantitative responsibilities of his profession. . . . [He] must demand quality of the highest order from the work of his pupils. It is not good teaching of the art of music to do otherwise. Yet *at the same time* . . . the standards set must be carefully and frequently measured so that

San Diego Public Schools, San Diego, California.

Fig. 16.4. The effective music teacher needs more than a knowledge of music. What additional desirable qualities does this teacher appear to have?

'musical education' is not the result for a few pupils, but that education through music is the result for all the pupils.[5]

The report states further that the good music teacher must be expert in human relationships, he must have intimate acquaintance with both subject matter and teaching methods, and he must be able to counsel wisely and to guide learning. For this he needs sound teacher-education preparation in his own field and in those of general education and general culture. Further, he must be able to sell his subject to pupils, teachers, administrators, and parents, and yet be able to see the pupil as an individual and the school program as a whole.

Truly this is a sizable order, but a challenging and stimulating one, and it is no more than what is expected of any good secondary-school teacher in any subject field. Of such people are fine schools made.

[5] "The Function of Music in the Secondary School Curriculum," in the *Bulletin of National Association of Secondary School Principals*, November, 1952, pp. 8–9.

Scheduling

The scheduling of organizations and ensembles has been discussed in Chapter 11. We shall be concerned with scheduling here chiefly from the administrator's standpoint. We look at music's place in the total school program and include music subjects as well as organizations.

Generally speaking, most music subjects in the secondary school are elective. The principal exception is General Music in the junior high school. This is recommended for a minimum of 90 minutes per week in two periods as a required subject at the seventh- and eighth-grade levels.[6] In Grade 9, one semester should be required if possible, but in present practice General Music classes above Grade 8 are usually elective.

An elective course theoretically presents no scheduling problems. It can be fitted in where it conflicts least with required courses. In practice, however, an elective status for General Music tends to defeat its purpose since relatively few pupils may be free to take it should they wish to do so.

The problem of scheduling such elective courses as music theory and music literature in small high schools where it is difficult to get sufficient enrollment for a class each year, is frequently solved by scheduling these classes in alternate years. Sometimes when even this cannot be done, the General Music course is used as a place to teach music theory and music literature. Under this arrangement it is desirable to section the General Music class, one section being set up for pupils with a musical background, the other for those without prior musical experience. In general, the placing of band, orchestra, and vocal group meetings before school, after school, or at noon is avoided by school administrators whenever possible. They recognize that such scheduling penalizes pupils interested in music and tends to keep music participation in the category of extracurricular activities. In a six-period day, academic subjects normally take four periods and physical education the equivalent of another half period. This leaves one and one-half open periods per day. The following plan is suggested by an experienced music director who has worked successfully with it under these circumstances:

1. Let orchestra alternate with band the same period every other day. During the football season let band meet three times and orchestra twice; second semester, during the concert season, let orchestra meet three times and band twice.
2. Mixed chorus can be scheduled in the remaining two and one-half periods left open by physical education. As many as three sections of girls' glee clubs and two sections of boys' glee clubs may then be staggered during other periods.
3. Keep the orchestra, band, and chorus periods free of single section classes insofar

[6] *Function of Music in the Secondary-School Curriculum*, *op. cit.*, p. 10.

as possible. Place in these periods only those one section classes which seem to draw few musicians (such as shop and agriculture).
4. Obtain from the music director the names of music pupils before making individual schedules.
5. Stabilize the schedule from year to year for a wider choice. For example, if speech and physics conflict, a pupil may take speech during the junior year and physics as a senior.
6. Ensembles and small sectional groups will usually have to get together after school hours or in their homes. With proper incentive and a good start, they frequently do very well. Without a solid in-school schedule for music organizations, there will be few ensembles in any event.[7]

Another pattern is suggested in the following schedule for a minimum program in a senior high school with one music room, one music teacher, and six- or seven-period day.[8] Instrumental classes may be arranged for free periods. However, the tendency to fill *all* free periods with instrumental or other groups should be avoided. At least one free period per day should normally be set aside for planning and preparation. The following is just one example of music program scheduling:

Period	Monday	Tuesday	Wednesday	Thursday	Friday
1	Orchestra	General Music	Orchestra	General Music	Orchestra
2		Music Appreciation		Music Appreciation	
3	Choir Mixed Chorus		Choir Mixed Chorus		Choir Mixed Chorus
4	Lunch	Lunch	Lunch	Lunch	Lunch
5	Boy's Choir	Girl's Choir	Boy's Choir	Girl's Choir	Boy's Choir
6	Band		Band		Band
7		Theory		Theory	
Extra Period	Rehearsals, clubs, etc.				

Block-of-time scheduling, instead of rigid 50-minute periods, is being tried in a number of forward-looking secondary schools around the nation as part of a general overhaul of curriculum and reorganization to meet current educational needs. As developed by the high-school faculty in Holland, Michigan, the block system provides much flexibility and increased opportunity to accommodate both group and individual needs. Study halls are eliminated. In their place are open periods during which pupils carry on individual or small-group work in the library, arts center, field house, music building, shop building, and laboratories. Music instructors use these open periods for work with ensembles or individuals.

[7] Harold Lickey, "Scheduling the Music Program in the Small or Middle-Sized School," *N.E.A. Journal*, January, 1955, p. 30.
[8] Lawler, Vanett (Ed.), *The Function of Music in the Secondary School Curriculum*, Bulletin of the Music Educators National Conference, 1952, p. 11.

As shown in the sample student schedule below, music organizations have substantial periods for rehearsal time. The orchestra strings meet Monday, Wednesday, and Friday from 8:00 to 10:00 A.M.; the full orchestra from 9:00 to 10:00 A.M. on Tuesday and from 2:15 to 3:15 on Wednesday. The band rehearses from 10:00 to 12:00 on Monday, Wednesday, and Thursday. Team teaching is used with sectional rehearsals, if desired, in strings, woodwind, brass, and percussion. The periods are long enough to accommodate both full organization and sectional rehearsals. In fact, a two-hour period makes a change of pace essential. A similar pattern is followed for vocal groups at other hours.

A SAMPLE SCHEDULE OF A HOLLAND (MICH.) HIGH SCHOOL JUNIOR

Time	Monday	Tuesday	Wednesday	Thursday	Friday
8:00	11th Gr. English	Open (for all students)	11th Gr. English	Chemistry	11th Gr. English
9:45					
10:00	Guidance	Guidance	Guidance	Guidance	Guidance
11:45	Band	Chemistry	Band	Band	Chemistry
12:25	Lunch	Lunch	Lunch	Lunch	Lunch
2:10	U.S. Hist.	Phys. Ed.	U.S. Hist.	Phys. Ed.	Open
2:15	Alg. III	Alg. III	Open (for all students)	Alg. III	U.S. Hist.
4:00					

Renewed Support for Music Programs

The importance of the arts in a modern school curriculum has been receiving increased emphasis since the early 1960s even as heavy pressures for academic and "basic" education have threatened the very existence of aesthetic experience for students in many secondary schools. This threat has been felt in reduced time schedules, decreased budgets, and loss of facilities and even of positions in extreme instances. Fortunately strong voices have been raised in defense of the arts and a balanced program of education. In 1962 the National Association of Secondary School Principals adopted an official position in a paper which stated that:

> Neither an outstanding nation nor a worthy individual can be intellectually mature and aesthetically impoverished. School programs should reflect a balanced image of social and artistic values. Every secondary school needs to provide well-trained personnel, adequate facilities, definite time during the school day, and broad curricular offerings in the arts for all students.[9]

[9] *The Arts in the Comprehensive Secondary School,* National Association of Secondary School Principals, 1962, p. 30.

The NEA's far-reaching Project on Instruction included among its priorities for the school the teaching of "fundamental understanding of the humanities and the arts . . . appreciation of and discriminating taste in literature, music, and the visual arts," and proceeded to affirm that, where federal and private foundation support were not forthcoming for such endeavors, state and local educational authorities "will have to give priority, in budget and program, to fields neglected by other sources of support."[10]

An encouraging evidence of foundation support came in 1963 in the Ford Foundation's grant of some 1.4 million dollars to the Music Educators National Conference for a six-year music project focused on creativity in the elementary and secondary schools. Other evidences of awakening public interest in music as a cultural force in modern living are exemplified in the Lincoln Center in New York, and in the unprecedented number of community symphony orchestras now found across the nation. It is also worthy of note that none of the supporting agencies, or the many prominent educators who have publicly defended music-education programs, have advocated a return to former programs and methods. The challenges of change and the need for new solutions to old and new problems will be the unquestioned order of the day for some time to come.

The place to begin in music, as in other subject areas, is in a thorough reassessment of our present educational objectives, a restatement of them in precise behavioral terms which everyone can understand, and a clear statement of priorities which can give direction to the total program of the school. How music education will fare in the current revolution in American education will depend in large measure on how well music educators can perform this task.

Suitable Class Size

The size of classes is a problem in many high-school subjects, and the music director with an intelligent understanding of this fact is in a better position to resolve it than one with little concern for the total school program. Class size is a problem particularly in schools where General Music is a required subject and teaching space is limited. The important factor, as always, is the welfare of the individual student. A class of 35 or 40 pupils is the practical maximum under which a teacher can get to know and work with the individual pupil. Large numbers of students can be interested in General Music, but if the class is large it should be sectioned as indicated earlier.

The size of music organizations may present similar difficulties. Talented youngsters are handicapped without sectioning, while the less gifted inevitably

[10] *Schools for the 60's*, National Education Association, 1963, p. 32.

must receive most of the director's attention. Thus it would be better to have a junior-high-school band or chorus of 60 students rather than 100. The practical solution when large numbers are to be accommodated is training bands or choirs. Both classes and music organizations should provide outlets and challenges for the gifted as well as the average child, but the same organization need not necessarily serve both (Fig. 16.5).

Credit for high school music study has long been a topic of concern for both administrators and music educators. Fifty years ago music was regarded purely extracurricular in the school program. As the quantity and quality of music offerings increased, music theory and harmony were given credit toward graduation.[11] Later, in accordance with the North Central Association proposal of credit calculations for high-school subjects on a time-unit basis, credit for music came to be allowed in terms of time spent in class and preparation. The North Central Association plan called for one unit of credit per year for each subject studied

Milwaukee Public Schools, Milwaukee, Wisconsin.

Fig. 16.5. The junior orchestra is excellent training for those who have little experience. It also permits the senior orchestra to progress at a faster rate.

[11] See Harry R. Wilson, *Music in the High School*, Silver Burdett, 1941, pp. 299–301.

200 minutes each week for 36 weeks, with an equivalent amount of time required for outside preparation. Laboratory work under the above plan receives half as much credit as work which is prepared.

Thus music organizations are allowed ¼ to ½ credit per year toward graduation, depending upon the amount of time involved in rehearsals. Some high schools grant up to four credits for music organization participations, though the more frequent maximum is two credits of the sixteen normally required for graduation. This credit, in many instances, includes credit for private music study under properly qualified teachers.

Reasonable Teacher Load

Teacher load is a problem throughout the educational system. The nature of the good teacher's work is such as to make difficult the weighing and equating of the many intangibles involved. This is particularly true of the music teacher's activities which include considerable work outside of assigned instructional duties. In consequence, no thoroughly equitable system of determining teacher load has yet been devised. In spite of this, some judgment of what constitutes a reasonable load is necessary. The quality of instruction inevitably suffers when the teacher is consistently overloaded. Both pupil and teacher need protection from situations which reduce the effectiveness of the learning experience. From this standpoint, crowded classrooms, overlarge classes, and unreasonable teacher loads are important professional concerns of the administrator and teacher alike.

A thorough study was made in 1954 of the work loads of 345 Michigan senior-high-school music teachers.[12] The study reveals that the average instrumental or vocal-instrumental music teacher in Michigan spends in excess of 50 hours per week on his duties if public performances and preparation related thereto are included. Class instruction accounts for only about half of his total load, with community service, out-of-class instructional duties, and public performances accounting for the remainder.

According to a national study of the work loads of 2200 teachers in 1950, the average time expenditure of 47.9 hours per week was regarded as too heavy as well as too uneven.[13] With this figure as a criterion, it is clear that the work load of many music teachers in Michigan is extremely heavy. It is a tribute to these teachers that, in spite of such loads, more than 50 percent reported enjoying their work very much.

Solutions to the teacher load problem will be reached only through the coop-

[12] Olaf W. Steg, "The Total Work-Load of High School Music Teachers in Michigan," *Journal of Research in Music Education*, Fall, 1955, pp. 101–118.

[13] *NEA Research Bulletin*, February, 1951, p. 14.

erative efforts of educational associations, colleges and universities, and of the administrators and of the teachers themselves. The complexities and practical implications of the problem point to the need for a series of coordinated studies designed to isolate and evaluate the numerous intangibles involved in good teaching. The role of the music teacher in this cooperative endeavor is defined by Steg:

> The ultimate responsibility for continuing a study of teaching load lies with the music teachers themselves. If studies, eventually to be followed by recommendations for action, are to be initiated by colleges or by state and national music associations, the stimulus must come from the teachers. If such studies are eventually to bear fruit in more equitable teaching loads, the music teachers must continue to cooperate in the studies, just as they have in this one.[14]

PHYSICAL FACILITIES FOR MUSIC INSTRUCTION

The music teacher, coordinator, and director naturally have a high degree of interest in the instruments and equipment used in their work. They readily accept responsibility and leadership, therefore, in the recommendation and selection of such equipment. Not so commonly recognized, but of equal if not greater importance, is the close cooperation with the superintendent and school architect concerning appropriate music rooms and facilities (Fig. 16.6). When it is considered that a building will be used for 40 to 50 years; that the specific characteristics and location of the music rooms have a considerable influence on the instructional program which will be carried on there; and that superintendents and architects do not automatically know what provisions need to be made for music spaces, the need for the music person to know as much as possible about these requirements becomes evident.

Music Facilities in New Buildings

It is not within the scope of this book to go into extensive detail on the subject of building requirements. Such information is available in an excellent publication devoted specifically to that subject.[15] We can, however, direct your attention to several primary considerations and suggest a few practical solutions to problems commonly faced in planning new schools.

The music teacher need feel no hesitancy in making suggestions for music

[14] Steg, *op. cit.*, p. 118.

[15] See *Music Buildings, Rooms and Equipment,* a revision of Music Education Research Council *Bulletin* No. 17, prepared by the 1952–1954 Committee on Music Rooms and Equipment, Music Educators National Conference, National Education Association, 1955.

Warren Holmes Co., Lansing, Michigan.

Fig. 16.6. Music facilities like these must be planned well in advance of construction. What features of this instrumental room are particularly good?

requirements in a new school building. In fact, long before construction begins, the superintendent is likely to request help from the faculty in making plans for such a building. He knows that the new school will more likely serve its primary function well if teachers are involved in the planning from the outset. We shall discuss some of the primary considerations to be kept in mind:

The Music Curriculum

We must know what functions are to be carried out in the spaces to be planned. These include consideration of what subjects are to be taught, what activities are to be carried on, and what their relationship is to the total school program. This is where we start.

Present and Future Needs

What we are doing now, what we *ought* to be doing, and what probable expansion will take place in the future are the essential considerations here. Perhaps one music room is enough at the moment, but unless enrollment is static or falling, it is better to construct two or more and use the extras for other classes until they are needed for music. Remember—you're building for 40 or 50 years.

Location of Music Rooms

Accessibility to the auditorium and to the outside is important. So is isolation from other classroom areas. Much cost can be saved, for example, by locating music rooms near cafeterias or shops rather than adjacent to other classrooms (Fig. 16.7). The cost of sound-deadening construction in walls and ceilings comes high.

Sound Insulation

Some insulation is necessary wherever music areas are located. For example, it is needed between practice rooms or between the band and vocal rooms, if you have both. Plastered cinder block is twice as effective as unfinished cinder block for reducing sound transmission; and split partitions with air spaces between them are about as effective and are less costly than solid partitions (see Fig. 16.8).

At this point a statement by Richard Bolt, head of Acoustics Laboratory at Massachusetts Institute of Technology, is well worth noting:

> The preceding discussion of sound insulation should serve to emphasize the importance of functional analysis and careful planning for segregation. It is difficult and costly to obtain 60 db. transmission loss in a single partition but easy to obtain this reduction through two walls separated by a corridor or storage space. A classroom directly under a band room could be made quiet only by a complicated multiple ceiling-floor construction; but putting a locker room under there would solve the problem without structural elaboration. *Good control cannot be put in as an after-thought.*[16]

Sound Absorption—Reverberation Control

A room should be neither too "live" nor too "dead" for the type of music to be played or sung there. This is a matter of avoiding excessive echo on the one hand and too much absorption on the other. Herein is good reason why the gymnasium is a very poor location for band practice because of its multiple hard reflecting surfaces, whereas areas suitable for band may be unsuited for chamber music or vocal groups.

The subject of reverberation control is complex but important. Fortunately, acoustical engineers have found excellent solutions to reverberation problems in sound-absorbent materials, nonparallel wall and corner construction, wall splaying, and sound traps of various types. They need to know, however, the principal kinds of uses to which the various spaces are to be put. It is the music person's job to supply this information and to encourage the superintendent to employ an acoustics engineer to help in planning for good hearing conditions in auditoriums, classrooms, and practice rooms. This is far too important to be overlooked or neglected in a modern school building.

[16] *Music Buildings, Rooms and Equipment, op. cit.*, p. 40.

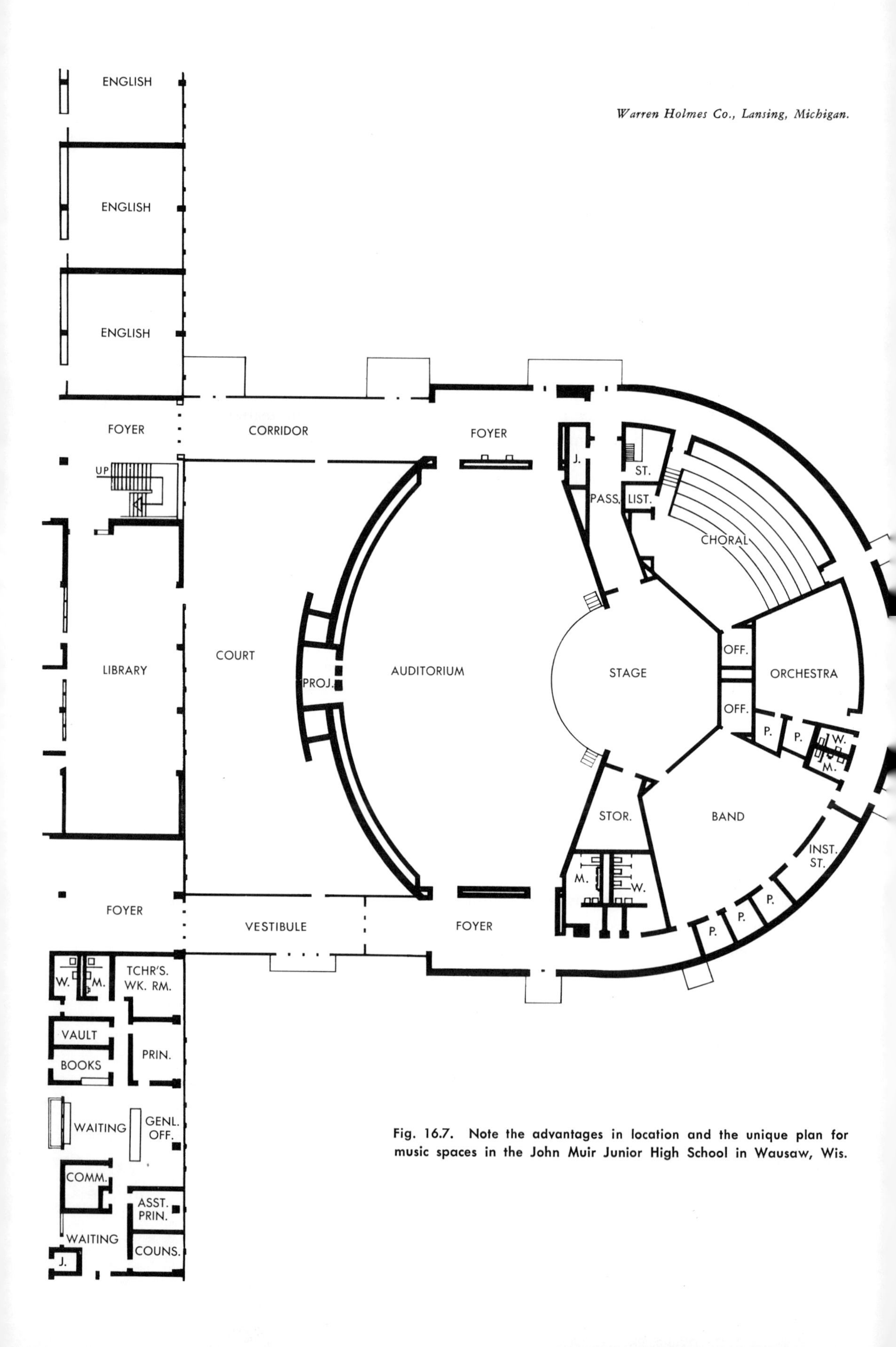

Warren Holmes Co., Lansing, Michigan.

Fig. 16.7. Note the advantages in location and the unique plan for music spaces in the John Muir Junior High School in Wausaw, Wis.

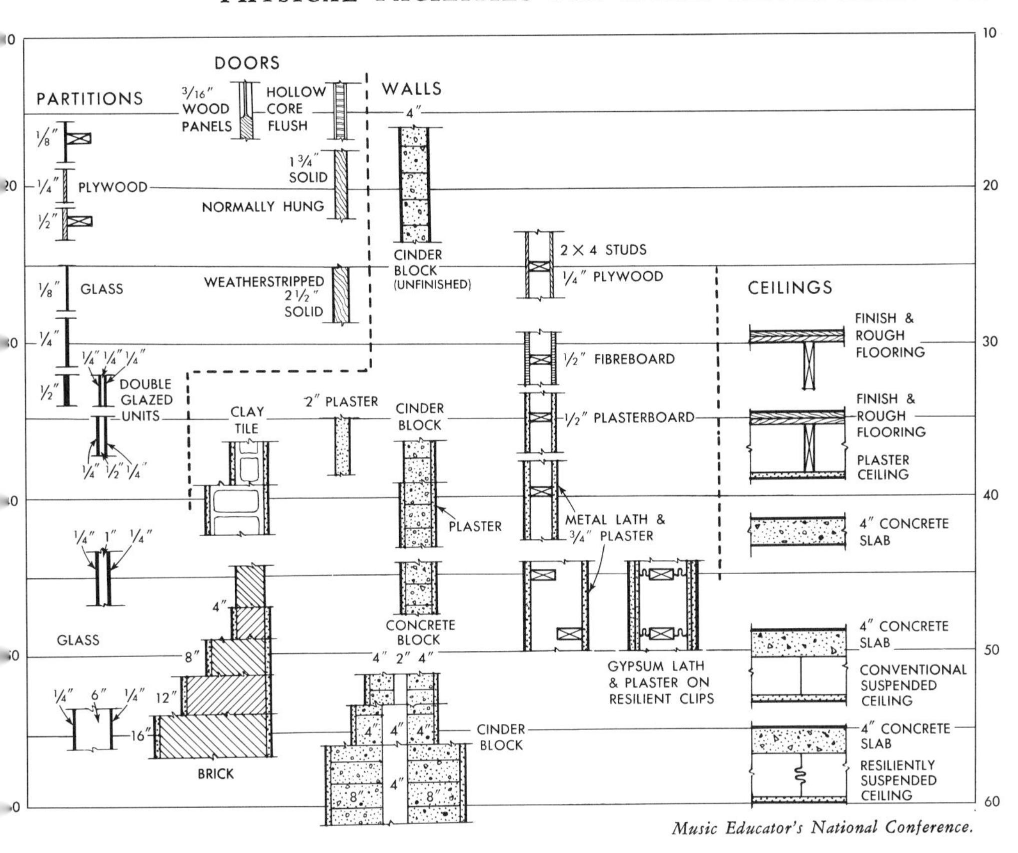

Fig. 16.8. This chart shows the relative sound-reduction (transmission loss) characteristics of various types of door, wall, and ceiling construction. On the basis of this information, what kinds of construction appear to be most suitable?

Compact Arrangement of Music Rooms

All music rooms should be close together so as to form an easily manageable unit. This is particularly important where there is only one music teacher. Practice rooms, rooms for instrumental and/or vocal music, and storage areas should be planned for convenient access and efficient supervision. Examples of compact planning are given in Fig. 16.9.

Equipment Selection and Financing

The importance of good equipment for the success of a music program would be difficult to overestimate. Assuming a competent music teacher and suitable music rooms, adequacy and quality of equipment have a direct bearing upon the

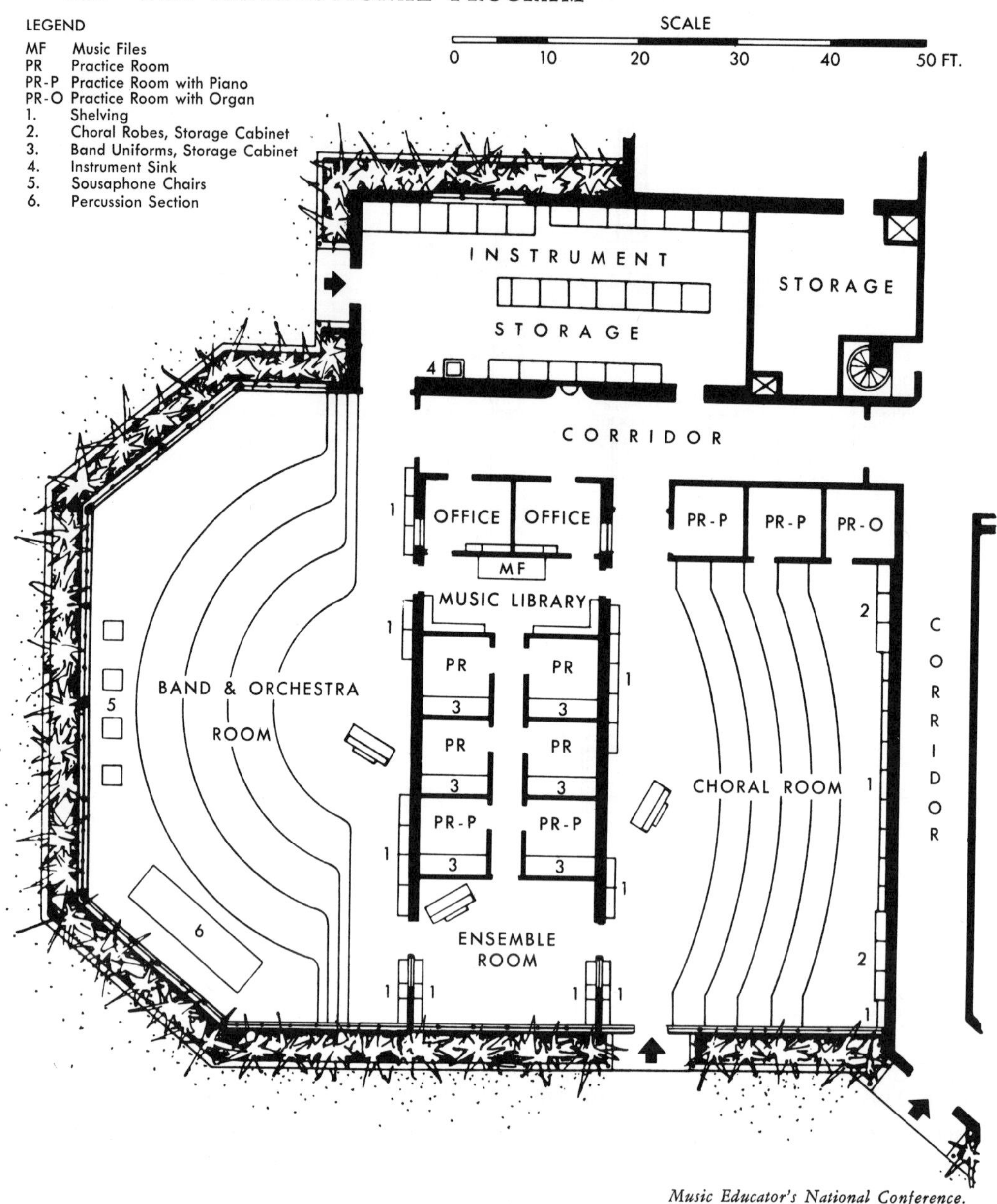

Music Educator's National Conference.

Fig. 16.9. These two illustrations show a number of factors which should be included in a good music facilities plan. See how many you can identify.

progress and success of music activities. Music teachers, coordinators, and directors have the important responsibilities of selection, recommendation, and care of large amounts of music equipment. Certain kinds of equipment should be built into music rooms. Provisions should be made for storage cabinets for instruments, music library racks, risers, display boards and chalkboards. Sug-

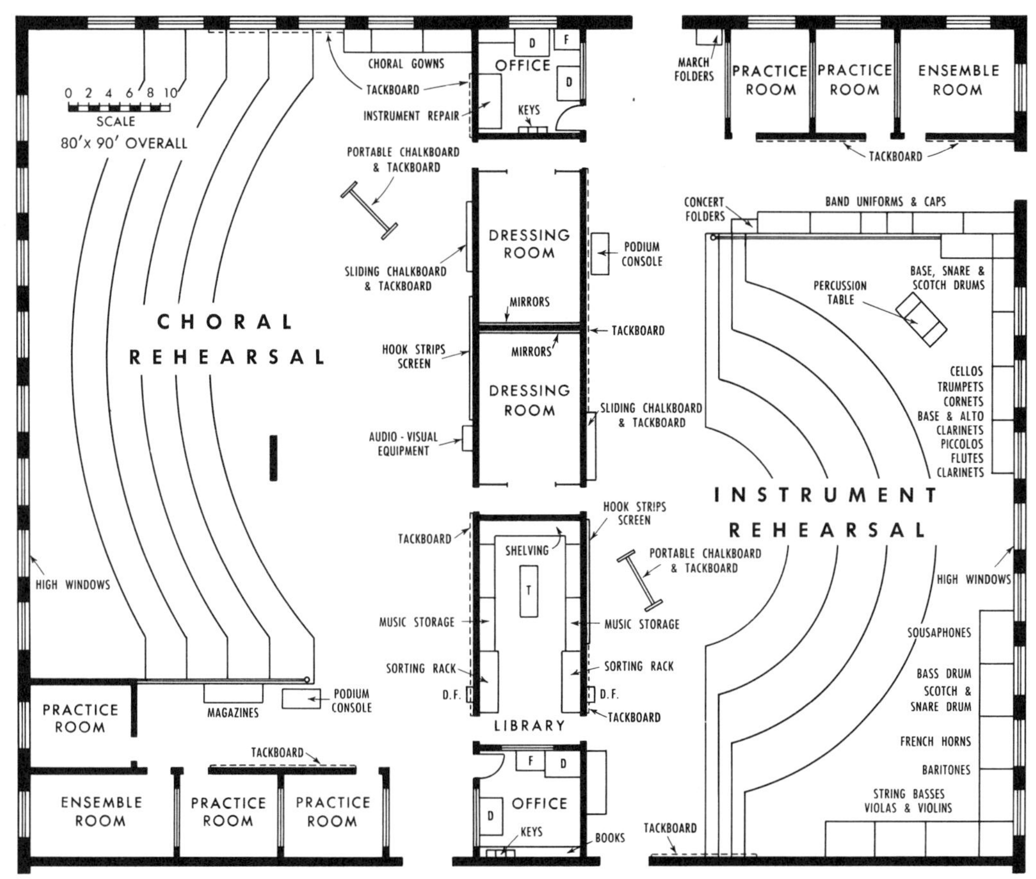

Music Educator's National Conference.

gested specifications for equipment of this nature are included in *Music Buildings, Rooms and Equipment* and should be incorporated in initial building plans (see Fig. 16.10).[17]

Other types of equipment and materials such as pianos, band and orchestral instruments, band uniforms and choir robes, and service items like the Stroboconn and Electrotuner, represent a considerable portion of the annual music budget.

Since the success of the music program depends heavily upon having an adequate supply of operational equipment, it should be planned for carefully. Annual budget moneys are more likely to be available in sufficient amounts if planning is done for several years in advance. School administrators are much more likely to go along with a coordinated and intelligent plan than to follow through on frequent isolated requests which show little comprehension of the overall financial problems of the school.

[17] See *Music Buildings, Rooms and Equipment, op. cit.*, pp. 52–64.

Lyons Township H. S., La Grange, Illinois.

Detroit Public Schools, Detroit, Michigan.

Fig. 16.10. Some facilities should be built into music areas of the school. Permanent risers allow for convenient placement of players or singers (top); private practice rooms are an important feature (middle); and special facilities should be planned for neat and accessible storage of music, instruments, and choral robes (facing page).

Muskegon Public Schools, Muskegon, Michigan.

Muskegon Public Schools, Muskegon, Michigan.

Port Huron Public Schools, Port Huron, Michigan.

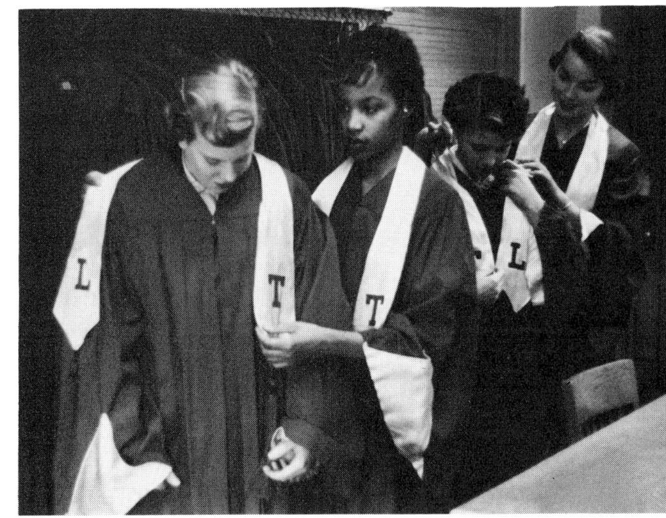

Lyons Township H.S., LaGrange, Illinois.

The five-year plan presented below is suggested in a study by five music directors in Michigan.[18] The plan is based upon an assumption that a band program is to be initiated in a small or medium-sized high school with no instruments or instrumental equipment on hand. Modifications of various types may be made to meet varying needs. For example, preband melody instruments might be purchased by the students or omitted if they are not feasible. Also it might be desirable to purchase for training purposes a number of the smaller instruments, such as flutes, clarinets, cornets, or trombones. In any case, the plan is illustrative of the type of long-range budget planning which is needed.

[18] Lorin Richtmeyer, Earl Gunsalus, Howland Fisk, Paul Shank, and Richard Foor, "An Administrator's Guide to the Instrumental Music Program in the Public Schools," unpublished seminar report, Michigan State University, 1955 (revised, 1964).

SAMPLE FIVE-YEAR PLAN

First Year	Budget of $4742
20 music stands @ $9 ea.	$180
40 preband melody instrs. @ $.80 ea.	32
1 bass drum (34″ x 16″)	85
2 snare drums (8″ x 15″) @ $60 ea.	120
1 pair of cymbals (16″)	50
1 sousaphone	500
1 baritone	300
2 French horns @ $280 ea.	560
1 baritone saxophone	390
music	250
35 uniforms @ $65 ea.	2275

Second Year	Budget of $2940
1 oboe	$325
1 bass clarinet	500
1 tenor saxophone	300
1 baritone	300
1 sousaphone	500
2 parade drums (12″ x 15″) @ $75 ea.	150
1 Scotch bass drum (10″ x 28″)	80
1 pair of cymbals (14″)	45
5 additional music stands	45
music and marching folios	45
10 additional uniforms @ $65 ea.	650

Third Year	Budget of $2455
1 French horn	$280
1 baritone	300
1 bassoon	500
1 set of tympani	450
1 piccolo (C)	110
1 set of bells	90
music	250
repairs	150
5 additional uniforms @ $65 ea.	325

Fourth Year	Budget of $2430
1 French horn	$280
1 sousaphone	500
1 oboe	325
1 bass clarinet	500
music	250
repairs	250
5 additional uniforms @ $65 ea.	325

Fifth Year	Budget of $2430
1 piccolo (C)	$110
1 sousaphone	500
1 bassoon	500
1 alto clarinet	350
5 additional music stands @ $9 ea.	45
music	300
repairs	300
5 additional uniforms @ $65 ea.	325

Instrument rental plans may be employed to increase the number of instruments available at a given time on a limited music budget. Arrangements for instrument rental to schools can occasionally be made through dealers or manufacturers. In such cases insurance, maintenance, and depreciation costs are assumed by the rental agency and become a part of the rental charge. Rental plans of this nature are fairly common in the instrument field, and will probably become more so in the future.

Whether to rent or to buy outright is, in any case, a matter to discuss with your superintendent or music supervisor, since many factors are apt to be involved including fiscal policies of the school system. By and large, the basic question is one of getting the best educational returns from the dollars invested. If more instruments would significantly enhance the amount and quality of music learning, you have a sound basis for investigating deferred-payment plans. Thus, if under the five-year purchase plan cited above instruments of the same quality could be made available in one or two years under rental (or rent-to-own) contracts with comparable average expenditures each year, this could be a significant enough advantage to your program to warrant serious consideration. Typewriters and office machines for business education classes are typically secured by high schools on a lease or rental basis, so there is ample precedent for such arrangements.

Insurance plans for instruments owned by the school are available to cover such hazards as loss or serious damage. Insurance is a means of covering risks of this kind and, like maintenance costs, is a legitimate educational expenditure. Large schools systems frequently carry their own insurance—i.e., they take the risks involved—because the risk is spread among many buildings and any single loss would represent a comparatively small proportion of the total budget. In smaller systems, the risk is proportionally greater and insurance protection more necessary. This is another matter to discuss with your music supervisor or superintendent if instruments in your charge are not already insured.

Insurance on student-owned instruments is also available. The cost is relatively low if a school plan is established with the insurance company, and numerous companies offer this coverage. Should your school not have such a plan in effect, it would be worth suggesting to your principal or superintendent. Claims for loss or damage are typically placed directly with the local agent by the student or his parent. While rates will vary somewhat from time to time, the following sample costs are fairly representative:

Instrument Value	Annual Rate
Under $100	$1.00
150	1.35
200	1.80
300	2.70
400	3.60
500	4.50

Quality control normally refers to a manufacturer's production and to the means taken to assure that minimum standards are met. We use the term here to refer to the *purchase* of equipment by the school and, more specifically, to the purchase of musical instruments. Experienced music directors know that good instruments are necessary for good results in band or orchestra. It is better to secure first-line instruments from a reliable manufacturer than to risk a questionable bargain at lesser cost. Most such bargains are apt to be somewhat inferior in workmanship and material, both of which result in poor intonation, more rapid deterioration, and increased maintenance costs.

If funds are limited, it is usually better to purchase good, rebuilt, first-line instruments in preference to new, second-best, or imported makes. Top-grade instrument manufacturers stand behind their products with guarantees, dependable service, and assurance of spare parts when needed. While used musical instruments, like used cars, involve certain risks to the purchaser, an instrument which was good to begin with can normally be restored by a reliable company to a condition almost as good as new.

EQUIPMENT DISTRIBUTION AND CONTROL

Equipment issue and record-keeping are important functions of the music teacher. Various systems have been developed to assist in the maintenance of accurate records with a minimum of effort and a maximum of efficiency. Most of these have been developed by music teachers themselves. Some good index systems are available commercially, but whatever system is used should function so as to accomplish two objectives: (1) a complete and accurate record of each piece of equipment for which the music department is responsible (Fig. 16.11); and (2) complete and accurate distribution control (Fig. 16.12).

The manner in which any distribution and control system is operated is as important as the system itself. The one reason for having instruments, music, and uniforms is to have them used by students. Thus, that system is best which facilitates optimum use while assuring proper care of the equipment. In this way the maximum number of students can be served at the lowest cost and with the greatest benefit to the music program.

A card system of some type is preferred by most music directors. Common to all such systems is an inventory card containing a complete description of each piece of equipment. Inventory cards are frequently made up in several colors for easier filing and identification. One might have a buff card for instruments, for example, pink for uniforms, and blue for special equipment. Each card should have a number which matches the school inventory number that is assigned and affixed to each piece of equipment. A white card is typically used for check-out purposes, and contains the same information as on the inventory card plus the pupil's and parent's signatures to a loan or rental agreement. Inventory and loan cards can be filed together when equipment is in and separately when it is out.

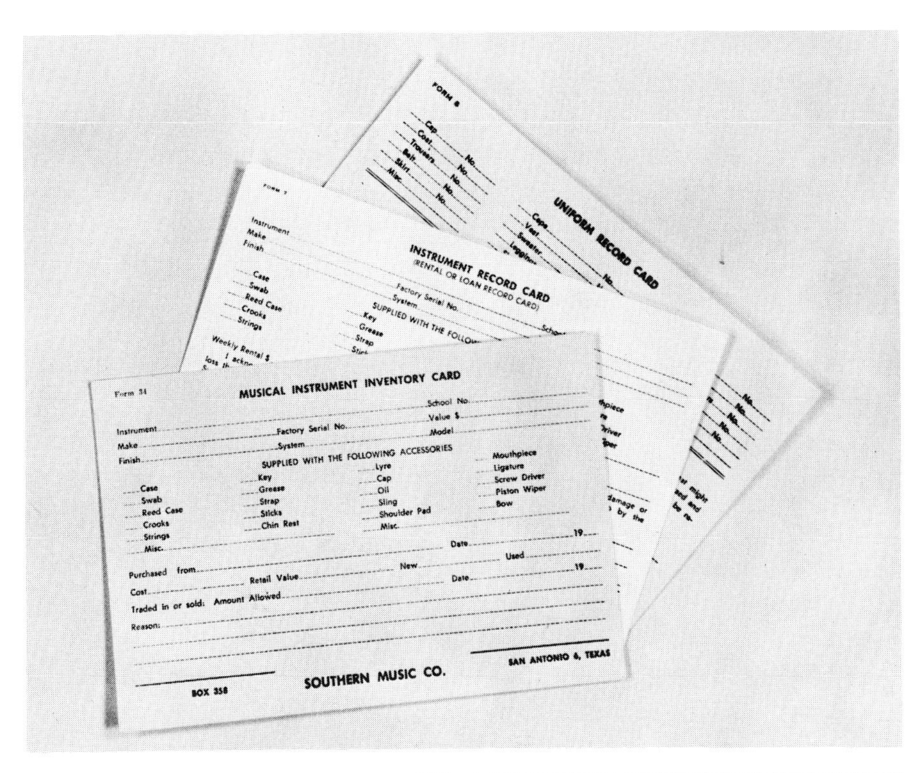

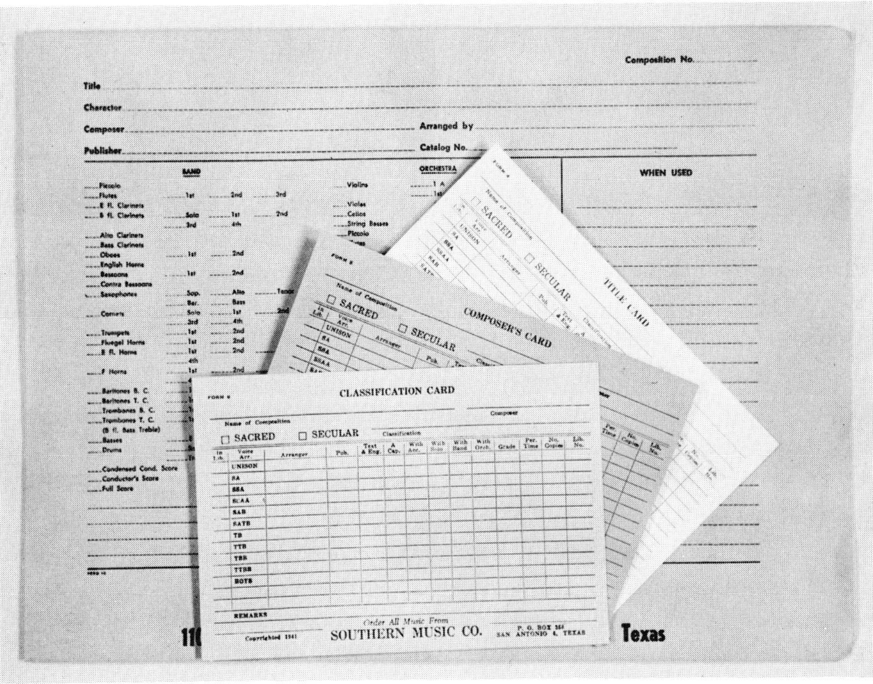

Southern Music Company

Fig. 16.11. Cards and envelopes of this type are helpful for easy location and circulation of music, uniforms, and equipment.

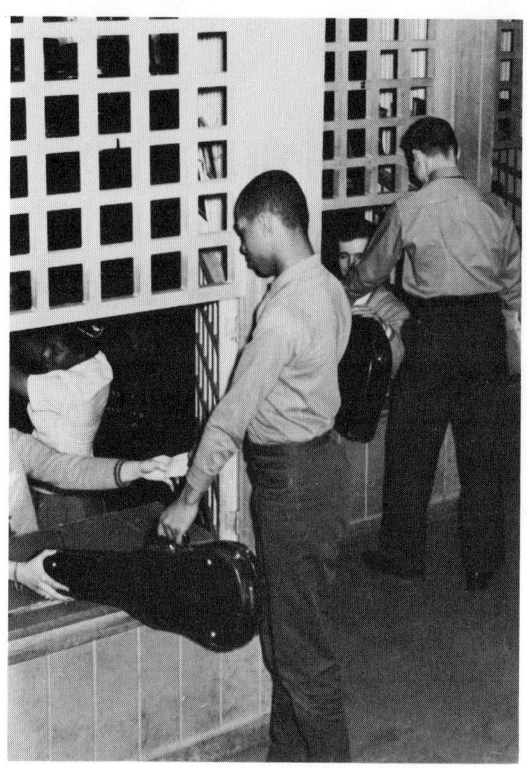

Fig. 16.12. High schools with large enrollments in band and orchestra may find an instrument check-room an asset to both teachers and students.

Detroit Public Schools, Detroit, Michigan.

One good system uses an envelope for each student. All loan cards signed by him are kept in his envelope until the materials are checked in, at which time the loan card is initialed and placed back in the master file with its corresponding inventory card. This necessitates a loan card with a series of signature spaces and has the advantage of avoiding the making up of a new loan card each time equipment is issued.

A simple and highly effective system of equipment issue and accounting has been developed at the University of Iowa. Called the Duo-Card system, it is based on the idea of having a matched pair of cards for each item of equipment. The inventory card is colored; the student card is white. *Both* are signed when equipment is issued, and both are receipted when the material is checked in. In the interim all loan cards are filed in a student envelope. While a larger number of cards are involved in the paired-card system than in some others, its flexibility and accuracy commend it particularly for use with large musical organizations (Fig. 16.13).[19]

[19] For a detailed account of the Duo-Card system see C. B. Richter, "Equipment Issue and Accounting," *Educational Music Magazine,* March–April, 1957, pp. 8 ff.

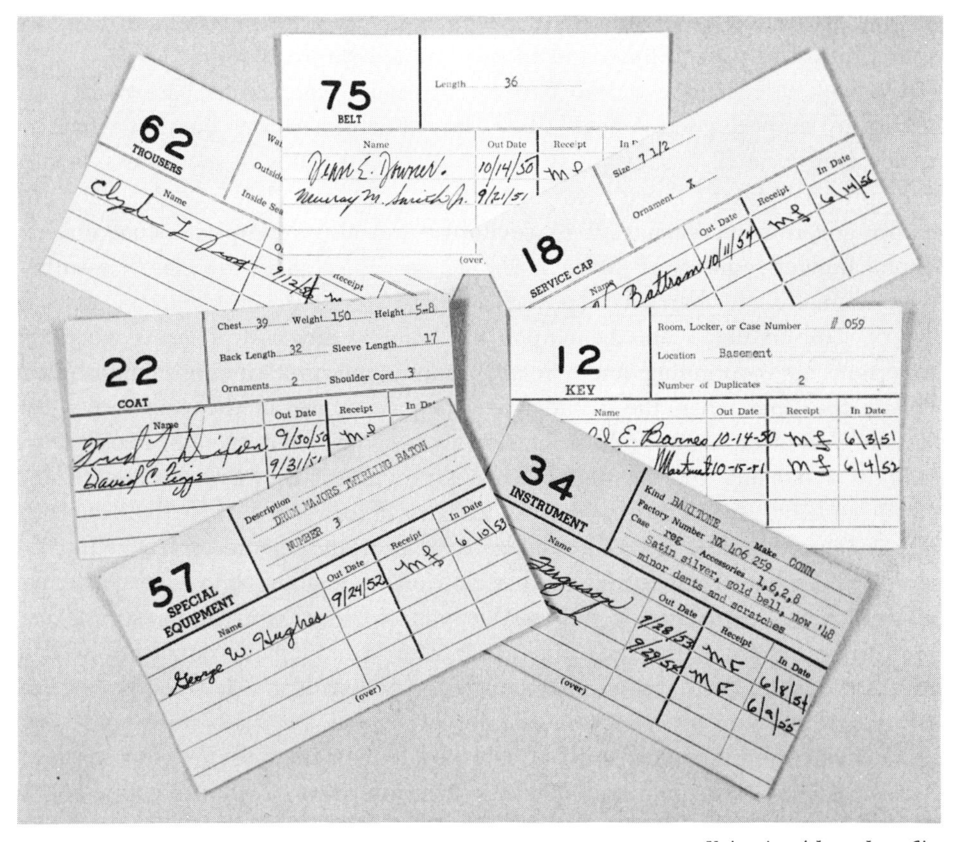

University of Iowa, Iowa City.

Fig. 16.13. A paired-card system for distribution of uniforms and equipment involves more cards than some systems, but it provides excellent control.

Considerable work is involved in setting up an effective system for equipment distribution and control, but the benefits are worth the effort. Once the system is established, it works *for* you. With a reasonable amount of supervision, reliable students can do much of the work and you have the assurance of an important administrative responsibility being properly cared for.

FINANCING THE MUSIC PROGRAM

The school administrator is concerned equally with securing the necessary funds for an adequate educational program and with securing the best educational results for each dollar spent. The teacher is an important factor in both endeavors. In the first instance, the teacher needs to inform his administrator of what is needed and why it is needed; in the second, he needs to produce results to justify expenditures and to substantiate future requests.

It is well to recognize at the outset that, while communities are ready and willing to support good schools, they do not automatically provide whatever money is requested. A substantial portion of school funds in most states comes from property taxes. These taxes are also a primary source of other city and county government revenue. It is inevitable—and also appropriate—that governmental budget requests of all kinds should be subjected to the closest scrutiny.

Occasionally, the harried taxpayer, or more frequently a taxpayers' association of some nature, seems bent upon tax relief at any cost. Then is when the importance of continuing and effective public interpretation is demonstrated. This is the time when the music teacher's past efforts in the community can pay off. Too often a good job in the schools is of itself not enough. People have to know about and approve of the school's program if they are to actively support it and the expenditures necessary to carry it forward.

It is important for you as a teacher to understand the factors affecting the size of the school budget and of that portion of it going into your particular subject. Such understanding will enable you to assist your administrator and your own program at the same time. It is wise to anticipate your needs well in advance, and to have a coordinated plan for acquiring needed equipment and supplies from year to year. You should, of course, be ready to supply your principal or superintendent with good and adequate reasons for your requests. And you should keep him well and regularly informed of what is happening in the music program so that he may be in a position to assess both your progress and your needs. These actions are important for other reasons as well, but they have a particular bearing on your music budget.

In 1957, the present authors studied secondary music-program expenditures, other than salaries, in 42 school systems across the country. Among other findings, it was determined that—on the average—expenditures increased 16 percent over the three-year period from 1954 to 1957. This represented an increase from $1.57 per pupil in the total secondary enrollment of these schools in 1953–1954 to $1.81 per pupil in 1955–1956. A spot check of ten of the same systems in 1963–1964 and 1964–1965 shows that average expenditures per pupil for secondary music-education programs have risen to $2.52 and $2.74, respectively. To the extent that the spot check is representative, this means an approximate 50 percent increase in the nine-year period between 1956 and 1965.

However, while such average expenditures as these may show a trend, they should not be regarded as standards with which to compare your own music budget. Several important factors—e.g., the relative stage of development of the music program and the size of the total enrollment—must also be considered. A school just starting a new program will require much larger expenditures than one already well equipped with instruments, music uniforms, and other items. A school program which emphasizes band but which has no orchestra will naturally cost less than a well-balanced music program. Programs must be comparable in many ways if their budgets are to be compared. Total enrollments must also be comparable for budget comparisons to have validity. The authors' 1957 study showed that music expenditures per pupil were significantly and consistently higher in secondary schools with enrollment under 1100 than in larger school systems.[20]

The most important consideration in assessing music budget requirements in any school is the quality of program desired. While money alone will not assure an excellent music program, a lack of sufficient funds to carry out soundly based, long-range plans for development will effectively prevent the attainment of excellence. Good education costs money in music as well as in other aspects of the school curriculum. Consequently, the effective music administrator places a high priority on efforts to secure sufficient financial support to keep his program moving forward.

SUMMARY

Education is primarily a function of the state government which establishes standards, supplies some financial support, and regulates certain aspects of the school's administration. The state usually delegates a large amount of authority for actual operation of the schools to local school districts of some type. The board of education establishes local policy and employs a superintendent of schools to administer the educational program. Each school, in turn, is administered by the school principal. Supervisors, including music coordinators, are not administrative officers. They achieve effective results largely through the degree of cooperation they can engender among the principals and teachers with whom they work.

The music teacher's work involves certain administrative responsibilities such as planning schedules, preparing the music budget, and requisitioning equipment and supplies. He also has an important role in planning music rooms and facilities for new school buildings. To be competent in this area as well as in his teaching, a music teacher should be thoroughly familiar with vocal and instrumental work, and he should be aware of the physical requirements of both areas.

Class size and teacher load are problems of particular concern to school music teachers. Sectioning of certain large classes and organizations is needed to pro-

[20] In 1955–1956, for example, 22 class AA schools (1100 and over) spent $1.41 per pupil on their music programs, while 9 class A (650–1099) and 8 class B (300–649) schools averaged $3.34 and $5.15 per pupil, respectively. All of these systems were selected as having good music programs.

vide appropriate experience for the gifted student as well as for the average or inexperienced pupil. The many intangible factors in good teaching make difficult the determination of equitable teaching loads. Solutions will be found only with the stimulus and active cooperation of teachers and administrators in studies initiated by their professional organizations and by colleges and universities.

School-building requirements for music programs must be based, first of all, upon the music curriculum. Present and future needs, location and arrangement of music rooms, sound insulation and absorption, and music equipment are other factors with which the music teacher should be concerned.

The purchase of instruments, uniforms, and other costly items needs to be planned over a period of time to assure a sound, developing program. An efficient system of distribution and control of equipment, uniforms, and music supplies is essential for their optimum use and proper care.

Music expenditures in selected secondary schools with good music programs have risen somewhat during the past decade in spite of financial problems in many communities across the nation. Those in charge of school music programs have a primary responsibility to make sound plans for long-range development and to work for the financial support necessary for their attainment.

SUGGESTED ACTIVITIES

1. Assume that you are in your first year in a position as music coordinator in a small school system. The superintendent has asked you to prepare a budget request for the high-school music program for the following year. Outline the steps you would take in setting up such a budget.
2. Set up several role-playing situations in which one student takes the role of the superintendent, another the music coordinator, another the principal, etc. Be ready to take any one of several roles in situations such as the following, or devise other situations suggested by topics in this chapter.
   a. The music teacher comes into the superintendent's office to request the purchase of two sousaphones for the band—an item not in the budget for this year.
   b. The principal and the superintendent are discussing the strong and weak points of a new high-school music teacher who is not present.
   c. A music teacher and three teachers of other subjects are comparing their teaching loads while they wait for a faculty meeting to start.
   d. The music teacher is conferring with the high-school principal concerning a student whose mother has complained because he's playing with the second rather than the first band.
3. Have a committee from the class visit a high-school music director in the vicinity, or several of them if possible, in order to get copies of their teaching and activity schedules and their suggestions on solutions to music scheduling problems. The

committee should then discuss its findings and its own reactions with the class. (Note: Ask your instructor to arrange with the schools for this activity.)

4. Invite a school superintendent or principal to come to a class session for a discussion of the kind of assistance he likes to have from teachers on such matters as budget planning, public relations, PTA's, Music Boosters, etc.
5. Have another committee visit one or more new junior- or senior-high-school buildings in the vicinity and find the strong points of the music rooms and facilities. The committee, as part of its report, should prepare for the class a list of features to be recommended in planning music facilities in new buildings.
6. In a situation where the administrator is only casually interested in the school music program, consider various possibilities as a teacher in his system for increasing his interest in a knowledge of your work and its importance.
7. The board of education in your school system is strongly in favor of the band, but doesn't appear to be concerned with the rest of your program, including the vocal music. How might you go about increasing its interest and support of a well-rounded program of music education?

SELECTED READINGS

Albright, A. D. *et al.*, *School Administration and the Human Sciences*, University of Kentucky, 1961.

Basic Concepts in Music Education, 57th Yearbook, Part I, National Society for the Study of Education, 1958.

Beranck, Leo L., *Music Acoustics and Architecture*, Wiley, 1962.

Brown, Glenn E., "The Dual Progress Plan in Music Education," *Music Educators Journal*, September–October, 1962, p. 62.

Culbertson, Jack, and Steven Hencley (Eds.), *Preparing Administrators–New Perspectives*, University Council for Educational Administration, 1963.

Dykema, Peter W., and Gehrkens, Karl W., *The Teaching and Administration of High School Music*, C. C. Birchard, 1941, pp. 436–447.

Engleman, Finis E., "Music and Public Education," *Music Educators Journal*, February–March, 1961, pp. 35–39.

Foff, Arthur, and Grambs, Jean D., *Readings in Education*, Harper, 1956, pp. 200–218.

Flora, Frank E., "Successful Administrative Relationships Make Successful Music Programs," *Music Educators Journal*, April–May, 1961, pp. 66–67.

Law, Glen C., "Music Administration During Transition," *Music Educators Journal*, September–October, 1963, pp. 52–55.

Music Buildings, Rooms, and Equipment, Music Education Research Council *Bulletin No. 17*, 1952–1954, Committee on Music Rooms and Equipment, Music Educators National Conference, 1955, pp. 5–95.

Music in American Education, Music Educators National Conference, Music Education Source Book No. 2, 1955, pp. 18–40.

Singleton, Ira C., *Music in Secondary Schools*, Allyn and Bacon, 1963, pp. 12–18, 356–395.

Snyder, Keith, *School Music Administration and Supervision*, Allyn and Bacon, 1959.
Stiles, Lindley J., *Theory & Practice of Supervision*, Dodd, Mead, 1961.
Tipton, Gladys, "Music Education in the Changing World," *Music Educators Journal*, June–July, 1961, pp. 32–35.
Titzroy, Dariel, and John Lyon Reid, *Acoustical Environment of School Buildings*, Educational Facilities Laboratories, 1963.
Weyland, Rudolph H., *A Guide to Effective Music Supervision*, Brown, 1960, pp. 127–189.
Willis, Benjamin, "Education–Challenge and Opportunity," *Music Educators Journal*, February–March, 1961, pp. 35–39.

3M Company, Minneapolis, Minnesota.

CHAPTER

17

Audio Experiences in Music Learning

Few of us recall the details of *how* our best teachers taught us. In trying to remember, we are likely to recall their enthusiasm for their work, the interest they had in us as individuals, their sense of humor, and their general competence. Most of them seemed to have a genuine liking and respect for their students, a feeling which was usually returned in kind. They were always fair, but seldom "easy." They made us work hard, but somehow to enjoy it. They were assured themselves and seemed to inspire confidence in us. Among other things, they each had that fine combination of qualities we call a good personality.

Yet, was this all? As we think about it, there was one vitally important ability which all of our best teachers seemed to possess. This was the ability to communicate effectively, to make meanings clear to us. *How* they did it would be difficult to describe. Each had his own way of getting ideas across, and his methods varied to suit the many different situations arising from day to day. We begin to see what is meant by those who call teaching an art.

REQUIREMENTS OF GOOD TEACHING

Good teaching begins with a thorough knowledge of one's subject. Clearly one cannot teach what he does not know. Yet knowledge of the subject itself is only a beginning. The abilities and characteristics of our best teachers as listed above are extremely important. Back of these abilities, however, and fundamental to them, is an understanding of how people learn plus an ability to apply that knowledge in many different teaching and learning situations. Fundamental, also, is an understanding of young people at various stages of development and of the reasons why they act as they do.

Coupled with these needs is the development of skills in the selection and application of methods suitable to the learning situation. With these methods, in turn, we must incorporate and make effective use of appropriate instructional materials so that the resultant learning experience is as stimulating and successful as we can make it. An important group of these instructional materials and methods is the subject of this and the following chapter, namely, audio and visual materials of instruction.

Audiovisual materials and methods are the core of a specialized and rapidly growing professional field in education known variously as "instructional communications," "educational technology," or "educational media." Pending standardization of terminology, we shall use the term *educational media.* This term refers particularly to *those methods of instruction which emphasize visual and auditory methods of making meanings clear to the learner.* Words—spoken or written—play an important part in good communication, but we have considerable evidence that appropriate combinations of verbal, visual, and listening experience are much more effective for learning than any one of these by itself. Teachers need, accordingly, to become familiar with a wide variety of such materials and to become skilled in their use in order to achieve the substantial benefits inherent in the educational media.

The music teacher thinks at once of phonograph records and tape recordings as examples of valuable media for getting important musical ideas across to their classes. A bit more reflection may suggest such additional examples as large charts of instruments or the piano keyboard, diagrams of the band and orchestra, the chalkboard staff, and pictures or slides of artists and composers as further examples of useful tools for teaching. Add instructional television, films, radio, programed instruction, and electronic tuners and timers and you begin to understand more of the scope and potential of the educational media field. It shall be our purpose in this and the following chapter to consider specific applications of the educational media in music teaching.

The Place of Educational Media in Music Teaching

It is well at the outset for us to recognize that audio and visual materials in the schools, along with books and reference materials, have but one reason for being there—to help pupils learn. The good music teacher is constantly on the alert for better ways of helping pupils to learn, for teaching and learning are essentially two sides of the same process. Whatever can help the learning process is important to both teacher and pupils.

Good teachers use a *variety* of teaching tools and, frequently, several in combination. For example, in a music literature unit on Schubert, you will doubtless use a number of good recordings in addition to a reading assignment in the music text. Several students may go to the library and study reference materials for special reports to the class about significant aspects of Schubert's life and work (Fig. 17.1). A student committee might develop a display board using pictures and articles about Schubert from the library and from your files. Perhaps you will play some illustrative passages on the piano or have talented stu-

Interlochen Arts Academy, Interlochen, Michigan.

Fig. 17.1. A good music library has music, recordings, and books pertaining to music subjects. It might also have a selection of pictures, filmstrips, and films relating to topics being currently taught.

dents do so for the class. A student ensemble might play a selection while the music they are playing is projected on a screen for the class to follow. This could easily be done, also, while a recording is being played. At an appropriate time you might wish to project a sound motion picture dramatizing Schubert's life.

These and many other activities and materials might be used with excellent results in a series of lessons on great composers. Note that the materials are used in combination in your class activities and that each reinforces the others. Neither you nor the class has a feeling at any point in a good lesson that the lesson is being interrupted by using the display, the recording, the projected music, or the film. Each has its contribution to make and each fits naturally into a well-ordered series of learning experiences about Schubert.

As another example, in teaching basic music you naturally will make considerable use of music staffs on the chalkboard. You may use flash cards for drill purposes and the piano keyboard for note and time identification exercises (Fig. 17.2). The feltboard is helpful for showing such items as note values, staff signatures, and chord structure. Student exercises on mimeographed or dittoed scores will provide necessary individual participation activity and an opportunity to check progress. You may have the students sing or play notes in unison at various stages to apply and fix learning. You and your class will discuss,

College of the Desert, Palm Desert, California.

Fig. 17.2. The electronic keyboard makes it possible for individual students to develop their musicianship more rapidly.

explain, demonstrate; and, again, you will use whatever techniques and materials will best accomplish the desired results.

Many of the methods and materials used in these two examples are audio-visual in character but of much greater importance is the fact that they are tools and techniques of good teaching. Anything which helps the learner to learn better, likewise helps the teacher to teach better. This is the whole point of educational media.

How do you determine which of the many types of instructional materials to use in a particular instance? How do you go about evaluating and selecting specific materials for a lesson? Finally, how do you use audio or visual media to get the best results? These and similar questions confront teachers daily in the normal course of their work.

In order to get at some of the answers, it will be helpful to consider the nature of the several types of educational media. In so doing, the particular instructional advantages of each type will be pointed up, their applications in music teaching will be illustrated, and some suggestions for their effective use will be noted.

RCA Victor.

Fig. 17.3. Attractive and artistic covers are found on most recordings. Sometimes the effect is purely decorative; often, however, the result is an interesting visual representation of the nature of the music or artist.

RECORDS AND PHONOGRAPHS

Aside from music and instruments, phonograph records are probably the most familiar type of instructional material in music teaching. Their convenience of use, availability in great numbers on virtually all types and levels of music instruction, and their high quality are familiar to all students and teachers of music. Through the use of recordings, virtually the entire field of music literature can be brought into the classroom (Fig. 17.3).

Records

School record collections have become standardized in the 33⅓ rpm (revolutions per minute) speed and 12-inch disk size in long-play, microgroove stereo or monaural recordings.[1] The 10-inch L.P. record and the older 78 rpm recordings of value have been reproduced on the 12-inch hi-fi record. The 45 rpm, 7-inch record is used chiefly for popular music.

Research in the recording and electronics industries has resulted in durable plastic records with excellent tonal quality and range and little surface noise. The quality of sound produced from such records is equally dependent, however, on having a phonograph or record player of comparable quality to that of the recording. Both are essential components in the reproduction of high-fidelity music from recordings.

Phonographs

Numerous good record players are available in both portable and console cabinets (Fig. 17.4). Lightweight tone arms are essential, and a jeweled stylus is recommended. Even a diamond stylus is not permanent, however, and must be replaced occasionally. A worn stylus quickly damages the tiny grooves on records and spoils their reproduction quality. A good phonograph has high quality component parts throughout. These include an amplifier (and a preamplifier in high-fidelity equipment), a turntable, preferably with a manual-type tone arm, variable speed control—frequently with a stroboscope light attachment for precision adjustment—and two or more speakers in sound chambers of appropriate size. These parts are carefully matched for uniform balance and performance. The cabinet is unimportant aside from the need for a sound chamber and an enclosure for the above parts. Frequently too much of the cost of a phonograph is tied up in an attractive cabinet.

Care of Records

A few precautions will greatly lengthen the life and maintain the quality of your records. The importance of avoiding the use of a worn needle or stylus has been mentioned. Second only to this in importance is keeping the record surface free of dust and finger marks. Handle records only by the edges and clean the surface as needed with a soft damp cloth or tissue by wiping in the

[1] The distinction between monaural and binaural or stereophonic recordings is discussed under "Tape Recording" on pp. 424–425.

Newcomb Audio Products Company, Hollywood, California.

Audiotronics Corp., North Hollywood, California.

Fig. 17.4. High-fidelity record players are available in portable, monophonic, or stereo models.

direction of the grooves (Fig. 17.5). Dust acts as an abrasive in the grooves and should be avoided as much as possible. This is complicated by the fact that the disk becomes charged with static electricity and tends to attract dust particles in the course of normal use. An antistatic brush is helpful in reducing dust, but occasional cleaning and proper handling are the chief means of protecting your records.

One useful tip is to buckle the cardboard envelope slightly when removing or inserting a record. Most record albums have an inner paper or plastic envelope which provides further protection in handling and inserting or removing from the outer cover. Uncovered records should *never* be piled on top of one another. Records should be stored on edge in a vertical position (Fig. 17.6). Since they warp easily, it is desirable that they be stacked snugly to provide lateral support. Piling records flat avoids warping problems but makes removal or replacement difficult. These precautions may imply that records are fragile and easily damaged. Actually, plastic records are relatively unbreakable, but they scratch easily. However, they are quite easily cared for and their high quality and fidelity makes the necessary effort well worthwhile.

Evaluation and Selection of Records

Because recordings are so much a part of any student's experience, some aspects of their selection and effective use will readily be apparent to you. For example, quality of performance as a factor in evaluation is basic and needs no dis-

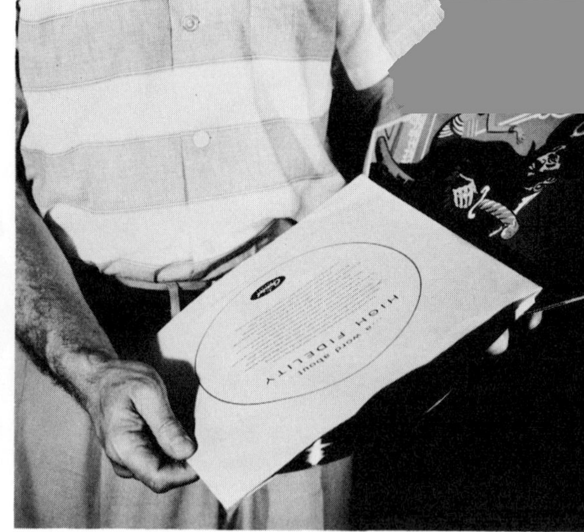

Michigan State University.

Fig. 17.5. These photographs show how to insert or remove records from covers. The inner envelope provides additional protection and makes buckling the outer cover unnecessary. Note how the fingers are kept off the record surface.

cussion. Less obvious, perhaps, but understandable to the teacher of music is the importance of objectives in selecting any kind of teaching material. The recording must suit your particular teaching needs to be of value, regardless of its other merits. For example, a New York Philharmonic recording of the Brahms *Variations on a Theme by Haydn* is less suitable than a tape recording of the same composition played by a good high-school orchestra when the purpose you have in mind is to let your high-school orchestra hear what their performance ought to sound like. Similarly, for a Music Literature class, where appreciation and enjoyment are the objectives, the Philharmonic would normally be preferable.

Limitations of Recordings

The advantages of recordings for teaching purposes are numerous. Yet, as with any other teaching material, there are also certain limitations. It is quite difficult to locate desired portions of a recording without bands or strips between sections. It is also difficult to set the stylus down on a microgroove playing surface without damage to a groove unless your player is equipped with a special counter-balanced tone arm which lowers gently at its own rate when operated manually. This type of manual tone arm is currently unavailable on

Both photographs from Neumade Products Corp., New York, New York.

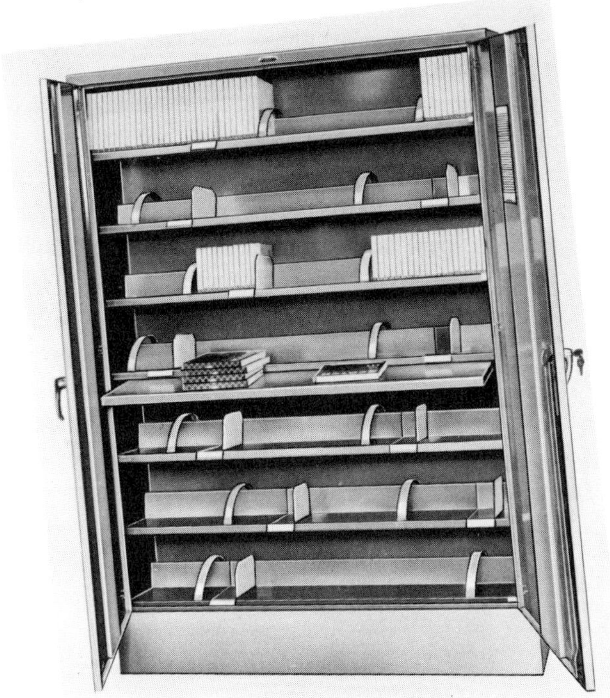

Fig. 17.6. Cabinets for records and tapes conserve space, provide protection, and simplify storage and retrieval problems. Two of many types available are illustrated above. The left cabinet will accommodate 600, 12″ records; the right, 306 5″ or 7″ tapes.

most cabinet-type phonographs and is not included with automatic record-changer mechanisms. It is, however, found on practically all professional play-back equipment.

Effective Use of Recordings

Discrimination in listening skills is a product of experience, and learning through listening proceeds much more readily with careful direction. Without such direction, each music student in a class tends to hear somewhat different things while listening to a record. The kind and extent of prelistening activity depends upon the purpose of the lesson. For pure enjoyment or recreation, teacher direction may be unnecessary or even undesirable. The "dissection" technique is as unsuited to music appreciation as it is to literature or poetry. However, for analysis of how a particular phrase is performed, of tonal balance between woodwinds and strings, or of the subtle elements in a crescendo or a pianissimo passage, specific direction as well as repetitive listening may be required.

Several elements must be present in any successful lesson as the capable music teacher knows. The first is *interest*, which must be motivated before significant learning of any kind can take place. You arouse interest in various ways depending upon the situation, the level of experience of your group, and the degree of interest already present. Your own enthusiasm and interest, your personality, and the relationship you have developed with your pupils are important factors. In any case, it is well to keep in mind that the starting point of an effective listening experience lies in the desire which each student brings to it.

The second necessary element in good listening is a *clear idea of what to listen for.* Unless we listen for general appreciation or for relaxation, some selective listening is required and this is where prelistening activities come in. Suggestions for listening may be teacher or pupil directed, depending again upon the purposes of the lesson, the interest and experience of the group, and similar factors. In any event, the effective listener always has some purpose or plan in mind as he listens to a recorded presentation.

Third, good listening is enhanced by *good listening conditions.* High quality in the phonograph and the recording contribute materially to effective listening. The acoustics of the room and proper location of the phonograph speaker in front of the group are likewise important. Close attention should be encouraged, casual conversation or other distractions avoided, and everything focused as much as possible on the listening experience.

Finally, the teacher and class do something *about* the listening experience when it is completed. The *follow-up* may apply to what has been learned, measure its effectiveness, or determine further steps needed. In an orchestra rehearsal, for example, several playings of a recorded passage on which the horns have had difficulty, should result in detectable improvement in execution. Results from listening to a Bach concerto in a Music Literature class may be detected in some measure from the intentness of the class as the recording is being played and in the nature of the following reactions.

TAPE RECORDINGS

Most of the virtues of good records are also found in tape recordings, plus certain unique benefits which make tape recorders valuable for music instruction at all levels. Among these advantages are the ease of recording by teachers or students, the possibility of immediate playback of such recordings, and the excellent quality and permanence of prerecorded tapes.

Recording for classroom use is by no means new. Before World War II, teachers were using disk recorders, modern versions of which are still employed for some purposes. Magnetic wire recorders, developed for communications purposes during the war, came into use during the late 1940s for music and speech work in spite of rather poor quality by modern standards. Both disk and wire recordings were rapidly superseded by the development of an improved recording process using quarter-inch tape.

How the Tape Recorder Works

While it is unnecessary for the instructor to understand the technical aspects of magnetic recording, an elementary comprehension is interesting as well as helpful in using the recorder. The surface of the tape is evenly coated with an iron oxide, the molecules of which readily rearrange themselves in accordance with electronic impulses received from a microphone. When the tape is rewound and played back, the process is reversed. Electronic impulses are received now from the tape, fed into the amplifier where they are strengthened and transmitted to a loud-speaker which changes the electrical impulses to sound waves. A simple diagram of what happens is shown in Fig. 17.7.

Whenever you record, an erase head located alongside of the recording head, automatically neutralizes any previously recorded patterns on the tape. This erasure takes place just before the tape passes over the recording head where new magnetic patterns are then recorded.

Two factors regarding the physical attributes of tape recordings are particularly important to the music teacher. The first is that, unlike records, tapes can be played an infinite number of times without any noticeable wear of the tape or loss in sound quality. The second is that the fidelity of tapes recorded with good equipment is superior to the fidelity which can be achieved by any other method. Accordingly, virtually all original recordings for phonograph records and motion picture sound tracks are now made on magnetic tape and later transferred to disk or film. Tape recording has literally taken over the sound-recording field.

Tape Recording and Playback Equipment

The quality of recording and playback equipment is a key factor in the excellence of a recording or its reproduction (Fig. 17.8). Equipment standards for music recording are necessarily higher than those for nonmusical purposes and several of these standards are worth noting.

Speed

Radio programs were initially recorded at a tape speed of 15 inches per second (IPS). During the mid-1950s recorders had improved sufficiently to reduce

3M Company, Minneapolis, Minnesota.

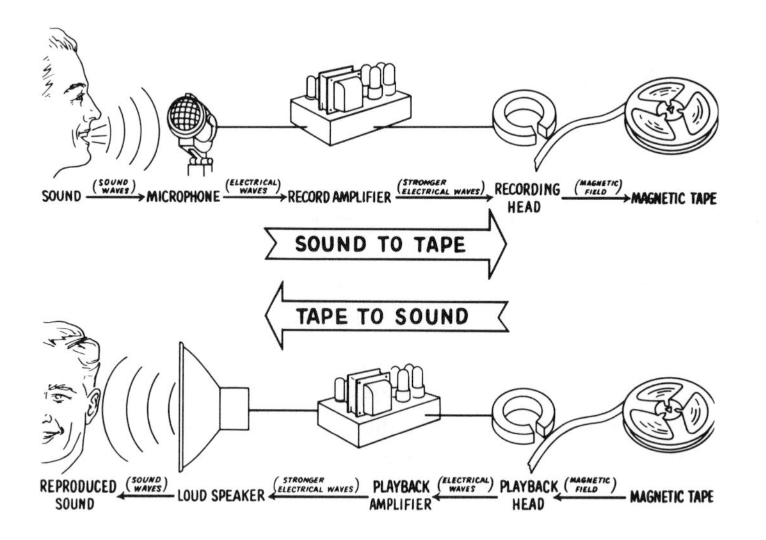

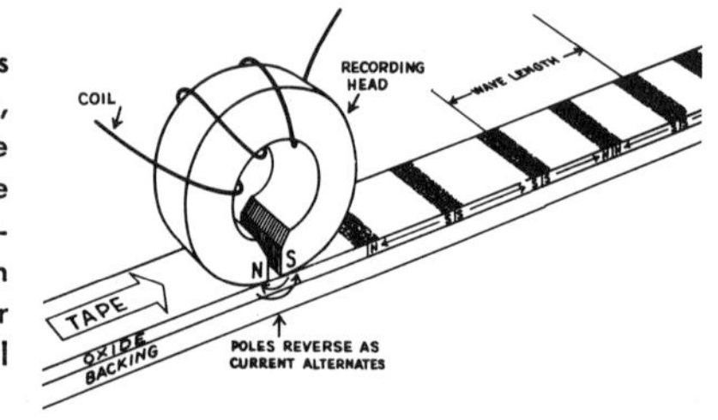

Fig. 17.7. When recorded on magnetic tape, sound waves are converted to electrical waves by the microphone, strengthened by an amplifier and transferred to the tape by means of a recording head as shown above. When the tape is played back, the process is reversed, with a playback head picking up magnetic impulses, converting them to electrical waves which are strengthened by the amplifier and fed to a loud speaker which converts the electrical waves to sound waves.

the speed to 7½ IPS. Advances in electronics have been so rapid that a tape speed of 3¾ IPS, or even 1⅞ IPS, can produce music recordings of excellent quality with professional recording equipment. For speech work (as in the Talking Books series) speeds of 15/16 IPS prove adequate. These rather remarkable improvements have been due to extensive research and development work both on recorders and on the tapes used in them.

Molectronics (a condensation of "molecular electronics") is a new field of scientific research created by demands of the space age. It has given rise to such spectacular developments as the transistor and to complete television circuits printed on a card smaller than the palm of your hand. It has made new magnetic recording and playback systems possible to the point where current forms will probably become obsolete in a few years. By then, you may have complete symphonies printed on a small card which can be inserted into a machine slot no larger than a parking meter and achieve sound quality equal or superior to the best equipment available in the mid-1960s.

The following table shows the reel sizes and tape lengths currently available.

UNINTERRUPTED RECORDING TIME
FOR VARIOUS MAGNETIC TAPE SPEEDS AND TAPE LENGTHS

Reel Size	Tape Length	Tape Speed (inches per second) 1⅞	3¾	7½
5″	600′	1 hour	30 min.	15 min.
5″	900′ [a]	90 min.	45 min.	22½ min.
7″	1200′	2 hours	1 hour	30 min.
7″	1800′ [a]	3 hours	90 min.	45 min.
7″	2400′ [a]	4 hours	2 hours	1½ hours

[a] Special base extra long play.
NOTE: All recording times are computed on basis of single track only. For dual track recording, time is doubled.

Quality of Recording and Reproduction

There are several factors in the sound quality of tape recordings of which the music teacher should be aware. These include motor-speed constancy, the quality and capacity of the amplifier, and the quality of the loud-speaker.

Motor-speed variation beyond very small limits produces unpleasant changes in pitch and tone called "wows" or "flutter." These cannot be tolerated in most music work, although they normally cause little difficulty in nonmusic applications.

Amplifier quality, as in a phonograph or radio, has marked influence on the range and accuracy of tonal response. Along with tape speed, the quality of the amplifier determines the degree of fidelity of either recording or reproduction. An output capacity of 10 to 15 watts is necessary for classroom work and a 25-watt amplifier is recommended for playback purposes in large areas such as auditoriums. While these outputs are in excess of what will normally be used, a reserve of power is necessary to avoid the distortion caused by using an amplifier at close to its capacity.

The *loud-speaker* is another important factor in the quality of your tape recorder. In playback of recorded tapes, the speaker is the "voice" of the instrument. Dual or multiple speakers with a "woofer" for low frequencies and a "tweeter" for high treble frequencies give excellent reproduction if located in baffles of suitable design and size. Such speakers are provided only with high-priced recorders, but one can be purchased separately and plugged in for use with any tape recorder, phonograph or radio.[2] Electronic developments have improved small speakers to the point where such speakers may be well suited to certain noncritical music uses.

Some additional considerations in the selection of tape recorders are suggested by the following questions.

[2] A detailed and helpful guide for selecting recording and reproduction equipment is given in MENC's *Music in American Education*, Source Book No. 2, 1955, pp. 230–232.

3M Company, Minneapolis, Minnesota.

Ampex Corporation, Redwood City, California.

3M Company, Minneapolis, Minnesota.

Ampex Corporation, Redwood City, California.

North American Philips Co., Inc., New York, New York.

3M Company, Minneapolis, Minnesota.

1. Is the recorder easy to operate? Threading and controls need not be complex and most tape recorders can be operated efficiently with a brief period of instruction. There should be a fast-forward and a fast-rewind mechanism and some kind of counter to simplify the location of desired portions on a reel of tape. Some kind of safety device is also desirable in order to prevent the accidental erasing of recorded materials.

2. Is the recorder readily portable? Flexibility of use is one of the real instructional advantages of the tape recorder. Thus it should be compact and sufficiently light in weight to be carried easily from one location to another. High-fidelity recorders are apt to be slightly less portable than general purpose equipment.

3. Is reliable and prompt repair service available? This consideration may well be the determining factor in selection between two good tape recorders. Occasional servicing and repairs are certain to be required and, other factors being relatively equal, you should purchase that equipment on which the best service can be assured. Many dealers are willing to loan a recorder or projector while one is being repaired in order to avoid interruption of use. It is wise to inquire about service when considering any type of audiovisual equipment.

Microphones and Microphone Techniques

Regardless of how good a recorder may be, it can record only what it "hears." Thus the microphone and the manner of its use are important considerations for the music teacher. Many types of microphones are available (Fig. 17.9). Familiarity with some nontechnical principles will help the music teacher in recording work. The first of these is that the microphone must be matched with the recorder for best results. For this reason, the simple crystal microphone supplied with many tape recorders is likely to be more satisfactory than a better microphone which is not matched with the recorder.

The best microphones for music work are the low impedance, directional type. Low impedance permits use of a cable up to 75 feet in length between the mike and the recorder, whereas high impedance circuits allow for only a short connecting cable. Nondirectional microphones pick up sounds from all directions. A wide-angle (120 degrees) unidirectional microphone provides sufficient spread for pickup of a performing group without catching undesirable echoes or other background noise. A second directional pickup is occasionally used for a soloist.

Fig. 17.8. Six representative, high-quality tape recorders, suitable for school music recording and reproduction are shown here. Most models have three speeds—7½, 3¾ and 1⅞ ips—will record and play dual-track monophonic tapes, and play two- and four-track stereo tapes. Certain models record stereo, provide an automatic reverse multiple-tape capacity and automatic threading.

Michigan State University.

Fig. 17.9. Microphones of various types are used in recording work. Top: directional microphone; middle: standard and finger types; lower: lavolier and crystal mikes.

The "mike" is nonselective and monaural. It picks up all sounds without discriminating between them as we would discriminate when listening to a concert or rehearsal, and it does so through a single "ear." Accordingly, care is necessary in placing the microphone to achieve the best balance and the most natural sound. The position selected needs to be sufficiently forward of the performing group to receive an equal balance from all sections. Experimentation is necessary to find this spot where the best focus of sound is found. Close one ear to get the monaural effect which the microphone will pick up.

Tape Care and Repair

Audio tape is readily cared for since it is wound on reels, and handling of the tape itself is seldom necessary except when threading on the tape recorder.

Storing the reels of tape in labeled cartons when not in use keeps them free of dust and makes them easy to locate. Colored reels and cartons are further aids to classification of tapes according to the types of material recorded on them.

Should a tape be accidentally torn or should you wish to remove or rearrange sections of it, splicing is a simple matter, as shown in Fig. 17.10.

Prerecorded Tapes

An important and rapidly expanding development in the tape field is that of prerecorded tapes for teaching purposes. Services have been established in many universities, colleges, and state departments of education whereby significant educational radio programs on tape are rerecorded, for a small fee, on rolls of tape sent in by schools. Catalogues are available from the above agencies, some of which also have a tape rental service.[3] The Department of Audiovisual Instruction of the National Education Association has prepared an excellent composite catalogue of such materials.[4] The finest taped programs in music and other areas are selected by a national committee of educators and made available to educational tape services or to schools on a rerecording or sale basis.

A steadily increasing number of high-fidelity tape recordings of symphonic, concert, and opera materials are likewise being offered for sale by record companies. In addition, several companies specialize in the sale of recorded tapes in music and other subjects.[5] The quality and permanence of these tape recordings make them of particular value to the music educator.

Suggested Uses for the Tape Recorder

Effective use of the tape recorder for prerecorded materials follows the principles discussed earlier with respect to records. In addition, however, there are numerous unique applications of tape recording in day-to-day music instruction. Zahrt, for example, lists the following uses which are pertinent to the secondary school:

1. Solo, ensemble, and group performances so that students may evaluate performance and check progress.
2. Vocal and instrumental compositions (solo, ensemble, orchestra, band, chorus) of festival music or required works for compositions to set standards of performance.
3. Artistically played piano accompaniments which soloists may use for rehearsal, or folk dance groups for performance.

[3] See the source list on pp. 578–579.

[4] Department of AudioVisual Instruction, *National Tape Recording Catalog* (2nd ed.), National Education Association, 1963.

[5] See the source list on p. 579.

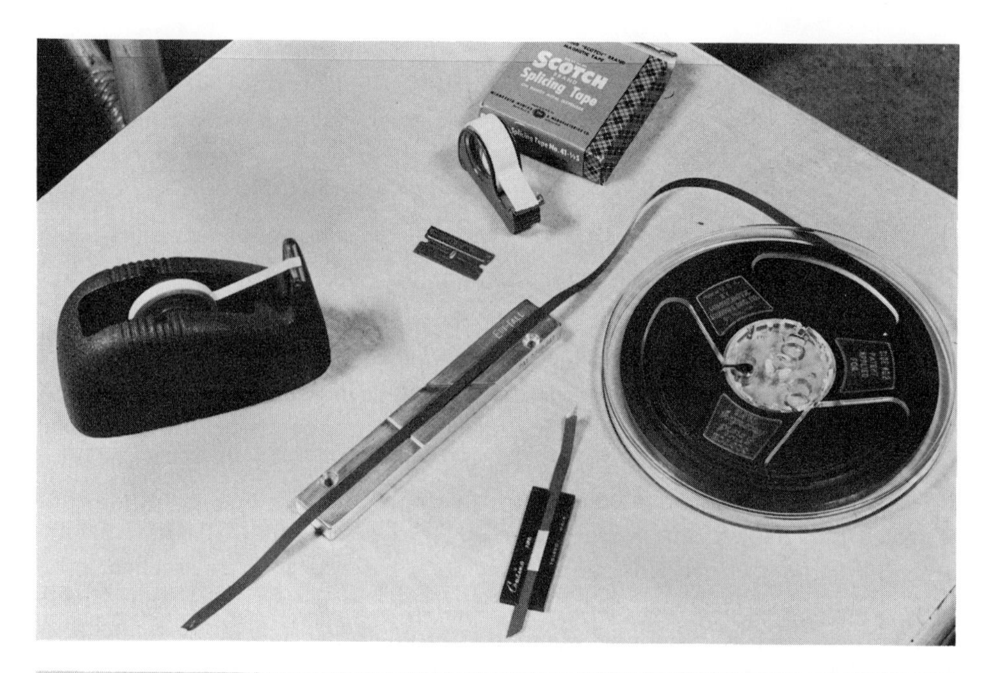

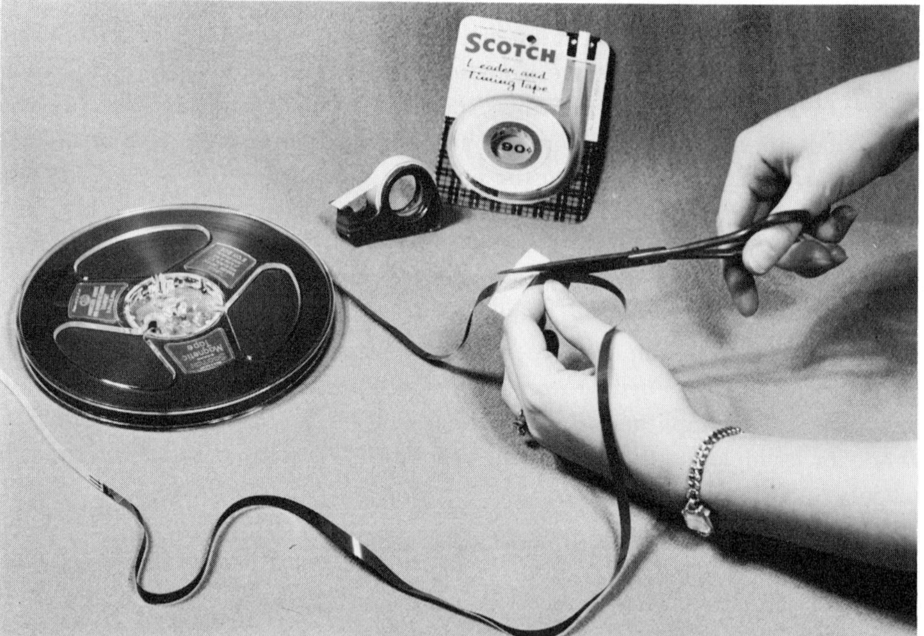

Both photographs from 3M Company, Minneapolis, Minnesota.

Fig. 17.10. To splice recording tape, place tape in cutting block and cut with razor in angled groove. Align both ends of tape with the uncoated (shiny) side up· Cover joined ends with splicing tape and trim edges as in lower illustration.

3M Company, Minneapolis, Minnesota.

Fig. 17.11. Radio programs can be recorded while the broadcast is going on, or recorded on tape beforehand and edited if necessary.

4. Programs for radio broadcast [Fig. 17.11].
5. Radio programs for future use in the classroom.
6. Programs for exchange between grades and between schools.
7. Classroom activities for playback at PTA meetings.
8. Demonstration lessons for reference of classroom teachers.
9. Rote songs, music for rhythmic activities for use by classroom teacher.
10. Lessons taught by practice teachers.
11. Concerts by visiting groups.
12. Voices of out-of-tune singers for sake of record and to identify progress.
13. Tone quality of voices; boys' changing voices, etc.
14. One or two parts of part-songs as an aid to teaching part-singing.
15. Rehearsal of music for mixed choirs when schedule will not permit combined rehearsals. Separate recordings are made of the girls' group and the boys' group. In rehearsal the missing parts are supplied by playback of the tape.
16. Auditions for placement in orchestras, bands, choirs, and ensembles.[6]

Another instructor points out the value of the tape recorder in permitting the director to hear a performing group as it really sounds. This is sometimes neces-

[6] Merton S. Zahrt, "Use of Tape Recordings," *New York State Music News*, October, 1951, pp. 3–4.

sary because the good director instinctively translates a phrase or chord into sounds in his mind—sounds which his group may not actually be achieving.[7]

Other uses which readily appeal to the busy music director include the taping of accompaniments for operetta rehearsals so that the cast has the benefit of the orchestra without the orchestra having to be present; taping of drum cadences for marching so new band members may practice by themselves; and the use of taped selections, not available on records, to prepare the General Music classes or the student body for a concert which is to be played.

The uses of the tape recorder in music teaching are virtually without limit. It is at once a timesaver, a convenience, and a powerful instructional tool for the music teacher and pupil.

Stereophonic Sound

The phenomenon of stereo sound recording and reproduction is worthy of special attention. Because of its marked superiority in realism, even over high-fidelity recordings as we know them, stereo sound has a promising future in music education.

The principle of stereo sound is a simple one. We hear through two ears and the sound which reaches one ear is slightly different from that heard by the other. This difference is due in part to the location of the ears on opposite sides of the head. Sounds from the left are heard better by the left ear and vice versa. This is the reason why a person with normal hearing can rather readily detect the direction from which a sound is coming. If we had only a single ear, such detection would be much more difficult.

As we listen to a "live" musical performance, that is, if we are actually present at a concert, we are actually hearing more than those who are listening to the same concert on the radio. The reason for this is that the radio listeners are hearing sounds emanating from a single microphone. (Even if more than one microphone is used, the sounds are mixed and transmitted as a single series of sounds.) In effect, therefore, the radio listener receives monaural sound while those in attendance at the concert hear binaurally.

Some metropolitan radio and television stations are now broadcasting symphony concerts stereophonically by transmitting one sound source on FM and the other on AM radio frequencies. With two corresponding radio sets tuned in, the listener receives stereophonic sound. Stereo broadcasting is now primarily done, however, on FM stations alone, through multiplexing. This means that the broadcast signal is split into two parts. The listener then uses a standard FM set in combination with a special FM unit to pick up both signals for stereo sound. Some manufacturers have combined the two units in one assembly. The difference be-

[7] See Herbert J. Phillips, "The Tape Recorder," *Journal of Education*, January, 1955, p. 15.

tween the two types of sound must be heard to be appreciated. It is a difference in realism and dimension, sometimes slight but frequently striking.

Stereophonic recordings have been made on both disks and tape. Two or more microphones are used, with the sound impulses from each going into separate amplifiers and onto separate tracks on a tape (Fig. 17.12). Played back simultaneously through dual speakers or through headphones with separate sound sources for each ear, the effect, in richness, in fullness of tone, and in presence, is unforgettably vivid.

Stereophonic sound is now commonly used in many advanced types of motion picture presentations. As many as seven separate sound tracks are heard, for example, in Cinerama. In stereo tape recorders and phonographs, the resourceful educator has tools with potential for marked new developments in the field of music education.

Listening Centers

A feature of materials centers and music areas in new school buildings is the listening center. This may be a group of small, sound-proofed, acoustically treated rooms where small groups or individuals can listen to recordings. The advantages of a listening center, however, may be secured without special rooms by means of ear phones plugged into record players or tape recorders. By means of jack boxes (Fig. 17.13), as many as six headsets may be used. Such an arrangement, makes it possible even in an ordinary classroom, library, or study area to provide excellent listening facilities at low cost. It makes feasible individual or small group listening exercises without disturbing others in the same room. Stereo listening is achieved by using dual instead of single connections with separate sound tracks then being played to each ear.

It is as important that good quality earphones be used for music listening as it is to have good speakers in a hi-fi or stereo system. Otherwise the quality of sound of which the system is normally capable cannot come through to the listener. Sponge rubber or synthetic cushions around each earphone are frequently used to protect headsets from accidental damage. These cushions also serve to screen out exterior noise and thus further improve the listening experience.

Telelectures

Electronic developments in the telephone industry have brought many new features, including one of particular interest to teachers—the *telelecture,* or *telecourse.* As these terms suggest, the telephone is used to bring learning ex-

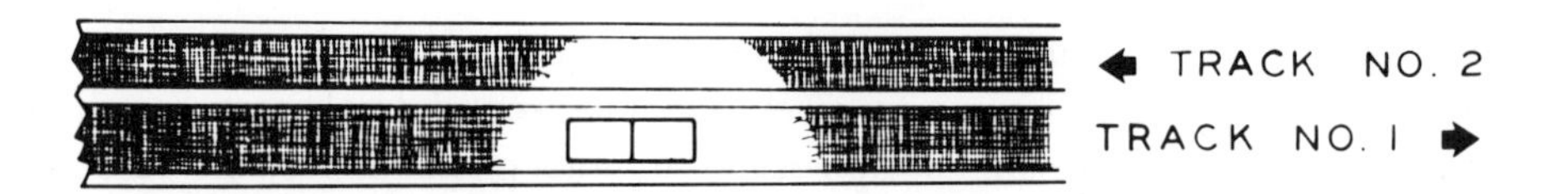

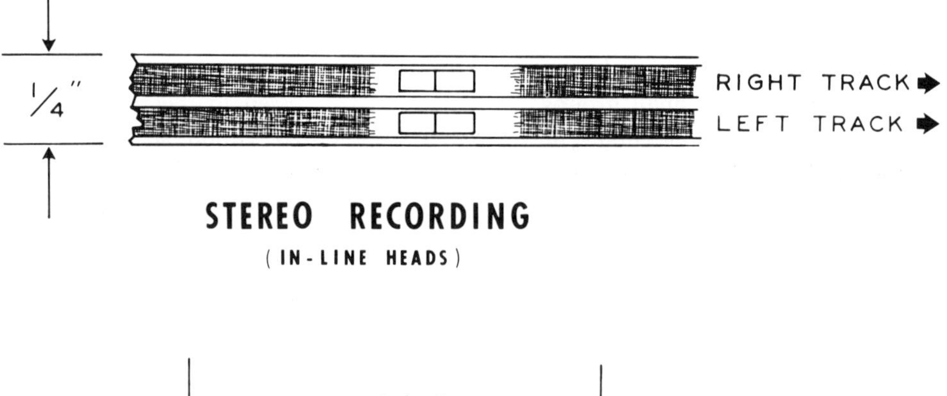

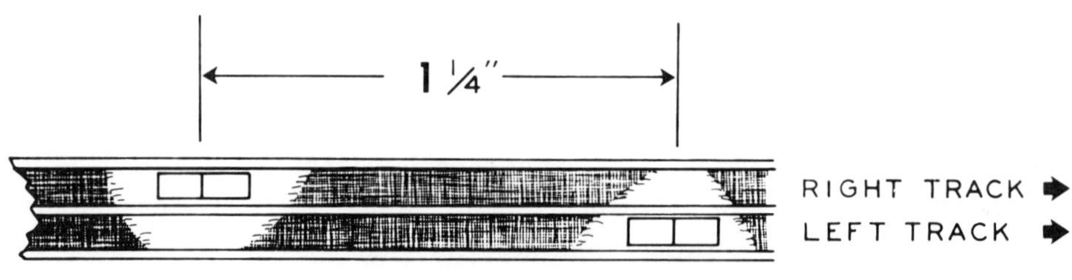

3M Company, Minneapolis, Minnesota.

Fig. 17.12. The difference between monophonic and stereo recording. Top: Dual-track monophonic recording; Middle: Stereo recording (in-line heads); Bottom: Stereo recording (staggered heads). The top recording is from a single microphone on on track; the bottom two are two methods of recording simultaneously from two microphones.

Fig. 17.13. By means of jack boxes such as these, a number of headphones can be plugged into a record player or tape recorder for individual or small-group listening without disturbing others. What differences in assignments and methods are made possible by this device?

Michigan State University.

periences—such as interviews with subject experts, or personalities in some area of public life—into the classroom (Fig. 17.14).

Special equipment supplied by the telephone company is used which consists of an amplifier and loud-speaker system that enables a whole class or assembly

Michigan Bell Telephone Company.

Fig. 17.14. An audience listens to a Telelecture from an authority at a remote point. Lecturer's photo is locally projected on the screen as he speaks—as are key points being made, a score being played or discussed, or other related scenes.

to listen to the person speaking on the other end of the line. Costs approximate long-distance telephone charges plus a fee for the equipment. The instructor or his students can ask questions or carry on conversations with the distant speaker so that the whole arrangement can be tailored to the specific interests of the group. Arrangements are made in advance with speakers and a time is set. For best results, these arrangements should be quite specific as to topics to be covered, objectives to be achieved, and the types of questions likely to be raised by the class members. Consider the value to a music class of a discussion with Leonard Bernstein on modern music or with other noted musicians or composers on their particular areas of interest. While such people could hardly be expected to provide a private concert, it might be possible to arrange to listen in on a practice period or a portion of a rehearsal. Faculty members of the school of music in your state university can also be reached via the telelecture as can performers and directors in other school systems.

ELECTRONIC TUNING AND ANALYZING DEVICES

In light of the importance of public performance in the music education program and the values of good musicianship, we should note several helpful tuning devices now available to the teacher of instrumental music. The earliest of these electronic tuners, called the Lecktro Tuner, provides a continuous A or B flat at two different volume levels for use in tuning instruments before rehearsals (Fig. 17.15). A later, more comprehensive development is a stroboscopic, tonal device which rapidly and accurately measures the pitch of any note in the scale. The device, commonly known as the Stroboconn, reacts both audibly and visually when a performer plays off pitch even slightly. It can be used to correct intonation of entire chords. A more portable modification called the Strobotuner provides similar results for sections and individuals. The Dynalevel provides electronic responses to vocal or instrumental tones in the form of color patterns in a tube. The instrument is a simplified oscilloscope which indicates visually the dynamic range of tones played or sung into it. Regular use of such devices tends to make the students more conscious of pitch and consequently to improve intonation and performance.

RADIO AND TELEVISION IN MUSIC EDUCATION

As the cultural historian of A.D. 2000 deals with the early and mid-twentieth century, he will doubtless note the tremendous impact upon American life of the electronic media of mass communication. In the midst of the present communications revolution, teachers may fail to appreciate both the challenges and the opportunities facing them in the realm of radio and television.

A second factor to be recognized about television in the current cultural scene lies in its general effectiveness. Depending upon the point of view, this effectiveness may be either good or bad. One may decry, with good reason, the level of much of the entertainment fare which our students find attractive. Yet, if we are to be candid with ourselves, this level is one measure of the past effectiveness of education on the buying public's tastes. The improvement of these tastes is a particular challenge to teachers of music.

On the other hand, the picture has its favorable side. Today, more people are seeing and hearing good drama in one year than in the whole history of the theater before television. In varying degrees, the same can be said for orchestra, concert artists, and ballet. Key figures of the cultural, political, and entertainment worlds have never been so intimately known to millions of people as they are today. In short, standards of many kinds *have* been raised by commercial tele-

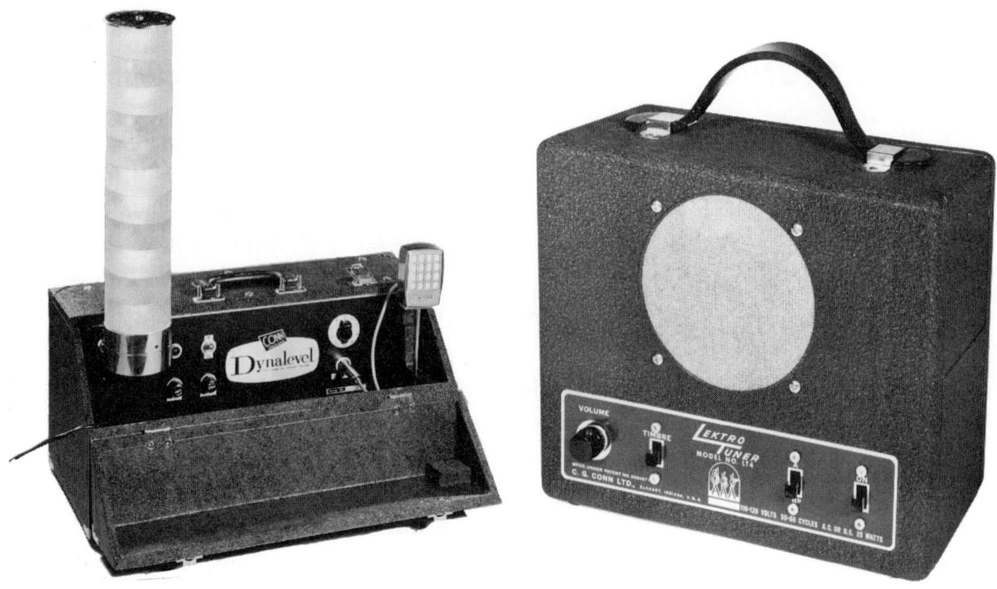

All photographs from Conn Corporation, Elkhart, Indiana.

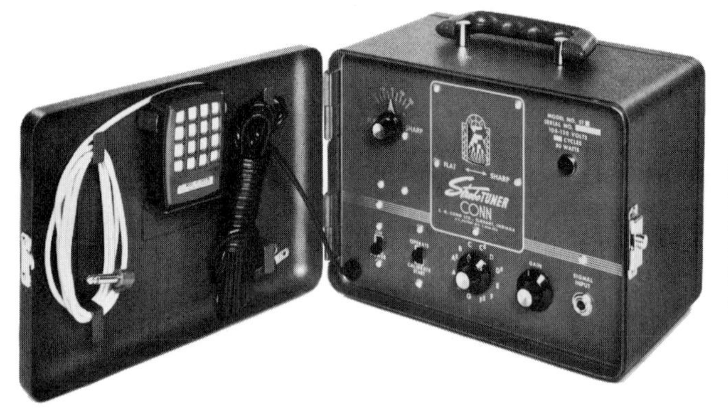

Fig. 17.15. These examples of electronic aids to music instruction can save time for the director and enable the music student to learn important music elements by himself.

vision programs. The fact that this phenomenon has been brought about by competition for viewing audiences rather than by a desire to improve public tastes may in itself be a tribute to the educational system. Poor programs by any standards do not last for long when the mere flick of a dial can tune them out.

The music educator has gained more than most from television. Excellent musical performance is the rule rather than the exception when music is played as part of a program, either in concert or as accompaniment. Even hillbilly music is played in tune these days, and the tributes regularly paid to their orchestra and choral conductors by prominent television stars are noted by budding musicians everywhere. MacLean and Lee summarize the overall benefits of electronic communications to the music field on the following page.

> In a quarter of a century, from the days of the crystal and pickle-tube radio sets to elaborate TV-FM radio and high-fidelity phonograph combinations, more advance has been made in bringing music to everybody than in all the past history of mankind. . . . Perhaps in no other field has an out-of-school agency of education made so great a contribution to the school itself and been so little in conflict with its purposes.[8]

The nature of commercial radio has changed considerably since the advent of television. Whereas the big shows of a few years ago have disappeared for the most part, radio has continued to sustain itself very well on a diet of recorded music, sports, newscasting, and occasional outstanding variety shows such as "Monitor." The "disk jockey" has developed in importance as recorded popular music has taken over the major portion of broadcast time on most AM stations.

A significant increase in FM (frequency modulation) stations marked the late 1950s and early 1960s. This development has continued in both commercial and educational stations and has provided opportunity for much flexibility and creativity in programing. Short-range FM stations suitable for moderate-sized school systems can be installed at relatively low cost (under $2000) and can serve both teaching and community relations purposes for the school system.

Educational Radio and Television in Music Instruction

The relation of educational radio to music instruction is too obvious to require elaboration. In areas where educational radio exists (Fig. 17.16) and music programs are available, the tape recorder provides an ideal means of making such programs available for class use when and where they can best be used. This removes one of the basic limitations of educational radio, namely, the fixed time schedule of broadcasts. The same limitation applies to television at the present time and a similar practical solution may be in prospect.

Professional videotape recorders such as those used in broadcasting stations record both sound and picture on a 2-inch magnetic tape at a speed of 15 IPS. A 14-inch accommodates a full-hour program. Newer, portable, transistorized models, designed for CCTV, use 1-inch tape at 7½ IPS and a 10½ inch reel will record 96 minutes of program material (Fig. 17.17). Tapes can be rewound and played back immediately on the videotape recorder. Quality of picture and sound are excellent and are good for 100 uses or more. As with ¼-inch sound tapes, videotapes can be erased when desired and used for new recordings.

New electronic developments are occurring so rapidly that videotape recorders are certain to become practicable for classroom use in terms of both size and cost. At this writing, prototype videotape recorders are in existence using ¼-inch

[8] Malcolm S. MacLean and Edwin A. Lee, *Change and Process in Education*, Holt, Rinehart and Winston, 1956, pp. 53–54.

National Association of Educational Broadcasters, Washington, D.C.

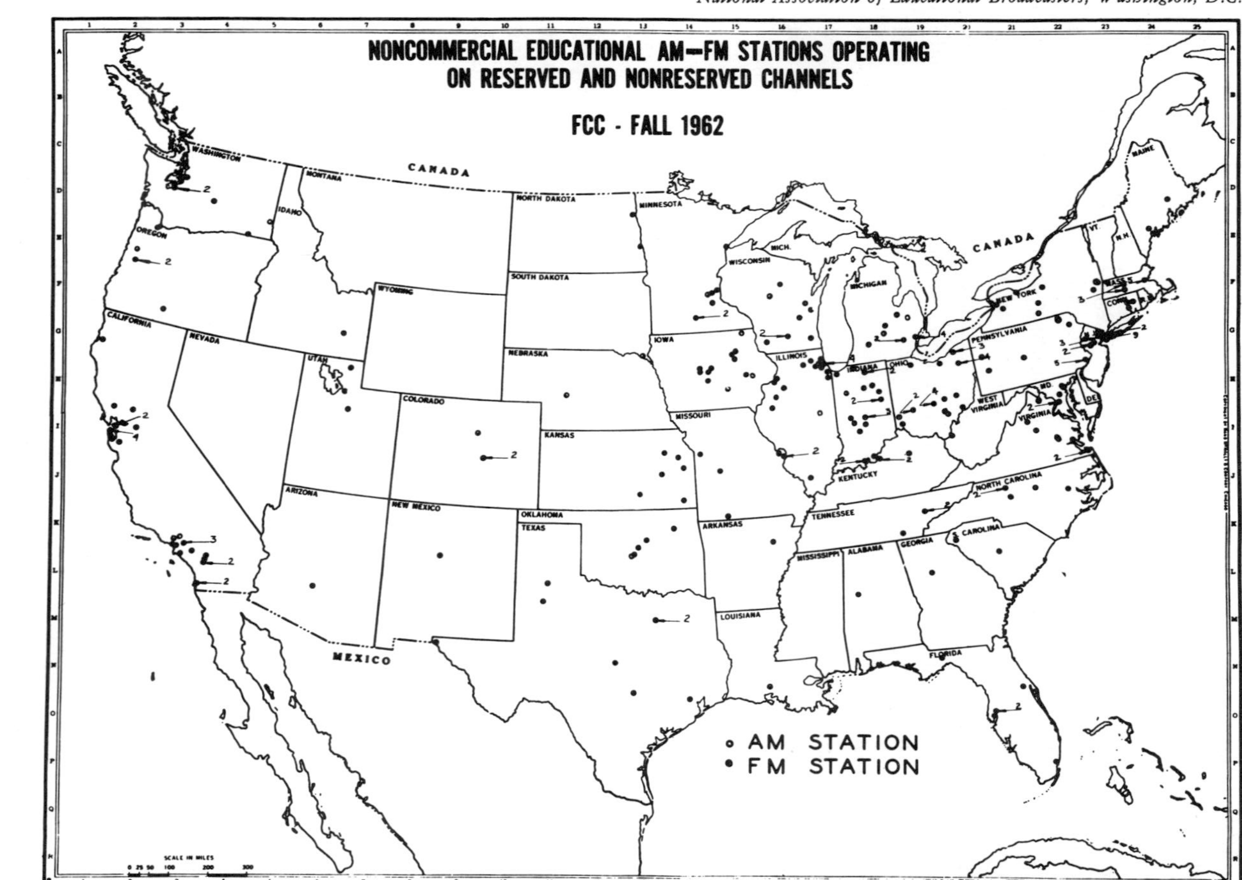

Fig. 17.16. Instead of having been eliminated by television, educational radio stations have steadily increased in number during the recent years. What are the reasons for this?

Fig. 17.17. Portable videotape recorders such as this presage the classroom videotape recorder of the future. Of what advantage will such recorders be to the music teacher?

Precision Instrument Company, Palo Alto, California.

tape and planned to sell for under $1000. It is only a question of time until such recorders become regularly used in classrooms for color as well as black and white recording. When this occurs the teacher will be able to record programs and use them whenever desired.

Extensive experimentation with closed- and open-circuit television, including music-education programs, has demonstrated the effectiveness of this medium both for supplemental and for direct instruction. Hagerstown, Maryland and Anaheim, California after several years of experimental programs have incorporated CCTV as a permanent part of their educational programs. Among many broadcast ETV programs across the nation, the Midwest Program in Airborne Television Instruction (MPATI) is unique. Programs are transmitted from a plane flying at 23,000 ft. altitude to an area covering parts of six states, 13,000 schools and over 5,000,000 students.

While a shortage of expert teachers in some subject areas can be relieved to an extent by instructional television, the more important benefits of the medium lie in the opportunities it provides for better and more complete educational programs in the schools and colleges of the nation. Imagine the music assembly of the future in which, on wide screen and with high-fidelity stereophonic sound, the great orchestras, concert performers, and musical plays of the world can be brought in whenever desired by means of video tape. Closed-circuit television can bring to any or all homerooms selected features such as an outstanding community song leader, the school orchestra, and soloists or ensembles playing their music festival numbers. Highlights of the festival itself in a distant town as well as other outstanding musical events from afar can be telecast from the scene and viewed in the school or taped for later use (Fig. 17.18).

It behooves us to consider carefully the role which television can play to best advantage in vitalizing and expanding music programs in the years ahead. Both radio and television have the educational advantages of immediacy, of introducing music specialists to any classroom, and of emotional stimulation through fine programs expertly presented. Both, as we have seen, also share certain limitations. But, along with other audiovisual materials, radio and television present challenging opportunities to the teacher prepared to take advantage of them.

An MENC report of the mid-1950s predicted that, in time, ETV would find its rightful place among the teaching tools available to music teachers.[9] This observation has proved to be substantially correct though somewhat conservative. Some of the more exceptional ETV programs are in music education which lends itself particularly well to the dissemination of outstanding teaching and of musical performance.

During the years ahead we may expect continued improvement in the quality of lessons on TV as we learn more how to use its particular capabilities. The development of inexpensive videotape recorders with which schools can record programs for replay whenever desired promises to remove the principal remaining barriers to sophisticated and extensive use of this powerful medium of instruction.

Copyright Law and the Schools

An important consideration in extending television use in schools and colleges, on the other hand, is that of protecting the rights of producing agencies. This is part of a broader national problem created by the development of elec-

[9] See Richard Berg in *Music in American Education,* Music Educators National Conference, 1955, p. 221.

National Association of Educational Broadcasters, Washington, D.C.

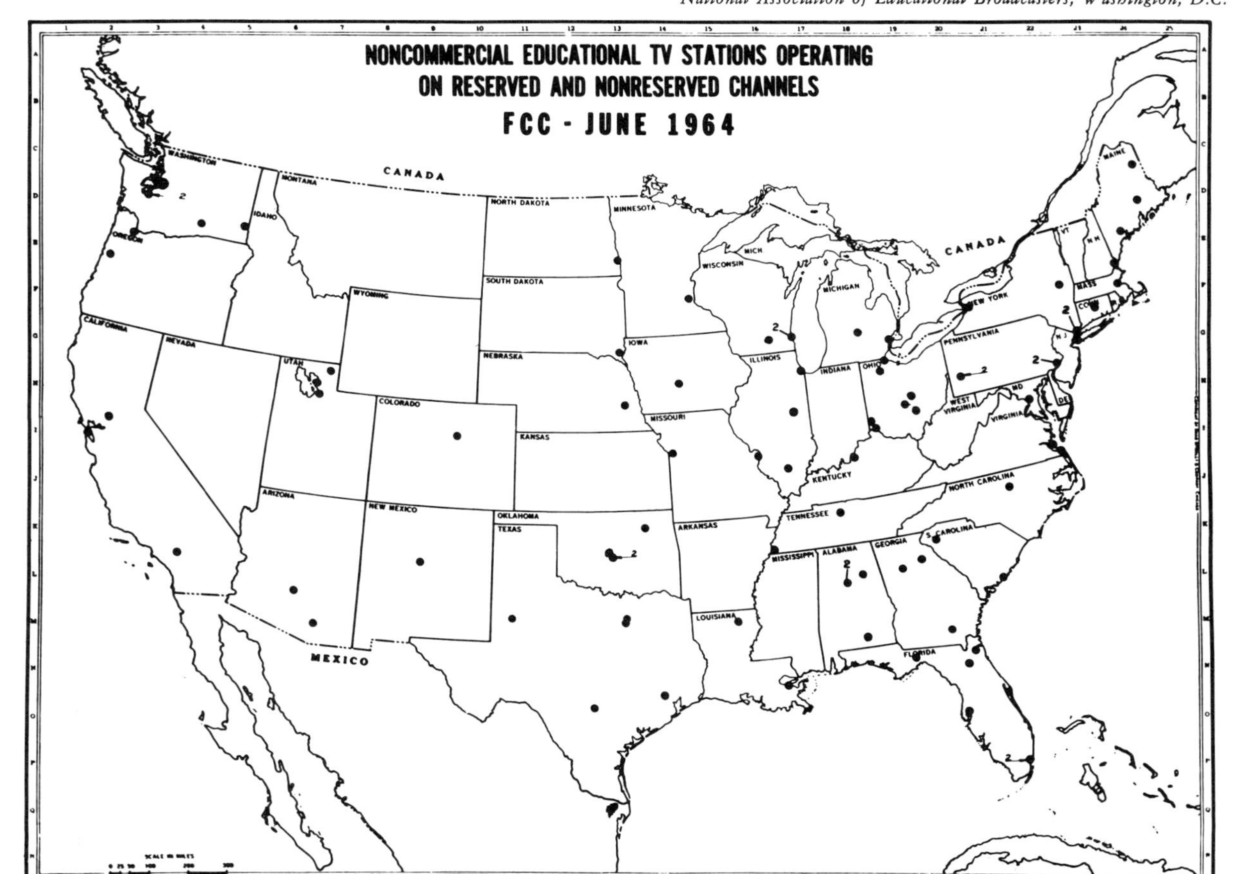

Fig. 17.18. Educational Television stations will one day blanket the nation. How can ETV benefit the music program in your school?

Music Educator's National Conference.

Fig. 17.19. Portable and relatively inexpensive TV cameras and equipment are used for CCTV programs in the Chicago Public Schools and in many other cities. How can music teachers use such facilities and programs to advantage?

tronic copying devices which can quickly reproduce printed or visual materials in whatever amounts are desired. Quite clearly, the public interest requires reasonable protection for writers, publishers, and producers lest the well-springs of creativity be cut off at their source. Just as clearly, the interests of public education must be protected against rigorous controls which would make the best teaching and learning materials economically impractical for most of our nation's schools. Congress must find an equitable solution as it revises the antiquated Copyright Law of 1909. Educators have an important stake in the outcome and a professional responsibility to participate intelligently and effectively in helping to shape it.

SUMMARY

Educational media in music instruction have one purpose: to improve learning. They are selected first in terms of suitability to teaching objectives and, second, in terms of quality of the media themselves.

Audio materials include such valuable tools as phonograph records, tape recordings, prerecorded tapes, stereo records and tapes, and radio programs. Television is included here also because, although strongly visual in nature, its educational characteristics and programing requirements have much in common with those of radio.

Effective use of audio materials, like all teaching methods, must be based upon well-defined teaching objectives. While there are numerous good methods of using phonograph records, prerecorded tapes, and radio and television programs in music teaching—all require careful planning, direction of listening, and appropriate listening conditions for good results. Equipment of high quality, and prompt, dependable repair service are likewise essential.

Uses of the tape recorder in music are both numerous and valuable. It is at once a timesaver, a convenience, and a powerful instructional tool. Music teachers should become skilled in its use and in the use of microphones to secure satisfactory recordings.

Radio and television are important media both for reception and broadcast activities in music education. Broadcasting has rather stringent requirements which must be met in order to realize significant educational or public-relations benefits from its use. The music teacher needs, also, to keep abreast of significant developments in stereo sound, video tape, electronic tuners, and other pertinent devices, and should apply them educationally as such application becomes feasible.

SUGGESTED ACTIVITIES

1. Have a committee from the class write for the latest catalogues of phonograph records and tape recordings. Then (1) make a simple evaluation of the sources in terms of suitability of materials, accessibility, and prices; and (2) prepare a display of catalogues to be used when reporting to the class. If possible, secure sufficient copies so that each student may have a set.
2. Follow the same procedure for audio equipment, including phonographs, tape recorders, school-type radios and television receivers. Have representative types of equipment available for demonstration to the class. Your audiovisual service center can be helpful here.

3. Arrange with a dealer for a class demonstration of stereo tape or records. Discuss where and how stereo sound can best be used in music classes.
4. Plan for three different uses of the tape recorder in music teaching situations. Include a statement of objectives and a description of the recording activity you will use. Also describe the proper physical and mechanical arrangements for using the tape recorder to best advantage.
5. Compare the way you would use records with the way you would use school broadcasts in a General Music class.
6. Arrange to view a televised music program (or a filmed recording of such a program) in your music education class. Describe (1) the utilization technique you would use with this lesson in a high-school class; (2) the unique values of the televised lesson seen; and (3) ways in which the program could be improved.
7. Have several representatives of your class confer with a television station program manager. Get his recommendations on the major considerations and the details involved in planning for a school music telecast over a local station.
8. Write your Congressman for the latest information available on revision of the Copyright Law of 1909. Study and discuss those aspects affecting school use of materials and prepare a position paper to send to your Congressman.

SELECTED READINGS

Cypher, Irene, "100 Audiovisual Ideas: Music," *Instructor*, January, 1960, pp. 69–70.

Doyle, E. J., "Teaching via TV," *Music Educators Journal*, January, 1961, pp. 90–91.

Hall, David, "The Nonavailable Recording," *Music Educators Journal*, September–October, 1963, pp. 136–138.

Hansen, Helge, "A Guide To High Fidelity in the Music Department," *Music Educators Journal*, September–October, 1963, pp. 111–112.

Hartshorn, Wm. C., "The Role of Listening," in *Basic Concepts in Music Education, Fifty-seventh Yearbook*, National Society for the Study of Education, University of Chicago Press, 1958, pp. 261–291.

Lewis, Philip, "Teaching Machines Have the Beat," *Music Educators Journal*, November–December, 1962, pp. 94–98.

Molnar, John W., "Teaching with a Tape Recorder," *Music Journal*, May, 1961, pp. 44 ff.

Music in American Education, Source Book No. Two, Music Educators National Conference, National Education Association, 1955, pp. 220–232.

Department of Audiovisual Instruction, *National Tape Recording Catalog*, National Education Association, 1963.

Page, Eleanor, "Music on Educational Radio and Television," in Department of Music, *Current Trends in Music Education*, University of Texas, 1962, pp. 49–55.

Raymer, D., "Tape Recorder: a Second Teacher," *Music Educators Journal*, January, 1961, pp. 90–91.

Schramm, Wilbur, Jack Lyle, Ithiel de Sola Pool, *The People Look at Educational Television*, Stanford University Press, 1963.

Schroeder, Duane, "Audio-Unit for Music Theory Classes," *Music Educators Journal*, February–March, 1960, pp. 92–93.

Sherburn, Merrill L., "Music in the Language Laboratory," *Music Educators Journal,* January, 1964, pp. 109–110.

Thiel, John, "Technical Media in the Academy of Music and the Creative Arts," *Music Educators Journal,* June–July, 1961, pp. 59–64.

Webster, Frank W., "Music Education by Television," *Music Educators Journal,* January, 1955, pp. 21–22.

Wittich, Walter A., and Charles F. Schuller, *AudioVisual Materials: Their Nature and Use* (rev. ed.), Harper & Row, 1962.

Films and Filmstrips:

Lessons from the Air, B & W, 14 min., British Information Services.

Listen Well, Learn Well, Color, 11 min., Coronet.

Magnetic Recorder: Its Operation and Uses, B & W, 19 min., University of Iowa.

Tape Recording for Instruction, B & W, 20 min., Indiana University.

The Tape Recorder: an Effective Teaching Instrument, B & W, 10 min., University of Texas.

Increasing the Effectiveness of Teaching with Tape Recording (filmstrip), sound, B & W, 10 min., Minnesota Mining & Mfg. Co.

San Diego Public Schools, San Diego, California.

CHAPTER

18

Music in the Visual Dimension

We tend to think of music primarily as an auditory experience. Yet the world of music, and particularly of music learning, involves much that is visual. The instruments themselves and how they are played, the musical score and how it is read, the conductor and how he directs, the performers and the manner of their performance—all have visual elements of great significance. The experienced listener even sees in his mind's eye some kind of picture of what the composer intended to express through his music.

In the final analysis, all learning takes place through the physical senses, and, in general, the more adequate the sensory experience, the better the learning. There is much evidence that seeing is the most efficient of the channels through which learning experience is acquired. We tend to learn best and remember longest those things which we can see as compared with those things which we can only hear, or read, or talk about. Thus, where visualization is pertinent and feasible, good teachers visualize.

Good teachers also know that a combination of materials and methods is normally better than any one type alone. In a lesson on instruments of the orchestra, for example, appropriate charts, films, recordings and demonstrations of the instruments themselves may be used along with related readings and discussion. In a music lesson on Mozart, emphasis may be placed on listening, reading, discussion, and a film on Mozart's life. The experienced teacher chooses those learning methods and materials which will best achieve the objectives of the lesson (Fig. 18.1). Since the visual element is important in the learning process, let us look more closely at some of the possibilities of visualization in music.

CHALKBOARDS AND STUDY DISPLAYS

Among the visual devices which are most readily available for use by the music teacher are the chalkboard, the display board, and the felt board.

From the Encyclopaedia Britannica Film, The Brass Choir *(2nd ed.).*

From the Encyclopaedia Britannica Film, The Woodwind Choir *(2nd ed.).*

From the Encyclopaedia Britannica Film, The Woodwind Choir *(2nd ed.).*

From the Encyclopaedia Britannica Film, Playing Good Music, The String Quartet—Techniques.

Fig. 18.1. These scenes showing professional musicians at work represent one of numerous types of sound motion pictures available to the music teacher.

The Chalkboard

One of the most familiar and convenient teaching tools is the chalkboard (Fig. 18.2). It is also commonly one of the most misused in spite of the fact that good use is largely a matter of a little care plus the application of a few simple principles:

1. Keep it clean. This is not only a matter of cleanliness, but primarily one of providing good contrast and visibility for materials placed on the chalkboard.

Fig. 18.2. One of many uses for the chalkboard in music instruction.

Lansing Public Schools, Lansing, Michigan.

Uniform downward strokes of the eraser, rather than a circular motion, will produce the best results when erasing.

2. Write or draw for the back row. Use heavy lines and characters large enough to be read easily anywhere in the music room. Test your technique by checking occasionally from the rear of the room. Remember that two-inch letters at 30 feet appear to be about the size of eight-point newspaper type at a normal reading distance of 18 inches.[1] This principle applies also to lettering on charts, displays, maps, posters, and other visuals.

3. Avoid crowding. Notes, signatures, and staff symbols which are large enough will still be difficult to read easily if crowded. Plan to use generous space. If necessary, erase and start over. If it's worth putting on the board, it's worth making readable.

4. Avoid glare. Sunlight or bright light hitting the board at the right angle can make the best work difficult, if not impossible, to see from some parts of the room.

5. Practice. Writing large letters and characters with heavy lines requires some practice for most people, but a little practice pays big dividends in visibility and effectiveness of chalkboard work.

Music staffs are commonly painted on chalkboard surfaces. These are usually located on one or more of the panels to the side of the board so as not to interfere with other uses of the board. Reasonable care in the formation of notes, clefs, key, and time signatures takes little additional time for the teacher and makes for better visual comprehension. Careless work by the instructor, tends to make the information on the chalkboard appear less important as well as less clear to the student.

[1] See Arthur Robinson, "The Size of Lettering for Maps and Charts," *Surveying and Mapping*, January–March, 1950, pp. 37–44.

Additional staffs can, of course, be drawn with the *staff liner.* Few people can draw a straight line on a sheet of paper, much less on a chalkboard, without a guide of some kind. A faint guide line is helpful and a heavy yardstick used with the staff liner can provide a series of level, uniform staffs when needed. Be sure that all of the five pieces of chalk in the liner are of the equal length and thickness. Sandpaper the tips if necessary to produce broad, even lines.

Many teachers find the *hidden drawing technique* to have useful applications in some music exercises.[2] This consists of revealing one segment of the board at a time on which, for example, a series of augmented and diminished chords or a musical phrase has been placed and covered in advance. The reverse side of a spring roller mounted map or chart may be used, or lightweight drapery material hung on a wire so that it can be pulled sideways. At the appropriate point in the lesson, the teacher removes the covering from the part of the exercise to be identified or discussed. A similar effect can be accomplished by covering sections of the chalkboard with strips of paper mounted horizontally with masking tape or Styx.[3] The strips are pulled off easily at the right moment. These techniques have the advantage of focusing the attention of the class sharply on the prepared chalkboard materials without having them in evidence until the best psychological point in the lesson has been reached.

Colored chalk may be useful on some occasions where it is desirable to direct attention to a particular note in a series of chords, to the several voices in a vocal score, or to sectional placement in a marching band formation. Different colors might be used for strings, reeds, brasses, and the percussion group in a chalkboard diagram of a symphony orchestra. Pastel rather than art-type colored chalks should be used to avoid later difficulty in cleaning the board.

Methods of cleaning chalkboard surfaces vary with the type and quality of boards. Water cannot be used on some, and abrasive cleaners should rarely be used on *any* chalkboard. Make it your business to find how the chalkboards in your room can be cleaned to best advantage and use that method. Clean erasers and clean boards provide the proper starting point for use of this effective and versatile medium.

Magnetic chalkboards are a relatively recent development with useful applications in a number of subjects. The magnetic chalkboard consists of a metal backing coated with a chalkboard surface. Small bar magnets on which symbols are mounted can be used to represent individuals or groups in a marching band. The magnets hold to the board surface, but can easily be moved around to demonstrate such concepts as band maneuvers.

[2] See Walter A. Wittich and Charles F. Schuller, *Audiovisual Materials: Their Nature and Use* (rev. ed.), Harper & Row, 1962, chap. 3, for a detailed discussion of this and other chalkboard techniques.

[3] See the source list on p. 575 ff. for this and other materials indicated in this chapter.

Study Displays

"The study display includes a variety of devices: two- and three-dimensional objects, and collections of graphics, pictures, and news clippings, displayed on bulletin, felt, or magnetic boards; mobiles; and floor exhibits that present a classroom's current learning plans or accomplishments in visualized form."[4] The display may take a variety of forms and may apply in music to anything from a decorative motif (Fig. 18.3) to examples of student compositions.

The ingenious teacher can devise many ways to stimulate interest and learning through effective displays. Roggensack suggests such titles, for example, as a "Concert Recording, Radio and Television Artists" board; "Places Suggest Music" with appropriate pictures, travel posters, and other illustrative items; "What's My Name?" for recognition or identification exercises; "The Evolution of Musical Instruments"; "Primitive Music"; "The World Dances," and others.[5]

Characteristics of Effective Study Displays

A good display for any purpose has certain characteristics which help make it effective. The following are particularly important:

1. *A good title.* Several good titles are suggested above. Titles which suggest action and involve the viewer are best. To be effective, any title needs to be read easily from across the room. This usually requires letters three inches or more in height. Teachers and students can make their own letters, or a variety of commercially prepared letters are available, many at low cost.
2. *Adequate blank space.* Space is necessary to set off the material displayed to best advantage. A cluttered display board is rarely effective and often takes more work than a good one. Usually the best results are obtained by leaving as much or more empty area than that covered by the display material.
3. *Strong center of interest.* The eye should travel naturally to a focal point in your display. This point may be prominent by reason of its size, its position, or a series of pictures or lines leading to it. It might be the largest item on the board or it may be on the largest mounting. It might be the title itself or a prominent background design such as a large treble clef. Nearly always, the center of interest is located above, below, or to one side of the actual center of the display.
4. *Interesting arrangement.* This is usually a product of experimentation. It is a good idea to try out several arrangements of your material on a desk or table top, or on paper before putting it up. This saves times and ensures satisfying

[4] Wittich and Schuller, *op. cit.*, p. 151.
[5] Delinda Roggensack, *Eyes and Ears for Music*, Educational Publishers, 1954, p. 18.

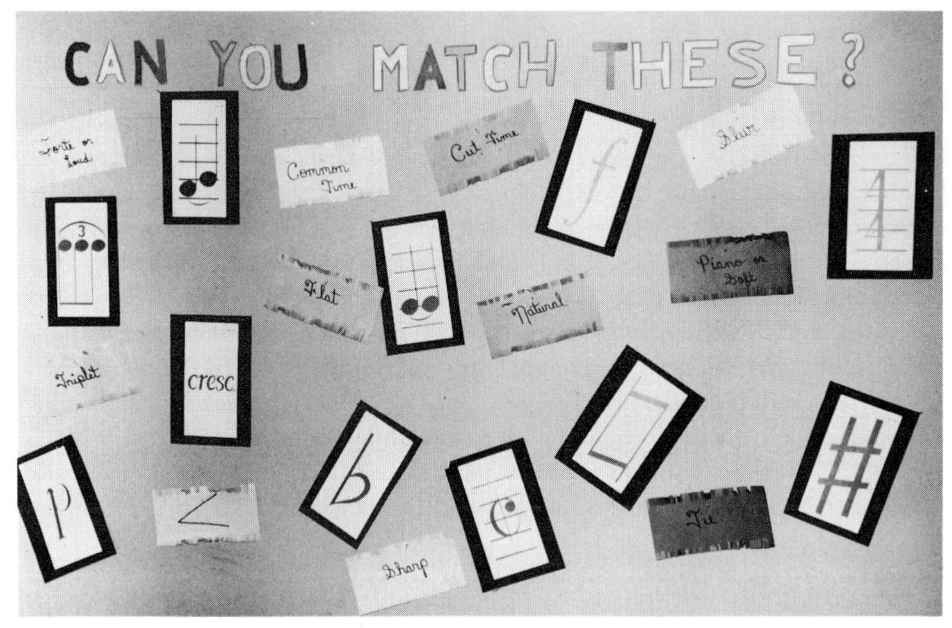

Kalamazoo Public Schools, Kalamazoo, Michigan.

Fig. 18.3. With a bit of imagination, the music display board can be made to involve the student directly.

results. With a little practice you will be able to develop interesting arrangements of the materials at hand. One caution: It is usually best to avoid regularly spaced rows of material. For more interest, break them up into related clusters.

5. *Suitable colors.* Good use of color in displays heightens attention-getting value and attractiveness and helps put across the message presented. Other than for holiday occasions such as Christmas, color should be used primarily to enhance the pictures, graphics or other materials in the display. Soft, blended colors are usually better than brilliant colors although the latter might be entirely suitable for a display on "Latin American Music" or "Indian Dances." In any case, colors used in a display should be selected to harmonize well with one another.

Appropriate Purposes for Displays

As with other types of teaching materials, the music teacher should use displays only when they can make a significant contribution to learning. Among the functions for which displays are particularly well suited are:

1. *Motivation.* An attractive display of record covers and pictures, for example, could serve to arouse interest in contemporary composers if a title such as

Detroit Public Schools, Detroit, Michigan.

Fig. 18.4. Extensive use of display space is made in this music room.

"Your Modern Masters" or "What Is Modern Music?" is used. A display entitled "Top Man with a Guitar" might serve as a starter for a worthwhile listening session and discussion on Andrés Segovia. Some means of arousing interest is essential to good teaching. The motivational display is one means of inciting initial interest. To accomplish this, it must be eye-catching, imaginative in design, and attractive in total effect. If your students stop to examine such a display more closely, it has at least some of the elements needed.

2. *Concept Illustration.* A second type of display can serve to illustrate work that is going on. In a series of general music lessons on instruments of the band and orchestra, a three-dimensional exhibit of disassembled instruments could be prepared by students in the class with the help of the instructor. Such materials can be safely mounted on peg board hooks or on table tops and used

to illustrate student reports on how instruments are constructed. Instrumental charts, pictures of instruments being played, and close-ups of correct embouchure are examples of good illustrative materials for study displays (Fig. 18.4). At a more elementary level, the felt board can be useful in illustrating note values, clef designations, and the construction of chords. It is also excellent for setting up note-reading exercises. Felt boards are discussed further on p. 449.

3. *Recognition of Pupil Work and Activities.* Display boards can also be used to feature and to give recognition to student work such as original compositions. Displays to advertise a forthcoming concert or operetta are familiar uses for corridor bulletin boards. Pictures of rehearsals, and posters and designs worked out by the students lend themselves well to the advertising display. An exhibit case in the corridor is a good spot for a diorama of the operetta stage or an interesting model of an orchestra (Fig. 18.5). Such displays not only stimulate attendance, but also provide opportunity for participation and worthwhile learning experiences for the students involved in their preparation.

Types of Display Surfaces

Display boards are constructed of materials such as cork, soft pressed-board, or peg boards. Most classrooms have built-in display boards of some type. In addition, almost any wall surface can be employed for display purposes if cer-

Washington Jr. High School, Duluth, Minnesota.

Fig. 18.5. Excellent displays such as this pipe-cleaner symphony orchestra can be made by students.

tain adhesive materials such as Styx or masking tape are used. When used properly, such adhesives are harmless to any surface and provide an almost unlimited amount of display space.

Peg boards are available in 4 × 8 foot sheets which can be cut to any desired size. The surface is perforated with rows of small holes about 2 inches apart into which brads or inexpensive fittings can be inserted. The fittings are hooks of various sizes which slip through the holes and brace against the back of the peg board. The board, accordingly, must be mounted so as to leave about one-half inch of space behind it. Golf tees can also be inserted part way into the holes and pictures or similar materials mounted on the projecting heads by means of an adhesive. Such mounting gives an interesting three-dimensional effect to any display.

Felt or flannel boards are portable boards covered with felt, flannel, or other material with a long nap. Lightweight materials with a sandpaper or felt backing will adhere to the flannel surface. One of the best backings is #2–0 sandpaper, but pieces of wool or cotton flannel will also adhere when placed on the felt board surface. Thus, staffs, signatures, and other musical symbols can be applied and moved about with ease (Fig. 18.6).

The ease and variety of uses of the felt board have made it a favorite device for drill and developmental work since materials can be readily shifted or rearranged. Both the director of a marching band and the teacher of basic music have numerous uses for this inexpensive and versatile device.

Materials for Study Displays

A number of suitable materials for study displays have already been suggested in the preceding discussion. Since the quality and, hence, the effectiveness of the display depends in substantial measure upon the quality of the pictures and other materials used, it will be worth while to consider several of these in more detail.

Flat Pictures

We live in an age of pictures. We find them everywhere—in newspapers, magazines, books, posters, even on our record albums. They have become an important medium of communication; they are of major importance in teaching.

The first requirement in selecting a picture is that it be suited to the purpose of your display. Those pictures which are best for use in study displays, have several characteristics:

1. A clear-cut center of interest (Fig. 18.7)
2. Effective color and techniques employed by the artist or photographer

Green Bay Public Schools, Green Bay, Wisconsin.

Fig. 18.6. What advantages are there in using a felt board for the type of work shown here?

3. Valid and accurate information or impression
4. A quality of genuine interest
5. For display purposes, a size large enough to be seen across the classroom.

Good pictures appear to best advantage when mounted. The mounting should be generous in size and proportioned to the shape of the picture or design somewhat as suggested in Fig. 18.8. The best color for mounting is normally a neutral shade or a minor color found in the picture itself. Rubber cement is a convenient adhesive for mounting since it permits a smooth surface, and excess cement around the edges of the picture is easily rubbed off with the fingers.

Graphics

The name "graphics" is applied to those visual materials in which drawing in some form is a prominent characteristic. Graphics include such materials as charts, diagrams, graphs, posters, cartoons, comics, and maps. Of these, charts, diagrams, and posters have particularly useful applications in music teaching at the secondary level.

Photo by Columbia Records.

Fig. 18.7. What qualities make this photograph of a musician and admiring child a good picture for display?

Walter A. Wittich and Charles F. Schuller.

Fig. 18.8. The width of margin depends upon the size and shape of the picture or design being mounted.

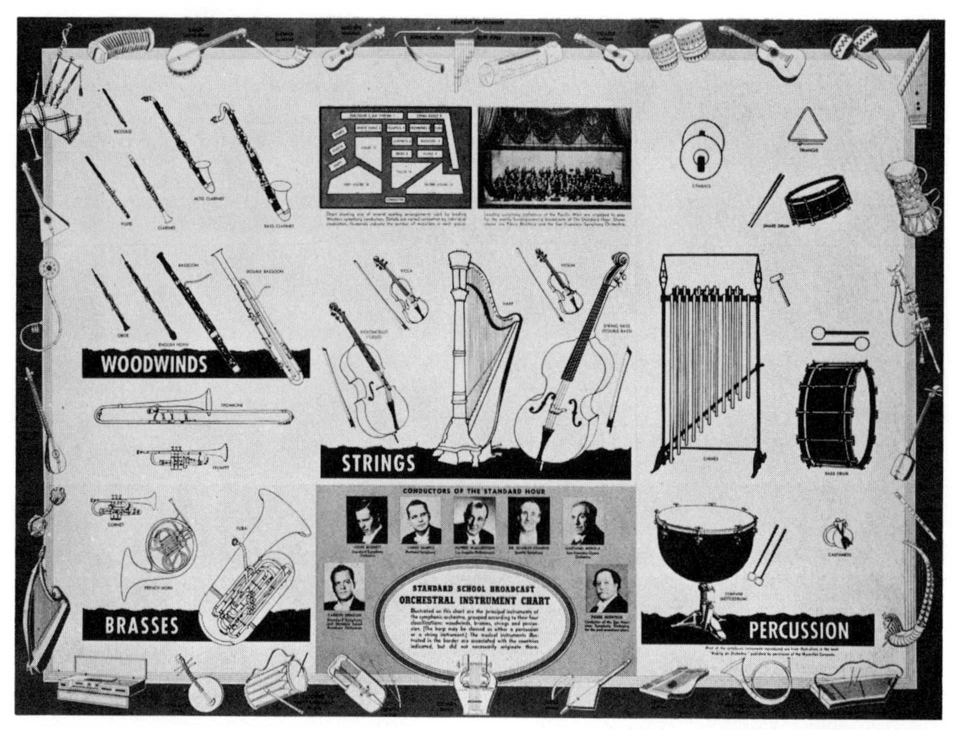

Standard Oil of California.

Fig. 18.9. What different media can you identify in this chart?

Charts are usually made up of a combination of several kinds of graphics. They often also contain photographs and printed matter in addition to diagrams, graphs, and other graphic materials. Their role is to show relationships of some kind in condensed, summarized form. A chart of a symphony orchestra, for example, may show pictures or sketches of the principal instruments plus a diagram of where the various sections of the orchestra are seated (Fig. 18.9).

Charts frequently contain considerable information. Commercially prepared charts are costly to print because of the large plates required. Thus there is a tendency to crowd the material and to include as much as possible in the available space. This reduces the size of illustrations on the chart and makes it difficult to read more than a few feet away. This type of chart is of value principally for individual or small group study. A good teaching chart presents *one* principal idea or comparison. It is uncluttered and the principal elements as well as the chart as a whole are large enough to be seen readily by an entire class.

It is readily possible to make your own charts. For example, a chart of various chords and progressions could show their likenesses and differences. Other simple and helpful charts might show comparative voice ranges; comparative instrument ranges; placement of bass, alto, and treble clefs; major and minor scales; and a series of different time signatures with a few bars of illustrative music.

Such charts can be worked out on a small sheet of paper such as staff paper. The headings and captions can be lettered or typed in and drawings or pictures added as desired. This sheet can then be placed in an opaque projector and traced on a large section of heavy wrapping paper, pieced together, and hung on a flat wall. After tracing, the letters, lines, and figures may be worked over to achieve a more finished effect. For example, black quarter-inch plastic gummed tape can be used for staff lines. Gummed paper letters are likewise available in various sizes and colors at low cost. Students can do much of this work. Once used, these "do-it-yourself" charts may be rolled up or folded and put away for future use. For more permanent charts, Cornell board, wide window shades on spring rollers, or the back of an old map may be used.

Good commercially prepared charts are available free or at low cost from most music and instrument companies. For example, a historical time-line chart, including developments in music, literature, art, and other fields is distributed by one music company. The map chart in Fig. 18.10 is distributed by the company responsible for the excellent Standard School Broadcast radio music programs. Most school systems now have lists of free and inexpensive materials sources, such as the Educator's Guide to Free Curriculum Materials, which include charts, posters, and other display materials.[6]

The *Educational Media Index* volume on Music and Fine Arts provides extensive listings of all kinds of audiovisual materials for music education including study display materials.[7] The listings are classified according to types of material, grade level, topics and sources. This valuable reference should be on every music teacher's desk.

Diagrams show relationships primarily by means of lines and symbols. A line of march or a band maneuver with a series of simple diagrams on the chalkboard and on mimeographed sheets can be laid out. The organization of the music department or the action of sound waves can be more easily explained with the aid of diagrams. Printed music is largely diagrammatic in nature, but we recognize that long experience is needed before one can read music well. To the beginner in music, the symbols of music have little more meaning than do the words of a strange language.

To some extent, all diagrams share this characteristic of abstraction. They require a degree of experience to be understood. Many people have difficulty in reading road maps accurately because they have not learned how to use them easily. This means that the teacher must be aware of the student's need for cer-

[6] P. A. Horkheimer *et al., Educator's Guide to Free Curriculum Materials,* Educator's Progress League (revised periodically).

[7] *Educational Media Index,* Vol. 3: *Music and Fine Arts,* McGraw-Hill, 1964.

Standard Oil of California.

Fig. 18.10. Various free or inexpensive visual materials such as this are available to the music teacher.

tain experiences before he can successfully interpret a given diagram. It is for this reason, true to some degree of charts and graphs as well, that diagrams are seldom used to introduce new material. They are much better suited to summary and review.

Posters like the one in Fig. 18.11, in contrast to diagrams, are very easily understood at first glance by most students who see them. Unless this is true, the poster fails in its purpose, for it is purely a fast-action device. It must convey its message at a glance. The design must be bold to get attention, the color striking, and the message as brief and sharp as possible. Posters are used regularly to call attention to coming attractions such as operettas, concerts, dances, and athletic events. They can be used also for such worthy reminders around the music rooms as "Music Hath Charms," "Musicians Practice," "Learn to Play an Instrument," "One Eye on the Director!" "Sing in Tune!" "Care for Your Instrument," and "Music Is for *You*." Given encouragement and incentive, students will make such posters for you and enjoy doing it.

Music and instrument companies, recording companies, and professional associations such as the American Music Conference and the Music Educators

(MENC) Music Educators National Conference.

Fig. 18.11. Good posters are often simple in design. Vivid colors add much to the effect.

National Conference are good sources of posters, as are travel agencies. The audiovisual center or the library in your school system may also have on file posters that you can use to advantage, as well as the guides to free and inexpensive materials mentioned earlier.

Three-Dimensional Materials

Materials such as models and objects when used in teaching do much to enliven curiosity and interest. Dioramas are highly appealing because of their lifelike realism in miniature. Three-dimensional materials, in general, have a high interest potential in teaching because most things in real life *are* three-dimensional. Thus a real violin is more naturally interesting than a picture of a violin. You can handle the instrument, get the feel of its weight and balance, and hear the sounds it makes as you draw the bow or pluck the strings. When you do this, the sensory experience is more complete and effective than when observing someone else demonstrate the violin or when looking at a picture of it.

On the other hand, if our purpose is to understand how a pipe organ works, the organ itself may be of little help. The important things are going on inside

Fig. 18.12. Simple objects often suffice for effective demonstrations.

Lansing Public Schools, Lansing, Michigan.

where we can't see them. In this case, a cut-away *model* plus a chart, a diagram, and some pictures will be much more useful than the organ itself. Music teachers frequently use varied lengths of rubber tubing or a series of partially filled glass jars to illustrate the effect on pitch of different lengths of the sound chamber (Fig. 18.12). These objects are helpful in understanding a wind instrument. Similarly a straight piece of tubing of the same length and diameter as that in a bugle is very useful in demonstrating that the coils in a brass instrument have no effect on its pitch.

A diorama is a three-dimensional scene incorporating objects and background in perspective. Usually the scene is done in miniature although museums use the diorama technique extensively in life size as well. Perspective is exaggerated in either case by tapering building or space dimensions from front to back and using progressively smaller figures and objects toward the background of the diorama. The background itself is usually drawn or painted so as to merge with the foreground. Dioramas may be used in music work to show such things as scenes from an opera or an operetta and scenes from the lives of famous composers. A scene like that in Fig. 18.13 from the high-school operetta "Snow Queen" would lend itself readily to diorama treatment for advertising the production as well as helping the director plan the stage settings and the movements of the performers.

STILL PROJECTION IN MUSIC TEACHING

The projected still picture in various forms has a variety of excellent applications in music teaching. Accordingly, every music teacher should become familiar with the possibilities of opaque, filmstrip, slide, and overhead transparency types of projection, and with the operation of the projectors for each of these types.

Riley Jania Senior High, South Bend, Indiana.

Fig. 18.13. Stage settings and dioramas have many elements in common.

Opaque Projection

Potentially, one of the most useful types of still projection for instructional purposes is opaque projection. It permits nontransparent materials such as flat pictures, book illustrations, tables, drawings, photographs, pupils' work, and even certain objects and specimens to be shown on a screen for group observation.[8]

The opaque projector is the *only* means by which student compositions can be projected for the class without special preparation. One writer points out that music structure, counterpoint, and orchestration can be presented on the opaque projector with significant advantage.[9] Among the educational advantages he finds are:

1. It focuses the attention of the entire class on the same problem
2. It allows the class to see and hear music at the same time

[8] Wittich and Schuller, *op. cit.*, p. 341.
[9] Mervin W. Whitcomb, "The Opaque Projector in Teaching Music," *Music Education Journal*, April–May, 1954, pp. 65–66.

Fig. 18.14. What advantages does the opaque projector have for the music teacher?

Charles Beseler Company, East Orange, New Jersey.

3. It helps to correct errors in student work through an open, frank democratic process
4. It allows students an opportunity to compare work with their classmates and to see their own creative work presented before the class
5. It speeds the development of techniques, skills, understandings, and appreciations.

In the latter connection, this music teacher finds the opaque projector useful in illustrations of manuscript writing, notation, melodic effectiveness, chord selection, musical form, style, and the like.

The opaque projector is a modern and much improved version of the old magic lantern. A 1000-watt lamp throws a powerful light on the material being projected. This light is reflected by means of mirrors through a series of lenses and onto a screen. A representative opaque projector is shown in Fig. 18.14. An efficient down-draft cooling system holds material in place without special mounting and also prevents scorching or damage to materials. An electric pointer device permits the instructor to indicate any specific point he wishes on the projected image without going up to the screen.

A square screen is highly desirable for best use of the opaque projector since most material used is longer vertically than it is wide horizontally. Since a square screen is also necessary for vertical slides and overhead transparencies and is perfectly satisfactory for motion pictures as well, there is no reason for schools to purchase the horizontal type screen. A square screen at least 60 × 60 inches, and preferably 70 × 70 inches, is recommended for classroom use.

The opaque projector is used in the front of the room. In order that it not block the student's view, it should be placed on a stand no more than 18 to 20 inches in height. Low stands with rubber casters are available which make it easy to move the projector from one room to another. The principal limitation of opaque projection is that it requires a well-darkened room for best results.

Filmstrips and Slides

Filmstrips and slides are sufficiently alike in basic structure and characteristics so that we may discuss them together. Both are small transparencies through which a strong light is projected to secure a brilliant image on the screen. Most filmstrip projectors, such as those in Fig. 18.15, will also project 2 × 2-inch slides. The principal difference lies in the fact that slides are separate while filmstrips contain a series of transparencies on a single strip of film (Fig. 18.16). Larger, 3¼ × 4-inch, slides have advantages which are discussed below.

Pictures and music supplement one another very well. A study by Reed of potential use of still pictures by some 60 music directors in widely scattered parts of the United States shows many applications of pictures for teaching, motivation, records, and publicity.[10] Among other uses in teaching, pictures of bowing techniques, embouchure formations, vowel sounds, baton twirling, wearing uniforms, and band formations are suggested by Reed as particularly helpful.

Several of these topics as they apply to individual instruments are available in filmstrip form. Filmstrips from various sources deal with such subjects as the several choirs of the orchestra—strings, brass, woodwinds and percussion—and with the benefits of a strong music program to the child and the community. Excellent filmstrips on individual instruments are available along with records of the instrument being played. New filmstrips are being released regularly and are noted in the professional music journals.

Anything which can be photographed can be put on a slide. Thus, most of the applications of still pictures in music teaching can be duplicated in slide form. In cases where a particular scene or a series of scenes, such as those of marching-band formations, close-up pictures of instruments, or song words for community sings, are apt to be used repeatedly, there is real value in having them on slides. One advantage of slides is that they are small, compact, and easily stored. Another is that they can be used in any desired order. Either slides or filmstrips can be projected onto a screen for as long a time as desired. Both are inexpensive; and the teacher with a 35 mm. camera can rather easily prepare his own slides in either black and white or in color.

An interesting and highly successful application of color slides in music listen-

[10] George Reed, *An Investigation of the Potential Use of Still Pictures by Directors of Music Organizations*, University of Southern California, 1954.

Viewlex.

Viewlex.

Eastman Kodak, Rochester, N.Y.

Fig. 18.15. Various good filmstrip and 2 × 2 slide projectors are used in music instruction today.

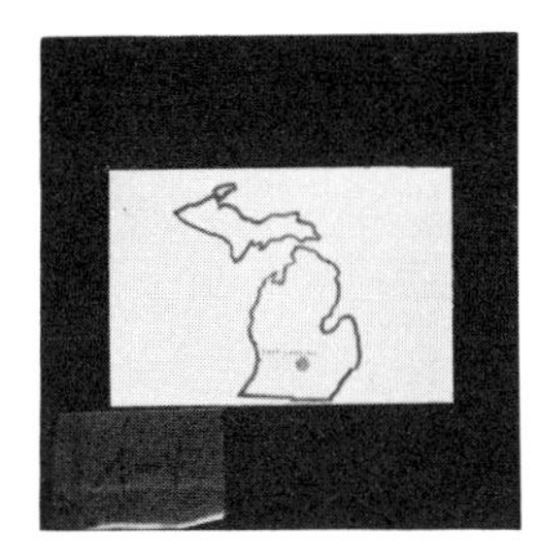

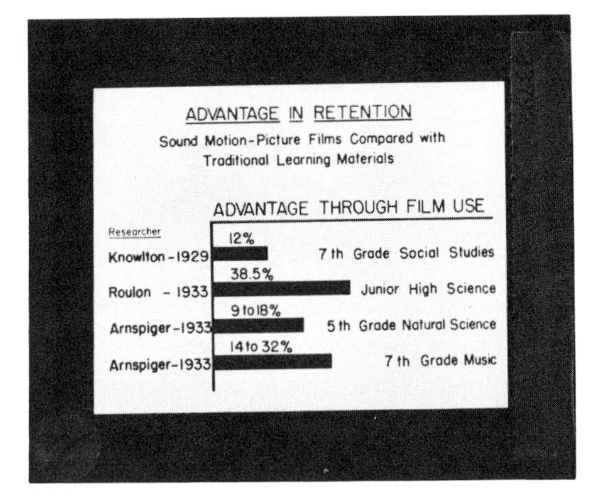

Fig. 18.16. A 2 × 2 inch and 3¼ × 4 inch slide with a double-frame and single-frame filmstrip.

Michigan State University.

ing is reported by DeBernardis and Ernst. Color scenes of sunsets, mountains, flowers, trees, and gardens, chosen to fit the mood of the music, were projected as recordings were played. The order of the pictures and the length of time they were left on the screen were adapted to the music. "Almost without exception, the audience expressed genuine pleasure from the experience. Teachers were invariably amazed at the power of the combination of still pictures and music in holding the sustained attention of a class for 20 minutes."[11]

Slide and filmstrip projectors should be operated from behind the group or class to avoid distraction. With a 500- or 750-watt lamp, classroom projection of black-and-white slides or filmstrips can be carried on without darkening the room. Color projection is more effective when the room is darkened, because extraneous light on the screen fades the colors of the projected picture.

Slide and filmstrip projectors come equipped with 5-inch lenses. If the projector is to be used with larger than class-size groups, a 7-inch lens should also be purchased. The lens of greater focal length permits the projector to be moved

[11] Amo DeBernardis and Karl Ernst, "Pictures and Music," *NEA Journal*, November, 1949, p. 616.

3M Company, Minneapolis, Minnesota.

Fig. 18.17. The overhead projector has most of the values of the chalkboard plus greater convenience and versatility. It also has certain unique capabilities some of which are suggested by these photos.

further from the screen so as to project from behind the group. Auditorium showings require a large screen and a projector with a 1000-watt lamp or arc light. The 3¼ × 4-inch slide has the advantage of being sufficiently large to permit hand drawing and lettering on the slide surface. Various methods used in preparing handmade slides are clearly demonstrated in a motion picture film which is available from most film libraries.[12] The 3¼ × 4-inch slide has a further advantage in that its size permits excellent photographic slides of subjects requiring great detail. A Polaroid camera film is now available with which the teacher can take pictures and have them ready for projection as slides within a few minutes.[13]

[12] *How to Make Handmade Lantern Slides,* 16 mm., sound, color, 20 min., Indiana University.
[13] See Richard Dryden, "Slides a la Carte," *Music Educators Journal,* January, 1961, pp. 94–95.

Overhead Transparencies

The overhead transparency projector has achieved wide popularity among teachers of all subject areas and grade levels because of its convenience, versatility, and ready application to a host of teaching needs. The teacher of music will find many uses for this means of visualizing information for vocal and instrumental groups as well as for classes.

The overhead transparency projector is actually a horizontal slide projector which operates from the front of the room and accommodates a very large slide (Fig. 18.17). The transparency can be as large as 100 square inches. The teacher faces the class while operating the projector which throws the projected image on the screen behind him. A 100-foot roll of cellophane in the projector can be used like a chalkboard. You write or draw on the plastic with a grease or China marking pencil and erase with a piece of cleansing tissue. Drawings and tests or exercises prepared beforehand can be rolled on and off the projection stage at will. For most uses the overhead transparency projector does not require a darkened room. A square screen is necessary, however, as well as a low stand as for the opaque projector.

The most outstanding and unique advantage of the overhead transparency projector is the fact that it makes possible the projection of transparent overlays (Fig. 18.18). This is the only projector on which the overlay technique can be employed. By means of overlays the instructor with preprepared materials can develop, step by step, each part of a composition. He can reveal the parts of an

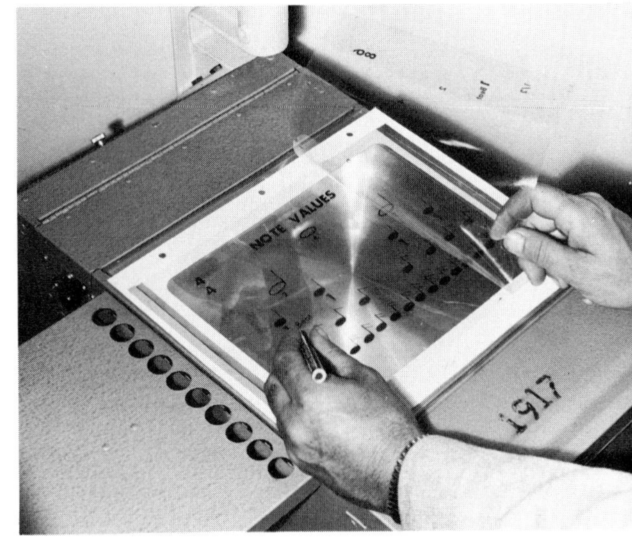

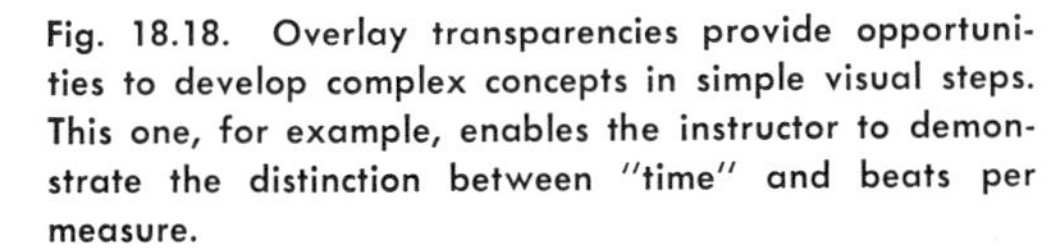
Fig. 18.18. Overlay transparencies provide opportunities to develop complex concepts in simple visual steps. This one, for example, enables the instructor to demonstrate the distinction between "time" and beats per measure.

Don Borg, Saginaw, Michigan.

instrument, build diagrams of band maneuvers, or place music on a large screen as it is being played for a class. Staffs can be applied photographically to sensitized plastic sheets, used for student exercises which are projected, erased, and used again. Songs can be typed on clear plastic sheets by means of special carbon paper and projected for assembly singing.

One music instructor describes successful uses of overhead transparencies in exercises on names of notes, rhythm training, and key signatures: "One slide can be made of all sharp- and flat-key signatures in the clefs desired and from this slide, the rules for determining the key name, the number and name of sharps and flats in each key signature, and positions of sharps and flats on the staff can be taught."[14]

MOTION PICTURES IN MUSIC TEACHING

As we have seen, there are many types of audiovisual instructional materials having useful applications in the teaching of secondary-school music. We have left until last that medium which is commonly thought of first; namely, the 16 mm. sound instructional film. What music films are there? How do you select good films for teaching? Are there ways of using films so that they are a real help in teaching and learning?

The Nature and Characteristics of Good Films for Teaching

The term "movies" typifies the skeptical view of the teacher whose chief experience with educational films has been in the assembly where a number of classes, if not the whole student body, have come in for a "show." It may also typify the view of the disappointed administrator or supervisor who has seen instructional films used as a means to get *out* of teaching rather than as teaching tools. In both cases, the cause may well lie in a lack of understanding of what good instructional films are and what they can accomplish when used by informed and competent teachers.

Before going further, let us examine the evidence. It has been established for many years that well-designed motion pictures can be of substantial assistance in the learning of factual information. Given a good film which covers material directly related to immediate teaching objectives, and given a quality of use which capable teachers normally apply in their day-to-day teaching, the kind of improved learning occurs which is illustrated in Fig. 18.19.

Extensive studies in 70 Nebraska high schools with an enrollment of 20,000 students from 1946 to 1950 show that students receive considerably more enrich-

[14] James C. Beavers, "Music Overhead," *Educational Screen*, March, 1954, pp. 104–105.

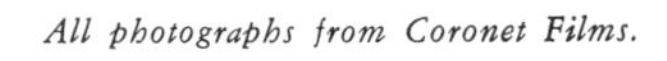

All photographs from Coronet Films.

Fig. 18.19. What advantages of film are illustrated by these scenes from the films *Brahms and His Music, Liszt and His Music*, and *Instruments of the Band and Orchestra: Percussion*?

ment from film use, in addition to doing as well or better on standard achievement tests, than do students not receiving film instruction. Other studies suggest that films can play a major role both in teaching skills and in influencing attitudes.

There are several types of films that are useful in teaching. The text or basic teaching film is perhaps the most familiar of these. It is most apt to be a straightforward presentation of visualized information. The basic teaching film employs environmental sounds where these are appropriate, as in *Brass Choir,*[15] *Science in the Orchestra,*[16] and other music films. Supplementary films include documentary films such as *Pacific 231,*[17] *The River,*[18] and *Morning Star,*[19] in which music plays a prominent role in portraying dramatic treatment of real life situations. Sponsored films may be basic teaching films, documentaries, or other types of films.

[15] Sound, B & W, 11 min., Encyclopaedia Britannica Films.
[16] Parts I, II, III, sound, B & W, McGraw-Hill Text Films.
[17] Sound, B & W, 10 min., Young America Films.
[18] Sound, B & W, 31 min., United States Department of Agriculture.
[19] Sound, color, 33 min., Encyclopaedia Britannica Films.

The term "sponsored" refers only to source, not to a type of film. Hollywood entertainment film excerpts of music teaching value have been made available to school through Teaching Films Custodians with the help of the MENC. Such titles as *Great Waltz, Naughty Marietta* and the *Schumann Story* are examples.

Finally there is a rapidly developing group of telefilms and kinescopes of television programs. Some of these, such as three series entitled *Music as a Language,*[20] *Music for Young People,*[21] and *Musical Forms*[22] are available through 16 mm. film libraries and can be used in the same manner as any other 16 mm. film.

Selecting Good Instructional Films

A good teaching film must be good in two different ways. The first of these is in terms of the teaching purpose and grade level. Regardless of how excellent a film may be in other respects, it is of little value unless it contributes directly and substantially to the specific lesson and group being taught. The purpose of the film and that of the teacher must coincide at least reasonably well before it should be considered. Second, the film should do well those things for which motion pictures are uniquely well suited. Is motion important? If so, is motion employed effectively? Does the film use its capacity to overcome time and distance? (Fig. 18.20) Does it add a significant life-like quality and realism to a learning situation in which this quality is important? In short, does the film do something of importance that you could not do as well without it? If the answer is "yes," the film should be seriously considered for use.

We need to consider, also, certain technical qualities of the film. Is the photography of good quality? In a historical or story-type film, is the performance convincing? In a techniques-type of film, are there sufficient close-up shots to give necessary details clearly? The sound quality in a music film is of the utmost importance, and the producer is very conscious of this fact. In consequence, poor sound quality is more apt to be the fault of the project amplifier system than of the film sound track. None the less, it is a good idea to check the sound quality on as good a projector as is available.

Using Films Effectively

The dynamic power of an excellent film brought into the lesson at the right time and used effectively can provide an exceptional learning experience. What factors are involved here? How *should* we teach with films? There is *no one*

[20] Series of seven films on composition, orchestration, and instrumentation. College and special adult use. University of Rochester.

[21] Series of thirteen films on major groups of instruments and music composed for them. Elementary through general adult use. Arts and Audiences, Inc.

[22] Series of six programs on development and illustration of musical forms. Senior High, College, and special adult use. University of Southern California.

best way. The first principle of good use of any instructional material might be termed flexibility of application. There is no one ideal method for use of a film, filmstrip, chart, book, recording, or sheet of music. Methods must be adapted to such factors as specific teaching objectives, the stage of the lesson reached, the level of musical competence of the group, and individual differences in such skills as observing and listening effectively.

For example, the use of a film on Mozart to introduce a study of the sonata form might differ considerably from the use of the same film in a General Music class to give a picture of Mozart's life. Similarly, and in either case, the procedure would differ when using the film for introduction or motivation as compared with its use for basic information or for summary purposes.

Similarly, a group which uses films regularly in an efficient manner is apt to require less complete direction than a class in which films are seldom a part of the lesson. Mature students may need less assistance than beginners on new names or vocabulary contained in a film, though just as much attention may be necessary on specifics to look for as the film is shown. The teacher's good judgment in terms of his class, its abilities and its needs, has much to do with how he uses films and other visual materials. Thus the skill and the creative ability of the teacher is still another variable in the pattern of effective use of audio-visual materials.

Within the framework of flexibility, there are several aspects of efficient film use of which the teacher should be aware:

1. *Preview and selection in terms of teaching objectives.* In order to teach effectively and with a film or filmstrip you need to know its content and how it is presented. This is essential, as well, for evaluation and selection as discussed above.
2. *Preparation of class and a focus on points to look for.* Generally speaking, your class needs to know why they are seeing this particular film, how it fits into the lesson, and what to look for. Coupled with this and implied by it is a need to arouse interest and a definite desire to see the film.
3. *Showing conditions as favorable as possible.* Light control, good ventilation, and good projection are the principal points here. If a film, filmstrip, or other projected material is to be shown, every reasonable effort should be made to assure that the image on the screen is as good as possible. The point of good projection is good learning.
4. *Follow-up discussion and application.* Assuming sound reasons for using a film, something must be done about it following the showing. Points to look for can be discussed, new learnings applied and measured, and reteaching, perhaps with a second showing or partial showing of the film, employed as needed.

Essentially, proper use of instructional materials is a question of perspective. Good teaching involves all kinds of appropriate materials and methods in combination. You use instruments, music, books, chalkboard, films, displays, and other available materials that will help do the job. You choose the methods, activities, and materials suited to the learning needs of your students. The experienced, capable instructor moves from one type of material and method to another, easily and naturally, because he knows the contribution which each makes to the learning situation. He integrates audiovisual materials with all of his other teaching materials because he is well aware that their greatest benefits can be realized by such coordination. He does so because he knows that meanings will be more clear and learning will be more permanent in the final outcome as a result of his effective application of audiovisual materials.

SUMMARY

Visual materials in various forms have an important part to play in music instruction. Chalkboards, study displays, still projection of several types, and motion pictures can be of significant value to the music teacher who is aware of their possibilities and of effective methods for their use.

The study display, for example, usually gives best results when provided with a good title, adequate blank space between materials, a strong center of interest, effective arrangement, and suitable use of color. These requirements also apply, in general, to the several forms of graphic materials and three-dimensional exhibits.

Opaque projection, filmstrips and slides, and the uniquely effective overhead transparency projector have particular advantages in illustrating music concepts. The motion picture is in many ways the most dynamic and potentially powerful audiovisual medium of instruction available to the music teacher. Like other teaching tools, the instructional music film requires skilled, intelligent use to accomplish the very real benefits of which it is capable.

SUGGESTED ACTIVITIES

1. Learn how to operate the still and motion picture projection equipment described in this chapter. This is a simple but essential skill to acquire.
2. Make a list of music activities in which visualization in some specific form could make a substantial contribution to effective learning in secondary-school music classes.

3. Assign a different visual described in Exercise 2 to each of six or more small committees for preparation and demonstration of effective use for the music methods class. Consult your college learning resources center for assistance if needed.
4. Arrange through your instructor to secure a number of good instrumental and vocal music films for preview and evaluation by several class committees. Prepare a classified list of good music films for distribution to the class.
5. Select a music film in an area of particular interest to you and plan for its effective use in a teaching situation. Note the responsibilities of the teacher in making this plan.
6. Arrange to put your plan into use. Either as a teacher in your own classroom, as a student teacher, or as a member of the music methods class, introduce, project, and guide follow-up activities related to the film experience. Evaluate the results with your classmates or colleagues.
7. Have committees study and suggest solutions to the class on such practical problems as:
   a. Light control for classrooms.
   b. Effective projection measures in classrooms with limited light control provisions.
   c. Caring for chalkboards.
   d. Increasing display space areas with temporary display boards, etc.
   e. Getting the best sound and picture in using a 16 mm. motion picture projector.
   f. Do's and Don't's in the proper care of motion picture films, filmstrips, and slides.

SELECTED READINGS

Arnspiger, Varney C., *Measuring the Effectiveness of Sound Pictures as Teaching Aids*, Contributions to Education, No. 565, Teachers College, Columbia University, 1933.

Brown, James, Richard Lewis, and Fred Harcleroad, *A-V Instruction Materials and Methods* (rev. ed.), McGraw-Hill, 1964.

Dale, Edgar, *Audio-Visual Methods in Teaching* (rev. ed.), Holt, Rinehart and Winston, 1954.

Music Educators National Conference, *Filmguide For Music Educators: Audio-Visual Aids In Music Education*, National Education Association, 1962.

Music Educators National Conference, *Music Buildings, Rooms and Equipment*, National Education Association, 1955, pp. 65–70.

Music Educators National Conference, *Music in American Education*, National Education Association, Source Book No. 2, 1955, pp. 216–220, 232–237.

Pace, Robert, "Keyboard Experience in The Classroom," *Music Educators Journal*, February–March, 1960, pp. 44–45.

Petts, L. B., *Handbook on 16 mm. Films for Music Education*, Music Educators National Conference, National Education Association.

Roggensack, Delinda, *Eyes and Ears for Music*, Educational Publishers, 1954.

Visual Instruction Bureau, University of Texas, 1962. Various pamphlets:
No. 1. *Bridges for Ideas*
No. 2. *Feltboards for Teaching*
No. 7. *Production of 2 × 2 Slides for School Use*

No. 8. *The Tape Recorder in The Classroom*
No. 9. *Educational Displays and Exhibits*
No. 10. *The Opaque Projector*
No. 11. *Better Bulletin Board Displays*

Wittich, Walter A., and Charles F. Schuller, *Audiovisual Materials: Their Nature and Use* (rev. ed.), Harper & Row, 1962.

Films and Filmstrips:

Better Bulletin Boards, color, 11 min., Indiana University.
Chalkboard Utilization, B & W, 15 min., Young America Films.
Felt Board in Teaching, color, 10 min., Wayne State University.
Film Learning and Research, B & W, 14 min., Walter A. Wittich.
Handmade Materials for Projection, color, 21 min., Indiana University.
How to Make Handmade Lantern Slides, color, 22 min., Indiana University.
Overhead Projector, B & W, 16 min., University of Iowa.
The Opaque Projector—Its Purpose and Use, B & W, 6 min., University of Iowa.
Teaching with a Filmstrip (filmstrip) 50 frames, B & W, Society for Visual Education, Inc.
Using the Slidefilm in Teaching (filmstrip) 46 frames, B & W, Young America Films.

Used by permission, Music Educators National Conference, Washington, D.C.

CHAPTER

19

The Care and Repair of Instruments

It is the day before the first band and orchestra concert in the fall. Carol breaks her violin bridge. Arthur finds that his cello soundpost is unaccountably rattling around in the bottom of his cello. Dick drops his clarinet and bends two keys. Johnny has a sticking key on his oboe. The children all come to the music teacher for help. The repairs are minor, but they are beyond the ability of the students to make. The town is small and there is no instrument repair service nearer than 70 miles. Someone must be able to make these repairs if the players are not to be lost to the orchestra.

Fortunately, the music teacher is able to make them. There is a need for similar small repairs nearly every day. Some of them the children can be taught to handle; some can be done by the teacher; still others need an expert repair man. This chapter will show the underlying causes of many instrumental problems and how they can be avoided by teaching the children proper care of their instruments.[1] It tells how the school instrumental teacher can make minor repairs and indicates which repairs need an expert service man. At the end of the chapter there is a list of some of the basic equipment and supplies the music teacher needs to keep instruments in good playing condition. He can add others to this list as his experience and competence grow.

STRINGED INSTRUMENTS

Care

All students must be impressed with the importance of the proper care of their instruments unless they wish to jeopardize their chances for progress at the very beginning. Merely because the stringed instruments do not have the moving parts common to brass and woodwind instruments is no reason to let students believe the instruments will take care of themselves.

[1] For the material in this chapter, the authors are grateful to Lorin Richtmeyer, Music Department, Northern Michigan University, Marquette, Mich.

The Bow

Before playing, tighten the bow just enough so that the hairs are taut, but not so much as to disfigure the natural curve of the stick. Loosen the bow before putting it away.

Pass the bow over the rosin two or three times before each use. Be careful not to use too much rosin, as too much is almost as bad as not enough.

Keep the hands off the hairs.

The Instrument

Using a dry cloth, wipe clean both the stick and violin after each use, being careful not to touch the hairs or the strings. Caked rosin may be removed with a finish cleaner and polisher made for that purpose. Too frequent use, however, will remove the varnish. Dust from the inside of the instrument may be knocked loose by putting a small amount of rice inside and shaking vigorously.

Keep the bridge straight. Loosen the strings slightly, if necessary, and gently pull into position.

Keep the instrument from sudden temperature or humidity changes to avoid unnecessary splitting. Have splits repaired promptly.

Do not loosen the strings when putting the instrument away.

Simple Repairs

Slipping Pegs

Slipping or sticking may be easily remedied by the application of a preparation called "peg dope." If this is not available, rub dry soap over the peg and add chalk dust.

Regluing

Remove all the old glue. Use sparingly only the best grade of cabinet-maker's glue. Hold work in place with wooden clamps and wipe off any excess glue with a damp cloth after clamping. Allow two or three days for drying.

Bridge-Fitting

New bridges should first be shaped to the size of the old. This may necessitate thinning the top by sanding. The feet should be cut roughly with a knife to fit the curve of the body. An exact fit may then be obtained by laying a strip of sandpaper midway between the F holes and rubbing the feet over it.

Soundpost Setting

This is most easily done with the soundpost setter (Fig. 19.1) but with patience it can be done with wires. The proper position is straight up and down immediately behind the right foot of the bridge (the foot under the smallest string). Bass soundposts are sometimes glued or tacked into place, but this is not recommended.

Cleaning Bow, Hairs

Loosen and wash in lukewarm water and mild soap. Rinse and allow to dry before tightening. Use powdered rosin first before applying cake rosin.

Reshaping Crooked Bows

Remove the frog. Grasp the bow firmly at either end and pass the stick back and forth through an alcohol flame, taking care not to burn the lacquer or singe the hairs. When it becomes sufficiently heated it will hold the desired shape.

WOODWIND INSTRUMENTS

Care

In general, all wooden instruments need the same type of care. They must be kept from sudden climatic changes. The student must take apart and swab his instrument *dry* after each use. Swabs should be washed frequently or they become hard and useless. Bore oil should be applied seasonally and used sparingly. On a new instrument this must be done once or twice a week for about six to eight weeks; then monthly for six to eight months, after which a seasonal application is all that is normally required. Small squares of waxed paper under the pads prevent the oil from harming them. Key oil should be applied monthly to the points of wear and to screws to prevent abnormal wear and rusting. The corked joints need cork grease occasionally or the instrument may go together with such difficulty that keys may be bent in the process. Instruct the student carefully in putting the Boehm system clarinet together so that the bridge key will not be bent or broken. Flute joints should not be greased. Usually occasional cleaning is all that is required. A stubborn joint may sometimes be eased by

Fig. 19.1. The soundpost can be seen being worked into proper position with a soundpost setter.

Michigan State University, East Lansing, Michigan.

rubbing graphite or a soft lead pencil over the joint. Saxophone neck pieces should be swabbed after each use. This is one of the most neglected practices.

Finally, concerning wooden instruments such as the clarinet and oboe family, if the instruments are kept in a room which has quite low humidity (this usually is true during the winter months when constant heating dies out the air) special care must be taken to prevent the wood from drying out and shrinking, thereby causing loose rings and sticking keys. The best remedy is to keep small humidifiers in the cases. These can be purchased commercially or made from small plastic "pill" tubes with holes inserted by a heated nail or pin and the tube then stuffed with cotton.

Cleaning

Nickel silver keys may be polished and kept shiny by use of a cleaning cloth similar to the "Blitz" cloth distributed by several instrument companies. Never use liquid or paste cleaners. If the student wipes the keys free from the perspiration of his hands after each use the tarnishing will be greatly retarded. Dust under the keys may be removed by use of a small soft-bristled paint brush.

Lacquer finishes need only a damp cloth for cleaning. Never use silver or other similar polishes as they will remove the lacquer. Special silicone lacquer cloths are available that add luster and a small degree of protection to the finish.

Mouthpieces should be washed about once a week in lukewarm water and mild soap to keep saliva, lipstick, and particles of dust from accumulating and hardening. Do *not* use hot water, as it may warp the mouthpiece. It is better to wipe the mouthpiece out with a tissue or cloth after playing rather than using the regular swab, since in time the cord may wear grooves in the tip rail of the facing. Reeds should be taken off the mouthpiece after playing, wiped clean, and laid against a flat surface to dry. Special plastic holders are available and recommended. Girls should be particular in removing lipstick before playing as this soaks into the pores of the reed and deadens its playing qualities. A reed that has become soiled can and should be washed with soap and water. Oboe and bassoon reeds should be rinsed out with clear water after playing, if possible.

Simple Repairs

Bent Keys

Particularly in the cheaper instruments, soft keys cause considerable trouble. Much of it can be avoided, however, if the student is shown how to take proper care of his instrument and made to assume responsibility for it. When using a vise or pliers the key must be protected so that it will not be marred. Thin pieces of cardboard will work for this purpose (Fig. 19.2). Better still, the purchase of a regular key bending plier is recommended since its use will be required many times. When bending the key, use firm pressure but move slowly. A broken key must be silver soldered and requires special equipment.

Sticking Keys

On an older instrument, failure to clean and oil, bent keys or post, and weak or broken springs may cause sticking keys. In the first two cases the solution is obvious and usually not too difficult. If the spring must be replaced, the old spring or broken piece must first be pushed back through the post. This is not difficult unless the spring has broken off flush with the post, in which case the spring punch is used to drive out the broken piece. To insert a new spring, select the largest size that will slide through the post opening freely. With the key in place, push the spring through until the point is approximately one-eighth of an inch beyond the spring catch, and mark the proper length by bending the spring behind the post. Then remove the spring, cut at the marked length, and flatten the large end slightly with a hammer. When reinserted in the post, the enlarged end should fit snugly and hold the spring firmly in place.

On new instruments, sticking keys are sometimes caused by wood shrinkage or low temperature. Before making any adjustments, allow the instrument to warm up to room temperature, and add humidifiers to the case if needed. This

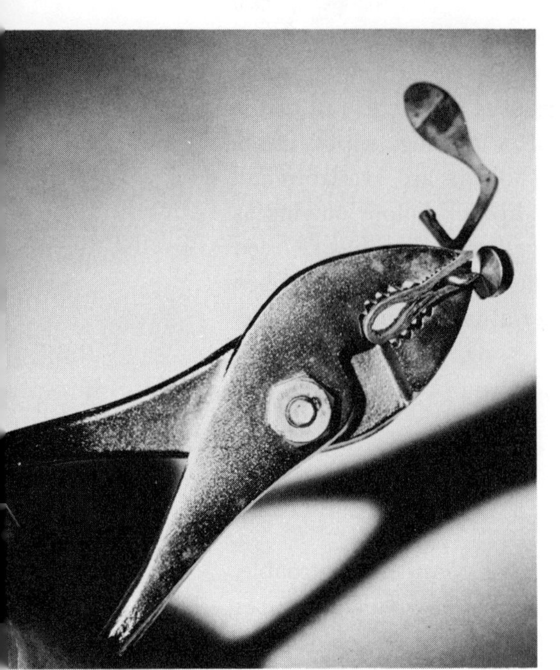

Michigan State University, East Lansing, Michigan.

Fig. 19.2. Cardboard in the plier jaws protects the finish on a key that is being straightened.

may necessitate waiting one or more days to allow the wood to expand to its normal dimensions. If the keys still stick, the following procedure is recommended: Take a small stick of wood about five inches long and a quarter of an inch wide and thick. Place one end against a cross arm nearest to the post of the sticking key and tap sharply, but not hard, with a mallet (Fig. 19.3). If this does not free the key, repeat the process at the other end of the key in the opposite direction. Alternate until the key moves freely. If the binding between posts is so great that this does not suffice, remove the key and carefully take off a small amount of metal from the end with a fine file or a hinge cutter designed for this purpose.

Locating Leaking Pads

There are several accepted ways of testing for leaks, depending on the particular instrument to be tested. One of the most common methods is to plug up one end of the instrument with a cork, hold the keys down, and blow. If air escapes there is, of course, a leak. With the free hand, apply additional pressure to individual keys to locate the exact spot. Some repair men blow smoke through the instrument to aid in finding the leak, but this method is not recommended since the odor lingers and is objectionable to the student. Another method, best

Fig. 19.3. Here is one way to loosen a sticking key on a woodwind instrument.

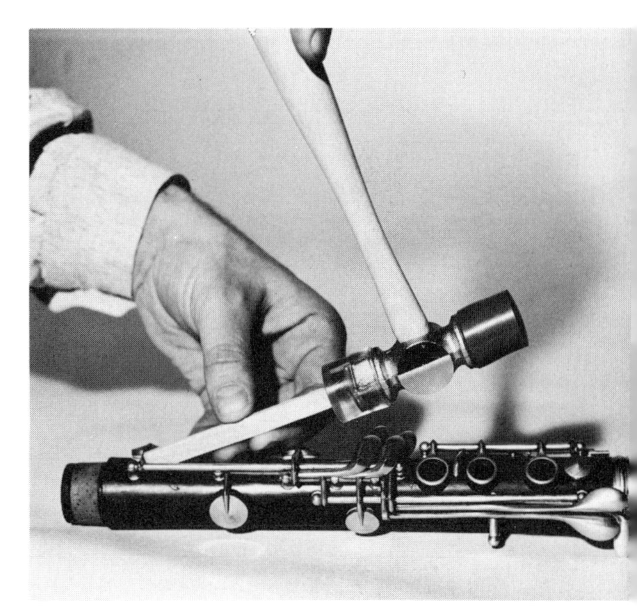

Michigan State University, East Lansing, Michigan.

suited to clarinets and flutes, is to use a "feeler," a small strip of tissue glued to the end of a small stick. With the key open, insert the tissue over the tone hole. Using a light pressure, close the key and slowly draw the paper out (Fig. 19.4). If there is much drag, the pad is covering properly. If there is very little or no drag at all, the pad is leaking. With this method it is possible to determine which side of the pad is leaking, and therefore it is perhaps the most accurate method of all.

Still another method, better suited to the saxophone, is the light test. Using a small electric light suspended in the instrument at the tone hole to be tested, a leak can be detected by the light showing under the pad.

Repadding

This is a job that requires considerable practice before a reliable technique can be acquired. There are, however, tricks of the trade that will make the job easier:

1. First remove the key from the instrument and take off the old pad by heating the key over an alcohol lamp.
2. When working with skin pads, such as those found on the clarinet, first puncture the new pad on the edge with a needle (Fig. 19.5). This prevents the pad from swelling when it is heated.

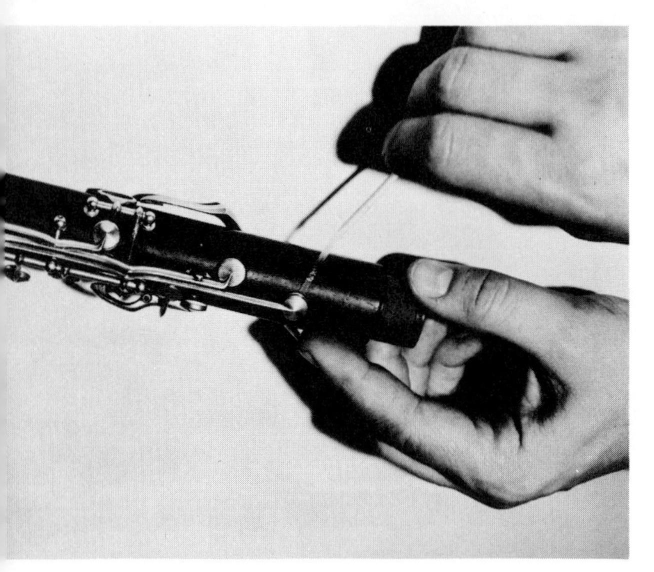

Michigan State University, East Lansing, Michigan.

Fig. 19.4. This photo shows the "feeler" technique of locating a leaking pad and the part that is leaking.

3. Harden all pads by laying them on a hard flat surface (jeweler's anvil) and tapping them lightly with a mallet.
4. Heat the pad cup and melt a small amount of shellac inside. When this cools to the consistency of thick syrup, place the pad in the cup, turn over and place the pad side down on a flat surface and hold down firmly until shellac hardens. Make sure pad is seated evenly in the cup. If shellac oozes out, either too much was used, it was too hot, the pad might have been the wrong size, or the pressure was applied unevenly. If it does not stick, either the shellac was too cold or not enough was used.
5. Replace the key on the instrument and check to see if the pad touches the tone hole evenly on all sides. If it does, the pad is then "seated" by heating the cup slightly (only soften the shellac, not melt it) and pressing down on the key a little harder than normal playing pressure. This should leave an even imprint of the tone hole on the pad.
6. If, when replacing the key, the pad does not touch the tone hole evenly, first check to see if the pad is level. If it is, and the correct thickness of pad has been used, it is better to bend the key so that the pad will set level than shift the pad. There may be cases, however, where a thicker or thinner pad will have to be used, or the pad moved. When the pad is leveled it is then seated as described before.
7. No shellac is needed on most flutes commonly used today. Instead, the pad is held in place by a center screw and washer. Paper or cardboard washers are used underneath the pad to build it up to the right thickness. The flute

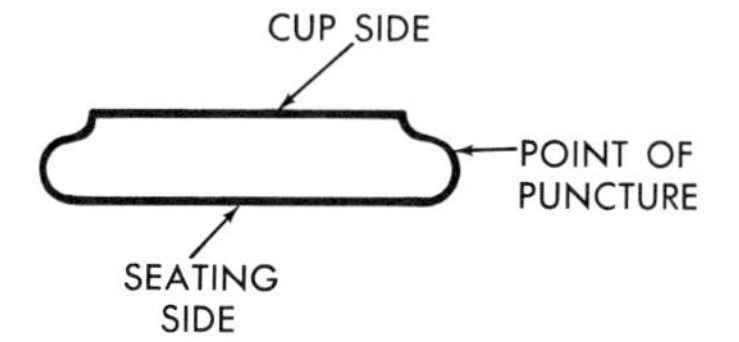

Fig. 19.5. This diagram shows the point at which to puncture a new skin pad before fitting, to prevent swelling when heated.

Michigan State University, East Lansing, Michigan.

requires delicate adjustment for good response, so the pad must be set perfectly level before seating.

We cannot leave the subject of repadding without mentioning the plastic pads that are now available and gaining much favor, particularly at the student level. While they are much more durable, they, unfortunately, are also more difficult to use correctly. The pads are easily fasened in with a plastic cement, but they require a carefully controlled amount of heat to seat properly. Complete instructions come with the kits, however, and with a little practice satisfactory results can be obtained.

Recorking Joints

Remove all the old cork and glue by scraping. Then cut a strip of cork the proper width from a sheet 3/32 of an inch in thickness. Make this just a little longer than necessary to go around the joint and bevel each end so that a smooth lapping will be obtained. On a metal instrument the joint may be heated and a melted coating of stick shellac applied. Allow to cool, then place the cork in position and wrap tightly with twine. By carefully slipping the open end of the instrument over a low alcohol flame, the inside of the bore will be heated and the shellac melted (Fig. 19.6). When this cools, the twine may be removed and the cork sanded down to the proper thickness.

An even easier method—particularly recommended for wood or ebonite joints—is to apply the cork with "contact cement," available at most hardware stores. With this method it is important that the cork is measured for proper fit beforehand, then the cement applied to both the joint and the cork. After they are dry to the touch (about 15 minutes) the parts are pressed together, and are ready to file or sand down immediately.

Loose Posts

On wooden instruments where the posts are screwed into the body, check first to see if the threads are still good. If they are but the post turns past the desired position, one or more thin, paperlike washers (post shims) can be

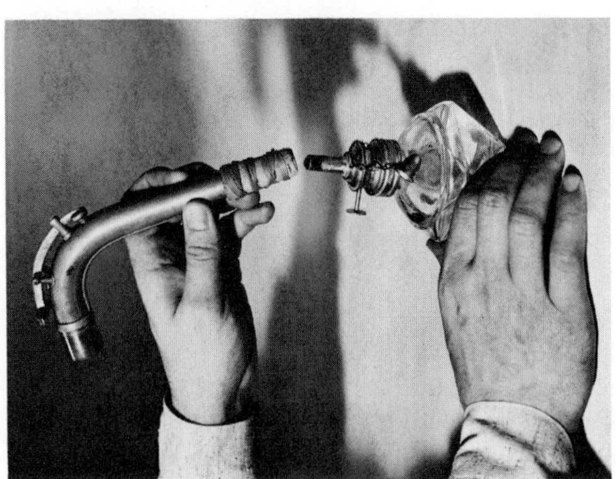

Michigan State University, East Lansing, Michigan.

Fig. 19.6. This photo shows how to melt the shellac in fitting on a new cork sleeve.

inserted between the body and the post flange. If there is less play than this, a drop of liquid shellac in the hole will hold the post in place.

Loose Rings

Loose rings on the joints of wooden instruments are caused by wood shrinkage and must be tightened to avoid splitting the instrument when it is put together. Since a satisfactory permanent repair requires special equipment that will actually shrink the metal ring to the proper tightness, we are concerned here only with the temporary repair. The most obvious method is to insert thin strips of paper or fine sandpaper under the ring. However, a more satisfactory method is to make a cheesecloth sleeve and fit it around the groove for the ring, then slip the ring over the sleeve and tap into position with a mallet (Fig. 19.7). Finish the operation by trimming the cheesecloth with a razor blade. These are only temporary repairs and further shrinking or swelling due to humidity changes will not let them last indefinitely.

Cracks

Some cracks, particularly in the joint of the clarinet, will not extend past the cork into the body of the instrument, and need not be banded if careful watch is kept to see that they do not extend further. If a crack or split does appear in the body where the playing quality will be affected, it should be repaired by a professional repair man, who will either pin it or band it, or both, depending upon its nature. For an emergency treatment of such a crack, one might get along until the instrument can be properly repaired by filling the crack with liquid shellac or wax. Banding or pinning as soon as possible is essential, however, to avoid having the split extend further.

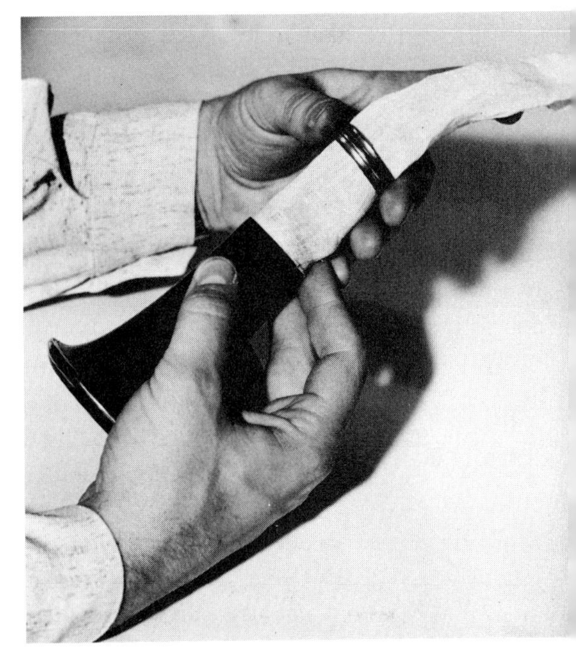

Fig. 19.7. Here is an excellent way to fasten a loose ring.

Michigan State University, East Lansing, Michigan.

BRASS INSTRUMENTS

Care

Because of their smaller number of intricate moving parts and because of their more sturdy appearance, the brass instruments are not as meticulously cared for by students as they should be. Unless cautioned about the possible consequences, dropped mouthpieces, dents, and corrosion do not seem important to the student (except that they spoil the beautiful finish) because nothing "breaks" and it still "blows." However, the following points of care should be stressed and the resulting consequences of neglect pointed out to the player.

Valve and Slide Care

The most obvious points of care for the brass instrument involve these two components. If the valves on Johnny's cornet or the slide on Jimmy's trombone refuse to respond, he is naturally made aware of this and may take some measures to correct it. With proper care, however, these situations should not arise. On a new valve instrument or trombone, the student should be impressed with the need for frequent cleaning out and lubrication. There is such close tolerance that unless kept properly oiled they will become unduly worn and will stick. Even with the best care, bits of metal will wear off at first, necessitating thorough and frequent flushing out. This period may last a few weeks, several months, or even as long as a year, depending upon the amount of use and the amount of valve tolerance to begin with. The same is true for the slide on the trombone. One cannot be too fussy with the care of valves and slides. Good valves or a good slide properly taken care of will last indefinitely. A satisfactory procedure for the student to follow is this:

1. On a new instrument, at least twice a week remove the valves or trombone slide and wash off with *lukewarm* water. (This does not apply to rotary valves.) Then flush out the valve casing or the outer casing on the trombone. Wipe clean with a lint-free cloth and lubricate with valve or slide oil. Use sparingly, as too much oil only gums up the action.
2. After the breaking-in period, the valve and slide of the instrument should be oiled frequently enough to insure good action and lasting protection.
3. Use a good grade of commercial oil specifically made for the instrument. Do *not* use saliva! It contains harmful corrosive acids. Some players prefer the fast action obtained by using a film of cold cream and water, but this is not recommended for the beginner since it requires even more frequent attention.
4. The tuning slides and valve slides should be pulled once a week and greased with ordinary white vaseline to avoid being "frozen" fast by corrosion. It is a good idea also to put a bit of vaseline on the threads of the top and bottom valve caps.

Rotary Valves

It should be mentioned here that the French horn rotary valves require additional information not covered by the preceding discussion of valve instruments. Two main points should be brought out concerning their care and maintenance:

1. By far the most common mishap for horn players occurs when a string breaks. The author has found that a very heavyweight waterproofed fish line serves as a satisfactory replacement. Use the other valves as a guide in replacing the string, being careful that it is tightened in the proper position to make the valve lever even with the others. The string should be pulled fairly tight so that there is no play.

2. The rotary-type valves also need frequent oiling; however, they need not be removed for oiling. Some horn valves may be oiled by removing the screw on the stop arm and inserting the oil there. Others must have the oil inserted underneath the stop arm. In either case, also remove the valve cap on the lever side and place a drop of oil on the shaft bearing. If the valves have become cor-

roded and stuck through a period of disuse, they can sometimes be freed by applying oil through the valve slides. If this is not successful, the valves must be removed and cleaned. This job should not be attempted unless the director is familiar with the instrument. For a detailed and illustrated procedure for disassembling and assembling the French horn it is suggested that the director refer to a directions booklet.[2]

Cleaning

The inside cleaning of a brass instrument should not be restricted to the valves and slides, as is often the case even with careful students. The saliva from the student's mouth is constantly collecting on the inside of the mouthpiece and tubing. If this is not removed frequently it will harden and become almost impossible to clean out by home methods. This accumulation will gradually increase until the diameter of the bore has been drastically changed, resulting in poor tone, faulty intonation, and difficult blowing. The years of research and scientific production methods that have resulted in producing the best bore sizes and taper, and the most resonant alloys, are for nothing if they are not kept clean. For this reason alone, students should not be allowed to eat, drink, chew, and play at the same time, as often happens at athletic events in which bands participate. Food particles and sugar from soft drinks or chewing gum all combine with saliva to present quite a formidable barrier to the job of keeping a brass instrument in its best playing condition.

The frequency with which the instrument should be cleaned depends upon the amount of playing and the conditions under which it is played. However, for an instrument that is used every day a conservative estimate would be at least every other week, with the mouthpiece being cleaned every week. The following suggestions will serve as a guide:

1. Remove all valves and slides. Flush out each part plus the main body of the instrument with *lukewarm* water, using a mild detergent if desired. (Remember, *hot* water may damage lacquer finishes.) The instrument and the disassembled slides should then be brushed out with a flexible brush, such as the Micro brush, and flushed a second time with clear water. A mouthpiece brush is also a good investment for the student.
2. After shaking and blowing out the excess water, wipe off and reassemble the instrument. Valves and slides must be oiled and greased as described on p. 484.

[2] See, for example, *How to Care for Your Instrument*, Elkhart, Ind., C. G. Conn.

Cleaning the Finish

Maintaining a sparkling finish should be a matter of pride with the student. It is a morale booster to play on a beautiful instrument, and in that respect it can actually help the student play better. Have the player learn the proper ways of polishing his instrument by following these suggestions:

1. Silver plated instruments: Use any good grade of silver polish, liquid or paste, and follow the directions on the label. Generally if the slides and valves are removed it is easier to work on the instrument and a better job can be done. Do not use any polish that is highly abrasive as the silver can be scratched easily.
2. Lacquer finished instruments: The same suggestions apply here as in the section on lacquered woodwinds. Do not use metal polishers or cleaners as they will remove the lacquer. A damp cloth is all that is needed.

Simple Repairs

The director does not have the multitude of repair problems with the brass instruments that he has with the woodwinds. The repairs that he is qualified to handle will require only one specific tool besides his regular equipment. That one tool is the mouthpiece puller, which, in the author's opinion, is an indispensable piece of equipment. The following discussion lists, in their seemingly most frequent occurrence, the repair problems and methods of handling them with which the director should be familiar.

Dents

Aside from the fact that dents in the instrument present an unsightly appearance, they may also greatly affect its playability. The metal alloy in the brass instruments, in order to respond with the right amount of resonance, must necessarily be soft and fairly thin. The slightest contact with hard or sharp objects will leave its mark. Students, therefore, should be cautioned about their own handling and particularly against passing the instrument around to less experienced or to careless fellow students. Any dent of major size should be handled by an experienced repair man as soon as possible; more harm than good usually results in the inexperienced and unequipped person's attempts in this area.

Dropping a mouthpiece often leaves the end somewhat flattened and, because it does not show, the flattening is often ignored. Not only can this cause the mouthpiece to stick in the shank, but it can cause serious difficulty in the blow-

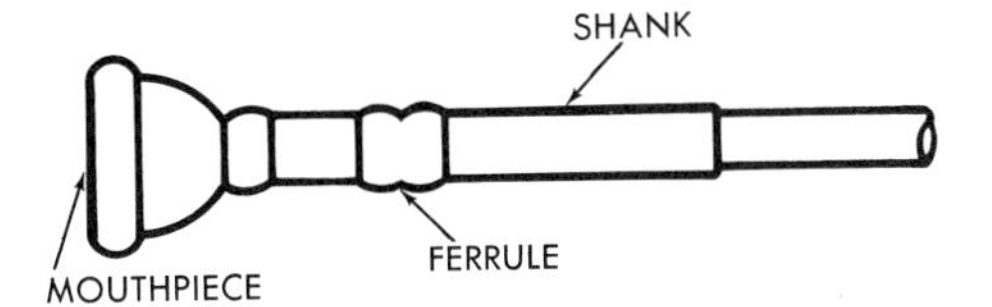

Fig. 19.8. Knowledge of such terms as those in this diagram permits precise identification of points which may require attention.

ing and intonation of the instrument (Fig. 19.8). A dent or nicks in the rim of the mouthpiece should be brought to the attention of the director. The sharp edges of a nick on the rim can be irritating to the lips of the player and should be corrected. A little vaseline on the shank of the mouthpiece will lessen any tendency to stick.

Stuck Mouthpieces

With a mouthpiece puller, this is a simple operation (Fig. 19.9). If one is not available, tap the mouthpiece receptacle lightly with a mallet. Strike at the end of the mouthpiece on the ferrule, turning it around as you do so. A few taps are usually all that are necessary. Above all, do *not* attempt to remove a stuck mouthpiece by use of a vise and pliers or by twisting in the hand. The mouthpiece will not only be badly marred but it may be twisted loose from the brace, making soldering necessary. Once the mouthpiece is loosened, clean and smooth the end with fine emery paper and apply a bit of vaseline. Check also to see if the end is dented. If so, it may be rounded out by working a metal rod in the opening. Several such rods of varying diameters will have a surprising variety of uses in repair work.

Removing Stuck Slides

When the instrument has not been properly cleaned and cared for, a "frozen" or stuck slide is the usual result. If the slide will not respond to a firm hand pressure, try the following technique:

1. Loop a leather thong, belt, or soft rope (at least two or three feet long) through the slide and fasten the other end in a vise or around a solidly embedded hook.
2. Hold the instrument so that it forms a straight line with the rope when it is pulled taut.
3. Move the instrument toward the vise and bring it back with a sharp jerk. Do not jerk too hard as you may pull the slide apart at its soldered joints. Several lighter jerks are better than one hard one.

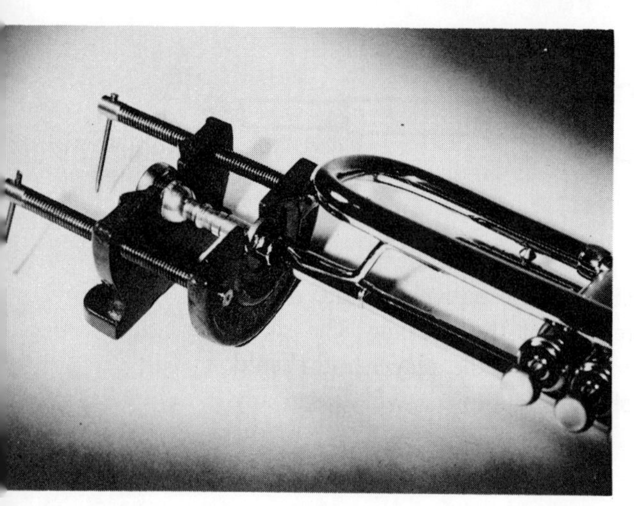

Michigan State University, East Lansing, Michigan.

Fig. 19.9. The mouthpiece is in position here to be removed without mar or damage to the instrument.

4. If this does not meet with success readily, and time is not too important, apply some penetrating oil to the inside and outside of the slide, let it set over night, and repeat the pulling process the next day.
5. If time is of the essence, apply heat to the slide and allow it to cool before pulling again. This may have to be repeated several times. Remember that the joints in the slide are only soft-soldered, so do not apply too much heat lest the solder melt or the lacquer finish burn.

Removing Corroded Valve Caps

Often on older instruments or even occasionally on newer ones when care has been grossly neglected, the top and bottom valve caps may be so corroded that the valves cannot be removed for cleaning. If firm pressure with the fingers fails to loosen them, apply the following methods:

1. Tap lightly with a mallet as in loosening a stuck mouthpiece (see p. 487).
2. If this does not loosen the cap, trying using penetrating oil or heating as in removing stuck slides (see above).
3. While the above methods should bring results, in very stubborn cases use pliers. However, be very careful to pad the jaws so that the finish is not marred.

Stuck Valves

When an instrument has not been in use for some time, or if it has been dented or otherwise damaged, stuck valves sometimes occur. If a valve cannot be moved with the hand, remove the top and bottom valve caps and the finger button. These procedures can then be tried:

1. Apply some penetrating oil at the top and bottom of the valve and also through the valve slide holes, trying to get the oil to soak in between the valve and the casing. If possible, let it set a few hours and try removing with the hand again.
2. If the valve still does not respond and is not already at the bottom of its stroke, try tapping the valve stem *lightly* (Fig. 19.10). Be careful to hit straight down so as not to bend or break the stem. Do *not* try this if the valve is already at the bottom.
3. If the valve is frozen at the bottom of the stroke, it is possible to drive it out from the bottom. To do this, get a piece of tubing, or a wooden rod, about the same size as the valve, and use to tap the valve upwards. The proper diameter of the tube or rod is important so that the force of the tapping will strike only against the outside edge of the valve. Do *not* push against the inside of the valve bottom, as in most cases this is only a thin disc soldered in place.
4. After removing the valve, check to find the cause of sticking. If it is only corroded, it may be cleaned by using penetrating oil and powdered pumice. Never sandpaper valves, as this will remove the plating.

Dented Valves and Slides

Sometimes sticking valves or dragging trombone slides are not caused by corrosion. If the valves and slides have been thoroughly cleaned and still do not work properly, check for minute nicks or dents in the valve casings or along the outer slide of the trombone. Nicks or dents must be tended to promptly or they will ruin the valve or inner slide. This is not a job for the inexperienced; the instrument should be sent to a reliable repair shop.

Replacing Spit-Valve Corks and Springs

A worn or leading spit-valve cork may be shaped and replaced in the same manner as a clarinet pad (see p. 479). It is possible to buy various sizes of these corks, and it is a good idea to have a quantity of the standard sizes in stock. From these any exact size may be easily shaped.

It is also a good idea to carry several kinds of spit-valve springs for easy and quick repairs, but if desired, a roll of spring wire may come in handy to make springs of any size. If nothing of this sort is available a rubber band makes a quick and simple temporary repair.

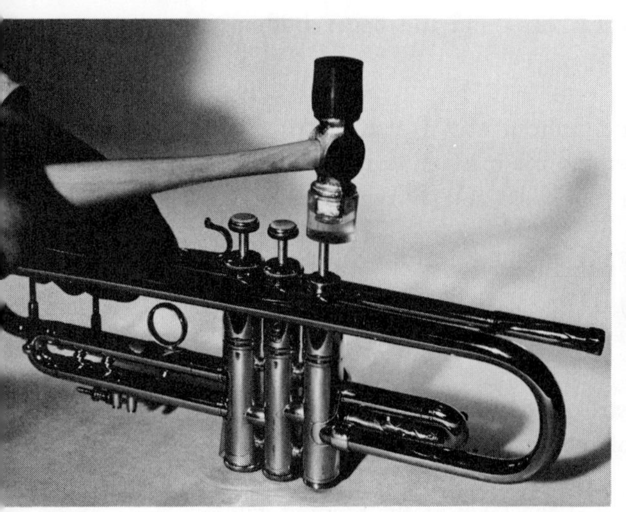

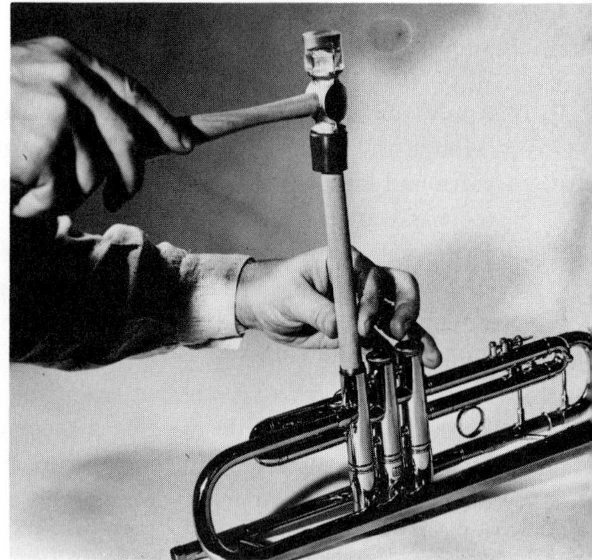

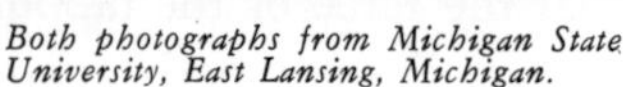

Both photographs from Michigan State University, East Lansing, Michigan.

Fig. 19.10. When other measures fail, tapping will loosen a stuck valve. What important precautions should be observed with this method?

Dents in General

As discussed in the section on care, dents can cause poor tone and intonation problems, and generally result in difficult blowing. However, while some nicks in mouthpieces can sometimes be smoothed by careful rubbing and buffing, most other dents in the brass instrument are outside the realm of the average music director. Unless one has the proper equipment and training, these dents are best taken to a good repair shop. A great deal more harm than good usually results in the inexperienced and unequipped person's attempts in this field. It is mentioned here only to emphasize the importance of having these repairs made.

PERCUSSION INSTRUMENTS

Care

The condition of the percussion instruments in many schools is enough in itself to discourage the ambitions of a budding drummer. Despite continued neglect and abuse it is expected that the student should be able to produce the characteristic sounds on the instruments, although, for example, in many cases tension rods on snare and bass drums are so rusted that adjusting the tension on the heads is impossible. Actually, keeping percussion instruments in repair and

Both photographs from Michigan State University, East Lansing, Michigan.

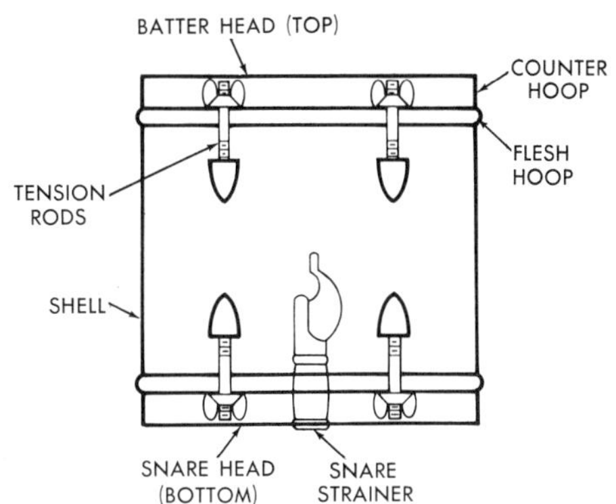

Fig. 19.11. How well do you know your drum parts? Cover the diagram and test yourself.

in good playing condition is a minor task if directors acquaint themselves with a few simple facts and then see that this information is relayed to the players. All that remains is to see that these instructions are carried out regularly by the students.

It would be a good idea for the director to provide both himself and his percussion students with the following check list and see that it is complied with at least twice a year:

1. Oil all moving parts and threads on the percussion instruments. This includes tension rods, snare strainers, tympani pedals, hand tuners, etc. (Fig. 19.11). Use a light machine oil and apply sparingly.
2. Protect the chrome and lacquer finishes with any good grade of wax cleaner.
3. Clean the dirt and grit from under the counter hoops, where constant pressure may damage the heads.
4. Tighten loose nuts and replace any missing nuts or washers either inside or outside the drum. Constant vibration causes frequent loosening.
5. Inspect all heads to see if the changes in weather have caused them to shrink or stretch to the point where they should be "wetted down" and reset.

Along with this check list may be included another list of general information that should be common knowledge to both the player and director:

1. Drum heads are affected primarily by humidity, and not by temperature. Dry weather, whether hot or cold, causes the heads to shrink and tighten.

When excessive moisture is in the air, during either warm or cold weather, the head is caused to stretch or loosen.

2. The best snare sound is obtained with the batter head fairly tight and the snare head a trifle looser. Do not loosen tension after playing except in damp weather when it becomes necessary to tighten the heads for playing. In this case, after playing they should be loosened to their original tension. In general, except in damp weather, it is better to leave the heads alone once the best playing tension has been determined.
3. The low tones on the tympani and bass drum are best obtained by tightening the heads somewhat after playing and returning them to their original tension before the next playing. In the case of the tympani, raising the pitch about a minor third after playing will subject the heads to enough tension to insure reaching the low notes the next time. This amount may vary, again according to the amount of moisture present in the air.
4. Creaking tympani heads should be corrected by applying paraffin to the part of the head which comes in contact with the edge of the bowl.
5. Cymbals should be kept polished. However, the polishing should *not* be done by heavy buffing as this wears down the tiny ridges in the metal, thereby destroying the tone. Use a nonabrasive metal polish such as Sears Roebuck Silicone Chrome Polish, or Western Auto Silicone Chrome Polish, following the directions on the label.
6. When they are not in use, cover tympani, bells, xylophone, and the like. This protects these instruments from curious fingers and keeps them free from dirt and grit.
7. The tone of the triangle may be improved by the use of a gut holder which is sold commercially and is equipped with a clip that enables the triangle to be suspended from the music rack until needed.
8. All the smaller percussion equipment, such as sticks, brushes, wood blocks, castanets, tambourine, sound effects, etc., should be kept in a cabinet out of reach of the nonpercussion players.
9. For appearance's sake alone, drum heads and drum slings should be cleaned as the need becomes apparent. The head may be easily washed with a mild soap and damp cloth. Take care that no water gets down along the edges of the counter hoop. Slings may be washed in soap and water with care taken afterwards to dry the metal fittings to prevent rusting.

Simple Repairs

If the care that has been outlined in the previous pages is followed faithfully there will arise few repairs that the average director will not be qualified to undertake. However, since broken heads constitute the majority of repairs, this problem will be discussed briefly, with the understanding that in most cases it is far better to turn broken heads over to the experienced drum shop.

Minor Breaks

Occasionally a small tear or cut may be observed in the head of a drum, usually around the rim. To prevent this from splitting wide open, a small bit of adhesive tape can be applied. This temporary repair may last for some length of time or only a short while, so it is best to have the head replaced at a time when it is convenient, to avoid having it split at an inconvenient time.

Retucking a Head

In this day of all plastic drum heads it is probably rare that a director will be called upon to tuck a skin head, and in the list of supplies (see p. 497) either a spare plastic head or a pretucked skin head is suggested as an answer to emergency repairs. However, since sometimes a director may face the problem of having to tuck a head himself, a brief outline of the method is:

1. Select a head large enough to allow for tucking around the hoop—4 inches for a small wooden hoop and 2 to 3 for a thin metal hoop. A bass drum or tympani head will require about 5 or 6 inches. For snare drums a heavy head is used for the batter side, and a thin transparent head for the snare side.
2. Soak the head in water of room temperature for about 15 to 20 minutes, depending upon the head thickness.
3. Lay on a flat surface, with flesh side up. This may be determined by testing with the fingernail; the flesh side will be soft and the hair side firm and smooth.
4. If the head to be tucked is a bass drum or tympani head, it should be tucked with slack in the middle to allow for excessive shrinkage. This may be formed by placing a pie plate or some similar object under the center of the head.
5. Place the flesh hoop in the exact center of the head and begin tucking at opposite sides as in Fig. 19.12. Continue this process until the entire head is tucked. A regular tucking tool or the handle of a spoon may be used. In the latter case the spoon should have a slight bend on the end so that the head may be tucked under and behind the flesh hoop.
6. Two methods of tucking are used. On a wooden flesh hoop it is usually sufficient merely to fold the head over the hoop and tuck underneath. On a metal hoop the tuck should continue under and up behind the hoop to hold it from slipping off.
7. Smooth out wrinkles as you go along and when the entire head is tucked, set it aside to dry for a few hours. Before it dries enough to begin pulling, put it on the drum shell and place the counter hoop in position. On a snare drum

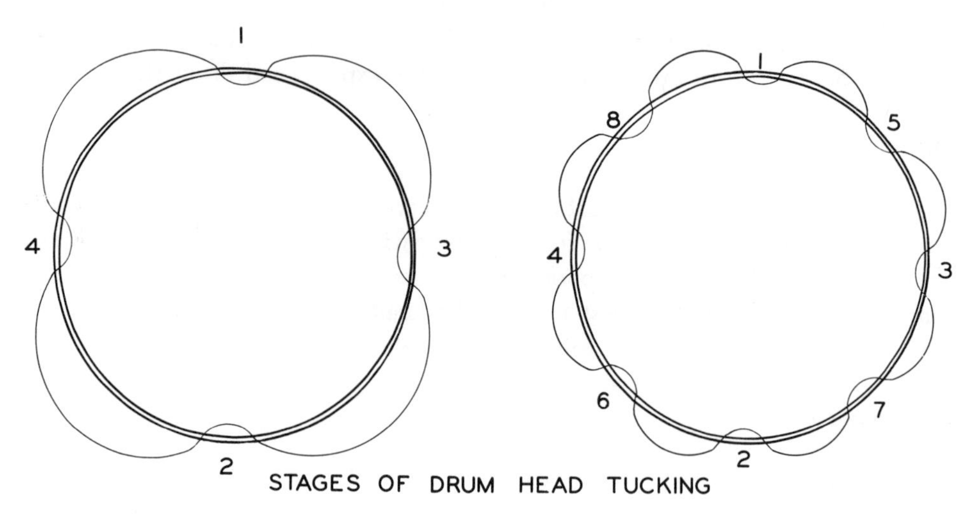

Michigan State University, East Lansing, Michigan.

Fig. 19.12. How to tuck a drum head. Using a tucking tool or spoon, work alternately from opposite sides so that tucking proceeds evenly.

the counter hoop should then be tightened down about a sixteenth to an eighth of an inch. On a bass drum this amount will be about an eighth to a quarter of an inch, and on tympani heads a quarter to a half of an inch.

8. If the weather is exceptionally dry, the center of the head dries too quickly, causing the head to tear at the rim where it may still be wet and soft. This is prevented by placing a damp towel in the center and allowing the rim area to dry first.

More specific details on the tucking and other repair techniques may be found in some of the references listed at the end of this chapter.

Resetting a Head

Because of excessive dryness or improper care of the head tension, the "collar" on the bass drum and tympani may be lost, thereby making it impossible to obtain the low tones desired. To correct this, remove the head and wet it down on both sides, being careful not to get any closer than an inch to the rim. When the head is thoroughly wet, replace it on the drum and pull the counter hoop down to the desired amount of collar.

Removing Dents in Tympani

Any dents in the bowl of the tympani can usually be removed satisfactorily by removing the head and gently tapping out the dents with a rawhide mallet or padded hammer.

EQUIPMENT FOR THE CARE AND REPAIR OF INSTRUMENTS

The life of a musical instrument depends largely upon its care and handling. It is up to the teacher to inspire in his students the respect and responsibility they should have toward their instruments.

Below is a checklist of the basic equipment needed for the care and repair of band and orchestra instruments; the music teacher may add other items according to his own experience (Fig. 19.13):

General equipment:

1. Well-lighted worktable
2. Bench vise
3. Mallet
4. Alcohol lamp
5. Set of pliers (long-nosed, flat duck-bill, and regular)
6. Set of small screwdrivers
7. Set of six-inch hand files (coarse, fine, flat, and rounded)
8. Knife
9. Single-edged razor blades
10. Sandpaper or emery cloth
11. All-purpose cement
12. Soldering iron, solid core solder and flux

String equipment and supplies:

1. Sound-post setters (large and small sizes)
2. Wood clamps
3. Good grade of cabinet-maker's glue
4. Assorted bridges
5. Assorted strings
6. Peg dope
7. Finish cleaner and polisher

Woodwind equipment and supplies:

1. Test light
2. Large and small spring hooks (can be made from crochet hooks)
3. Spring punch
4. Stick and liquid shellac
5. Assorted flute and piccolo pads
6. Assorted oboe and bassoon pads

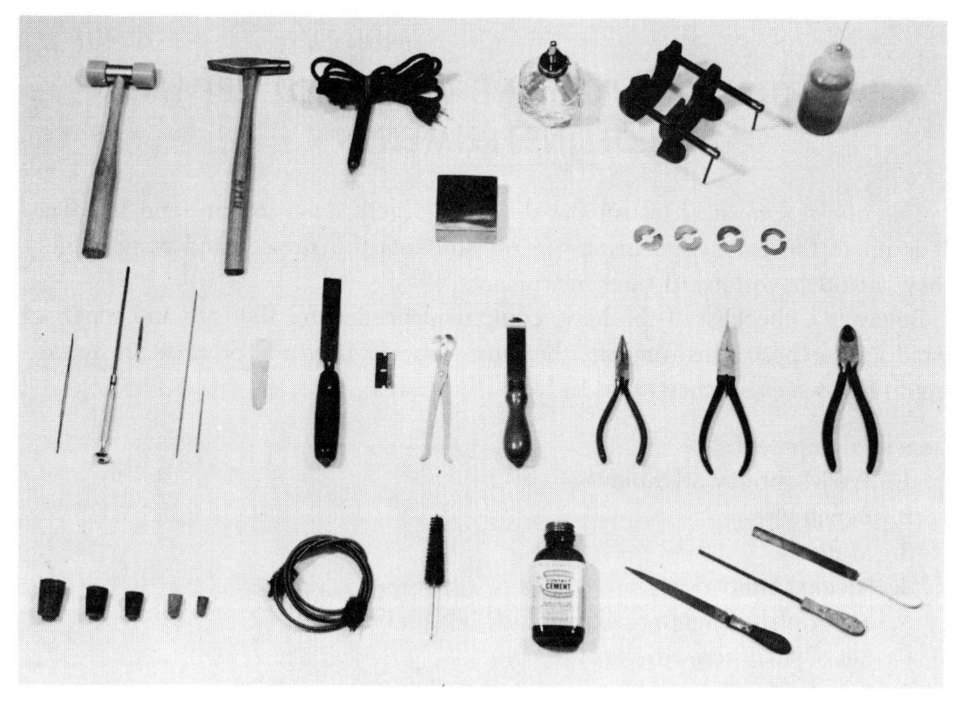

Northern Michigan University, Marquette, Michigan.

Fig. 19.13. Top row, left to right: Soft mallet, hardened steel hammer, leak test light, jeweler's anvil, alcohol lamp, mouthpiece puller with four sizes of adapter rings, bench oiler; Middle row, left to right Spring hook, screwdriver with long and short blades, spring punches, pad slick, cork knife, single-edged razor blade, soundpost setter, drumhead tucker, needle-nose pliers, key-bending pliers, wire cutters; Bottom row, left to right: Set of 5 leak-testing corks, flexible cleaning brush, mouthpiece brush, contact cement, cork files.

7. Assorted clarinet pads (most common sizes are 9½, 10, 12, 15, 16.5, and 17 millimeters)
8. Assorted saxophone pads
9. Assorted flute, clarinet, and saxophone pivot screws
10. Assorted flute, clarinet, and saxophone needle and flat springs
11. Assorted saxophone neck corks
12. Assorted thicknesses of sheet cork
13. Cork grease
14. Key and bore oil

Brass equipment and supplies:

1. Mouthpiece puller
2. Strap or strips of rawhide (for pulling slides)
3. Flexible brushes (for cleaning tubes and slides)
4. French horn valve string (heavy fishing twine will work)
5. Assorted spit-valve corks

6. Assorted spit-valve springs (or coil of spring wire)
7. Assorted valve springs and washers
8. Penetrating oil
9. Valve and slide oil
10. Vaseline

Drum equipment and supplies:
1. Head tucker (bent spoon handle will work)
2. Snare batter head (pretucked for emergencies)
3. Light machine oil
4. Paraffin

While the above seems like a lengthy list, the director will not suffer from an oversupply, and will want to add items of his own choice from time to time.

SUMMARY

The reader should keep in mind that all the points on care and repair included here represent knowledge for which he, as a band or orchestra director, should be responsible. The students look to him for help since they respect his judgment as their teacher. Helping them to learn proper care for their instruments is as important a part of his job as instructing them in the art of playing. Often a musical instrument is one of the most expensive possessions a child has been entrusted with thus far, and an emphasis on the responsibility for proper care may go a long way in helping the child appreciate the money invested in it.

The repairs discussed are of the nature that will test the director's ingenuity and patience, but such training can make for greater confidence in oneself as a teacher, and inspire the greater confidence of one's students, which in the final analysis makes all teaching methods more effective. Should the reader find his interest sparked by initial successes in repairing, he may desire more comprehensive information regarding these and other repairs. To date the most explicit book in this field is the *Selmer Band Instrument Repairing Manual* by Erick D. Brand. This and other reference materials are listed in the Selected Readings at the end of this chapter.

SUGGESTED ACTIVITIES

1. Remove and replace the sound post in a violin.
2. Shape and fit a new bridge to a violin.

3. Replace and seat several pads on a clarinet. Check for leaks using the methods discussed in this chapter.
4. Replace and seat several pads on a saxophone. Check for leaks with a light tester.
5. Recork the joint on a wood clarinet. Also recork a saxophone neck.
6. Using the cheesecloth-sleeve method, repair a loose ring on a clarinet.
7. Replace the string on a French horn valve.
8. Remove a stuck mouthpiece with the mouthpiece puller.
9. Disassemble, flush out, lubricate, and reassemble all parts on a cornet and on a trombone.
10. Remove the head of a snare drum, wet it down on both sides, and remount it.

SELECTED READINGS

Brand, Erick D., *Selmer Band Instrument Repairing Manual* (rev. ed.), E. C. Schirmer, 1946.

Conn, C. G., *How To Care for Your Instrument*, C. G. Conn.

Pascucci, Vito, *Care and Minor Repairs of the Clarinet*, G. Leblanc, 1959.

Price, Paul, "Care and Repair of Percussion," *The Instrumentalist*, January–February, 1951, p. 27.

Repair and Accessory Manual, Long Island City, N.Y., Penzel-Mueller Company.

Tiede, Clayton H., *The Practical Band Instrument Repair Manual*, Wm. C. Brown, 1962.

You Fix Them, Cleveland, O., Scherl and Roth, 1955.

Waln, George E., "Repair Your Own," *The Instrumentalist*, November–December, 1952, p. 33.

PART II

The Music Educator's Reference File

Michigan State University.

CHAPTER

20

Organizational Aids

OUTLINE OF A PROGRAM FOR MUSIC EDUCATION[1]

Preschool, Kindergarten, First Grade

Basic music activities (minimum time, 20 minutes daily):

1. *Singing*
   a. Learning songs by imitation
   b. Matching tones
   c. Playing singing games
2. *Rhythmic*
   a. Making free rhythmic responses to music suitable for activities such as walking, skipping, hopping, etc.
   b. Playing simple directed folk dances and games
3. *Listening*
   a. Distinguishing simple elements in music, such as mood, rhythm, instruments
4. *Playing*
   a. Learning to use rhythm instruments—triangle, drum, and simple melody instruments such as tone bells, marimba, etc.
5. *Creative*
   a. Giving opportunities for original responses in rhythms, songs, playing, listening

Grades Two and Three

Basic music activities (minimum time, 20 minutes daily):

1. *Singing*
   a. Learning songs by imitation
   b. Matching tones
   c. Playing singing games
   d. Attention to tonal and rhythmic characteristics of music, such as identifying high and low tones, like and unlike phrases, etc.
   e. Singing of rounds and descants

[1] Reprinted with permission from *Music in American Education*, a publication of the Music Educators National Conference, 1201 16th St., N.W., Washington, D.C., 20036.

   f. Using song books to introduce the musical score in familiar songs and in new songs when the group is ready and interested
2. *Rhythmic*
   a. Continuation of free rhythmic activity
   b. Responding to note groups heard
   c. Playing simple directed folk dances and games
3. *Listening*
   a. Distinguishing simple elements in music, such as mood, rhythm, instruments, themes
   b. Recognizing the use of music by different groups and peoples such as Indians, Mexicans, etc.
4. *Playing*
   a. Continuing use of rhythm instruments, adding simple melody instruments such as melody bells, xylophone, psaltery, etc.
5. *Creative*
   a. Giving opportunities for original responses in rhythms, songs, playing, listening

Grades Four and Five

Basic music activities (minimum time, 25 to 30 minutes daily):

1. *Singing*
   a. Learning songs by imitation
   b. Continuing note reading songs
   c. Continuing the use of song books and learning of the musical score in familiar and in new songs according to the skill and interests of the students, using both song and simple instrument activity
   d. Preparing for part singing by the use of rounds, descants, simple interval combinations and easy chording
   e. Singing two and three part songs when the group is ready and able to carry on such activities
   f. Large and small ensemble experience
2. *Rhythmic*
   a. Playing directed folk and square dances
   b. Playing rhythmic accompaniments to familiar songs using folk or standard rhythm instruments
3. *Listening*
   a. Distinguishing simple elements in music, such as mood, rhythm, instruments, themes, form
   b. Music of various peoples, operas of interest to children
4. *Playing*
   a. Class instruction in piano
   b. Rhythm instruments and simple melody instruments like marimba, song bells, and autoharp
   c. Exploratory instruments such as Flutophone, Tonette, Song Flute and recorder
   d. Class instruction on orchestral and band instruments

5. *Creative*
   a. Continuing opportunities for original responses in rhythms, songs, playing, listening
   b. Encouraging the composing of original melodies, rhythmic accompaniments to songs, simple harmonies to familiar songs

Grade Six

Basic music activities (minimum time, 25 to 30 minutes daily):

1. *Singing*
   a. Learning songs by imitation
   b. Continuing the reading program
   c. Singing two and three part songs
   d. Large and small ensemble experience
2. *Rhythmic*
   a. Playing directed folk and square dances
   b. Playing rhythmic accompaniments to familiar songs, using folk or standard rhythm instruments
3. *Listening*
   a. Distinguishing simple elements in music, such as mood, rhythm, instruments, themes, form
4. *Playing*
   a. Class instruction in piano
   b. Rhythm instruments and simple melody instruments, like marimba, song bells, autoharp
   c. Class instruction on orchestral and band instruments
   d. Large and small ensemble experience
5. *Creative*
   a. Continuing opportunities for original responses in rhythms, songs, playing, listening
   b. Encouraging the composition of original melodies, rhythmic accompaniments to songs, simple harmonies to familiar songs

Junior-High-School Grades (Seven, Eight, and Nine)

1. *General Music Course*
   Open to all students regardless of previous musical experience. A course offering a variety of musical activities, such as playing, singing, listening, reading music, creative activity, etc.
2. *Vocal Music*
   Boys' and girls' glee clubs, chorus or choir, small vocal ensembles, assembly singing for all students.
3. *Instrumental Music*
   Orchestra, band, small instrumental ensembles; class instrumental instruction in

wind, string, and keyboard, for beginners and more advanced students; credit for private lessons available in Grade 9.

4. *Special Electives in Music*
   In some junior high schools there is need for special elective classes in Music Appreciation and in Music Theory, especially in Grade 9.
5. *Relating and Coordinating Out-of-School Influences*
   Radio, television, motion pictures, church, and home music experiences should be coordinated in all possible ways with those of the classroom.

Senior-High-School Grades (Ten, Eleven, and Twelve)

1. *Vocal Music*
   Boys' and girls' glee clubs, chorus, choir, small vocal ensembles, voice classes, applied music credit for private lessons. Some of the large choral groups selective and others open for election by any interested student, unless the school is too small to allow for more than one group.
2. *General Music*
   Open to all students, regardless of previous musical experience. A course similar to that described under Junior High School, but adjusted in its content to Senior High School interests and needs.
3. *Instrumental Music*
   Orchestra, band, small ensembles; class instrumental instruction in wind, string, percussion and keyboard for beginning and advanced students; dance band. Orchestra and band should be divided into beginning and advanced sections, or first and second groups, if the enrollment warrants such division; applied music credit for private lessons.
4. *Elective Course Offerings*
   Music theory, music appreciation, music history. Many high schools find it feasible to offer several years of instruction in each of these fields.

For All Students in Elementary and Secondary Grades

1. *Assembly Programs*
   Music programs with singing by all the students, the appearance of school musical organizations, and appearance of outside artists and musical organizations.
2. *Recitals and Concerts by Student Performers*
3. *Educational Concerts*
4. *Music Clubs*
   Clubs devoted to those interested in certain phases of music study or related areas: Record Collectors Club, Conducting Club, Folk Dance Club, Recorder Club, etc.
5. *Musical Programs in the Community*

TESTING

Musical Aptitude Tests

Drake Musical Aptitude Test, Raleigh M. Drake, Science Research Associates, Inc., 57 W. Grand Ave., Chicago 60610, 1954.

K-D Music Tests, Jacob Kwalwasser and Peter W. Dykema, Carl Fischer, Inc., 1930.

Kwalwasser Music Talent Test, Jacob Kwalwasser, Mills Music Co., Form A: Secondary; Form B: Elementary.

Measures of Musical Talents, Carl E. Seashore, Don Lewis, and Joseph G. Saetveit, The Psychological Corporation, 304 E. 45th St., New York 10017, 1956. Six 78 rpm recordings.

Test of Musicality (4th ed.), E. Thayer Gaston, Odell's Instrumental Service, 925 Massachusetts, Lawrence, Kan., 1956.

Tilson-Gretsch Musical Aptitude Tests, Lowell M. Tilson, The Fred Gretsch Mfg. Co. Two LP recordings.

Whistler-Thorpe Music Aptitude Test, Series A, Harvey S. Whistler and Louis P. Thorpe, California Test Bureau, 5916 Hollywood Blvd., Los Angeles 8, Calif., 1950. Rhythm and pitch recognition.

Wing Standardized Tests of Musical Intelligence, Herbert Wing. Published by H. D. Wing and Cecelia Wing, Sheffield City Training College, Sheffield, England. Distributed by the National Foundation for Educational Research, 79 Wimpole St., London W1, England.

Musical Achievement Tests

Aliferis Music Achievement Test, James Aliferis, University of Minnesota Press, Minneapolis, 1954. Music theory, college. Tape.

Farnum Music Notation Test, Stephen E. Farnum, The Psychological Corporation, 304 E. 45th St., New York 10017, 1953.

Diagnostic Tests of Achievement in Music, M. Lila Kotick and T. L. Torgerson, California Test Bureau, 5916 Hollywood Blvd., Los Angeles 8, Calif., 1950.

Kwalwasser-Ruch Test of Musical Accomplishment, Jacob Kwalwasser and G. M. Ruch, Bureau of Educational Research and Service, State University of Iowa, Iowa City, Iowa, revised 1927.

Providence Inventory Test in Music, Richard D. Allen, Walter H. Butterfield, and Marguerite Tully, World Book Co., 313 Park Hill Ave., Yonkers, N.Y., 1932.

Watkins-Farnum Performance Scale for All Band Instruments, John G. Watkins and Stephen E. Farnum, Hal Leonard Music, Inc., Winona, Minn., 1954.

AMC AND MENC PUBLICATIONS

The American Music Conference[2]

Correlation and Integration of Music in the Classroom
Current Views on School Music
Elementary Music Workshops
Filmstrip Folder
Help Your Child Like Music
Keyboard Experience
Keyboard Experiences in the Classroom
Leaders Endorse Keyboard Experience for Pre-Band Students
Music Activities in Community Recreation
Music in the Jet Age
Music Is For Everyone
Organizing a Community Band
The Potential of Fretted Instruments in School Music
A Study of Instrumental Music in 322 School Systems
Why a Grade School Band
Why Have a School Band
You Can Give Your Child Music
You Too Can Make Music
Your Child and Music Lessons

Music Educators National Conference[3]

Administration and Supervision

Guiding Principles for School Music Group Activities
Music and Art in the Public Schools
Music Buildings, Rooms and Equipment
Prevailing Practices in the Supervision of Instrumental Music
The Music Educator's Business Handbook (See p. 508 for description.)
The Music Teacher and Public Relations

Philosophy of Music Education

The Child's Bill of Rights in Music
Creative Arts in Education
Music and Public Education

[2] The American Music Conference, 332 S. Michigan Avenue, Chicago, 60604, offers these publications in single quantities without cost. Nominal charge for titles requested in quantities.
[3] Check list of publications, with prices, may be obtained from Music Educators National Conference, 1201 16th St., N.W., Washington, D.C., 20036.

The Study of Music: An Academic Discipline
Will Earhart: Teacher, Philosopher, Humanitarian

Preschool and Elementary Education

An Autochthonous Approach to Music Appreciation
Music for Fours and Fives
Music Education for Elementary School Children
Music in Everyday Living and Learning
Teaching Music in the Elementary School: Opinion and Comment

Secondary School Music

Music for the Academically Talented Student in the Secondary School
The Music Curriculum in the Secondary Schools
Music in the Senior High School
Singing in the Schools

Curriculum—General

Music for Your School
Music in American Education (Source Book II)
Outline of a Program for Music Education

Comparative Music Education

The Arts in the Educational Program in the Soviet Union
How Can Music Promote International Understanding?
Music Education in a Changing World

Career Information

A Career in Music Education
Careers in Music
Post-Baccalaureate Grants and Awards in Music
Your Future as a Teacher of Music in the Schools

Teacher Education

Musical Development of the Classroom Teacher

Reprints

Afro-American Music
The Concertos for Clarinet

Lists and Bibliographies

Bibliography of Research Studies in Music Education (1932–1948)
Bibliography of Research Studies in Music Education (1949–1956)
Contemporary Music

Doctoral Dissertations in Music and Music Education (1957–1963)
Film Guide for Music Educators
Index to Americana in the "Musical Quarterly"
Music Education Materials—A Selected Bibliography

Strings

String Instruction Program in Music Education (Complete Set)
String Instruction Program No. 1 (SIP I)
Bibliography for String Teachers (SIP II)
String Teacher and Music Dealer Relations and Problems (SIP III)
Recruiting Strings in the Schools (SIP IV) Interesting String Majors in Music Education (SIP V)
Why Have a String Program? (SIP VI) Selection and Care of a String Instrument (SIP VII)
Basic Principles of Double Bass Playing (SIP VIII)
Basic Principles of Cello Playing (SIP IX)
Basic Principles of Violin Playing (SIP X)

Piano

Handbook for Teaching Piano Classes
Music Begins with the Piano
Traveling the Circuit with Piano Classes

Periodicals

Indexes to the Music Educators Journal
International Music Educator
Journal of Research in Music Education
Music Educators Journal

Copyright Agreement Forms

Copyright Agreement Forms I and II

Festival Materials and Music Lists

The Code for the National Anthem of the United States (see p. 513)
Materials for Miscellaneous Instrumental Ensembles
The NIMAC Manual
Selective Music Lists for Chorus, Orchestra, Band
Selective Music Lists for Instrumental and Vocal Solos, Instrumental and Vocal Ensembles
Official Adjudication Forms

The Music Educator's Business Handbook

A representative group of firms serving schools and the teaching profession has formed the Music Industry Council, an auxiliary of the Music Educators

National Conference. The council has published *The Music Educator's Business Handbook* which covers the business aspects of music education. The *Handbook* covers business correspondence, shipping instructions, "on approval" orders and credit, order forms, uniforms, instrument buying, addresses of member firms, and much more information that is extremely valuable to both the beginning and the experienced teacher. The *Handbook* is supplied without cost to teachers on request. Write to MENC, 1201 16 St., N.W., Washington, D.C. 20036.

PROFESSIONAL CODES[4]

A CODE OF ETHICS

The competition of school bands and orchestras in the past years has been a matter of grave concern and, at times, even hardship to the professional musicians.

Music educators and professional musicians alike are committed to the general acceptance of music as a desirable factor in the social and cultural growth of our country. The music educators contribute to this end by fostering the study of music among the children, and by developing an interest in better music among the masses. The professional musicians strive to improve musical taste by providing increasingly artistic performances of worthwhile musical works.

This unanimity of purpose is further exemplified by the fact that a great many professional musicians are music educators, and a great many music educators are, or have been, actively engaged in the field of professional performance.

The members of high school symphonic orchestras and bands look to the professional organizations for example and inspiration; they become active patrons of music in later life. They are not content to listen to a twelve-piece ensemble when an orchestra of symphonic proportions is necessary to give adequate performance. These former music students, through their influence on sponsors, employers and program makers in demanding adequate musical performances, have a beneficial effect upon the prestige and economic status of the professional musicians.

Since it is in the interest of the music educator to attract public attention to his attainments for the purpose of enhancing his prestige and subsequently his income, and since it is in the interest of the professional musician to create more opportunities for employment at increased remuneration, it is only natural that upon certain occasions some incidents might occur in which the interests of the members of one or the other group might be infringed upon, either from lack of forethought or lack of ethical standards among individuals.

In order to establish a clear understanding as to the limitations of the fields of professional music and music education in the United States, the following statement of policy, adopted by the Music Educators National Conference and the American Federation of Musicians, and approved by the American Association of School Administrators, is recommended to those serving in their respective fields.

[4] Reprinted with permission of the Music Educators National Conference.

I. Music Education

The field of music education, including the teaching of music and such demonstrations of music education as do not directly conflict with the interests of the professional musician, is the province of the music educator. It is the primary purpose of all the parties signatory hereto that the professional musician shall have the fullest protection in his efforts to earn his living from the playing and rendition of music; to that end it is recognized and accepted that all music to be performed under the "Code of Ethics" herein set forth is and shall be performed in connection with non-profit, non-commercial and non-competitive enterprises. Under the heading of "Music Education" should be included the following:

1. *School Functions* initiated by the schools as a part of a school program, whether in a school building or other building.
2. *Community Functions* organized in the interest of the schools strictly for educational purposes, such as those that might be originated by the Parent-Teacher Association.
3. *School Exhibits* prepared as a part of the school district's courtesies for educational organizations or educational conventions being entertained in the district.
4. *Educational Broadcasts* which have the purpose of demonstrating or illustrating pupils' achievements in music study, or which represent the culmination of a period of study and rehearsal. Included in this category are local, state, regional and national school music festivals and competitions held under the auspices of schools, colleges, and/or educational organizations on a non-profit basis and broadcast to acquaint the public with the results of music instruction in the schools.
5. *Civic Occasions* of local, state or national patriotic interest, of sufficient breadth to enlist the sympathies and cooperation of all persons, such as those held by the G.A.R., American Legion, and Veterans of Foreign Wars in connection with their Memorial Day services in the cemeteries. It is understood that affairs of this kind may be participated in only when such participation does not in the least usurp the rights and privileges of local professional musicians.
6. *Benefit Performances* for local charities, such as the Welfare Federations, Red Cross, hospitals, etc., when and where local professional musicians would likewise donate their services.
7. *Educational or Civic Services* that might beforehand be mutually agreed upon by the school authorities and official representatives of the local professional musicians.
8. *Audition Recordings* for study purposes made in the classroom or in connection with contest or festival performances by students, such recordings to be limited to exclusive use by the students and their teachers, and not offered for general sale or other public distribution. This definition pertains only to the purpose and utilization of audition recordings and not to matters concerned with copyright regulations. Compliance with copyright requirements applying to recording of compositions not in the public domain is the responsibility of the school, college or educational organization under whose auspices the recording is made.

II. Entertainment

The field of entertainment is the province of the professional musician. Under this heading are the following.

1. *Civic parades, ceremonies, expositions, community concerts, and community-center activities* (See I, Paragraph 2 for further definition); *regattas, nonscohlastic contests, festivals, athletic games, activities or celebrations, and the like; national, state and county fairs* (See I, Paragraph 5 for further definition).
2. *Functions for the furtherance, directly or indirectly, of any public or private enterprise; functions by chambers of commerce, boards of trade, and commercial clubs or associations.*
3. *Any occasion that is partisan or sectarian in character or purpose.*
4. *Functions of clubs, societies, civic or fraternal organizations.*

Statements that funds are not available for the employment of professional musicians, or that if the talents of amateur musical organizations cannot be had, other musicians cannot or will not be employed, or that the amateur musicians are to play without remuneration of any kind, are all immaterial.

Jointly Agreed to and Authorized by Executive Actions of the
Music Educators National Conference
American Federation of Musicians
American Association of School Administrators

A CODE FOR RELATIONS WITH MUSIC MERCHANTS

A Code of Ethics between the Ohio Music Education Association and the Music Merchants Association of Ohio:

Whereas, both organizations are primarily interested in the music education of the school children of Ohio, and in furthering the interest of these young people in the art of music; and

Whereas, in this common effort, harmony and understanding should prevail;

Now the following Code of Ethics is adopted and approved:

First. The retail music merchant shall sell musical instruments and merchandise, of good quality at fair prices, to the public-school pupils of Ohio; and he shall, at all times, assist and help the community public-school music teacher in promoting an interest in the study of vocal and instrumental music.

Second. The public-school music teacher shall confine his activities to the teaching of music, as required by the laws of the State under Section 7718 G. C., and the regulations of the Educational Department, to the public-school pupils of Ohio; and he shall not sell musical instruments or merchandise directly or indirectly, to the pupils, or accept commissions of any kind, in any manner whatsoever, from any manufacturer, jobber, or music merchant for recommending any kind, brand, or make of musical merchandise.

Third. It shall be the prerogative of every public-school music teacher in Ohio to examine and test the suitability of all musical instruments and merchandise purchased by pupils for use in school study, and, if found deficient, to communicate with the retail merchant selling the same, looking to the immediate adjustment of the difficulty, but the public-school music teacher in Ohio shall not recommend to his pupils or their parents any single make or brand of instrument exclusively.

Fourth. It shall be the duty of every retail music merchant in Ohio, readily and quickly to assist all public-school music teachers in his community, to see that pupils have proper and suitable instruments, by exchange or otherwise; to stock such musical intruments and merchandise for sale to pupils as the teachers may request or recommend to the dealer; to arrange for the renting or loaning of instruments to talented pupils upon the recommendation of the teacher; and generally to cooperate with the public-school music teachers along these lines. In the event any local retail music merchant fails, neglects, or refuses so to cooperate with his public-school music teachers, then, and in that event, the teachers shall have the right and privilege, without violating this Code, to seek and find other retail sources for the musical instruments and merchandise necessary and required by the pupils in the proper study of music.

A CODE FOR RELATIONS WITH THE PRIVATE MUSIC TEACHERS

To promote cooperation in and understanding of the interrelating fields of music teaching the Ohio Music Teachers Association and the Ohio Music Education Association adopt the following statement of policy:

I. Music Education

The school music teacher is a public employee and is obligated to serve the interests of the whole community. It shall be his privilege and responsibility to advise parents on questions pertaining to the private instruction of pupils under his jurisdiction. At all times the best interest of the pupil is of first importance. It shall be the obligation of the public-school music teacher to give to parents, upon request, the names of private teachers who are competent. In so doing, the school music teacher shall avoid recommending a single private teacher above all others, but shall suggest two or more, the final choice to be made by the parents. In communities where the choice is limited, it shall be incumbent upon the school music teacher to serve the interests of the student within the limitations of the resources available in the community.

II. Music Studio Instruction

Music studio instruction is defined as lessons given for a consideration by individual music teachers or groups of teachers who are not employed by, or under the jurisdiction of, a public school or institution supported by public taxation.

As a citizen, the studio teacher shall cooperate in the support of public education, including music instruction at elementary music levels in the schools for the general good of the community.

III. Agreement

It is mutually agreed, between the aforesaid organizations that it is unethical for any music teacher, whether teaching in school or in a private studio:

a. To discuss with parents or pupils the works of another teacher in such manner as will injure the professional reputation of any teacher;

b. To claim sole credit for the achievement of pupils under separate or cooperative instruction, when such claim shall reflect or imply discredit upon a preceding or cooperating teacher.

It is the common purpose of music teachers to cooperate:

a. In raising standards of music instruction;
b. In promoting interest in active participation in music performance;
c. In developing wide appreciation of music;
d. In establishing opportunities for elementary music instruction under the auspices of the school for exploratory purposes;
e. In encouraging study with private teachers at the end of the period of exploratory instruction;
f. In extending opportunities for music study to the underprivileged child through scholarships or extension of school instruction in individual instances;
g. In encouraging regularity of attendance at both school and private lessons, rehearsals, recitals, and performances;
h. In operating an organized plan for giving credit toward graduation study with recognized studio teachers;
i. In alleviating the influence and practice of unethical methods of music instruction.

It is further agreed that each organization will maintain a permanent Code of Ethics Committee. These committees shall meet together during the month of May of each year.

THE CODE FOR THE NATIONAL ANTHEM OF THE UNITED STATES OF AMERICA

The Star-Spangled Banner should be sung or played only on programs and in ceremonies and other situations where its message can be projected effectively.

Since the message of the Anthem is carried largely in the text, it is essential that emphasis be placed upon the *singing* of The Star-Spangled Banner.

The leader should address himself to those assembled and invite their participation. If an announcement is necessary, it might be stated as follows: "We shall now sing our National Anthem," or "So-and-So will lead you in singing our National Anthem."

On all occasions the group singing the National Anthem should stand facing the flag or the leader, in an attitude of respectful attention. Outdoors, men should remove their hats.

It is suggested that, when it is not physically inconvenient to do so, the members of a band or orchestra stand while playing the National Anthem.

If only a single stanza of the National Anthem is sung, the first should be used.

Our National Anthem is customarily sung at the opening of a meeting or program, but special circumstances may warrant the placing of it elsewhere.

In publishing the National Anthem for general singing, the melody, harmony, and syllable divisions of the Service Version of 1918 should be used. In publishing for vocal groups, the voice-parts of the Service Version should be adhered to. (The Service Version in A-flat is reproduced on the pages following.) For the purposes of quick identification, the words "Service Version" should be printed under the title.

It is not good taste to make or use sophisticated concert versions of the National

The Star-Spangled Banner

stream - ing! And the rock - ets' red glare, the bombs burst - ing in
clos - es? Now it catch - es the gleam of the morn - ing's first
na - tion. Then con - quer we must, for our cause it is
air, Gave proof thro' the night that our flag was still there.
beam, In full glo - ry re - flect - ed now shines on the stream;
just, And this be our mot - to: "In God is our trust."
Chorus (♩= 96)
O say, does that Star-Span - gled Ban - ner yet
'Tis the Star-Span - gled Ban - ner, O long may it
And the Star-Span - gled Ban - ner in tri - umph shall
wave O'er the land of the free and the home of the brave?
wave O'er the land of the free and the home of the brave!
wave O'er the land of the free and the home of the brave!
broaden
broaden

Anthem, as such. (This does not refer to incorporating the Anthem, or portions of it, in extended works for band, orchestra, or chorus.)

For general mass singing by adults, and for band, orchestra, or other instrumental performances, the key of A-flat is preferable. For treble voices, the key of B-flat may be used.

If an instrumental introduction is desired, it is suggested that the last two measures be used.

When the National Anthem is sung unaccompanied, care should be taken to establish the correct pitch.

The National Anthem should be sung at a moderate tempo. (The metronome indications in the Service Version are quarter note = 104 for the verse and quarter note = 96 for the chorus.)

The slighting of note value in the playing or singing of the National Anthem seriously impairs the beauty and effectiveness of both music and lyric. Conductors should rehearse painstakingly both instrumental and vocal groups in the meticulous observance of correct note values.

This Code for the National Anthem is intended to apply to every mode of civilian performance and to the publication of the music for such performance.

The Service Version of the National Anthem was prepared in 1918 by a joint committee of twelve, comprising John Alden Carpenter, Frederick S. Converse, Wallace Goodrich, and Walter R. Spalding, representing the War Department Commission on Training Camp Activities; Hollis E. Dann, Peter W. Dykema (Chairman), and Osbourne McConathy, representing the Music Educators National Conference (then known as Music Supervisors' National Conference); Clarence C. Birchard, Carl Engel, William Arms Fisher, Arthur E. Johnstone, and E. W. Newton, representing the music publishers.

COPYRIGHT LAW

A COPYRIGHT LAW GUIDE FOR MUSIC EDUCATORS[5]

A. Even though music is protected by copyright under the United States Copyright Law there are various things which you can do without securing permission of any type and without fear of infringing.

You may purchase a copyrighted musical composition, orchestration or other form of published music and do the following with it:

1. You may sell it or give it away.
2. You may perform it in private, or in public for non-profit.
3. You may use it for teaching in a classroom, at home or in a pupil's home. Solely for teaching purposes you may write symbols and indicate instructions upon it.
4. Provided the composition has already been recorded by others, under the authorization of the copyright owner, for the manufacture of phonograph records serving to

[5] Copyright © 1960 and 1962 by MUSIC PUBLISHER'S PROTECTIVE ASSOCIATION, INC. and MUSIC PUBLISHERS' ASSOCIATION OF THE UNITED STATES, INC. This guide may be reprinted in its entirety without permission, provided the above copyright notice and this notice appear in each reprint. Permission to reprint excerpts from this guide must be secured from the copyright owners.

reproduce the same mechanically, and provided further that you notify the copyright owner by registered mail of your intention to make such use (with a duplicate of such notice to the Copyright Office, Washington 25, D.C.), you may make similar use thereof upon making monthly payments of the statutory royalty, to the copyright owner.

B. If you wish to make some other type of use which is not described above, you should write to the copyright owner for specific permission in each instance. The following are some of the things you may not do without specific permission:

1. Reprinting or copying the work or any part of it by any method or means whatsoever.
2. Arranging, adapting, orchestrating, translating or making any versions of the work or any part of it.
3. Photographing or reproducing the work or any part of it by any method or means, including on film or slides or by opaqūe projector.
4. Performing the work in public for profit.
5. Recording the work by any method or means or for any use or purpose, other than as provided in "A.4" above, including in synchronization with motion pictures or for television, and whether on records, film or tape.
6. Writing of parodies upon lyrics.

To avoid infringement, the right to do each or any of these acts must be cleared, and the clearance of one particular right does not clear any of the other rights. All rights are separate, distinct and independent. For instance, the clearance for broadcast does not carry with it the right to copy, or to arrange, or to record; clearance of the right to record does not carry with it the right to perform. The obligation is upon you to make certain that the right involved in the act you intend to do, has been cleared.

C. If you have occasion to perform the composition publicly for profit, guide yourself as follows:

1. If the performance is to be in a theatre or over a radio or television station, in all likelihood the theatre, radio or television station will have a license for you to perform the musical composition publicly for profit. However, it is your obligation to make certain of this and to secure a license if there is none.
2. If the performance is to take place elsewhere, there is less likelihood that the establishment has a license for you to perform publicly for profit and in such event a license must be secured. There are three important performing rights societies which license the great majority of copyrighted works: American Society of Composers, Authors and Publishers (usually referred to as "ASCAP"), 575 Madison Avenue, New York 22, New York; Broadcast Music, Inc. (usually referred to as "BMI"), 589 Fifth Avenue, New York 17, New York; and SESAC, Inc., 10 Columbus Circle, New York 19, New York.
3. If you have occasion to present a musical play or other dramatic work on the stage at your school or elsewhere, whether for profit or non-profit, you must secure a license from the owner of the work or his agent.

D. When you see the word "Copyright" or the distinctive © printed on a piece of music, it is the notice that protects the copyright owner of the work and authorizes him to exclusively exercise and enforce all rights secured to him under the United States Copyright Law, and at the same time it is the notice that informs *you* that the exercising by you of any such acts, including those described in B and C above, *unless authorized*, will subject you to liability under such law.

A printed copy of a musical composition published in the United States, bearing no copyright notice, indicates that the composition is in the public domain in the United States and may be used freely. However, if an arrangement, adaptation or other version of such a work has been copyrighted, utmost caution must be exercised in treating the same as you would any other copyrighted work. But notwithstanding such copyrighted arrangement, adaptation or other version, of a work in the public domain, you are still free to treat the basic composition as being in the public domain. A work in the public domain reprinted in a compilation is not protected, even though the compilation itself is copyrighted, unless the reprint is a copyrightable or copyrighted arrangement, adaptation or other version thereof.

FORMS[6]

Permanent Music Record

The form on p. 520 provides a cumulative record of the student's participation in all music activities other than regular classroom or general music. They are returned to a central file at the close of the school year and referred to the following year.

Year indicates school year such as 1950–1951, 1951–1952, etc.
School indicates name of the school attended that year.
Code numbers 1 to 10 are used as follows:

An entry on the long line after grade 4 might read as follows: 1 violin; 8 Trinity Methodist S; indicating that the student used his own violin to play in an elementary string class and sang soprano in a Trinity Methodist organized choir.

An entry for the same student in his fifth year might be as follows:

2 cello; 3 piano, Cummings; 4 alto; 10 cello II, indicating that the student changed to cello using a school owned instrument; was studying piano privately with Cummings; sang alto in his elementary school glee club; played a cello solo in a recognized festival and received a II rating.

[6] Courtesy of the Pomona Unified School District, Pomona, California.

POMONA CITY SCHOOLS
Pomona, California

Dear Parents:

This information is being sent to you at this time so that you may know the progress which your child is making in the instrumental classes. The ease or difficulty with which children play an instrument is determined by many factors such as:

1. Music talent.
2. Physical coordination.
3. Quality of the instrument including proper equipment and adjustment.
4. Attention to details of instruction and assignments in class.
5. Enough regular daily practice with some adult supervision to thoroughly establish the necessary skills.
6. Learning the names and meanings of notes, rests, key signatures, time signatures, music terms and other symbols.

You will always be welcome to visit the classes so that you may know the best way to give help in home practice. However, since teaching time is scheduled so closely, conferences can be arranged more satisfactorily at other than class meeting time.

Please sign the second page and return to the instructor.

Yours truly,

John R. Keith
Consultant in Music Education

PERMANENT MUSIC RECORD

Last Name	First	Middle
Address	Phone	
Parent's Name		

Grade	Year	School	Grade	Year	School	Grade	Year	School
3			7			10		
4			8			11		
5			9			12		
6								

1 Own instrument—Kind of Instrument
2 School instrument—Kind of instrument
3 Private lessons—Instrument or voice—Name of teacher
4 School Glee Club or Chorus—Indicate part—SATB
5 A, B, or Elementary All-City Band or Orchestra
6 Community Band—Instrument—Part
7 Pomona Valley Symphony—Instrument—Part
8 Church or other choir—Indicate part—SATB
9 Other music classes—Identify
10 Solo and Ensemble experience and ratings
Add your comments on citizenship, talent, ability, cooperation, work habits, suggestions for improvement.

Grade	
3	
4	
5	
6	
7	
8	
9	
10	
11	
12	

PROGRESS REPORT OF STUDENTS IN INSTRUMENTAL CLASSES

School ______________________ Student ______________________

______ Progress has been excellent

______ Progress has been satisfactory but recommend attention to these items:

______ better instrument

______ instrument needs repair, adjustment

______ equipment needed

______ better class attention

______ adult supervision of practice

______ learn note names, values, symbols and terms

______ Progress has been unsatisfactory. Student should continue only if these recommendations have immediate attention:

______ good quality instrument ______________________

______ repairs and adjustments ______________________

______ equipment ______________________

______ regular attendance with instrument

______ adult supervision of enough practice

______ learn note names, values, symbols and terms

______ better attention to instruction assignments

______ Student should not continue.

This recommendation is primarily for those who are renting an instrument for a trial period and will want to decide soon whether or not to purchase. If you own the instrument and would like your child to continue in the class will you please call 9–3081 and ask that the teacher contact you for a conference.

____
Instructor's signature

Parent's comments:

____
Parent's signature

POMONA CITY SCHOOLS
Pomona, California

School

Owned by ______________________ In use at ______________________

Agreement For Loan of Musical Instrument

Instrument	Make	Serial Number
______________	______________	______________

Condition: Excellent_____ Good_____ Fair_____ Poor_____ Value____________

Accessories included:

_____ Case	_____ Bow	_____ Cap	_____ Strap
_____ Mouthpiece	_____ Chin Rest	_____ Swab	_____ Stand
_____ Ligature	_____ Shoulder pad	_____ Lyre	_____ Key
_____ Extension pipe	_____ Mute	_____ Crooks	_____ Sticks
______________	______________	______________	______________

The above described instrument and accessories are being loaned to ______________

______________ a student of the Pomona City Schools for use only in the regularly organized school groups and those activities specifically listed below:

_____ Private lessons

_____ Municipal Band

_____ Pomona Valley Symphony Orchestra

__________ Groups sponsored jointly by the Recreation Department and the Pomona City Schools.

The undersigned student and parents, jointly and severally, agree to keep the instrument in good playing condition, to reimburse the Pomona City Schools for any damage due to negligence or misuse and to return it promptly when requested by an authorized school representative.

______________________ ______________________

Date Student's Signature

____

Approved by: Parent's Signature

______________________ ______________________

Authorized representative of the Pomona City Schools

Address Phone

SUMMER VACATION LOAN (*Only*)

The five dollar ($5.00) deposit acknowledged by receipt number ________________ will be returned to the depositor when the instrument is returned in as good a condition as when received less reasonable depreciation due to normal usage.

____
Date

____
Authorized School Representative

____
Parent or Student

The above described instrument and accessories returned this date and refund of the five dollar ($5.00) deposit acknowledged less $______________ deduction for damage.
Additional charges paid $________________
Instrument returned in good condition ______

Michigan State University.

CHAPTER

21

Books

CARE AND REPAIR OF INSTRUMENTS

Care and Minor Repairs of the Clarinet, Vito Pascucci, G. Leblanc, 1959.
How To Care for Your Instrument, C. G. Conn, Elkhart, Indiana.
The Practical Band Instrument Repair Manual, Clayton H. Tiede, Wm. C. Brown, 1962.
Repair and Accessory Manual, Penzel-Mueller Co., Long Island City, N.Y.
Selmer Band Instrument Repairing Manual (rev. ed.), Erick D. Brand, E. C. Schirmer, 1946.
You Fix Them, Scherl and Roth, Inc., Cleveland, Ohio, 1955.

CAREERS IN MUSIC

A Career in Music Education, Music Educators National Conference, 1962.
Careers and Opportunities in Music, Alan Rich, Dutton, 1964.
Your Future in Music, Robert E. Curtis, Richards Rosen Press, 1962.

CHORAL AND VOCAL TEXTS FOR TEACHERS[1]

The Art of Conducting, Michal Bowles, Doubleday, 1959.
The Art of the Choral Conductor, William J. Finn, Summy-Birchard, Vol. II, 1960.
Artistic Choral Singing: Practical Problems in Organization, Technique, and Interpretation, Harry R. Wilson, G. Schirmer, 1959.
The Choral Director's Handbook, Walter Ehret, Marks, 1959.
Choral Teaching at the Junior High School Level, G. A. Rorke, Schmitt, Hall & McCreary, 1957.
The Chorus and Its Conductor, Max T. Krone, Neil A. Kjos, 1945.
Conducting Choral Music (2nd ed.), Robert L. Garretson, Allyn and Bacon, 1965.
Expressive Conducting, Max T. Krone, Neil A. Kjos, 1945.
Fundamentals of Choral Expression, Hayes M. Fuhr, University of Nebraska Press, 1944.
The Grammar of Conducting, Max Rudolf, G. Schirmer, 1950.
NIMAC Manual, The Organization and Management of Interscholastic Music Activities, National Interscholastic Music Activities Commission, MENC, 1963.
Opera Production: A Handbook, Quaintance Eaton, University of Minnesota Press, 1961.

[1] Books for use by the teacher. Choral materials for the student are found in Chapter 23.

Organizing and Directing Children's Choirs, Madeline D. Ingram, Abingdon, 1959.
The School Music Conductor, P. Van Bodegraven and H. R. Wilson, Schmitt, Hall & McCreary, 1942.
Technique and Style in Choral Singing, George Howerton, Carl Fischer, 1957.
Training the Boy's Changing Voice, Duncan McKenzie, Rutgers University Press, 1956.

THE EXCEPTIONAL CHILD

Common Sense about Gifted Children, Willard Abraham, Harper & Row, 1958.
Education of the Gifted, Merle Sumption and Evelyn M. Luecking, Ronald, 1960.
The Psychology of Exceptional Children, Karl C. Garrison and Dewey G. Force, Jr., Ronald, 1959.
Teaching the Gifted Child, James J. Gallagher, Allyn and Bacon, 1964.

THE GENERAL MUSIC CLASS

Books for Use by the Teacher and for Reference by the Students

All about the Symphony Orchestra, Dorothy P. Commins, Random House, 1961.
A Book of Christmas Carols (piano score and guitar chords), Haig and Regina Shekerjian, Harper & Row, 1963.
The Country Blues, Samuel B. Charters, Holt, Rinehart and Winston, 1960 (Afro-American music, recordings by Folkways).
Discovering Music, Howard D. McKinney and W. R. Anderson, American Book, 1952.
Drums through the Ages, Charles L. White, Sterling, 1960.
Exploring Science, Six, Walter A. Thurber, Allyn and Bacon, 1960.
First Book of Sound, David C. Knight, Watts, 1960.
Folk Music, USA, Howard Grafman and B. T. Manning, Citadel, 1962.
The Folk Songs of North America, Alan Lomax, Doubleday, 1960.
Great Symphonies, How To Recognize and Remember Them, Sigmund Spaeth, Garden City, 1936.
Guiding Junior High School Pupils in Music Experiences, Frances Andrews and Joseph A. Leeder, Prentice-Hall, 1953.
The Instruments of Music (3rd ed.), Robert Donington, Barnes & Noble, 1962.
Instruments of the Modern Symphony and Band, Arthur E. Johnstone, Carl Fischer, 1948.
A Junior High School Music Handbook, Sally Monsour and Margaret Perry, Prentice-Hall, 1963.
Music and Man, Howard D. McKinney, American Book, 1948.
A Music Educator's Introduction to Barbershop Harmony, SPEBSQSA, Inc.
The Music in Your Life, Delos Smith, Harper & Row, 1957.
Music Makers of Today, Percy M. Young, Roy Publishers, 1958.
Music To Remember, Lillian Baldwin, Silver Burdett, 1951.
The Nutcracker, Warren Chappell, Knopf, 1958.
Pennsylvania Songs and Legends, George Korson (Ed.), University of Pennsylvania Press, 1949.
The Reading Singer, Irvin Cooper, Allyn and Bacon, 1964.

Science and Music: From Tom-Tom to Hi-fi, Melvin Berger and Frank Clark, McGraw-Hill, 1961.
The Trapp-Family Book of Christmas Songs, Franz Wasner (arr.), Pantheon, 1950.
A Treasury of Jewish Folksong, Ruth Rubin (Ed.), Schocken Books, 1950.
Tune Up: Instruments of the Orchestra and Their Players, Harriet E. Huntington, Doubleday, 1945.
The Weavers' Song Book, Folk Songs of Many Lands, The Weavers, Harper & Row, 1960.
Young People's Concerts, Leonard Bernstein, Simon and Schuster, 1962.

Books for Use by Students

Birchard Music Series, Books 7 & 9, Ernst, Grentzer, Housewright, Summy-Birchard, 1962.
General Music for the Junior High School (four books with teacher's manuals), Belwin, 1955.
Growing with Music, Books 7 & 8 (with workbooks), Ehret, Barr, Blair, Prentice-Hall, 1959.
Living with Music, Allen Richardson and Mary E. English, Witmark, 1956.
Music for Living, Books 7 & 8, Cooper, Freeburg, Imig, Nordholm, Rhea, Serposs, Silver Burdett, 1959.
Music for Young Americans, Books 7 & 8, Berg, Hooley, Wolverton, Burns, American Book, 1960.
Music for Young Listeners, Lillian Baldwin, Silver Burdett, 1951.
Music in Our Heritage, Ira C. Singleton and Emile H. Serposs, Silver Burdett, 1962.
Music in Our World, Alice M. Snyder, Mills Music, 1962.
Our Singing World, Books 7 & 8, Pitts, Watters, Glenn, Wersen, Ginn, 1951–1959.
People and Music, Thomasine C. McGehee and Alice D. Nelson, Allyn and Bacon, 1963.
This Is Music, Books 7 & 8, Sur, DuBois, Nye, Allyn and Bacon, 1963.
Together We Sing, Books 7 & 8 (rev.), Wolfe, Krone, Fullerton, Follett, 1960.

THE HUMANITIES

Sources of Course Development

The Allied Arts, A High School Humanities Guide for Missouri, Publication No. 128G, 1963 edition, Commissioner of Education, State of Missouri, Jefferson City, Missouri.
Fine Arts Adventure, Art and Music for Senior High School, The Board of Education of the City of Detroit, 1963.
An Introduction to the Arts, Humanities I Handbook (4th ed.), University of Chicago Press, 1950.

Music

The Beautiful in Music, Edward Hanslick, Liberal Arts Press, 1957.
Berlioz and His Century (rev. ed.), Jacques Barzun, Meridian, 1956.
Biblical Chant, Abraham W. Binder, Philosophical Library, 1959.

The Book of Modern Composers (2nd ed.), David Ewen (Ed.), Knopf, 1950.
Church Music: Illusion and Reality, Archibald T. Davison, Harvard University Press, 1952.
A Composer's World—Horizons and Limitations, Paul Hindemith, Harvard University Press, 1952.
The Cultured Man, Ashley Montagu, World, 1958.
From the World of Music, Ernest Newman, John Calder (London), 1956.
Fundamentals of Music Appreciation, Hummel Fishburn, Longmans Green, 1955.
Great Composers Through the Eyes of Their Contemporaries, Otto Zoff (Ed.), Dutton, 1951.
Harvard Brief Dictionary of Music, Willi Apel and Ralph T. Daniel, Washington Square Press, 1960.
A History of Musical Thought (3rd ed.), Donald N. Ferguson, Appleton-Century-Crofts, 1959.
A History of Western Music (new shorter edition), Donald Jay Grout, Norton, 1964.
How Opera Grew, Ethel Peyser and Marion Bauer, Putnam, 1956.
The Importance of Music, Sigmund Spaeth, Fleet, 1963.
Literature and Music as Resources for Social Studies, Ruth Tooze and Beatrice P. Krone, Prentice-Hall, 1955.
The Main Stream of Music and Other Essays, Donald Francis Tovey, Oxford, 1949.
The Making of Music, Ralph Vaughan-Williams, Cornell University Press, 1955.
Men of Music: Their Lives, Times, and Achievements, Wallace Brockway and Herbert Winstock (rev. ed.), Simon and Schuster, 1958.
Music: A Design for Listening, Homer Ulrich, Harcourt, Brace, 1956.
Music and Literature: A Comparison of the Arts, Calvin S. Brown, University of Georgia Press, 1948.
Music History and Ideas, Hugo Leichenstritt, Harvard University Press, 1938.
Music and Man, Howard D. McKinney, American Book, 1948.
Music in the Baroque Era, Manfred F. Bukofzer, Norton, 1950.
Music in the Romantic Era, Alfred Einstein, Norton, 1947.
Music in Western Civilization, Paul Henry Lang, Norton, 1941.
The Music of Early Greece, Beatrice Perham, Neil A. Kjos, 1937.
Music Through the Ages, Marion Bauer and Ethel Peyser, Putnam, 1946.
Music Through the Centuries, Nick Rossi and Sadie Rafferty, Bruce Humphries, 1963.
The Opera: A History of Its Creation and Performance, Wallace Brockway and Herbert Weinstock, Simon and Schuster, 1941.
Our Musical Heritage: A Short History of Music (2nd ed.), Curt Sachs, Prentice-Hall, 1955.
Patterns of Culture, Ruth Benedict, Mentor Books, New American Library, 1934.
People and Music, Thomasine C. McGehee and Alice D. Nelson, Allyn and Bacon, 1963.
Pleasures of Music, Jacques Barzun (Ed.), Viking, 1951.
The Reluctant Art, The Growth of Jazz, Benny Green, Horizon, 1963.
Shaw on Music: A Selection from the Music Criticism of Bernard Shaw Made by Eric Bentley, George Bernard Shaw, Doubleday, 1955.
The Story of Jazz, Marshall W. Stearns, Oxford, 1956.
The Stream of Music (rev. ed., paperback), Richard Anthony Leonard, Doubleday, 1962.
Vast Horizons (Crusades), Mary Seymour Lucas, Viking, 1943.
What To Listen for in Music, Aaron Copland, McGraw-Hill, 1957.

Literature

The Basis of Criticism in the Arts, Stephen C. Pepper, Harvard University Press, 1946.
Brave New World, Aldous Huxley, Bantam Books, 1932.
Bulfinch's Mythology, Thomas Bulfinch, Modern Library, Random House, 1934.
Candide, Voltaire, Norman L. Torrey (Ed.), Appleton-Century-Crofts Classics, 1964.
Classical French Drama, Wallace Fowlie (Ed.), Bantam Books, 1962.
Classic Myths in English Literature and in Art, Charles Mills Gayley, Ginn, 1911.
Common Sense and the Crisis, Thomas Paine, Dolphin, Doubleday, 1959.
Complete Poetry and Selected Prose, John Milton, Modern Library, Random House, 1947.
Crime and Punishment, Dostoyevsky, Modern Library, 1963.
The Daughter of Time, Josephine Tey, Berkley, 1959.
The Dialogues of Plato, J. D. Kaplan (Ed.), Washington Square Press, 1961.
Faust—Parts I & II, Goethe, Penguin, 1959.
Four Great Tragedies, William Shakespeare, Washington Square Press, 1956.
Golden Bough, James George Frazer (Ed.), Macmillan, 1922.
Good Reading, Atwood H. Townsent (Ed.), Mentor Books, New American Library, 1960.
The Great Critics, James Harry Smith and Edd Winfield Parks (Ed.), Norton, 1939.
Gulliver's Travels, Jonathan Swift, Dolphin, Doubleday, 1959.
Henry the Fifth, William Shakespeare, Louis B. Wright and Virginia LaMar (Eds.), Washington Square Press, 1958.
History of the English Language, Albert C. Baugh, Appleton-Century-Crofts, 1935.
A History of English Literature, E. Legouis and L. Cazamian, Macmillan, 1957.
The Humanities in Contemporary Life, Robert F. Davidson, Sarah Herndon, J. Russell Reaver, and William Ruff (Eds.), Holt, Rinehart and Winston, 1960.
Immortal Poems of the English Language, Oscar Williams (Ed.), Washington Square Press, 1960.
The Inheritors, William Golding, Harcourt, Brace & World, 1962.
An Introduction to Poetry, Raymond Macdonald Alden, Holt, Rinehart and Winston, 1931.
Lives of Saints, Alban Butler, R. J. Kenedy & Sons, 1956.
Madame Bovary, Gustave Flaubert, Modern Library, Random House, 1955.
A Modern Book of Esthetics, Melvin M. Rader (Ed.), Holt, Rinehart and Winston, 1935.
Mythology, Edith Hamilton, Little, Brown, 1942.
Oedipus Plays of Sophocles, Paul Roche, New American Library, 1960.
Our Heritage of World Literature, Stith Thompson and John Gassner, Dryden, 1942.
Out of the Silent Planet, C. S. Lewis, Collier, 1961.
Outlines of English Literature, Alonzo C. Hall and Leonard B. Hurley, Heath, 1930.
The Pocket Aristotle, Justin D. Kaplan (Ed.), Washington Square Press, 1962.
Practical Criticism, I. A. Richard, Harcourt, Brace, 1935.
The Prince, Niccolo Machiavelli, Mentor Books, New American Library, 1952.
The Principles of Aesthetics, Dewitt H. Parker, Silver Burdett, 1920.
Six Great Modern Plays, Dell.
The Story of Philosophy, Will Durant, Washington Square Press, 1962.
Types of World Literature, Percy Hazen Houston and Robert Metcalf Smith, Odyssey, 1930.

Understanding Poetry, Cleanth Brooks and Robert Penn Warren, Holt, Rinehart and Winston, 1950.

The Visual Arts

An American Architecture, Frank Lloyd Wright, Horizon, 1955.
American Skyline, Christopher Tunnard and Henry Hope Reed, New American Library, 1960.
Architecture: An Art for All Men, Talbot Hamlin, Columbia University Press, 1947.
The Architecture of America, John E. Burchard and Albert Bush-Brown, Little, Brown, 1961.
Architecture Today and Tomorrow, Cranston Jones, McGraw-Hill, 1961.
Art and Civilization, Bernard Myers, McGraw-Hill, 1957.
Art and Life in America, Oliver Larkin, Holt, Rinehart and Winston, 1960.
Art Has Many Faces, Katherine Kuh, Harper & Row, 1959.
Art in the Western World, David M. Robb and J. J. Garrison, Harper & Row, 1953.
Art Search and Self-Discovery, J. A. Schinneller, International Textbook, 1961.
Art Through the Ages (4th ed.), Helen Gardner, Harcourt, Brace, 1959.
Arts and Ideas, W. Fleming, Holt, Rinehart and Winston, 1955.
The Arts and Man, Raymond S. Stites, McGraw-Hill, 1940.
Collection: Palettes: Van Gogh, Louvre, Gaugin, Utrillo, Degas, Klee, E. S. Herman, Herman, 1948–1950.
Exhibition Catalog: Form Givers, Time Magazine for the American Federation of Arts, 1959.
50 Great Artists, Bernard Myers, Bantam Classic, Bantam Books, 1959.
Good Taste in Home Decorating, Donald D. MacMillan, Holt, Rinehart and Winston, 1954.
The Great American Art Series: Albert P. Ryder, Thomas Eakins, Winslow Homer, Willem de Kooning, Stuart Davis, Jackson Pollock, Pocket Books, 1960.
The Harper History of Painting, David M. Robb, Harper & Row, 1951.
A History of Architecture, Bannister Fletcher, (17th ed.), Scribner, 1961.
History of Art, College Outline Series, Jane Anne Vincent, Barnes & Noble, 1955.
History of Engraving and Etching, A. M. Hind, Houghton Mifflin, 1923.
The History of Impressionism, John Rewald, New York, Museum of Modern Art, 1946.
A History of Modern Architecture, Jurgen Joedicke, Frederick A. Praeger, 1960.
History of Modern Painting, Herbert Read and Maurice Raynal, Skira, 1950.
The History of Western Art, Erwin Christensen, Mentor Books, New American Library, 1959–1960.
History of World Art, Upjohn, Wingert, Mahler, Oxford, 1949.
The Horizon Book of the Renaissance, Horizon (New York periodical), Doubleday, 1961.
An Illustrated Handbook of Art History, Frank J. Roos, Macmillan, 1937.
Introduction to Modern Architecture, J. M. Richards, Penguin, 1956.
Italian Painting, Frank Jewett Mather, Jr., New York, Holt, Rinehart and Winston, 1951.
Key Monuments of the History of Art, H. W. Jansen (Ed.), Prentice-Hall, 1959.
Looking Into Art, Frank Seiberling, Holt, Rinehart and Winston, 1959.
Mainstreams of Modern Art, John Canaday, Simon and Schuster, 1959.
Masters of World Architecture: LeCorbusier, Frank Lloyd Wright, Pier Luigi Nervi,

Antonio Gaudi, Ludwig Mies Van der Rohe, Alvar Aalto, Pocket Books, 1960.
Metropolitan Seminars in Art, Series I and II: *Great Periods in Painting*, John Canaday, New York, Metropolitan Museum of New York, 1961.
Modern American Painting and Sculpture, Sam Hunter, Dell, 1956.
Modern French Painting, Sam Hunter, Dell, 1956.
Old Masters, Herman Wechler (Ed.), Pocket Books, 1949.
Origins of Modern Sculpture, W. R. Valentiner, Whittenborn, 1946.
The Picture History of Painting, H. W. and Dora J. Janson, Washington Square Press, 1957.
The Praeger Picture Encyclopedia of Art, Frederick A. Praeger, Praeger, 1958.
Printmaking Today, Jules Heller, Holt, Rinehart and Winston, 1958.
Readings in Western Civilization (3rd ed.), George H. Knoles, Lippincott, 1960.
Sculpture Through the Ages, Lincoln Rothschild, McGraw-Hill, 1942.
Signs and Symbols of Christian Art, George Wells Ferguson, Oxford, 1954.
The Story of Art, E. H. Gombrich, Phaidon, (New York Graphic), 1951.
The Story of Painting for Young People, H. W. and Dora J. Janson, Abrams, 1952.
The Story of Sculpture, Agnes Allen, Roy, 1958.
The Tastemakers, Russell Lynes, Harper & Row, 1954.
Understanding the Arts, Bernard Myers, Holt, Rinehart and Winston, 1958.
Vision in Motion, Lasloz R. Moholy-Nagy, Theobald, 1947.
The Visual Arts, Wallace S. Ballinger, Holt, Rinehart and Winston, 1960.
The Visual Arts Today, Gyorgy Kepes (Ed.), Wesleyan University Press, 1960.
The Way of Western Art, 1776–1914, E. P. Richardson, Harvard University Press, 1938.
World History of the Dance, Curt Sachs, Norton, 1937.
The World of Great Architecture: From the Greeks to the 19th Century, Robert F. Jordan, Viking, 1961.

The Related Arts

The Arts, Hendrick Willem Van Loon, Simon and Schuster, 1937.
The Creative Process, Brewster Ghiselin (Ed.), New American Library, California, 1960.
The Humanities, Louise Dudley, McGraw-Hill, 1960.
The Humanities, Applied Aesthetics (3rd ed.), Louise Dudley and Austin Faricy, New York, McGraw-Hill, 1960.
An Introduction to Music and Art in the Western World, Milo Wold and Edmund Cykler, Wm. C. Brown, 1958.

INSTRUMENTAL MUSIC

The Art of French Horn Playing, Philip Farkas, Summy-Birchard, 1956.
The Art of Handbell Ringing, Nancy Poore Tufts, Abingdon, 1961.
The Band Yearbook, Hal Leonard, Hal Leonard, issued annually.
Basic Guide to Trumpet Playing, Byron L. Autrey, M. M. Cole, 1963.
Basic Guide to Violin Playing, Jack Pernecky, M. M. Cole, 1963.
Bassoon Technique, Archie Camden, Oxford, 1962.
Brass for Beginners, J. R. McKenna and W. H. Swinburne, Oxford, 1960.

The Brass Instruments: Performance and Instructional Techniques, James H. Winter, Allyn and Bacon, 1964.
Clarinet Technique, Frederick Thurston, Oxford, 1962.
Contemporary Brass Technique, Vernon E. Leidig, Highland, 1960.
Flute Technique (3rd ed.), F. B. Chapman, Oxford, 1962.
Guide to Teaching Percussion, Harry R. Bartlett, Wm. C. Brown, 1964.
Guide to Teaching Woodwinds, Frederick W. Westphal, Wm. C. Brown, 1962.
The High School Band Director's Handbook, W. Clyde Duvall, Prentice-Hall, 1960.
Horn Technique, Gunther Schuller, Oxford, 1962.
Instrumental Music, Principles and Methods of Instruction, Wolfgang Kuhn, Allyn and Bacon, 1962.
Instrumental Music in Today's Schools, Robert House, Prentice-Hall, 1964.
Instrumentalists' Handy Reference Manual, Clarence V. Hendrickson, Carl Fischer, 1959.
Marching Band Fundamentals, Al Wright, Carl Fischer, 1963.
Marching Band Maneuvers, Richard L. Schilling, Instrumentalist, 1958.
Marching for Marching Bands, Don R. Marcouiller, Wm. C. Brown, 1958.
Marching Fundamentals and Techniques for the School Bandsman, William D. Revelli and George R. Cavender, LesStrange, 1961.
The Modern Conductor, Elizabeth A. H. Green, Prentice-Hall, 1961.
Modern Marching Band Technique, Jack Lee, Hal Leonard, 1955.
Musicianship and Repertoire, Elizabeth A. H. Green, Theodore Presser, 1963.
NIMAC Manual, The Organization and Management of Interscholastic Music Activities, National Interscholastic Music Activities Commission, MENC, 1963.
Oboe Technique (2nd ed.), Evelyn Rothwell, Oxford, 1962.
Orchestra Percussion Technique, James Blades, Oxford, 1962.
Orchestra Planning Guide, National School Orchestra Association, High School, Benton Harbor, Mich., 1962.
Orchestral Bowings and Routines, Elizabeth A. H. Green, Ann Arbor Publishers, 1957.
Patterns of Motion Series, Book I: "Patterns"; Book II: "Kaleidoscopes," William E. Moffitt, Hal Leonard, 1964.
Percussion Manual for Music Educators, Joel T. Leach, Henry Adler, 1964.
Playing and Teaching Brass Instruments, Robert W. Winslow and John E. Green, Prentice-Hall, 1961.
Playing and Teaching Percussion Instruments, Myron D. Collins and John E. Green, Prentice-Hall, 1962.
Playing and Teaching Stringed Instruments, Parts I and II, Ralph Matesky and Ralph Rush, Prentice-Hall, 1963.
Playing and Teaching Woodwind Instruments, Clarence Sawhill and Bertram McGarrity, Prentice-Hall, 1962.
Prelude to Brass Playing, Rafael Mendez, Carl Fischer, 1962.
Principles of Violin Playing and Teaching, Ivan Galamian, Prentice-Hall, 1962.
Recruiting the String Section, National School Orchestra Association, High School, Benton Harbor, Mich., 1962.
Teaching Instrumental Music, Charles Boardman Righter, Carl Fischer, 1959.
Violin Gymnastics, Maxim Jacobsen, London, Bosworth, 1960.
Vital Brass Notes, Charles Colin, Leblanc, 1955.
The Woodwinds: Performance and Instructional Techniques, Everett Timm, Allyn and Bacon, 1964.

LIBRARY REFERENCE

In junior and senior high schools of all sizes, the school library should develop a varied and extensive catalog of books on music and musicians. The following list will suggest some titles which might be added to the library for reference material and for reading by interested students.

Belafonte, An Unauthorized Biography, Arnold Shaw, Chilton, 1960.
Charles Ives and His Music, Henry Cowell and Sidney Cowell, Oxford, 1955.
Chopin, A Pictorial Biography, Andre Boucourechliev, Viking, 1963.
Composers of Operetta, Gervase Highes, St Martin's, 1962.
Dictionary of Popular Music, Peter Gammond and Peter Clayton, Philosophical Library, 1961.
Encyclopedia of Jazz, Leonard Feather, Horizon, 1960.
Famous Negro Music Makers, Langston Hughes, Dodd, Mead, 1957.
Gilbert and Sullivan Song Book, Malcolm Hyatt and Walter Fabell, Random House, 1955.
Harvard Dictionary of Music, Willi Apel, Harvard University Press, 1944.
A History of Music, Theodore M. Finney, Harcourt, Brace, 1935.
In the Big Time, Katherine L. Bakeless, Lippincott, 1953.
A Journey to Greatness: The Life and Music of George Gershwin, David Ewen, Holt, Rinehart and Winston, 1958.
Lighter Classics in Music, An Encyclopedia of Musical Masterworks in the Lighter Style, David Ewen, Arco, 1961.
The Listener's Dictionary of Musical Terms, Helen L. Kaufmann, Grossett & Dunlap, 1960.
Mozart, Manuel Komroff, Knopf, 1956.
Music and Imagination, Aaron Copland, The New American Library of World Literature, 1959.
Music of the Americas, North and South, Paul H. Apel, Vantage, 1960.
The New College Encyclopedia of Music, J. A. Westrup and F. Fl. Harrison, Norton, 1960.
The New Oxford History of Music, Egon Wellesz (Ed.), Oxford, 1959.
A Panorama of American Popular Music, David Ewen, Prentice-Hall, 1957.
A Portrait of Bach, Jo Manton, Abelard, 1957.
A Short History of Music (9th printing), Alfred Einstein, Random House, 1961.
A Short History of Music in America, John Tasker Howard and George Kent Bellows, Thomas Y. Crowell, 1957.
Short History of Opera (2 vols.), Donald Jay Grout, Columbia University Press, 1947.
Story Lives of American Composers, Katherine L. Bakeless, Lippincott, 1953.
The Story of Jazz, Rex Harris, Grosset & Dunlap, 1960.
The Story of Siegfried, James Baldwin, Scribner, 1956.
The Story of the Trapp Family Singers, Maria Augusta Trapp, Dell, 1960.
Through An Opera Glass, Irene Gass and Herbert Weinstock, Abelard, 1958.
What Jazz Is All About, Lillian Erlich, Julian Messner, 1962.

MUSICIANSHIP

Aural Tests for Schools, Ieuan Rees-Davies, Gray, 1961 (teachers).
Backgrounds in Music Theory, Maurice Whitney, G. Schirmer, 1954.
Band Scoring, Joseph Wahner, McGraw-Hill, 1960.
Basic Keyboard Skills, William Pelz, Allyn and Bacon, 1963.
Basic Music and Basic Music Workbook, H. Owen Reed, Mills, 1954.
Basic Principles of the Technique of the 18th- and 19th-Century Composition, Allen I. McHose, Appleton-Century-Crofts, 1951.
Chords in Action, Dorothy Bishop, Carl Fischer, 1956.
The Composer's Point of View, Robert Stephen Hines (Ed.), University of Oklahoma Press, 1963.
Creative-Analytical Theory of Music, Books 1 and 2, Earl Bigelow, Frank Cookson *et al.*, FitzSimons, 1949.
Creative Harmony and Musicianship, Howard Murphy and Edwin J. Stringham, Prentice-Hall, 1951.
Creative Orchestration, George Frederick McKay, Allyn and Bacon, 1963.
Elementary Musicianship, Alvin Bauman and Charles W. Walton, Prentice-Hall, 1959.
Essentials of Elementary Music Theory, George Rushford, Rubank, 1955.
Folk Song Sight Singing Series, Edgar Crowe, Annie Lawton and Gillies Whittaker, Oxford, 1933.
Foundations of Music, Wayne Barlow, Appleton-Century-Crofts, 1953.
Foundations in Music Theory, Leon Dallin, Wadsworth, 1962.
Fundamentals of Music, Raymond Elliott, Prentice-Hall, 1955.
Fundamentals of Music Reading, Paul Harder, Mills, 1950.
Graded Music Reading, Ieuan Rees-Davies, Gray, 1961.
Harmonic Practice, Roger Sessions, Harcourt, Brace, 1951.
Intervals, Scales and Temperaments, Ll. S. Lloyd and Hugh Boyle, St Martin's, 1963.
Introduction to the Theory of Music, Howard Boatwright, Norton, 1956.
Keyboard and Dictation Manual, Allen McHose and Don White, Appleton-Century-Crofts, 1949.
Keyboard Training in Harmony, Parts 1 and 2, Arthur Heacox, Arthur Schmidt, 1917.
Learn To Read Music, Howard Shanet, Simon and Schuster, 1956.
Measurement and Evaluation in Music, William E. Whybrew, Wm. C. Brown, 1962.
More Music for Sight Reading, John Vincent, Mills, 1943.
Musical Form, Robert E. Tyndall, Allyn and Bacon, 1964.
Music for Sight Reading, John Vincent, Mills, 1943.
Music for Sight Singing, Robert W. Ottman, Prentice-Hall, 1956.
Music Fundamentals, Howard Murphy, Chandler, 1962.
Music Fundamentals Through Song, Louise Myers, Prentice-Hall, 1956.
Practical Ear Training, Janet McLoud McGaughey, Allyn and Bacon, 1961.
Practical Harmony, Hans Tischler, Allyn and Bacon, 1964.
Preparing Music Manuscript, Anthony Donato, Prentice-Hall, 1963.
The Reading Singer: Graded Melodies for Music Reading and Ear Training, Irvin Cooper, Allyn and Bacon, 1965.
Rudiments of Music, Jeannette Cass, Appleton-Century-Crofts, 1956.
Rudiments of Music, John Castellini, Norton, 1962.

Sight Singing Manual, Allen McHose and Ruth N. Tibbs, Appleton-Century-Crofts, 1944.
A Song Approach to Music Reading, Charles Leonhard, Silver Burdett, 1963.
Theory and Musicianship (with work sheets), Edith McIntosh, Carl Fischer, Bk. 1, 1955, Bk. 2, 1956.
A Workbook in the Fundamentals of Music, H. Owen Reed, Mills, 1947.

MUSIC EDUCATION TEXTS FOR TEACHERS

Reference books for the classroom teacher and for the teacher of elementary music.

Basic Music for Classroom Teachers (2nd ed.), Robert E. Nye and Bjornar Bergethon, Prentice-Hall, 1962.
The Craft of Music Teaching in the Elementary School, Inez Schubert and Lucille Wood, Silver Burdett, 1964.
Foundations and Principles of Music Education, Charles Leonhard and Robert W. House, McGraw-Hill, 1959.
Guiding Children's Growth Through Music, Eileen L. McMillan, Ginn, 1959.
Guiding Junior High School Pupils in Music Experiences, Frances Andrews and Joseph A. Leeder, Prentice-Hall, 1953.
Help Yourself To Music, Beatrice P. Krone and Kurt R. Miller, Howard Chandler, 1959.
How To Help Children Learn Music, Madeleine Carabo-Cone and Beatrice Royt, Harper & Row, 1955.
A Junior High School Music Handbook, Sally Monsour and Margaret Perry, Prentice-Hall, 1963.
Keyboard Experiences and Piano Class Instruction, William R. Sur (Ed.), MENC, 1956.
Let's Make Music (workbook), Maurine Timmerman, Summy-Birchard, 1958.
Let's Teach Music, Maurine Timmerman, Summy-Birchard, 1958.
Making and Playing Classroom Instruments, Marcella Vernazza, Fearon, 1959.
Music Curriculum Guides, Harold W. Arberg and Sarah P. Wood, U.S. Department of Health, Education, and Welfare, Office of Education, 1964.
Music Education in the High School, J. A. Leeder and W. S. Haynie, Prentice-Hall, 1958.
Music Fundamentals for the Classroom Teacher, Gene C. Wisler, Allyn and Bacon, 1961.
Music in the Elementary School (2nd ed.), Robert E. and Vernice T. Nye, Prentice-Hall, 1964.
NIMAC Manual, National Interscholastic Music Activities Commission of the Music Educators National Conference, 1963.
Piano for Classroom Music, Robert Pace, Prentice-Hall, 1958.
The Playground as Music Teacher, Madeleine Carabo-Cone, Harper & Row, 1959.
Procedures and Techniques of Music Teaching, Richard H. Werder (Ed.), Catholic University of America Press, 1962.
Professional Imperatives: Expertness and Self-Determination, National Commission on Teacher Education and Professional Standards, N.E.A., Washington, D.C., 1962.
School Music Administration and Supervision, Keith D. Snyder, Allyn and Bacon, 1959.
Teaching Children Music in the Elementary School (3rd ed.), Louise Kifer Myers, Prentice-Hall, 1961.

Teaching Junior High School Music: General Music and the Vocal Program, Irvin Cooper and Karl Kuersteiner, Allyn and Bacon, 1965.
Teaching Music, Raymond Elliot, Merrill, 1960.
Your School Music Program, Frances M. Andrews and Clara E. Cockerille, Prentice-Hall, 1958.

MUSIC LITERATURE[2]

The Art of Enjoying Music, Sigmund Spaeth, McGraw-Hill, 1933.
Beethoven, Reba P. Mirsky, Follett, 1957.
Complete Stories of the Great Operas, Milton Cross, Doubleday, 1949.
Composers Eleven, Neville Cardus, George Braziller, 1959.
The Enjoyment of Music, Joseph Machlis, Norton, 1956.
The Great Masters Series, Roth, Rosenberry, Young, Hall, Raynor, and Holst, Boosey and Hawkes, 1961 (7 booklets, paperbound).
Harmony for the Listener, Robert L. Jacobs, Oxford, 1958.
Introduction to Contemporary Music, Joseph Machlis, Norton, 1963.
An Introduction to Twentieth Century Music, Peter S. Hansen, Allyn and Bacon, 1961.
History's 100 Greatest Composers, Helen L. Kaufman, Grosset and Dunlap, 1957.
The Joy of Music, Leonard Bernstein, Simon and Schuster, 1959.
Leonard Bernstein, David Ewen, Chilton, 1960.
A Listener's Anthology of Music, Lillian Baldwin, Silver Burdett, 1950.
Listening to Music Creatively (2nd ed.), Edwin J. Stringham, Prentice-Hall, 1959.
Metropolitan Opera Guild Stories of the Operas, Robert Laurence, Silver Burdett, 1945.
People and Music, Thomasine C. McGehee and Alice D. Nelson, Allyn and Bacon, 1963.
Understanding Music, William S. Newman (rev. ed.), Harper & Row, 1961.
The Way of Music, William E. Brandt, Allyn and Bacon, 1963.
The Wonderful World of Music. (A Primer of Musicology), Benjamin Britten and Imogen Holst, Garden City Books, 1958.

PROGRAMMED TEACHING

For the teacher and possibly for advanced high-school students.

Basic Materials in Music Theory, A Course of Programmed Learning, Paul Harder, Allyn and Bacon, 1965.
Introduction to Music Fundamentals, J. Austin Andrews and Jeanne Foster Wardian, Appleton-Century-Crofts, 1964. A programmed textbook for the elementary classroom teacher.
Perceiving Music: Problems in Sight and Sound. (Programmed Teaching), Guy Alan Bockman and William J. Starr, Harcourt, Brace, 1962 (with records).
Scales, Intervals, Keys and Triads, John Clough, Norton, 1964.

[2] See also lists of books for the library, in the humanities, and general music.

RECREATIONAL MUSIC

AGBOR: A Guide to Books on Recreation, National Recreation Association, Dept. MU, 1959 Journal.
The American Square Dance, Margot Mayo, Sentinel, 1948.
The Ballad Book of John Jacob Niles, John Jacob Niles, Houghton Mifflin, 1961.
The Ballad Mongers, Oscar Brand, Funk and Wagnalls, 1962.
The Book of Bells, Satis Coleman, John Day, 1938.
Creative Music for Children, Satis Coleman, Putnam, 1922.
Directions for Making the Bass Shepherd's Pipe, James, Schuberth, 1947.
The Drum Book, Satis Coleman, John Day, 1931.
Drums Through the Ages, Charles L. White, Sterling, 1960.
A Few References on Singing Games, M.P. #647, National Recreation Association.
Folksongs and Footnotes, Theodore Bikel, Meridian, 1960.
Folk Dancing, Richard Kraus, Macmillan, 1962.
Forty Approaches to Informal Singing, National Recreation Association.
Handy Folk Dance Book, Cooperative Recreation Service, 1951.
Handy Square Dance Book, Cooperative Recreation Service, 1951.
Having Fun with Music, Doron K. Antrim, Thomas Y. Crowell, 1958.
How To Make Music on the Harmonica, P. V. Planta, Sentinel, 1957.
How To Make and Play a Shepherd Pipe, Augustus Zanzig, National Recreation Association, 1950.
Introduction to Recreational Education, John H. Jenny, Saunders, 1955.
Let's Play the Recorder, Robert Bouchard, Bruce Humphries, 1962.
Make Your Own Musical Instruments, Muriel Mandell and Robert E. Wood, Sterling, 1957.
The Marimba Book, Satis Coleman, John Day, 1930.
Music Activities in Community Recreation, American Music Conference.
A Music Educator's Introduction to Barbershop Harmony, SPEBSQSA.
Music in Recreation: Social Foundations and Practices, Kaplan, Stipes, 1955.
Music Skills for Recreation Leaders, Forrest J. Baird, Wm. C. Brown, 1964.
Notes for Song Leaders, Janet Tobitt, Girl Scouts.
Piper's Guild Handbook, James, Schuberth, 1939.
Playing the Piano for Pleasure, Charles Cooke, Simon and Schuster, 1941.
The Recorder: Its Tradition and Its Task, Hildemarie Peter, D. F. Peters, Agents, 1958.
Recorder Technique, A. Rowland-Jones, Oxford, 1961.
Recreation Through Music, C. Leonhard, Ronald, 1952.
Song Sampler, Quarterly Publication, Cooperative Recreation Service.
A Treasury of Living, C. Braucher, National Recreation Association, 1950.

Michigan State University.

CHAPTER

22

Films and Recordings

FILMSTRIPS

For use in the teaching of General Music, Humanities, Musicianship, Music Literature, and other music classes and activities. The key to symbols for producers or distributors may be found on pp. 579–580. Filmstrips accompanied by records or tapes are identified.

Title	Source	Sound	Frames	Use
Aida	JAM	yes	34	J–S
America the Beautiful	SVE	no	33	J–S
The Art of Bow Making	SCH	yes	49	J–S
The Barber of Seville	JAM	yes	34	J–S
Bells at Christmas	SVE	yes	43	J–S
Carmen	MET	no	45	J–S
The Chesapeake and the Shannon (folk)	BOW	yes	92	J–S
Christmas Carols	CATH	no	23	J–S
Christmas in Folk Music	SVE	yes	41	J–S
Christmas in Sacred Music	SVE	yes	37	J–S
Community Songs (slides 3½ × 4)	SIMS	no		J–S
Coppelia	JAM	yes	34	J–S
Folk Music of Our Pacific Neighbors (2)	BOW	yes	38, 40	J
Folk Songs of California and the Old West (2)	BOW	yes	95	J
Great Composers (6: J. S. Bach; Mozart; Beethoven; Schubert; Brahms; Sousa)	EBF	no	51 ea.	J
Great Composers and Their Music (6: Johann Sebastian Bach; George Frederic Handel; Franz Joseph Haydn; Wolfgang Amadeus Mozart; Ludwig van Beethoven; Franz Peter Schubert)	JAM	yes	35 ea.	J–S
Hansel and Gretel	JAM	yes	34	J
How We Got Our Christmas Carols	SVE	yes	43	J–S
Huron Indian Christmas Carol	BOW	no	37	J–S
Instrumental Instructional Filmstrips (14 filmstrips available for all orchestral instruments)	UNEB, CONN	no	50	J

Title	Source	Sound	Frames	Use
Instruments of the Symphony Orchestra (6: String Instruments; Woodwind Instruments; Brass Instruments; Percussion Instruments; Melodious Percussion Instruments; The Orchestra)	JAM	yes	30 ea.	J–S
Jack Was Every Inch a Sailor (2 versions)	BOW	yes	58	J
	BOW	no	38	J
Learn to Play the Autoharp	BOW	yes	40	J–S
Lohengrin	JAM	yes	34	J–S
The Magic Flute	JAM	yes	34	J–S
The Mastersingers	JAM	yes	34	J–S
Meet the Instruments of the Symphony Orchestra	BOW	yes		J–S
Meet the Orchestra	CMC	yes		J–S
A Midsummer Night's Dream	JAM	yes	34	J–S
Moving Ahead with Music	AMC	yes	104	J–S
Music in Our School	AMC	yes	40	J–S
Music Stories (6: Peter and the Wolf; Hansel and Gretel; The Nutcracker; Peer Gynt; The Firebird; The Sorcerer's Apprentice)	JAM	yes	29–31	J
The Nutcracker and the Mouse-King	EBF	no	48	J–S
Opera and Ballet Stories (6: Lohengrin; The Magic Flute; Aida; The Barber of Seville; The Mastersingers; Coppelia)	JAM	yes	35–40	J–S
Our American Heritage of Folk Music (6: Songs of the Sea; Songs of the Cowboy; Songs of the Mountains; Songs of the Plains; Songs of the Railroad; Songs of the Civil War)	SVE	yes	50	J–S
Our National Anthem	YAF	no	40	J–S
Percussion Performance (3: Tambourine; Castanets; Triangle)	LYON	yes		J–S
The Raftsmen (Canadian Folk)	BOW	yes	99	J
Songs of the American Revolution	SVE	yes	51	J–S
Songs of the Mississippi Valley	SVE	yes	53	J–S
Songs of the Old South	SVE	yes	54	J–S
Songs of the Old Southwest	SVE	yes	55	J–S
Songs of Pioneer Mid-America	SVE	yes	55	J–S
Songs of the Western Frontier	SVE	yes	54	J–S
Stories of Music Classics (6: The Sleeping Beauty; William Tell; Midsummer Night's Dream; Swan Lake; The Bartered Bride; Sheherazade)	JAM	yes	32–33	J
The Story of Handel's Messiah	SVE	yes	58	J–S
The Story of the Nutcracker	SVE	yes	75	J–S
Tosca	MET	no	45	J–S
Violin Making in Europe and Violin Adjusting in the U.S.A.	SCH	yes	71	J–S

William Tell	JAM	yes	34	J–S
You Can Make Music	AMC	yes	40	J

MOTION PICTURE FILMS (16 MM.)

For use in Assemblies, General Music, Humanities, Choral and Instrumental Music, Musicianship, Music Literature, and other classes and activities. The films are classified according to special interest areas, but see also the other categories. Available in black and white and/or color. Key to producers and distributors can be found on pp. 580–582.

Band

TITLE	SOURCE	COLOR	MIN.	USE
Band Attention	OST	color	10	J–S
Band on the March	OST	b/w or color	10	J–S
Baton Directing	OST	b/w	10	J–S
Baton Twirling	OST	b/w or color	10	J–S
Drum Major	OST	b/w or color	10	J–S
Here Comes the Band	McGH	b/w	19	J–S
Holiday for Bands	PAR	color	26	J–S
How To Twirl a Baton	McGH	b/w	12	J–S
Instruments of the Band and Orchestra: Introduction	COR	b/w or color	11	J
The King's Musick	BIS	b/w	18	J–S
Maneuvers for Field and Street	OST	b/w or color	10	J–S
Marching Band Fundamentals	INDU	b/w or color	21	J–S
Military Drill	INDU	b/w or color	10	J–S
Mister B Natural	CONN	b/w or color	27	J–S
Musical Performance Improvement for the Snare Drum	UWIS	b/w	22	J–S
National Anthem	NAVY	b/w	2	J–S
On Wisconsin	UWIS	color	30	J–S
Overland with the Spartan Band	MSU	color	18	J–S
Purdue University Marching Band Series (30 films)	PU	color	14–20	J–S
Saturday Spectacle (Illinois)	UILL	color	30	J–S
Tribute to Sousa	OSU–MPD	color	17	J–S
Trojan Tempo	USC	color	17	J–S
United States Army Band	FILMS	b/w	10	J–S
University of Illinois Concert Band	UILL	b/w	22	J–S
University of Michigan Marching Band	UM	color	13	J–S
Your Marine Band from Then Till Now	USM	b/w	27½	J–S

Choral and Vocal Music

Title	Source	Color	Min.	Use
Anthems of the Church (3 parts)	CATH	b/w	10 ea.	J–S
Australian Folk Song Series (4 films)	BF	b/w	vary	J–S
Choral Concert	NFB	b/w	10	S
Folk Music Festival Series (11 films)	BF	b/w	vary	J–S
Folk Song Fantasy	IFB	color	8	J–S
George London	MTP	b/w	55	J–S
Glasgow Orpheus Choir	BIS	b/w	12	J–S
Glee Club	BWNU	b/w or color	5	S
Hail Alma Mater	USAR	b/w	6	S
Human Throat	BRAY	b/w	12	S
Hymn of the Nations	UWF	b/w	28	J–S
Improving Your Posture	COR	color	10	J–S
It's Fun To Sing	STE	b/w	11	J–S
Lady from Philadelphia (M. Anderson)	CON	b/w	60	J–S
Let's All Sing Together (6 films)	LIBF	b/w	9–11	J–S
Let's Make Music Series (4 films, Folk Songs)	BF	b/w	7	J–S
The Lord's Prayer	UW GOV	b/w	4	J–S
Marian Anderson	MIL	b/w	27½	J–S
Mechanics of Breathing	EBF	b/w	11	S
Negro Spirituals—Helen Tamiris	CON	b/w	17	J–S
Selected Negro Spirituals	EBF	b/w	11	J–S
Selected Negro Work Songs	EBF	b/w	9	J–S
Sing a Little (Folk)	STE	b/w	9	J–S
Singing Champions (male chorus)	NFB	b/w	10	J–S
Singing in the General Music Class	UIA	b/w	30	J–S
Snowdonia (Welsh songs)	BIS	color	17	J–S
Songs of Nova Scotia	CON	b/w	11	J–S
Songs of the Auvergne	RFL	b/w	20	J–S
Songs of the Campus	McGH	b/w	15	J–S
Stephen Foster and His Songs	COR	b/w or color	16½	J–S
A Time for Bach	FI	b/w	26	J–S
Vocal Music (vocal study)	EBF	b/w	11	J–S
Voice of a Choir	UW GOV	b/w	24	S
World of Songs	OSU–MPD	color	13	J–S
Your Posture	McGH	b/w	10	J–S
Your Voice	EBF	b/w	11	J–S
Youth and Music in Detroit	WSU	color	24	J–S

General Interest

Title	Source	Color	Min.	Use
An A B C for Music	PIC	b/w	11	J–S
The American Square Dance	COR	b/w	11	J–S
Ballad of the West	EBF	b/w	15	J–S
Begone Dull Care (jazz)	NFB	color	6	J–S

Title	Source	Color	Min.	Use
Bernstein in Berlin	FORD	b/w	50	J–S
Bernstein Concert Series (4 films)	FORD	b/w	60	J–S
Billy the Kid (And Little Mohee)	BF	b/w	7	J
Classic Guitar: Miniature Orchestra	NET	b/w	23	J–S
Concert Hall Favorites	ALM	b/w	15	J–S
Concert on Film	MIL	b/w	26	J–S
Correlating Music with Social Studies in the General Music Class	UIA	b/w	30	J
Norwegian Folk Dances	AMF	color	11	J–S
One Life for Music	MIL	b/w	26	J–S
Our Country's Song	COR	b/w or color	10	J–S
Piano Encores	FILMS	color	10	J–S
Recording with Magnetic Tape	UMIN	b/w	8	J–S
Science of Sound and Musical Tone	HAM	color	20	J–S
Six Basic Categories	NET	b/w	29	S
The Sounds of Music	COR	b/w or color	10	J–S
Spanish Gypsies	AF	b/w	10	J–S
Spreewald Folks (German folk)	TFC	b/w	10	J–S
Stephen Foster and His Songs	COR	b/w or color	16	J–S
Tales from the Vienna Woods	SMUSA	b/w	10	J–S
Tanglewood	UWF	b/w	21	J–S
Three Rs and the Arts (Interlochen)	NMC	color	20	J–S
Toot, Whistle, Plunk and Boom	CONN	color	20	J–S
The Trio (Rubinstein, Heifetz, Piatigorsky)	MIL	b/w	29	J–S
Unfinished Symphony: First Movement	SMUSA	b/w	12	J–S
Unfinished Symphony: Second Movement	SMUSA	b/w	12	J–S
A World Is Born	DIS	color	20	J–S

Humanities

Title	Source	Color	Min.	Use
The Age of Sophocles	EBF	color	28	S
Appalachian Spring (ballet)	CON	b/w	31	J–S
Architecture West	AM	b/w	22	S
Architecture U.S.A.	AIA	color	36	S
Aristotle's Ethics, Book I—The Theory of Happiness	EBF	color	30	S
Art: What Is It? Why Is It?	EBF	color	30	S
Art of The Middle Ages	EBF	color	30	S
Athens—The Golden Age	EBF	color	30	S
Ballet Festival	NFB, CON	b/w	11	J–S
Ballet Girl	BF	b/w	23	J–S
Ballet of the Dolls (Coppelia)	HOFF	b/w	15	J–S
Boogie-Doodle (Jazz)	IFB, CON	color	4	J–S
Boundary Lines	McGH	color	10	S

Title	Source	Color	Min.	Use
Chartres Cathedral	EBF	color	30	S
The Character of Oedipus	EBF	color	28	S
A Dancer's World	CON	b/w	27	S
Design: Composition, Light and Shade, Line, and Shape	McGH	b/w	40	S
Design to Music	IFB	color	6	J–S
Early Victorian England and Charles Dickens	EBF	color	34	S
The Earth Sings	BF	b/w	15	J–S
Edinburgh Festival of Music and Drama	BIS	b/w	11	J–S
Elements of the Visual Arts	STEPH	color	30	S
The Engulfed Cathedral	AVIS	color	10	J–S
Frank Lloyd Wright	JOUR	color	21	S
French Tapestries Visit America	FII	color	30	S
From Clay To Bronze	UMO	b/w	20	S
Great Expectations I	EBF	color	34	S
Great Expectations II	EBF	color	34	S
Greek Lyric Poetry	EBF	color	30	S
Hamlet–The Age of Elizabeth	EBF	color	28	S
Henry Moore	FII	color	17	S
How To Make an Etching	ALM	b/w	30	S
The Humanities: What They Are and What They Do	EBF	color	45	S
Images from Debussy	AF	b/w	14	J–S
Invitation to Music	IFB, OFF	b/w	14	J–S
Leonardo da Vinci	EBF	color	10	S
The Magic Fiddle (ballet)	CON	color	15	J–S
Magic Flute	HOFF	b/w	13½	J–S
Making a Mural	EBF	b/w	5	S
Man and God	EBF	color	28	S
Modern Sculpture	STEPH	b/w	20	S
Moor's Pavane	FCI	color	27	S
Music and Architecture Through the Ages	UWF	b/w	19	S
Mystic Lamb	MMA	b/w	9	S
A Night Journey	CON	b/w	30	S
The Novel, What It Is, What It's About, What It Does	EBF	color	34	S
Oedipus Rex	EBF	b/w	90	S
Orpheus and Euridice	STEPH	b/w	30	S
Our Town and Our Universe	EBF	color	28	S
Our Town and Ourselves	EBF	color	28	S
Pagliacci	BF	b/w	89	S
Picasso	CON	color	50	S
Picture in Your Mind	McGH	color	16	S
Plato's Apology–The Life and Teachings of Socrates	EBF	color	30	S

Title	Source	Color	Min.	Use
The Poisoned Kingdom	EBF	color	28	S
The Readiness is All	EBF	color	28	S
The Recovery of Oedipus	EBF	color	28	S
Rediscovered Harmonies	FII	b/w	22	J–S
Rembrandt	EBF	color	27	S
The Renaissance	IF	color	21	S
Rodin	UWF	b/w	23	S
Satin Slippers (ballet)	BF	b/w	32	J–S
Speaking of the Arts	STEPH	b/w	27	S
Stars of the Russian Ballet	BF	color	80	S
Steps of the Ballet	EBF	b/w	25	J–S
The Stone Wonders of Naumberg	MMA	b/w	17	J–S
Symphonies in Stone	ASSN. F.	b/w	10 ea.	J–S
The Theatre—One of The Humanities	EBF	color	28	S
The Titan	NBC	b/w	90	S
Van Gogh	MGM	color	20	S
A Visit with Henry Matisse	FACSEA	b/w	25	S
What Is Modern Art	MMA	color	20	S
What Happens in Hamlet	EBF	color	28	S

Keyboard Instruments

Title	Source	Color	Min.	Use
The Alphabet in Black	NET	b/w	29	S
The Alphabet in White	NET	b/w	29	S
Artur Rubinstein (2 films)	MIL	b/w	26 ea.	J–S
Concert Miniatures (2 films)	STE	b/w	10 ea.	J–S
Grieg: Piano Concerto in A Minor	SG	b/w	21	J–S
The Harpsichord	ALM	b/w	10	J–S
Jose Iturbi (2 films)	MIL	b/w	10	J–S
Music in the Wind (organ)	STE	b/w	10	J–S
Myra Hess (piano)	CON	b/w	10	J–S
New Horizons: The Building of a Piano	BALD	color	14	J–S
Paderewski Concert	OFF	b/w	10	J–S
Vronsky and Babin (two pianos)	AF, MIL	b/w	20	J–S
Wanda Landowska (harpsichord)	EBF	b/w	30	J–S

Musicianship

Title	Source	Color	Min.	Use
Casals Master Class Series (Programs 1–25)	NET	b/w	30	S
Colors in Music	NET	b/w	29	S
Conducting Good Music	EBF	b/w or color	13	J–S
Dance Form in Classical Music	MIL	b/w	26	S
Elements of Composition	INDU	b/w	27	J–S
An Essay in Sound	NET	b/w	29	S
Forms of Music: Instrumental	COR	b/w or color	16	J–S
Harmony in Music	COR	b/w or color	13½	J
Haydn's Farewell Symphony	FILMS	color	9	J–S

Title	Source	Color	Min.	Use
Meter and Rhythm	NET	b/w	29	s
Modern Music	NET	b/w	29	s
Music and Emotion	NET	b/w	29	s
Music As Sound	NET	b/w	29	s
Musical Notes	UWIS	b/w	12	J–S
Musical Words	NET	b/w	29	s
Narrative Music	NET	b/w	29	s

Music Literature

Title	Source	Color	Min.	Use
Andre Segovia	EBF	b/w	30	J–S
Andre Segovia (Festival of Performing Arts)	MTP	b/w	55	J–S
Artur Rubinstein	MIL	b/w	26	J–S
Beethoven and His Music	COR	b/w or color	10	J–S
Brahms and His Music	COR	b/w or color	13½	J–S
Casals Master Class Series (Programs 1–25)	NET	b/w	30	s
Concerts on Film Series (40 films)	LES	b/w	vary	J–S
Finlandia	STE	b/w	9	J–S
Fifth Symphony in C Minor	SMUSA	b/w	10	J–S
First Piano Quartet	FILMS	color	10	J–S
George Frederick Handel	UWF	b/w	20	J–S
The Great Waltz	TFC	b/w	20	J–S
Handel and His Music	COR	b/w or color	13½	J–S
Igor Stravinsky	EBF	b/w	29	s
Images from Debussy	AF	b/w	14	J–S
Immortal Bizet	ALM	b/w	26	J–S
Liszt and His Music	COR	b/w or color	13	J–S
Maestro Franz Liszt at Weimar	TFC	color	10	J–S
Man of Music (Healey Willan)	NFB	b/w	18	J–S
Mozart and His Music	COR	b/w or color	10	J–S
Musical Antiques	PARA	color	6	J–S
Musical Forms	NET	b/w	29	J–S
Musical Terms Melodrama	WSU	color	11	J–S
Music as a Language Series: University of Rochester (13 films)	NET	b/w	29	s
Nadia Boulanger	EBF	b/w	30	J–S
Overture to Orpheus in Hades	SMUSA	b/w	10	J–S
Overture to Rosamunde	SMUSA	b/w	10	J–S
Pablo Casals (Festival of Performing Arts)	MTP	b/w	55	J–S
Rediscovered Harmonies	FII	b/w	22	J–S
Schubert and His Music	COR	b/w or color	11	J–S
The Schumann Story	TFC	b/w	32	J–S
Serenata Notturna	SMUSA	b/w	13	J–S
Sibelius	STE	b/w	10	J–S
Tchaikowsky's Symphony No. 4	FILMS	color	6	J–S

Title	Source	Color	Min.	Use
Thieving Magpie	FILMS	color	9	J–S
Virtuoso Franz Liszt as Composer	TFC	color	14	J–S
Visit with Darius Milhaud	BF	color	31	J–S
Wanda Landowska	EBF	b/w	30	J–S

Opera and Operetta

Title	Source	Color	Min.	Use
The Barber of Seville	OFF	b/w	21	S
Carmen	SMUSA	b/w	13	J–S
Carmen—Andalusian Nights	STE	b/w	13	J–S
Castle in Seville (Don Giovanni)	HOFF	b/w	13½	J–S
Christmas Slippers (Russian operetta)	BF	b/w	32	J–S
Don Pasquale	OFF	b/w	25	S
Eugene Onegin	BF	color	102	J–S
Gypsy Princess	HOFF	b/w	90	J–S
H.M.S. Pinafore	HOFF	color	70	J–S
Inside Opera with Grace Moore	TFC	b/w	25	J–S
La Traviata	DYN	b/w	30	J–S
Lucia di Lammermoor	IFB, OFF	b/w	22	J–S
The Marriage of Figaro	HOFF	b/w	15	S
The Medium	ATH	b/w	81	J–S
Merry Mount	NET	b/w	29	S
Merry Wives of Windsor	HOFF	b/w	28	J–S
The Music of Great German Composers: Stories of Operas and Ballets (series of 13 films)	HOFF	b/w	13	J–S
Naughty Marietta	TFC	b/w	33	J–S
A Night at the Peking Opera	FII	color	20	J–S
On Such a Night	CON	color	35	J–S
Opera School	NFBC	b/w	36	J–S
Three Penny Opera	BF	b/w	112	J–S
Trumpet, Horn, and Trombone	COR	b/w or color	11	J–S
William Tell	IFB	b/w	25	J–S
Willie the Operatic Whale	FILMS	color	15	J–S

Orchestra

Title	Source	Color	Min.	Use
Basic Violin Playing: Tone Production	P. COX	b/w	16	J–S
Bolero	AVIS	b/w or color	8	J–S
Conducting Good Music	EBF	b/w or color	13	J–S
David Oistrakh Playing (1) "Slavonic Dance in E Minor" by Dvorak-Kreisler	BF	b/w	5	J–S
David Oistrakh Playing (2) "Mazurka" by Zarzycki	BF	b/w	5	J–S
Emperor Waltz	STE	b/w	10	J–S
Fifth Symphony	STE	b/w	9	J–S
Fingal's Cave	AVIS	color	9	J–S

Title	Source	Color	Min.	Use
Instruments of the Band and Orchestra: Introduction	COR	b/w or color	11	J
Instruments of the Orchestra	CON	b/w	20	J–S
La Gazza Ladra (Rossini)	FILMS	color	10	J–S
Little Fugue in G Minor	TFC	b/w	5	J–S
Merry Wives of Windsor	FILMS	color	9	J–S
Midsummer Night's Dream	SG	b/w	17	J–S
Mozart and Barrios on Six Strings	FII	b/w	10	J–S
New York Philharmonic Orchestra	MIL	b/w	13	J–S
Peer Gynt Suite	OFF	b/w	20	J–S
Poet and Peasant Overture	FILMS	color	19	J–S
Rehearsal (Montreal Orchestra)	NFB	b/w	12	J–S
Romantic Symphony	NET	b/w	29	S
Rudolf Serkin and the Budapest String Quartet (Festival Performing Arts)	MTP	b/w	55	J–S
Science in the Orchestra: Part I, Exploring the Instruments; Part 2, Hearing the Orchestra; Part 3, Looking at Sounds	McGH	b/w	12, 13, 10	J–S
The Sound and the Story (recording the orchestra)	IVT	color	22	J–S
The Symphony Orchestra	EBF	b/w or color	14	J–S
Tchaikowsky's Fourth Symphony	STE	b/w	10	J–S
Toccata and Fugue	AVIS	color	10	J–S
Venice Concert (Philharmonic, Bernstein)	FORD	b/w	59	J–S
Vienna Philharmonic (11 films)	STE	b/w	10–11	J–S
Young Peoples Concert Series—Leonard Bernstein (3: What is a Sonata? (Mozart's Jupiter Symphony), Young Performers (Ravel's Mother Goose Suite), Sibelius 100th Anniversary Concert (Finlandia and parts of Symphony No. 2) (Additional programs planned for release)	BELL TEL (free)	b/w	60 ea.	J–S

Seasonal

Title	Source	Color	Min.	Use
Chantons Noel	NFB	color	10	J–S
Christmas Carols	STE	color	8	J–S
Christmas Song	COR	b/w	20	J–S
Christmas Music of the Southwest	UA	b/w	14	J–S
Merry Christmas	STE	b/w	12	J–S
On the Twelfth Day (Christmas)	BF	color	22	J–S
Silent Night: Story of the Christmas Carol	COR	b/w or color	13	J–S
Song of Christmas	PORT	color	10	J–S

Strings

Title	Source	Color	Min.	Use
Andante et Rondo (cello)	HOFF	b/w	8	J–S
Andrés Segovia (guitar)	MIL	b/w	13	J–S
Basic Violin Playing: Tone Production	COAST	b/w	16	J–S
Cello Concert (Leonard Rose)	STE	b/w	10	J–S
Chamber Music Is Fun	BRIG	b/w or color	30	J–S
Coolidge Quartet	MIL	b/w	10	J–S
David Oistrakh Playing (violin, 2 films)	BF	b/w	5 ea.	J–S
Eine Kleine Nachtmusik	STE	b/w	12	J–S
Emanuel Feuermann (cello)	MIL	b/w	9	J–S
Gregor Piatigorsky (cello)	MIL	b/w	26½	J–S
Hollywood String Quartet	MIL	b/w	26	J–S
Instruments of the Orchestra: Strings	COR	b/w or color	11	J
Jascha Heifetz (2 films)	MIL	b/w	26	J–S
Listening to Good Music, The String Quartet	EBF	b/w	14	J–S
Malaguena (violin)	HOFF	b/w	6	J–S
Mozart and Barrios on Six Strings (guitar)	FII	b/w	10	J–S
Pablo Casals, A Legend Come to Life (cello)	MIL	b/w	26	J–S
Paganini Caprices (violin)	ART	b/w	10	J–S
Playing Good Music (string quartet)	EBF	b/w	14	J–S
The Story of Chamber Music	BRIG	b/w or color	29	J–S
The Story of a Violin	NFB	color	21	J–S
The String Choir	EBF	b/w or color	11	J–S
String Quartet and Its Music	NET	b/w	28	J–S
The String Trio	COR	b/w	11	J–S
Tchaikovsky Concert (cello)	STE	b/w	10	J–S
To Hear Your Banjo Play	BF	b/w	10	J–S
The Voices of the String Quartet	NET	b/w	25	J–S
William Primrose (viola)	PICT	b/w	10	J–S

Wind and Percussion Instruments

Title	Source	Color	Min.	Use
Basic Snare Drum Technique (additional film loops)	TROX	b/w	10	J–S
A Beethoven Sonata (horn)	CON	b/w or color	18	J–S
The B Flat Clarinet	McMG	b/w or color	9	J–S
The Brass Choir	EBF	b/w or color	11	J–S
Flute, Clarinet, and Bassoon	COR	b/w or color	11	J–S
Flute and Harp: Melody and Polyphony	NET	b/w	23	J–S
Instruments of the Band and Orchestra: The Brasses	COR	b/w or color	11	J
Instruments of the Band and Orchestra: The Percussions	COR	b/w or color	11	J

Title	Source	Color	Min.	Use
Instruments of the Band and Orchestra: The Woodwinds	COR	b/w or color	11	J
Introducing the Brasses	NET	b/w	23	J–S
Introducing the Woodwinds	NET	b/w	23	J–S
Musical Performance Improvement for the Snare Drum	UWIS	b/w	10	J–S
The Percussion Group	EBF	color	11	J–S
Percussion, the Pulse of Music	NET	b/w	21	J–S
Rafael Mendez (trumpet)	MIL	b/w	27	J–S
The Saxophone in Concert	ART	b/w	11	J–S
The Snare Drum	UWIS	b/w	19	J–S
The Woodwind Choir	EBF	color	11	J–S

INSTRUCTIONAL TELEVISION MATERIALS FOR BROADCAST USE[1]

Accent on Music (8 lessons, 30-min. each, kinescope)
Concerts and commentary designed to supplement secondary-school music course. Symphony orchestra, jazz, ancient instruments, concert band, the conductor, the oratorio, and boys changing voices. Commentator: Dr. Edward Gilday.

How to Make Music (two series of 14 lessons, 30-min. each, kinescope)
Supplementary instruction in musical theory, history, and appreciation for intermediate grades. Demonstration and participation format. State University of Iowa.

Keys to Music (20 lessons, 15-min. each, kinescope)
Instruction in music fundamentals for middle and upper grades using keyboard as the major teaching device. Thomas Organ Co.

Music for You (64 lessons, 20-min. each, videotape)
Supplementary instruction in the understanding and appreciation of music for intermediate grades. Midwest Program on Airborne Television Instruction.

Music for Young People (13 lessons, 30-min., film)
Enrichment instruction designed to introduce the instruments of an orchestra and with music composed specifically for the various sections. Pupils and such noted musicians participate as Yehudi Menuhin, Thomas Scherman, Julliard String Quartet, and the Stradivarius Society. National Educational Television and Radio Center (NETRC)

Musical Forms (6 lessons, 30-min. each, kinescope)
Designed to introduce the student to "sonata," "scherzo," "theme," and similar terms with illustrations in the form of complete movements from the work of Schumann, Schubert, Brahms, Haydn, Franck, Grieg, and Beethoven. (NETRC)

[1] For rates and additional information address the National Center for School and College Television, Box A, Bloomington, Indiana 47402.

RECORDINGS—LISTS AND CATALOGS

People and Music, McGeehee-Nelson, Allyn and Bacon, 1963. Lists of recordings at ends of chapters.

School Records Catalog, Children's Music Center, 5373 W. Pico Blvd., Los Angeles 19, California.

Folk Music of the United States and Latin America, A catalogue of available phonograph records, Division of Music, Library of Congress, 1948.

RCA Victor Educational Record Catalog, RCA Victor Education Dept., 155 E. 24 St., New York 10010.

Recordings of Latin American Songs and Dances, Chase, Gilbert, Music Division, Pan-American Union, Washington, D.C., 1950.

Record-Filmstrip Catalog, Educational Record Sales, 157 Chambers St., New York 10007.

Muskegon, Michigan.

CHAPTER

23

Music

ASSEMBLY SINGING

Choral Collections

Title	Composer-Arranger	Publisher
Catch That Catch Can (rounds)	Taylor	ECS
Chorus and Assembly	Thiel-Heller	SCHM
Community and Assembly Singing	Zanzig	NRA
The Ditty Bag	Tobitt	JT
Golden Book of Favorite Songs (Orch. acc. available)		SCHM
Gray Book of Favorite Songs		SCHM
Let's Sing	Jones	SCHM
New American Song Book		SCHM
New Blue Book of Favorite Songs		SCHM
Noels	Oberndorfer	FITZ
One Hundred Songs You Remember	Buchtel	NK
Our Singing Nation	Heller	SCHM
Singing Time (unison or mixed)		SCHM
Sing Together		GS
Song Sessions	MacLean	REM
Songs We Sing		SCHM
Universal Folk Songster (mostly unison)		GSCH
Work and Sing, Music of One World, One Tune More, Handy Play Party Book, Songs of Many Nations, We Sing, Twelve Carols, Look Away, Guiana Sings, Joyful Singing, Swing High, 15 Austrian Folk Songs, Merry Hours, Bridge of Song, and many others. Send for list of booklets.		CRS

Cumulative Song List

I. Songs that are physically stimulating and which arouse, therefore, a strong emotional response:

Anchors Aweigh
The Army Air Corps
Battle Hymn of the Republic
The Caissons Go Rolling Along
The Marines' Hymn
Over There
Stout Hearted Men
There's Something About a Soldier
When Johnny Comes Marching Home

II. Songs with the sense of fun and vigorous, salty humor characteristic of a young and vigorous people:

Billy Boy
Camptown Races
Cindy
The Glendy Burke
Jingle Bells
Oh! Susanna
Old Dan Tucker
She'll Be Comin' 'Round the Mountain
Turkey in the Straw
Yankee Doodle
Yankee Doodle Dandy

III. Simple, heartwarming songs of love and longing—emotions which are shared by young and old, high and low, regardless of race, color, or creed:

Carry Me Back to Old Virginny
Deep River
Home on the Range
The Home Road (Carpenter)
Home, Sweet Home
Keep the Home Fires Burning
The Long, Long Trail
My Old Kentucky Home
Old Folks at Home

IV. Songs of loyalty to our country, tributes testifying to our confidence and devotion:

America
America (Bloch)
America the Beautiful
American Hymn (Speed Our Republic)
America, My Own (Cain)
Columbia, the Gem of the Ocean
God Bless America
Hail Columbia

V. Songs asserting courage upheld by the strength of unified purpose:

God of Our Fathers
Hail, Land of Freedom (Turner)
Onward Christian Soldiers
Land of Our Birth (Lowell Mason-Kipling)
Song of Freedom
The Star-Spangled Banner
This Is My Country

VI. Songs attesting man's persistent faith in the ideals of human worth and the right to freedom:

Chester (Early American, by Billings)
Faith of Our Fathers
Go Down Moses (Negro Spiritual)
Netherlands Hymn
On, Thou Soul (Slavic)
Song of Hope (Hebrew)

VII. Songs expressing the serenity and peace that come from confident faith in things of the spirit:

Brother James' Air (The Lord Is My Shepherd)
Faith of Our Fathers
The Lord's Prayer (Malotte)
A Mighty Fortress
Now Thank We All Our God
Now the Day Is Over
O God, Beneath Thy Guiding Hand
O God, Our Help in Ages Past

VIII. Songs that convey the stability and sense of belonging that derive from the sheltering, protective quality of family affections:

All Through the Night
At the Gates of Heaven
Golden Slumbers
Lullaby (Brahms)
Sleep and Rest (Mozart)
Sweet and Low

IX. Songs that promote friendliness among a group of people through their sharing the delight of singing beautiful melodies together:

A Cuba (Cuban)
Beautiful Dreamer (U.S.)
Carmela (Mexican)
Drink to Me Only (English)
La Golondrina (Mexican)
I Dream of Jeanie (U.S.)
Londonderry Air (Irish)
La paloma azul or Cielito linda (Mexican)
The Rose of Tralee (Irish)
Santa Lucia (Italian)
Scarlet Sarafan (Russian)

X. Popular songs, i.e., songs which are popular because of common acceptance, songs of the people:

Bicycle Built for Two
East Side, West Side
Irish Eyes Are Smiling
I Want a Girl
Let Me Call You Sweetheart
(and appropriate current favorites)

CHORAL

It is suggested that all choral materials recommended be secured on approval and the selection of music be in terms of the experience and vocal resources of the students who will sing the music. Catalogs of octavo music may be secured from the music publishers listed on p. 585, and lists of materials are suggested from sources on p. 573. Examination of music before purchase is imperative.

Choral Collections, Junior High School[1]

Title	Composer-Arranger	Parts	Publisher
Achievement Choral Collection	Isaac	Boys	CF
Boys in Song	Guettler	Boys	MPH
Boy's Own Chorus Book	Baker-Daniel	Boys	BM
Choral Adventures	Heller	B–G	SCHM
Chorus Book for Boys	Probst-Bergquist	Boys	GSCH
Choruses for Changing Voices	Vernon-Trimingham	B–G	SCHM
Close Harmony for Boys	Baker-Daniel	Boys	BM
Descants and Easy Basses	Krone	B–G	NK

[1] Choral collections for singing in the General Music Class, for junior-high-school boys, girls, and mixed choruses and glee clubs. See also listings for senior-high-school choral groups and for assembly singing. Key to publishers, p. 585.

Title	Composer-Arranger	Parts	Publisher
Descants for Junior High Singing	Cooper	B–G	CF
Descants To Sing for Fun	Foltz-Murray	2-pt.	MILL
A Dozen Songs of the Americas	Pitcher	SA	BEL
From Descants to Trios	Krone	B–G	STA
Four in Harmony	Ehret-Gardner	4-pt.	NK
Glee Club Book for Boys	Glenn	Boys	OD
Great Songs of Faith	Krone	B–G	NK
Hi and Lo	Ehret-Gardner	B–G	STA
The Junior A Cappella Chorus Book	Christiansen-Pitts	B–G	OD
Just for Fun (unison, 2-pt.)		B–G	MPH
Let's Sing	Hood-Perry	B–G	CF
Let's Sing Parts (unison, 2- or 3-pt.)	Staples	B–G	MILL
Listen To Our Songs (unison with descant)	Grant	B–G	BM
Melody and Harmony	Ehret-Gardner	B–G	STA
Mills Collection of 2-part Sacred and Secular Choruses	Howorth	2-pt.	MILL
More Descants To Sing for Fun	Foltz-Shelley	2-pt.	MILL
More Melody, Rhythm and Harmony	Slind	2-3-4-pts.	MILL
Music for Young Chorus	Vance-Kjelson	SA, TB	BEL
My Gal Sal	Yoder	B–G	NK
The New Blue Book of Favorite Songs	Beattie *et al.*	B–G	SCHM
Our Third Book of Descants	Krone	B–G	NK
Part Songs for Changing Voices	Vernon *et al.*	Boys	SCHM
Patterns in Song	Richardson-Frackenpohl	B–G	MPH
People and Song	Pitcher	SSA	HF
Relax and Harmonize	Goward	Boys	BM
Rounds and Canons	Wilson	SATB	SCHM
Sing Joyfully (Catholic song texts)	Sister Mary Philomena, O.P.	B–G	FOL
Singing Down the Road	Siegmeister-Wheeler	Boys	GI
Singing Time	Heller-Goodell	B–G	SCHM
Songs for Boys	Gibb	Boys	WOOD
Songs for Junior High School Boys	Wright-Lester	Boys	REM
Songs for Pre-Teentime	Cooper	B–G	CF
Songs of Hills and Plains	Wilson	B–G	SCHM
Songs of Many Nations	Krone	B–G	NK
Teen Age Songs	Cooper	B–G	CF
Teen Trios	Ehret-Gardner	SAB	STA
Teen Tunes for S.A. (cambiata)	Ehret	Boys	BOOS
Three in Song	Ehret-Gardner	3-pt.	STA
Troubadours (rev. ed., 4-pt., limited range)	Nightingale	B–G	CF

TITLE	COMPOSER-ARRANGER	PARTS	PUBLISHER
Tune Time for Teen Time	Cooper	Boys	CF
Tunes for Teens	Wheeler-Siegmeister	B–G	TP
Unison Songs for Boys	Cooper	Boys	CF
When Voices Are Changing	Breach	Boys	TP
Youth Sings		SB, SAB	SHAW

Music Series Texts for Grades 7 and 8

Allyn and Bacon, *This Is Music*, Books 7–8, Sur, DuBois, Nye, 1963.
American Book Co., *Music for Young Americans*, Books 7–8, Berg, Hooley, Wolverton, Burns, 1960.
Follett, *Together We Sing*, Books 7–8 (rev.), Wolfe, Krone, Fullerton, 1960.
Ginn & Co., *Our Singing World*, Books 7–8, Pitts, Watters, Glenn, Wersen, 1951–1959.
Prentice-Hall, *Growing With Music*, Books 7–8, Ehret, Barr, Blair, 1959.
Silver Burdett, *Music for Living*, Books 7–8, Cooper, Freeburg, Imig, Nordholm, Rhea, Serposs, 1959.
Summy-Birchard, *Birchard Music Series*, Books 7–8, Ernst, Grentzer, Housewright, 1962.

Choral Collections, Senior High School

TITLE	COMPOSER-ARRANGER	PARTS	PUBLISHER
The A Cappella Chorus, in *Three Centuries of Choral Music*:	Jones-Krone		WIT
Vol. 1		SA, TB	
Vol. 2		SAB, SATB	
Vol. 3		SAB	
Vols. 4–7		SATB	
The A Cappella Chorus Book	Christiansen-Cain	SATB	OD
The A Cappella Singer for Men's Voices	Clough-Leighter	TTBB	ECS
Achievement Choral Collection	Isaac	SAB	CF
The Art of A Cappella Singing	Smallman-Wilcox	SATB	OD
Barber Shop Classics, Vols. 1 & 2	Spaeth	TTBB	REM
Choral Musicianship Series, Bk. 4	Wilson	SAB	SB
Choral Program Book, Vols. 1 & 2	Christiansen	SATB	AUG
The Choral Program Series	Wilson	SATB	SB
Christmas Carols for Male Voices		TTBB	SCHM
Christmas Carols for Treble Voices			SCHM
The Clarendon Book of Songs for Senior Schools		2-pt.	OX
Descants on Christmas Carols			SCHM
Descants to Songs for Fun	Foltz-Murphy	TB	MILL
Eight Negro Spirituals, Bks. 1 & 2	Brown	2-pt.	OX
Festival Program Book		SSA	NK

Title	Composer-Arranger	Parts	Publisher
The Festival Song Book	Bell	2-3-pt.	MILL
For Four or More (barbershop)	House	TTBB	BEL
Four in Harmony	Ehret-Gardner	SATB	STA
Fred Waring Song Book		SSA, SATB, TTBB	SHAW
Gentlemen Songsters		TTBB	SHAW
Harmony and Rhyme	Grant	SSA	BM
Have Songs Will Sing		SAB	SHAW
Holiday Montage	Ades	SATB	SHAW
The Junior A Cappella Chorus Book	Christiansen-Cain	SATB	OD
Krone Chorus Album for Mixed Voices	Krones	SATB	BEL
Let There Be Song!	Siegmeister-Ehret	SSA	BOU
Madrigals and A Cappella Choruses	Cain	SATB	SCHM
Master Choruses	Ross-Smallman-Matthew	SATB	OD
Music For Moderns	Stickles	SATB	EHM
Negro Spirituals and Folk Songs	Hairston-Wilson	SATB	BOU
Old and New Christmas Carols	Pitcher	SATB	GSCH
Old and New Christmas Carols	Pitcher	SSA	GSCH
The Oxford Book of Carols	Dearmer-Williams-Shaw	SATB	OX
The Oxford SAB Song Book	Jacques	SAB	OX
Prentice-Hall Choral Series: Bks. 1–4	Wilson-Ehret-Glarum	SATB	PREN
Relax and Harmonize	Coward	TB, TTB, TBB	BM
Rounds and Canons	Wilson	SATB	SCHM
Sacred Choral Music	Pitcher	SAB	BM
Salute to Music	Ehret-Wilson	SAB	BOOS
Schirmer's Favorite Four-Part A Cappella Choruses		SATB	GSCH
Select A Cappella Choruses	Cain	SATB	SCHM
Selected Songs for Men	Christiansen-Wycisk	TTBB	AUG
Sing, Girls, Sing!	Andersen	SSA	SCHM
Sing, Men, Sing!	Andersen	TTB	SCHM
Sing We Noel!	Stone	SAB	PRO
Sing Ye!	Cookson	TTBB	FITZ
Singable Songs for Male Voices	Grant	TTBB	SCHM
Sixteen Chorales	Bach	SATB	GSCH
Songfest	Simeone	SATB	SHAW
Songs for the Chorus	SPEBSQSA	TTBB	SP
Sugar and Spice	Ades	SSA	SHAW
Teen Trios	Ehret-Gardner	SAB	STA
Three In Song	Ehret-Gardner	SSA	STA
The Three-Way Chorister	Gardner	SA, SAT, SATB	STA
Treble Clef Song Series	Overby	SSA	AUG

TITLE	COMPOSER-ARRANGER	PARTS	PUBLISHER
Tunes for Three or Four	Gardner	SAT, SATB	STA
Tunes for Two or Three	Gardner	2-3-pt.	STA
Twelve Compositions by Twelve Composers	Krone	SA	BEL
Twelve Moravian Chorales	Antes	SATB	BOOS
Twenty Sea Shanties	Hugill-Clements	U, parts	OX
The Two-Way Chorister (treble)	Gardner	2-3-pts.	STA
The Young Choralier (folk)	Gardner	SAATB, SAAT	STA

Madrigals

TITLE	COMPOSER-ARRANGER	PARTS	PUBLISHER
Adieu, Sweet Amaryllis	Wilbye		ECS
Ah, Look Upon These Eyes	Palestrina	SSA	GRAY
All Creatures Now	Bennett	SSATB	ST
April Is in My Mistress' Face	Morley		ECS
Ave Verum Corpus	Byrd		ECS
Awake Sweet Love	Dowland	SATB	EMB
Begone Dull Care	Jacob		MILL
Cease Sorrows, Now	Weelkes	SSA	ECS
Come Again, Sweet Days	Dowland	SATB	GRAY
Come, Let's Be Merry	Traditional		BOOS
Come to Me Grief Forever	Byrd	SSATB	ST
Come Tune Your Voice	Gastoldi-Stanton		JF
Dainty Fine Sweet Nymph	Morley	SSATB	ECS
Dancing and Springing	Hassler	SSATB	CF
Fair Maid Thy Loveliness	Hassler		EMB
Fair Phyllis I Saw	Farmer		GAL
Fine Knacks for Ladies	Dowland	SATB	GRAY
Fire and Lightning from Heav'n	Morley	SS, TT	OX
Fire, Fire My Heart	Morley	SSATB	GSCH
Flora, Wilt Thou Torment Me?	Morley	TT	OX
Flow My Tears	Dowland	SB, TB	OX
A Galliard	Staden	SATB	CF
Good-day, Sweetheart	Lassus	SATB	OD
Go Ye My Canzonets	Morley	SS	OD
Hard By a Fountain	Waelrant	SATB	GRAY
Hark All Ye Lovely Saints	Weelkes		ECS
The Holly and the Ivy	Boughton		GSCH
I Behold the Streamlet Run	Costeley	SATB	K
I Go Before My Charmer	Morley	SA	ECS
I Love My Love	Holst		GSCH
Il Bianco E Dolce Digno	Arcadelt	SATB	K
In the Merry Month of May	Wilson	SATB	OD
In These Delightful Pleasant Groves	Purcell	SATB	WIT

Title	Composer-Arranger	Parts	Publisher
Innsbruch, I Now Must Leave Thee	Isaac	SATB	CF
Invitation to Madrigals (20)	Dart	SATB	GAL
It Was the Frog in the Well	Ravenscroft	SATB	OX
Lost Is My Quiet Forever	Purcell	SA	ECS
Love Learns by Laughing	Morley	SSA	ST
Love Me Truly	Lefevre	SATB	K
Lullaby, My Sweet Little Baby	Byrd		GAL
Matona, Lovely Maiden	Lassus	SATB	GRAY
My Bonnie Lass She Smileth	German		GRAY
My Heart Doth Beg You'll Not Forget	Lassus	SATB	ECS
The Nightingale	Weelkes	SSA	ECS
Now Is the Month of Maying	Morley	SATTB	OD
Now Let Us Lift Our Youthful Voices	Hassler		CF
O Care, Thou Wilt Despatch Me	Weelkes	SSATB	ST
O Eyes of My Beloved	Lassus	SATB	ECS
O Lonely Night	Praetorius	SSA	GRAY
On the Banks of the Tebro	Palestrina	SATB	GSCH
Rest Sweet Nymph	Pilkington	SATB	ST
She Is So Dear	Praetorius	SATB	OD
Shoot, False Love, I Care Not	Morley		ECS
The Silver Swan	Gibbons	SSATB	GRAY
Since First I Saw Your Face	Ford	SATB	WIT
Since My Tears and Lamenting	Morley		CF
Sing a Merry Madrigal	Sullivan-Treharne		BM
Sing, Sing a Song for Me	Vecchi		BOU
Sing We and Chant It	Morley	SSATB	ECS
Some Men Desire Spouses	Weelkes	SSA	ST
So Well I Know Who's Happy	Vecchi	SATB	ECS
Stay, Time Awhile Thy Flying	Dowland	SATB	OX
Student Song	Schein	SSATB	CF
Sweet Day	Vaughan-Williams		MILL
There Were Three Ravens	Ravenscroft	SATB	OX
Though Your Strangeness	Jones	SA, TB	OX
To Shorten Winter's Sadness	Weelkes	SSATB	ST
To Woodland Glades I Must Fare	Tessoer	SATB	ECS
Weep, O Mine Eyes	Bennet		TP
Weep You No More, Sad Fountains	Dowland	SATB	HF
Welcome, Sweet Pleasure	Weelkes	SSA	OD
Welcome, Sweet Pleasure	Weelkes	SSATB	GSCH
When Allen-A-Dale Went A-Hunting	DePearsall		TP
When Shall My Sorrowful Sighing?	Tallis	SATB	OX

Title	Composer-Arranger	Parts	Publisher
Whither Runneth My Sweetheart	Bartlet	SA, TB	WIT
The Willow Song	Williams		MILL
With Drooping Wings	Purcell		ECS
With Love My Heart Is Ringing	Hassler	SATB	CF

Choral Music with Instrumental Accompaniment[2]

Title	Composer-Arranger	Parts	B–O	Publisher
An Abraham Lincoln Song	Damrosch	SATB	B–O	MPH
All Glory Laud and Honor	Teschner	SSA, SATB	B–O	HF
All Out America	Cailliet-Krone	SATB, SSA, SA	B	NK
America	Moore	SATB	B	MILL
America the Beautiful	Ward-Wilson-Grasso	SATB, SAB	B–O	SCHM
America, Our Heritage	Steele-Ades	SATB	B–O	EMB
American Panorama	Williams	SATB	B	NK
American Thanksgiving	Yoder	SATB	B	NK
Arioso Cantabile	Bach-Lester	SATB	O	MPH
An Autumn Day in an 18th Century Village	Handel	2-pt.	piano, recorders, strings, flutes, oboes	OX
Battle Hymn of the Republic	Wilhousky	SATB	B–O	EMB
Battle Hymn of the Republic	Waring (ed.)	SATB, TTBB	B–O	SHAW
Born To Be Free	Williams	SATB	B	NK
Canticle of Praise	Neander	SSA, SAB, SATB	O	MILL
Children's Prayer	Humperdinck-Johnson	SATB	B	EMB
Choral Procession	Kountz	SATB, SAB, SSA	B	MPH
Christmas Fantasy	Verrall	SATB	B	EMB
The Christmas Story	Yoder	SATB	B	NK
Come if You Dare, from *King Arthur*	Purcell	SATB	B	BOOS
The Crusaders Overture	Buchtel	SATB	B	NK
The Desert Song	Romberg-MacLean		B–O	MPH

[2] (B = Band; O = Orchestra)

Title	Composer-Arranger	Parts	B–O	Publisher
Dry Bones	Yoder	SATB	B	NK
Ever Onward	Williams	SATB	B	NK
Father of All	R. Dvorak	SATB	B–O	NK
Festival Finale	Maddy	SATB	B–O	NK
Festival Prelude	Frank	SATB	trumpet trio	SCHM
Festival Song of Praise	Mendelssohn-Harris	SATB	O	EMB
Forever Thy Word	Whear	SATB	B–O	EMB
Freedom	Quilter	SATB	B–O	BOOS
From Sea to Shining Sea	Whitney	SATB	B–O	MPH
Glory and Honor	Rachmaninoff-Houseknecht	SATB	B	NK
God of All Nations	Leisring-Houseknecht	SATB	B	NK
God of Our Fathers	Warren-Johnson	SATB	B	EMB
Hail Bright Abode	Wagner	SATB	O	FITZ
Hallelujah Chorus, *Messiah*	Handel	SATB	O	JF
Hallelujah Chorus, *Mt. of Olives*	Beethoven	SATB	O	JF
Holy, Holy, Holy	Liedzen	SATB	B	BOU
Honor and Glory	Bergh	SATB	B–O	MPH
How Lovely Are the Messengers	Mendelssohn	SATB	O	JF
Hymn of Freedom	Brahms-Tolmage	SATB	B	EMB
Hymn of Praise	Mozart-Tolmage	SATB	B	EMB
Hymnus	Lillya	SATB	B–O	BOU
Inland Sea	Williams	SATB	B–O	NK
Jesu, Joy of Man's Desiring	Bach-Wilson	SATB	O	SUMB
Joshua	Yoder	SATB	B	NK
Land of Hope and Glory	Elgar-Luckhardt	SATB SSA, SA, SATB	B	BOOS
Lift Up Your Heads	Coleridge-Taylor	SATB	B	EMB
Mannin Veem	Haydn	SATB	B	BOOS
March of Freedom	Myrow	SATB	B–O	SO
May the Good Lord Bless and Keep You	Wilson	SATB, SSA, TTBB	B–O	EMB
A Mighty Fortress	Luther	SSA, TTBB, SATB	B–O	BOOS
A Mighty Fortress Is Our God	Bach-Damrosch	SATB	B–O	MPH
My Own America	Wrubel-Isaac	SATB	B–O	EMB

Title	Composer-Arranger	Parts	B–O	Publisher
Nation's Creed	Williams	SATB	B	SCHM
A Nation's Prayer (Panis Angelicus)	Franck	SATB, SSA, TTBB	B–O	EMB
No Man Is An Island	Clarke	SATB	B	EMB
Now Let All Sing	Kirk	SATB	piano, trumpets, trombone, tympani	SHAW
Now Thank We All Our God	Cruger-Cailliet	SSA, SATB	B–O	BOOS
O Brother Man!	Ringwald-Ades	SATB	B	EMB
O Come All Ye Faithful	Baldwin	SATB, TTBB	O	JF
Ode to America	Canterbury	SATB	B–O	FITZ
Ode to Democracy	Kleinsinger	SATB with solo baritone	B	EMB
One World	O'Hara	SATB	B	EMB
Onward Christian Soldiers	Simeone	SATB, TTBB	B–O	SHAW
Onward Ye Peoples!	Sibelius	SSA, SA, TTBB, SATB	O	GAL
Our Beloved Land	Warren	SATB	O	TP
Pilgrim's Chorus from *Tannhauser*	Wagner-Aliferis-Sperry	SATB	B	SCHM
Praise Ye The Father	Gounod	SATB	O	JF
Praise Ye The Lord of Hosts	Saint-Saens-Jurey	SA, SAB, SSA, SATB	O	MILL
Prayer for the United Nations	Moore	SATB	O	GRAY
Psalm 150	Franck	SSAA, TTBB, SATB	O	JF
Rose Marie	Friml-MacLean	SATB	B–O	EMB
Salute to America	Youse	SATB	B–O	EMB
Salvation Is Created & Awake	Tschesnokoff-Wagner-Houseknecht	SATB	B	NK
Selection from Naughty Marietta	Herbert-MacLean		B–O	MPH
The Singers	Longfellow-York	SATB	B–O	MPH
A Song of Music	Hindemith	SSA	O	AMP
Steamboat Comin'	Cornwell-Myers	SATB	B	EMB
Stouthearted Men	Romberg	SATB, TTBB, SSA	B	EMB
Strong Is Thy Strength	Bach-Cailliet	SATB, SSA	B	BEL

Title	Composer-Arranger	Parts	B–O	Publisher
Sweet Spirit, Comfort Me	Bratton	SATB	O	AMP
Testament of Nations	Williams	SATB	B	SCHM
Thanks Be to Thee	Handel-Houseknecht	SATB	B	NK
They Call It America	Grant-Isaac	SATB	B–O	EMB
This Day We Honor	Williams	SATB	B	NK
Three Christmas Chorales	Yoder	SATB	B	NK
To Music	Davenport-Walters	SATB	B	EMB
To Music	Schubert-Wilson	SATB, SAB, SSA	strings	SCHM
Toyland! Toyland!	Herbert-Jurey	SSA, SA, SATB	O	MILL
Tribute to Romberg	Beeler-Watson	SATB	B–O	EMB
Victor Herbert Favorites	Herbert-Lake	SATB, TTBB	B–O	EMB
Voice of Freedom	Rubinstein-Cailliet	SSA, SATB, TTBB	B–O	BOOS

OPERETTAS

Junior High School

Title	Composer-Arranger	Publisher
Annie Laurie	Lawrence-Lee	MPH
The Band Wagon	Clark-Penn	EMB
The Belle of the West	George	EMB
Buccaneers	Steckel-Williams	MPH
The Familiar Stranger	Lawrence-Lee	MPH
Galloping Ghost	Wilson	EMB
The Geografoof	Gorney	EMB
Gondoliers, Iolanthe, Mikado, Patience, Trial By Jury (abridged)	Gilbert & Sullivan	SUMB
Hansel and Gretel	Humperdinck-Elsmith	SUMB
The Hither and Thither of Danny Dither	North	EMB
Hold That Curtain	Gregory & Gurski	EMB
The Magic Castle	Benotzky	EMB
On the Range	Farr	EMB
Pinafore	Gilbert & Sullivan—Grayson	EMB
Pirates of Penzance	Gilbert & Sullivan—Stevens	EMB
Polished Pebbles	Carrington	EMB
Roaring Camp	Lawrence-Lee	MPH
Sliding Down the Moon	House	HOFF
Sourwood Mountain	Underwood-Perry	SUMB
Young Handel of Hanover	Boswell-Clark	MPH

Senior High School

Title	Composer-Arranger	Publisher
Babes in Toyland (rev. ed.)	Herbert-Wilson	MPH
The Bartered Bride	Smetana-Bartusek	MPH
Bastien and Bastienna	Mozart	EBM
Beautiful Dreamer	Foster-Grey	EMB
Chimes of Normandy	Planquette-Cornwall	EMB
Chonita	Liszt-Wilson	EMB
The Emperor's New Clothes	Simeone	SHAW
Forest Prince	Tschaikowsky-Wilson	EMB
The Fortune Teller (rev. ed.)	Herbert-Wilson	MPH
Frantic Physician	Gounod	SB
The Gondoliers	Gilbert & Sullivan-Treharne	EMB
Green Cheese	Wilson	EMB
Hi-Fi Follies (TV satire)	Don Wilson	MPH
It's a Small War	Blake-Owen-Tysh	OX
Joys of Youth	Fall	EBM
The Lantern Marriage	Offenbach-Kahn	EBM
The Lowland Sea	Wilder-Sundgaard	GSCH
Martha	Von Flotow	SUMB
Magic Flute	Mozart-Elsmith	EMB
Masquerade in Vienna (Die Fledermaus adapt.)	Strauss-House	EMB
The Mighty Casey	Schuman-Gury	GSCH
The Mikado	Gilbert & Sullivan	EMB
Pinafore	Gilbert & Sullivan	EMB
Pirates of Penzance	Gilbert & Sullivan	EMB
The Prince of Pilsen (rev. ed.)	Luders-Pixley-Bradley-Wilson	MPH
Purple Towers	Wilson	EMB
Robin and Marion	Milhaud	EBM
Robin Hood	DeKoven-Wilson	EBM
Rosamunde	Schubert	SB
Shreds and Patches	Gilbert & Sullivan-Wilson	EMB
The Singing Freshmen	Bennett	BM
Smoky Mountain	Hunkins	EMB
Springtime	Reinhardt-Steiner	EMB
Stars and Stripes Forever	Sousa-Grey	EMB
The Stingiest Man in Town (Scrooge)	Spielman-Torre-Wilson	MPH
Sunday Excursion	Wilder	GSCH
The Tall Trees (lumberjack)	Dodge	EMB
Tune In	Wilson	EMB
Up On Old Smoky	Lorenz	EMB
A Waltz Dream	Strauss-Wilson	EMB
Words and Music	Lee	EMB

INSTRUMENTAL

Instrumental music should be secured on approval, for examination. In addition to the collections listed, catalogs for other instrumental music may be secured from the music publishers listed on p. 585. Lists of materials are also suggested from sources on p. 573. Key to publishers is on p. 585.

Collections of Band Methods and Materials

Title	Composer-Arranger	Publisher
Adventures in Clarinet Playing, Bks. 1 & 2	Van Bodegraven	STA
The Band Booster	Kinyon	MPH
Band Ensemble Folio "For Young Bands"	Kinyon	BEL
The Band in Formation	Beeler	EBM
Band Fundamentals in Easy Steps	Taylor	MILL
Band Method	Skornicka-Bergeim	BOOS
The Band Reader	Freeman-Whitney	EHM
Belwin Band Builder	Douglas-Weber	BEL
Belwin Elementary Band Method	Weber-Hovey	BEL
Bennet Band Book, 4 vols.	Bennet	FILL
The Breeze Easy Series of Separate Methods	Kinyon	MPH
Bridging the Gap	Cheyette-Roberts	CF
Concert Band Varieties	Buchtel	MILL
Concert Folio for Younger Bands	Schoenfeld	MPH
Daily Drills	Yoder	NK
Dixieland on Parade	Ward	GSCH
Easy Steps to Band	Taylor	MILL
Ensemble Band Method	Smith-Yoder-Bachman	NK
Exercises for Ensemble Drill	Fussell	SCHM
First Adventures in Band	Weber	BEL
First Class Band Folio	Kinyon	MPH
First Division Band Course	Weber	BEL
First Performance Book for Band	Peters-Yoder	NK
First Program Music for Beginning Bands	Prescott-Phillips	PAS
The Gridiron March Book	Weeks	MPH
Hi-Fi Band Book	Barnard	PAS
Instrumental Course	Skornicka	BOOS
Master Method for Band	Peters-Yoder	NK
Our Band Class Book	Herfurth-Stuart	CF
Our First Band Folio	Cheyette	RU
Play Away	Beeler	GSCH
Round-The-World Band Book	Yoder	EBM
Rubank Elementary Band Course	Van Deusen *et al.*	RU
Scale Etudes	McLeod-Staska	SCHM
Symphonic Themes for Band	Hiden	MPH
Unique Chorales	Prescott	PAS

Collections of String Methods and Materials

Title	Composer-Arranger	Publisher
Academic Album	Pochon	CF
Academic String Orchestra Series		CF
The Aeolian String Ensemble Method	Dasch-Bennet	FITZ
Chamber Music Album	Pochon	CF
Concert Repertoire	Ginsburgh	NK
Easy Steps to the Orchestra, Bk. 1	Keller-Taylor	MILL
Ensemble Album	Pochon	CF
Famous Composers String Ensemble, Folio, vol. 1	Zamecnik	SF
First String Ensemble Album	Johnson	CF
Four Elizabethan Madrigals	Davis-Weems	GSCH
From Third to First (beginning violin method)	Angis	CF
Gamble's Class Method for Strings	Fischel-Bennett	MPH
Graded Masterworks for Strings	Fischel-Wilson	MPH
Harms String Americana	Sopkin	MPH
Introduction to String Quartets	Clarke	BM
Junior Masterworks for Strings	Fischel-Wilson	MPH
Merle Isaac String Class Method	Isaac	COLE
Muller-Rusch String Method, Bks. 1, 2, 3	Muller-Rusch	NK
Music For String Instruments	Rush	BOOS
Palmer House Ensemble Collection	Ginsburgh	NK
Rhythm Master Method Series	Lesinsky	MPH
String Music of the Baroque Era	Clarke	BM
Strings From the Start	Jones-Dasch-Krone	CF
Symphonic String Course	Maddy	NK
A Tune a Day	Herfurth	BM
Twenty-Five Christmas Carols	Clarke	BM
University String Orchestra Album	Stoessel	CF
Victor Herbert String Americana	Campbell-Watson	MPH
Waller String Method, Bks. 1, 2	Waller	NK

Orchestra Folios

Title	Composer-Arranger	Publisher
Advancement Orchestra Folio	Isaac	CF
All Season Orchestra Folio	Barnard-Floyd	SCHM
At the Court of Maria Theresa	Gluck-Kahn	GSCH
The Belwin Orchestra Builder	Muller-Weber	BEL
Cardinal Orchestra Folio	Wilson	MPH
Concert Hall	Isaac	EMB
Curtain Raiser	Gordon	EBM

Title	Composer-Arranger	Publisher
Distinguished Music for School Orchestras	Taylor	GSCH
Easy Steps to the Orchestra, Bk. 2	Keller-Taylor	MILL
Encore Orchestra Folio	Herfurth	EMB
Festival Orchestra Book	Wilson	MPH
Junior Classics for Orchestra	Wilson	MPH
Lerner & Loewe Orchestra Folio	Hayman	CHAP
The Lockhart Orchestra Class Method	Lockhart	MPH
Merle Isaac Orchestra Folio	Isaac	EMB
Mills Concertmaster Orchestra Album	Weaver-Spangler-Lindsay	MILL
Music Educator's Elementary Orchestra Album	Skornicka-Koebner	MILL
Music for Young Orchestras	Herfurth	CF
Orchestra Is Fun	Herfurth	EMB
Orchestra Performance No. 1 & 2	Muller-Rusch	NK
Orchestral Transcriptions	Weaver	MILL
Our Easy Orchestra Folio	Herfurth	CF
Our Famous Favorites for Orchestra	Herfurth	CF
Our Junior Symphony Orchestra Folio	Watters	EMB
Our Own Orchestra Folio	Watters	CF
Our School Orchestra Folio	Isaac	EMB
Second Orchestra Program Album	Jurey	MILL
Symphonic Themes	Hiden	MPH
Third Orchestra Program Album	Jurey	MILL
Tuning Method for Orchestra	Righter-Dasch	MPH
West Side Story Selection for Orchestra	Bernstein-Mason	GSCH
The Williams' Orchestra Series	Rowley	MILL

RECREATIONAL MUSIC MATERIALS

Instrumental

A wide selection of instrumental materials is available for all the simple instruments. Charts and slides designed by the teacher and made in the school have proven to be very useful aids, particularly at the start of instruction. The list which follows is merely suggestive and in most instances represents only a small percentage of the instructional material and compositions suitable for use in the junior and senior high schools.

Title	Author-Composer	Publisher
Autoharp:		
Autoharp Practice Cards		NAS
Golden Autoharp Harmonies	Spaeth	NAS
Harmony Fun with the Autoharp	Krone	NK

TITLE	AUTHOR-COMPOSER	PUBLISHER
Sing 'n Strum (Autoharp chords)	Waldrop	WJS
A Teacher's Guide for the Golden Autoharp	Watters	NAS
Banjo:		
The Five-String Banjo American Folk Styles	Seeger	HAR
Drums:		
Drums, Tom-Toms and Rattles	Mason	A. S. BARNES
Guitar:		
EZ Method for Guitar		WJS
The Active Spanish Guitarist (2 vols.)	Sweetland	PER
Guitar Method and Song Folio	White	PER
Spanish Guitar Course (4 vols.)	Sweetland	PER
Harmonica:		
Harmonica Favorites for Chromatics		MILL
Instructor for the Harmonica	Perry	HOH
Modern Harmony for Harmonica	Perry	BOOS
Harmolin:		
Harmony Fun with the Harmolin	Krones	NK
Melodica:		
Teacher's Guide and Beginners Lesson Plan for the Hohner Soprano Melodica		HOH
Ocarina:		
The Ocarina Book	Shoemaker	GRETCH
Piano:		
The Adult Explorer	Ahearn-Blake-Burrows	WILL
House of Music Piano Method	Mattos	NK
The Oxford Piano Course	Haake-McConathy-Schelling	OX
Young America at the Piano	Burrows-Ahearn	SUMB

Recorder:

Sources for recorder music—Catalogs available from Hargail Music Press, C. F. Peters, Oxford U. Press, Peripole, Witmark, E. B. Marks, Mills Music.

Title	Author-Composer	Publisher
Dance Movements by Old Masters (treble, tenor)	Handel, Purcell	SCHO
Dexterity Exercises and Dances for Recorders	G. Rooda	HAR
800 Years of Music for Recorders (Bks. 1 & 2)	Hess (ed.)	AMP
Elizabethan Dances and Ayres (descant)	Hunt	SCHO
Melody Method for the Recorder	Melody Flute Co.	
Music of the Hebrew People—Israeli and Jewish Songs	Newman (arr.)	HAR
The New Recorder Tutor, Bks. 1 & 2	Goodyear	MILL
One and All, Harmonica Method for Recorders	Richardson	WIT
A Practical Method for the Recorder	Hunt & Donnington	CF
A Practice Book for the Treble Recorder	Rowland-Jones	OX
School Recorder Book, Bks. 1 & 2	Priestly & Fowler	HAR

Pipes:

Charts for Pipe Making, Cabrera, Available from Aranka Balint, Pipers', 94 Hamilton Place, New York, N.Y., 10031.

Title	Author-Composer	Publisher
First Book of Tunes for Pipes (3-, 4-, 5-parts)	Holst	SCHU
Graded Tunes for Treble Pipes (8 leaflets)	Blockridge	SCHU
A Tutor for Bamboo Pipes for Alto and Tenor	James	SCHU
Volkslied and This Old Man, and Shepherd's Lullaby	James	SCHU

Song Flute:

Title	Author-Composer	Publisher
Game of Music Building, Bk. II	Owen	SFL
Songs from Everywhere (tunes arr. for Song Flute)	Owen	SFL
Tonette Tunes and Techniques (beginning)	Davis	RU
You Can Play (Song Flute)	Sterrett-Wilkinson	CF

Ukulele:

Title	Author-Composer	Publisher
EZ Method for Ukulele		WJS
Five Minute Guaranteed Ukulele Course		COLE
Songs and Solos for the Ukulele	Smeck	HA
Ukulele Pleasures	Petz	BEL

TITLE	COMPOSER-ARRANGER	PUBLISHER
Combinations of Instruments:		
Ten Minute Self-Instruction for Tonette, Ocarina, Harmonica and Ukulele, W.D. Pamphlet #28–16, Government Printing Office, Washington, D.C.		
Easy Steps for Melody Instruments (Flutophone, Song Flute, Tonette, Ocarina)	Taylor	MILL
Melody Method for Pre-Instruments (Song Flute, Tonette, Ocarina, Fife, Recorder)	Perkins	CF
My Musical Instrument Book	Boyter	CF
O, Say Can You Hear? (5 vols.)	House	MILL
You Can Play (Tunes for Tonette, Song Flute, Ukulele, Autoharp, separately or together)	Sterrett-Wilkinson	CF

Vocal

Song Collections

TITLE	COMPOSER-ARRANGER	PUBLISHER
America Sings	Carmer	KNOPF
Barber Shop Classics, Vols. 1 & 2	Spaeth	REM
Best Loved Hymns		SCHM
Botsford Collection of Folk Songs (3 vols.)		GSCH
Christmas Carols, Customs, Legends		SCHM
Descants on Favorite Hymns		SCHM
Dett Collection of Negro Spirituals (4 vols.)		SCHM
A Festival of Freedom (patriotic songs–tableau, story)		NRA
A Fireside Book of Favorite American Songs	Boni & Lloyd (eds.)	S&S
A Fireside Book of Folk Songs	Boni & Lloyd (eds.)	S&S
Forty Approaches to Informal Singing		NRA
Great Hymns with Descants		SCHM
Joyous Carols (2-part)	Whitner	CF
Lift Every Voice	Siegmeister-Wheeler	CF
More Barber Shop Classics	Spaeth	REM
Noels		SCHM
101 Best Loved Songs	Moorehead	POCKET BKS
O Sing Me Your Song, O		JT
Parade and Afterglow of Barbershop Harmonies		SCHM

Title	Composer-Arranger	Publisher
Singing America (North, South & Central American songs)		NRA
Stories of the Christmas Carols		NRA
Tumbalalaika	Schwartz & Kevess	HAR
Uncommon Christmas Carols		SCHM
Work and Sing, Amigos Cantando, Good Fellowship Songs, Sing a Tune, Happy Meetings, Open Road Song Book, Pagoda, Pocket Songs, Swiss Alpine Songs, A Little Carol Book, Songs for Harvest and Thanksgiving Festivals, and many others. Send for list of booklets.		CRS

Vocal and Instrumental

Songs with Simple Instrumental Accompaniment

Title	Composer-Arranger	Publisher
Autoharp Accompaniments to Old Favorite Songs	Blair	SUMB
Jolly Come Sing and Play	Rowan-Simon	CF
Sing and Strum	Snyder	MILL
Sing or Play Sight Reading Fun (with Symphonet, Flutophone, Tonette, Song Flute)	Vandre	MILL
Songs of the Hills and Plains	Wilson	SCHM
Songs To Sing with Recreational Instruments	Cheyette & Renna	PER

Games, Dances, Mixers

Title	Composer-Arranger	Publisher
Action Songs (P 89)		NRA
The Christmas Book		NRA
Dramatized Ballads	Tobitt & White	DUTTON
A Few References on Singing Games (M.P. #647)		NRA
Handy Folk Dance Book, Handy Party Book, Handy Square Dance Book		CRS
Musical Mixers and Simple Square Dances		NRA
Sing and Dance		SCHM
Skip To My Lou (17 singing games)		GS
Songs of the Hills and Plains		SCHM
Swing Your Partner (SATB with dancers)	Pitcher	HF
Yours for a Song		JT

SOURCES OF LISTS OF MATERIALS

Band Music Guide, The Instrumentalist, 1418 Lake St., Evanston, Ill.
Catalogs from music publishers.
Conducting Choral Music, Robert L. Garretson, Allyn and Bacon, 1965 (lists of choral and octavo publications, choral collections, extended choral works).
E.M.B. Guide, Educational Music Bureau.
Equipment, Supplies and Teaching Aids, EMB.
Film Guide for Music Educators, Donald Shetler, MENC, 1961.
Folk Music, Library of Congress, Washington, D.C., 1959 (listing of folk songs from Archives).
The Instrumentalist (lists of materials and excellent coverage of new materials).
Lists and Suggestions for Piano Teaching, & *Supplement I*, Polly Gibbs, Baton Rouge, La., 1961 (mimeographed, graded materials).
Lists of Songs and Songs with Descants for Boys, M.P. #172, National Recreational Ass'n.
Materials for Miscellaneous Instrumental Ensembles, MENC (listings of music for unusual combinations).
Music Education Materials, MENC, 1959 (a selected bibliography of books, choral and instrumental materials, audiovisual aids, music theory texts, etc.).
Music Instruments, The Instrumentalist.
The Opera Directory, London, John Calder (also available from Sterling Publishing House, New York, 1961) list of contemporary operas.
People and Music, McGehee-Nelson, Allyn and Bacon, 1963 (lists of songs, books, and recordings at ends of chapters).
Reviews and lists of materials in state music education periodicals.
Reviews of new materials, *Music Educators Journals*, MENC.
Selective Music Lists, NIMAC, MENC, 1963 (instrumental and vocal solos and ensembles).
"The Show Band," Rayburn Wright, *The Instrumentalist.*

MUSIC SERIES TEXTS FOR ELEMENTARY GRADES

Allyn and Bacon, Inc., *This Is Music*, Books 1–6, Sur, McCall, Tolbert, Fisher, Pitcher, DuBois, Nye, 1961–1962.
American Book Company, *Music for Young Americans*, Books 1–6, Berg, Burns, Hooley, Pace, Wolverton, 1959–1960.
Follett Publishing Company, *Together We Sing*, Books 1–6 (rev.), Wolfe, Krone, Fullerton, 1959–1960.
Ginn & Co., *The Magic of Music*, Books 1–6, Watters, Wersen, Hartshorn, McMillan, Gallup, Beckman, 1965.
Prentice-Hall, Inc., *Growing with Music*, Books 1–6, Wilson, Ehret, Snyder, Hermann, Renna, 1963.
Silver Burdett, *Making Music Your Own*, Books 1–6, Landeck, Crook, Youngberg, Luening, 1964.

Michigan State University.

CHAPTER

24

Audiovisual Material and Equipment Sources

DISPLAY MATERIALS

Chalkboard Supplies

Time-Saving Specialities, 2922 Bryant Ave., S. Minneapolis, Minn. Blackboard Marking Set, Chalkboard ink, cleaning solvent.
Lea Audio-Visual Service, 182 Audley Dr., Sun Prairie, Wis. Styx, adhesive wax.

Charts

C. G. Conn, Ltd., Elkhart, Indiana. Variety of instrument charts, Music Instrument clip Sheet, Music Educational Aids, and Music Masters.
Educational Music Bureau, Inc., 434 South Wabash Ave., Cleveland 3, Ohio. Visual-demonstration boards.
Music-Graph, The Ohio Flock-Cote Co., 5713 Euclid Ave., Cleveland 3, Ohio. Visual-demonstration boards.
J. W. Pepper and Sons, Inc., 1423 Vine St., Philadelphia 2, Pa.

Display Surfaces

Demco Library Supplies, 2120 Fordemn Ave., Madison 4, Wis. Pegboards for wall, floor, or pedestal; hardware.
Follett Publishing Co., 1010 W. Washington Blvd., Chicago 7, Ill. Kling-Tite Paper.
Holt, Rinehart and Winston, Inc., Publishers, 383 Madison Ave., New York, N.Y. Coheragraph.
Match-a-Tach, 26 E. Pearson St., Chicago 11, Ill. Magnetic display boards, with letters, numbers, objects.
Oravisual Co., Inc., 321 15th Street, St. Petersburg, Fla. Oravisual Folding Flannel Board and Display Tripod.

Fine Art Reproductions

Artext Prints, Inc., Westport, Conn.

Flat Pictures

Art Institute of Chicago, Museum Store, Michigan Ave. and Adams St., Chicago, Ill. Also, color slides, postcards, reproductions, price lists available on request.
Colonial Art Co., 1336-8 N.W. First St., Oklahoma City 4, Okla.
C. G. Conn, Ltd., Elkhart, Ind. Music Instrument Clip Sheet, Music Educational Aids, Music and the Masters.
Educational Music Bureau, Inc., 434 Wabash Ave., Chicago, Ill.
Informative Classroom Picture Publishers, 31 Ottawa Ave., N.W., Grand Rapids, Mich., 49502.
Instructor Magazine, Normal Park, Dansville, N.Y.
Instrumentalist, The, 1418 Lake St., Evanston, Ill.
Keyboard, Jr. Magazine, 1346 Chapel St., New Haven 11, Conn.
Metropolitan Museum of Art, Fifth Ave. at 82nd St., New York, N.Y.
Music Educators Journal, 1201 Sixteenth St., N.W., Washington, D.C., 20036.
National Geographic Magazine, 16th St. and M Street, Washington, D.C.
Picto-Chrome Publishing Co., 1428 V St., N.W., Washington, D.C.
Schmitt, Hall and McCreary, 527 Park Ave., Minneapolis, Minn., 55415.
Steinway Collections, 45-02 Ditmars Blvd., L.I. 5, N.Y.
Theodore Presser C., Bryn Mawr, Pa.
University Prints, Box 244, Cambridge 38, Mass. Fine Arts & Architecture *prints*, 5½ × 8 inches, 2½¢ in black & white, 5¢ in color.

Graphics

Dick Blick Co., Galesburg, Ill. Source of art supplies, papers, etc.
Chart-Pak, Inc., Lincoln Ave., Stanford, Conn. Self-adhering tapes and symbols.
Chettfield-Clarke Co., 24 Roberts St., Pasadena 3, Calif. Magnetic board.
Craftint Manufacturing Co., 1615 Collamer Ave., Cleveland 10, Ohio; La Salle Sign and Artist Supply Co., 8411-13 Linwood Ave., Detroit 6, Mich. Self-adhering color, *craft color*, tone, *craftone*, and letters, *craftype*, full line of art supplies.
Don Jer Products Co., 51-47 69th St., Woodside, Long Island, N.Y. Source of flocking material for flannelboards.
Florex, Inc., 815 Bates Street, Detroit, Mich. Flannel backing material, *Flock-Tite.*
Friendship Press, 475 Riverside Dr., New York, N.Y., 10027.
Upson Co., Cut-Out Letter Alphabet Division, Lockport, N.Y. Cut-out Letters 3½ to 8″ high (excellent for exhibits), special cut-out names or phrases.
Visual Specialties Co., 21 Sawmill River Rd., Detroit, Mich. Prepared feltboard materials and colored felt pieces.

Letters

Artype, Inc., 549 W. Randolph St., Chicago 6, Ill. Self-adhering letter, ARTYPE.
Glassoloid Corp. of America, 32 Wellington Ave., Clifton, N.J. Plastic lamination material and laminating presses. Also, laminating presses. Laminations processed in sizes up to 23″ × 50″ and 29″ × 39″.
Graforel, 77 Fifth Ave., New York, N.Y. Cork letters.
Hernard Manufacturing Co., 923 Old Nepperham Ave., Yonkers, N.Y.; Mitten's Display Letters, 345 Fifth Ave., Redlands, Calif. Plaster letters.
Hilary Co., 141 Hilary Circle, New Rochelle, N.Y.; Mitten's Display Letter Co., 345

Fifth Ave., Redlands, Calif.; Redikut Letter Co., South Prairie Ave., Hawthorne, Calif. Pasteboard letters.
Manhattan Wood Letter Co., 151 W. 18 Street, New York, N.Y.; New York Wood Letter Co., 18 Green Street, New York, N.Y. Wood letters.
Mutual Aids, Department 455, 1946 Hilihurst Ave., Los Angeles 27, Calif. Colored cardboard letters.
Poster Products, Inc., 3401 W. Division Street, Chicago 51, Ill.; Tablet and Ticket Co., 1021 W. Adams Street, Chicago 1, Ill. Gummed paper letters.
Redikut Letter Co., 185 N. Prairie Ave., Hawthorne, Calif. Cardboard letters.
W. L. Stensgaard & Assoc., 346 N. Justine Street, Chicago 7, Ill.; Sturgis Plastic Letters, Box 552, Sturgis, Mich. Plastic letters.
Tablet & Ticket Co., 1021 W. Adams St., Chicago, Ill. Source of stick-on type of letters, figures, etc.

Lettering Equipment

Keuffel and Esser Co., 5535 Woodward Ave., Detroit, Mich.; E. Kietzgen C., 2455 N. Sheffield Ave., Chicago, Ill. Payzant lettering pens.
Mark-Tex Corp., 161 Coolidge Ave., Englewood, N.J. Tech-pen for inking glass, metal, porcelain, paper, plastic, cloth, etc., in colors.

Posters

American Music Conference, 332 S. Michigan Ave., Chicago 4, Ill.
Carl Fischer, Inc., 62 Cooper Square, New York 3, N.Y. Rhythm notation posters; music symbol posters.
Cunard Line, 25 Broadway, New York, N.Y.
Pan American Airways, PO Box PAA, Jamaica, N.Y.

Sensitized Plastic Sheets

Charles Beseler Co., 219 S. 18 St., East Orange, N.J.
Ozalid Co., Johnson City, N.Y.
Technifax Corp., 195 Appleton St., Holyoke, Mass.

Transparencies

Charles Beseler Co., 219 South 10th Street, East Orange, N.J.
Robert J. Brady Co., 2355 M. St., N.W., Washington 7, D.C. Acetate ink.
ColorLure, Inc., 5745-47 S. Western Ave., Chicago, Ill. Color transparencies.
Ozalid Co., Johnson City, N.Y.; Technifax Corp., 195 Appleton Street, Holyoke, Mass. Overhead transparencies.

RECORDING AND LISTENING MATERIALS

Records

Instructor Magazine, Normal Park, Dansville, N.Y.
Spoken Arts Records, Inc., 95 Valley Road, New Rochelle, N.Y.

Recordings and Transcriptions

Allyn and Bacon, Inc., 150 Tremont St., Boston, Mass., 02111.
American Book Co., 55 Fifth Ave., New York, N.Y., 10003.
Max V. Bildersee, Box 1771, Albany 1, N.Y. Audio cardalog.
Columbia Records, Educational Dept., 799 Seventh Ave., New York, N.Y., 10019.
Educational Audio-Visual, Inc., 29 Marble Ave., Pleasantville, N.Y.
Folkway Records and Service Corp., 121 W. 47 St., New York, N.Y., 10036.
Follett Publishing Co., 1010 Washington Blvd., Chicago 7, Ill.
Ginn & Company, Statler Bldg., Boston 17, Mass.
Sam Goody, 235 W. 49 St., New York, N.Y., 10019.
Keyboard Jr. Magazines, 1346 Chapel Street, New Haven 11, Conn.
Materials For Learning, Inc., 1376 Coney Island Ave., Brooklyn, N.Y., 11230
The Metropolitan Opera Guild, Inc., 654 Madison Ave., New York, N.Y., 10021.
NBC Radio-Recording Division, RCA Bldg., Radio City, New York, N.Y.
Silver Burdett Co., Morristown, N.J., 07960.
Sound Book Press Society, Inc., 36 Garth Road, Scarsdale, N.Y., 10583.

Tape Recording Services and Libraries

Arizona State University, Central Arizona Film Cooperative, Tempe, Ariz.
Audiovisual Section, State Department of Education, 600 Mt. Pleasant Ave., Providence, R.I. (services limited to R.I.).
Audio-Visual Service, State Department of Education, Atlanta, Ga.
Brigham Young University, Bureau of Audio-Visual Communications, Provo, Utah.
Commonwealth of Virginia, Bureau of Teaching Materials, State Board of Education, Richmond 16, Va.
Cornell University, Roberts Hall, Radio and Television Service, Department of Extension, Teaching and Information, Ithaca, N.Y.
Division of Supervised Study, State University Station, Fargo, N.D.
Indiana University, Audio-Visual Center, Bloomington, Ind.
Kent State University, Audio-Visual Center, Kent, Ohio.
Massachusetts Department of Education, Office of Communications and Public Relations, 200 Newbury St., Boston 16, Mass.
Missouri Tapes for Teaching Program, Department of Audio-Visual Education, 7220 Waterman Ave., St. Louis 5, Mo.
National Education Assoc., Department of Audiovisual Instruction, 1201 Sixteenth St., N.W., Washington, D.C., 20036
New Jersey State Department of Education, Audio-Visual Bureau, Trenton, N.J.
Oklahoma A & M College, Audio-Visual Center, Stillwater, Okla.
Oregon School of the Air, Radio Station KOAC, General Extension Division, Oregon State System of Higher Education, Corvallis, Ore.
Pennsylvania State University, Audio-Visual Library, University Park, Penn.
Schwann, Long Playing Record, Catalog—A Guide to Monaural and Stereo Long Playing Records, 137 Newbury St., Boston 16, Mass.
South Dakota School of the Air, Tape Library, Radio Station KUSD, Vermillion, S.D.
Tapes for Teaching, Department of Education, Centennial Bldg., St. Paul 1, Minn. (service available only to Minn. schools).
Texas School of the Air and Tapes, Texas Education Agency, Austin, Tex.

University of Colorado, Bureau of AV Instruction, Boulder, Col.
University of Connecticut, Audio-Visual Center, Storrs, Conn.
University of Illinois, Audio-Visual Aids Service, Division of University Extension, Champaign, Ill.
University of Iowa, Bureau of Audio-Visual Instruction, Iowa City, Iowa.
University of Michigan, Audio-Visual Education Center, Frieze Bldg., 721 E. Huron, Ann Arbor, Mich.
University of Nebraska, Bureau of Audio-Visual Instruction, Lincoln, Neb.
University of New Hampshire, Audio-Visual Center, Durham, N.H.
University of North Carolina, Bureau of Visual Education, Extension Division, Chapel Hill, N.C.
University of Oklahoma, Educational Materials Services, Norman, Okla.
University of Utah, Audio-Visual Bureau, Extension Division, Salt Lake City, Utah.
University of Washington, The Film Center, Seattle 5, Wash.
University of Wyoming, Adult Education and Community Service, Laramie, Wyo.
Wisconsin School of the Air, Recording Service, Radio Hall, Madison, Wis.

Stereophonic Tapes

RCA Victor, 30 Rockefeller Plaza, New York, N.Y.
Revere-Wollensak, Division 3M Company, St. Paul 19, Minn.

Monophonic

RCA Victor, 30 Rockefeller Plaza, New York, N.Y.

Records

Spoken Arts Records Inc., 95 Valley Road, New Rochelle, N.Y.

FILMSTRIPS, SLIDES, AND TRANSPARENCIES

Symbol	
AMC	American Music Conference, 332 S. Michigan Ave., Chicago, Ill., 60604
BOW	Bowmar Records, 10515 Burbank Blvd., N. Hollywood, Calif., 91601
CATH	Cathedral Films, Inc., 2921 W. Alameda Ave., Burbank, Calif.
CMC	Children's Music Center, 2858 Pico Blvd., Los Angeles 6, Calif.
CONN	Conn Corp., Educational Services Dept., 1101 E. Beardsley Ave., Elkhart, Ind., 46514
EBF	Encyclopaedia Britannica Films, Inc., 1150 Wilmette Ave., Wilmette, Ill.
FRP	Friendship Press, 475 Riverside Drive, New York, N.Y., 10027
JAM	The Jam Handy Organization, 2821 E. Grand Blvd., Detroit, Mich., 48211
LYON	Lyons Bank Instrument Co., 223 W. Lake, Chicago, Ill., 60606
MET	Metropolitan Opera Guild, Inc., 654 Madison Ave., New York, N.Y., 10021

SCH	Scherl & Roth, Inc., 1729 Superior Ave., Cleveland, Ohio
SIMS	Sims Visual Aids Co., Quincy, Ill.
SVE	Society for Visual Education, Inc., 1345 Diversey Parkway, Chicago, Ill., 60614
UNEB	University of Nebraska, Bureau of Audio-Visual Instruction, Lincoln, Neb.
YAF	Young America Films, McGraw-Hill Book Co., Text-Film Dept., 330 W. 42nd St., New York, N.Y., 10018

MOTION PICTURE FILMS SOURCES

SYMBOL	
ACA	Academy Films, 800 N. Seward St., Hollywood, Calif.
AF	A. F. Films, Inc., 1600 Broadway, New York, N.Y.
AIA	American Institute of Architects, Inc., 1741 New York Ave., N.W., Washington, D.C., 20006
ALM	Almanac Films, Inc., 41 Union Square W., New York, N.Y., 10003.
AM	Allen-Moore, Inc., 7936 Santa Monica Blvd., Hollywood 46, Calif.
AMF	American Film Registry, 24 E. 8th St., Chicago, Ill., 60605
ART	Artists Films, Inc., 8 W. 45th St., New York, N.Y., 10017
ASSN. F.	Association Films, Inc., 347 Madison Ave., New York, N.Y., 10017
ATH	Athena Films, Inc., 165 W. 46th St., New York, N.Y., 10019
AVIS	Avis Films, P.O. Box 643, Burbank, Calif.
BALL	Baldwin Piano Co., 1801 Gilbert Ave., Cincinnati 2, Ohio
BELL TEL	Bell Telephone Co. (Contact local Business Office)
BF	Brandon Films, Inc., 200 W. 57th St., New York, N.Y., 10019
BIS	British Information Services, 45 Rockefeller Plaza, New York, N.Y.
BREY	Bray Studios, Inc., 729 Seventh Ave., New York, N.Y., 10019
BRIG	Brigham Young University, Dept. of Audio-Visual Communications, Provo, Utah
BRNU	Brown University, Brown Photo Lab., Providence 12, R.I.
CATH	Cathedral Films, Inc., 2921 W. Alameda Ave., Burbank, Calif.
COAST	Coast Visual Education Co., 5620 Hollywood Blvd., Hollywood 28, Calif.
CON	Contemporary Films, 267 W. 25th St., New York, N.Y.
CONN	C. G. Conn Ltd., Educational Services Dept., 1101 E. Beardsley, Elkhart, Ind.
COR	Coronet Films, 65 E. South Water St., Chicago, Ill. 60601
CUE	University of California Extension, Educational Films Sales Dept., Berkeley 4, Calif.
DIA	Walt Disney Productions, 16MM Films, 350 S. Buena Vista, Burbank, Calif.
DYN	Dynamic Films, Inc., 405 Park Ave., New York, N.Y.
EBF	Encyclopaedia Britannica Films, 1150 Wilmette Ave., Wilmette, Ill.
FCI	Film Center, Inc., 64 W. Randolph St., Chicago, Ill., 60601
FII	Film Images, Inc., 1860 Broadway, New York, N.Y., 10023
FILMS	Films Incorporated, 5625 Hollywood Blvd., Hollywood 28, Calif.
FORD	Ford Motor Co., Motion Picture Dept., The American Road Department of Education, Dearborn, Mich.

SYMBOL	
FACSEA	Society for French-American Cultural Services & Educational Aid, Audio-Visual Dept., 972 Fifth Ave., New York, N.Y., 10021
HAM	Hammond Organ Co., 4200 W. Diversey Ave., Chicago, Ill., 60639
HOFF	Hoffberg Productions, Inc., 362 W. 44th St., New York, N.Y., 10018
IF	Instructional Films, 65 E. South Water Street, Chicago, Ill., 60601
IFB	International Film Bureau, Inc., 332 S. Michigan Ave., Chicago, Ill., 60604
INDIA	Consulate General of India, 417 Montgomery St., San Francisco, Calif.
INDU	Indiana University, Dept. of Journalism, Bloomington, Ind.
IVT	Institute of Visual Training, Inc., 40 E. 49th St., New York, N.Y., 10017
JOUR	Erven Jourdan, 411 S. Western Ave., Los Angeles, Calif.
LES	Irving Lesser Enterprises, 527 Madison Ave., New York, N.Y., 10022.
LIB	Library Films, Inc., 723 Seventh Ave., New York, N.Y., 10019
McGH	McGraw-Hill Book Co., Text-Film Dept., 330 W. 42nd St., New York, N.Y., 10018
McMG	McMurray-Gold Productions, 275 S. Beverly Drive, Beverly Hills, Calif.
MGM	Metro Goldwyn Mayer, Educational Film Department, Hollywood, Calif.
MIL	Mills Picture Corp., 6533 Hollywood Blvd., Hollywood 28, Calif.
MMA	Museum of Modern Art, Film Library, 11 W. 53 St., New York, N.Y., 10019
MSU	Michigan State University, East Lansing, Mich.
MTP	Modern Talking Picture Service, Inc., 3 E. 54th St., New York, N.Y., 10022.
NAVY	Navy, United States Navy, Washington, D.C.
NBC	N.B.C. Film Department, Rockefeller Center, New York, N.Y., 10019
NET	National Educational Television, Indiana University, Bloomington, Ind.
NFB	National Film Board of Canada, 680 Fifth Ave., New York, N.Y., 10019
NMC	National Music Camp, 303 S. State St., Ann Arbor, Mich.
OFF	Official Films, Inc., 25 W. 45th St., New York, N.Y.
OST	Ostwald Band Films, Division of "Uniforms by Ostwald," Staten Island 1, N.Y.
OSU–MPD	Ohio State University, Motion Picture Division, 1885 Neil Avenue, Columbus 10, Ohio
OWI	Office of War Information, distributed by United World Films
PAR	Parthenon Pictures, 2625 Temple St., Hollywood 26, Calif.
PARA	Paragon Productions, 191 Brady Lane, Bloomfield Hills, Mich.
P. COX	Paul Cox, Coast Visual Education Co., 5620 Hollywood Boulevard, Hollywood 28, Calif.
PIC	Pictura Films Distribution Corp., 41 Union Square W., New York, N.Y., 10013
PICT	Pictorial Films, Inc., 105 E. 106 St., New York, N.Y.
PORT	Portafilms, Orchard Lake, Mich.
PU	Purdue University, Audio-Visual Center, Lafayette, Ind.
RFL	Rembrandt Film Library, 267 W. 25th St., New York, N.Y., 10001.
SCI	Scientific Films Co., 6804 Windsor Ave., Berwyn, Ill.
SG	Screen Gems, Inc., 711 Fifth Ave., New York, N.Y.
SMUSA	Sterling Movies, U.S.A., 375 Park Avenue, New York, N.Y., 10022
STE	Sterling Educational Films, Inc., 6 East 29 St., New York, N.Y., 10016
STEPH	Stephens College, Columbia, Mo.
SUEF	Sutherland Educational Films, 201 North Occidental Blvd., Los Angeles, Calif.

Symbol	
TFC	Teaching Film Custodians, Inc., 25 W. 43 St., New York, N.Y., 10036
TROX	Troxel Music Enterprises, 2744 W. San Juan, Phoenix, Ariz.
UA	University of Arizona, Bureau of Audio-Visual Services, Tucson, Ariz.
UIA	State University of Iowa, Iowa City, Iowa
UILL	University of Illinois, Champaign, Ill.
UM	University of Michigan, Audio-Visual Education Center, Freize Bldg., 720 E. Huron, Ann Arbor, Mich.
UMIN	University of Minnesota, A-V Education Service, Wesbrook Hall, Minneapolis 14, Minn.
UMO	University of Missouri, Columbia, Mo.
USAR	U.S. Army Pictorial Service Division, Motion Picture Branch, Washington, D.C.
USC	University of Southern California, Dept. of Cinema, Film Distribution Div., 3518 University, Los Angeles 7, Calif.
USM	U.S. Marine Corp. Director, 100 Harrison St., San Francisco 6, Calif.
UW–GOV	United World Films, Inc., Government Films Dept., 1445 Park Ave., New York, N.Y., 10029
UWF	United World Films, Inc., 1445 Park Ave., New York, N.Y., 10029
UWIS	University of Wisconsin, 600 N. Park St., Madison, Wis.
WMSBG	Colonial Williamsburg, Film Distribution Section, Box 516, Williamsburg, Va.
WSU	Wayne State University, Audio-Visual Production Center, 680 Putman, Detroit 2, Mich.

Arsenal Technical High School, Indianapolis, Indiana.

CHAPTER

25

Sources of Literature and Music Equipment and Supplies

MUSIC PUBLISHERS

SYMBOL	
AB	Allyn and Bacon, Inc., 150 Tremont St., Boston, Mass., 02111
ABC	American Book Company, 55 Fifth Ave., New York, N.Y., 10003
AMP	Associated Music Publishers, 1 W. 47th St., New York, N.Y., 10036
AUG	Augsburg Publishing House, 426 S. 5th St., Minneapolis, Minn., 55415
BEL	Belwin, Inc., 250 Maple Ave., Rockville Center, N.Y.
BM	Boston Music Co., 116 Boylston St., Boston, Mass., 02116
BOOS	Boosey and Hawkes, Inc., Oceanside, N.Y., 11572
BOU	Bourne Company, 136 W. 52nd St., New York, N.Y.
CF	Carl Fischer, 56-62 Cooper Square, New York, N.Y., 10003
CHAP	Chappell & Co., 609 Fifth Ave., New York, N.Y., 10017
COLE	M. M. Cole, 823 S. Wabash Ave., Chicago, Ill.
CRS	Cooperative Recreation Service, Delaware, Ohio
EBM	E. B. Marks Music Corp., 136 W. 52nd St., New York, N.Y., 10019
ECS	E. C. Schirmer Music Co., 221 Columbus Ave., Boston, Mass., 02116
EHM	Edwin H. Morris & Co., 31 W. 54th St., New York, N.Y., 10019
EMB	Educational Music Bureau, 434 S. Wabash Ave., Chicago, Ill., 60605
FILL	Fillmore Music Co., c/o Carl Fischer, 56-62 Cooper Square, New York, N.Y., 10003
FITZ	H. T. FitzSimons Co., 615 N. LaSalle St., Chicago, Ill., 60610
FOL	Follett Publishing Company, 1010 W. Washington Blvd., Chicago, Ill., 60607
GAL	Galaxy Music Corp., 2121 Broadway, New York, N.Y., 10023
GI	Ginn and Co., Statler Building, Boston, Mass., 02117
GRAY	H. W. Gray Co., Inc., 159 E. 48th St., New York, N.Y., 10017
GS	Girl Scouts, 155 E. 44th St., New York, N.Y.
GSCH	G. Schirmer, Inc., 609 Fifth Ave., New York, N.Y., 10017
HA	Harms, Inc., 619 W. 54th St., New York, N.Y., 10019
HAN	Handy-Folio Music Co., 7212 W. Fond du Lac Ave., Milwaukee 18, Wis.
HAR	Hargail Music Press, 157 W. 57th St., New York, N.Y., 10019
HF	Harold Flammer, Inc., 251 W. 19th St., New York, N.Y., 10011

Symbol	
HOFF	Raymond A. Hoffman Co., 1615 Briggs Ave., Wichita 3, Kan.
HOH	Hohner, Inc., Andrews Rd., Hicksville, N.Y., 11802
JF	J. Fischer & Bros., Harristown Road, Glen Rock, N.J., 07452
JT	Janet E. Tobitt, 5 Tudor Place, New York, N.Y., 10017
K	Kalmus Music Co., 421 W. 28th St., New York, N.Y., 10001
MILL	Mills Music, Inc., 1619 Broadway, New York, N.Y., 10019
MPH	Music Publishers Holding Corp., 488 Madison Ave., New York, N.Y., 10022
NAS	National Autoharp Sales Co., Box 1120, Des Moines, Iowa
NK	Neil A. Kjos Music Co., 525 Busse, Park Ridge, Ill.
NRA	National Recreation Association, 8 W. 8th St., New York, N.Y.
OX	Oxford University Press, 417 Fifth Ave., New York, N.Y., 10016
PAS	Paul A. Schmitt, now Schmitt, Hall & McCreary
PER	Peripole, 51-17 Rockaway Beach Blvd., Far Rockaway, Long Island, N.Y., 11691
PET	C. F. Peters Corp., 373 Park Ave. South, New York, N.Y., 10016
PREN	Prentice-Hall, Inc., Englewood Cliffs, N.J., 07632
PRO	Pro Art Publications, Inc., 469 Union Ave., Westbury, N.Y., 11591
REM	Remick Music Corp., RCA Building, Rockefeller Center, New York, N.Y.
RU	Rubank, Inc., 5544 W. Armstrong Ave., Chicago, Ill., 60646
SB	Silver Burdett, Park Avenue and Columbia Rd., Morristown, N.J., 07960
SCHM	Schmitt, Hall & McCreary, 527 Park Ave., Minneapolis, Minn., 55415
SCHO	Schott and Co., Ltd., London, c/o AMP
SCHU	Edward Schuberth and Co., 240 W. 55th St., New York, N.Y., 10019
SF	Sam Fox Publishing Co., 1841 Broadway, New York, N.Y., 10023
SFL	Song Flute Co., 630 S. Wabash Ave., Chicago, Ill.
SHAW	Shawnee Press, Inc., Delaware Water Gap, Pa., 18327
SO	Southern Music Co., 1100 Broadway, Box 329, San Antonio, Tex., 78206
SP	SPEBSQSA, Inc., 20619 Fenkel Ave., Detroit, Mich.
S&S	Simon & Schuster, 630 Fifth Ave., New York, N.Y., 10020
ST	Stainer and Bell, c/o Galaxy Publishing Co.
STA	The Staff Music Publishing Co., 374 Great Neck Rd., Great Neck, N.Y.
SUMB	Summy-Birchard Co., 1834 Ridge Ave., Evanston, Ill., 60204
TOM	Gordon V. Thompson, Ltd., 32 Alcorn Ave., Toronto 7, Ontario, Canada
TP	Theodore Presser Co., Bryn Mawr, Pa., 10910
WILL	Willis Music Co., 440 Main St., Cincinnati 2, Ohio
WIT	M. Witmark & Sons, c/o MPH
WJS	William J. Smith Music Co., 254 W. 31 St., New York, N.Y., 10001
WOOD	B. F. Wood Co., Inc., 1619 Broadway, New York, N.Y., 10019
YA	Young Audiences, Inc., 115 E. 92nd St., New York, N.Y., 10028

BOOK PUBLISHERS

Abelard-Schumann Ltd., 6 W. 57 St., New York, N.Y., 10019
Abingdon Press, 201 Eighth Ave., S., Nashville 3, Tenn.

Harry N. Abrams, Inc., 6 W. 57 St., New York, N.Y., 10019
Henry Adler Publishing Co., 130 W. 46 St., New York, N.Y.
Allyn and Bacon, Inc., 150 Tremont St., Boston, Mass., 02111
American Book Co., 55 Fifth Ave., New York, N.Y., 10003
American Music Conference, 332 S. Michigan Ave., Chicago, Ill., 60604
Ann Arbor Publishers, Ann Arbor, Mich.
Arco Publishing Co., Inc., 480 Lexington Ave., New York, N.Y., 10017
Augsburg Publishing House, 426 Fifth St., Minneapolis, Minn., 55415
A. S. Barnes, 11 E. 36 St., New York, N.Y., 10016
Barnes & Noble, 105 Fifth Ave., New York, N.Y., 10003
George Braziller, Inc., 214 Fourth Ave., New York, N.Y., 10003
Wm. C. Brown Company, 135 S. Locust St., Dubuque, Iowa
Carl Fischer, Inc., 62 Cooper Square, New York, N.Y., 10003
Catholic University of America Press, 620 Michigan Ave. N.E., Washington, D.C., 20017
Howard Chandler, 660 Market St., San Francisco, Calif.
Chandler Publishing Co., 604 Mission St., San Francisco 5, Calif.
Citadel Press, 222 Fourth Ave., New York, N.Y., 10003
M. M. Cole, 823 S. Wabash Ave., Chicago, Ill.
P. F. Collier & Son Corp., 640 Fifth Ave., New York, N.Y., 10019
Columbia University Press, 2960 Broadway, New York, N.Y., 10027
Cornell University Press, Ithaca, N.Y.
Dell Publishing Co., Inc., 750 Third Ave., New York, N.Y., 10017
Dodd, Mead & Co., 432 Park Ave. S., New York, N.Y., 10016
E. P. Dutton & Co., 300 Fourth Ave., New York, N.Y., 10010
Fearon Publishers, 2263 Union St., San Francisco 23, Calif.
Fleet Publishing Corp., 230 Park Ave., New York, N.Y., 10017
Follett Publishing Co., 1010 W. Washington Blvd., Chicago, Ill., 60607
Funk and Wagnalls, 360 Lexington Ave., New York, N.Y., 10017
Garden City Books, Doubleday & Co., Garden City, N.Y.
Ginn & Co., Statler Bldg., Boston, Mass., 02117
H. W. Gray Co., Inc., 159 E. 48 St., New York, N.Y., 10017
Grosset & Dunlap, Inc., 1107 Broadway, New York, N.Y., 10010
Harcourt, Brace & World, 750 Third Ave., New York, N.Y., 10017
Harper & Row, 49 E. 33 St., New York, N.Y., 10016
D. C. Heath & Co., 285 Columbus Ave., Boston, Mass., 02116
Holt, Rinehart and Winston, Inc., 383 Madison Ave., New York, N.Y., 10017
Horizon Press, Inc., 220 W. 42 St., New York, N.Y., 10036
Houghton Mifflin Co., 2 Park St., Boston, Mass., 02107
Bruce Humphries, Publishers, 48 Melrose St., Boston, Mass.
Interlochen Press, Interlochen, Mich., 58943
International Textbook Co., Scranton 15, Pa.
P. J. Kenedy & Sons, 12 Barclay St., New York, N.Y., 10008
Neil A. Kjos Music Co., 525 Busse, Park Ridge, Ill.
G. Leblanc Co., 7019 30th Ave., Kenosha, Wis.
Hal Leonard Music, Inc., 64 E. Second St., Winona, Minn., 55987
J. B. Lippincott Co., E. Washington Sq., Philadelphia, Pa., 19105
Little, Brown & Co., 34 Beacon St., Boston, Mass., 02106
Longmans, Green & Co., 119 W. 40 St., New York, N.Y., 10018
McGraw-Hill Book Co., Inc., 330 W. 42 St., New York, N.Y., 10036

Mentor Books, New American Library, 501 Madison Ave., New York, N.Y., 10022
Meridian Books, Inc., 12 E. 22 St., New York, N.Y., 10010
Charles E. Merrill Books, Inc., 1300 Akum Creek Dr., Columbus 16, Ohio
Julian Messner, Inc., 8 W. 40 St., New York, N.Y., 10018
Mills Music, Inc., 1619 Broadway, New York, N.Y., 10019
Modern Library, Random House, Inc., 457 Madison Ave., New York, N.Y., 10022
Music Educators National Conference, 1201 16 St. N.W., Washington, D.C., 20036
National Recreation Association, 8 W. 8th St., New York, N.Y., 10011
New American Library of World Literature, Inc., 501 Madison Ave., New York, N.Y., 10022
W. W. Norton & Co., Inc., 55 Fifth Ave., New York, N.Y., 10003
The Odyssey Press, Inc., 55 Fifth Ave., New York, N.Y., 10003
Oliver Ditson Co., Bryn Mawr, Pa.
Oxford University Press, 417 Fifth Ave., New York, N.Y., 10016
Pantheon Books, Inc., 22 E. 51 St., New York, N.Y., 10003
Penguin Books, Inc., 3300 Clipper Mill Rd., Baltimore, Md., 21211
C. F. Peters Corp., 373 Park Ave. S., New York, N.Y., 10016
Phaidon Publishers, Inc., 575 Madison Ave., New York, N.Y., 10022
Philosophical Library, Inc., 15 E. 40 St., New York, N.Y., 10016
Frederick A. Praeger, Inc., 15 W. 47 St., New York, N.Y., 10036
Prentice-Hall, Inc., Englewood Cliffs, N.J., 07632
Theodore Presser Co., Bryn Mawr, Pa., 19010
G. P. Putnam's Sons, 210 Madison Ave., New York, N.Y., 10016
Random House, 457 Madison Ave., New York, N.Y., 10022
Richards Rosen Associates, 13 E. 22 St., New York, N.Y., 10010
The Ronald Press Co., 15 E. 26 St., New York, N.Y., 10010
Roy Publishers, Inc., 30 E. 74 St., New York, N.Y., 10021
W. B. Saunders Co., W. Washington Sq., Philadelphia, Pa., 19105
G. Schirmer, Inc., 609 Fifth Ave., New York, N.Y., 10017
Schmitt, Hall & McCreary Co., 527 Park Ave., Minneapolis, Minn., 55415
Schocken Books, Inc., 67 Park Ave., New York, N.Y., 10016
Charles Scribner's Sons, 597 Fifth Ave., New York, N.Y., 10017
Sentinel Book Publishers, Inc., 112 E. 19 St., New York, N.Y., 10003
Silver Burdett Co., Park Ave. & Columbia Rd., Morristown, N.J., 07960
Simon and Schuster, Inc., 630 Fifth Ave., New York, N.Y., 10020
Skira, Inc., Publishers, 381 Fourth Ave., New York, N.Y., 10016
St Martin's Press, 175 Fifth Ave., New York, N.Y., 10010
Summy-Birchard Co., 1834 Ridge Ave., Evanston, Ill., 60204
University of Georgia Press, Athens, Ga.
University of Pennsylvania Press, 3436 Walnut St., Philadelphia, Pa., 19104
University Publishing Co., 1126 Q St., Lincoln, Neb.
Wadsworth Publishing Co., Inc., Belmont, Calif.
Washington Square Press, Inc., 630 Fifth Ave., New York, N.Y., 10020
Franklin Watts, Inc., 575 Lexington Ave., New York, N.Y., 10022
Wesleyan University Press, Middletown, Conn.
World Publishing Co., 2231 W. 110 St., Cleveland, Ohio, 44102

MUSIC MAGAZINES

The Instrumentalist, 1418 Lake St., Evanston, Ill.
Journal of Research in Music Education, Music Educators National Conference, 1201 16th St. N.W., Washington, D.C., 20036
Keyboard Jr., 1346 Chapel St., New Haven, Conn., 06511
Music Educators Journal, Music Educators National Conference 1201 16th St. N.W., Washington, D.C., 20036
The Music Journal, 1776 Broadway, New York, N.Y., 10019
Musical America, 111 W. 57th St., New York, N.Y., 10019

BAND, ORCHESTRA, AND RECREATIONAL INSTRUMENTS

Artley, Inc., 2000 Middlebury St., Elkhart, Ind.
Buescher Band Instrument Co., 225 E. Jackson Blvd., Elkhart, Ind.
Continental Musical Instrument Co., 717 Chicago Ave., Evanston, Ill.
Conn Corp., 1101 E. Beardsley Ave., Elkhart, Ind., 46514
The Cundy-Bettoney Co., Inc., 96 Bradlee St., Hyde Park, Boston, Mass., 02136
Elkan-Vogel Co., Inc., 1712-16 Sansom St., Philadelphia, Pa., 19103 (recorders)
The Getzen Co., Inc., 431 E. Geneva St., Elkhorn, Wis.
The Fred Gretsch Mfg. Co., 60 Broadway, Brooklyn 11, N.Y.
Hargail Music Press, 157 W. 57th St., New York, N.Y., 10019 (recorders)
The Harmolin Co., Box 244, La Jolla, Calif.
The Harmony Co., 4610 Kolin Ave., Chicago, Ill., 60632 (guitars)
Wm. S. Haynes Co., 12 Piedmont St., Boston, Mass., 02116 (flutes)
Hershman Musical Instrument Co., Inc., 53 W. 23rd St., New York, N.Y., 10010
Hohner, Inc., Andrews Rd., Hicksville, N.Y., 11802 (glockenspiel, Melodica, harmonica)
Frank Holton & Co., Elkhorn, Wis., 53121
G. C. Jenkins Co., 1014 E. Olive, Decatur, Ill., 62525 (percussion, marimba, chimes)
Kay Musical Instrument Co., 1640 W. Walnut St., Chicago, Ill., 60612
George Kelischek Workshop for Historical Instruments, 2725 Knox St. N.E., Atlanta 17, Ga.
B. F. Lotching & Co., Inc., 8947 Fairview Ave., Brookfield, Ill., 60513 (bells)
C. Leblanc Co., 7019 30th Ave., Kenosha, Wis.
William A. Lewis & Son, 30 E. Adams St., Chicago, Ill., 60603 (stringed instruments)
Linton Mfg. Co., Inc., 919 Nappanee St., Elkhart, Ind., 46518
Lyon-Healy, 243 S. Wabash Ave., Chicago, Ill., 60604
Lyons Band Instrument Co., 223 W. Lake St., Chicago, Ill., 60606
Martin-Freres, 5-9 Union Square, New York, N.Y., 10003
The Martin Band Instrument Co., 431 Baldwin St., Elkhart, Ind.
The Melody Flute Co., Laurel, Md.
Musser, Inc., 8947 Fairview Ave., Brookfield, Ill., 60513 (marimbas)
National Autoharp Sales Co., Box 1120, Des Moines, Iowa

F. E. Olds & Sons, Inc., 350 S. Raymond Ave., Fullerton, Calif.
The Pedler Co., 431 Baldwin St., Elkhart, Ind.
Peripole, Inc.—Carl Van Roy Co., 51-17 Rockaway Beach Blvd., Far Rockaway, L.I., N.Y.
Remo, Inc., 12904 Raymer St., N. Hollywood, Calif. (Weather King drum heads)
Scherl & Roth, 1729 Superior Ave., Cleveland, Ohio, 44114 (stringed instruments)
Oscar Schmidt-International Inc., 87 Ferry St., Jersey City, N.J., 07307 (Autoharps)
Edward Schuberth & Co., 240 W. 55th St., New York, N.Y., 10019 (shepherd's pipes)
Schulmerich Carillons, Inc., Carillon Hill, Sellersville, Pa.
H. & A. Selmer, Inc., 1119 N. Main St., Elkhart, Ind., 46515
Slingerland Drum Co., 6633 N. Milwaukee Ave., Niles 48, Ill.
Song Flute Co., 630 S. Wabash Ave., Chicago, Ill.
Steinway & Sons, Steinway Place, Long Island City 5, N.Y.
Targe & Dinner, Inc., 425 S. Wabash Ave., Chicago, Ill., 60605 (Tone bells)
David Wexler & Co., 823 S. Wabash, Chicago, Ill., 60605 (bells)
The H. N. White Co., 5225 Superior Ave., Cleveland, Ohio, 44103
W. F. L. Drum Co., 1728 N. Damon Ave., Chicago, Ill., 60647
Avedis Zildjian Co., 39 Fayette St., N. Quincy, Mass., 02171 (cymbals, gongs)

BAND UNIFORMS AND CHOIR GOWNS

Academic Church and Choir Gown Mfg. Co., 5870 Hollywood Blvd., Hollywood, Calif.
Bentley & Simon, Inc., 7 W. 36th St., New York, N.Y., 10018
Brooks-Van Horn Costume Co., Inc., 232 N. 11th St., Philadelphia, Pa.
Collegiate Cap & Gown Co., 1000 N. Market St., Champaign, Ill.
Craddock Uniforms, 1209 Grand Ave., Kansas City 6, Mo.
DeMoulin Brothers & Co., Greenville, Ill.
Fechheimer Bros. Co., 4th St. & Pike St., Cincinnati, Ohio
Ireland Needlecraft, 3661 San Fernando Rd., Glendale 4, Calif.
E. R. Moore Co., 923 Dakin St., Chicago, Ill., 60613
Nelson Knitting Mills, Inc., 2105 W. Superior St., Duluth 6, Minn. (sweater uniforms)
Northwestern Theatre Associates, 2540 Eastwood Ave., Evanston, Ill.
Thomas A. Peterson Co., 501 E. 33rd St., Kansas City 9, Mo.
Robert Rollins Blazers, Inc., 252 Park Ave. S., New York, N.Y., 10003
Saxony Uniforms, 230 Canal St., New York, N. Y., 10013
Stanbury & Co., 720 Delaware St., Kansas City 5, Mo.
Uniforms by Ostwald, Inc., Ostwald Plaza, Staten Island, N.Y., 10301
C. E. Ward Co., New London, Ohio

MUSICAL EQUIPMENT AND SUPPLIES

Award Emblem Mfg. Co., 3534 W. 51st St., Chicago, Ill., 60632
Berntsen Brass & Aluminum Foundry, 2334 Pennsylvania Ave., Madison, Wis. (Porta-Stage Risers)

Brewer-Titchener Corp., Furniture and Equipment Div., Cortland, N.Y.
Bruce Humphries, 48 Melrose St., Boston, Mass. (Staffwriter)
Clarin Mfg. Co., 4640 W. Harrison St., Chicago, Ill., 60644 (music chairs)
Educational Music Bureau, Inc., 434 S. Wabash Ave., Chicago, Ill., 60605
Franz Mfg. Co., 53 Wallace St., New Haven, Conn. (Flash-Beat Metronome)
Haldeman-Homme Mfg. Co., 2580 University Ave., St. Paul 14, Minn. (choral risers)
Krauth & Benninghofen, 940 Symms Ave., Hamilton, Ohio (music stands)
Mitchell Mfg. Co., 2740 S. 34th St., Milwaukee 46, Wis. (band and orchestra risers)
The Monroe Co., 353 Church St., Colfax, Iowa (standing choral risers)
Morren Mfg. Co., 2220 Foothill Blvd., Pasadena 8, Calif. (steel music files)
M. Payson Mfg. Co., Box 136, Fairbury, Neb. (risers)
Peery Products Co., Box 8156, Portland 7, Ore. (risers)
S. & H. Mfg. Co., 316 Summit St., Normal, Ill. (Sherrart roll-away musical instrument racks)
H. & A. Selmer, Inc., Elkhart, Ind. (Selmer concert band stands)
Sice, Inc., 5215 Eden Ave. S., Minneapolis, Minn., 55424 (proscenium curtains for portable stage)
Stagecraft Corp., 25 Belden Ave., Norwalk, Conn. (portable acoustic shell)
Strayline Products Co., Dobbs Ferry, N.Y. (battery-operated safety candles)
Wallach & Associates, Inc., Box 3567, Cleveland, Ohio, 44118 (record cabinets)
Wenger Music Equipment Co., Owatonna, Minn. (risers, portable stages, sousaphone chairs)
Wiese Mfg. Co., Box 72, Davenport, Iowa (music stands and lights)

Index

Format by Jeanne Ray Juster
Set in Linotype Caledonia
Composed by The Haddon Craftsmen, Inc.
Printed by The Murray Printing Company
Bound by The Haddon Craftsmen, Inc.
HARPER & ROW, PUBLISHERS, INCORPORATED

68 69 70 7 6 5 4 3 2